Progress in IS

Progress in IS encompasses the various areas of Information Systems in theory and practice, presenting cutting-edge advances in the field. It is aimed especially at researchers, doctoral students, and advanced practitioners. The series features both research monographs, edited volumes, and conference proceedings that make substantial contributions to our state of knowledge and handbooks and other edited volumes, in which a team of experts is organized by one or more leading authorities to write individual chapters on various aspects of the topic. Individual volumes in this series are supported by a minimum of two external reviews.

The Series is SCOPUS-indexed.

Jorge Marx Gómez · Antoine Gatera ·
Devotha Godfrey Nyambo
Editors

Advancement in Embedded and Mobile Systems

Proceedings of the 2nd ICTA-EMOS Conference, 19–20 September 2024, Kigali, Rwanda

Springer

Editors
Jorge Marx Gómez
University of Oldenburg
Oldenburg, Niedersachsen, Germany

Antoine Gatera
Faculty of Education
UTAB
Byumba, Rwanda

Devotha Godfrey Nyambo
NM-AIST
Arusha, Tanzania

ISSN 2196-8705 ISSN 2196-8713 (electronic)
Progress in IS
ISBN 978-3-031-99218-6 ISBN 978-3-031-99219-3 (eBook)
https://doi.org/10.1007/978-3-031-99219-3

This Springer imprint is published by the registered company Springer Nature Switzerland AG
The registered company address is: Gewerbestrasse 11, 6330 Cham, Switzerland

Foreword

The International Conference on Technological Advancement in Embedded and Mobile Systems (ICTA-EMoS 2024), hosted by the University of Technology and Arts of Byumba (UTAB) in Kigali, Rwanda, convenes researchers and practitioners engaged in advancing embedded and mobile system technologies within the broader context of sustainable development.

Under its central theme, ICTA-EMoS 2024 highlights the growing role of emerging technologies in addressing contemporary economic, social, and environmental challenges. The conference scope reflects the interdisciplinary nature of modern technological innovation, encompassing areas such as artificial intelligence, robotics, mobile computing, the Internet of Things, and related digital systems that contribute to sustainable technological progress.

As embedded and mobile systems increasingly underpin digital infrastructures across sectors, scholarly dialogue that bridges foundational research and applied innovation becomes essential. ICTA-EMoS provides a platform for such exchange, fostering collaboration among researchers working at the intersection of technological advancement and societal impact.

This volume brings together selected contributions presented at ICTA-EMoS 2024, reflecting current research directions and ongoing efforts to harness emerging technologies responsibly and effectively. We extend our appreciation to the authors and organisers whose commitment to advancing research in this domain has shaped this publication.

It is our hope that the work presented herein will stimulate further inquiry, collaboration, and innovation in embedded and mobile systems, particularly in contexts where technological advancement contributes to sustainable development objectives.

Jorge Marx Gómez
Carl von Ossietzky Universität Oldenburg

Acknowledgements

The Organizing Committee of the 2nd International Conference on Technological Advancement in Embedded and Mobile Systems (2nd ICTA-EMoS) 2024 thanks all the implementing partners of the dSkills@EA Project for support and collaboration to host the conference.

Carl von Ossietzky Universität Oldenburg

CENIT@EA

University of Technology and Arts of Byumba (UTAB)

The East African Community (EAC)

The Inter University Council of East Africa (IUCEA)

The Nelson Mandela Institution of Science and Technology (NM-AIST)

Deutsche Gesellschaft für Internationale Zusammenarbeit (GIZ)

Contents

Development of a Digi-Face Cross-Platform Mobile App for Online Teaching, Learning and Research: A Case Study of African Higher Education Communities

Innocent V. Kitauka, Loyani Loyani, Sinde Ramadhani, and Musa Ally Dida

Abstract This project report explores the design, development, and implementation of an innovative cross-platform mobile application, tailored for online teaching, learning, and research within the context of African higher education communities. Building upon the existing Digi-Face platform, which serves as a foundation for online education, this study addresses a technical gap by extending the capabilities to a mobile interface. This project report aims to bridge this gap by developing a cross-platform mobile app, optimizing the Digi-Face experience for mobile devices. The primary objective is to develop a cross-platform Mobile App for online teaching, learning, and research within the African Centers of Excellence in East Africa by providing an intuitive and accessible mobile interface. The study employs a comprehensive methodology, incorporating both qualitative and quantitative research methods. The development process involves utilizing industry-standard tools and frameworks for cross-platform mobile app development, ensuring compatibility across various devices and operating systems such as Android and IOS. Upon implementation, the results demonstrate a substantial improvement in the accessibility and usability of the Digi-Face platform through the mobile app. The application facilitates streamlined access to educational materials, collaborative features, and research resources. Comparative analysis with existing methodologies reveals a marked enhancement in user engagement, resource utilization, and overall learning experiences.

I. V. Kitauka (✉) · L. Loyani · S. Ramadhani · M. A. Dida
Nelson Mandela African Institution of Science and Technology, Arusha, Tanzania
e-mail: innocent.kitauka@nm-aist.ac.tz

L. Loyani
e-mail: loyani.loyani@nm-aist.ac.tz

S. Ramadhani
e-mail: Ramadhani.sinde@nm-aist.ac.tz

M. A. Dida
e-mail: mussa.ally@nm-aist.ac.tz

J. Marx Gómez et al. (eds.), *Advancement in Embedded and Mobile Systems*, Progress in IS, https://doi.org/10.1007/978-3-031-99219-3_1

Keywords Digi-face · Mobile app · Online learning

1 Introduction and Background

Online learning has emerged as an effective approach to education, combining the benefits of both face-to-face and online learning. The integration of mobile technology into online learning has opened up new opportunities for learners to access course materials, interact with their instructors and peers, and complete assignments and assessments. Mobile apps are increasingly being used to support and enhance the online learning experience.

According to a study by [1], mobile apps can facilitate communication between learners, instructors, and peers, allowing for increased interaction and collaboration. Moreover, a study by [1, 2] found that mobile apps can improve the quality of interactions and the level of engagement among learners. Mobile apps can also support the learners' preferences and individual differences in different settings of study environments, which is essential for success in academic and professional settings.

Furthermore, a study by [3] found that mobile apps can enhance self-directed learning by providing learners with access to a wide range of learning resources, allowing them to set their own learning goals, and providing opportunities for self-assessment.

The Digi-Face mobile app, developed as a case study for this master's project, aims to provide learners with access to course materials, opportunities for interaction and collaboration, and support for self-directed learning. The app has been designed to enhance the online learning experience by providing learners with a user-friendly interface and seamless integration between face-to-face and online learning. A study by [4] found that Mobile apps can also support the development of digital literacy skills as well as intercultural competence, which are increasingly important in today's digital age. So mobile apps can facilitate the development of digital literacy skills by providing learners with opportunities to use digital tools and resources with opportunities to interact with peers from diverse cultural backgrounds.

Overall, the development of the Digi-Face mobile app for online learning has the potential to make a significant contribution to the field of education by providing learners with a more engaging, interactive, and personalized learning experience.

As the previous studies show, mobile apps have a significant impact on different aspects of education, such as communication, critical thinking, self-directed learning, digital literacy, intercultural competence, and academic achievement. The development of the Digi-Face mobile app for online learning can build upon these findings and contribute to the ongoing research on mobile learning in education.

Online learning, which combines traditional face-to-face instruction with online learning, has become an increasingly popular approach in education [5]. With the proliferation of mobile devices and mobile technology, mobile learning has become an important tool for supporting online learning and enhancing student engagement [6]. However, the development of effective mobile learning applications that can support online learning is not without challenges. For example, mobile learning applications must be designed to effectively integrate with traditional classroom instruction and meet the specific needs of individual learners [7]. Additionally, ensuring the quality and effectiveness of mobile learning applications requires careful planning, design, and implementation [8].

1.1 Objectives

The main objective of this study is to develop Digi-Face cross-platform mobile apps for online teaching, learning, and research, to be used by all Centers of Excellence to facilitate these processes. Specifically, the study aims to identify system requirements for Digi-Face cross-platform mobile apps tailored for online teaching, learning, and research. Additionally, it seeks to develop these apps for use by African higher education communities. Finally, the study includes validating the developed system to ensure its effectiveness and reliability.

2 Related Works

2.1 Online Learning Systems

This project examined the key features and best practices for developing mobile apps for online learning, as well as the challenges and limitations associated with their implementation. Finally, I will also review the existing literature on the specific context of Digi-Face, the case study for this project, to identify the unique requirements and challenges of implementing online learning using a mobile app in this educational context. The literature review provided a foundation for the design and development of a mobile app for online learning at Digi-Face and will inform the evaluation of its effectiveness in enhancing learning outcomes and promoting student engagement.

In a series of studies, researchers explored the impact of mobile learning apps in diverse educational settings. Kaliisa and Picard investigated the effects of a mobile learning app in an online learning environment, revealing a significant improvement in students' academic performance and engagement [9]. Despite this success, the study highlighted a technological limitation due to limited data on students' learning preferences, emphasizing the need for comprehensive insights into personalized learning materials.

Similarly, Fisher et al. conducted a case study on a mobile app for online learning, discovering enhanced student engagement and satisfaction. However, the study also noted limited access to technology for some students, raising concerns about the equitable use of mobile apps and prompting further investigation into their impact on learning outcomes [10].

Sung et al. developed a mobile app for collaborative learning, demonstrating improvements in collaboration skills and satisfaction. Yet, the study identified a technological limitation related to insufficient data on students' learning preferences, suggesting a potential hurdle in optimizing personalized learning materials. Notably, the app's impact on academic performance remained unexplored [11].

Ziraba Godwill et al. delved into the effects of a mobile app for collaborative learning in higher education, reporting increased student participation and engagement. But, the study highlighted a technological limitation attributed to the scarcity of high-quality digital learning resources. This limitation raises questions about the app's effectiveness in contexts with diverse resource availability and prompts consideration of its impact on individual learning outcomes [12].

Sung et al. developed a mobile app for promoting active learning, resulting in heightened student engagement and satisfaction [11]. Nevertheless, the research revealed a technological constraint concerning the accessibility of superior digital learning materials, underscoring possible obstacles to optimizing the app's efficacy [13]. In their research of the efficacy of a mobile app in a Malaysian university, Muzaffar et al. discovered improvements in student performance and satisfaction. Nevertheless, the study only included a small amount of information on students' preferred methods of learning, failing to investigate how the mobile app would affect group learning [14].

Pektaş and Gürel improved group project participation and cooperation skills by creating a mobile app for collaborative learning. However, because the study was limited to a particular educational setting, its conclusions could not be applied to specific learning objectives [15]. Goundar and Kumar looked into the use of mobile apps to raise English language competency in an online learning setting and found notable increases in both competency and engagement. Despite this achievement, the study highlighted how some students and teachers had restricted access to technology, which raised concerns about the app's wider application to other fields of study [16].

Dias and Bidarra investigated the use of a smartphone app to encourage self-regulated learning, noting improvements in academic achievement and self-regulation abilities. However, the study also found a technological constraint that prevented some pupils from having full access to technology, which could affect its general acceptance. The app's long-term effects on learning outcomes were not explored [17].

Damyanov and Tsankov developed a mobile app for active learning, significantly improving students' engagement and satisfaction. Yet, the study was limited to a specific educational context, leaving open questions about the app's effectiveness in different subject areas [1].

2.2 *Technology in Online Learning*

In the ever-evolving landscape of online learning, Lim et al. [18] confronted the pressing challenge of low engagement and motivation exacerbated by the COVID-19 pandemic. Their response was a mobile app seamlessly with interactive quizzes and social learning elements, aiming to elevate student engagement and motivation. Yet, woven into their findings was the acknowledgment of technological limitations—a stark reality of limited access to technology for some students, potentially casting a shadow over the app's full potential.

This online companion was designed to deliver personalized learning materials and interactive features, envisaging a future where student engagement takes center stage. However, amidst the optimism, a technological hurdle emerged—the limited availability of data on students' learning preferences and performance, subtly challenging the app's envisioned impact.

Concluding this digital tapestry, [19] stood at the intersection of feedback and support, seeking to elevate engagement and motivation. Their mobile app, aspired to bridge the gap. Yet, etched into their findings was the recognition of technological limitations—the scarcity of data on students' preferences and performance, a lingering shadow on the path to personalized support.

The system is designed to provide a comprehensive and effective online learning experience by utilizing various technologies. It aims to provide students with access to course materials, notifications, and communication channels, as well as tools for creating and delivering assessments and interactive learning resources as described in Fig. 1. One of the key features of the proposed system is its ability to personalize the learning experience for each student. The system will collect data on student performance, behavior, and preferences and use this data to provide personalized recommendations and feedback. This will enable students to receive the support and guidance they need to succeed in their studies.

3 Materials and Methods

3.1 *Study Area and Scope*

The case study of the project entitled "Development of Digiface Cross-Platforms Mobile App for Online Teaching, Learning, and Research: A Case Study of African Higher Education Communities" for CENIT@EA at NM-AIST highlights the importance of utilizing technology in education to improve the learning experience for students in East Africa. CENIT@EA is a regional center of excellence for information and communication technology (ICT) located in Dar es Salaam, Tanzania.

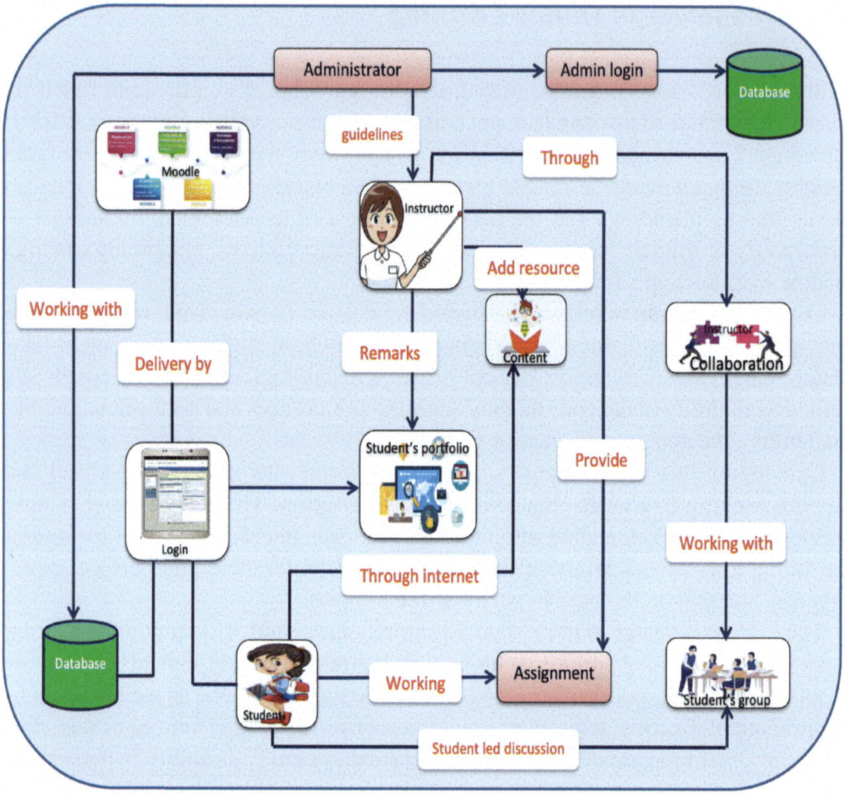

Fig. 1 The proposed system

3.2 System Architecture

Agile software development methodology was used in the creation of a DIGI-FACE mobile application. The Agile methodology is an adaptable approach to system development that encourages continual collaboration with stakeholders at all levels and continuous development and testing throughout the software development process. Agile is a software development methodology that prioritizes collaborative, adaptable, and iterative approaches, as illustrated in Fig. 2. It involves completing frequent testing and feedback loops as well as breaking things down into little, manageable pieces.

The study followed the Agile Extreme Programming (XP) methodology paradigm for gathering requirements, developing systems, and testing. It was employed to expedite the system's delivery within the designated time frame. It stresses a very short development cycle by providing a high-quality system at lower development costs

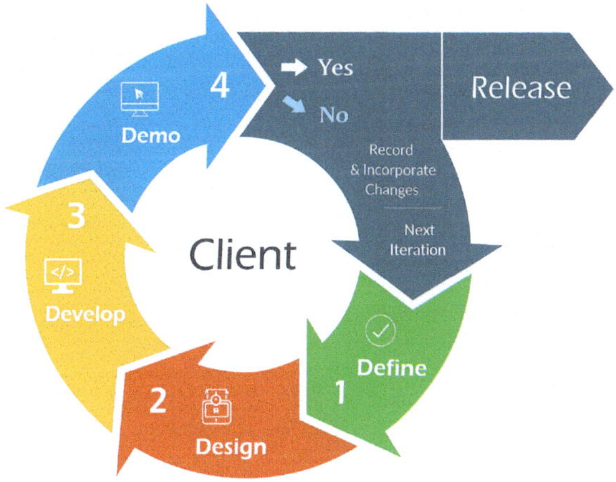

Fig. 2 Agile methodology diagram (source)

than other traditional approaches. It emphasizes teamwork, input, and customer-focused priorities. Additionally, as shown by Fig. 3, it highlights methods for developing high-quality software, including pair programming, test-driven development (TDD), and continuous integration.

The gathered system requirements will be examined using graphical languages based on the Unified Modeling Language (UML) rules and artifacts. System modeling will be done using StarUML, a UML diagram modeling tool. To map the acquired requirements into each of this diagram, the user case diagram, class diagram,

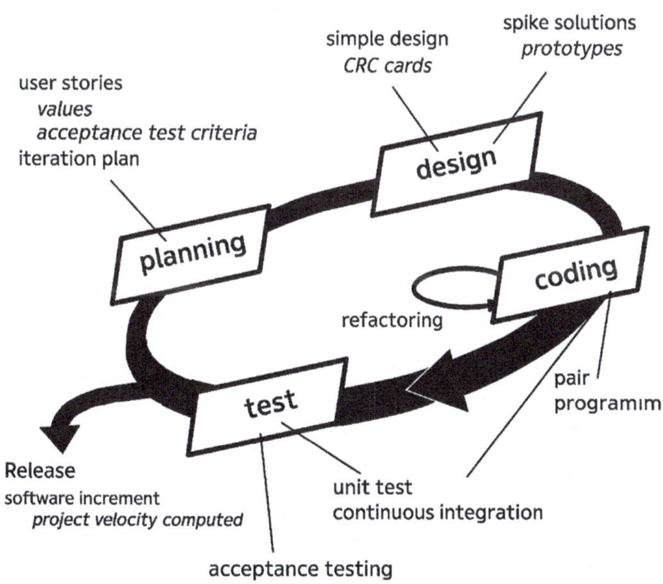

Fig. 3 Agile framework extreme programming (source)

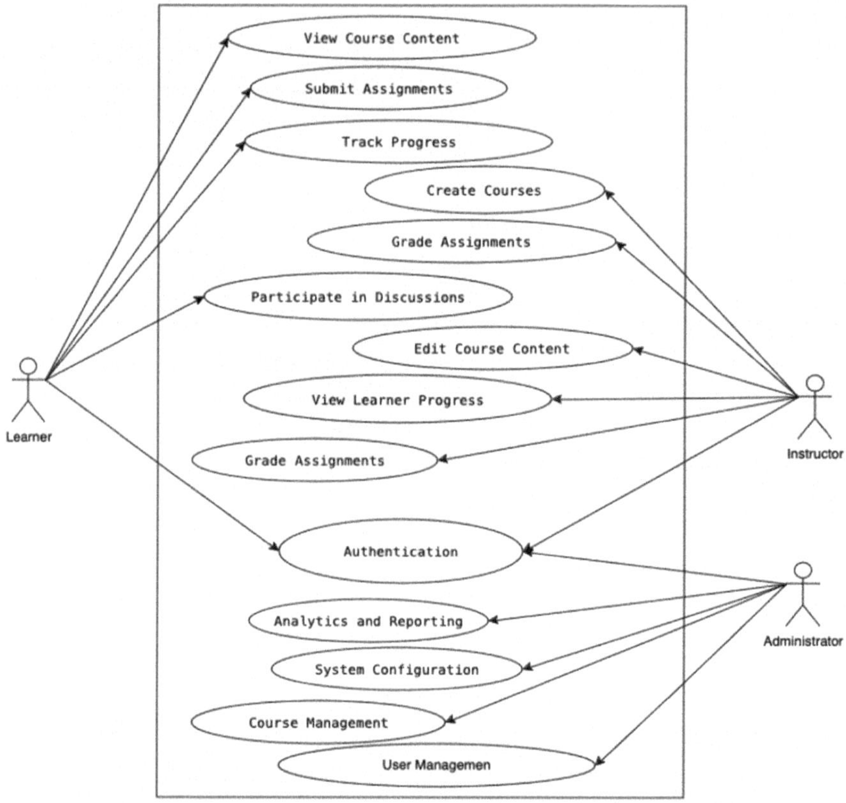

Fig. 4 Use case diagram

data flow diagram (DFD), state diagram, sequence diagram, and ER-Diagram will be utilized.

This diagram (Fig. 4) illustrates the interactions of different users with the system, starting from the authentication process and beyond. Since the actor is identified as a user, each user has the ability to carry out all the actions performed by the actor.

The workflow illustration shows how the online learning process will be carried out from the outset to the conclusion, including the assessment. Upon logging in, students will have multiple options and be required to supply different papers based on their level, as seen in Fig. 5.

3.3 Data Collection and Analysis

A precisely constructed online questionnaire was then distributed to a limited group of 55 key stakeholders closely engaged with the online learning process. We used

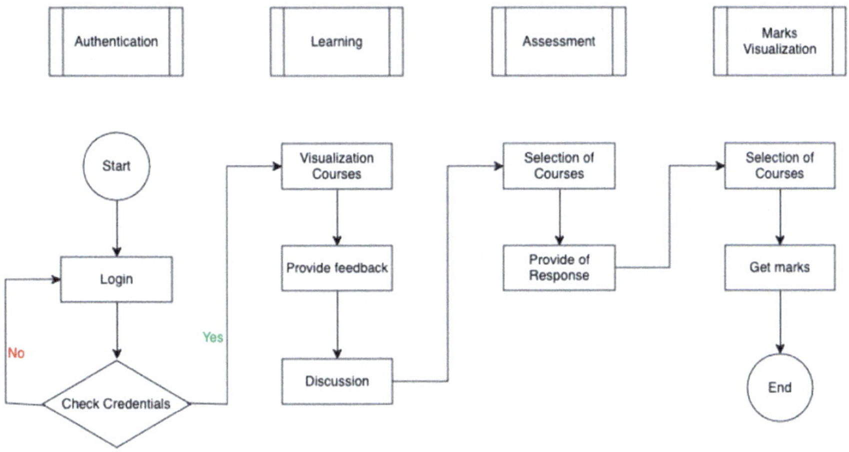

Fig. 5 System workflow diagram

an organized strategy to obtain nuanced feedback by using Google Survey forms, interviews, and focus group discussions. User interface preferences, feature priorities, and expectations from the online learning experience were all addressed by stakeholders. This information, acquired as a result of a joint effort, not only gives a comprehensive understanding of stakeholder perspectives but it also serves as the foundation for extracting essential requirements critical to the development of our system.

The purpose of this comprehensive questionnaire was to gather the various needs and perspectives of our online learning stakeholders. After that, a thorough evaluation of the data gathered led to the identification and classification of both functional and non-functional requirements, as indicated in Tables 1 and 2.

3.4 User Interface

The adopted methodology provides an easy-to-use interface designed to make the accrediting process easier for student seeking for a learning platform. To protect data, we use strong security methods such as encryption with the MD5 algorithm combined with user IDs, which ensures authentication is secure and data integrity is preserved.

To ensure data security throughout the authentication procedure, the login page leverages encryption techniques. With the user in mind, we developed it to be responsive, easily responding to different screen sizes and devices. As users begin their certification journey, the login page sets the tone for a user-friendly and secure online learning experience, emphasizing trust and ease of use.

Table 1 Functional requirements

S/N	Functional requirements	Description
1	Course creation	Our application will simplify the creation of courses by offering instructors with an easy interface for efficient management and delivery of interesting information, effortlessly satisfying varied learning demands
2	Course enrollment	Students will benefit from an easy-to-use course enrollment experience on the app. This interface will provide a smooth and intuitive experience, allowing students to easily browse available courses, enroll with a few clicks, and access their preferred learning resources. This shortened course enrollment process maintains accessibility and improves overall user happiness for app users
3	Creation of account	Users will be able to quickly set up their profiles thanks to the app's simple account setup process. Users can input information, modify preferences, and have fast access to the app's capabilities through a simple and secure interface
4	Blog	The app will contain a simple blog feature that will allow users to contribute observations, articles, and educational content
5	Authentication and registration	Users will have a safe way to complete registration and authentication tasks through the app, guaranteeing a customized and safe access to our online learning environment

Table 2 Non-functional requirements

S/N	Non-functional requirement	Description
1	Security	The system is secure, and access requires proper authentication and authorization. System data are also kept in a secure database and accessed through SSL
2	Performance	The system is relatively fast as indicated in the user acceptance testing
3	Reliability and availability	The system operates efficiently and effectively over time
5	Usability	End users can use the system with very few instructions

The system provides a specific user with specific rights to visualize the Course management' feature, which allows users to efficiently track and manage courses as shown in Fig. 6.

For students who are interested in concentrating on their well-being in the Health Center sector, the application provides a plethora of options. This area offers helpful

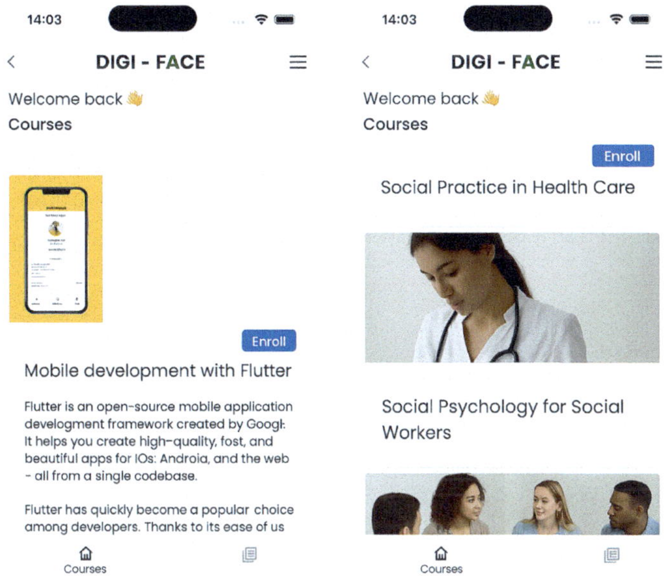

Fig. 6 The course enrollment interface

information about fitness regimens, mental wellness efforts, and health recommendations. Students can look into choices for their mental and physical health, encouraging a well-rounded approach to their academic career.

4 Results and Discussions

4.1 Results

The application validation findings demonstrate a high level of user satisfaction, with 76.4% of the sampled 55 people saying they are "very satisfied" with accessing and sharing learning resources via our mobile app. Furthermore, 12.7% said they were "satisfied," indicating a strong overall sentiment. A small 1% expressed a neutral view, highlighting the app's functionalities' overwhelmingly positive reception. These validation findings validate our app's success in satisfying user expectations and promoting a rewarding learning experience. And among the 55 people polled, a whopping 80% reported a strong capability and readiness to work with others on learning initiatives via our mobile app. Another 12.7% reported sporadic collaboration, indicating continuous participation in group learning activities. A lesser proportion of 6% reported infrequent instances of collaboration, while the remainder of participants stated that they had never participated in collaborative endeavors.

Remarkably, on a scale of 1–10, 63.6% of respondents said a straightforward user interface in our mobile learning app was very high important. Furthermore, 16.4% said it was very significant, stressing the importance of user-friendly design. Another 16.4% said it was less important. According to the majority of respondents, a straightforward interface plays a key role in user pleasure and app usage. The mobile application also greatly improves collaboration among stakeholders, according to a large majority of participants (92.7%). Less than 3% more people likely agreed, and the same portion was indifferent to such an assertion.

5 Discussion

The main objective of this study is to develop Digi-Face cross-platform mobile apps for online teaching, learning, and research to be used by all Centers of Excellence to facilitate these processes. Specifically, the study aims to identify system requirements for Digi-Face cross-platform mobile apps tailored for online teaching, learning, and research. Additionally, it seeks to develop these apps for use by African higher education communities. The Flutter framework, with its Dart programming language, has been instrumental in crafting a visually appealing and cross-platform interface. This choice of technology empowers our app with the flexibility to run seamlessly across various devices, providing users with a consistent and engaging learning experience. Flutter's prowess in creating intuitive and interactive user interfaces aligns perfectly with the 63% of users who emphasized the importance of such design features. Validation results, notably the 76.4% expressing high satisfaction in accessing and sharing learning materials, signify the successful integration of these technologies. The app's ability to meet user needs is further underscored by the collaborative aspect, with 80% of users indicating a willingness to engage in group projects. The use of advanced technologies has not only met but exceeded user expectations, creating a technologically advanced and adaptive mobile app for online learning. On a scale of 1–10, where 63% emphasized the importance of an intuitive user interface, Flutter's contribution is paramount. Its capacity to deliver a user-friendly design complements the innovative use of Moodle, PHP, and APIs, resulting in a harmonious blend of technology that resonates with users. The dual approach of using Google Form surveys and group discussions for requirement gathering aligns with best practices in user-centered design.

According to Alammary et al. [20], surveys and group discussions are effective in eliciting user needs and preferences, providing a comprehensive understanding of user expectations. This approach ensures that the app development is grounded in real user feedback, which is crucial for creating a user-centric solution. The choice of PHP and Moodle as the technological backbone is supported by the robustness and flexibility these platforms offer. Moodle, a widely used learning management system (LMS), is praised for its capability to organize educational content efficiently [3]. The integration of PHP enhances this with a responsive and intuitive user interface, crucial for an engaging user experience. Sung et al. [21] highlight that the combination of a strong LMS like Moodle and a flexible programming language like PHP can significantly improve the functionality and usability of educational platforms. APIs play a vital role in enabling real-time communication and collaborative features within the app. Real-time chat functionality, powered by APIs, enhances user engagement by facilitating dynamic discussions, which is critical in a learning environment. Research by Rezvan [22] emphasizes that real-time communication tools significantly enhance collaborative learning, supporting the effectiveness of this feature in the Digi-face app.

Again, according to research by Ziraba Godwil et al. [12], Flutter's ability to create intuitive and interactive user interfaces makes it a preferred choice for mobile app development. The study found that Flutter's cross-platform capabilities significantly enhance user experience by providing a seamless and engaging interface, which is corroborated by 63% of users who emphasized the importance of an intuitive user interface. The validation results, indicating high satisfaction levels, underscore the successful integration of these technologies. A significant 76.4% of users expressing high satisfaction in accessing and sharing learning materials highlights the effectiveness of the app's features. Research by Manyengo [23] supports this, suggesting that user satisfaction in online learning platforms is closely tied to the ease of accessing and sharing educational content. Additionally, the collaborative aspect of the app, with 80% of users willing to engage in group projects, is consistent with findings by Cavus and Uzunboylu [24], who found that collaborative tools in educational apps significantly boost user engagement and learning outcomes.

6 Conclusion and Future Works

The development of our mobile app for online learning, based on the Digi-Face platform, has significantly transformed traditional educational practices. By integrating a blend of online and offline learning resources with interactive elements, we have created an engaging and dynamic learning environment. This transformation allows students to access learning materials anytime and anywhere, fostering a flexible and personalized learning experience. Key features such as real-time collaboration, discussion forums, and multimedia content have enhanced the overall effectiveness of the learning process. The app's user-friendly interface ensures accessibility for users of varying technological proficiency, promoting inclusivity in education. Our case study revealed positive outcomes in student engagement, information retention, and overall satisfaction with the learning experience. The app's analytics provide valuable insights into user behavior, enabling educators to tailor content and interventions to meet diverse student needs. However, by giving students constant access to excellent learning resources and motivating cooperation among them, the app promotes long-term involvement and deeper understanding of educational content. Monitoring and evaluating user data help teachers to make better decisions and implement focused interventions that over time raise academic performance.

Again, the creation of our mobile app for online learning represents a significant advancement in educational practices and sets the stage for future innovations in the field. The Digi-Face platform has proven to be a cornerstone in making learning more accessible, engaging, and effective. Moving forward, it is crucial to develop a strategic approach to resource allocation, anticipate scalability needs, and invest in scalable infrastructure to accommodate a growing user base. Implementing a user-friendly feedback mechanism, collaborating with educators to adapt content to specific educational needs, providing regular training programs, and emphasizing data security will further enhance the app's adaptability, user experience, and trustworthiness.

Acknowledgements The authors would like to acknowledge the Nelson Mandela African Institution of Science of Technology (NM-AIST) for providing facilities and a conducive environment that helped to complete the project successfully.

References

1. I. Damyanov and N. Tsankov, "Mobile apps in daily learning activities," *International Journal of Interactive Mobile Technologies*, vol. 12, no. 6, pp. 133–140, 2018, https://doi.org/10.3991/IJIM.V12I6.9659.
2. A. Efendi and T. S. Qodr, "Improving critical thinking skills of high school students through the implementation of mobile-based game applications," *International Journal of Education and Practice*, vol. 11, no. 3, pp. 613–626, Apr. 2023, https://doi.org/10.18488/61.V11I3.3440.
3. T. H. Morris, "Self-directed learning: A fundamental competence in a rapidly changing world," *International Review of Education*, vol. 65, no. 4, pp. 633–653, Aug. 2019, https://doi.org/10.1007/S11159-019-09793-2/METRICS.
4. X. Zhang and M. Zhou, "Information and digital technology-assisted interventions to improve intercultural competence: A meta-analytical review," *Comput Educ*, vol. 194, p. 104697, Mar. 2023, https://doi.org/10.1016/J.COMPEDU.2022.104697.
5. C. Glahn, M. R. Gruber, and O. Tartakovski, "Beyond Delivery Modes and Apps: A Case Study on Mobile Blended Learning in Higher Education," 2011.
6. Dario Antonelli *et al.*, "A Virtual Reality Laboratory for Blended Learning Education: Design, Implementation and Evaluation," *MDPI*, 2023.
7. J. Machii, J. Murumba, and E. Micheni, *Predictive Analytics and Artificial Intelligence in Blended Learning: A New Dawn for Institutions of Higher Learning*. 2021. [Online]. Available: https://www.researchgate.net/publication/355819835.
8. R. Shemahonge and J. S. Mtebe, "Using a mobile application to support students in blended distance courses: A case of Mzumbe University in Tanzania," 2018.
9. R. Kaliisa and M. Picard, "A Systematic Review on Mobile Learning in Higher Education: The African Perspective," 2017.
10. R. Fisher, Á. Perényi, and N. Birdthistle, "The positive relationship between flipped and blended learning and student engagement, performance and satisfaction," vol. 22, no. 2, pp. 97–113, Oct. 2018, https://doi.org/10.1177/1469787418801702.
11. Y. T. Sung, J. M. Yang, and H. Y. Lee, "The Effects of Mobile-Computer-Supported Collaborative Learning: Meta-Analysis and Critical Synthesis," *Rev Educ Res*, vol. 87, no. 4, pp. 768–805, Aug. 2017, https://doi.org/10.3102/0034654317704307.
12. Ziraba Godwill, Abdallah, G. Chenyuei Akwene, A. nee Alemanjoh Mariana Nkea, and S. Charles Lwanga, "The Adoption and Use of Moodle Learning Management System in Higher Institutions of Learning: A Systematic Literature Review," Online, 2020. [Online]. Available: http://www.ajpojournals.org.

13. RD Balaji, Fatma Ali Al-Mahri, and Malathi Balaji, "A Perspective Study on Content Management in E-Learning and M-Learning," 2020.
14. A. W. Muzaffar, M. Tahir, M. W. Anwar, Q. Chaudry, S. R. Mir, and Y. Rasheed, "A systematic review of online exams solutions in e-learning: Techniques, tools, and global adoption," 2021, *Institute of Electrical and Electronics Engineers Inc.* https://doi.org/10.1109/ACCESS.2021.3060192.
15. Ş. T. Pektaş and M. Ö. Gürel, "Blended learning in design education: An analysis of students' experiences within the disciplinary differences framework," *Australasian Journal of Educational Technology*, vol. 30, no. 1, pp. 31–44, 2014, https://doi.org/10.14742/ajet.372.
16. M. S. Goundar and B. A. Kumar, "The use of mobile learning applications in higher education institutes," *Educ Inf Technol (Dordr)*, vol. 27, no. 1, pp. 1213–1236, Jan. 2022, https://doi.org/10.1007/s10639-021-10611-2.
17. S. B. Dias and J. Bidarra, "A/B/C-TEACH Framework: The Application of AI in Blended Learning," 2020. [Online]. Available: https://www.researchgate.net/publication/341043925.
18. M. Arsenovic, M. Karanovic, S. Sladojevic, A. Anderla, and D. Stefanovic, "Solving Current Limitations of Deep Learning Based Approaches for Plant Disease Detection," *Symmetry 2019, Vol. 11, Page 939*, vol. 11, no. 7, p. 939, Jul. 2019, https://doi.org/10.3390/SYM11070939.
19. D. Mathew Lashayo and M. Gapar Md Johar, "A REVIEW OF E-LEARNING SYSTEMS' ADOPTION IN TANZANIA UNIVERSITIES," *South East Asia Journal of Contemporary Business, Economics and Law*, vol. 13, no. 2, 2017.
20. A. Alammary, J. Sheard, and A. Carbone, "Blended learning in higher education: Three different design approaches," *Australasian Journal of Educational Technology*, vol. 30, no. 4, pp. 440–454, 2014, https://doi.org/10.14742/ajet.693.
21. Y. T. Sung, K. E. Chang, and T. C. Liu, "The effects of integrating mobile devices with teaching and learning on students' learning performance: A meta-analysis and research synthesis," *Comput Educ*, vol. 94, pp. 252–275, Mar. 2016, https://doi.org/10.1016/j.compedu.2015.11.008.
22. Rezvan Nazempour and Houshang Darabi, "Personalized Learning in Virtual Learning Environments Using Students' Behavior Analysis," 2023.
23. P. R. Manyengo and P. Renatus Manyengo, "Background report Digitalization in teaching and education in the United Republic of Tanzania Digitalization," 2021. [Online]. Available: www.ilo.org/publns.
24. N. Cavus and H. Uzunboylu, "Improving critical thinking skills in mobile learning," *Procedia Soc Behav Sci*, vol. 1, no. 1, pp. 434–438, 2009, https://doi.org/10.1016/j.sbspro.2009.01.078.

A Data-Driven Web-Based System for Regional Program Accreditation: The Case of Inter-University Council for East Africa (IUCEA)

Carmel Nkeshimana, Ben Ruhinda, Devotha G. Nyambo, and Shubi F. Kaijage

Abstract In response to the evolving landscape of regional program accreditation, we undertook the development of a user-centric Regional Program Accreditation System (RPAS). This system was meticulously designed to cater to the diverse needs of accreditation bodies, educational institutions, and expert reviewers within the East African Region. Our journey commenced with an extensive requirement-gathering phase, engaging end-users to shape the system's design and functionality. The RPAS was built using cutting-edge technologies, including ReactJs, Django, API integration, Tailwind CSS, and MySQL, ensuring scalability, security, and flexibility. Agile methodologies, particularly Extreme Programming, were used, enabling expedited development and fostering close collaboration, ensuring adaptability to users' evolving needs. The RPAS streamlines the accreditation process with a user-friendly interface and real-time collaboration features, thereby enhancing transparency and operational efficiency. Robust authentication mechanisms were implemented to ensure data security. Additional user-friendly features, such as night mode, QR code-based certificate verification, and automated notifications, were introduced for convenience. In the future, RPAS can be enhanced by implementing Machine

C. Nkeshimana (✉) · D. G. Nyambo · S. F. Kaijage
Computational and Communication Science and Engineering (CoCSE), The Nelson Mandela African Institution of Science and Technology (NM-AIST), Arusha, Tanzania
e-mail: carmelnkeshimana2020@gmail.com

D. G. Nyambo
e-mail: devotha.nyambo@nm-aist.ac.tz

S. F. Kaijage
e-mail: shubi.kaijage@nm-aist.ac.tz

B. Ruhinda
Inter-University Council for East Africa, Kampala, Uganda
e-mail: bruhinda@iucea.org

J. Marx Gómez et al. (eds.), *Advancement in Embedded and Mobile Systems*, Progress in IS, https://doi.org/10.1007/978-3-031-99219-3_2

Learning for Document Content Analysis, enhancing Reporting and Analytics Capabilities, and establishing Automated Reminders and Notifications. These enhancements will further empower RPAS, making it a valuable tool for streamlining accreditation processes and contributing to the elevation of program quality and educational excellence in the region.

Keywords Process automation · Regional accreditation · Data-driven · Programme accreditation

1 Introduction and Background

External Quality Assurance (EQA) is a phenomenon that has received widespread attention by higher education institutions (HEIs) worldwide. In order to ensure that the education offered by HEIs meets labour market requirements, many countries have established national higher education commissions and councils to regulate the provision of higher education in their respective countries. Accreditation of programmes is universally accepted as a means of quality assurance. Thus, as it is the case elsewhere across the globe, in the East African Community (EAC) region, it is a best practice that before a programme is offered, it must be accredited by the respective National Commission/Council or any other accrediting body using prescribed quality assurance standards and guidelines. The benefits of accreditation are widely known and may include, but not be limited to advancing standards, enhancing excellence, good reputation building, creating public accountability, safeguarding the interests of higher education stakeholders, acceptability of credits transfers, acceptability of qualifications by employers and other higher education stakeholders and increasing the possibility for securing support from funding agencies.

In recognition of the importance of enhancing the mobility of students [1] and labour by enhancing recognition of qualifications [2], several initiatives have been undertaken at the East African level. For example, under Article 102 of the EAC Treaty, Partner States agreed to coordinate their human resources development policies and programmes and also to harmonize curricula, examination, certification, and accreditation of education and training institutions through the joint action of their relevant national bodies. Equally, they agreed to exchange information and experience on issues common to their educational systems, from which they would collaborate in establishing appropriate education and training programs. To facilitate these processes, IUCEA was re-established as an EAC Institution in accordance with Article 102 (2) (f) and mandated to play a coordinative and oversight role in the Community for the enhancement of education quality and sustainable development of higher education systems and research for purposes of supporting the region's socio-economic development and regional integration [3]. The establishment of the EAC Common Market Protocol (EACMP) in 2010 and the declaration of the EAC as a Common Higher Education Area in 2017 expanded the mandate of IUCEA to provide for among other things, harmonized quality assurance and accreditations systems that would allow comparability, compatibility and synchronization of higher education and training systems, and the qualifications attained to facilitate mobility of learners and labour [3]

Over the past several decades, there has been an increasing trend for HEIs to seek international reputation by subjecting their programs and institutions to accreditation by non-national accrediting agencies. Examples of this include non-USA business schools that have obtained accreditation from the US Association to Advance Collegiate Schools of Business (AACSB), and business schools from a range of countries that have sought accreditation under the EQUIS scheme in Europe or from the Association of MBAs in the UK [3].

In a variety of scenarios, data management is frequently supported by information systems. Sifiullin et al. have made an important contribution to this subject by providing an effective data management solution that is accessible from anywhere, addressing the changing needs of current research contexts. Sifiullin et al. showed how researchers have been hard at work on a variety of novel ways to create energy-efficient servers with intelligent designs. These structures are optimized for power consumption during operation and are accompanied with real-time energy consumption monitoring, which is crucial in today's technologically driven environment [4]. There is also an agency in Germany's higher education system AQAS (Agency for Quality Assurance by Accreditation of Study Programs) that aims to guarantee the calibre of educational programs and establishments, AQAS carefully develops and executes accrediting procedures. The agency determines whether study programs meet defined requirements and criteria utilizing methodical reviews. In addition to evaluating specific programs, AQAS also does institutional assessments, which encourages higher education institutions to be dedicated to ongoing improvement [5].

In the EAC region, there is currently no regional accreditation management system. Accreditation is done by National Commissions/Councils for higher education at the national level. However, some potential international funding agencies of higher education (e.g. World Bank, KFW, GIZ, DAAD) request evidence of regional/international accreditation as one of the requirements in their funding protocols [3]. A practical and most recent example is of programs from 24 Centers of Excellence that are hosted by 16 universities in eight countries namely Ethiopia, Kenya, Malawi, Mozambique, Rwanda, Tanzania, Uganda, and Zambia. These centres were required by the funding agencies to have international accreditation as one of the disbursement-linked indicators. The absence of regional accreditation in the EAC region has necessitated some HEIs to consider seeking international accreditation from agencies in developed countries, which have well-established and recognized quality assurance systems. In many cases, the programs are subjected to tools available in the region and evaluated by experts such as the ones that are already in the region and for astronomically high prices.

It is against the above background, that the Inter-University Council for East Africa (IUCEA) considered it necessary and beneficial to establish a regional accreditation system that would provide appropriate mechanisms to guide the accreditation process of programs at the EAC regional level. Therefore, this paper presents the development of a data-driven accreditation management system for the Inter-University Council for East Africa with the main goal of automating the existing process, reduces feedback loops, and minimizes paperwork for higher efficiency and expert use within and outside of the region.

1.1 Objectives

In the scope of the Inter-University Council for East Africa (IUCEA), the main goal of this project is to develop a customized, data-driven web application for regional program accreditation. It aims to accomplish each of these particular objectives. First and foremost, it seeks to methodically determine and specify the requirements for creating the application in compliance with IUCEA criteria. The project then concentrates on creating, developing, and implementing a strong system that perfectly satisfies the particular needs of regional program accreditation. Afterwards, there is an obligation to thoroughly verify the effectiveness, functionality, and performance of the program. The application's compliance with the necessary standards and smooth alignment with the unique requirements of the IUCEA's certification procedures are guaranteed by the validation process. These goals, which centre on the conception, development, and validation of a data-driven online application for regional program accreditation at IUCEA, essentially serve as the project's foundation.

2 Related Works

2.1 Accreditation in Education

Accreditation is a formal process that recognizes an organization or program for satisfying set quality requirements. Accrediting authorities conduct rigorous evaluations to guarantee conformity with particular standards [6]. And when we talk about regional programme accreditation, we refer to the process of reviewing and acknowledging the quality and efficacy of educational programs within a specified geographic region. It entails analysing programs against predetermined standards and criteria to ensure they fulfil established excellence benchmarks [3].

In the grand tapestry of our evolving society, the role of higher education shines as a beacon of transformation. It's a journey that begins with the recognition that education possesses the power to elevate individuals from mere beings to invaluable human resources. This journey is not solitary; it intersects with the dynamic forces of technology, accreditation systems, and the changing paradigms of education [7].

As we navigate the labyrinth of modernity, we encounter automation, a technological titan reshaping industry. Developers of automation platforms [8] invest significantly in cloud computing infrastructure, forming strategic alliances with Enterprise

Resource Planning Systems (ERPSs). Guruge and Kadel take us on this quest, highlighting how automation's embrace has catalyzed the evolution of ERPs and its influence on sustainability accounting and reporting within higher education. Here, the story intertwines technology and education, showing us the importance of data management and reporting for academic progress [9].

Every journey encounters crossroads and debates, and so does higher education. Andreani et al. offer us an intriguing twist. They introduce the possibility of reforming accreditation systems, spotlight criticisms of accreditation systems, possibly validating the need for change, and act as a compass, guiding us to identify and rectify flaws within these systems. This subplot underscores the essential role of quality assurance mechanisms in higher education [10].

As the plot thickens, we come face to face with a villain—contract cheating. Guruge and Kadel propose a comprehensive framework to combat this menace within academic institutions. Their plan hinges on three key principles: awareness, monitoring, and evaluation. This narrative exposes the dark side of academia, where contract cheating thrives in the shadows, and calls for the heroes of education to step forward. It reveals the necessity for proactive measures in safeguarding academic integrity [9].

The story then shifts its focus to a different locale—Taiwan. Yahn-Shir et al. unveil the empirical impact of higher education policies on the establishment of institutes and graduate schools. Here, the tale underscores the ripple effect of education policies, showing how they impact professional organizations and audit firms' performance. The narrative weaves together the strands of policy, economics, and education, highlighting the intricate dance of societal and economic forces [10].

As the story unfolds, we delve into the digital age. Chakroun leads us through the transformative effects of digitalization on various professions and education systems. His narrative advocates for equipping TVET teachers with professional development opportunities to adapt to evolving demands, offering a glimpse into the ever-shifting landscape of education in the digital era [11].

Now, we approach a climax. Romanowski brings into focus the role of accreditation, casting it as a potentially neocolonialist tool. The research suggests that accreditation processes can impose specific understandings of teacher education, affecting non-US teacher education programs and shaping the landscape of higher education. Here, we confront the tension between global standardization and localized educational practices [12].

Nazemi et al. have reached a crossroads in their effort to comprehend the broad narrative of higher education's impact on social, economic, cultural, scientific, and political growth. It's a time when everyone needs to work together. We are on the verge of harmonizing educational approaches, curriculum designs, scientific issues, and learning outcomes. This coherence allows for meaningful comparisons of study programs and institutions across European higher education. It's the point at which the strands of technology, accreditation, ethics, politics, and globalization all come together [13].

This tale reminds us that higher education is not just a chapter in our history; it's an ongoing story, with each research endeavour adding a new layer to its rich narrative.

The plot may twist and turn, but the essence remains—education as a catalyst for development, ever-evolving to meet the challenges of the times [14].

In conclusion, the narrative of higher education's role in our society unfolds through the lens of technology, ethics, policy, and globalization [10]. Each research contribution enriches the storyline, emphasizing the intricate interplay between education and societal transformation. As we journey through this narrative, we recognize the need to harmonize methodologies and outcomes, fostering a shared understanding among European higher education institutions and beyond. Thus, the story of higher education continues, an ever-evolving saga of progress and development.

2.2 *Technology in Accreditation*

In today's world, data are like a treasure chest waiting to be unlocked. It's not just numbers and facts; it's a powerful tool that can guide us in making crucial decisions in various fields. This valuable resource has the potential to revolutionize the way we operate, making it as essential as oil in the future [15].

Dew and their team recognized the significance of data when it comes to managing complex processes. They developed a web-based solution that streamlines the engineering accreditation process. This system brings together everything—curriculum analysis, course and instructor management, program information collection, report generation, and tracking graduation quality. It's a perfect example of how data-driven systems can simplify complex procedures [16].

Dalal Nikunj and his colleagues delved into the concept of practical wisdom, realizing that simplicity can be a powerful tool. They created a wisdom nexus framework with a smart simplification strategy, breaking it down into key components. This framework provides clarity and enables a deep understanding of complex situations through a wisdom lens. Their approach demonstrates the strength of simplifying complex concepts [17].

Moving on, Mark and his team explored the connection between blockchain technology and information systems. They took a close look at the history of blockchain and its relationship with information systems. By doing so, they shed light on how information systems can benefit from blockchain technology, demonstrating how a technological shift can bring new perspectives to well-established systems [18].

Dobslaw and his team tackled a practical challenge—evaluating the Return on Investment (ROI) of integrating automated graphical user interface testing into software projects. They introduced a stepwise replay approach, simplifying the process by breaking it down into clear steps. This method allows for a precise calculation of ROI, making it easier for developers and testers to assess the impact of their work [19].

Mayr-Dorn and their team presented a strategy to streamline the adherence to quality constraints in development activities. Their approach simplifies the process by separating quality assurance limitations from the development process. This separation enables engineers to focus on their work while receiving alerts about unmet quality constraints. It's a practical way to simplify the complex task of maintaining quality in development activities [20].

These studies show us how simplification and the effective use of data can lead to more efficient processes and better decision-making [15]. In the context of our research on a data-driven web-based system for regional program accreditation, they offer valuable insights into how simplicity and data can transform the landscape of accreditation systems, making them more effective and user-friendly.

2.3 Data-Driven Solutions

In our journey to develop a data-driven web-based system for regional program accreditation, several gaps and opportunities arise.

Mayr-Dorn and their colleagues emphasize the need of evaluating real effort reduction to evaluate the impact of our' prototype. They stress the need to investigate how frequently engineers might profit from our system. This study reveals a key gap in comprehending the practical decrease in effort and prospective areas for future improvements [20].

On another front, Susetyo and colleagues offered insight on the National Accreditation Board for Schools/Madrasah's move from compliance-based certification to performance-based certification. This transformation represents a substantial shift in the accrediting procedure. The hiring of assessors based on personality and cognitive ability demonstrates the necessity for a system that supports this new approach. As a result, their system was designed to serve primary and secondary schools in Indonesia [21].

Dew and the team's research reveal an important gap in user authentication and system administration. While they discuss the use of usernames and passwords for authentication, the absence of a way to change passwords or access user logs presents a notable limitation. System administrators currently hold the authority to decide how user login information is utilized, highlighting the potential for improvements in user management within our system [16].

Lvovich and their team offer future directions, proposing to investigate AGT test suites for systems with frequent GUI changes. This research is in alignment with our goals of efficiency and robustness. By identifying bugs early on and improving AGT frameworks, the value proposition of such systems can be strengthened. This research points to the need for technology that can adapt to changing environments and challenges, a core concept in our pursuit of an adaptable accreditation system [22].

Furthermore, to complete the accreditation procedure, documents must be filled out and essential documentation must be provided physically. Members of the IUCEA committee begin the accreditation process, which, as proven by Dew et al., requires

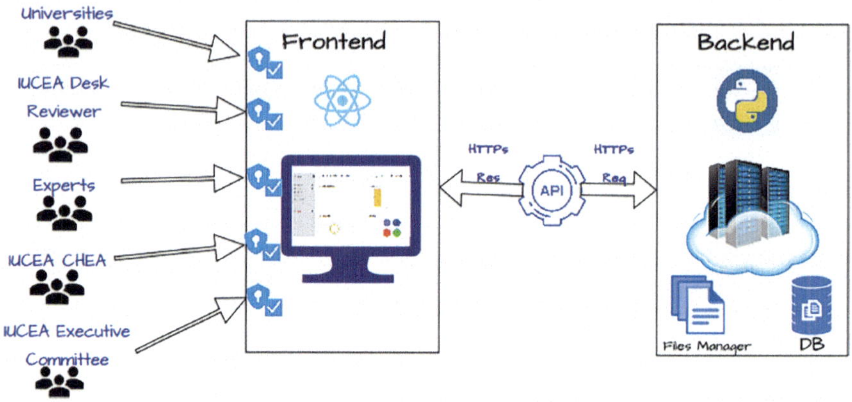

Fig. 1 The proposed solution

extensive information collecting, organization, and analysis, all of which takes time [16].

The proposed solution, illustrated in Fig. 1, is a comprehensive data-driven accreditation management system designed for the Inter-University Council for East Africa (IUCEA). This system aims to automate the accreditation process, thereby enhancing efficiency, reducing paperwork, and streamlining feedback mechanisms. Key features include real-time data access, integration of quality assurance standards, and robust reporting capabilities.

3 Materials and Methods

3.1 System Architecture

A data-driven web application for regional programme accreditation is developed using an agile software development approach. The Agile approach promotes continuous development and testing throughout the software development process as well as ongoing engagement with stakeholders at every level, making it a flexible system development technique. As shown in Fig. 2, agile is a technique for software development that emphasizes iterative, flexible, and collaborative approaches. It entails breaking tasks down into little, digestible chunks and doing frequent testing and feedback loops.

The research adheres to the Extreme Programming (XP) Agile methodology paradigm from requirement collecting to system development and testing. It utilizes to hasten the delivery of the system within the allotted time range. By offering a high-quality system at lower development costs than other conventional methodologies, it emphasizes a very quick development cycle. It places an importance on collaboration,

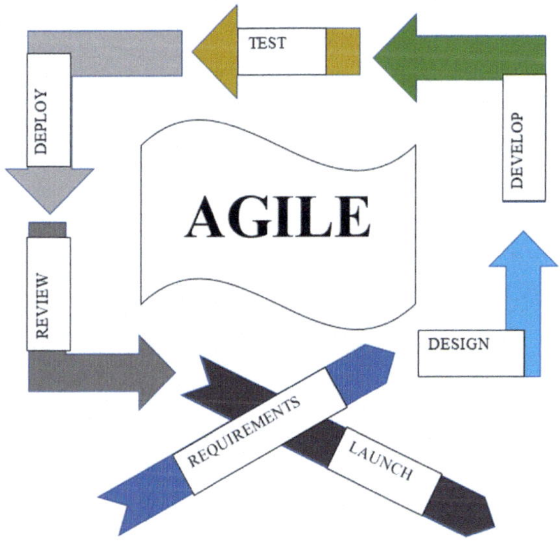

Fig. 2 Agile methodology diagram

feedback, and customer focus. It also emphasizes high-quality software development approaches such as continuous integration, test-driven development (TDD), and pair programming as described by Fig. 3.

Based on the rules and artefacts of the Unified Modeling Language (UML), graphical languages are used to examine the acquired system requirements. StarUML, a UML diagram modelling tool, is used for system modelling. It is used for the user

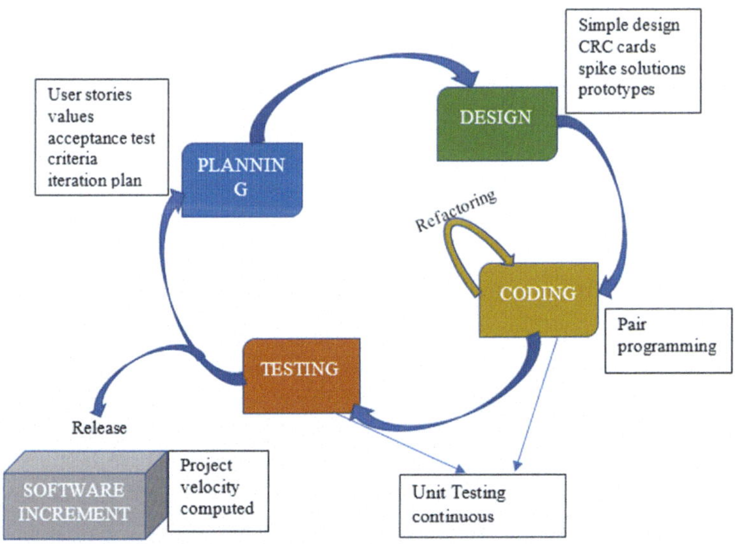

Fig. 3 Agile framework extreme programming

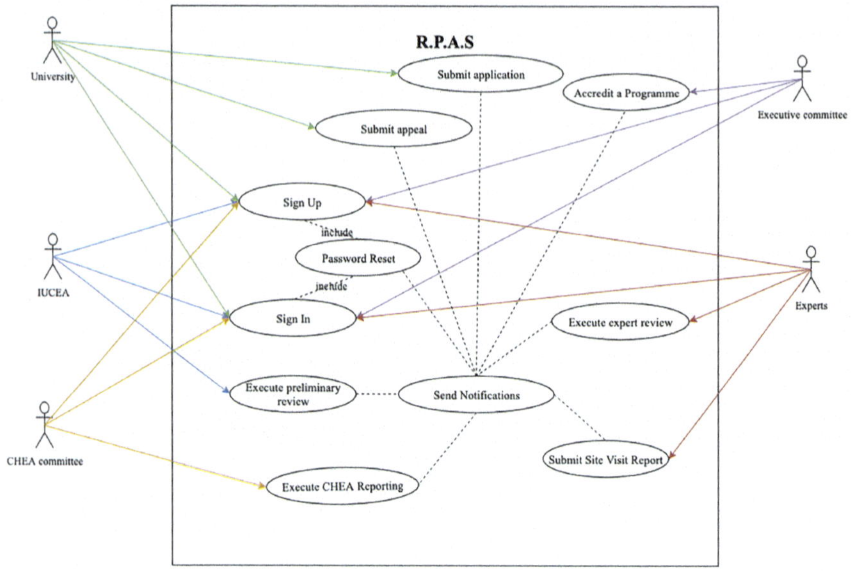

Fig. 4 Use case diagram

case diagram, class diagram, data flow diagram (DFD), state diagram, sequence diagram, and ER-Diagram in order to map the gathered requirements into each of these diagrams (Fig. 4).

This diagram depicts how various users interact with the system, beginning with authentication and others. Because the actor was designated as a user, each user is able to execute all the acts performed by the actor user.

The workflow diagram illustrates how, from the beginning of the accreditation process, documents and information are transferred between different system operations. As illustrated in Fig. 5, when the institution submits its documents for accreditation or appeal, the process proceeds, and the system delivers feedback by email and system notifications.

3.2 Data Collection and Analysis

A precisely constructed online questionnaire was then distributed to a limited group of six key stakeholders closely engaged with the regional accreditation process. The questionnaire included a mix of closed and open-ended questions that were methodically constructed to obtain valuable primary data. This information is critical in directing the continuing development and enhancement of our Regional

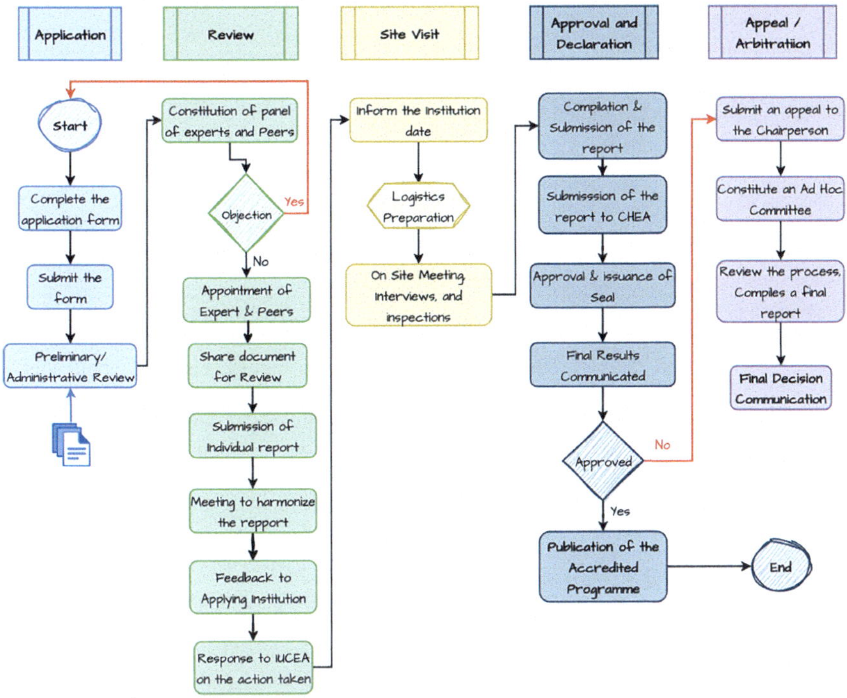

Fig. 5 System workflow diagram

Programme Accreditation System (RPAS), which ensures that the system is deliberately customized to the unique needs and objectives of our regional educational landscape.

This extensive questionnaire was created with the goal of capturing the different requirements and insights of our regional accreditation stakeholders. Following that, the collected data were carefully evaluated, resulting in the identification and categorization of both functional and non-functional requirements, as shown in Tables 1 and 2. These requirements serve as the foundation for the RPAS, ensuring that it effortlessly matches the expectations of our regional certification process.

3.3 User Interface

The adopted methodology provides an easy-to-use interface designed to make the accrediting process easier for higher institutions seeking program accreditation. The user-friendly 'Regional Programme Accreditation Portal' makes it simple for universities to handle submissions and track progress. To protect data, we use strong security methods such as encryption with the MD5 algorithm combined with user IDs, which

Table 1 Functional requirements

S/N	Functional requirements	Description
1	Submission of accreditation documents (application)	The system should be able to offer institutions a secure, user-friendly platform for uploading crucial accreditation-related documents, streamlining processes, and enhancing efficiency By ensuring that accrediting bodies have real-time access to structured document repositories, it simplifies evaluations and promotes transparency
2	Preliminary review and report	Within the RPAS, the system designed for the IUCEA Quality Assurance (QA) board provides a secure, user-friendly gateway for examining university submissions. It allows for real-time access to structured documents, speeding reviews and facilitating the development of complete preliminary reports, all of which improves transparency and decision-making
3	Expert review	The system allows multiple assessors access to provide expertise and deliver marks on various criteria to an application that was created and assigned to them
4	Site inspection	The system allows experts to be allocated to site visits and also provides an interface for them to submit their point of view after visiting the institution and marking certain criteria, after which it compiles a report
5	Common higher education area report submission	The system gives an interface for the CHEA Committee to login and visualize various submissions already made on the application, as well as send a report on to the executive committee for approval
6	Executive committee report	The system gives an interface for the Executive Committee to sign and visualize various submissions already made on the application, and also as well as send a provide an accreditation to the application or deferred it
7	User management	The system provides a login and registration interface for many types of users, including experts, universities, and others In the event that a password is lost, the system provides a password reset interface The system assists administrators in disabling accounts or granting further access to accounts
8	Notifications	The system promptly sends email notifications to the appropriate recipients following each important action taken

ensures authentication is secure and data integrity is preserved. This unified strategy improves both user experience and sensitive information protection, establishing a trusting and efficient environment for program certification in the region.

To ensure data security throughout the authentication procedure, the login page leverages encryption techniques. With the user in mind, we developed it to be responsive, easily responding to different screen sizes and devices. As users begin their

Table 2 Non-functional requirements

S/N	Non-functional requirement	Description
1	Security	The system is secure, and access requires proper authentication and authorization. System data are also kept in a secure database and accessed through SSL
2	Performance	The system is relatively fast as indicated in the user acceptance testing
3	Reliability and availability	The system operates efficiently and effectively over time
4	Usability	End users can use the system with very few instructions
5	Standards	The system complies with the IUCEA organization standards

certification journey, the login page sets the tone for a user-friendly and secure accreditation experience, emphasizing trust and ease of use.

The system has also a password reset interface that allows users to recover access to their accounts or change their passwords in a convenient and safe manner. Users simply input their registered email address in the event of a forgotten password or the need for a change. Following submission, they receive an email with a unique password reset link. This link allows users to securely reset their password, maintaining the security of their account information. This simple procedure encourages accessibility and data security, allowing users to handle their account credentials with simplicity and trust. And a link is sent to your email, and a reset password page is launched, where you enter your password and confirm it. Additionally, the system offers a dashboard that displays the overall number of certification applications, providing a quick overview of system activity. This holistic perspective improves decision-making and supports transparency, ensuring users remain informed and efficient in their jobs throughout the certification process. Also it can be customized in dark mode any time when the user wishes to do it.

The system provides to a specific user with specific rights to visualize the 'List Application' feature which allows users to efficiently track and manage applications, with each application displaying unique statuses such as 'Pending,' 'Preliminary Review Done,' 'Validation Review Pending for Preliminary Review,' 'Expert Review Submission,' 'Under Site Visit,' and 'Submitted to CHEA Committee.' This user-friendly page offers a centralized perspective of the certification process, encouraging transparency and informed decision-making (Fig. 6).

The Accreditation Certificate is a symbol of accomplishment within our accreditation system, representing the pinnacle of academic excellence. Each certificate attests to approved institutions' and programs' passion and commitment. The certificate includes a QR code to strengthen its legitimacy and authentication, allowing for rapid and easy verification.

The certificate carries the weight of authority, with signatures from major stakeholders such as the chairperson of the executive committee board. These signatures represent the accreditation program's collective acceptance and acknowledgement of its excellence and adherence to criteria. Our Accreditation Certificate, with its QR

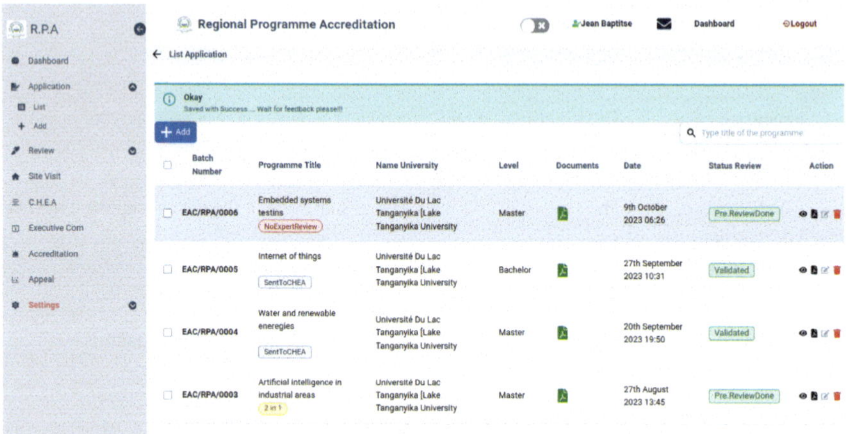

Fig. 6 The list of application after second review

code and signature, stands as a mark of confidence, transparency, and the region's unwavering dedication to academic excellence.

4 Results and Discussions

4.1 Results

The system underwent a comprehensive acceptance and validation process at IUCEA to ensure its seamless functionality and effectiveness in regional program accreditation. Utilizing a Google Form survey, we systematically evaluated the system's performance and usability, aligning it with the real-world needs and expectations of our end-users. The participants, comprising stakeholders and end-users, unanimously agreed that the system met the organization's specific needs and expectations, with 66.7% expressing high satisfaction, 16.7% indicating somewhat satisfied, and 16.7% indicating somewhat dissatisfied.

Remarkably, five out of six users rated the system as highly successful and user-friendly, highlighting its effectiveness and negating any apparent areas for improvement. However, one participant raised legitimate concerns about the system's pace and performance. The system's alignment with the organization was affirmed by the majority, with three out of six participants stating it aligns 'very well' and three agreeing that it aligns 'well.' This consensus reinforces the system's appropriateness for the organization's demands, enhancing operational efficiency and contributing to the achievement of objectives.

The system significantly enhances collaboration among stakeholders, as reported by 66.7% of participants, with an additional 33.3% agreeing with this statement. This broad agreement underscores the system's efficacy in promoting smooth communication and cooperation. Impressively, 83.3% of participants expressed a strong likelihood of recommending the system to other schools undergoing accreditation processes, indicating its potential to serve a broader community.

In terms of responsiveness and processing speed, a substantial proportion, 66.7%, expressed satisfaction with the system's performance, while 33.3% claimed it performs 'very well.' This strong agreement emphasizes the system's efficiency in delivering quick and responsive interactions, crucial for a seamless certification process. A notable outcome is the unanimous 100% agreement among participants regarding having appropriate training and support for using the system, reflecting our commitment to user education and empowerment.

Half of the respondents, 50%, acknowledged that the system significantly contributed to expediting the certification process, eliminating the need for manual labour. The remaining 50% acknowledged the system's positive impact but indicated that its significance might not have been as pronounced. In terms of functionality, 83.3% of participants expressed confidence in the system, attesting to its smooth alignment with accreditation standards. However, 16.7% made valid observations about areas where compliance gaps or adjustments may exist, highlighting the need for ongoing refinement to address potential challenges.

4.2 Discussion

The development of our regional program accreditation system stemmed from a robust understanding of user needs and requirements gathered during the early stages, aligning with Mayr-Dorn and colleagues' emphasis on evaluating real effort reduction in system impact assessment [20]. Our staff, comprising various stakeholders, expressed a strong interest in digitalizing the regional accreditation process, with 83.3% emphasizing the need for a system meeting accreditation requirement effectively. Reflecting on the limitations of the existing paper-based system, 66.7% noted minor compliance gaps, and 33.3% identified more significant compliance issues. This observation underscores the necessity for a system that streamlines processes and facilitates timely interactions, resonating with Dew and the team's insight on the challenges of information collecting, organization, and analysis in accreditation processes [16].

Our design and development approach, utilizing ReactJs, Django, Tailwind CSS, and MySQL database, reflects best practices for scalability and interoperability, as highlighted by Lvovich and the team's call for systems with frequent GUI changes and the need for technology adaptable to evolving challenges [22]. The integration of Djoser library for data security aligns with Dew and the team's identification of gaps in user authentication and system administration [16].

In response to our staff's preferences, our system incorporates features such as a night mode switch, QR code-based certificate verification, as shown in Fig. 7 and

Fig. 7 The certificate overview

email notifications at various stages, ensuring user-friendly functionality and real-time collaboration, in line with insights from related works, including Susetyo and team's transformation from compliance to performance-based certification [21]. The consideration of user guidelines and manuals, preferred by 83.3% of our staff, echoes Dew and team's identification of a limitation in user management and authentication [16]. Additionally, our system offers a comprehensive solution to document management, reporting, and insightful dashboards, addressing the needs expressed by our staff and supporting the quest for systems that simplify adherence to quality constraints in development activities, as proposed by Mayr-Dorn and team [20].

The related works highlight various challenges and innovative solutions within the realm of information systems and technology. Mark and team's exploration of blockchain technology underscores the potential for technological shifts to bring new perspectives to established systems [18]. Dobslaw and team's practical approach to evaluating Return on Investment (ROI) in automated graphical user interface testing aligns with our focus on efficiency and impact assessment [19]. The regional program accreditation system is not only aligned with the specific needs and preferences of our end-users but also draws inspiration from related works to deliver a comprehensive, user-centric, and technologically advanced solution that addresses the challenges highlighted in the existing literature on accreditation systems and technology integration.

5 Conclusion and Future Works

The road to develop the regional program accreditation system has been guided by the critical input of our end-users. Their requirements and preferences served as the foundation for developing a strong, secure, and user-friendly solution. The technology improves collaboration, transparency, and data management while also streamlining the certification process. The incorporation of cutting-edge technologies such as ReactJs, Django, API, Tailwind CSS, MySQL, and Djoser has enabled us to build a dynamic and adaptable platform that satisfies the diverse needs of certifying organizations, institutions, and specialists alike. Furthermore, the addition of real-time notifications, certificate verification, and a night mode option indicates our dedication to providing a comprehensive solution that answers our consumers' unique difficulties.

We continue to refine and expand our accreditation system in response to ongoing user feedback and emerging best practices in the sector. Our goal is to continue promoting educational quality in the region by providing accreditation organizations and institutions with a tool that not only fits their immediate demands but also adapts to meet future difficulties. This approach, we feel, plays a critical role in improving program quality, fostering openness, and streamlining the accrediting process, ultimately contributing to the growth of education in our region.

We actively seek ways to improve the user experience, strengthen security measures, and optimize system performance in the spirit of continuous improvement. Our commitment to training, support, and comprehensive documentation ensures that end users can fully utilize the system's capabilities. We envision a future in which certification processes are more efficient, accessible, and data-driven, eventually enhancing our region's educational landscape.

Finally, the development and execution of this regional program accreditation system marks an important step forward in our continued goal to promote and elevate educational institutions. We are enthusiastic about the good impact it has on program quality, accreditation efficiency, and stakeholder collaboration, and we look forward to the revolutionary role it plays in defining our region's educational future.

Acknowledgements The authors would like to acknowledge the Centre of Excellence for East Africa (CENIT@EA) and DAAD GIZ's scholarship program for funding the project, and the Nelson Mandela African Institution of Science of Technology (NM-AIST) for providing facilities and a conducive environment that helped to complete the project successfully.

References

1. Roy, A., Newman, A., Ellenberger, T., Pyman, A.: Outcomes of international student mobility programs: a systematic review and agenda for future research. Studies in Higher Education. 44, 1630–1644 (2019). https://doi.org/10.1080/03075079.2018.1458222
2. Civera, A., Meoli, M., Paleari, S.: International student mobility: onset for a future career or an experiential opportunity? International Studies in Sociology of Education. 32, 559–578 (2023). https://doi.org/10.1080/09620214.2021.2007417
3. IUCEA: Guidelines – Inter-University Council of East Africa, https://www.iucea.org/guidelines/
4. Safiullin, R., Marusin, A., Safiullin, R., Ablyazov, T.: Methodical approaches for creation of intelligent management information systems by means of energy resources of technical facilities. (2019). https://doi.org/10.1051/e3sconf/201914010008
5. Programme Accreditation – AQAS e.V., https://www.aqas.eu/programme-accreditation/
6. Minh Ngoc, N., Minh Hieu, V., Hoang Tien, N., Doan Minh Duc, L.: Impact of accreditation policy on quality assurance activities of public and private universities in Vietnam. Int. J. Public Sector Performance Management. (2023)
7. Kumar, P., Shukla, B., Passey, D.: Impact of Accreditation on Quality and Excellence of Higher Education Institutions. (2021)
8. Zutshi, A., Grilo, A., Nodehi, T.: The value proposition of blockchain technologies and its impact on Digital Platforms. Comput Ind Eng. 155, 107187 (2021). https://doi.org/10.1016/J.CIE.2021.107187
9. Guruge, D.B., Kadel, R.: Towards an Holistic Framework to Mitigate and Detect Contract Cheating within an Academic Institute—A Proposal. Education Sciences 2023, Vol. 13, Page 148. 13, 148 (2023). https://doi.org/10.3390/EDUCSCI13020148
10. Andreani, M., Russo, D., Salini, S., Turri, M.: Shadows over accreditation in higher education: some quantitative evidence. High Educ (Dordr). 79, 691–709 (2020). https://doi.org/10.1007/S10734-019-00432-1/METRICS
11. Chakroun, B.: National Qualifications Framework and TVET teacher competence frameworks: A neglected dimension of qualifications reforms? Eur J Educ. 54, 370–388 (2019). https://doi.org/10.1111/EJED.12359
12. Romanowski, M.H.: CAEP Accreditation: Educational Neocolonialism and Non-US Teacher Education Programs. Higher Education Policy. 35, 199–217 (2022). https://doi.org/10.1057/S41307-020-00205-X
13. Nazemi, E., Tarokh, M.J., Djavanshir, G.R.: ERP: A literature survey. International Journal of Advanced Manufacturing Technology. 61, 999–1018 (2012). https://doi.org/10.1007/S00170-011-3756-X
14. Dumitru, V.F., Ionescu, B. Ştefan, Rîndaşu, S.M., Barna, L.E.L., Crîjman, A.M.: Implications for Sustainability Accounting and Reporting in the Context of the Automation-Driven Evolution of ERP Systems. Electronics 2023, Vol. 12, Page 1819. 12, 1819 (2023). https://doi.org/10.3390/ELECTRONICS12081819
15. Nolin, J.M.: Data as oil, infrastructure or asset? Three metaphors of data as economic value. Journal of Information, Communication and Ethics in Society. 18, 54–69 (2020). https://doi.org/10.1108/JICES-04-2019-0044/FULL/XML
16. Dew, S.K., Lavoie, M., Snelgrove, A.: An Engineering Accreditation Management System. (2020)
17. Dalal, N., Pauleen, D.J.: The wisdom nexus: Guiding information systems research, practice, and education. Information Systems Journal. 29, 224–244 (2019). https://doi.org/10.1111/ISJ.12196
18. Berdik, D., Otoum, S., Schmidt, N., Porter, D., Jararweh, Y.: A Survey on Blockchain for Information Systems Management and Security. Inf Process Manag. 58, 102397 (2021). https://doi.org/10.1016/j.ipm.2020.102397

19. Dobslaw, F., Feldt, R., Michaelsson, D., Haar, P., De Oliveira Neto, F.G., Torkar, R.: Estimating Return on Investment for GUI Test Automation Frameworks. Proceedings - International Symposium on Software Reliability Engineering, ISSRE. 2019-October, 271–282 (2019). https://doi.org/10.1109/ISSRE.2019.00035
20. Mayr-Dorn, C., Vierhauser, M., Bichler, S., Keplinger, F., Cleland-Huang, J., Egyed, A., Mehofer, T.: Supporting quality assurance with automated process-centric quality constraints checking. Proceedings - International Conference on Software Engineering. 1298–1310 (2021). https://doi.org/10.1109/ICSE43902.2021.00118
21. Susetyo, B., Soetantyo, S.P., Sayuti, M., Nur, D.: The Innovation and the Transformation of Indonesian Schools Accreditation Management System. Indonesian Journal on Learning and Advanced Education (IJOLAE). 4, 128–139 (2022). https://doi.org/10.23917/ijolae.v4i2.17113
22. Lvovich, I.Y., Lvovich, Y.E., Preobrazhenskiy, A.P., Preobrazhenskiy, Y.P., Choporov, O.N.: Modelling of information systems with increased efficiency with application of optimization-expert evaluation. J Phys Conf Ser. 1399, 33079 (2019). https://doi.org/10.1088/1742-6596/1399/3/033079

Connecting Manufacturing Sector Data Ecosystems with Federated Learning

Jonas Kallisch and Jorge Marx Gómez

Abstract This paper explores the potential of combining Data Ecosystems in the manufacturing sector with Federated Learning, to benefit from intercompany data analytics, while maintaining sovereignty. The paper starts with an overview on the state-of-the-art of data sharing and Data Ecosystems in the manufacturing sector. The benefits, challenges, and the main reason for the current lack of intercompany data exchange and the use of Data Ecosystems are described. As the main barrier to join Data Ecosystems of the manufacturing companies seems to be the data sovereignty, the paper investigates into Federated Learning, as a solution to this issue. The research investigates existing Data Ecosystems to determine their readiness for integrating Federated Learning. Through literature reviews and practical experiments, the study finds that while many ecosystems recognize the potential of Federated Learning, none currently enables the use of Federated Learning inside the system. The paper proposes architectures for integrating Federated Learning into these ecosystems, highlighting the benefits and feasibility of such integration. The findings suggest that enabling Federated Learning in Data Ecosystems can enhance cross-company data analysis, leading to improved operational efficiency and innovation in the manufacturing sector. Further research and development are essential to realize these benefits.

Keywords Federated learning · Data sharing · Data ecosystems · Data analytics

J. Kallisch (✉)
OFFIS Institute for Information Technology, Oldenburg, Germany
e-mail: Jonas.kallisch@offis.de

J. Marx Gómez
Carl Von Ossietzky University Oldenburg, Oldenburg, Germany
e-mail: jorge.marx.gomez@uol.de

J. Marx Gómez et al. (eds.), *Advancement in Embedded and Mobile Systems*, Progress in IS, https://doi.org/10.1007/978-3-031-99219-3_3

1 Data Ecosystems and Intercompany Data Analytics

1.1 Opportunities of Data Sharing and Data Ecosystems

In recent years, data and the analysis of data have become a major production factor for the industry sector [1]. Companies harvest data to improve their production system, quality of goods and services, and thereby increase the operational efficiency [2]. With more data, they unlock new business opportunities, like virtual services for physical goods [3, 4]. Data Ecosystems (DE) have evolved that support the interactive use of the products and by that deliver benefits for the customer.

In this paper, the authors define a DE as a complex socio-technical network that enables collaboration between actors in order to share, analyze, and monetize data [5]. A DE, therefore, is an infrastructure that enables interaction between independent actors on individual basis and motivation [6].

While these infrastructure environments have become common for many Businesses to Consumer (B2C) applications, like Cloud-Software-Services, APPs, or other digital services, data sharing and utilization between Businesses (B2B) in DEs are not that usual [7].

However, there are some existing and evolving ecosystems with the aim to connect those companies and enable them to collaboratively analyze their data and enrich it with services. These B2B DEs offer synergies for participants by optimizing the collaboration between them and, in some cases, lead to the development of new business models [8].

According to this, companies would benefit from the exchange and analysis of data in the DE. Especially, the opportunity to include data from companies that are not first-tier suppliers or customers in the own data analysis can provide new insights into the life cycle of the product or even enable the company to improve their products. This could lead to a reduction in waste, energy consumption, and costs in the overall production system.

However, as studies have shown that the sharing of data between companies is not commonly applied in Supply Chains (SC). In addition, many companies only share data from certain parts of their information systems, like logistic and finance [9]. Small and medium enterprises (SME) often do not share data with their customers and suppliers on a regular basis and also do not participate in DEs [10].

1.2 Reasons for a Lack of Intercompany Data Exchange in the Manufacturing Sector

Despite the advantages, companies in the manufacturing sector have significant reservations about sharing their data. These concerns are related to data security and privacy issues [10]. Recent studies and surveys have shown that the biggest fear of most companies is that the sharing of data from their manufacturing systems could expose intellectual property and therefore endanger their competitive position [11]. A leak of sensitive data from the shop floor could even threaten the existence of a company, as competitors could use the information to improve their own production systems with decades of gained knowledge [12].

Even within their SC, many companies have concerns to share data, since the relevant data come from their main value-creating processes and could be used by their partners to gain advantages in the business relation [13]. These concerns lead many companies to be reluctant to contribute their data to a shared DE, posing a significant hurdle to the development and implementation of DEs and limiting their potential.

According to surveys, other factors that explain companies' reluctance to participate in DEs are a lack of expertise within their own company, a lack of clarity about the expected value gained and uncertainties regarding the legal consequences of sharing data [10]. Nevertheless, the fear of losing intellectual property remains the biggest hurdle in establishing DEs.

1.3 Solutions to Overcome the Lack of Intercompany Data Sharing

As previous work has shown, the fear of losing control over valuable data is the main reason for a lack of data sharing in DEs. The question remains: are there possible solutions to solve this issue? Solutions that are able to counter companies' concerns about the loss of intellectual property can be divided into organizational, contractual, and technical measures.

Organizational measures, data sharing can be carried out via a mediator, a so-called data trust [14]. In a DE, this can be a service provider that is outside the SC and therefore has no interest in the utilization of the data. This guarantees that the data will not be passed on and provides cross-company analysis results. In this scenario, participants retain some of their sovereignty, but lose control over the security of the shared data, as the independent service provider stores them.

In addition, contracts can be concluded to secure intellectual property rights that safeguard data ownership rights [15]. These are generally suitable for safeguarding interests, but also offer additional risks due to the additional storage locations.

Finally, technical measures are an option to protect sensitive company data from loss and misuse. These are of particular interest to many entrepreneurs, as they enable data ownership rights to be protected more reliably. These options include, for example, differential privacy and federated learning. In the context of ecosystems, however, technical protection concepts are not widespread.

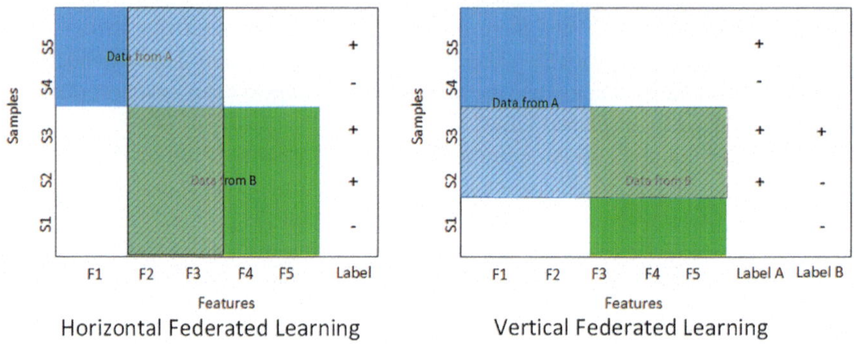

Fig. 1 Difference between types of federated learning

1.4 Federated Learning as a Solution to Preserve Data Sovereignty

Federated learning (FL) offers a promising solution to the fear of loss of control of data sovereignty. FL is a concept to analyze data sets distributed over different devices connected with a central station [16]. It can be divided into horizontal FL, vertical FL, and transfer Learning. The difference between vertical and horizontal FL is the selection of elements they share, while in Transfer Learning, a pre-trained model designed to perform one task, like detecting faults, is trained on another data set to do something else, like identify fraud in an organization [17].

As Fig. 1 shows, horizontal FL shares features, e.g. temperature measuring or other data points, but not the samples—a concrete case of measurement, while vertical FL shares samples but not features.

2 Research Question

2.1 Existence and Support of Data Ecosystems for Federated Learning

The first research question aims to identify existing DEs that enable or support FL use. It is crucial to understand which ecosystems have already implemented mechanisms for integrating FL and which technologies and infrastructures are being utilized. DEs such as GAIA-X, Project 44, and similar initiatives provide interesting use cases and platforms for integrating FL. These systems need to be analyzed in terms of their architecture, security mechanisms, and integration capabilities.

2.2 Integration of Federated Applications into Existing Data Ecosystems

This paper's second research question is how FL applications can be applied in the identified DEs. The main questions should be answered: whether DEs can make use of FL, how do the systems support FL, and what effort is needed to include FL applications in the identified DEs.

3 Methodology

3.1 Literature Review to Identify Relevant Data Ecosystems

The first research question aims to identify existing DEs that enable or support the use of FL. It is important to understand if any ecosystems have already implemented mechanisms for integrating FL. Therefore, the authors decided to use a structured literature review to identify relevant ecosystem that are adopting or might be able to adopt methods of FL. The Heß model is used as the basis for this literature analysis [18].

In order to identify relevant papers, the portals ScienceDirect and Google Scholar have been used. ScienceDirect's extensive research collection, mostly fully accessible papers, and extensive literature base for manufacturing and logistics management make it a preferred choice. Google Scholar adds the opportunity to get papers, books, and journals from more publishers since it lists a wide range of sources, including academic publishers, universities, and institutional repositories. This extensive coverage increases the likelihood of finding relevant research materials.

For the research, the search terms "Federated Learning" and "Federated Machine Learning" in combination with the terms "supply chain", "value chain", "data ecosystem", and "data space". This search was supplemented with "data environment", "intercompany", and a combination of the terms "manufacturing network", "cooperation", and "third party". We linked the terms individually with an AND. The result helped to get an overview of the landscape of DEs and how each of them may interact with the concept of FL. The most promising ecosystems are then analyzed to determine whether FL can be used in experiments.

3.2 Experiments to Test the Feasibility of Federated Learning

Building on the insights from the literature review, practical experiments are conducted. The purpose of these experiments is to evaluate the efficacy of FL in the identified DEs. We will set up a simple application with a platform connector for the different identified ecosystems and try to identify ways to integrate a FL analysis based on data the authors received from a manufacturing company. We can use the data set in the context of vertical FL and divide it into subsets to simulate horizontal FL. To understand the difference between those two methods of FL, the paper will give a short overview of the concepts in the upcoming section.

4 Analyzing Data Ecosystems

4.1 Data Ecosystems and Federated Learning

The conducted literature review provides an overview of the use of FL in the domain, along with a list of relevant ecosystems for further investigation. Firstly, we will provide an overview of the current integrations of FL within DEs in non-manufacturing sectors. Afterwards, we will describe the state of use of FL in the manufacturing-related DEs.

4.1.1 Health Care Ecosystems

Health Care (HC) ecosystems have been among the most active in utilizing FL because data sharing raises significant privacy concerns. A more recent publication from Darzidehkalani et al. [19] describes the implementation of FL in the multi-center HC setting. The used ecosystems have a focus on enabling privacy-preserving techniques. However, by studying the work of Abreha et al. [20] and Patel et al. [21], it is obvious, the architectures of the FL applications cannot work as a role model for manufacturing ecosystems, as they create single solutions for certain broadly appearing problems in the sector. The single application is not combined in a broader architecture and therefore is not interconnected or supplied on a single platform. The need for such an FL platform to combine the existing applications with open data is expressed in a current meta study by Teo et al. [22]. For the manufacturing sector, this means that no direct models can be derived, and the existing best practices of the healthcare sector can only be used for individual use cases.

4.1.2 Open Banking

Another emerging domain for FL is open banking ecosystems. According to Long et al. [23], the use of FL in the open banking context is when the sharing of the financial data between organizations improves innovation and individualized services. FL assists these institutions in co-developing and improving ML models based on the collected user data while also respecting users' privacy and legal requirements like General Data Protection Regulation (GDPR).

The banking sector provides an ideal basis for the use of FL due to the standardized data structures between banks. However, as in the HC sector, these are not bundled in a centralized ecosystem but are instead oriented towards individual applications between members. Examples of this are the work of Yang et al. [24] or Li and Wen [25]. They describe the use of FL in the area of fraud detection and credit risk management. It can therefore be stated that the sector and its applications cannot be used as an example for application in the manufacturing industry due to the non-transferable prerequisites.

4.1.3 IoT and Smart Cities

The Internet of Things (IoT) and smart cities are the novel domain for the FL to address data from different sources. Concentrating on the IoT context, Kholod et al. [26] provide a comparison of the state-of-art open-source frameworks for FL. Smart devices generate vast amounts of data to feed into a smart city communication system. For this reason, FL is ideal for such settings because while it enables the devices to teach each other, it does not gather all the information within a single place. This has the beneficial side of preserving privacy and consumption of latency and bandwidth over the data centralization.

Even though the IoT sector and the handling of IoT devices in the area of FL are very similar to that of manufacturing, the application requirements are not comparable in many fields. The generation and format of the data used differ significantly, as in the area of smart cities and public DEs, the data structures of all those involved are similar and often openly accessible [27]. In the manufacturing sector, on the other hand, the systems differ in many ways and platforms, and DEs must take the individual architectures of heterogeneous systems more into account than in the area of smart cities. Finally, it can be noted that there is a huge contrast to the field of smart cities in the area of manufacturing in that the sector is strongly characterized by small to medium-sized enterprises, while strong players are more dominant in public spaces [28].

4.2 Federated Learning in Manufacturing Data Ecosystems

As the focus of this paper is the question of whether and how DEs in the manufacturing sector can make use of the concept of FL, this section will evaluate the available ecosystems. We will take a look at the individual positions of the ecosystems and see if there are any available products that contain FL.

4.2.1 Big Data Value Association

The Big Data Value Association (BDVA) is a European organization dedicated to support the development of big data and AI-associated technologies across Europe [29]. The BVDA is an ecosystem of ecosystems as the member ecosystems, called i-spaces, are providers of Ecosystems by itself. The Association thereby is difficult to evaluate, since 29 subsystems, deliver 29 different solutions [30]. The subsystems, called i-Spaces, are categorized in the groups, platinum, gold, silver, and bronzes depending on the readiness level of their ecosystem. The criteria of the evaluation are the used infrastructure, the services provided, projects and applications delivered, the impact to the overall ecosystem, the business strategy and sustainability, the federation capabilities and the applied ethics in the system. The different sub-ecosystems have different domains and approaches. Some of the ecosystems are not plant to enable interaction, but create a platform to publish open data, methods or concepts.

The position of the BDVA on FL is published in a recent document [31]. The BDVA describes the need on privacy-preserving analytics in big DEs, as it enables more participants to take advantage of the methods provided. FL is described in the paper as a solution to overcome GDPR issues as well as to reduce the amount of data being transferred. The published document closes with a call to action to the members and other DEs to develop tools and systems to enable the use of FL. Therefore, it can be predicted that the ecosystem might enable the use of FL in the near future but did not present any concepts or architectures now.

4.2.2 International Data Spaces

The International Data Spaces (IDS) initiative focuses on creating secure and trusted data exchange ecosystems, maintaining data sovereignty and fostering interoperability across industries [32]. Its reference architecture model includes connectors, data usage control policies, and a certification mechanism to ensure secure data exchange. The whole concept of the IDS relies heavily on open data sharing and monetization of the data provided. There are some approaches, like the MUSKETEER project, that have brought ideas of using FL within the ecosystem, but the IDS by itself did not deliver any statements suggesting to go further in the direction of privacy preserving in their ecosystem [33].

4.2.3 GAIA-X

GAIA-X is a European project developing a federated and secure data infrastructure, emphasizing data sovereignty and interoperability across cloud services [34]. Its decentralized architecture supports cloud and edge computing resources, promoting transparency and data portability. GAIA-X aims to create a unified European data infrastructure, reducing dependency on non-European providers. Like the BDVA

GAIA-X is an ecosystem of ecosystems, containing a subset of data spaces for different sectors, that are interconnected by the GAIA-X infrastructure.

GAIA-X provides a range of technologies that could support the application of FL in the ecosystem. Firstly, there is the Self Sovereign Identity (SSI), which provides a guarantee of the authenticity of the business partner [35]. This is necessary in order to avoid the exploitation of federated services and thus gain the trust of the participants. For the integration of FL applications, the SC can thus be uniquely identified first and an analysis can be efficiently supplemented with additional participants. In addition to this service, another FL-supporting element is the federated catalogue [35]. This allows the contents of the ecosystem to be listed and allows participants to request them. This service could therefore be used to automatically include public data in the analysis, while the protected information is included by FL. It may be possible to use the federated catalogue only to share labels and data structures. This would essentially be a misuse of the system, so it is understandable that the GAIA-X Association does not currently offer FL services.

Nevertheless, in a recent publication, the GAIA-X Association recognizes the need for applications to protect sensitive information [36]. It also specifically mentions the concept of FL. It should be noted that the GAIA-X derivatives, such as Catena-X, have individual concept deviations. In the following section, we will therefore provide a brief overview of important work on the FL of these DEs.

4.2.4 GAIA-X Subsystems

The subsystems of GAIA-X have different sectors and aims. For this part of the paper, we will focus on the manufacturing sector and have found multiple interesting ecosystems. As most of them are still in the phase of concepts for this paper, we will just examine the lighthouse projects Catena-X [37] and Data4Industry-X [38].

First of these is Catena-X, an architecture within the GAIA-X ecosystem, which facilitates peer-to-peer data exchange, ensuring data sovereignty for all participants. One of the key components of Catena-X is the Eclipse Data Connector (EDC), which is already employed in various applications to minimize the transfer of sensitive data [39]. EDC allows for secure, controlled data exchanges, enabling organizations to collaborate without compromising their data integrity and confidentiality. Therefore, the participants of Catena-X have already been investigating the possibilities of using FL within the EDC [40]. Some works have listed the barriers of using FL within the structures, and some participants have presented concepts to integrate FL in the future [41]. However, as the concepts heavily rely on future integration of new services in the ecosystem, those are not applicable right now.

Another approach from the GAIA-X ecosystem is Data4Industry-X, an initiative aimed at fostering data-driven innovation in the industrial sector. It benefits from FL by facilitating the development of industry-wide models for predictive maintenance, quality control, and SC optimization [38]. The project aims to increase transparency between participants, enable data exchange, reduce the carbon footprint, analyze environmental impact, and generate performance indicators on SC efficiency. Therefore, it is not surprising that FL use is outside the scope of the project.

4.2.5 EuProGiant

EuProGiant seeks to establish a European infrastructure for secure, scalable, and flexible data processing to boost industrial competitiveness and innovation [42]. The platform relies on an open architecture, using GAIA-X and a system of nodes, run and maintained by the participants of the system. Therefore, it could also be seen as a derivate of GAIA-X, but the authors found that the relation to GAIA-X is smaller than the other projects.

The system enables the enrichment of the nodes to include data services, collect, and enrich data outside of the GAIA-X ecosystem [43]. This means that the nodes enable the participants to create a second stream of data outside of the GAIA-X ecosystem, without losing the ability to include data from the federated catalogue. While the project and ecosystem have not published any papers on the usage of FL or other privacy-preserving technologies, it might be a feasibly candidate to elaborate the possibility of enriching the open architecture with an FL service component.

4.2.6 Project44

Project44 is a global logistics and supply chain visibility platform that provides real-time tracking and predictive analytics to optimize supply chain operations [44]. As the only non-Europe-based approach, the open DE allows the interaction of logistic systems. Its cloud-based architecture integrates various data sources from logistics networks to offer enhanced transparency and predictive insights [45]. The aim of the project is to provide more transparency and to improve the collaboration in the logistics sector. Therefore, FL as a concept is not in the scope of the project, and no publications mentioning FL in Project44 have been found.

4.3 Conclusion

The literature review provided insight into ongoing work on the identified systems and showed that many of the ecosystems already evaluate the options of using FL to enable collaboration between participants without violating GDPR or the intellectual property of companies.

Although the authors cannot guarantee that they have provided a complete overview of all existing ecosystems, it can be assumed that the significant systems have been identified and evaluated. They currently do not have any accessible applications to use FL in the system. Therefore, possible architectures for using FL are discussed in the next section of this paper.

5 Architectures of Federated Learning in Data Ecosystems

5.1 *Use-Case for the Integration of Federated Learning in Data Ecosystems*

As the last section of this paper has shown that none of the evaluated DEs applies FL to their concepts, this section will describe options to integrate FL into the DEs. To reduce the complexity of the prototyping stage, the authors decided to investigate the ecosystems of GAIA-X and EuProGiant. Since those two DEs have published papers mentioning FL, they might be feasible candidates to evaluate the usage of FL in DEs.

To test the usability of FL in DEs, a data set from a manufacturing SC was used. It contains information from three stages of a SC of an aluminum product. This data set includes data from tool design, workpiece preparation data, the actual die-casting process, finishing, and quality analysis of the finished component. The data set contains time-series data with temperature and pressure curves, master data of machines, analysis data of raw materials, as well as data on the parameters used at the machines and faults or events. The data set comprises the elements of 8400 products, so a large amount of data was available for the experimental design. Flower was used to create a data analytics setup in two scenarios. By analyzing the data set, we followed the method of Joseph [46].

5.2 *Options for Using Federated Learning in GAIA-X*

The investigation into GAIA-X found that the integration of FL might be possible in two ways [35]. The most promising is to set up a federated analysis services, which interacts with the GAIA-X federated catalog. Based on the SSI, this service could enable companies to run their own clients to process data from the company data platforms across companies. On the one hand, this service could facilitate the integration of data from new partner companies into the analysis and, on the other hand, automatically include data from third-party data providers in the analysis of SC data through a direct connection to the federated catalog. The architecture can thus combine the data sovereignty of FL with the openness of a DE. To test this method, we would have to create an own data space inside of the GAIA-X DE. Therefore, we just evaluated the possible scenarios for this type of solution. The architecture of the solution is shown in Fig. 2 as the Scenario Federated Learning as a Service.

The second identified option to integrate FL in GAIA-X is to use the federated catalogue to manage the shared data without transferring actual data to the platform. Therefore, a client–server architecture outside of the GAIA-X environment must fulfill the framework for FL. The structure is shown in Fig. 2, described as third party-based Federated Learning Application.

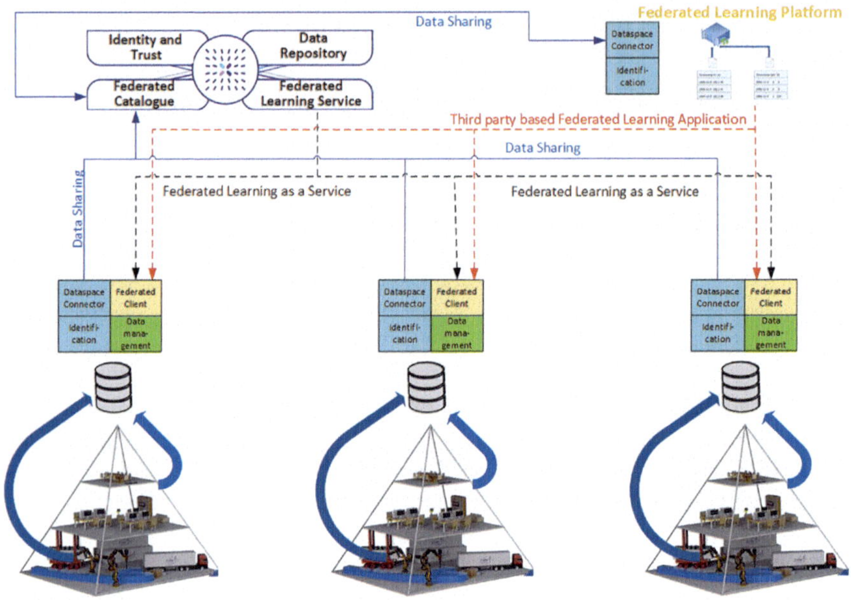

Fig. 2 Two scenarios to integrate federated learning in data ecosystems

The tested architecture is able to create a connection between different parties but comes with some major shortcomings. First of all, since the process of FL is outside of the DE environment, services like the self-sovereign identity (SSI) of GAIA-X are no longer available. Therefore, a trusted party must perform the authentication. Second, the gain of this solution is limited to the public availability of the data structures. This means that the client–server model of the FL framework can access the overall data structure without getting it from the cooperating companies. Finally, it is important to note that this solution did not facilitate the seamless integration of new suppliers or customers into the FL application, as they would initially need to establish a connection with the environment outside of the DE. As a result, the first untested solution should be preferred and further investigated in the future.

5.3 Options for Using Federated Learning in EuProGiant

As described earlier, EuProGiant is a project with the aim of creating an industrial DE to connect industrial partners and support the resilience of SCs through data-driven analytics. While taking advantage of GAIA-X federation services, the project and platform are able to connect individual data owners and consumers on a broader scale. While the EuProGiant platform does not directly support FL, it does allow users to upload data or algorithms to the existing test network. Like in GAIA-X,

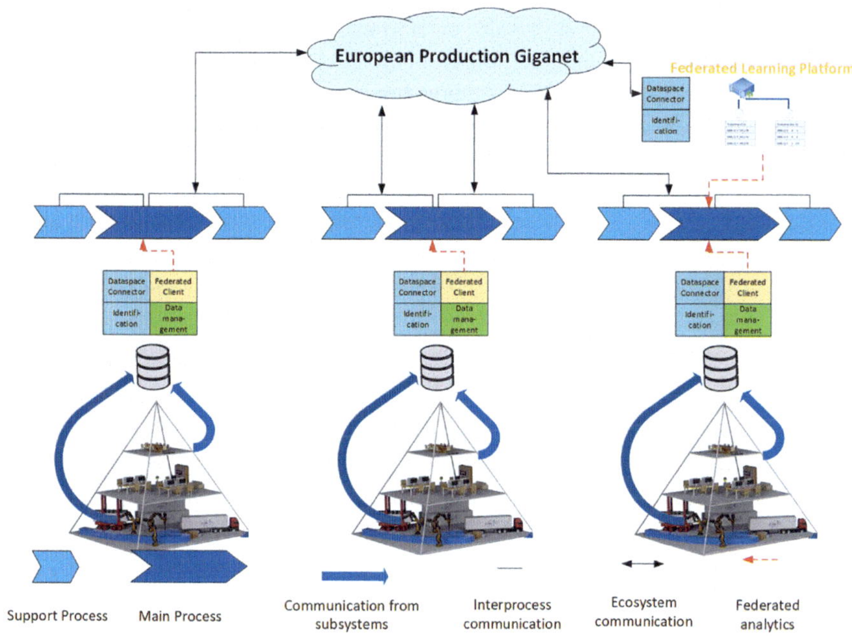

Fig. 3 Integrating federated learning in EuProGiant (based on [47])

the ideal solution would be to provide a service to connect and distribute federated clients between the partners.

However, the open architecture of EuProGiant allows sharing federated learning algorithms, and we created a data subset to see if the training updates from the not-connected clients were able to make use of the repository to update their individual models. Figure 3 shows how the interaction between the FL application and the data space of the ecosystem worked. As the graphic shows, the interaction between the DE and the data owners.

The way the ecosystem works makes the use of horizontal FL applicable even if it does not deliver a service. However, as the platform did not support the active training of algorithms, we were not able to create a working vertical FL application. The method we developed to incorporate FL into the system also has a drawback: it necessitates manual integration and requires incremental model updates. Therefore, the use of FL in the ecosystem is not practicable at the moment.

6 Conclusion

The paper has discussed the benefits and applicability of Federated Learning applications in Data Ecosystems. The literature review revealed the existence of numerous ecosystems, with some ecosystems' communities actively discussing the use of

Federated Learning. However, besides calls to action like the one from the BDVA and the mention of Federated Learning from the GAIA_X Association, the existing and accessible ecosystems did not support the use of Federated Learning. Beside the manufacturing sector, the authors find approaches to combining the concepts of Data Ecosystems and Federated Learning. These range from banking applications to health care data analysis to guarantee the data sovereignty of individuals. Nevertheless, it should be noted that the sectors have characteristics that make it difficult to transfer Federated Learning approaches to the manufacturing sector. These are, for example, significantly more standardized data structures, higher volumes of available data, and, in some cases, a better distribution of data between the players.

The paper therefore analyzed concepts for integrating Federated Learning into Data Ecosystems and tested them in two cases. The existing structures necessitated the execution of many parts of the application outside the provided ecosystems. The integration of services for federated data analysis would be much better for facilitating access and usability. For many companies, the authors believe that the usability of Federated Learning within a Data Ecosystem would facilitate the analysis of cross-company data and, in some cases, even make it possible in the first place. Further work, concepts, and application examples for Federated Learning in Data Ecosystems are therefore essential from the authors' point of view.

References

1. Marmolejo-Saucedo, J. A., Hurtado-Hernandez, M. u. Suarez-Valdes, R.: Digital Twins in Supply Chain Management: A Brief Literature Review. In: 2020 – Intelligent Computing and Optimization, pp. 653–661.
2. Weichert, D., Link, P., Stoll, A., Rüping, S., Ihlenfeldt, S. u. Wrobel, S.: A review of machine learning for the optimization of production processes. The International Journal of Advanced Manufacturing Technology 104 (2019) 5–8, pp. 1889–1902.
3. Qu, J., Meng, C. u. Hu, B.: Pricing and quality decisions in virtual product supply chains with information sharing. Journal of the Operational Research Society 74 (2023) 7, pp. 1746–1762.
4. Hermes Newsroom: 17. Hermes-Barometer: Kollaboration in der Supply Chain: Großes Potenzial, zahlreiche Hemmnisse | Hermes Newsroom, 2023. https://newsroom.hermesworld.com/17-hermes-barometer-kollaboration-in-der-supply-chain-grosses-potenzial-zahlreiche-hemmnisse-26381/, last accessed 2024/06/26.
5. Estevez, E., Janssen, M. u. Barbosa, L. S. (Hrsg.): Proceedings of the 8th International Conference on Theory and Practice of Electronic Governance. New York, NY, USA: ACM 10272014.
6. Zuiderwijk, A., Janssen, M. u. Davis, C.: Innovation with open data: Essential elements of open data ecosystems. Information Polity 19 (2014) 1,2, pp. 17–33.
7. McKnight, D. H., Lankton, N. K., Nicolaou, A. u. Price, J.: Distinguishing the effects of B2B information quality, system quality, and service outcome quality on trust and distrust. The Journal of Strategic Information Systems 26 (2017) 2, pp. 118–141.
8. Lade, P., Ghosh, R. u. Srinivasan, S.: Manufacturing Analytics and Industrial Internet of Things. IEEE Intelligent Systems 32 (2017) 3, S. 74–79.
9. Culot, G., Orzes, G., Sartor, M. u. Nassimbeni, G.: The future of manufacturing: A Delphi-based scenario analysis on Industry 4.0. Technological Forecasting and Social Change 157 (2020).

10. Södergren, F. u. Cartling Wallén, M.: Creating Value Through Information Sharing: Exploring the Transition Towards a Digital Supply Chain, 2022.
11. Kallisch, J., Marx-Gómez, J. u. Wunck, C.: Challenges and Opportunities of Intercompany Big Data Analytics in Supply Chains. Development Methodologies for Big Data Analytics Systems (2024), pp. 249–262.
12. Colicchia, C., Creazza, A., Noè, C. u. Strozzi, F.: Information sharing in supply chains: a review of risks and opportunities using the systematic literature network analysis (SLNA). Supply Chain Management: An International Journal 24 (2019) 1, pp. 5–21.
13. Panahifar, F., Byrne, P. J., Salam, M. A. u. Heavey, C.: Supply chain collaboration and firm's performance. Journal of Enterprise Information Management 31 (2018) 3, pp. 358–379.
14. Stachon, M., Möller, F., Guggenberger, T., Tomczyk, M. u. Henning, J.-L.: Understanding data trusts. 2023.
15. Kozlenkova, I. V., Hult, G. T. M., Lund, D. J., Mena, J. A. u. Kekec, P.: The Role of Marketing Channels in Supply Chain Management. Journal of Retailing 91 (2015) 4, pp. 586–609.
16. Yang, Q., Liu, Y., Chen, T. u. Tong, Y.: Federated Machine Learning: Concept and Applications.
17. Zhang, J., Guo, S., Qu, Z., Zeng, D., Wang, H., Liu, Q. u. Zomaya, A.: Adaptive Vertical Federated Learning on Unbalanced Features. IEEE Transactions on Parallel and Distributed Systems (2022).
18. Heß, J.: Strukturierte Literaturrecherche – ein Rahmenkonzept. Regionale Erfolgsfaktoren entlang des Gründungsprozesses (2021), pp. 125–139.
19. Darzidehkalani, E., Ghasemi-rad, M. u. van Ooijen, P. M. A.: Federated Learning in Medical Imaging: Part I: Toward Multicentral Health Care Ecosystems. Journal of the American College of Radiology : JACR 19 (2022) 8, pp. 969–974.
20. Abreha, H. G., Hayajneh, M. u. Serhani, M. A.: Federated Learning in Edge Computing: A Systematic Survey. Sensors (Basel, Switzerland) 22 (2022) 2.
21. Patel, N. P., Parekh, R., Amin, S. A., Gupta, R., Tanwar, S., Kumar, N., Iqbal, R. u. Sharma, R.: LEAF: A Federated Learning-Aware Privacy-Preserving Framework for Healthcare Ecosystem. IEEE Transactions on Network and Service Management 21 (2024) 1, pp. 1129–1141.
22. Teo, Z. L., Jin, L., Li, S., Di Miao, Zhang, X., Ng, W. Y., Tan, T. F., Lee, D. M., Chua, K. J., Heng, J., Liu, Y., Goh, R. S. M. u. Ting, D. S. W.: Federated machine learning in healthcare: A systematic review on clinical applications and technical architecture. Cell reports. Medicine 5 (2024) 2, pp. 101419.
23. Federated Learning for Open Banking, Long, G., Tan, Y., Jiang, J. u. Zhang, C., 2021.
24. Yang, W., Zhang, Y., Ye, K., Li, L. u. Xu, C.-Z.: FFD: A Federated Learning Based Method for Credit Card Fraud Detection. Big Data - BigData 2019. 8th International Congress, Held As Part of the Services Conference Federation, SCF 2019, San Diego, CA, USA, June 25–30, 2019, Proceedings. Lecture Notes in Computer Science Ser, v.11514. Cham: Springer International Publishing AG 2019, pp. 18–32.
25. Li, Y. u. Wen, G.: Research and Practice of Financial Credit Risk Management Based on Federated Learning 31 (2023).
26. Kholod, I., Yanaki, E., Fomichev, D., Shalugin, E., Novikova, E., Filippov, E. u. Nordlund, M.: Open-Source Federated Learning Frameworks for IoT: A Comparative Review and Analysis. Sensors 21 (2020) 1, pp. 167.
27. Banabilah, S., Aloqaily, M., Alsayed, E., Malik, N. u. Jararweh, Y.: Federated learning review: Fundamentals, enabling technologies, and future applications. Information Processing & Management 59 (2022) 6.
28. Khan, L. U., Saad, W., Han, Z., Hossain, E. u. Hong, C. S.: Federated Learning for Internet of Things: Recent Advances, Taxonomy, and Open Challenges. IEEE Communications Surveys & Tutorials 23 (2021) 3, pp. 1759–1799.
29. Curry, E., Tuikka, T., Metzger, A., Zillner, S., Bertels, N., Ducuing, C., Dalle Carbonare, D., Gusmeroli, S., Scerri, S., López de Vallejo, I. u. García Robles, A.: Data Sharing Spaces: The BDVA Perspective. In: Otto, B. (Hrsg.): Designing Data Spaces. The Ecosystem Approach to Competitive Advantage. Cham: Springer International Publishing AG 2022, pp. 365–382.

30. Zillner, S., Le Bars, L., Lama, N. de, Scerri, S., García Robles, A., Tonna, M. C., Kenneally, J., Mayer, D., Hahn, T., Caj, S., Seidl, R., Carbonare, D. D. u. Curry, E.: A Roadmap to Drive Adoption of Data Ecosystems. In: Curry, E. (Hrsg.): The Elements of Big Data Value. Foundations of the Research and Innovation Ecosystem. Cham: Springer International Publishing AG 2021, pp. 41–62.
31. BDV Big Data Value Association: BDVA and CoE DSC joint white paper on combining Data Spaces and PETs - BDV Big Data Value Association, 2024. https://bdva.eu/news/bdva-and-coe-dsc-joint-white-paper-on-combining-data-spaces-and-pets/, last accessed 2024/06/26.
32. Otto, B., Hompel, M. ten u. Wrobel, S.: International Data Spaces. In: Neugebauer, R. (Hrsg.): Digital Transformation. Berlin, Heidelberg: Springer Berlin / Heidelberg 2019, pp. 109–128.
33. Bonura, S., Carbonare, D. D., Díaz-Morales, R., Fernández-Díaz, M., Morabito, L., Muñoz-González, L., Napione, C., Navia-Vázquez, Á. u. Purcell, M.: Privacy-Preserving Technologies for Trusted Data Spaces. In: Curry, E., Auer, S., Berre, A. J., Metzger, A., Perez, M. S. u. Zillner, S. (Hrsg.): Technologies and Applications for Big Data Value. Cham: Springer Nature 2022, pp. 111–134.
34. Kraemer, P., Niebel, C. u. Reiberg, A.: Gaia-x and business models. 2023.
35. GAIA-X Association: GAIA-X: Technical Architecture, 2021. https://www.data-infrastructure.eu/GAIAX/Redaktion/EN/Publications/gaia-x-technical-architecture.html, last accessed 2024/06/26.
36. Niebel, C. u. Smoleń, A.: AI and Gaia-X. 2023.
37. Catena-X: Home | Catena-X, 2023. https://catena-x.net/en/, abgerufen am: 16.02.2023.
38. Data4Industry-X Bridging Industrial Data Ecosystems, 2024. https://www.dawex.com/en/news/data4industry-x-bridging-industrial-data-ecosystems, last accessed 2024/09/09.
39. Siska, V., Karagiannis, V. u. Drobics, M.: Building a dataspace: Technical overview. 2023.
40. Schöppenthau, F., Patzer, F., Schnebel, B., Watson, K., Baryschnikov, N., Obst, B., Chauhan, Y., Kaever, D., Usländer, T. u. Kulkarni, P.: Building a Digital Manufacturing as a Service Ecosystem for Catena-X. Sensors 23 (2023) 17.
41. Müller, T., Gärtner, N., Verzano, N. u. Matthes, F.: Barriers to the Practical Adoption of Federated Machine Learning in Cross-company Collaborations. Proceedings of the 14th International Conference on Agents and Artificial Intelligence. SCITEPRESS - Science and Technology Publications 2022.
42. Dumss, S., Weber, M., Schwaiger, C., Sulz, C., Rosenberger, P., Bleicher, F., Grafinger, M. u. Weigold, M.: EuProGigant – A Concept Towards an Industrial System Architecture for Data-Driven Production Systems. Procedia CIRP 104 (2021), pp. 324–329.
43. Hoffmann, F., Koch, T., Weber, M., Weigold, M. u. Metternich, J.: Development of Data-based Business Models to Incentivise Sustainability in Industrial Production. Hannover : publish-Ing 2023.
44. project44: High-Velocity Supply Chain Platform | project44, 2024. https://www.project44.com/, last accessed 2024/06/26.
45. Mass, T.: System Architecture at project44 - project44 TechBlog - Medium. project44 TechBlog (2022).
46. Joseph, V. R.: Optimal ratio for data splitting. Statistical Analysis and Data Mining: The ASA Data Science Journal 15 (2022) 4, pp. 531–538.
47. EuProGigant: Use cases - EuProGigant, 2022. https://euprogigant.com/en/use-cases/, last accessed 2024/08/10.

Secure and Efficient Teller Desk Transactions Through Biometric and RFID Technology

Pacifique Niyongabire, Kisangiri Michael, Judith Leo, and Martine Lyimo

Abstract This paper introduces a biometric banking system, a technological innovation that is set to transform cash withdrawals at CRDB Bank Burundi by eliminating paper-based transactions. The system's key features include biometric authentication methods, such as fingerprint and RFID card scanning, integrated with advanced encryption protocols for robust data security. It effectively addresses common banking inefficiencies, such as lengthy transaction times and security vulnerabilities associated with manual processes. Additionally, the system offers real-time transaction notifications via SMS, WhatsApp, or email, enhancing transparency, and customer satisfaction. Extensive testing with CRDB staff, customers, and other interested individuals has demonstrated the system's efficiency, reliability, and user acceptance. A statistical survey conducted with CRDB staff, customers, and other stakeholders revealed an 85% reduction in transaction times, a 90% increase in operational efficiency, and a significant improvement in security measures. The findings highlight significant reductions in transaction times, increased operational efficiency, and heightened security measures. This paper discusses the system's design, implementation, and testing phases, emphasizing its potential to revolutionize banking operations and set a precedent for digital transformation in the banking sector.

Keywords Biometric banking · Paperless transactions · Bank teller desk transactions

P. Niyongabire (✉) · K. Michael · J. Leo · M. Lyimo
School of Computational and Communication Sciences and Engineering, The Nelson Mandela African Institution of Science and Technology (NM-AIST), Arusha, Tanzania
e-mail: niyongabirep@nm-aist.ac.tz

K. Michael
e-mail: Kisangiri.michael@nm-aist.ac.tz

J. Leo
e-mail: judith.leo@nm-aist.ac.tz

M. Lyimo
e-mail: martine.lyimo@nm-aist.ac.tz

J. Marx Gómez et al. (eds.), *Advancement in Embedded and Mobile Systems*, Progress in IS, https://doi.org/10.1007/978-3-031-99219-3_4

1 Introduction

The banking industry has experienced substantial transformation in recent years, driven by integrating digital technology into various aspects of financial services [1]. Innovations such as Automated Teller Machines (ATMs), mobile banking, and online transactions have significantly streamlined processes and increased accessibility and convenience for customers [2]. Despite these advancements, a notable segment of clients continues to prefer face-to-face interactions with bank tellers for their financial transactions [3]. This preference stems from a desire for personalized assistance, a sense of security, familiarity with traditional banking practices, and the desire to conduct high-value or complex transactions [4]. CRDB Bank Burundi, recognizing the intricate relationship between customer preferences and digital banking technologies, has effectively incorporated modern digital solutions, including ATMs, mobile banking, and online services. However, many of its customers still opt for direct interactions with bank tellers, which involve manual form filling, the presentation of identity documents, and in-person transaction processing [5]. These manual processes present several challenges, including long waiting times, potential data entry errors, and security risks associated with handling physical documents.

This system is introduced to digitize face-to-face transactions at the bank teller desk to address these issues and balance the need for digital convenience with personalized service. This initiative aims to deliver a seamless, secure, and efficient transaction experience, leveraging advanced technology while maintaining the essential elements of human interaction that customers value. The proposed solution involves implementing a paperless cash withdrawal system utilizing RFID and biometric fingerprint verification. This system is designed to enhance security through biometric authentication and encryption, streamline the identification process, and eliminate the need for cumbersome form filling. It also aims to cater to a diverse customer base, including individuals with physical limitations and those seeking to minimize physical contact during health crises like pandemics. This initiative aligns with broader industry trends where financial institutions are rethinking their service models to meet evolving customer expectations, improve operational efficiency, and ensure robust data security in the digital era.

The success of this project has the potential to position CRDB Bank Burundi at the forefront of banking innovation in the region. It also offers valuable insights for other financial institutions striving to bridge the gap between customer preferences and digital transformation. The subsequent sections of this paper will delve into the development and implementation of the paperless cash withdrawal system, its technological underpinnings, expected benefits, and challenges. Through comprehensive analysis and empirical research, we will explore the efficacy of this solution in enhancing customer satisfaction, operational efficiency, and the future of in-person banking transactions.

1.1 Targeted Innovation for In-Person Transactions

While many advancements in banking technology have focused on streamlining processes through ATMs, internet banking, and mobile applications, a critical area remains overlooked: in-person transactions at the bank teller desk [6]. Despite efforts to digitize banking processes, teller desk transactions in many institutions still rely heavily on paper-based methods, resulting in inefficiencies and delays. This issue persists not only at CRDB Bank Burundi but also in numerous banks across different countries.

Unlike other banking innovations, such as ATMs and online banking, which cater to remote or self-service transactions, this system focuses on improving the customer experience at the teller desk. By offering an alternative to paper-based forms and manual processes, it ensures that even high-value or complex transactions can be completed efficiently and securely, meeting the preferences of customers who favor face-to-face service. Additionally, the potential for replication across other banking institutions is significant. Using APIs, this system can be easily integrated with existing banking platforms, extending its impact beyond CRDB Bank Burundi and providing a scalable solution for other banks seeking to modernize their teller desk operations.

2 Literature Review

2.1 Digital Transformation in Banking

The banking sector has witnessed a dramatic shift towards digitalization over the past few decades. The introduction of technologies such as ATMs, online banking, and mobile banking apps has significantly transformed how financial services are delivered and accessed [7]. These advancements have not only improved operational efficiency but also enhanced customer convenience and access to banking services [8]. However, despite these strides in digital banking, a significant portion of the customer base still prefers face-to-face interactions for their transactions. Studies have shown that many customers value personalized assistance and the perceived security of in-person services [9].

2.2 Transition from Paper-Based to Digital Transactions

The move towards paperless banking has been driven by the need to improve transaction efficiency, enhance security, and reduce environmental impact [10]. Digital signatures and electronic documents have become standard in many banking processes, reducing the reliance on physical paperwork. Yet, significant challenges remain, particularly in cash deposits and withdrawals at bank teller desks, where traditional, paper-based methods are still prevalent.

2.3 Existing Paperless Banking Solutions

Several initiatives have attempted to address the challenges associated with traditional, paper-based transactions in banking. The adoption of digital signatures and electronic documentation has been a significant step towards reducing paper use in banks [11]. Systems leveraging biometric authentication for ATMs and online banking have also been explored to enhance security and user convenience [12]. For instance, biometric ATMs using fingerprint or facial recognition technology have been deployed in various regions, aiming to provide secure and convenient access to cash withdrawals and other services [13]. However, these solutions primarily focus on ATMs and online banking, leaving the paper-based processes at bank teller desks largely unaddressed.

In the study by Prihodova and Hub, the authors developed a hand-based biometric system using convolutional neural networks (CNNs) to enhance secure user authentication in mobile banking applications. While this approach significantly improves transaction efficiency and security in online banking, it primarily addresses mobile banking platforms. However, it does not directly address the unique challenges faced in in-person bank teller transactions, where paper-based processes and physical verification methods are still prevalent. Our system, by contrast, focuses on modernizing these in-person transactions by integrating biometric fingerprint authentication and RFID technology, offering a secure and paperless solution specifically tailored for bank teller desk environments [11].

Gokul et al. introduced a system that combines fingerprint biometrics with RFID technology for ATM authentication, significantly improving security by mitigating fraud and identity theft issues common in PIN-based systems. However, while their approach enhances security at ATMs, it is specifically limited to these environments and does not extend to bank teller transactions, where paper-based processes remain dominant. Our system expands upon this concept by applying similar security measures, fingerprint biometrics, and RFID authentication but targets in-person transactions at bank teller desks, offering a broader solution that addresses the overlooked area of paperless transactions in banks [12].

Aljuaid and Ansari proposed a cardless ATM authentication system that utilizes fingerprint, facial, and retina biometrics, significantly enhancing ATM security through a multidimensional approach. However, while their system improves the security of ATM transactions, it does not extend to in-person transactions at bank tellers, where paper-based processes are still prevalent. Our proposed system, by focusing on bank teller desk transactions, addresses this gap, offering a secure and efficient alternative for paperless withdrawals and in-person interactions [13].

Chigada explored biometric authentication to prevent credit fraud in South African banking. The study highlighted the potential of biometric systems but noted infrastructure challenges and did not focus on bank teller desks. RFID technology has been extensively used in various applications, including asset tracking and payment systems. The RC522 RFID module, for example, offers an efficient and cost-effective solution for proximity-based authentication. However, its application in bank teller transactions remains underexplored [14].

Alzamel et al. explored using fingerprint biometrics in point-of-sale (POS) networks to combat fraud and identity theft. While their study highlighted the benefits of biometric security in POS transactions, it did not address bank teller operations or the necessary data security measures for these types of in-person transactions. Our system extends biometric security to bank teller desk transactions, filling this gap and ensuring both enhanced security and data protection in this overlooked area of banking [15].

Hublikar et al. proposed a biometric authentication system for online banking, suggesting a three-part architecture for registration, authentication, and management. Despite its potential, the study did not consider real-time notifications and did not address bank teller operations [16].

Badovinac and Simic introduced a multimodal biometric authentication (MBA) system for cardless payments, combining fingerprint, voice, and face recognition for enhanced accuracy. However, their system lacked real-time transaction alerts, a feature our system incorporates to ensure that customers are instantly informed of account activities [17].

2.4 *Biometric and RFID Technologies*

Biometric authentication, including fingerprint, facial recognition, and iris scanning, has emerged as a robust method for enhancing security in various applications, including banking [16]. Integrating these technologies into banking systems aims to reduce fraud and ensure that only authorized individuals can access sensitive financial information or perform transactions. Additionally, RFID technology has been widely used for asset tracking, access control, and payment systems due to its ability to quickly and accurately identify and authenticate users [18].

Despite extensive use in different domains, these technologies' applications in bank teller transactions remain limited. Most current implementations are in self-service contexts, such as ATMs and point-of-sale (POS) systems, rather than direct teller-assisted transactions.

2.5 Real-Time Transaction Notifications

Providing real-time transaction alerts is an essential feature that enhances transparency and trust in banking transactions. While many existing systems offer only SMS notifications, they often lack the flexibility to cater to diverse customer preferences [19]. This limitation can decrease customer satisfaction, as some users may prefer alternative communication methods such as email or instant messaging apps like WhatsApp.

2.6 Addressing the Gaps

The proposed biometric banking system at CRDB Bank Burundi aims to bridge these gaps by introducing a comprehensive solution for paperless cash withdrawals at bank teller desks. This system utilizes biometric fingerprint verification and RFID card authentication to ensure secure and efficient transactions. Additionally, it will offer real-time transaction notifications through SMS, email, and WhatsApp, allowing customers to choose their preferred method of communication. This project focuses on the bank teller desk, addressing the challenges of in-person banking transactions that existing digital solutions have largely overlooked. Integrating these advanced technologies aims to enhance security, reduce waiting times, and improve overall customer satisfaction.

3 Study Methods and Approach

3.1 Research Design

This study employs a multimethod research design, combining both qualitative and quantitative approaches to comprehensively investigate the effectiveness and security of a paperless cash withdrawal system at bank teller desks. The primary objective was to develop and evaluate a system that integrates RFID technology, biometric authentication, customer preference notification, and AES encryption to enhance transaction security and efficiency.

3.2 System Development and Integration

The development of the paperless cash withdrawal system involved meticulous selection and integration of both hardware and software components to ensure a robust, secure, and user-friendly solution.

Hardware Tool Selection and Integration

The hardware components include the ESP32 microcontroller, chosen for its Wi-Fi and Bluetooth capabilities and support for AES encryption. A fingerprint scanner adds a second layer of security, using biometric authentication to verify users. AES encryption ensures that data transmitted from the ESP32 to the database remains secure [20]. RFID card authentication offers an alternative for clients with disabilities or those who prefer contactless transactions, especially in emergencies like pandemics [8]. Figure 1 illustrates the circuit diagram of the hardware tools used.

Software Tool Selection and Integration

On the software side, MySQL was chosen for managing client and transaction data due to its reliability and open-source nature. CodeIgniter, a PHP framework, handled server-side processes like user authentication and database interactions, with built-in AES encryption for added security. Draw.io was used to create diagrams for visualizing system flow and user interactions, while WebSocket technology enabled real-time communication between the web app and the embedded device for smooth data transmission. After authentication, the teller completes the transaction, and customers are notified via SMS, WhatsApp, or email. Figure 2 illustrates the implemented system, highlighting features designed to enhance functionality and effectiveness.

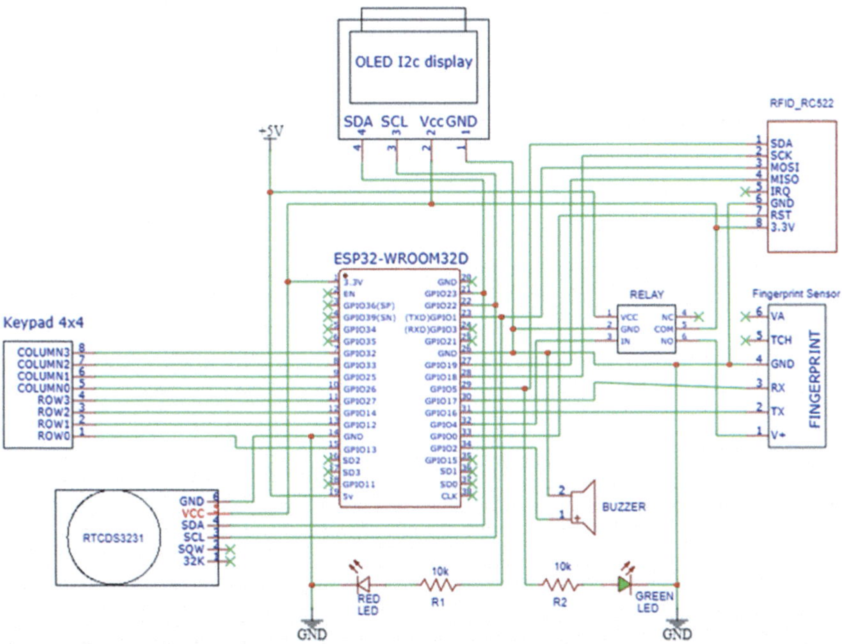

Fig. 1 Circuit diagram

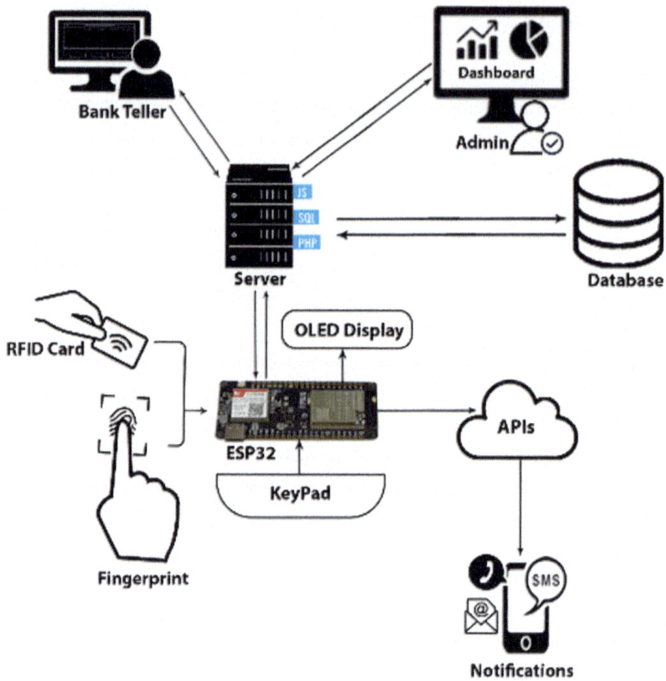

Fig. 2 Design of the proposed system

3.3 System Architecture

Integrating sophisticated biometric and RFID technology, the biometric banking system is intended to enable safe, paperless cash withdrawals. At the heart of the system lies an ESP32 microcontroller, which controls data processing and communication between different components, such as biometric verification, user interaction, and transaction feedback. The system design ensures that these components integrate seamlessly to provide a seamless user experience while upholding the greatest degree of security.

3.4 Data Flow Diagram

The data flow within the biometric banking system follows a structured sequence designed to ensure secure and efficient transactions. Bank tellers initiate the process by allowing customers to authenticate themselves using either a registered fingerprint or an RFID card. The system then verifies the customer's identity against stored biometric data. Upon successful verification, the customer is prompted to enter the desired withdrawal amount. If the requested funds are available, the bank teller

Fig. 3 Data flow diagram

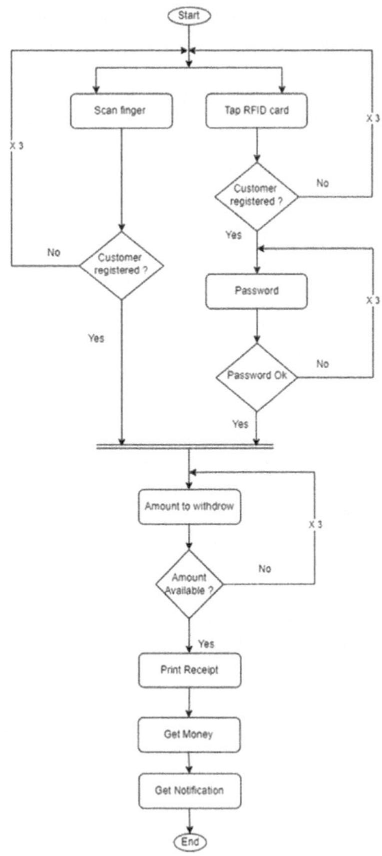

disburses the money, and the transaction details are securely recorded. Customers receive real-time transaction alerts via SMS, WhatsApp, or email, ensuring they are promptly informed of their account status. This systematic approach to data flow enhances transaction security and improves transparency and customer communication, making the biometric banking system both reliable and user-friendly. Figure 3 depicts the flowchart diagram of the fully operating system in minute detail, describing the customer's journey during the withdrawal process.

3.5 Security Measures

Ensuring the security of transactions and sensitive customer data is paramount in designing the biometric banking system. This section outlines the various security measures implemented to safeguard against potential threats and vulnerabilities.

1. Biometric Authentication

Biometric fingerprint scanning provides a robust and reliable method of user authentication. Unlike traditional PINs or passwords, biometric data are unique to each individual and difficult to replicate, significantly reducing the risk of unauthorized access.

2. RFID Authentication

For enhanced accessibility, particularly for customers with physical disabilities who may struggle with traditional fingerprint-based authentication, RFID card authentication is offered as an alternative method. The system was implemented with a dual authentication system to mitigate concerns about potentially misusing a lost or stolen RFID card. Once an RFID card is presented, the system prompts the user to enter a personal password to complete the transaction. This two-step verification ensures that even if the RFID card is lost or stolen, unauthorized access is prevented, as the system requires both the card and the correct password for authentication. In addition, all RFID transactions are logged and linked to real-time notifications, enabling customers to monitor any unauthorized attempts immediately [18].

3. Advanced Encryption Standard (AES)

AES encryption protects data during transmission from the embedded ESP32 microcontroller to the database. This ensures that sensitive information, such as biometric data and transaction details, remains confidential and is protected against interception and unauthorized access [21].

4. Secure Communication Protocols

The system employs Advanced Encryption Standard (AES) encryption to safeguard data during transmission. Data are encrypted at the embedded end (ESP32) before being sent to the database. This ensures that even if data are intercepted during transmission, it remains unreadable to unauthorized parties. With its strong cryptographic properties, AES encryption is highly effective in preventing data breaches and ensuring secure communication between devices.

5. Real-Time Transaction Notifications

The current system at CRDB Bank Burundi offers SMS notifications only for transactions, but this approach needs more flexibility and caters to evolving customer preferences. To enhance transparency and security, a new feature that allows customers to choose their preferred notification channel: SMS, WhatsApp, or email was introduced. This enhanced system integrates with the bank's core banking system through secure APIs. Once a transaction is completed at the teller desk, the system triggers real-time notifications via the customer's selected channel.

6. Secure Server-Side Processing

PHP and the CodeIgniter framework are employed for server-side processing, handling data validation, user authentication, and business logic securely. CodeIgniter's built-in support for AES encryption further reinforces the security measures implemented within the system, ensuring secure and efficient data management.

7. Physical Security Measures

The hardware components, including the ESP32 microcontroller, RFID module, and fingerprint scanner, are housed in a tamper-resistant enclosure to prevent unauthorized access and physical tampering. Additionally, the bank teller initiates the withdrawal process in the web application, after which the customer can scan their finger or RFID card and enter the amount to withdraw. The customer device is fixed in front of the bank teller desk, adding another layer of security by ensuring that bank staff closely monitor and control transactions.

4 Results and Discussion

4.1 Introduction to Results

Findings from our study on the biometric-based banking system, including user and staff feedback, system performance metrics, and the effectiveness of security measures, are discussed here. The figures provided visual representations of key aspects of the system's functionality and user interaction.

4.2 User Perceptions of the Benefits of a Biometric-Based System

Customers who used the biometric banking system were surveyed and interviewed. The results indicated that most respondents perceived the system's convenience and security positively. Users reported that the biometric authentication process was quick and seamless compared to traditional methods (Fig. 4).

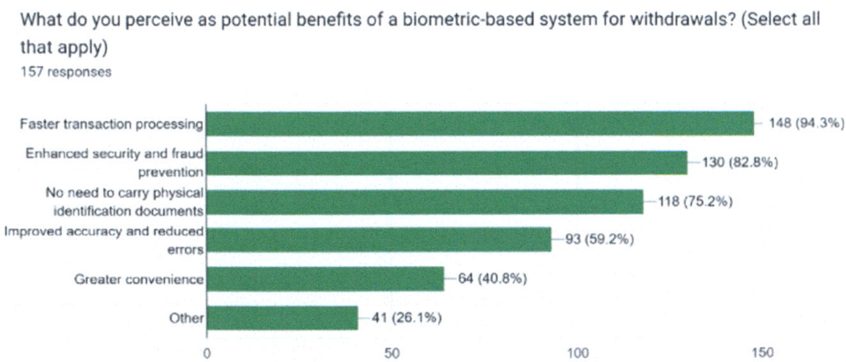

Fig. 4 User satisfaction survey results

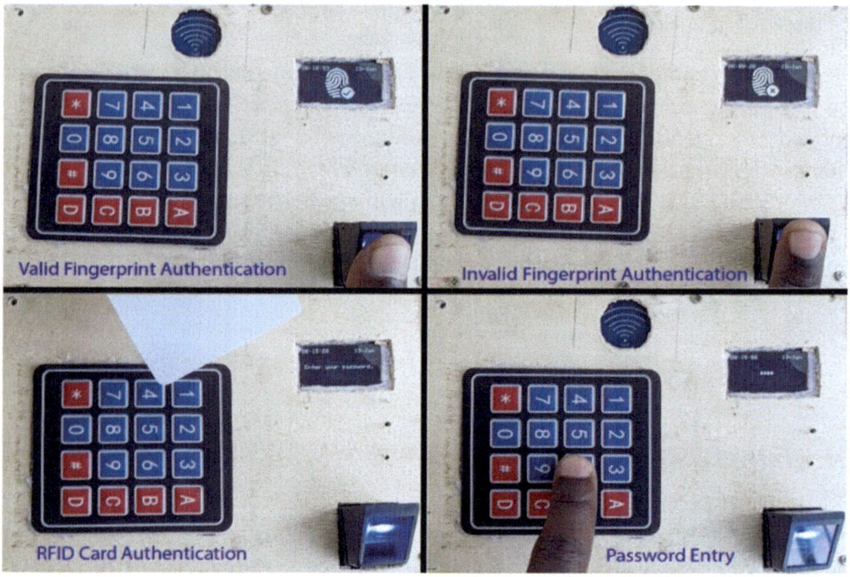

Fig. 5 Authentication process using fingerprint or RFID reader

4.3 *System Development Results*

The development results are categorized into key areas, each illustrating different aspects of the system's operation and user interface.

Authentication Process Using Fingerprint or RFID Reader

The authentication process begins when a user scans their fingerprint or RFID card. The system verifies the scanned data against stored records, ensuring secure and accurate identification. The dual authentication method provides an RFID card alternative with a secondary password layer (Figs. 5 and 6).

Transaction Completion and Receipt Generation

After processing the transaction, the system generates a receipt detailing the transaction details. Afterwards, notifications are automatically delivered via SMS, WhatsApp, or email, providing multiple channels for user convenience (Figs. 7 and 8).

4.4 *Comparative Analysis*

Compared to traditional banking systems, the biometric-based solution shows significant improvements in security and user experience. Integrating AES encryption

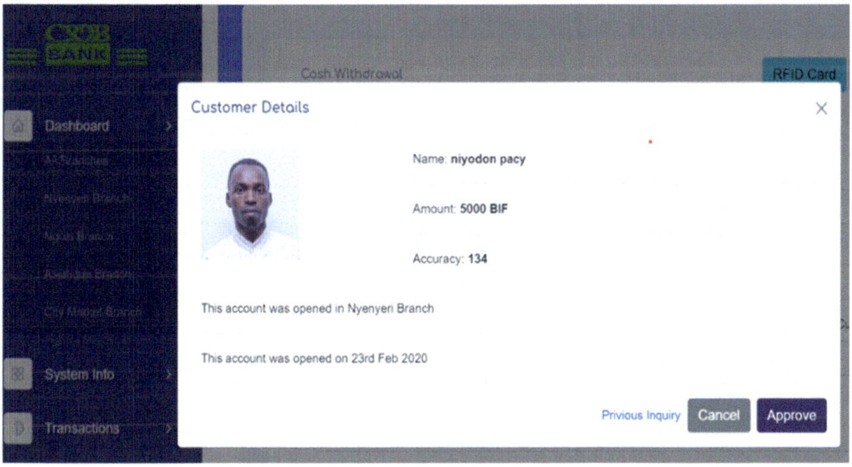

Fig. 6 Transaction processing interface

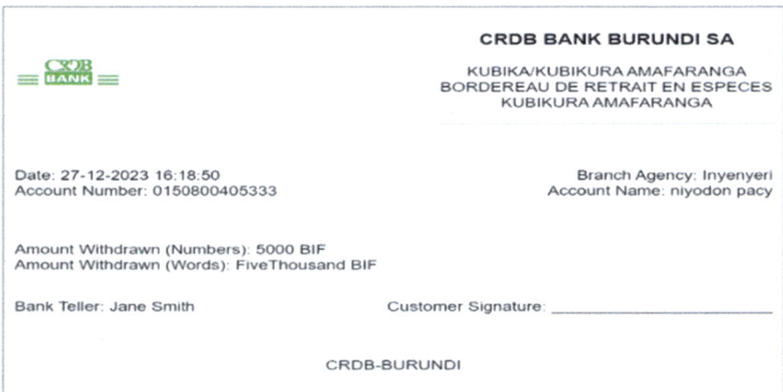

Fig. 7 Printed receipt

ensures secure data transmission, while biometric and RFID authentication methods provide robust protection against unauthorized access (Table 1).

4.5 Discussion of Key Findings

The experiments and real-world applications of the biometric banking system showcase its effectiveness in addressing key challenges in banking. Figure 1 highlights the successful integration of components like fingerprint scanning, RFID authentication, OLED display, keypad, and buzzer. Using either a fingerprint or RFID card, the client authentication system proved reliable, ensuring quick and secure access

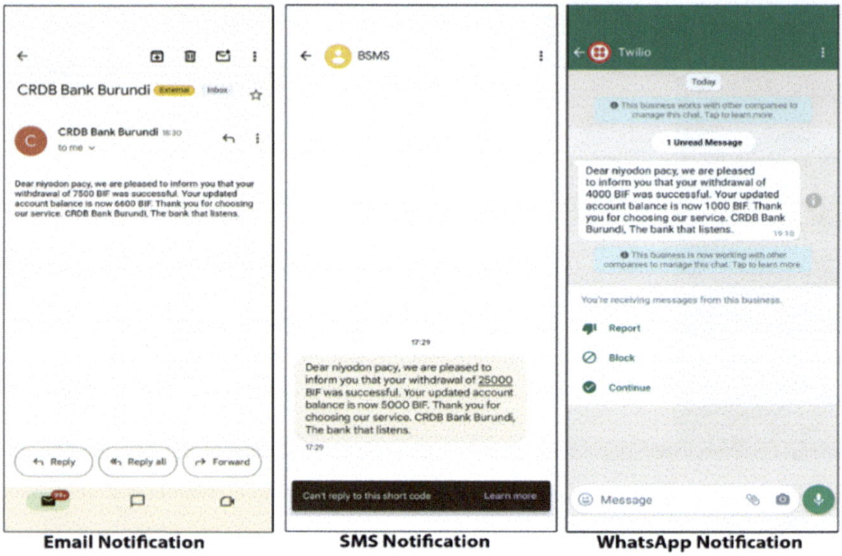

Fig. 8 Email, SMS, and WhatsApp notification

Table 1 Security comparison chart

Performance metric	Developed system	Existing paper-based system
Transaction speed	Faster	Slower
User convenience	Higher	Lower
Security	Enhanced	Limited
Accuracy	Higher	Lower
Cost effectiveness	Efficient	Inefficient
Documentation handling	Paperless	Paper-based
Data integrity	Reliable	Prone to errors
Customer satisfaction	Improved	Reduced
Processing time	Reduced	Longer
Transaction errors	Fewer	More
System maintenance	Simplified	Complex

to withdrawal services. This aligns with findings from similar research that highlights biometric authentication as a key factor in enhancing security and reducing transaction time. The Transaction Processing Interface further ensures safe and transparent transactions, with customers entering withdrawal amounts and receiving teller approval after authentication.

5 Conclusion and Future Work

In conclusion, this system effectively modernizes bank teller transactions by integrating biometric and RFID technologies, enhancing security, and streamlining the withdrawal process. However, a key limitation is the absence of deposit functionality. While the focus has been on developing a secure and user-friendly withdrawal platform, adding deposit options in the future would provide clients with a more complete and satisfying banking experience.

Acknowledgements We extend our heartfelt thanks to the Center of Excellence in East Africa (CENIT@EA) for their essential support through the scholarship fund, which was crucial for this research. We also appreciate CRDB Bank Burundi for its collaboration and the invaluable input from its technical and administrative staff, which was key to refining the biometric banking system. Additionally, we are grateful for the feedback from users and staff that contributed to the system's success and to our institutions for their support and resources throughout the project.

References

1. S. J. Kaur, L. Ali, M. K. Hassan, and M. Al-Emran, "Adoption of digital banking channels in an emerging economy: exploring the role of in-branch efforts," *Journal of Financial Services Marketing*, vol. 26, no. 2, pp. 107–121, Aug. 2021, https://doi.org/10.1057/S41264-020-00082-W/TABLES/3.
2. L. K. Osei, Y. Cherkasova, and K. M. Oware, "Unlocking the full potential of digital transformation in banking: a bibliometric review and emerging trend," *Future Business Journal 2023 9:1*, vol. 9, no. 1, pp. 1–18, Aug. 2023, https://doi.org/10.1186/S43093-023-00207-2.
3. D. Bradley, D. A. Finer, M. Gustafson, and J. Williams, "When Bankers Go to Hail: Insights into Fed-Bank Interactions from Taxi Data," *SSRN Electronic Journal*, Aug. 2022, https://doi.org/10.2139/SSRN.3141240.
4. M. S. Alnsour, "Online relationship marketing for banks in face-to-face economies," *Journal of Marketing Analytics*, vol. 6, no. 3, pp. 105–116, Aug. 2018, https://doi.org/10.1057/S41270-018-0032-Z/METRICS.
5. S. Chauhan, A. Akhtar, and A. Gupta, "Customer experience in digital banking: a review and future research directions," *International Journal of Quality and Service Sciences*, vol. 14, no. 2, pp. 311–348, Aug. 2022, https://doi.org/10.1108/IJQSS-02-2021-0027/FULL/PDF.
6. S. Zhang, L. Han, K. Kallias, and A. Kallias, "The value of in-person banking: evidence from U.S. small businesses," *Review of Quantitative Finance and Accounting*, vol. 57, no. 4, pp. 1393–1435, Nov. 2021, https://doi.org/10.1007/S11156-021-00982-5/TABLES/14.
7. P. Modiha, "Digital Transformation in the Finance and Banking Sector," pp. 95–117, 2024, https://doi.org/10.1007/978-3-031-52403-5_8.
8. W. Yang, S. Wang, J. Hu, G. Zheng, and C. Valli, "Security and Accuracy of Fingerprint-Based Biometrics: A Review," *Symmetry 2019, Vol. 11, Page 141*, vol. 11, no. 2, p. 141, Aug. 2019, https://doi.org/10.3390/SYM11020141.
9. Jemimah, "Designing a Biometric (Finger) Using Multispectral Imaging Biometric Authentication Measures for Enhancing ATM Security in Nigeria," 2019.
10. N. R. Cerdán, "The custody system in the dynamism of deposits and withdrawals from banking institutions with the BCRP," *SCIÉNDO*, vol. 26, no. 1, pp. 95–98, Aug. 2023, https://doi.org/10.17268/SCIENDO.2023.013.

11. K. Příhodová and M. Hub, "Hand-Based Biometric System Using Convolutional Neural Networks," *Acta Informatica Pragensia*, vol. 9, no. 1, pp. 48–57, 2020.
12. S. Gokul, S. Kukan, K. Meenakshi, S. S. V. Priyan, J. R. Gini, and M. E. Harikumar, "Biometric based smart ATM using RFID," *Proceedings of the 3rd International Conference on Smart Systems and Inventive Technology, ICSSIT 2020*, pp. 406–411, Aug. 2020, https://doi.org/10.1109/ICSSIT48917.2020.9214287.
13. S. M. Aljuaid and A. S. Ansari, "Automated Teller Machine Authentication Using Biometric," *Computer Systems Science and Engineering*, vol. 41, no. 3, pp. 1009–1025, Aug. 2021, https://doi.org/10.32604/CSSE.2022.020785.
14. J. M. Chigada, "A qualitative analysis of the feasibility of deploying biometric authentication systems to augment security protocols of bank card transactions," *SA Journal of Information Management*, vol. 22, no. 1, Aug. 2020, https://doi.org/10.4102/SAJIM.V22I1.1194.
15. , M. Alzamel, A. H. A., and M. Alsmadi, "Point of Sale (POS) Network with Embedded Fingerprint Biometric Authentication," *International Journal of Scientific Research in Science and Technology (IJSRST)*, vol. 6, Sep. 2019.
16. S. Hublikar, V. B. Pattanashetty, V. Mane, P. S. Pillai, M. Lakkannavar, and N. S. V Shet, "Biometric-Based Authentication in Online Banking," *Lecture Notes in Networks and Systems*, vol. 400, pp. 249–259, 2023, https://doi.org/10.1007/978-981-19-0095-2_26.
17. N. Badovinac and D. Simic, "A Multimodal Biometric Authentication (MBA) in Card Payment Systems," *Proceedings - 2019 International Conference on Artificial Intelligence: Applications and Innovations, IC-AIAI 2019*, pp. 23–29, Aug. 2019, https://doi.org/10.1109/IC-AIAI48757.2019.00011.
18. Y. Huang, B. Fu, N. Peng, Y. Ba, X. Liu, and S. Zhang, "RFID Authentication System Based on User Biometric Information," *Applied Sciences 2022, Vol. 12, Page 12865*, vol. 12, no. 24, p. 12865, Aug. 2022, https://doi.org/10.3390/APP122412865.
19. J. Wanner, L. V. Herm, K. Heinrich, and C. Janiesch, "The effect of transparency and trust on intelligent system acceptance: Evidence from a user-based study," *Electronic Markets 2022 32:4*, vol. 32, no. 4, pp. 2079–2102, Oct. 2022, https://doi.org/10.1007/S12525-022-00593-5.
20. M. Paradesi Priyanka *et al.*, "A Comparative Review between Modern Encryption Algorithms viz. DES, AES, and RSA," *Proceedings of International Conference on Computational Intelligence and Sustainable Engineering Solution, CISES 2022*, pp. 295–300, 2022, https://doi.org/10.1109/CISES54857.2022.9844393.
21. A. Olutola and M. Olumuyiwa, "Comparative Analysis of Encryption Algorithms", Accessed: Mar. 18, 2025. [Online]. Available: www.ajpojournals.org.

Internet of Things-Based System for Real-Time Monitoring of Margarine Production Process: A Case Study of SAVONOR in Burundi

Ezechiel Niyonzima, Shubi Kaijage, Elizabeth Mkoba, and Beatus Mbunda

Abstract This paper presents an Internet of Things (IoT)-based system developed to enhance the margarine production process by enabling real-time monitoring of critical production parameters such as temperature, pH levels, color, and humidity. The system addresses challenges faced by the margarine production department at SAVONOR, Burundi, particularly in the areas of temperature regulation, quality control, and the need for manual intervention. The system aims to improve production efficiency and quality by integrating IoT sensors and actuators through real-time data collection, automated alerts, and remote monitoring. This work provides insights into the system's reliability, sensor calibration, and integration with existing production infrastructure. Importantly, user acceptance testing (UAT) was conducted, and the results were 85%, demonstrating the system's high functionality and performance, and the satisfaction of the users.

Keywords Margarine production · Peltier cooling system · Internet of Things (IoT)

1 Introduction

In the context of margarine production, maintaining precise control over parameters such as temperature, pH levels, and ingredient quality is crucial for ensuring consistent product quality [1]. Traditional production systems often rely on manual interventions and visual inspections, which can result in inefficiencies and inconsistencies [2]. This paper presents an IoT-based solution designed to automate and optimize real-time monitoring of key production variables to address these challenges. The developed system, tailored for use in the SAVONOR margarine production plant in Bujumbura, Burundi, offers significant benefits. It incorporates sensors to capture

E. Niyonzima (✉) · S. Kaijage · E. Mkoba · B. Mbunda
Tanzania School of Computational and Communication Science and Engineering, The Nelson Mandela Africa Institution of Science and Technology (NM-AIST), Arusha, Tanzania
e-mail: niyonzimae@nm-aist.ac.tz

J. Marx Gómez et al. (eds.), *Advancement in Embedded and Mobile Systems*, Progress in IS, https://doi.org/10.1007/978-3-031-99219-3_5

temperature, pH, and color data, as well as automated actuators, such as a Peltier cooler, for dynamic control of the production process. The system also provides real-time alerts via email and SMS, ensuring that lab personnel and maintenance staff are promptly notified of any deviations in production conditions, thereby enhancing production efficiency and quality [3].

2 Related Works

Various methods have been employed to address challenges in food production processes, such as hydrogenation in margarine, fermentation process monitoring, and food quality monitoring. The following studies highlight the most relevant research in these areas.

An IoT-based beer fermentation monitoring system was developed to improve the quality and efficiency of beer manufacturing by continuously tracking parameters such as temperature, humidity, and CO_2 levels. However, while successfully monitoring these variables, the system lacks alert mechanisms for potential issues and does not account for additional parameters like pH or gravity [4]. Another study introduced an IoT system for real-time monitoring of CO_2 emissions during wine fermentation, providing winemakers with critical CO_2 level information throughout the process. However, it fails to monitor other key factors like humidity and temperature, which are crucial for optimal fermentation conditions [5].

Furthermore, a web-based IoT system was designed to control and monitor cocoa fermentation and drying processes, aiming to modernize traditional agricultural methods through process data collection. While effective for cocoa production, it does not address specific challenges in margarine production [6]. A PLC control system for small-scale fine chemical manufacturing, using beer fermentation as a case study, was developed to automatically manage temperature and pressure during fermentation [7]. This system improves output quality and reduces costs. An IoT-based system for tempeh production was successfully developed [8]. However, this system only manages temperature and humidity parameters.

Additionally, an IoT-based system for industrial applications enhances real-time data monitoring and control by integrating various IoT devices with traditional systems. It focuses on automating production line control and monitoring parameters like operating activities and downtime, with potential for future advancements using machine learning and broader monitoring variables such as vibration and power usage [9].

Fig. 1 Geographic location of SAVONOR in Bujumbura, Burundi

3 Materials and Methods

3.1 Case Study

This case study explores developing and implementing an Internet of Things (IoT)-based system for real-time monitoring of the margarine production process at SAVONOR, a leading manufacturing company located in Bujumbura, Burundi. The Project highlights integrating modern technological solutions to enhance operational efficiency and ensure product quality in the food manufacturing sector. The geographical location of SAVONOR is illustrated in Fig. 1.

3.2 System Development Approach

The agile software development methodology (ASDM) was applied throughout the project, covering all phases from problem identification to solution design, development, and assessment [10]. Because ASDM can quickly adjust to changes and provides a clear overview of project progression and functionality, it was specially selected to construct the Internet of Things (IoT)-based system for real-time monitoring of margarine production. It makes the ongoing development of systems easier at every stage of the process. Furthermore, the agile methodology's Extreme Programming (XP) proved to be especially useful for building prototypes when it came to planning, designing, coding, and testing activities that prioritize efficiency, feedback, and product quality [11].

3.3 System Architecture

The IoT-based system architecture, illustrated in Fig. 2, comprises several key components to ensure effective margarine production monitoring. Sensors including the DHT22 for temperature and humidity, a pH sensor for acidity levels, and a color sensor for visual quality assessment are strategically positioned in the production area to capture essential data. The system utilizes an ESP32 WROOM-32D microcontroller for its dual-core processing capabilities, enhanced GPIO options, and integrated Wi-Fi/Bluetooth, offering superior reliability and processing power compared to the ESP8266. Actuators, specifically a Peltier cooling system, automatically regulate temperature when it surpasses predefined thresholds. The user interface is designed for real-time data visualization through a web dashboard, complemented by a 20x4 LCD screen, enabling operators to efficiently monitor and manage production metrics.

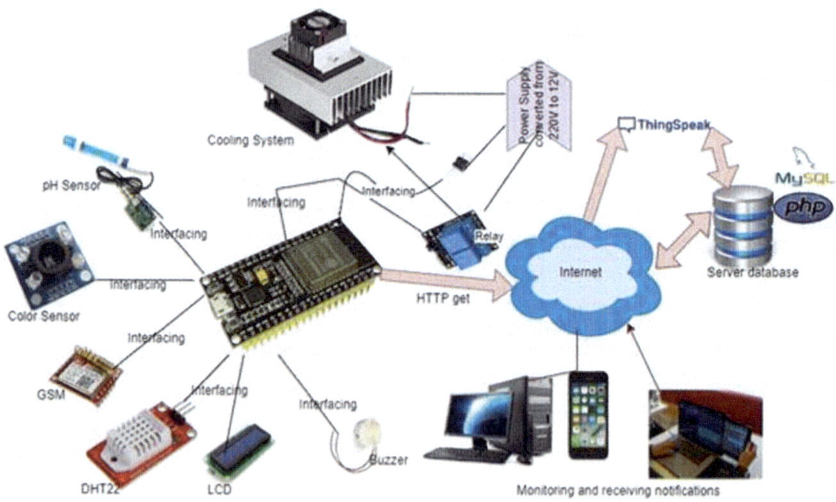

Fig. 2 System architecture

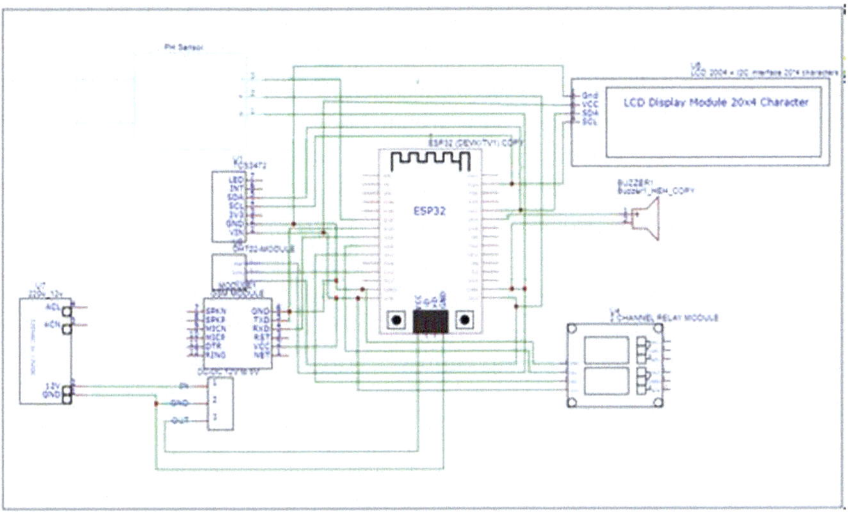

Fig. 3 Schematic diagram of the system

3.4 Hardware Tool Integration

The ESP32-WROOM-32 microcontroller was selected for its affordability, compatibility, and advanced features compared to its predecessor, the ESP8266. This microcontroller, equipped with a 32-bit Tensilica Xtensa LX6 processor, offers both single- and dual-core versions with integrated Bluetooth and Wi-Fi capabilities, making it a powerful choice for the IoT-based real-time margarine production monitoring system. The system's schematic integrates various components, including the ESP32-WROOM-32D microcontroller board, sensors, and actuators.

The sensor connects to pins 21 (SCL) and 22 (SDA), sharing the I2C bus with an LCD. The pH Sensor is linked to pin 32, the DHT22 Temperature and Humidity Sensor to pin 12, the Buzzer to pin 19, and the Relay Module (2 Channels) to pins 26 and 27. The relay module manages temperature control by activating to prevent overheating when temperatures exceed 60 degrees Celsius and deactivating when temperatures fall between 0 and 59 degrees Celsius. The GSM SIM800L Module's transmitter (Tx) is connected to pin 33, and its receiver (Rx) to pin 25. All sensors are powered by the 5V and 3.3V outputs from the ESP32-WROOM-32D, ensuring effective integration and power management, as depicted in Fig. 3.

3.5 Integration and Calibration of IoT Sensors

The IoT system was designed for seamless integration with existing production machinery and software, using standard industrial communication protocols to ensure compatibility and continuity of operations. Data from the system is centralized for historical analysis. To guarantee real-time accuracy and reliability, each sensor was carefully calibrated before deployment: the DHT22 temperature sensor was calibrated with a reference thermometer to within ±0.5°C; the pH sensor was adjusted using standard buffer solutions to within ±0.2 pH units; and the color sensor was calibrated with reference cards to detect specific shades. Regular recalibration and signal conditioning were implemented to maintain data accuracy and minimize noise.

4 Results and Discussion

4.1 The Functionality of the Developed System

The solution that has been designed effortlessly optimizes margarine production operations by integrating many components. Throughout the production process, sensors such as the DHT22, pH, and color sensor collect vital data points and send them to the ESP32 microcontroller for analysis. This microcontroller manages the temperature management process by keeping an eye on the data from the DHT22 sensor. When the temperature rises above the ideal range of 0–59 degrees Celsius, the Peltier cooler kicks in to start chilling the area until it returns to a comfortable level. The system evaluates pH levels and color changes at the same time. The GSM module notifies Lab Personnel via call, SMS, and email to come in for testing right away if the pH falls outside of the intended range of 6 to 8 and if the color sensor picks up a yellow tint. Furthermore, the plant manager is instantly notified of any irregularities by a buzzer alert. Maintenance Personnel are notified in the event of parameter deviations, such as variations in pH levels or color, so they can take immediate action. Suppose an abnormal condition, like the color becomes yellow and the pH level remaining out of the range for up to 50 minutes, is detected. In that case, the system notifies maintenance personnel through calls, SMS, and emails as shown in Fig. 4. Through web and mobile applications, real-time monitoring is visualized, giving stakeholders a thorough understanding of the production process. By maximizing operational effectiveness, reducing downtime, and enabling proactive maintenance, this integrated method eventually optimizes SAVONOR's margarine output. Additionally, Fig. 5 illustrates the proposed and working prototype for the IoT-based margarine production monitoring system, highlighting the integration of sensors, actuator, LCD, buzzer, jumper wires, and the ESP32 microcontroller to enable real-time monitoring and control.

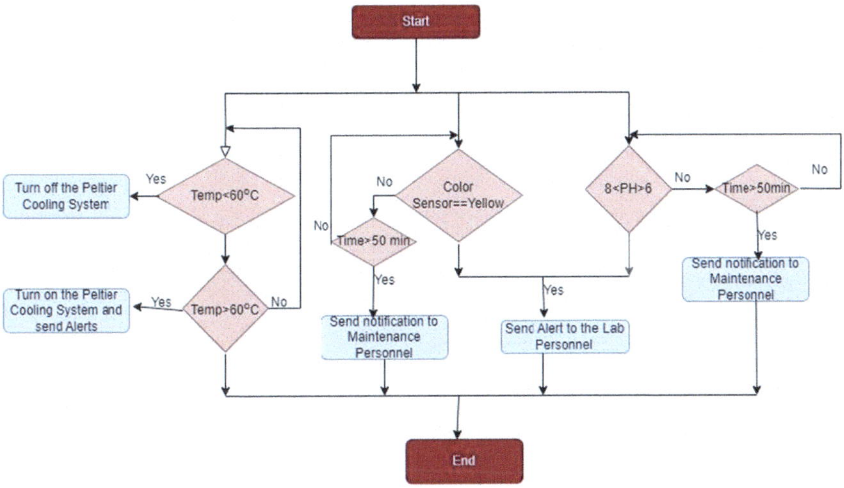

Fig. 4 Flowchart of the proposed system

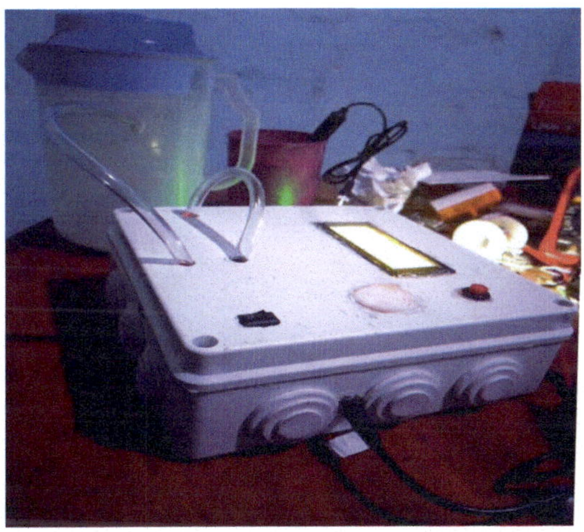

Fig. 5 The proposed prototype

4.2 System Reliability

The IoT system reliably captured real-time data for key production parameters, including temperature, pH levels, and color. Figure 6 shows the real-time monitoring interface where temperature, pH, and color data were visualized, along with trend analysis data displayed through the ThingSpeak cloud platform.

The system also featured a web application for remote monitoring. Figure 7 shows the login page, granting users access to view the production data remotely. Upon logging in, users are directed to the main dashboard (Fig. 8), where the system's key

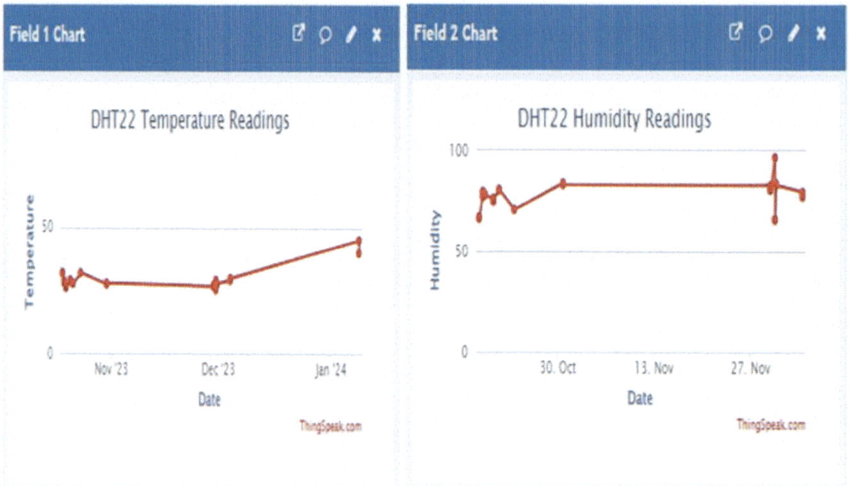

Fig. 6 ThingSpeak cloud platform

metrics, such as temperature data, are displayed (Fig. 9) for real-time monitoring and historical analysis.

During testing, the system demonstrated consistent accuracy in maintaining target temperature ranges using the Peltier cooling system. The automatic temperature regulation reduced the risk of overheating, thereby improving production efficiency.

Fig. 7 Login page

Fig. 8 Main page

IOT BASED SYSTEM FOR REAL TIME MARGARINE PRODUCTION PROCESS Accueil DHT22 Color Sensor PH Level

IOT BASED SYSTEM FOR REAL TIME MARGARINE PRODUCTION PROCESS

ID	Temperature	Humidity	Record Time
1	0.00	0.00	2023-09-27 17:36:00
2	0.00	0.00	2023-09-27 17:47:21
3	30.80	81.00	2024-05-07 20:03:18
4	30.90	80.90	2024-05-07 20:03:31
5	31.00	80.60	2024-05-07 20:03:43
6	30.50	80.30	2024-05-07 20:09:35
7	30.60	79.60	2024-05-07 20:10:19
8	30.60	79.80	2024-05-07 20:10:29
9	31.20	79.00	2024-05-07 23:10:12
10	31.40	79.60	2024-05-07 23:10:29

Fig. 9 Temperature and humidity data

4.3 Notifications and Alerts

The IoT system features a proactive notification mechanism that alerts personnel when critical parameters deviate from predefined norms. Lab personnel received an email and SMS alerts when pH levels exceeded 60°C or when the color sensor detected unacceptable deviations (Fig. 10). This reduced response times and minimized production delays, resulting in improved product consistency.

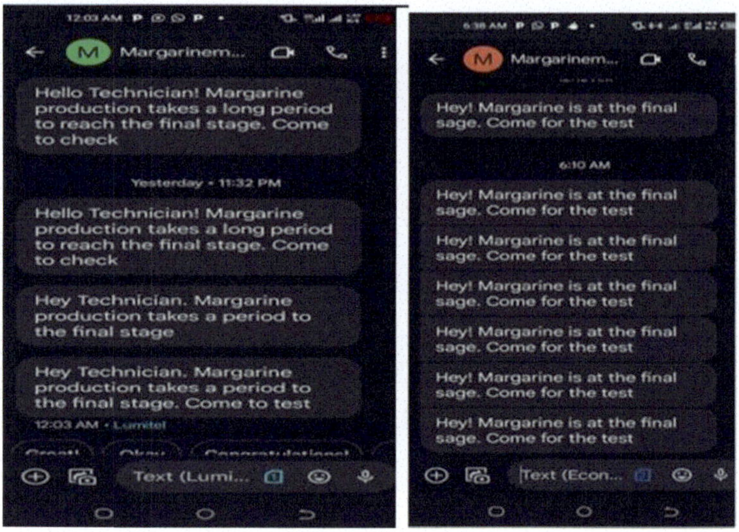

Fig. 10 Notification and alerts

4.4 User Acceptance Testing (UAT)

User Acceptance Testing was conducted with 20 respondents, including plant managers, lab personnel, and maintenance staff. Feedback was collected via Google Forms, with 85% of respondents expressing satisfaction with the system's ease of use, real-time monitoring capabilities, and automated alerts. Many highlighted that the system significantly improved their ability to manage production conditions without manual intervention. The details of the testing phase are illustrated in Fig. 11.

4.5 Integration Challenges and Technical Considerations

During the integration of the IoT system with existing production machinery, several challenges were encountered. Compatibility issues arose, necessitating the development of custom adapters to enable seamless communication between the machinery and the IoT system. Additionally, initial tests identified data transmission delays, which were mitigated by optimizing the Wi-Fi network and adjusting sensor polling intervals. Despite these hurdles, the system was successfully deployed, and no major compatibility issues were reported during the final implementation phase.

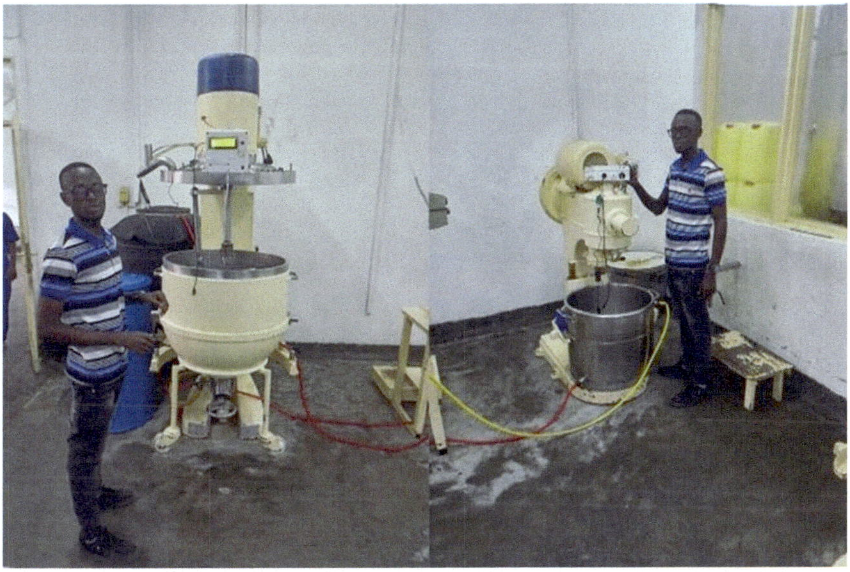

Fig. 11 System testing

4.6 Comparison with Existing Systems

The developed IoT system was compared with the existing manual monitoring system used at the plant. The new system significantly reduced human error, improved data accuracy, and shortened response times for temperature deviations and quality control issues. After the implementation of this IoT-based system, a comparison of the performance metrics was done before and after deployment to evaluate its impact.

5 Conclusion and Future Work

This paper presents an IoT-based system designed to enhance SAVONOR's margarine production by enabling real-time monitoring and control of key production parameters. The system integrates seamlessly with existing machinery and provides reliable, automated alerts, improving production efficiency and quality. Future work will focus on expanding the system to cover additional production metrics such as ingredient levels and viscosity. Further testing will be conducted to evaluate the system's performance in long-term operation and its impact on overall production outcomes.

Acknowledgements I would like to express my sincere gratitude to the Center of Excellence in East Africa (CENIT@EA) for its steadfast support of the scholarship fund. During my internship, my academic and industrial host supervisors provided invaluable guidance, support, and encouragement. Their facilitation and assistance were crucial to the project's success.

References

1. S. Berdiansyah and F. Arifan, "Evaluation of the effect of sesame lecithin emul- sifier generated from sesame oil water degumming process on margarine pro- duction," *Food Res*, vol. 7, no. 1, pp. 236–243, Feb. 2023, https://doi.org/10.26656/fr.2017.7(1).553.
2. M. D. Álvarez, B. Herranz, A. Saiz, and S. Cofrades, "Functionality of Puff Pastry Olive Pomace Oil-Based Margarines and Their Baking Performance," *Foods*, vol. 12, no. 11, Jun. 2023, https://doi.org/10.3390/foods12112138.
3. A. R. Yanes, P. Martinez, and R. Ahmad, "Towards automated aquaponics: A review on monitoring, IoT, and smart systems," Aug. 01, 2020, *Elsevier Ltd*. https://doi.org/10.1016/j.jclepro.2020.121571.
4. D. Buonocore, G. Ciavolino, D. Di Caro, and C. Liguori, "An IoT-based beer fermentation monitoring system," in *2021 IEEE International Workshop on Metrology for Agriculture and Forestry (MetroAgriFor)*, IEEE, 2021, pp. 263– 267.
5. E. Canete-Carmona, J. J. Gallego-Martinez, C. Martin, M. Brox, J. J. Luna- Rodriguez, and J. Moreno, "A Low-Cost IoT Device to Monitor in Real-Time Wine Alcoholic Fermentation Evolution through CO2 Emissions," *IEEE Sens J*, vol. 20, no. 12, pp. 6692–6700, Jun. 2020, https://doi.org/10.1109/JSEN.2020.2975284.
6. C. A. Gutiérrez, Institute of Electrical and Electronics Engineers, and IEEE Communications Society., *2019 IEEE Latin-American Conference on Communications (LATINCOM) : proceedings : 11–13 November 2019, Salvador, Brazil.*
7. Y. Yongfeng and T. Ying-Xin, "Beer fermentation control system design based on S7–1200PLC," in *2022 International Conference on Computer Engineering and Artificial Intelligence (ICCEAI)*, IEEE, 2022, pp. 849–851.
8. I. Riadi and R. Syaefudin, "Monitoring and Control Food Temperature and Hu- midity using Internet of Things Based-on Microcontroller," *Jurnal Ilmiah Teknik Elektro Komputer dan Informatika*, vol. 7, no. 1, p. 108, Apr. 2021, https://doi.org/10.26555/jetski.v7i1.20213.
9. M. Ninawe, S. Patil, A. Ojha, S. Bawane, and P. Kawale, "REAL TIME DATA MONITORING & CONTROLLING BY USING IoT," JETIR, 2020. [Online]. Available: www.jetir.org
10. M. Zorzetti, I. Signoretti, L. Salerno, S. Marczak, and R. Bastos, "Improving agile software development using user-centered design and lean startup," *Inf Softw Technol*, vol. 141, p. 106718, 2022.
11. A. Fruhling and G.-J. De Vreede, "Field experiences with eXtreme programming: Developing an emergency response system," *Journal of Management Information Systems*, vol. 22, no. 4, pp. 39–68, 2006.

Design and Development of an Internet of Things (IoT)-Based Smart Monitoring System for Community Water Wells in Rwanda

Uwamahirwe Yvonne, Jean Claude Habimana, Colombe Yves Ishimwe, Philbert Nsengiyumva, and Omar Gatera

Abstract Community water wells are essential for providing clean and safe drinking water in many rural and urban areas. However, maintaining their reliability and efficiency can be challenging due to maintenance issues, water quality concerns, and environmental factors. This paper proposes an Internet of Things (IoT)-based smart monitoring system to address these challenges. The system aims to enhance the monitoring, management, and maintenance of water wells through real-time data collection, analysis, and remote control capabilities. By leveraging IoT technologies, sensor networks, Actuators and cloud computing, the proposed solution enables efficient monitoring of key parameters such as turbidity and pH levels. Additionally, it facilitates proactive maintenance and timely interventions by alerting stakeholders, including those with disabilities, about potential issues or anomalies through

U. Yvonne · J. C. Habimana (✉)
Internet of Things Embedded Computing Systems at the Africa Centre of Excellence of Things (ACE-IoT), College of Science and Technology, University of Rwanda, Kigali, Rwanda
e-mail: claudeacademic@gmail.com

U. Yvonne
e-mail: mahirwe91@gmail.com

C. Y. Ishimwe
College of Science and Technology (CST), University of Rwanda(UR), Kigali, Rwanda
e-mail: ishimwe92@gmail.com

P. Nsengiyumva
Electrical Engineering, University of Sherbrooke, Quebec, Canada

Electrical Engineering From the Central University of Technology, Free State, Bloemfontein, South Africa

P. Nsengiyumva
e-mail: nsenga_philibert@yahoo.com

O. Gatera
Department of Electrical and Electronics Engineering Head of PhD Studies and Research, African Center of Excellence in Internet of Things (ACEIoT), College of Science and Technology, University of Rwanda, Kigali, Rwanda
e-mail: ogatera@gmail.com

J. Marx Gómez et al. (eds.), *Advancement in Embedded and Mobile Systems*, Progress in IS, https://doi.org/10.1007/978-3-031-99219-3_6

various actuators. These alerts aid in decision-making regarding water use based on its status. The experimental results demonstrate that the system is promising and can be effectively used for health improvement.

Keywords Community water wells · Smart monitoring system · Sensor networks · Actuators and water quality

1 Introduction

Seventy per cent of the earth is covered with water, making it one of the most significant and ubiquitous elements in our planet [1]. It is necessary to the survival of all living things [2].

Life as we know it would not be possible on Earth without water. The availability of clean, safe water is a major global difficult. Many people from urban areas face issues of bad water quality. The availability of pure and safe drinking water is essential for maintaining public health and welfare. Traditional monitoring methods are often manual and infrequent in all aspects, making it challenging to detect changes in water quality or respond promptly to contamination incidents; thus its result affects Population negatively mostly in Urban areas [3]. Water pollution is cause by many factors. Including human activities [4, 5]. Water pollution raises human beings' problems including diseases that affect their lives and thus lead to economic growth impacts [6, 7]. Overall, utilizing dirty water can have detrimental effects that are substantial, thus, it's crucial to make sure that all water sources or supplied water are adequately treated and kept up to assure their security and cleanliness [8, 9].

The proposed system aimed to mitigate the risks of water pollution by ensuring the reliable, safe, and efficient management of water resources through the use of IT Technology. Various sensors were used to measure water parametres like turbidity and pH to assess their levels at the end-user side. Water with High turbidity can have harmful pathogens and clog filters, while high pH can cause skin irritation, gastrointestinal issues, and pipe corrosion. Both factors affect water taste and quality, making it essential to maintain them within safe limits. The proposed system uses various notifications like Liquid Crystal Display (LCD), Light emitting diode (LED), buzzers, and global system for Mobile communication(GSM) alerts to ensure timely action, benefiting all users, including those with disabilities. Water supply authorities can access water quality data online via the GSM module, enabling proactive maintenance. This IoT-based smart monitoring system for community water wells enhances clean, safe, and sustainable access to drinking water.

By leveraging IoT technology, communities can overcome the challenges of water pollution and work towards a future where water contamination are no longer barriers to a healthy life.

2 Review of Related Work

Numerous projects and research studies have been carried out in this area, concentrating on various facets of water monitoring. In order to measure the pH levels of water, Moparthi et al. built a water quality monitoring system-using IoT. The potential of IoT in water quality monitoring is highlighted by the use of variety IoT devices. Arduino was used in the connectivity with sensors (pH sensor) was used in its implementation. One potential workaround for this would be adding communication means Water supply authorities and other stakeholders could have access to the water quality data regardless of where they are.

Fadel and Shujaa created another water quality monitoring method [10]. While it was a commendable decision to implement the system using the ESP32 and a variety of sensors, including pH, turbidity, temperature, and humidity, it appears that the system has certain limitations when it comes to informing water management authorities and guaranteeing the security of the water supply for communities.

To address the issue of failure to notify authorities, it may be necessary to incorporate a reliable communication mechanism to the system. This could involve integrating a notification system to notify the appropriate authorities about water quality changes. Overall, it is crucial to consider both the effective notification of water management authorities and the security of the water supply when designing and implementing water quality monitoring systems. By addressing these concerns, Fadel and Shujaa's system can significantly contribute to safeguarding water quality and ensuring the well-being of the communities it serves. In that respect, Lakshmikantha and A. Hiriyannagowda, [11] stated that water quality should be detected or identified in real-time to make certain the supply of clean water. Smart solutions for monitoring water pollution were used where innovative sensors, communication, and Internet of Things (IoT) technology has been used. With all interrelated and interconnected technologies, data was recorded by using sensors, processed with the help of an Arduino board, and a Wi-Fi-module was used to transmit data to the cloud. However, the system does not permit messaging to communities as end users.

Hakimi and Jamil [12] developed a system to monitor and manage water quality by using various sensors based on the analysis on water quality monitoring models that gather water properties during live experiments. The precisions done tend to develop that system and be implemented using IoT although it is not suitable for best communication between water manufacturing authorities and communities. Vijayakumar [13] developed a system for monitoring water quality by using technology. The system indicated the acidity or alkalinity of the water. Pure water has a pH of 7, whereas acidic or alkaline water has a pH higher than 7. The pH ranges from 14 to 0. Drinking water should have a pH between 6.5 and 8.5. The amount of invisible suspended particles in water was measured using turbidity. The likelihood of getting sick rises with water turbidity. Based on the turbidity level, the system could indicate if the water was clean enough to use or if it needed to be cleansed. Arduino module have been used to implement the project and data gathered by sensors viewed on internet by the help of Wi-Fi technology.

Pokhrel [14] explored Kolora meter as alternative to the existing commercial monitoring devices. It was developed using the open-source platform Arduino UNO model and Node MCU board as the microcontroller to process measured parameters and Wi-Fi connection. Its main purpose was identifying water status before being supplied. Leveraging IoT in water resource management offers significant benefits, but there are key technical challenges to address.

Accessibility for individuals with disabilities is often limited due to current communication channels. Additionally, unreliable network connectivity in rural areas hampers effective data transmission and monitoring. To overcome these issues, innovative solutions are needed to ensure inclusivity and explore alternative communication methods that work in areas with limited connectivity, ultimately improving the efficiency of IoT-based water monitoring systems for community benefit.

3 System Design and Methodology

3.1 Embedded System Block Diagram

This block diagram illustrates the connectivity and flow of information and control between the various components of the project. This block diagram outlines the connections and interactions between these components, ensuring effective monitoring and communication of water quality information.

This project comprises several components including sensors, actuators and communication module (Fig. 1).

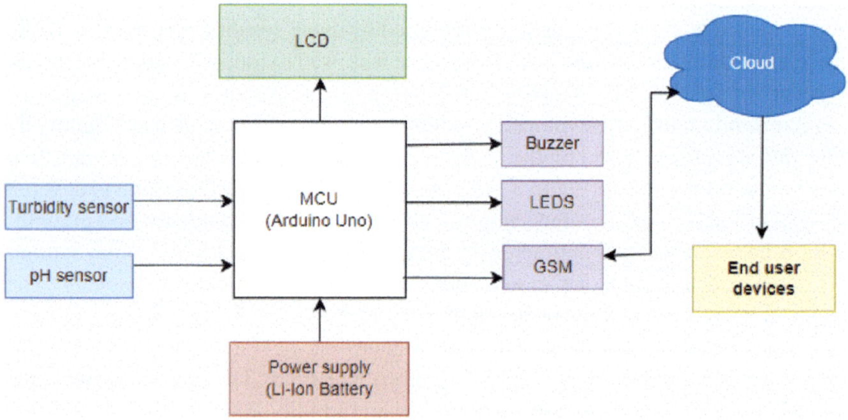

Fig. 1 System block diagram

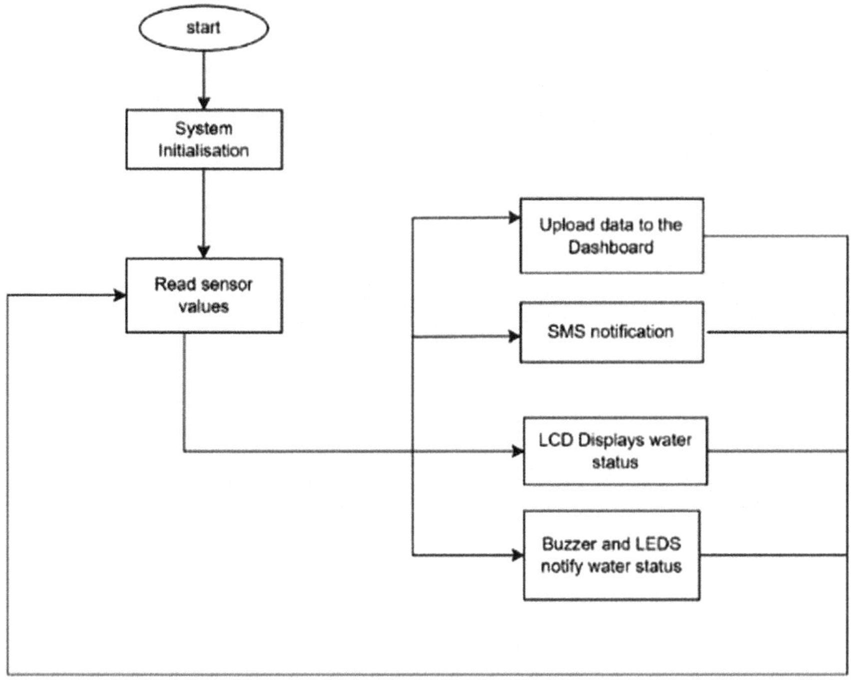

Fig. 2 System flow chart

3.2 System Flow Chart

Figure 2 provides a visual representation of the processes and steps involved in monitoring water parameters as Turbidity and pH.

3.3 Methodology

The study used a quantitative approach, starting with a literature review to identify gaps in current water monitoring methods. The research involved creating An IoT system equipped with necessary devices for providing water quality realtime information to users including people with disabilities and Stakeholders but focusing on rural areas of Muhanga District, Rwanda. Staff from water and sanitation corporation (WASAC) participated, and a sample of 384 households was calculated using sample size formula. Data was collected via an online questionnaire and analyzed with SPSS. The Agile model was chosen for system development due to its iterative and flexible nature, allowing for adaptability and continuous refinement during the project (Fig. 3).

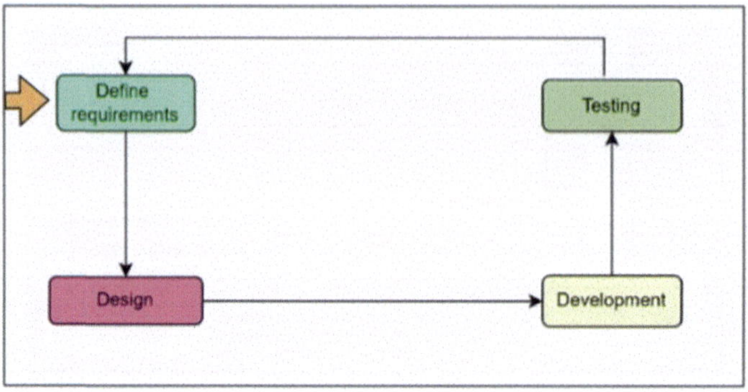

Fig. 3 Agile model

4 Result and Discussion

4.1 Embedded Device Set up

A prototype water monitoring system including sensors (pH, turbidity) and actuators (LEDs, LCDs, buzzers) is shown in Figs. 4 and 5. Using these sensors, the system creates a visual representation of the water's condition and signals any contamination using audio and visual cues. Users are alerted to low water quality by the buzzer going off, the LCD warning, and the red light coming from the LEDs when the sensors identify contamination.

The IoT-based smart monitoring system for community water wells is designed to continuously assess and communicate the quality of water in real-time. The system utilizes a network of sensors as pH and Turbidity to collect and transmit data. It

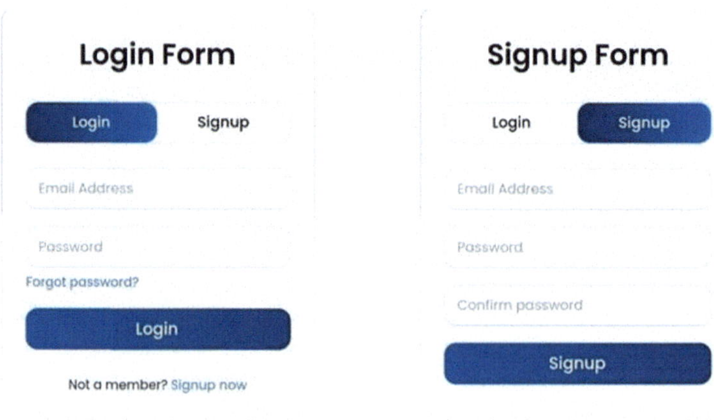

Fig. 4 Hardware connectivity

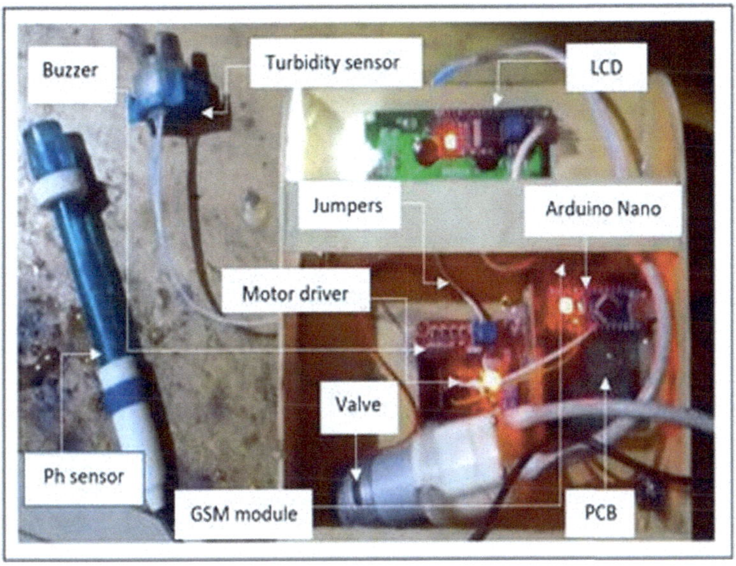

Fig. 5 Login and sign up

also use actuators LCDs, LEDs, buzzers, and GSM provided real-time water quality alerts and communication modules to provide accurate information about key water parameters to dashboard.

Multiple notification methods ensured inclusivity for all community members, including those who are blind, deaf, or illiterate. Additionally, water providers can monitor water quality online.

4.2 User Registration and Login Process

This is a login form for system users. The system users must create account and the login to access the dashboard that holds informations transmitted from sensors visualized on Dashboard.

4.3 Web Dashboard Development

The web dashboard development employs Bootstrap, JavaScript, HTML, and CSS for a responsive user interface.

Django connects the interface to MySQL for efficient data management, ensuring seamless functionality. MySQL supports robust database design and management,

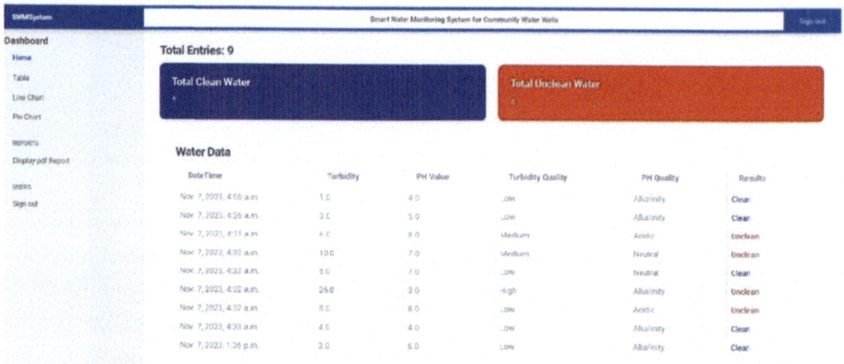

Fig. 6 Data visualisation

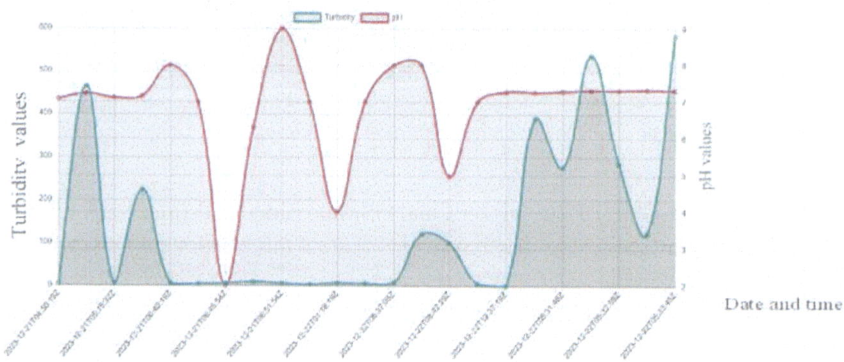

Fig. 7 pH and turbidity variation

enabling effective data storage and retrieval, resulting in a dynamic dashboard for monitoring and analyzing data effectively (Figs. 6, 7, 8 and 9).

From here, Users Can take an appropriate decision of water uses based on visualized data (Figs. 10 and 11).

4.4 Discussions

From the above Figs. 6, 7, and 8, the line graph shows changes in turbidity and pH over time, with fluctuations in both indicating water quality. Upward trends in turbidity suggest increased cloudiness, while changes in the pH line reflect shifts in water acidity or alkalinity. Intersections of pH and turbidity lines at normal levels, with a pH around 7 and acceptable turbidity, signal clean water. Data labels allow

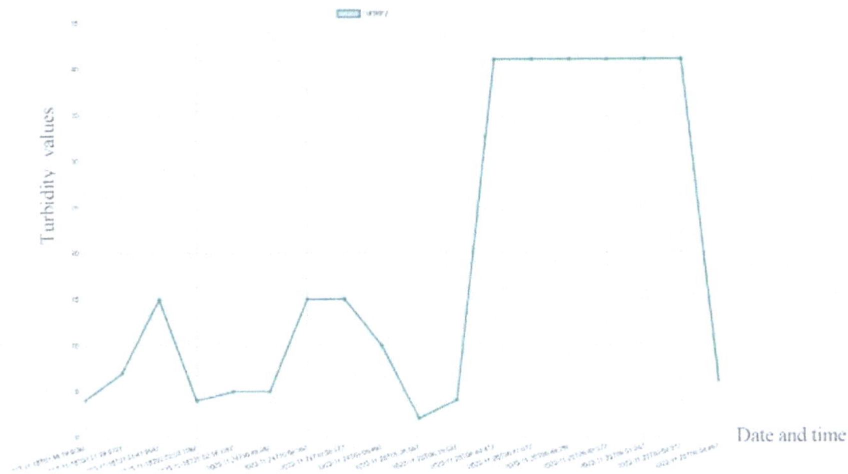

Fig. 8 Turbidity variation levels

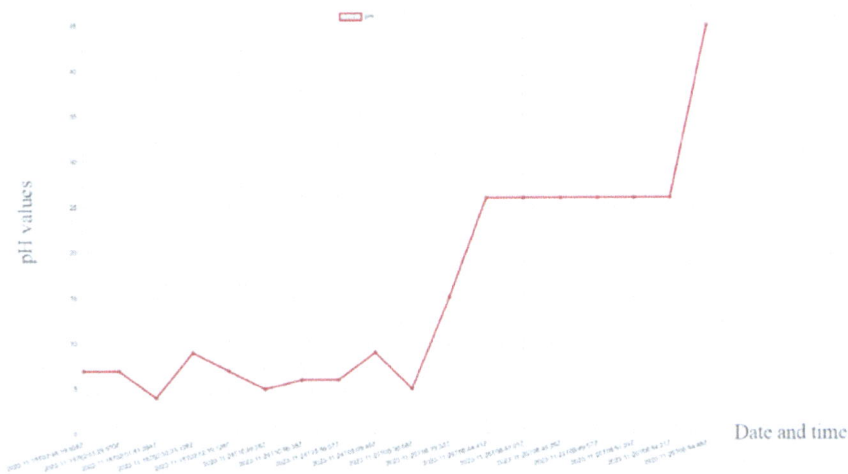

Fig. 9 pH variation

precise monitoring, providing key insights for effective water resource management. Therefore, it's, will significantly improve community health and water management.

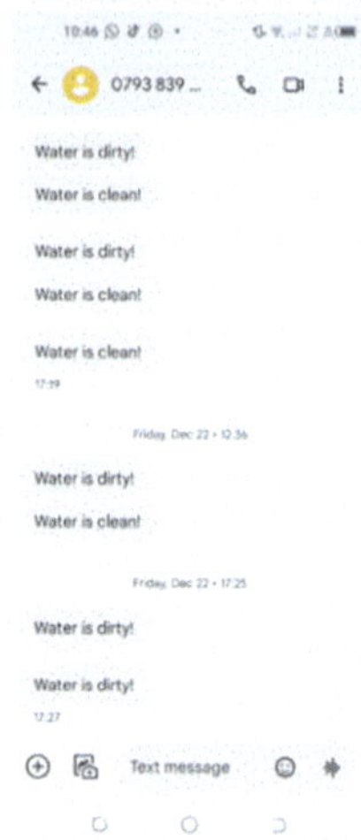

Fig. 10 LCD, LED, and Buzzer notification

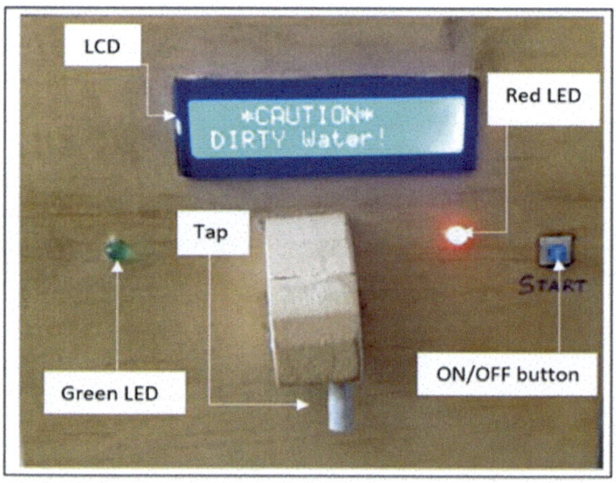

Fig. 11 SMS notification

5 Conclusion and Future Study

5.1 Conclusion

Implementing an IoT-based smart monitoring system for community water wells enhances community health and water supply efficiency. Sensors measure turbidity and pH, allowing for timely detection of contaminants. Remote monitoring enables continuous oversight without physical presence, and the data collected aids authorities in resource allocation and planning. This integration leads to a more sustainable and resilient water infrastructure, benefiting the entire community, including people with disabilities, and improving management practices.

5.2 Conclusion and Future Study

I recommend water provider to deploy an IoT technology for monitoring community water wells incorporate alert devices. This initiative would enhance community health and empower water supply authorities to effectively monitor and maintain water resources. The system will incorporate alert devices to facilitate real-time monitoring, enabling quick detection of changes in water quality. Additionally, the system will provide valuable information to individuals with disabilities, empowering them to make informed decisions regarding water usage based on notifications received [15].

References

1. D. K. Banerjee, "Water pollution and human health," Water Sanit. Mid-Decade Proc. 12th WEDC Conf., no. December 2021, pp. 47–50, 1986, https://doi.org/10.4066/2529-8046.100020.
2. Z. KILIÇ, "Su Kirliliği Nedenleri, Olumsuz Etkileri ve Önleme Yöntemleri," İstanbul Sabahattin Zaim Üniversitesi Fen Bilim. Enstitüsü Derg., no. 3, 2021, https://doi.org/10.47769/izufbed.862679.
3. Barnes J M, "The impact of water pollution from formal and informal urban developments along the Plankenbrug river on water quality and health risk," no. December, p. 240, 2003.
4. F. W. Owa, "Water Pollution: Sources, Effects, Control and Management," Int. Lett.Nat. Sci., vol. 8, pp. 1–6, 2014, https://doi.org/10.56431/p-gk4d9j.
5. L. Lin, H. Yang, and X. Xu, "Effects of Water Pollution on Human Health and Disease Heterogeneity: A Review," Front. Environ. Sci., vol. 10, no. June, 2022, https://doi.org/10.3389/fenvs.2022.880246.
6. C. E. Closmann, "Water Pollution and Economic Upheaval," vol. 33, no. 5, pp. 1919–1923, 2007.
7. J. Leju Celestino Ladu, A. L. Athiba, S. Tombe Venusto Lako, and M. Lomoro Alfred, "Investigation on the Impact of Water Pollution on Human Health in Juba County, Republic of South Sudan," J. Environ. Pollut. Hum. Heal., vol. 6, no. 3, pp. 89–95, 2018, https://doi.org/10.12691/jephh-6-3-2.
8. C. Sciences, "Polluted Water Borne Diseases: Symptoms, Causes, Treatment and Prevention," vol. 2019, no. 2, pp. 21–26, 2019, https://doi.org/10.26655/jmchemsci.2019.6.4.
9. S. Desbureaux, R. Damania, A.-S. Rodella, J. Russ, and E. Zaveri, "The Impact of Water Quality on GDP Growth," Impact Water Qual. GDP Growth, no. February 2020, 2019, https://doi.org/10.1596/33071.
10. A. A. Fadel and M. I. Shujaa, "Water Quality Monitoring System Based on IOT Platform," IOP Conf. Ser. Mater. Sci. Eng., vol. 928, no. 3, 2020, https://doi.org/10.1088/1757-899X/928/3/032054.
11. V. Lakshmikantha, A. Hiriyannagowda, A. Manjunath, A. Patted, J. Basavaiah, and A. A. Anthony, "IoT based smart water quality monitoring system," Glob. Transitions Proc., vol. 2, no. 2, pp. 181–186, 2021, https://doi.org/10.1016/j.gltp.2021.08.062.
12. I. M. Hakimi and Z. Jamil, "Development of Water Quality Monitoring Device Using Arduino UNO," IOP Conf. Ser. Mater. Sci. Eng., vol. 1144, no. 1, p. 012064, 2021, https://doi.org/10.1088/1757-899x/1144/1/012064.
13. N. Vijayakumar and R. Ramya, "The real time monitoring of water quality in IoT environment," ICIIECS 2015 - 2015 IEEE Int. Conf. Innov. Information, Embed. Commun. Syst., vol. 1, no. 9, pp. 156–158, 2015, https://doi.org/10.1109/ICIIECS.2015.7193080.

14. S. Pokhrel, A. Pant, R. Gautam, and D. B. Kshatri, "Water Quality Monitoring System Using IOT," J. Innov. Eng. Educ., vol. 3, no. 1, pp. 155–164, 2020, https://doi.org/10.3126/jiee.v3i1.34337.
15. V. Strang, "The Meaning of Water," Mean. Water, 2020, https://doi.org/10.4324/9781003087090.

A Mobile-Based Machine-Learning Model for Predicting Maintenance of Dental Machines for Health Facilities: A Case of Ministry of Health in Uganda

Famina Ayebare, Shubi Felix Kaijage, Neema Mduma, Liston Kiwoli, Hillary Kaluuma, Lambert Byarugaba, and Lydia Ssanyu

Abstract The health sector remains underfunded, falling short of the 15% budget allocation recommended by the Abuja Declaration of which Uganda is a member. Between 2010 and 2016, the budget of the health sector was an average of 7.8% of the national budget. In 2020/2021, it accounted for 5.1% of the national budget, from the previous 7.9% in the previous financial year. Major issues facing the health system include grossly underpaid health practitioners, scarcity of health workers, and necessary equipment in government facilities. The concept of machine learning is ubiquitous, and different algorithms have been used to train and build models to come up with different solution in the health sector. The objective of this project was to come up with a mobile-based machine-learning model for predicting the maintenance of dental machines based on the failure type to determine whether the machine is in good condition to work on patients efficiently or needs repair and maintenance. The project used both quantitative and qualitative methods of data collection.

F. Ayebare (✉) · S. F. Kaijage · N. Mduma · L. Kiwoli
Computational and Communication Science and Engineering (CoCSE), The Nelson Mandela African Institution of Science and Technology (NM-AIST), Arusha, Tanzania
e-mail: ayebaref@nm-aist.ac.tz

S. F. Kaijage
e-mail: shubi.kaijage@nm-aist.ac.tz

N. Mduma
e-mail: neema.mduma@nm-aist.ac.tz

L. Kiwoli
e-mail: liston.kiwoli@nm-aist.ac.tz

F. Ayebare · H. Kaluuma · L. Byarugaba · L. Ssanyu
Infectious Diseases Institute, Makerere University, Kampala, Uganda
e-mail: hkaluuma@idi.co.ug

L. Byarugaba
e-mail: lbyarugaba@idi.co.ug

L. Ssanyu
e-mail: lssanyu@idi.co.ug

J. Marx Gómez et al. (eds.), *Advancement in Embedded and Mobile Systems*, Progress in IS, https://doi.org/10.1007/978-3-031-99219-3_7

Random Forest and XG boost classifiers were used to train and test the model using structured data. The dataset contained 8 features, which were the product ID, type of machine, UDI (unique identifier), air temperature, process temperature, rotational speed, torque, and tool wear. Heat dissipation, power failure, random failure, overstain, and no failure were labels used to predict the type of failure that could occur, XG boost classifier emerged as the best with accuracy score of 97.3% in comparison with Random Forest after the accuracy score and confusion matrix of the two algorithms.

Keywords Mobile-based · Machine-learning model · Predictive maintenance · Failure type · Ministry of Health

1 Introduction

Medical supply and asset management are key components of delivering healthcare. Asset management is one of the most important yet sometimes disregarded [1]. A health facility's assets include medical equipment, which are maintained, repaired, and upgraded through the process of asset management [2]. Major issues facing the health system include grossly underpaid health practitioners, scarcity of health workers, inadequate supplies of medicines and necessary medical assets in government facilities, insufficient hospital beds, accumulated costs, and poor accessibility to health services, especially in rural areas [2]. Poor management and maintenance of medical equipment, such as dental machines, pose significant challenges [3]. Delayed maintenance of dental machines often leads to unforeseen downtimes, increased repair costs, and potential disruptions in patient care.

2 Literature Review

Using Mobile Phones and Web-Based Technology to Improve Community Health Workers' Performance in Low and Middle-Income Countries

In the study conducted by Feroz et al. [4], their study proposed the use of mobile technology by community health workers in low- income countries to report health-related issues like maternal and child health, sexually related issues, respiratory issues, and many more. The limitation in this project was the internet connectivity [4].

Information Systems in Medical Equipment Management

Fuaddi et al. proposed a web-based maintenance information system in medical equipment management that aimed to facilitate hospital management in monitoring and supervising the maintenance and calibration activities of medical equipment [5].

This helped to solve the process of recording the management of maintenance and calibration of medical equipment conducted manually or conventionally with the book as the media. This meant that all activities were conducted without the help of a computer so it could provide records of various data maintenance and calibration lost or damaged; however, there was no machine learning embedded [5].

Application of Predictive Maintenance in the Health Facilities Environment

Gonzalo et al. developed a model to predict the maintenance of the air conditioning facilities in hospitals like the air conditioners by analyzing the equipment failures by applying the condition-based maintenance technique, however, only one algorithm-based technique was used [6].

3 Technical Gap

Numerous systems have been developed regarding medical assets information systems using different technologies, which include web-based information systems with access controls like password authentication, bar code scanning, and QR. However, the developed solution builds on the foundational work of other researchers in predictive maintenance, and it adapts these principles to the context of dental machines with a mobile-based approach. The developed solution used a mobile-based machine-learning model for predicting the maintenance of dental machines for health facilities.

4 Proposed Solution

The proposed system involved three users: the clinical engineers, the Ministry of Health decision-makers, and the health head officers. The clinical engineers under the supervision of the Village Health Teams (VHTs) will add the data to the system, which will be captured and submitted through the application. The model will be utilized to make predictions about the maintenance of dental machines Secondly, the information will be stored in a database that is accessed by Infectious Diseases Institute (IDI). The Ministry of Health (MoH) will access the information via the Application Programming Interface (API). The proposed solution, as shown in Fig. 1.

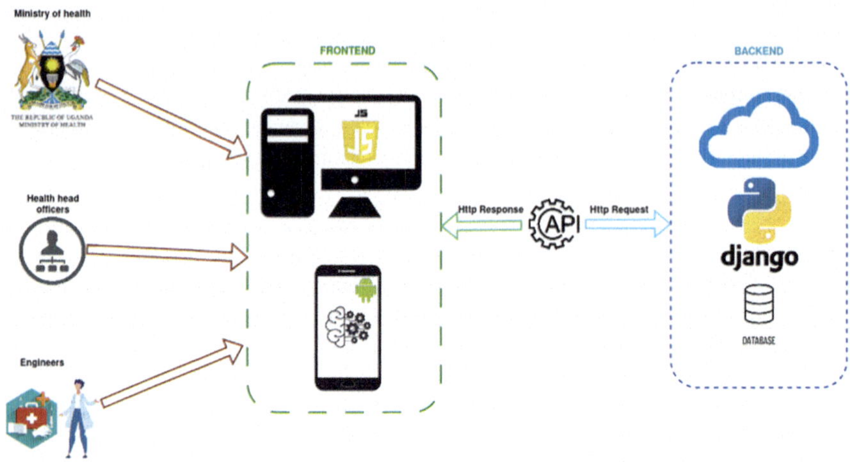

Fig. 1 Proposed solution of the system

5 Materials and Methods

This chapter examines the necessary materials and tools, as well as the requirements-gathering techniques used to develop the proposed mobile-based model machine-learning model for predicting dental machines with an asset information system for health facilities.

6 Data Collection Methods

The process of gathering data is frequently crucial to a research project's success. How data is gathered and handled can greatly influence how the study is conducted. [7]. Secondary data (https://www.kaggle.com/datasets/shivamb/machine-predictive-maintenance-classification) was obtained online to train and test the machine-learning model, which contained 8 features, namely:

Product ID
Type of Machine
UDI (Unique Identifier)
Air Temperature
Process Temperature
Rotational Speed
Torque
Tool wear

One hot encoding teh Type column

```
[ ] # Perform one-hot encoding with drop_first=True
    df_encoded = pd.get_dummies(df, columns=['Type'], prefix='Type', drop_first=True)
    df_encoded.head()
```

	Air temperature [K]	Process temperature [K]	Rotational speed [rpm]	Torque [Nm]	Tool wear [min]	Target	Failure Type	Failure Type_encoded	Type_L	Type_M
0	298.1	308.6	1551	42.8	0	0	No Failure	1	0	1
1	298.2	308.7	1408	46.3	3	0	No Failure	1	1	0
2	298.1	308.5	1498	49.4	5	0	No Failure	1	1	0
3	298.2	308.6	1433	39.5	7	0	No Failure	1	1	0
4	298.2	308.7	1408	40.0	9	0	No Failure	1	1	0

Fig. 2 Dropped two features from the data set

Failure Type	Heat Dissipation Failure	No Failure	Overstrain Failure	Power Failure	Random Failures	Tool Wear Failure
Type						
H	8	979	1	5	4	6
L	74	5757	73	59	12	25
M	30	2916	4	31	2	14

Fig. 3 Labels from the data set

The target was the failure type, and the labels included heat dissipation, power failure, random failure, overstrain, no failure, and tool wear failure. The total size of the dataset was 10,000. The independent variable was the failure type, and the rest of the features were the dependent variables. However, two of the above features were dropped: the product ID and the unique identifier (UDI). Figure 2 shows features that were considered in the development of the model after dropping the two features that never had an impact on the model.

Figure 3 below shows the labels of the target feature (failure type), and they included heat dissipation, no failure, overstrain failure, power failure, random failure, and tool wear.

7 System Development Approach

The agile process model was used in the development of the system because of its core values, which helped to deliver the exact system the customer wanted, and extreme programing was used.

System Design

Use Case Diagram

The use case diagram is a schematic illustration of the way an actor communicates with a developed system [8]. The system starts with the user logging in, depending on the user's role. The clinical engineer enters information to predict whether a dental machine requires maintenance or is still operational and also enters other information

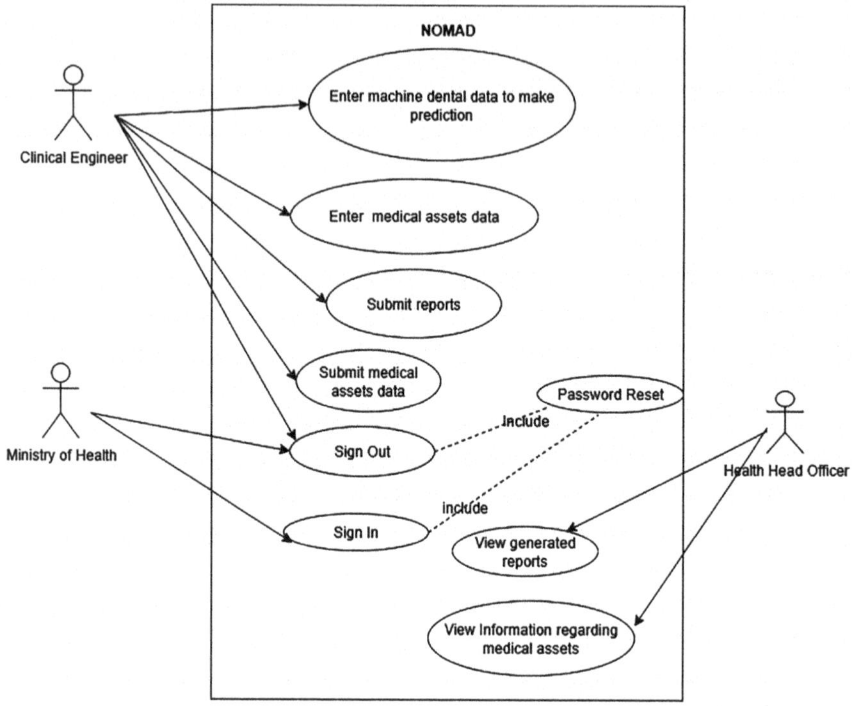

Fig. 4 Use case diagram of the developed solution

about other medical assets regarding their status, whether they are available in good condition or need to be discarded as obsolete. The health head officer, on the other hand, views the information entered by the clinical engineer at the district level to plan. The Ministry of Health will view all information from different regions in the different parts of the country at the regional level and come up with formal decisions and plans effectively. Figure 4 shows the developed solution's use case diagram.

8 System Architecture

The logical design of the software architecture in Fig. 5 illustrates the detailed components of the system. The Android components are put in a package named Dart and plugin. The Dart object-oriented programming language is used to design the interfaces, and Python is used to interact with the activities. The logical design package provides an example of what goes into developing Android applications. It also displays the elements of the server environment, which include the scripts used for the server-side scripting and the file formats handled by the scripts, such as jpeg and php. The Apache web server in this architecture is frequently used to run Hypertext

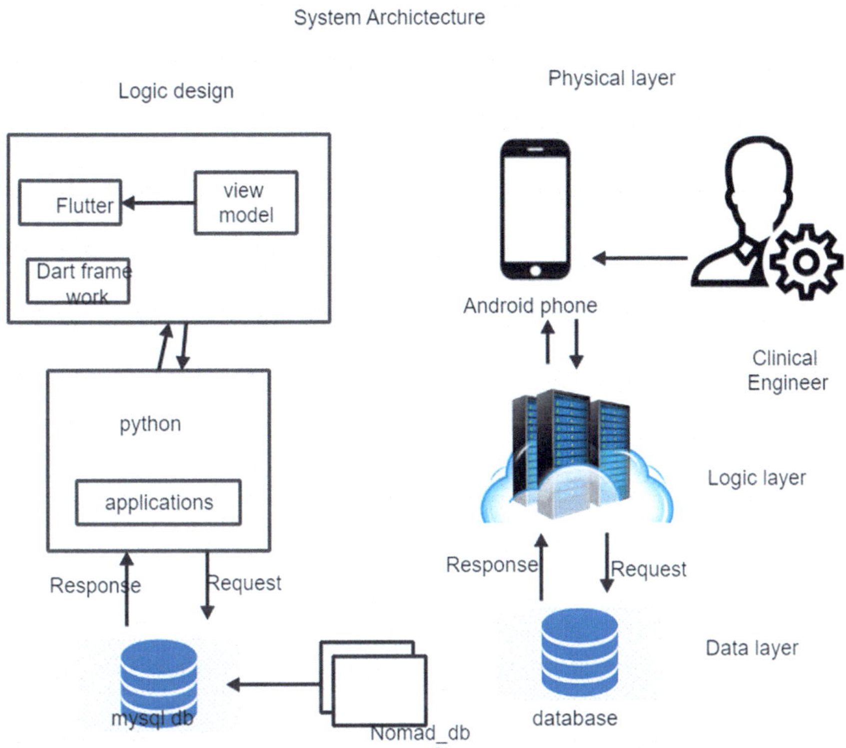

Fig. 5 System architecture diagram

Pre-processor scripts, which were used to create the API. It also hosts the database as well as the data components. The database name is Nomad_db, and it was created using MySQL.

9 Data Preprocessing for the Model

This involved importing all the necessary libraries, which included matplotlib for data visualization, the NumPy, Pickle, Seaborn, and Panda's libraries. Rows and columns in a tabular format to estimate the likelihood of failure on each machine. The target feature was the Failure Type column, which was used to predict the specific failure of the machine to solve the Multiclassification problem. The dataset was heavily imbalanced; therefore, a balancing technique to the Type column was applied to predict the specific failure of the machine to solve the Multiclassification problem.

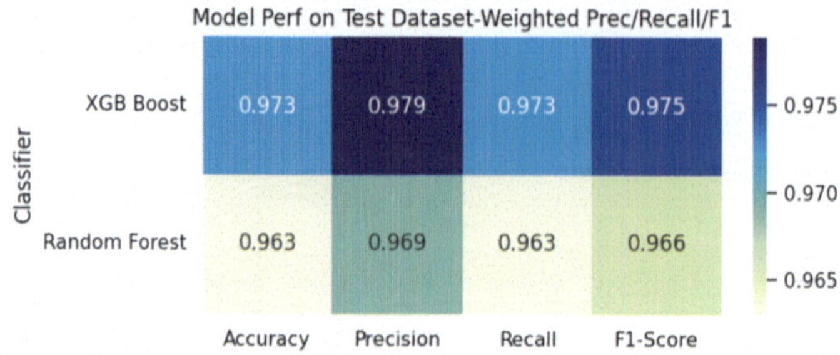

Fig. 6 Model performance on the test dataset

10 Model Training and Testing

A multi-class classification model was used to predict the maintenance needs of the dental machines since it was a classification problem to be solved. Depending on the type of failure encountered, whether it was due to random failure, power failure, or heat dissipation predicted. This was developed using the XG boost algorithm, which performed better than the Random Forest. 70% of the dataset was used for training the model, and those were 7,000 records, 10% was used for validating and 20%, which were 2,000, were used for testing the model. Figure 6 shows the model's performance on the test data.

11 Results and Discussion

11.1 Results

We were able to come up with an application that can facilitate the clinical engineers' predictive maintenance of dental machines. The mobile app was tested through User Acceptance Tests by the different stakeholders who expressed their opinions on it. The Mobile app is available on "https://appetize.io/app/w6hg6awajyf5bzxnp3omo g4p7y". Some of the different pages of the application are displayed in Table 1.

On top of the application that we produced, we carried out a survey on the project and the application. The User Acceptance tests had 10 respondents that interacted with the mobile application and shared this feedback in a survey form; some of the results are shown in Fig. 7.

Table 1 Shows the interface appearance of some of the pages in the App

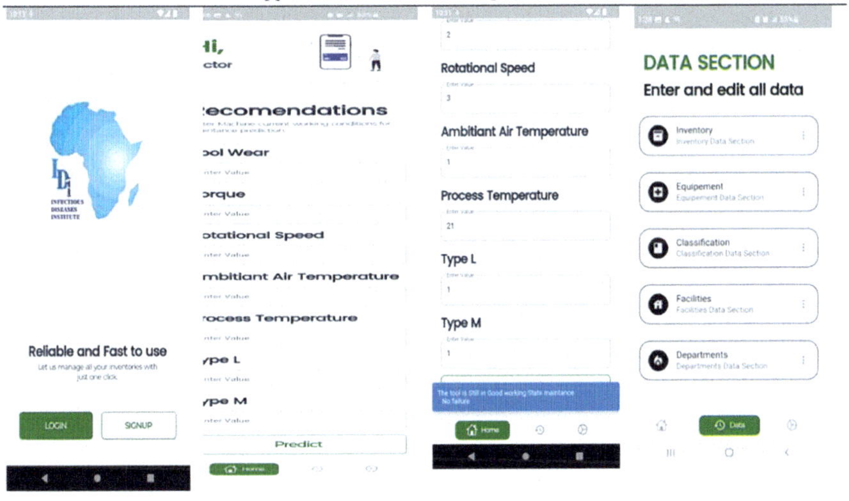

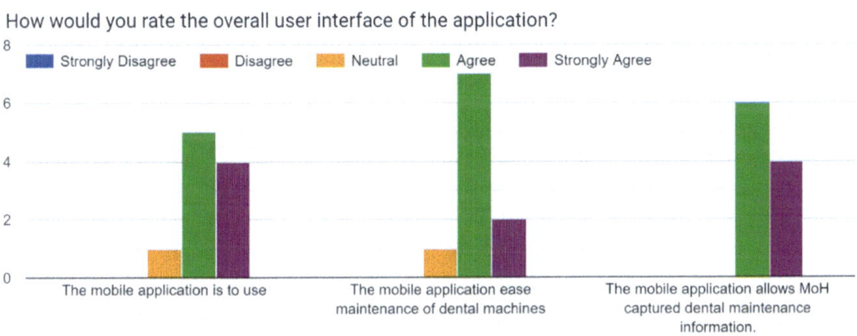

Fig. 7 Rating of the user interface of the application

12 Discussion

Compared to the previous related works, some studies have explored predictive maintenance for medical equipment, focusing on critical machines like MRI machines, air conditioners, and ventilators. However, the developed solution builds on the foundational work of other researchers in predictive maintenance, and it adapts these principles to the context of dental machines with a mobile-based approach. The emphasis of the developed system is that it offers flexibility and ease of access, catering to the dynamic environments of dental practices where mobility can be a significant advantage. These efforts highlight the potential for machine learning to enhance equipment reliability and patient safety in the health Sector.

13 Conclusion

System requirements were gathered from the stakeholders for the developed system using interviews, and snowballing was the sampling technique used. After categorizing the requirements into functional and non-functional requirements, reviewed the literature about existing systems and came up with the technical gap after the design and development of the system commenced. Online data (https://www.kaggle.com/datasets/shivamb/machine-predictive-maintenance-classification) was obtained to train and test the machine-learning model that contained the dataset of 8 features, and the analysis of data was carried out using Google Forms, and Matplotlib was used for data visualization for the machine-learning model. In conclusion, the developed system was taken to the users to ascertain whether the system worked according to the functional and non-functional requirements.

14 Recommendations

Future Works

Due to limited time constraints and data, two algorithms were trained and tested, that was XG boost and Random Forest; however, if more data is obtained, then other algorithms like artificial neural networks can be trained and tested. The application may be extended to iOS users since the developed solution only applies to Android phone users. The feature of storing data offline should be incorporated, and the data should sync when the internet is accessed. The model was trained and tested particularly for dental machines only for this particular project, but there is always room for expansion to train the model for other medical equipment.

References

1. Lugada, E., Komakech, H., Ochola, I., Mwebaze, S., Olowo Oteba, M., and D. Okidi Ladwar, D., "Health supply chain system in Uganda: current issues, structure, performance, and implications for systems strengthening," J. Pharm. Policy Pract., 15(1),1–11 (2022). https://doi.org/10.1186/s40545-022-00412-4.
2. "https://www.ncbi.nlm.nih.gov/pmc/articles/PMC5837176/".
3. Lugada, E., Komakech, H., . and Ochola, I. et al, "Health supply chain system in Uganda: current issues, structure, performance, and implications for systems strengthening. J of Pharm Policy and Pract 15, 14 (2022). https://doi.org/10.1186/s40545-022-00412-4".
4. Feroz, A., Jabeen, R., and Saleem, S., "Using mobile phones to improve community health workers performance in low-and-middle-income countries," BMC Public Health, vol. 20, no. 1, pp. 1–6, 2020, https://doi.org/10.1186/s12889-020-8173-3.
5. Fuaddi, M., and Sabarguna, B., S., "Web-based maintenance information system in medical equipment management," AIP Conf. Proc., vol. 2092, no. April, 2019. https://doi.org/10.1063/1.5096736.

6. Application of Predictive Maintenance in Hospital Heating, Ventilation and Air Conditioning Facilities Gonzalo Sánchez-Barroso a, Justo García Sanz-Calcedo (2019).
7. Wilcox, A., B., Gallagher, A., B., Boden-Albala, K., D., and Bakken, S., R., "Research Data Collection Methods from Paper to Tablet Computers," Med. Care, (50) 68–73 (2012). https://doi.org/10.1097/MLR.0b013e318259c1e7.
8. Aleryani, A., & Aleryani, A. Y. (2016). Comparative Study between Data Flow Diagram and Use Case Diagram Some of the authors of this publication are also working on these related projects: 1000 Researchers FCIT View project A MODEL TO MEASURE THE IMPACT OF CULTURE ON E-READINESS FOR E-GOVERNMEN. International Journal of Scientific and Research Publications, 6(3), 124.

Digitization of End-To-End Value Streams: Conceptualizing a Data Model Based on Complex Graph Networks for AI-Based Tools

Mick Geisthardt, Lutz Engel, and Jorge Marx Gómez

Abstract Value stream analysis and design are central elements of lean management, employed globally by industrial improvement teams to facilitate sustainable value creation. As value stream analysis and design evolve to incorporate material flow cost accounting, information logistics, and external influence factors, increasing data volumes and calculation complexity are driving up the expenses of method application. Traditional pen-and-paper approaches become impractical and non-value-adding. While research within the problem domain focuses primarily on analyzing current value streams, integrating real-time data, and facilitating ad-hoc optimization, the actual site of value creation—the target value stream design and corresponding improvement strategies for implementation—remains largely overlooked. To address this gap, this paper introduces a novel data model that translates value streams from physical whiteboards to the digital realm via complex value stream graph networks (CVSGN). This data model represents value stream structures as complex graph networks with nodes and edge feature vectors, providing a foundation for pattern-based digital value stream analysis and design through artificial intelligence-based tools. The data model offers industry practitioners practical benefits like optimized workflows, data-driven decision-making, and scalability, making it powerful for enhancing operational efficiency and supporting continuous improvement across diverse industries.

Keywords Value stream analysis and design · Data model · Complex value stream graph networks (CVSGN) · Artificial Intelligence · Decision transformer

M. Geisthardt (✉) · J. Marx Gómez
Department of Computing Science, Business Information Systems/Very Large Business Applications, Carl von Ossietzky University of Oldenburg, Oldenburg, Germany
e-mail: mick.geisthardt@jade-hs.de

J. Marx Gómez
e-mail: jorge.marx.gomez@uni-oldenburg.de

M. Geisthardt · L. Engel
Department Management, Information, Technology, Institute for Production and Service Systems, Jade University of Applied Sciences, Wilhelmshaven, Germany
e-mail: lutz.engel@jade-hs.de

J. Marx Gómez et al. (eds.), *Advancement in Embedded and Mobile Systems*, Progress in IS, https://doi.org/10.1007/978-3-031-99219-3_8

1 Introduction

In industrial production of capital and consumer goods, like machinery or food, improvement teams are tasked with enhancing value creation and eliminating waste. They achieve this by applying globally established lean management techniques, such as value stream analysis and design. By advancing the methodology of value stream analysis and design [1] to include material flow cost accounting [2], the consideration of information logistics [3], and external influential factors [4], new opportunities as well as challenges arise.

Overall methodological advancement removes the traditional lead time centricity [1], thereby major aspects such as material and energy-based waste, digitalization, but also the sales market, labor market, and other external aspects like policy and trends can be included through advanced key performance indicators. Emerging diversity across the methodology additionally results in an aggregate growth in application complexity and available data volumes, which questions traditional pen-and-paper approaches and changes how improvement teams should learn, think, and operate. New solutions are required to empower improvement teams in their increasingly complex duties.

Existing research as well as approaches from practice concentrate on conceptual design of digital solutions with a predominant focus on analyzing and simulating current value streams, integration of real-time data, and ad-hoc optimization [5–10]. Yet, the actual place of value creation—the target value stream design and resultant improvement strategies for implementation—remains largely overlooked. To address this gap, this paper presents the conceptualization of a data model that enables end-to-end value streams to be transferred from the physical world of industrial whiteboards to the digital world of artificial intelligence (AI). More precisely, this new model represents value stream structures as complex graph networks with node and edge feature vectors and provides a basis for pattern-based digital value stream analysis and design through AI. To showcase the data model's potential, besides the presentation of the data model, this paper includes an example for the data model's conceptual application in an AI-based tool particularly for value stream design, i.e., the identification of resource-efficient end-to-end value streams.

This paper initially introduces the theoretical background of advanced value stream analysis and design, related work on digital value stream analysis and design, and complex graph networks from graph theory. Subsequently, the methodology of this paper is presented. Next, results with concentration on the data model and its conceptual application in value stream analysis and design is presented. Lastly, conclusion and an outlook on further research is revealed.

2 Theoretical Background

2.1 *Advanced Value Stream Analysis and Design*

A end-to-end value stream can be defined abstractly as a process chain that includes all value-adding and non-value-adding activities that are essential for the main flow of a company's products from procurement to the customer [1]. An illustrative example of a value stream can be found in the production of an automobile. The value stream begins with the procurement of raw materials, energy, and components, such as sheet steel for the car body, engines, gearboxes, and electronics. These materials pass through various production processes such as body construction, painting, component assembly, and final assembly, right through to shipping the car to the customer. The value stream includes all value-adding activities (e.g., engine assembly) as well as all non-value-adding activities (e.g., waiting times between production steps). By analyzing and designing the end-to-end value stream of a company, inefficiencies can be identified and optimized to increase overall value creation and eliminate waste.

When applying value stream analysis and design, initially an improvement team maps the current value stream of a relevant product family and illustrates it with standardized value stream elements on a whiteboard (value stream analysis) [1]. The concepts of "Muda", "Mura" and "Muri" can be used to identify inefficiencies. "Muda" translates to waste and refers to any activity that consumes resources but does not add value to the product or service from the customer's perspective. "Mura" means unevenness and refers to variations or inconsistencies in production processes that lead to waste. This can manifest as fluctuations in production volume, timing, or quality. "Muri" means overburden and refers to placing excessive strain on employees, equipment, or processes. This can result from unrealistic demands, poor planning, or inefficient resource utilization [11]. By eliminating the identified inefficiencies and applying the value stream design guidelines, the improvement team designs a target value stream that is resource-efficient and optimized in terms of lead time (value stream design) [12]. Thereby, the encompassing philosophy for all activities is the ideal state, known from the Toyota Production System (TPS). It is also known as the "north star" and includes the aspects of zero defects, 100% value creation, one-piece flow according to customer demand, and safety for people [13].

The value stream analysis and design method has been advanced by diversification of input and output characteristics by research [14–16]. In this paper, advanced value stream analysis and design refers to the advancements through material flow cost accounting [2], information logistics [3], and the consideration of external influence factors [4]. Figure 1 illustrates an example of a current value stream of this advanced form of value stream analysis and design and clarifies the methodological complexity that is to be conveyed via the complex graph network-based data model (see Sect. 4). The detailed explanation of the advanced value stream follows the figure.

The lead time-centered elements of the traditional value stream analysis with suppliers (S), processes (P), inventories (I), customers (C) and the lead time ladder (LT) are indicated in black, grey, and orange. To resolve the fact of incomplete

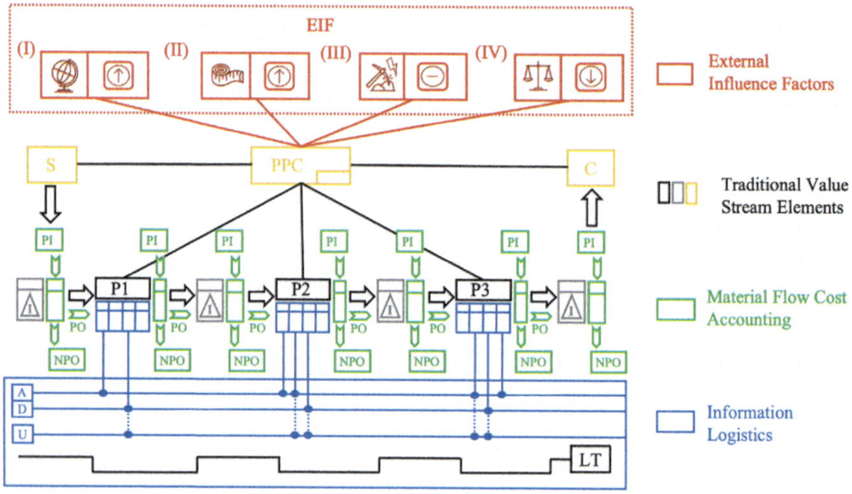

Fig. 1 Example of an end-to-end value stream in current situation utilizing advanced value stream analysis and design [17]

improvements in favor of the lead time, the consideration of material and energy waste is realized via material flow cost accounting according to DIN EN ISO 14051:2011 [18]. Presented in green, the input and output of a process is differentiated into product input (PI), product output (PO) and non product output (NPO). In the exemplary case of processing sheet metal on a punching press, the sheet metal would be the PI, the stamped parts for further processing represent the value-adding PO, and the resulting offcuts are considered non-value-adding NPO. The costs of product input, product output and non product output are broken down into costs of material, energy, system, and disposal. In addition, key performance indicators such as absolute monetary value creation or degree of value creation can be used for in depth insights [2].

By incorporating information logistics, it becomes possible to track activities and key performance indicators of the information flow via analog (A) and digital storage media (D) with their utilization (U), exhibited in blue. Evaluation can be performed using the metrics of digitization rate, data availability, and data usage. Media discontinuities between the storage media become visible and thus enable the initiation of targeted optimization projects in context of digitization [19].

Focusing primarily on internal factors is not always effective. For example, if major suppliers' geopolitical situations are critical (I) and supply chains are long (II), a lack of material availability (III) and regulatory restrictions (IV) can quickly lead to costly production limitations. Therefore, the external influence factors (EIF) displayed in red from the sales market, the labor market, the procurement market, and other external influences such as politics, the social field, technology, and general trends can be included to facilitate holistic optimization [4].

2.2 Related Work

Value stream analysis and design in the context of digitization can basically be interpreted in two directions. First direction involves enhancing the value stream analysis and design method to explicitly support the digitization of production processes. Second direction pertains to the digitization of the value stream analysis and design methods themselves, using digital tools to simplify both theoretical tasks and real-world activities. Thus, current research can be differentiate in value stream analysis and design for digital production and digital value stream analysis and design [20]. This paper addresses the second research direction. Current concepts from the literature emphasize the importance of digitization, simulation, key performance indicators, and continuous improvement in the context of digital tools for value stream analysis and design. Thereby, current concepts concentrate on the conceptual design of digital tools focusing on analyzing and simulating current value streams, integration of real-time data, event-based frameworks, dynamic systems, digital twins, and ad-hoc optimization [5–10]. Yet, most work focuses on analyzing and improving current value streams with value stream analysis rather than designing resource-efficient target value streams with value stream design guidelines. To address this gap, this paper presents a data model for end-to-end value streams that is based on graph theory and can be used in AI-based tools to, e.g., identify resource-efficient target value streams.

2.3 Complex Graph Networks

Graph theory is a branch of mathematics that explores the properties and applications of graphs. A graph is fundamentally a collection of points, called nodes, and lines connecting these points, called edges. Graphs are important tools used to model relationships and interactions in various fields, including computer science, biology, sociology, and transportation [21]. Graphs as data structures can be represented in a wide variety of ways, which often include adjacency matrix or incidence matrix [22].

Different concepts of graphs exist such as directed graphs (digraphs) or weighted graphs. The primary difference between undirected and directed graphs lies in the directionality of their edges. In undirected graphs, edges imply a mutual relationship, whereas, in digraphs, relationships are directional, indicating a one-way connection. Undirected graphs are often used to model symmetric relationships like friendships or connections in social networks. Digraphs are used in scenarios where direction matters, such as web page linking, where one page links to another but not necessarily vice versa, or in representing workflows and processes. In weighted graphs, edges carry a weight, which represents the cost, distance, or strength of the connection between vertices. Weighted graphs are used in applications like finding the shortest path in a transportation network or the least expensive connection in a communication network [21].

The concept of the complex graph network of this paper, also referred to as a complex network, is a specific type of graph that displays non-trivial topological properties—properties that are not present in simple networks. These networks are characterized by their large size and intricate structure, often observed in natural and man-made systems such as social networks, biological systems, and technological networks. The networks size makes it complex and, thus, makes it impossible to comprehend or predict their overall behavior by examining the actions of individual nodes or edges [22].

3 Methodology

Objective of this paper is the conceptualization of a data model dedicated to the digitalization of end-to-end value streams. This data model is intended to be applicable in the context of AI-based tools for value stream analysis and design to support improvement teams from industry, especially in the less research-addressed design of resource-efficient value streams.

To achieve this objective, this paper transfers concepts from graph theory to the construct of the end-to-end value stream (see Fig. 1) to make it digital representable as a complex graph network via node and edge feature vectors. Subsequently, the potential of the data model in value stream analysis and design is considered. Lastly, the conceptual application of the data model in an AI-based tool based on decision transformers [23] (sequence modeling approach) for the identification of resource-efficient end-to-end value streams is demonstrated—Interpreting value stream design as a prediction task. Thus, this paper offers not solely a data model, but also a potential concept for its value-adding application in industrial practice.

4 Results

4.1 Data Model

To transfer end-to-end value streams from the physical world of whiteboards in industry to the digital world of artificial intelligence, a clear, understandable, and interpretable data model is required. The data model is subject to the premise that its data structure must be comprehensible for humans i.e., the improvement team and at the same time can be utilized in a value-adding way within the scope of AI-based tools.

As part of the conceptualization, the data model of this paper is based on the implementation of graph-theoretical concepts [21, 22], which are used to capture

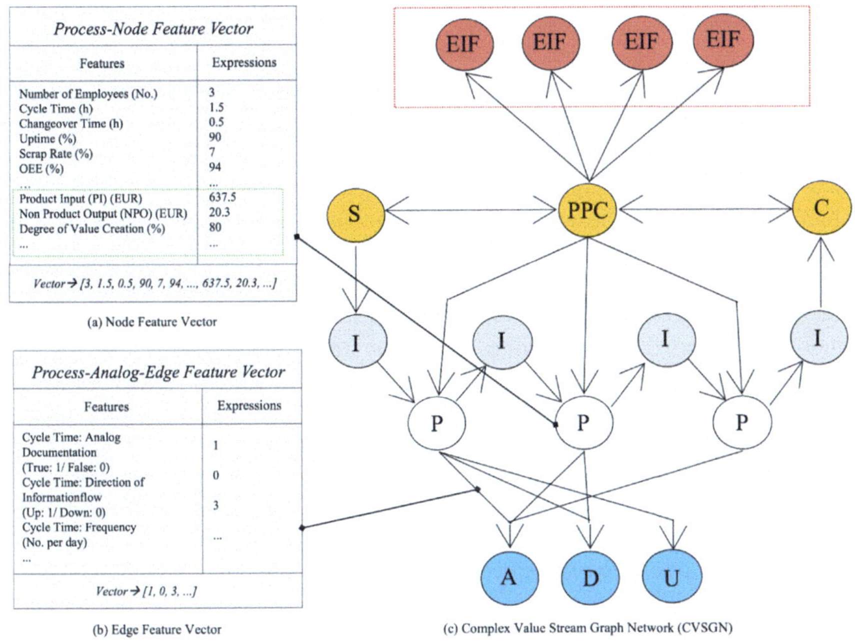

Fig. 2 Example of an End-To-End Value Stream as a Complex Graph Network Composed of Node and Edge Feature Vectors—(a) Example of a Node Feature Vector Representing a Process, (b) Example of a Edge Feature Vector Representing the Directed Linkage between Process and Analog Memory Media, and (c) Structure of the Complex Value Stream Graph Network (CVSGN)

and holistically map the value stream structure with its features and expressions. As exemplified in Fig. 2, a value stream can be represented by a large complex graph network, this complex network can be referred to as a complex value stream graph network (CVSGN). The detailed explanation of the CVSGN data model follows the figure.

The nodes within the graph represent the structural components of the value stream described in Sect. 2.1. This includes traditional components [1] such as suppliers (S), processes (P), inventories (I), production planning and control (PPC), customers (C), components of information logistics [3] such as information flow via analog (A) and digital storage media (D) with their utilization (U) and also external influence factors (EIF) [4]. The features and expressions of each node are specified through a vector, which also integrates the aspect of material flow cost accounting into the data model [2]. The edges within the graph represent connections between structural components of the value stream and thus the flow of material, energy, information and costs. The edges are directed, meaning that the graph is a so-called digraph. The features and expressions of each edge are also expressed via a vector. Overall, the structure of the CVSGN data model enables to represent value stream structures as complex graph networks with node and edge feature vectors.

4.2 Application

The CVSGN data model can be applied by industrial improvement teams in both value stream analysis and value stream design. In value stream analysis, the data model can be used as a simulation environment for analysis. It is also feasible to design the data model dynamically with real-time data via Internet of Things (IoT) technology and thus enable ad-hoc optimization. Ultimately, it would be possible to use the data model within a digital twin.

Due to its structure, the data model can be utilized particularly in the context of value stream design to identify resource-efficient value streams through the application of value stream design guidelines supporting improvement teams in their work. Thereby, the process and the dynamics of value stream design can be interpreted within reinforcement learning (RL) as a control problem or as a prediction problem that is to be realized online or via training batches (offline) [24]. The following Fig. 3 shows the conceptual application of the data model in an AI-based tool based on the architecture of the decision transformer, also referred to as transformer reinforcement learning. In contrast to conventional more complex RL methods, where a policy or a value function is learned, decision transformer considers the selection of action as a conditional sequence prediction task [23]. To implement the decision transformer architecture as part of the value stream design for the prediction of steps in the direction of the next value stream, training sequences consisting of states (s), actions (a) and associated rewards (r) are required. The states of the value stream can be mapped using the described CVSGN data model. The actions are the established value stream design guidelines from research and practice [1, 12]. The rewards are represented numerically and include the gains of the implemented action, but also the associated resource consumption. As part of the data collection, it is sufficient for the improvement team to collect small quantities of sequences with high quality and then to augment these using a simulation game for value stream analysis and design such as that developed by Geisthardt et al. [17, 25].

After training, the decision transformer can utilize the stacked input sequences to autoregressively predict optimal next action sequences (implementation strategies) within value stream design and thus potentially support improvement teams in the industry in the iterative development and identification of resource-efficient end-to-end value streams.

4.3 Discussion

The CVSGN data model presented in this paper holds advantages, limitations, and implications for generalization. Utilizing a graph theory-based data model, the complex interrelations and dependencies within a value stream can be captured in highest detail, providing a comprehensive overview that is not attainable through existing approaches. The structure of the data model, with its node and edge feature

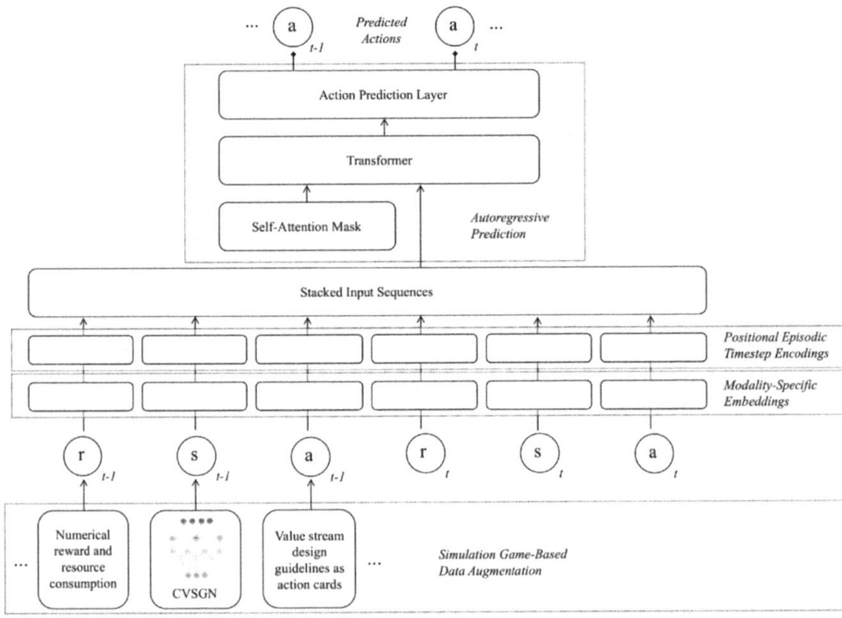

Fig. 3 Concept of a Decision Transformer Architecture [23] for the Prediction of Next Action Sequences in Value Stream Design Utilizing the CVSGN Data Model

vectors, is highly conducive to AI applications. By providing a detailed and structured dataset, the model can enable pattern-based digital value stream analysis and value stream design. The data model can support ongoing monitoring and improvement efforts. By providing a unified view on the value stream, the data model encourages different departments and teams to work together towards common objectives. This leads to more collaborative, holistic, and effective improvement strategies.

Limitations include that overall implementation of the data model requires extensive data collection and precise modeling of each component and its interactions. This process can be time-consuming and resource-intensive, potentially hindering the adoption of the model in organizations with limited resources. Also, the accuracy and effectiveness of the data model is heavily dependent on the quality of the data collected. Inaccurate or outdated data can lead to erroneous analyzes and suboptimal decision-making.

The data model can be generalized and applied across various industries. Any industry confronted with production of capital and consumer goods relies on end-to-end value streams, and thus, can benefit from this model due to its flexibility to be tailored to the specific needs and features of different sectors. The data model is also scalable, meaning it can be adapted to both small-scale operations and large, complex systems. This scalability ensures that organizations of different sizes and complexities can implement the model and reap its benefits. The ability to scale the model up or down as needed makes it a versatile tool for continuous improvement.

5 Conclusion and Future Work

This paper presented the conceptualization of a data model for the digitization of end-to-end value streams. The purpose of this data model is to be applicable in the context of AI-based value stream analysis and design tools to support industrial improvement teams, especially in the less research-addressed design of resource-efficient value streams.

For this purpose, concepts from graph theory were transferred to the end-to-end value stream construct to make it digitally representable as a directed complex graph network with node and edge feature vectors. Based on these concepts, the data model presented is referred to as a complex value stream graph network (CVSGN) data model. In addition, the potential of the data model in value stream analysis and design was considered. This involved the conceptual application of the data model in an AI-based tool utilizing the decision transformer architecture for the sequence-driven identification of resource-efficient end-to-end value streams.

The CVSGN data model offers advantages, limitations, and implications for generalization. Its graph theory-based structure captures complex interrelations within a value stream in high detail, aiding AI-based applications and enabling comprehensive digital value stream analysis and design. Thereby, the data model's implementation requires extensive data collection and precise component modeling, which can be resource-intensive. Additionally, the model's effectiveness hinges on data quality; inaccurate or outdated data can compromise analyzes and decision-making. Despite these challenges, the model's flexibility and scalability make it applicable across various industries, from small-scale operations to large, complex systems. Its ability to adapt to different sectors ensures its utility in driving continuous improvement efforts, making it a versatile tool for companies of all sizes.

In continuation of this paper, the CVSGM data model is to be applied and examined in detail experimentally in the laboratory utilizing simulations and in real industrial practice. Furthermore, the data model needs to be tested in AI-based applications such as the decision transformer described above. Thereby, the presented advantages, limitations, and implications for generalization should be iteratively extended, proofed or negated.

References

1. Rother, M., Shook, J.: Sehen lernen, Mit Wertstromdesign die Wertschöpfung erhöhen und Verschwendung beseitigen. Lean Management Institut GmbH (Workbooks für Lean Management), Mülheim (2011).
2. Engel, L., Kranhold, M.: Lean Management wird zum Green Management, Um Materialflusskosten erweiterte Wertstromanalyse. Deutsches Ingenieurblatt 2021, 1–6 (2021).
3. Meudt, T.: Wertstromanalyse 4.0 – Eine Methode zur integrierten Erfassung und Analyse von Material- und Informationsflüssen in Wertströmen, Dissertation Technische Universität Darmstadt. Shaker Verlag, Düren (2020).

4. Zanker, C., Reisen, K.: Stabilitäts- und Flexibilitätsanforderungen an Produktionssysteme. In: Kötter, W., Schwarz-Kocher, M., Zanker, C. (eds.) Balanced GPS, Ganzheitliche Produktionssysteme mit stabil-flexiblen Standards und konsequenter Mitarbeiterorientierung. Springer Fachmedien, Wiesbaden (2015).
5. Balaji, V., Venkumar, P., Sabitha, M., Amuthaguka, D.: DVSMS: dynamic value stream mapping solution by applying IIoT. Sādhanā 45, 1–13 (2020).
6. de Assis, R.F., de Santa-Eulalia, L.A., Ferreira, W.d.P., Armellini, F., Anholon, R., Rampasso, I.S., Santos, J.G.C.L.d.: Translating value stream maps into system dynamics models: a practical framework. The International Journal of Advanced Manufacturing Technology 114, 3537–3550 (2021).
7. Frick, N., Metternich, J.: The digital value stream twin. Systems 10, 102 (2022).
8. Lu, Y., Liu, Z., Min, Q.: A digital twin-enabled value stream mapping approach for production process reengineering in SMEs. International Journal of Computer Integrated Manufacturing 34, 764–782 (2021).
9. Meudt, T., Kaiser, J., Metternich, J., Spieckermann, S.: Wertstrommodellierung und-simulation im Zeichen von Digitalisierung und Industrie 4.0. Zeitschrift für wirtschaftlichen Fabrikbetrieb 112, 865–868 (2017).
10. Teriete, T., Böhm, M., Sai, B.K., Erlach, K., Bauernhansl, T.: Event-based framework for digitalization of value stream mapping. Procedia CIRP 107, 481–486 (2022).
11. Ohno, T.: Das Toyota-Produktionssystem. Campus Verlag GmbH, Frankfurt/Main (2013).
12. Erlach, K.: Wertstromdesign, Der Weg zur schlanken Fabrik. Springer-Verlag GmbH, Berlin (2010).
13. Rother, M.: Toyota Kata: Managing People for Improvement, Adaptiveness and Superior Results. McGraw-Hill Global Education Holdings LLC, New York (2009).
14. Balsliemke, F.: Kostenorientierte Wertstromplanung, Prozessoptimierung in Produktion und Logistik. Springer Gabler, Wiesbaden (2015).
15. Braglia, M., Carmignani, G., Zammori, F.: A new value stream mapping approach for complex production systems. International Journal of Production Research 44, 3929-3952 (2006).
16. Cai, Y., You, J.: Research on value stream analysis and optimization methods. In: 4th International Conference on Wireless Communications, Networking and Mobile Computing, (2008).
17. Geisthardt, M., Engel, L., Schnegelberger, M.: Towards Gamification of Advanced Value Stream Analysisand Design: A Game-Based Learning Concept. In: Volker Wohlgemuth, V., Kranzlmüller, D., Höb, M. (eds.) EnviroInfo 2023: Lecture Notes in Informatics (LNI). Gesellschaft für Informatik e.V. (GI), Bonn (2023).
18. Deutsches Institut für Normung e.V. (DIN): DIN EN ISO 14051:2011–12, Umweltmanagement – Materialflusskostenrechnung – Allgemeine Rahmenbedingungen (ISO 14051:2011). Beuth Verlag GmbH, Berlin (2011).
19. Meudt, T., Metternich, J., Abele, E.: Value stream mapping 4.0, Holistic examination of value stream and information logistics in production. CIRP Annals 66, 413–416 (2017).
20. Erlach, K., Böhm, M., Gessert, S., Hartleif, S., Teriete, T., Ungern-Sternberg, R.: Die zwei Wege der Wertstrommethode zur Digitalisierung: Datenwertstrom und WertstromDigital als Stoßrichtungen der Forschung für die digitalisierte Produktion. Zeitschrift für wirtschaftlichen Fabrikbetrieb 116, 940-944 (2021).
21. Knauer, U., Knauer, K.: Algebraic graph theory: morphisms, monoids and matrices. Walter de Gruyter GmbH & Co KG (2019).
22. Van Steen, M.: Graph theory and complex networks. An introduction 144, (2010).
23. Chen, L., Lu, K., Rajeswaran, A., Lee, K., Grover, A., Laskin, M., Abbeel, P., Srinivas, A., Mordatch, I.: Decision Transformer: Reinforcement Learning via Sequence Modeling. In: Neural Information Processing Systems (2021).
24. Sutton, R.S., Barto, A.G.: Reinforcement learning: An introduction. MIT press, Cambridge (2018).
25. Geisthardt, M., Engel, L., Schnegelberger, M.: Simulation Game Concept For AI-Enhanced Teaching Of Advanced Value Stream Analysis And Design. In: Herberger, D., Hübner, M.

(eds.) Conference on Production Systems and Logistics: CPSL 2023-2. publish-Ing., Hannover (2023).

IoT-Based System for Maintaining Constant Taste of Ginger-Flavoured Alcohol: A Case of Eden Business Center, Rwanda

Speciose Ingabire, Godfrey Naman, Ramadhani Sinde, and Judith Leo

Abstract The beverage industry, particularly the flavoured alcohol sector, plays a role in the development of Rwanda since most of people consume ginger beer due to its lower cost, demand, spacy medicine, and small alcohol volume. Regardless the increase of several this approach proposes to address these challenges however; it does not fully solve the issue. In this paper, a smart IoT-based system monitoring proposes to address the flavour consistency issue faced by the beverage industries. The proposed solution aims to enhance the monitoring and controlling the production and fermentation process through real-time data collection and remote control capabilities. By leveraging IoT technologies, sensor networks, cloud computing, and mobile application were used. The proposed study enables efficient monitoring of key parameters such pH, temperature, alcohol and concentration. Moreover, it facilitates rapid control and timely interventions by altering the user about the active data on the ginger beer status. The experimental results prove that the system has great prospect and it is for beverage industries usage. The ginger industry is seeing improvements and evolution in today's technology. Ginger is an upright perennial plant that grows to a height of three feet and a width of 1.5–6 cm. It thrives in well-drained soil and in areas that receive some shade. Ginger may be cultivated in both irrigated and rain-fed environments.

Keywords Taste consistency · Ginger-flavoured alcohol · GSM alerts

S. Ingabire (✉) · G. Naman (✉) · R. Sinde (✉) · J. Leo (✉)
Computational and Communication Science and Engineering (CoCSE), The Nelson Mandela Africa Institution of Science and Technology (NM-AIST), Arusha, Tanzania
e-mail: ingabires@nm-aist.ac.tz

G. Naman
e-mail: godfrey.naman@nm-aist.ac.tz

R. Sinde
e-mail: ramadhani.sinde@nm-aist.ac.tz

J. Leo
e-mail: judith.leo@nm-aist.ac.tz

J. Marx Gómez et al. (eds.), *Advancement in Embedded and Mobile Systems*, Progress in IS, https://doi.org/10.1007/978-3-031-99219-3_9

1 Introduction

Ginger has been widely used as medicine's properties. It contains bioactive compounds with anti-inflammatory, antioxidant, and antimicrobial effects, aiding in the treatment and prevention of various health conditions [1]. Its distinct taste makes it versatile for many applications [2]. Ginger used in beers like ginger wine, whisky, liqueur, and flavoured alcohol [3]. Ginger-flavoured alcohol has become increasingly popular in the beverage industry in recent years. This is due to the growing demand for craft cocktails and unique flavour combinations among consumers. Ginger beverage industries are facing the different challenge during production process due to inadequate way of preparation of ginger alcohol, which can result to certain error while using Manuel techniques in monitoring and controlling the production process. This can result to get unstable alcohol taste. The EBC is the local beverage industry situated in Kigali Rwanda, which is a homegrown venture, started in 2005 as a backyard of flavour soft drink made from Ginger plant. EBC, a popular ginger-flavoured alcohol beverage, expanded from homemade soft drink to widely accepted varieties in Rwanda, Uganda, Zambia, Tanzania, and Mozambique [4]. The EBC is facing the challenge of the inconstant alcohol Taste due to no real-time system to monitor and maintain taste parameters such as humidity, temperature, gas level, pH level, and weight which can cause danger to this company as well as less about quality of product [5]. However, concepts related to the internet of things (IoT) are pervasive in nature. It has the ability to link several parts together over the internet, which can stimulate innovation. In order to achieve the flavour consistency test of the ginger beer, an IoT-based system proposes. The objective of the project was to develop an IoT based-system for maintaining the constant Taste of Ginger-flavoured alcohol in order to monitor the production of the Ginger Alcohol at low cost.

2 Related Works

A new system structure and HTTP communication method was suggested for the process of monitoring the fermentation conditions of the Debina varietal sparkling wine produced in the region of Zitsa Epirus, Greece, dubbed Wine-SBS. The technology consists of microcontroller devices known as CBS-sensor transceivers, which disperse throughout the debina fermentation tanks and have sensors to track wine characteristics and storage conditions. Periodically, measurements are transmitted and received by a central cloud system application service. After being gathered by a CBS-sensor collector, the multiplexed HTTP flows of an HTTP/2 request are sent to a distant application server. The measures of transmission, which obtain periodically, are sent to the cloud using HTTP protocol. Therefore, the system implemented does not provide the user should receive remote notifications via messages. A system for testing the quality of Fermented Ginger Drink (Ginger Ale) made from different Indonesian ginger varieties was developed by [6]. It focused on assessing Ginger Beer quality based on the ginger type used. The study applied an experimental method, testing various ginger factors during fermentation, including organoleptic properties, probiotic microorganism isolation, alcohol level measurement, reducing sugar content, and phenolic compound identification. However, it did not account for other ingredient quantities or technologies that could provide real-time data on aspects such as alcohol content. The real-time analysis of diacetyl perception in beer samples was conducted using MOX sensors. Voltametric detection and chromatographic analysis techniques were adapted, making use of metal oxide sensors (MOS) for a faster, cost-effective evaluation of diacetyl concentration through resistance variation. The S3+ (Nano Sensor Systems s.r.l.; Reggio Emilia, Italy) device was used to detect volatile compounds via a custom array of materials. Principal Component Analysis (PCA) facilitated production process management within an IoT-integrated system. Electrochemical sensors enabled testing different beer typologies, validating this approach for diacetyl evaluation while also differentiating beer types. However, the study did not explore technology for monitoring alcohol levels and temperature. A model for alcohol fermentation in a brewing-integrated approach for continuous fermentation control was developed [7]. It employed an integrated system for managing continuous beer fermentation with immobilized yeast. Experimental results were used to develop dependencies for calculating real extract and ethanol at varying fermentation stages and dilution rates. Proper fermentation was critical for high-quality ginger beer production, as sugars in the water were converted by yeast into ethanol, carbon dioxide, and other by-products. In industrial systems, fermenters were equipped with sensors for monitoring fermentation parameters, main parameters of the fermentation process with taste containing management. This kind of systems were usually too expensive for craft breweries, therefore verifying the fermentation conditions was achieved with off-line measurements, taking beer samples from each fermenter at regular intervals of time. Low-cost systems would be ideal for this system, in order to permit monitoring of the fermentation process. The device's electronics consist of a Fire Beetle 2 ESP32-E dev board for communications and processing, along with an MPU6050 to determine the hydrometer's angle in the water. An optional DS18B20 sensor monitors the brew temperature, and an 18,650 cell provides power [8].

3 Material and Methods

3.1 A Case Studies

The study conducted in Eden Business Center limited, which locates in Kigali city in the Republic of Rwanda. Eden Business Center Limited contributes to the economic development of Rwanda by promoting local entrepreneurship, generating employment opportunities, and supporting the growth of small and medium enterprizes (SMEs). Through its production and distribution of ginger-flavoured alcoholic beverages, the company stimulates agricultural demand, benefiting local farmers and suppliers. Additionally, Eden Business Center fosters innovation in the beverage industry, enhances Rwanda's industrial output, and contributes to the national economy through tax revenues and export potential. This positions the company as a key player in driving sustainable economic growth within the country. However, Eden business Center was facing the issue of maintaining product consistency in the case of variable production conditions. By ensuring product quality through technology, the system will help to monitor ginger beer taste constant using pH, temperature and refractometer display data via lcd, buzzer, GSM notification and a mobile application ensuring the constant quality of ginger beer. The data sent to the web application (ThingSpeak) for analysis, visualization and control ensuring the safety fermentation of ginger beer and proactive control intervention.

3.2 Research Methods

Both qualitative and quantitative methods were used to carry out data gathering, analysis, and interpretation in this paper. This was necessary due to it was a need to understand the behaviour and opinion of participant and how they should adjust to the IoT remote system, as well as show the system's capabilities experiments and obtain further system design concepts.

3.3 System Development Approach

The V-Model, a software development model that shows the relationships between every phase of the software development life cycle (SDLC) and its associated phase, was used in this study. In this case, the V-Model was chosen given that it is the best approach for industrial projects as it requires testing from the start and eliminates defects at every stage, making the products stronger and reducing rework [9]. Furthermore, the strategy emphasized testing and evaluating, offered a framework system for development, increased team communication, and ensured product quality.

3.4 Software Tools Integration

The system was designed and simulated using EasyEDA (version 6.4.31), [10] with a microcontroller integrated to manage sensors and actuators. The ESP32-WROOM-32D [11] microcontroller was programmed using the Arduino IDE, which includes libraries for connecting to cloud platforms and APIs for data storage, visualization, and remote relay automation. SQL and PHP were utilized for backend development, and HTML, CSS, and JavaScript for frontend development. ThingSpeak was used for visualizing sensor data related to pH, temperature, and concentration, as well as providing remote control via a mobile application.

3.5 Hardware Component Integration

The developed system was composed of an ESP32 microcontroller board, one buzzer, GSM SIM800L, PH sensor, and temperature sensor. The PH sensor was connected to pin 14 of the microcontroller, buzzer was connected to pin 23 is used to alert the nearest environment if the drinks are ready. Furthermore, temperature attached and mounted to pins18 and 22 of microcontroller, also connected to pin 18 of ESP 32 microcontroller. The transmitter (TX) and receiver (Rx) pins of GSM module attached to pins 16 and 17 of ESP 32. GSM SIM800L powered by 5V DC supply and other components to 3.3V from the ESP32. Figure 1 shows the systematic integration of microcontroller, all sensing and actuating units.

3.6 The Algorithm Workflow of IoT—Based System for Maintaining Constant Taste

The system developed based on three main inputs, pH level, Temperature and concentration monitoring. When the ph. Level, Temperature reached Threshold, the system will notify the user and if the Fermentation Process completed Alert will send to the person in charge. The diagram below presents the algorithm flowcharts of the IoT—Based System for Maintaining Constant Taste (Fig. 2).

4 Results and Discussion

This section provides a summary of the results and discussion of the developed smart Monitoring Taste by identifying system units. The methods and materials used resulted in the development of an IoT-based system for ensuring consistent taste and real-time notification.

4.1 Sensing Unit and Developed Prototype

The sensing operation unit effectively interfaced, yielding the expected digital data output for the processing unit. Parameters such as pH, alcohol content, and concentration levels of the ginger beer e successfully monitored, data transmitted to the

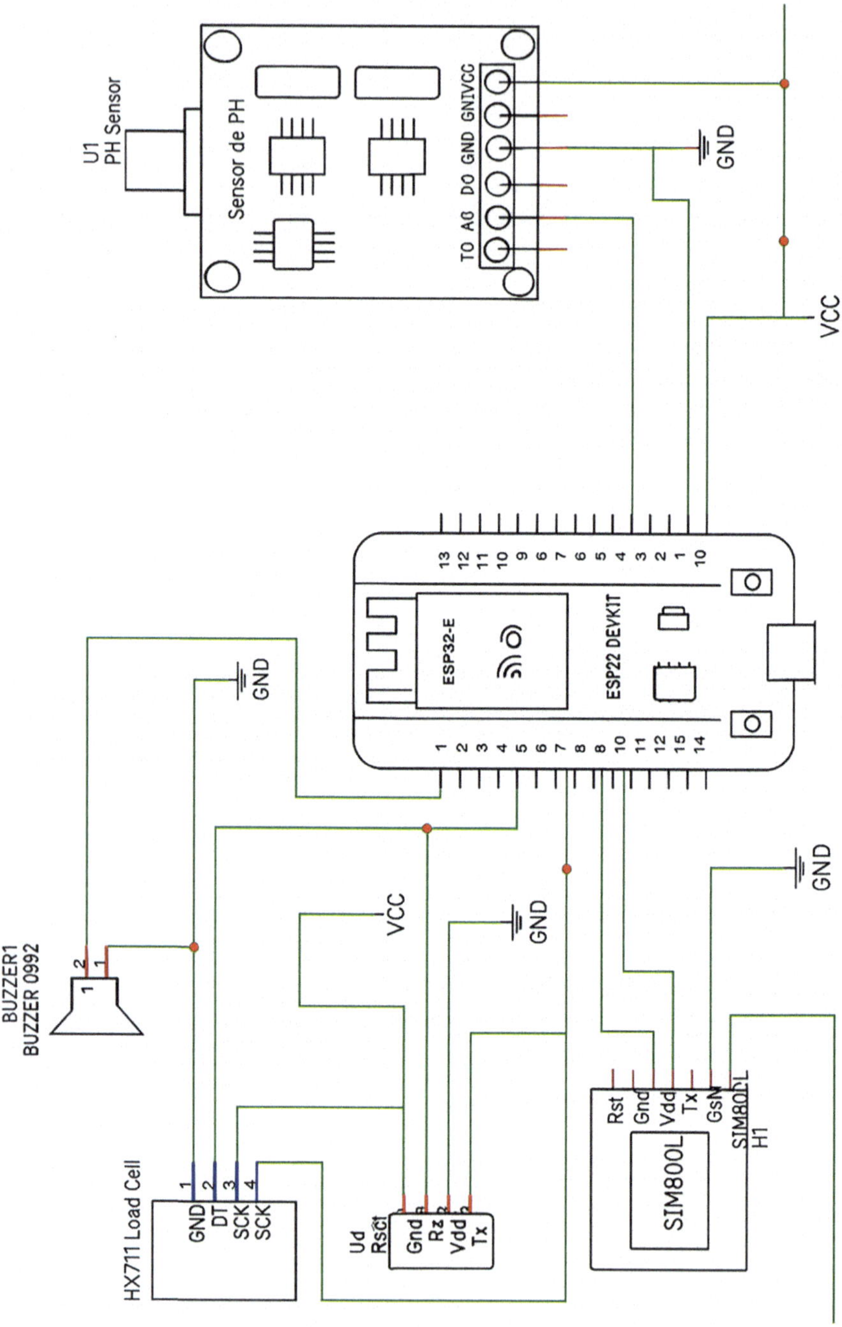

Fig. 1 Circuit schematic diagram

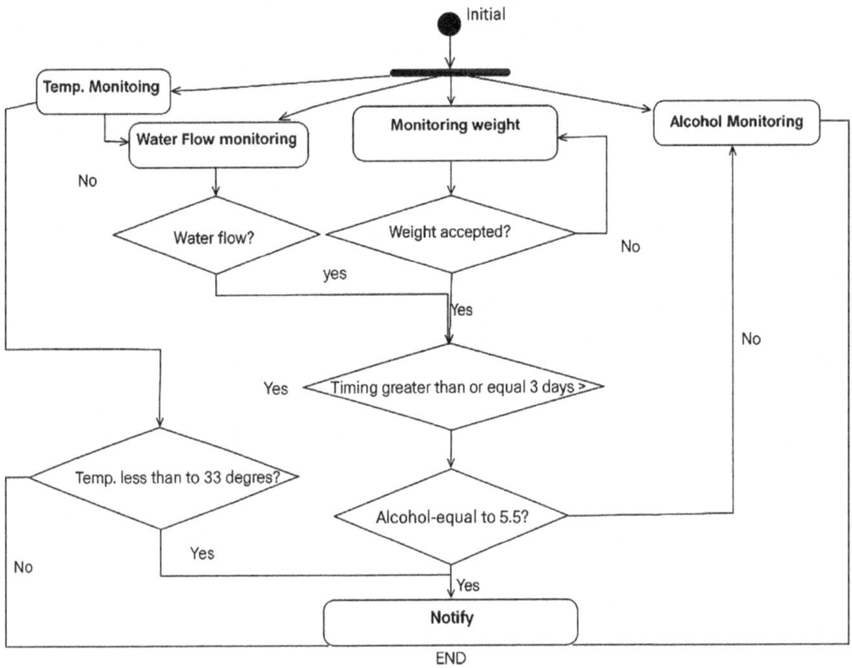

Fig. 2 Flowchart of the developed system

processing unit for further analysis. The data visualized in real-time through ThingSpeak, demonstrating the system's capacity for continuous monitoring. The processing unit, functioning as the core of the smart taste monitoring system, executed tasks including data segmentation, classification, and generating output signals to the notification unit. The following graphs illustrate the variations in ginger beer pH and temperature detected by the sensors over time (Figs. 3, 4, and 5).

4.2 *The Notification Unit*

The notification device properly interfaced and could notify the user to the desired results. In addition, the notification device could deliver a Short Message Service (SMS) to display the production process status (pH, temperature, concentration, and alcohol level). Figure 6 shows a Smart taste constantly monitored display and a short message service (SMS) provided over the Global System for Mobile (GSM) connected.

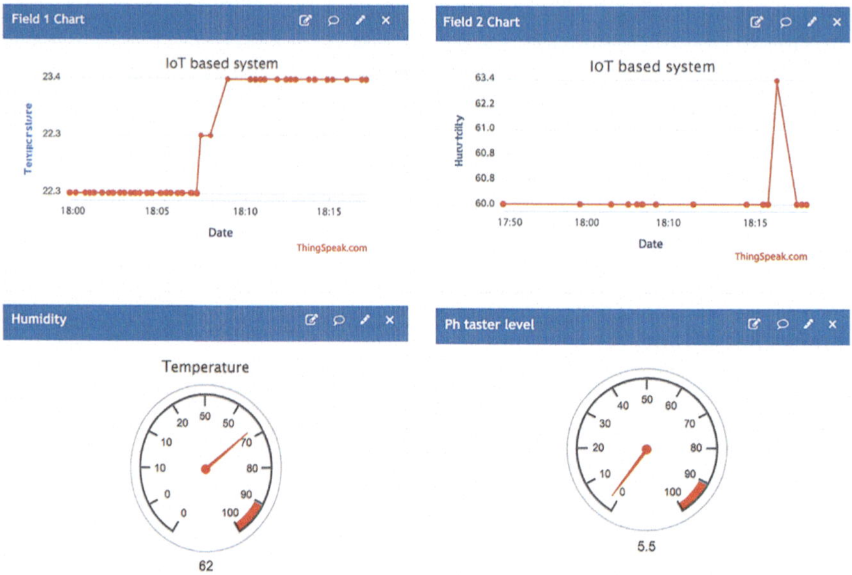

Fig. 3 Variation of pH and temperature

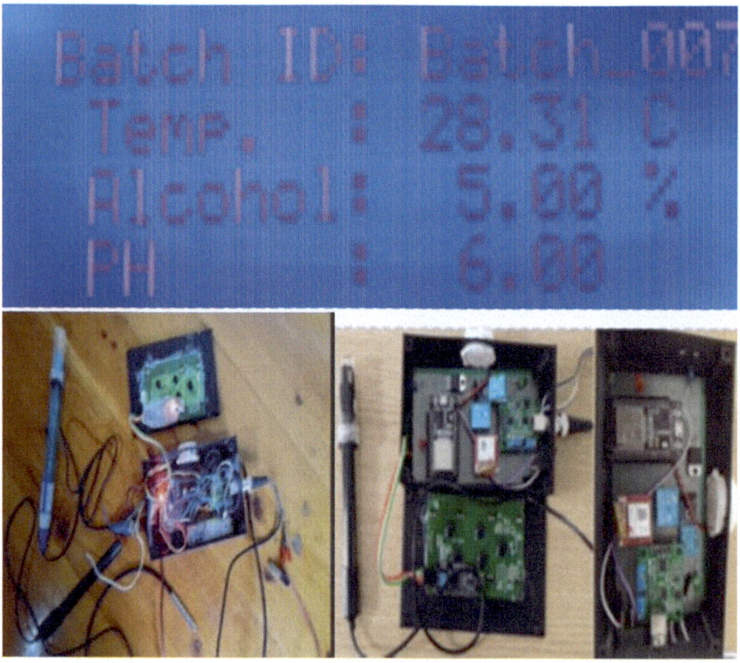

Fig. 4 Developed prototype

Fig. 5 Notification message

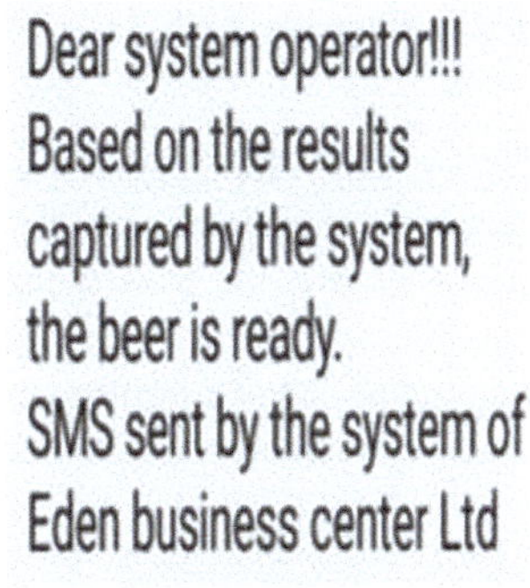

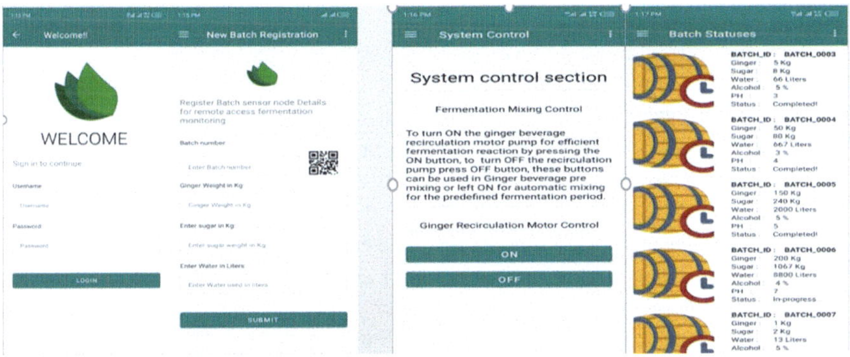

Fig. 6 Mobile application results

4.3 Mobile Application Results

The mobile application developed in this project includes login and dashboard. Users, such as operators or operation managers, are assigned login credentials to access the application. On the login page, users need to enter their username and password to proceed to the main interface. The dashboard page displays information related to the ginger beer taste maintaining and fermentation process. This information is accessible after the user scans a QR code of a batch or enters the batch number. The dashboard visualizes key parameters such as temperature, pH level, alcohol level, and concentration level. Finally, the mobile application includes a sign out/logout page, allowing users to securely exit after observing and analyzing the data.

4.4 System Validation and Testing

The system validated using a questionnaire to validate the produced flavoured ginger beer taste maintaining and monitoring system, Furthermore, utilizing a systematic questionnaire; the constructed system evaluated and validated. The system was also scalable verified with effective responsive checking. The hardware and software functionalities and combination of all individual units were included during system validation and communicated together to provide the working system (Fig. 7).

4.5 Discussions

The tests and experiments performed during system prototype development have shown that the components were communicated each other. The developed system should communicate with a mobile application and provides the real-time flavoured ginger beer data during ginger beer production process on the system itself. The flavoured ginger beer taste maintaining with data conditions was automatically displayed on LCD The developed prototype also proposed another alternative of SMS communication via GSM technology to send flavoured ginger beer taste data to the operator or operation manager to assist and support easiness of ginger beer monitoring in the assigned time wherever. After validating and test performance, the result strongly appreciated and satisfied with the developed and prototyped system. The developed IoT ginger-flavoured beer taste maintaining system provides a safe operational aspect with a remote ginger beer taste maintaining parameters monitoring. In addition, the system is cost effective, efficient with user friendly interactive, and provides higher performance to any assigned engineer. Users must have internet access and login using the username and password created during the registration process. Rendering to the study, the developed system has successfully operated to provide the real-time ginger beer data.

5 Conclusion and Future Works

5.1 Conclusions

The proposed IoT-based system for monitoring and controlling the production and fermentation process in the beverage industry, specifically for ginger beer, has shown promising results. By leveraging IoT technologies, sensor networks, cloud computing, and mobile applications, the system effectively monitors key parameters such as pH, temperature, alcohol concentration, and more. The real-time data collection and remote control capabilities facilitate rapid control and timely interventions, ensuring flavour consistency and improving overall production efficiency.

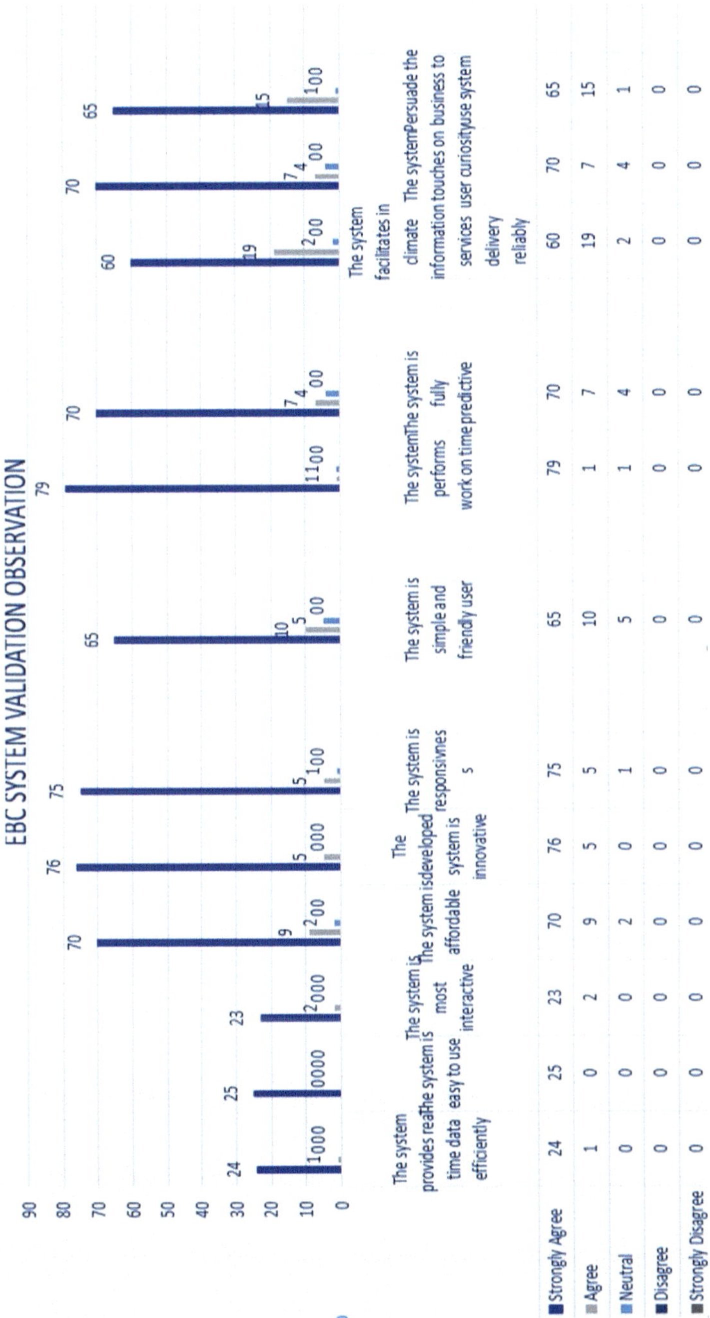

	The system provides real time data efficiently	The system is easy to use	The system is most interactive	The system is affordable	The developed system is innovative	The system is responsiveness	The system is simple and friendly user	The system performs work on time	The system is fully predictive	The system facilitates in climate services delivery reliably	The information touches on business to user curiosity	The system Persuade the use system
Strongly Agree	24	25	23	70	76	75	65	79	70	60	70	65
Agree	1	0	2	9	5	5	10	1	7	19	7	15
Neutral	0	0	0	2	0	1	5	1	4	2	4	1
Disagree	0	0	0	0	0	0	0	0	0	0	0	0
Strongly Disagree	0	0	0	0	0	0	0	0	0	0	0	0

Fig.7 System validation

The successful implementation of this system indicates its potential for significant economic improvement in the beverage industry. I recommend the beverage industries, particularly those producing flavoured alcoholic beverages like ginger beer, should consider adopting IoT-based monitoring systems to enhance production quality and efficiency and utilize the data collected by the IoT system for advanced analytics to predict trends, optimize processes, and improve product quality.

5.2 Future Works

Future research can explore the integration of advanced analytics and machine learning algorithms to further enhance the predictive capabilities of the IoT system and try to expand the range of monitored parameters to include additional quality indicators such as microbial content and flavour profiles.

Acknowledgements I would like to express my sincere appreciation to the Centre of Excellence in ICT in East Africa for the scholarship sponsorship. I am also deeply grateful for my academic and industrial supervisors' guidance, support, and encouragement. Special thanks to the Eden Business Center Limited management for the great insights and facilitation provided during my internship while working on this project.

References

1. Mashadi NS, Ghiasvand R, A. G, H. M, D. L, and Mofid MR., "Anti-Oxidative and Anti-Inflammatory Effects of Ginger in Health and Physical Activity: Review of Current Evidence," *Int. J. Prev. Med.*, pp. 36–42, 2013.
2. D. G. Nam, M. Kim, J. S. Choe, and A. J. Choi, "Effects of HighPressure, Hydrothermal, and Enzyme-Assisted Treatment on the Taste and Flavor Profile of Water-Soluble Ginger (Zingiber Officinale) Extract," *Foods*, vol. 11, no. 4, 2022, https://doi.org/10.3390/foods11040508.
3. M. R. Jangra, R. Kumar, S. Jangra, A. Jain, and K. S. Nehra, "Production And Characterization Of Wine From Ginger, Honey And Sugar Blends," *Glob. J. Bio-Science Biotechnol.*, vol. 7, no. 1, pp. 74–80, 2018.
4. Rwanda FDA, "Rwanda Food and Drugs Authority," pp. 1–21, 2022, [Online]. Available: https://www.rwandafda.gov.rw/home.
5. M. Leonel, L. Torres, E. Garcia, T. Santos, and M. Mischan, "Production of Alcoholic Beverage from Ginger: Study of Fermentation Process and Final Product Quality," *Br. J. Apple. Sci. Technol.*, vol. 9, no. 4, pp. 318–326, 2015, https://doi.org/10.9734/bjast/2015/17704.
6. Pujiati, A. Sulistyarsi, and N. F. Prafitasari, "The Quality Test of Fermented Ginger Drink (Ginger Ale) Produced from Various Types of Indonesian Ginger," *Proc. 2nd Int. Conf. Educ. Technol. (ICETECH 2021)*, vol. 630, no. Icetech 2021, pp. 152–159, 2022, https://doi.org/10.2991/assehr. k. 220103.023.
7. S. Vassilev, V. Iliev, V. Shopska, M. Kaneva, and G. Rostov, "Modeling of alcohol fermentation in brewing-integrated approach for control of continuous alcohol fermentation," *Proc. - 29th Eur. Conf. Model. Simulation, ECMS 2015*, vol. 8, no. 10, pp. 286–291, 2015, https://doi.org/10.7148/2015-0286.

8. D. Buonocore, G. Ciavolino, S. Dello Iacono, and C. Liguori, "Online Identification of Beer Fermentation Phases," *Fermentation*, vol. 10, no. 8, 2024, https://doi.org/10.3390/fermentation10080399.
9. S. Balaji, "Waterfall vs. v-model vs. agile: A comparative study on SDLC," *WATEERFALL Vs. V-MODEL Vs. Agil. A Comp. STUDY SDLC*, vol. 2, no. 1, pp. 26–30, 2012.
10. V. K. Abdrakhmanov, R. B. Salikhov, and S. A. Popov, "Experience of using EasyEDA to develop training boards on the PIC16f887 microcontroller," *J. Phys. Conf. Ser.*, vol. 2096, no. 1, 2021, https://doi.org/10.1088/1742-6596/2096/1/012098.
11. E. Systems, "Datasheet ESP32-WROOM-32D & ESP32WROOM-32U," pp. 1–3, 2023, [Online]. Available: https://www.espressif.com/sites/default/files/documentation/esp32wroom-32d_esp32-wroom-32u_datasheet_en.pdf.

The Interconnection Between Artificial Intelligence (AI) and the Film Industry

Atenya Gichuki and Jonathan K. Ngugi

Abstract The advent of Artificial Intelligence (AI) has ushered in a transformative era for the film industry, revolutionizing the creative landscape from pre-production to distribution. This paper explores the multifaceted role of AI in filmmaking, examining its impact on script analysis, cinematography, editing, and beyond. AI tools such as StoryFit enhance script analysis in pre-production, improving character development and audience engagement. During production, AI facilitates precise cinematography and innovative techniques like markerless 3D motion capture. In post-production, AI streamlines editing, color grading, sound design, and VFX while creating realistic crowd behaviors through advanced software. AI also reshapes film distribution by leveraging predictive analytics to forecast box office performance, as demonstrated by companies like Warner Bros. Beyond these technical contributions, the paper situates AI in the broader context of sustainable development, addressing its alignment with key Sustainable Development Goals (SDGs). AI fosters innovation and infrastructure growth in line with SDG 9 (Industry, Innovation, and Infrastructure), supports inclusive economic growth through job creation (SDG 8), and promotes ethical practices in casting and diversity (SDG 5: Gender Equality). Furthermore, AI's efficiency in resource management contributes to SDG 12 (Responsible Consumption and Production), and its evolving ethical considerations reflect the importance of peace and justice in SDG 16 (Peace, Justice, and Strong Institutions). Through case studies, this paper delves into the interconnection between AI and filmmaking across all phases and the speculative future of AI's integration, highlighting the need for a balanced approach that fosters creativity, efficiency, and sustainability in the film industry.

Keywords Artificial Intelligence (AI) · Film industry · Pre-production · Production · Post-production · Sustainable Development Goals (SDGs)

A. Gichuki (✉) · J. K. Ngugi
University of Lay Adventist of Kigali, Kigali, Rwanda
e-mail: paulatenya@gmail.com

J. Marx Gómez et al. (eds.), *Advancement in Embedded and Mobile Systems*, Progress in IS, https://doi.org/10.1007/978-3-031-99219-3_10

1 Introduction

The dawn of the digital age has brought forth a synergy between technology and creativity, with Artificial Intelligence (AI) emerging as a pivotal force in the realm of cinema. The film industry, known for its perpetual quest for innovation, has embraced AI, not merely as a tool but as a collaborator, reshaping the art of storytelling and the technical finesse of movie-making. AI's infiltration into the cinematic world is not a futuristic prophecy but a present reality. From the germination of an idea to the final cut that graces the screens, AI's touchpoints are manifold. In pre-production, AI algorithms dissect scripts, offering various insights into character arcs and plot dynamics, thereby augmenting the creative intuition of writers and directors. As the lights dim and cameras roll, AI's role becomes even more pronounced. It assists cinematographers in capturing the essence of a scene with precision, and its advanced algorithms facilitate remote motion capture, thus broadening the horizons of visual storytelling. The post-production phase witnesses AI's capability to streamline workflows, where it meticulously refines edits, orchestrates special and visual effects, and fine-tunes audio, ensuring that the director's vision is translated into an immersive experience for the audience. The integration of AI into filmmaking not only revolutionizes the production process but also contributes to global sustainability objectives. AI's role in innovation and infrastructure development aligns with the United Nations' Sustainable Development Goals (SDG 9), which emphasizes fostering innovation and building resilient industries and infrastructure. By enhancing productivity in areas such as script analysis, production, and post-production, AI technology fosters efficiency, helping to modernize the creative sector and drive economic growth in the film industry. Beyond the creative process, AI extends its prowess to the business side of cinema. It analyzes market trends and audience preferences, predicting a film's success with remarkable accuracy. This predictive analysis informs strategic decisions regarding release dates, marketing campaigns, and distribution channels, ultimately influencing a film's journey from the studio to the audience. As AI continues to evolve, its interconnection with film promises to unlock new dimensions of creativity and efficiency. However, this convergence also raises profound ethical questions, challenging us to redefine the boundaries between human ingenuity and machine intelligence. The film industry stands at the cusp of this technological renaissance, poised to explore the vast potential of AI while navigating its ethical landscape with discernment and responsibility. This paper seeks to answer the question: *How has AI transformed the filmmaking process across its various stages—pre-production, production, and post-production?*

2 Literature Review

This research adopts a qualitative approach, drawing insights from existing case studies and a literature review of AI applications in the film industry.

2.1 AI in the Pre-production Phase of Filmmaking

A critical stage of the filmmaking process, pre-production entails careful planning and organization prior to the start of real filming. The first step is to establish a production company, which is required for financial and legal control. The screenplay is dissected to determine every component that is required, including settings, actors, and props. The production is led by key professionals, such as the department heads and directors. A thorough budget is made to control expenses, and a shooting plan is made to guarantee that time and resources are used effectively. Location scouting is the process of identifying potential shooting locations. Casting directors choose performers based on their auditions for the different parts. While obtaining licenses and insurance guarantees that the production follows all legal requirements, storyboarding and shot lists serve as visual guides for filming. During the pre-production phase of filmmaking, the integration of Artificial Intelligence (AI) is significantly altering the landscape of film conceptualization and planning. The influence of AI is particularly evident in scriptwriting, storyboarding, and casting areas where it brings a transformative touch. Utilizing Natural Language Processing (NLP) algorithms, AI can dissect scripts to identify key elements such as emotional tones, character development, and plot structure. These insights are invaluable to filmmakers, aiding them in honing their narratives to captivate audiences more effectively [1]. Tools empowered by AI, such as ScriptBook and ScriptHop, are pioneering the use of predictive analytics to forecast audience responses, offering filmmakers a lens to fine-tune their stories. These tools not only expedite the development process but also foster a more inventive storytelling method. In the realm of casting, AI's role is expanding, with systems designed to align actors with roles that complement their profiles and previous work, thereby broadening the horizons for discovering new talent and assembling diverse casts [1].

Artificial Intelligence (AI) is increasingly being utilized in the casting process of filmmaking, where it serves as a powerful tool for casting directors. By leveraging machine learning algorithms, AI can analyze extensive data sets to identify actors who best fit specific roles based on their skills, experience, and past performances. This not only streamlines the casting process but also enhances the potential for discovering new talent and creating more diverse casts. For instance, AI platforms like Casting Droid and Largo. AI utilize these algorithms to match actors with roles that align with their attributes and previous work, thereby opening up exciting possibilities for talent discovery and fostering inclusivity in casting decisions. The use of AI in pre-production processes in casting and script analysis contributes to (SDG 8) by creating new job opportunities in AI technology, software development, and creative industries. Additionally, AI's objective data-driven approach in casting helps promote gender equality (SDG 5) by reducing biases, thereby fostering inclusivity and diversity in film representation. AI-powered platforms can ensure that actors are chosen based on talent and suitability for roles rather than entrenched gender or racial stereotypes, promoting fair representation in the film industry. The integration of AI in casting is a testament to the technology's potential to revolutionize traditional processes in the film industry. It exemplifies how AI can contribute to the creative aspects of filmmaking, ensuring that the right talent is chosen to bring stories to life. As AI continues to evolve, its applications in casting and other areas of filmmaking are expected to become more sophisticated, further transforming the industry. Schank [2] contributions to the field of Artificial Intelligence (AI) through his development of script theory in the 1970s have been pivotal. His innovative framework for representing sequences of actions within specific contexts known as scripts has provided a foundational structure for AI systems to simulate human-like understanding and interaction in script analysis. Schank [2] work has been instrumental in advancing the field of cognitive science and has had a profound impact on the development of AI technologies that require an understanding of human behavior and language processing. Schank [2] script theory posits that our understanding of the world is based on a series of scripts, which are structured sequences that describe stereotypical human activities. For example, a restaurant script would include sequences such as entering the restaurant, ordering food, eating, and paying the bill. These scripts are stored in our memory and are triggered by relevant cues in the environment, allowing us to anticipate and interpret events. In AI, this concept has been utilized to create systems that can predict and understand human actions by recognizing and following these scripts. The application of script theory in AI extends beyond simple recognition of patterns; it enables machines to engage in more sophisticated interactions with humans. By incorporating [2] scripts into AI programming, developers can create systems that not only recognize sequences of events but also understand the roles, props, and entry conditions associated with them. This has led to advancements in natural language processing, chatbot development, and even the creation of narrative-generating algorithms. Schank [2] influence is evident in the way modern AI can process complex language and engage in contextually relevant dialogue, making interactions with machines more natural and intuitive. Schank [2] script theory has been a cornerstone in the evolution of AI especially in the film industry, particularly in areas that involve language understanding and human-like interaction. His work continues to inspire and inform the development of AI systems that are capable of complex, context-aware processing and interaction in the filmmaking industry.

Yi [3] asserts that the utilization of Natural Language Processing (NLP) algorithms in scriptwriting marks a significant advancement in the intersection of AI and creative writing. Scholars in this domain have emphasized AI's role in text generation, particularly in its ability to produce scripts based on specific themes or topics. This technological support is not meant to supplant human creativity but rather to bolster it, providing screenwriters with a powerful tool to enhance and streamline their creative processes. NLP algorithms can analyze vast amounts of literary data, recognize patterns in successful scripts, and suggest new combinations of plot elements and dialogue that might not be immediately apparent to human writers. This capability allows for the generation of fresh content that maintains the essence of human storytelling while introducing novel perspectives and ideas. The collaborative synergy between human writers and AI tools can lead to the creation of scripts that are both innovative and resonant with audiences. Moreover, the application of

AI in scriptwriting extends to the refinement of dialogue and character development. By processing the complexities of language and character interaction, AI can offer suggestions that enhance the depth and authenticity of characters, making them more relatable and compelling. The contributions of scholars in this field have laid the groundwork for a new era of scriptwriting, where AI acts as a co-creator, aiding writers in crafting narratives that captivate and engage.

Hermann [4] posits that the intersection of Artificial Intelligence (AI) and fiction, particularly within the genre of science fiction, has been a fertile ground for scholars to explore how AI narratives influence public perception. These narratives often serve as a mirror, reflecting societal hopes, fears, and ethical concerns regarding the development and integration of AI technologies. Science fiction has long been a reference point in discussions about the ethics and risks surrounding AI, with stories portraying AI in various lights from benevolent assistants to rogue entities thus shaping the public's understanding and expectations of AI. Scholars like Isabella [4] have analyzed the role of AI in science fiction as part of a larger corpus of 'AI narratives.' These narratives are not just stories but are also seen as metaphors that delve into the human condition and socio-political issues beyond technology. By portraying AI as human-like or autonomous, science fiction can sometimes paint a distorted image of the technology's current potential, distracting from the real-world implications and risks of AI, such as discrimination, exploitation, and surveillance by AI technologies. Furthermore, the work of scholars in this field has highlighted the importance of understanding the impact of these narratives on AI policy and development. How AI is depicted in fiction can influence the general public and researchers, policymakers, and industry leaders. As AI technologies become more advanced and commonplace, the ethical considerations presented in science fiction offer valuable insights into the potential consequences of AI's trajectory in society [4]. The contributions of scholars such as [5–7], have been instrumental in showcasing the capabilities of Artificial Intelligence (AI) in enhancing language-related tasks. Zhou Yu's work at Columbia University, for instance, focuses on optimizing human–machine communication through multimodal sensing and analysis, speech and natural language processing, and machine learning. This research is crucial for developing AI systems that can effectively assist in language translation by understanding and interpreting user actions beyond spoken words, thus facilitating more natural and efficient communication [5], and Liu's [6] research delves into the realm of AI-assisted writing, particularly in educational settings. Their studies have shown that AI-supported English writing approaches can significantly improve the quality of university students' writing. By incorporating reflective thinking and AI tools, students are able to enhance their writing skills, demonstrating the potential of AI in supporting the creative writing process and aiding in the development of academic writing abilities [6]. Hsu [7] have contributed to the understanding of AI's role in story structure formulation. Their work highlights how AI technologies can assist writers in creating high-level and creative writing, inspiring new ideas and enhancing creativity. The use of AI in story-writing promotes human–robot interaction development and encourages users to interact with the story by manipulating props or characters, thus enriching the storytelling experience.

2.2 AI in the Production Phase of Filmmaking

The production phase of filmmaking is the stage where the actual filming of the movie takes place. This is when all the planning and preparation from the pre-production phase come into action. During production, the director works with the cast and crew to capture the scenes written in the script. It involves coordinating the actors, managing the set, and handling the technical aspects such as lighting, cinematography, and sound recording. This phase is critical because it's when the visual and audio elements of the film are created. The production team follows the shooting schedule, which outlines when and where each scene will be filmed. The director, along with the director of photography (DoP) and other key crew members, works to bring the script to life, ensuring that the artistic vision is realized on screen. It's a highly collaborative process that requires meticulous attention to detail and the ability to adapt to various challenges that may arise during filming. Vitrina [1] posits that artificial intelligence (AI) is revolutionizing the field of cinematography by introducing precision and efficiency in camera movements and scene optimization. AI-powered cameras and robotic cinematography solutions, such as those developed by ARRI and RED, are capable of automating various aspects of filming. These advanced systems can handle framing, focus, and exposure, allowing for consistent and precise shots that enhance the visual storytelling of a film. In addition to camera automation, AI assists in optimizing scenes to achieve the ideal lighting and composition. By analyzing data on historical production, weather patterns, and equipment availability, AI can predict potential bottlenecks and adjust schedules accordingly. This not only ensures a smoother production workflow but also contributes to the creative process by suggesting adjustments that enhance the visual aesthetics of each shot [5].

According to [8], the use of machine learning algorithms in AI-powered camera movement is another significant contribution to cinematography. These algorithms can analyze scenes and create dynamic camera movements that correspond with the emotion of the characters, the mood of the scene, and the overall story arc. This technology enables filmmakers to craft camera movements that are not only technically impressive but also emotionally resonant with the narrative. AI's role in cinematography extends to post-production, where it can automatically cut and assemble scenes, adjust color balances, and even suggest edits based on the narrative structure. This not only speeds up the editing process but also opens up new creative possibilities for filmmakers, enabling them to explore unique visual styles and effects that were previously difficult or time-consuming to achieve [9]. Davenport and Bean [10] posit that generative AI has become a focal point in Hollywood and the entertainment industry. They add that it impacts various aspects of film production, including scripting, shooting, and post-production. Their findings emphasize that generative AI can create outputs such as stories, scripts, ad copy, reviews, marketing campaigns, and both moving and static images. As filmmakers face economic pressures and seek productivity gains, generative AI offers a way to produce content more efficiently. Notably, AI tools can suggest storylines, character arcs, and dialogue, as demonstrated by ChatGPT. However, questions about image intellectual property rights arise, especially when AI generates new characters influenced by existing ones. AI's role in optimizing the production process extends to supporting (SDG12), which advocates for responsible consumption and production. By streamlining filming processes, reducing the need for physical sets, and enabling remote production through AI-enhanced technologies, filmmakers can minimize environmental impacts and resource wastage. AI-driven virtual production techniques reduce the need for on-location filming and large physical props, thereby contributing to a more sustainable film production process.

Taplin [11] asserts that AI's impact extends to predicting how unique storylines will resonate with viewers. By analyzing data, AI systems provide insights into audience preferences. While the technology is still evolving, it promises to guide filmmakers in making informed creative decisions. Variety Intelligence Platform's recent report highlights the need for regulation regarding material produced using AI or similar technologies. The film "*Everything Everywhere All at Once*" (2022) leveraged generative AI in its creation. Although generative AI-generated videos remain relatively short and primitive, they demonstrate the technology's potential. Researchers like Taplin discuss the ethical implications of AI-generated content, including questions about copyright and ownership [11]. Reddy et al. [12] assert that in the anime film "Coco," convolutional neural algorithms played a crucial role in analyzing visual effects. Reddy et al. [12] showcase how AI enhances visual storytelling and elucidate that by understanding the impact of AI on film aesthetics, filmmakers can harness its power to create captivating visuals. Motion Capture (MoCap) is a technique that has evolved significantly since its inception in the early 1970s. Initially used primarily for biomechanical research and motion analysis, it has now found widespread applications in various domains, including entertainment, sports analysis, virtual reality, and medical research. The fundamental idea behind MoCap is to capture the movement of real-world actors and apply that data to computer-generated 3D models, resulting in realistic animations.

Researchers [13], from Dongguk University in Korea have explored the current application of DEEPMOTION. Their study analyzes issues related to multi-person object motion capture and highlights the vast prospects for AI-enhanced motion capture. Chen and Chung [13] did a case study on AI-Driven DEEPMOTION Motion Capture Technology. DEEPMOTION represents a significant advancement in motion capture technology. By integrating artificial intelligence, DEEPMOTION recognizes and tracks complex movements and expressions more accurately and efficiently. Markerless motion capture, which relies on computer vision techniques, is likely to impact biomechanics significantly. Unlike traditional marker-based systems, markerless approaches do not require physical markers on actors. Challenges related to accuracy and robustness remain, but innovations in computer vision promise exciting developments in this field. Researchers have been exploring state-of-the-art methods that can track human movement without the need for cumbersome markers. The film industry now benefits from near real-time AI-driven motion capture. This technology enables filmmakers to rapidly capture and process motion data, enhancing production efficiency. Details about actors' movements, facial expressions, and even eye movements can be seamlessly integrated into digital form using AI-powered motion capture systems. Real-time feedback allows directors and animators to make immediate adjustments, improving the overall quality of animations. AI has developed an AI motion capture system that operates without physical markers. Instead, it uses image recognition and deep learning to automatically recognize key points in the human body and reconstruct a three-dimensional model. This approach eliminates the need for attaching markers to actors, making motion capture more accessible and efficient. The system's accuracy continues to improve as deep learning models learn from large datasets that have revolutionized filmmaking [14]. The ethical implications of AI's growing role in filmmaking, particularly regarding biases in casting and intellectual property rights of AI-generated characters and content, warrant further exploration.

2.3 *AI in the Post-production Phase of Filmmaking*

Post-production refers to the period after filming wraps, where the editing of visual and audio materials begins. It encompasses a collaborative process involving professionals such as editors, sound designers, colorists, and visual effects artists. The goal is to transform raw footage into a cohesive and engaging film or video. One of the most prominent contributions of AI in post-production is automated video editing. AI-powered tools can analyze footage and make editing decisions based on predefined criteria or learning from vast datasets of previously edited films. For instance, the AI tool "EditMate" uses machine learning to automate the editing process by selecting the best clips and arranging them in a coherent sequence. According to [15], this technology reduces the time and labor involved in traditional editing, allowing editors to focus on creative decisions rather than repetitive tasks. In their study, [16] explore the transformative role of artificial intelligence (AI) in the visual effects (VFX) and film industry. They highlight how AI, particularly when combined with machine learning, enhances various aspects of VFX production and filmmaking. The research provides a comprehensive analysis of AI's applications across different stages of film production, including pre-production, production, and post-production. Specific areas of impact include scriptwriting, motion picture production, character animation, final film composition, and tracking. The study also includes a survey indicating the current and future benefits of AI in VFX and filmmaking, showing that AI can significantly improve film quality and boost box-office returns. AI has also revolutionized the creation and integration of visual effects (VFX). AI algorithms can now generate realistic effects, such as explosions, weather phenomena, and digital creatures, with minimal human intervention. AI-driven VFX tools like "DeepFX" employ deep learning techniques to create high-quality effects that blend seamlessly with live-action footage. These advancements not only improve the visual quality of films but also significantly cut down the cost and time required for producing VFX.

Singh et al. [16] emphasize the critical contributions of AI in the post-production phase of filmmaking. AI technologies facilitate various post-production tasks, such as automated video editing, enhanced visual effects, sound design, and color grading. AI tools streamline the editing process by selecting and arranging the best clips, thereby saving time and effort for editors. These advancements also contribute to (SDG 4) by making film and video content more accessible as educational tools. AI-enhanced films, particularly in virtual reality and interactive media, offer new ways to deliver educational content, enhancing digital literacy and promoting interactive learning experiences for audiences across the world. These technologies create opportunities for more engaging and inclusive educational experiences, particularly in underserved regions. AI-driven VFX tools generate realistic effects and integrate them seamlessly into live-action footage. In sound design, AI improves audio quality and generates suitable soundscapes that complement visual elements. AI-powered color grading tools ensure consistent and precise color schemes, enhancing the overall visual appeal of films. By automating and optimizing these tasks, AI not only improves efficiency but also enhances the creative aspects of filmmaking, leading to higher-quality productions and better audience engagement. Sound design is another area where AI has made substantial contributions. AI tools can now enhance audio quality, remove unwanted noise, and even generate sound effects. They highlight the development of AI systems that can autonomously create soundscapes for films, ensuring that the audio complements the visual elements effectively. These systems use deep learning models trained on extensive audio datasets to predict and generate the most suitable sounds for different scenes. Color grading, a crucial step in post-production, has also benefited from AI advancements. AI-powered color grading tools can analyze the visual style of reference films and apply similar color schemes to new footage. These tools leverage machine learning algorithms to achieve consistent and aesthetically pleasing results across different scenes. This technology not only speeds up the color grading process but also ensures a high-level of precision and consistency.

Wan [17] in the article, the role of intelligent computer multimedia technology in the post-production of film and television is thoroughly examined. The research underscores the growing importance of high-quality visual design in the era of digital technology, particularly for short videos and major films. The study highlights how computer multimedia technology, integrated with artificial intelligence (AI), is revolutionizing video processing, thus fostering innovation within China's film industry. This technology is pivotal in expanding creative possibilities and enhancing the artistic expression of film and television works. Wan [17] elaborates on the unique contributions of computer multimedia technology across various stages of post-production, such as video editing, color rendering, and audio processing. AI-driven video editing significantly improves the quality and efficiency of editing processes. By automating tasks like object recognition, behavior analysis, and video content understanding, AI enables automatic video editing, reducing the time and effort required from human editors. This automation enhances the overall efficiency and accuracy of post-production work. One notable contribution of AI in post-production, as discussed by [17], is in the color rendering stage. AI can automatically process black and white video resources, enhancing their visual appeal. This automatic processing ensures consistent color quality across different scenes, thereby improving the visual coherence of the final product. Moreover, AI's ability to adjust lighting, color, and sound effects enhances the visual and auditory experience of film and television works, making them more immersive for audiences.

Wan [17] also emphasizes the economic benefits of using computer multimedia technology in film and television post-production. By compensating for shortcomings in the pre-filming process and shortening the production cycle, AI technology can improve the economic efficiency of film production companies. This efficiency is particularly evident in the ability to handle batch processing of similar videos and the flexibility in media storage, which reduces costs and enhances data retrieval during post-production. Wan [17] demonstrates that AI and computer multimedia technology play crucial roles in enhancing the artistic and economic aspects of film and television post-production. These technologies not only improve the efficiency and quality of video editing, color rendering, and audio processing but also contribute to the overall creative and economic success of film productions. AI platforms have become instrumental in predicting a film's success, and guiding critical decisions related to release dates, marketing strategies, and distribution plans. These predictive capabilities are primarily driven by analyzing large datasets that include historical box office data, social media trends, and audience sentiment. AI tools can assess a wide range of variables to forecast a film's potential success. Factors such as genre, cast, director, production budget, and release timing are analyzed to predict box office performance. Yuan and Shibasaki [18] demonstrated that multi-model ensembles, including algorithms like XGBoost and LightGBM, can predict box office outcomes with high accuracy by evaluating these diverse factors. This predictive capability helps producers and marketers optimize their strategies to enhance the film's financial success [19].

AI's ability to predict box office success extends to informing marketing and distribution strategies. For instance, by analyzing social media sentiment and trends, AI can identify the most opportune moments to launch marketing campaigns. This ensures that promotional efforts align with peak interest periods among potential audiences, thereby maximizing engagement and return on investment. This sentiment analysis helps in determining optimal release windows and tailoring marketing content to resonate more effectively with target demographics [18]. A case study by [17] on Warner Bros. reveals it as a prominent example of a studio leveraging AI to forecast box office performance. By integrating AI tools into their decision-making processes, they can predict the potential financial outcomes of films with significant accuracy. These predictions aid in determining release schedules that maximize profitability and ensure that marketing efforts are strategically aligned with expected audience responses. The integration of AI in these processes underscores its value in reducing financial risks and enhancing strategic planning [17]. AI also contributes significantly to the artistic and technical quality of films during the post-production phase. Techniques like automated CGI enhancements are increasingly managed by AI systems. These systems not only accelerate the post-production process but also ensure a higher consistency and quality in the final output. According to [17], intelligent multimedia technology in post-production improves both the efficiency and artistic expression of film projects. AI platforms are reshaping the landscape of film production and marketing by providing data-driven insights that inform critical decisions. From predicting box office success to optimizing marketing strategies and enhancing post-production quality, AI's contributions are making the film industry more efficient and adaptive to audience preferences. These advancements highlight the growing importance of AI in not only predicting but also shaping the future success of films.

2.4 Conclusion

The growing role of AI in the film industry also brings to light important ethical considerations, aligning with (SDG 16,) which calls for promoting peace, justice, and strong institutions. Issues such as AI bias in casting, copyright infringement of AI-generated content, and the potential marginalization of human creators need to be addressed to ensure that AI technology is used fairly and ethically. By fostering discussions on the responsible use of AI, the industry can work towards establishing guidelines that protect the rights of creators, actors, and audiences, while maintaining the integrity of the creative process. In conclusion, while AI continues to reshape the filmmaking industry, its impact extends beyond technological innovation. By aligning with various Sustainable Development Goals, such as fostering innovation and industry (SDG 9), promoting inclusive economic growth (SDG 8), advancing gender equality (SDG 5), and ensuring responsible production (SDG 12), the integration of AI in filmmaking supports broader global objectives. The ethical use of AI further contributes to creating just and equitable institutions, reinforcing the potential of AI as a force for sustainable development in creative industries.

References

1. Vitrina, "AI in filmmaking: revolutionizing the entire process from pre-production to distribution," Vitrina Blog, Aug. 2023. [Online]. Available: https://vitrina.ai/blog/ai-in-filmmaking/. Accessed: Sep. 12, 2024.
2. R. Schank, "Contextual dependency theory," InstructionalDesign.org, 1975. [Online]. Available: https://www.instructionaldesign.org/theories/script-theory/. Accessed: Sep. 12, 2024.
3. Yi, "AI in scriptwriting: enhancing creativity & streamlining process," Junia AI's Blog, 2023. [Online]. Available: https://junia.ai/blog/ai-in-scriptwriting/. Accessed: Sep. 12, 2024.
4. Hermann, "Artificial intelligence in fiction: between narratives and metaphors," AI & Society, vol. 38, pp. 319–329, 2023. [Online]. Available: https://link.springer.com/article/10.1007/s00146-023-01459-6. https://doi.org/10.1007/s00146-023-01459-6.
5. Z. Yu, "Multimodal sensing and analysis for human-machine communication," Columbia University, 2021. [Online]. Available: https://cs.columbia.edu/. Accessed: Sep. 12, 2024.

6. X. Liu, et al., "AI-supported English writing approaches for university students," Journal of Educational Technology & Society, 2021.
7. C. Hsu, et al., "AI technologies for story structure formulation," International Journal of Creative Writing and Storytelling, 2019.
8. M. Sheils, "The future of cinematography: AI-powered camera movement," Rivetai Blog, 2023. [Online]. Available: https://www.blog.rivetai.com/how-ai-is-rewriting-the-script-of-filmmaking/. Accessed: Sep. 12, 2024.
9. Rivetai, "How AI is rewriting the script of filmmaking," Rivetai Blog, 2024. [Online]. Available: https://www.blog.rivetai.com/how-ai-is-rewriting-the-script-of-filmmaking/. Accessed: Sep. 12, 2024.
10. T. H. Davenport and R. Bean, "The impact of generative AI on Hollywood and entertainment," MIT Sloan Management Review, 2023. [Online]. Available: https://sloanreview.mit.edu/. Accessed: Sep. 12, 2024.
11. J. Taplin, "Director Emeritus, Annenberg Innovation Lab, USC," Personal communication, 2023. [Online]. Available: https://www.jontaplin.com/about. Accessed: Sep. 12, 2024.
12. V. S. Reddy, M. Kathiravan, and V. L. Reddy, "Revolutionizing animation: unleashing the power of artificial intelligence for cutting-edge visual effects in films," Soft Computing, vol. 28, pp. 749–763, Jan. 2024. https://doi.org/10.1007/s00500-023-09448-3. [Online].
13. X. Chen and J. Chung, "A case study on AI-driven DEEPMOTION motion capture technology," The Institute of Internet, Broadcasting and Communication, 2024.Datta and R. Goswami, "The film industry leaps into artificial intelligence: scope and challenges by the filmmakers," in Rising Threats in Expert Applications and Solutions, V. S. Rathore, N. Dey, V. Piuri, R. Babo, Z. Polkowski, and J. M. R. S. Tavares, Eds. Springer, Singapore, 2021, vol. 1187, pp. 601–614. https://doi.org/10.1007/978-981-15-6014-9_80.
14. H. Wu, T. Santarra, M. Leece, R. Vargas, and A. Jhala, "Joint attention for automated video editing," in ACM International Conference on Interactive Media Experiences, 2020.
15. A. Datta and R. Goswami, "The film industry leaps into artificial intelligence: scope and challenges by the filmmakers," in *Rising Threats in Expert Applications and Solutions*, V. S. Rathore, N. Dey, V. Piuri, R. Babo, Z. Polkowski, and J. M. R. S. Tavares, Eds. Singapore: Springer, 2021, vol. 1187, pp. 601–614. https://doi.org/10.1007/978-981-15-6014-9_80.
16. H. Singh, A. Rastogi, and K. Kaur, "Artificial intelligence as a tool in the visual effects and film industry," in Recent Advances in Computing Sciences, 1st ed., vol. 1, CRC Press, 2023, pp. 312–316.
17. J. W. Wan, "The application strategy of intelligent computer multimedia technology in film and television post-production," Journal of Computers, vol. 35, no. 2, pp. 183–197, Feb. 2024.
18. W. Yuan and R. Shibasaki, "Utilizing AI for market trend analysis in film distribution," Journal of Marketing Analytics, vol. 9, no. 2, pp. 113–127, Jun. 2021. [Online]. Available: https://link.springer.com/article/https://doi.org/10.1057/s41270-021-00115-2.
19. Y. Ni, F. Dong, M. Zou, and W. Li, "Movie box office prediction based on multi-model ensembles," Information, vol. 13, no. 6, pp. 299, Jun. 2022. [Online]. Available: https://www.mdpi.com/2078-2489/13/6/299.

Design and Development of an At-Birth Detection and Monitoring Digital System for Children Born with Down Syndrome in Rwanda

Habimana Jean Claude, Murererehe Julienne, Rugema Joselyne, Ingabire Speciose, Uwamahirwe Yvonne, Nzayisenga Joselyne, Boniface Ntambara, Mutesa Leon, and Niyoyita Jean Paul

Abstract In Rwanda, enhancing awareness and early detection of Down syndrome at birth is crucial for healthcare providers, parents, and the community. Currently, the identification of Down syndrome symptoms in newborns is often delayed. To tackle this problem, we developed a web-based tracking system for Down syndrome. Through thorough analysis and surveys with 158 healthcare professionals from

---

H. J. Claude (✉) · N. Joselyne
College of Medicine and Health Sciences, University of Rwanda, Health Informatics Department at the Regional Centre of Excellence in Biomedical Engineering and eHealth, Kigali, Rwanda
e-mail: jhabimana@mifotra.gov.rw

N. Joselyne
e-mail: jnzayisenga@rp.ac.rw

M. Julienne · R. Joselyne · N. J. Paul
College of Medicine and Health Sciences, University of Rwanda, Kigali, Rwanda
e-mail: jmurerere@cartafrica.org

R. Joselyne
e-mail: jrugema@nur.ac.rw

N. J. Paul
e-mail: jpniyoyita@nursph.org

I. Speciose
The Nelson Mandela African Institute of Science and Technology, Embedded and Mobile Systems, Arusha, Tanzania
e-mail: ingabires@nm-aist.ac.tz

U. Yvonne
Internet of Things Embedded Computing Systems at the Africa Centre of Excellence of Things (ACE-IoT), College of Science and Technology, University of Rwanda, Kigali, Rwanda
e-mail: yuwamahirwe@fh.org

B. Ntambara
IEEE Tanzania Section, Europe, Middle East, and Africa, Arusha, Tanzania

Africa Center of Excellence in Internet of Things (ACEIoT), College of Science and Technology, University of Rwanda, Kigali, Rwanda

J. Marx Gómez et al. (eds.), *Advancement in Embedded and Mobile Systems*, Progress in IS, https://doi.org/10.1007/978-3-031-99219-3_11

various regions, including the Eastern Province and Kigali City. The findings indicated that healthcare providers are well-versed in health information systems and have access to the necessary technology and internet connectivity, which supports the system's feasibility. Our web-based application, built using HTML, CSS, JavaScript, PHP, and MySQL, enables authorized healthcare personnel to document suspected Down syndrome cases and coordinate referrals to district and referral hospitals for further evaluation and treatment. Feedback loops and treatment recommendations are efficiently managed, ensuring timely interventions. This system shows significant potential to enhance care and facilitate timely interventions for children with Down syndrome in Rwanda.

Keywords Down syndrome · Web application development · At birth detection · Monitoring

1 Introduction

Down Syndrome (DS), or trisomy 21, poses challenges and opportunities within Rwanda's healthcare system [1]. This genetic disorder is marked by physical features and congenital anomalies, including heart disease and gastrointestinal problems, along with conditions like hypothyroidism, celiac disease, diabetes, and developmental delays [2]. Chromosomal disorders like DS lead to disabilities and increased child mortality. The lack of data on DS in Rwanda hampers policy initiatives, highlighting the need for improved reporting to document DS prevalence and status [3]. Individuals with DS exhibit various symptoms impacting musculoskeletal, neurological, and cardiovascular functions. Common symptoms include short stature, muscle hypotonia, atlantoaxial instability, reduced neuronal density, cerebellar hypoplasia, intellectual disability, and congenital heart defects (CHDs) [4].

Atrioventricular septal defects (AVSDs) are common among people with DS, increasing their risk of health issues like hypothyroidism, autoimmune disorders, sleep apnea, epilepsy, sensory impairments, blood disorders, infections, anxiety disorders, and early-onset Alzheimer's disease. Interestingly, solid tumors are less frequent in individuals with DS compared to the general population [5, 6]. DS leads to intellectual disabilities and physical difficulties. Typical physical characteristics may include a shortened neck, excess skin, a flattened facial shape, and downturned mouth corners. However, people with DS can lead fulfilling lives and often live into their 60s with proper support and care. DS prevalence is consistent across different

B. Ntambara
e-mail: bonifacen@ieee.org

M. Leon
Centre of Human Genetics, College of Medicine and Health Sciences, University of Rwanda, Kigali, Rwanda
e-mail: lmutesa@nur.ac.rw

populations, occurring in approximately 1 in every 650 to 1,000 viable births globally. African data is limited, but South Africa and Nigeria report a prevalence of about 1 in 865 viable births [7]. In Rwanda, the incidence of DS is underestimated due to the absence of screening protocols. A 2010 study found 18.8% of 345 participants had DS, and by 2016, 600 children, mostly from Kigali, were registered with the Rwanda Down Syndrome Organization [8].

Newborns with DS are identifiable by physical traits such as reduced muscle tone, a distinct palm crease, a flattened facial profile, and upward-slanting eyes, but these features can also appear in infants without DS. A karyotype analysis of a blood sample is typically used to confirm the diagnosis [9]. Rwanda has made significant strides in addressing the medical needs of children with DS, including the establishment of specialized consultations and a University Medical Genetics Department in 2006, reflecting the country's commitment to improving DS healthcare services [10]. Additionally, a digital reporting method has been developed to enhance early identification and intervention, potentially improving the quality of life for individuals with DS [11].

2 Review of Related Works

The diagnosis of Down Syndrome (DS) relies on cytogenetic and genetic abnormalities, necessitating specialized expertise which delays timely detection. Enhancing access to experts and streamlining confirmation processes is crucial [12]. In resource-constrained countries like Rwanda, widespread internet and smartphone usage can improve the diagnosis and treatment of genetic conditions through accessible technologies like web-based or mobile applications [13]. A strong reporting system is needed to document new DS cases at birth or during health center visits, enabling early genetic disease detection and timely interventions [14]. DS detection systems, compatible with smartphones, use facial recognition to gather birth data and facilitate prompt referrals, improving detection efficiency [15]. Diagnostic imaging systems for smartphones and the web provide an accurate and affordable way to identify DS, though physical exams alone in low-resource areas can be challenging due to subtle anomalies [16]. Facial recognition systems, such as Face2Gene, offer promising screening techniques with accuracy rates between 60 and 69%, aiding early detection and reducing complications [17]. Telemedicine enhances DS detection and monitoring, though infrastructure limitations pose challenges. Remote detection can mitigate the need for physical transfers, making telemedicine essential in regions with limited specialized healthcare services [18, 19]. It is crucial to determine the acceptability of virtual health worker visits in place of in-person consultations [20]. Telemedicine allows healthcare professionals to collaborate on diagnoses and treatment plans, presenting significant opportunities for patient contact [21].

A modified Adaboost algorithm for DS detection uses facial expression images, extracting features with a robust geometric descriptor and classifying them with AdaBoost, training a Neural Network through Backpropagation [22]. Another method uses facial features and neural networks, incorporating nasal bone identification and texture analysis for disease detection [23, 24]. A novel face recognition approach employing kNN and SVM differentiates DS faces in digital images, utilizing datasets like FERET and LFW for automated DS detection [25]. A CNN-based Face Recognition System introduced architectures for recognizing DS and William syndrome, achieving up to 91% accuracy [26]. Abdolah Chalechale's framework for DS recognition uses local binary pattern (LBP) histograms and SVMs for classification, comparing first- and second-order directional derivative LBPs [27].

According to the study, using a monitoring system can enhance the standard of care and mitigate the number of transfers for patients with Down syndrome (DS). Electronic solutions facilitate quick initiation of actions by healthcare personnel in response to worrisome symptoms, hence mitigating the difficulties that come with patient transfers.

Implementing a digital strategy in healthcare institutions enables recording and tracking patient data related to Down syndrome, hence promoting prompt therapeutic interventions and early symptom diagnosis. It also emphasizes the possible advantages of combining continuous monitoring and automated DS detection into a fully digital solution for proactive action and smooth patient care. However, such computerized systems' accuracy and usefulness need to be carefully considered.

3 System Design and Methodology

3.1 Flowchart of the System

Newborns are quickly screened and diagnosed as the first step in the system. Newborns who exhibit symptoms suggestive of Down syndrome (DS) are sent to district hospitals (DH) for additional assessment. Referral or federal hospitals (RH) are contacted if DH suspects DS to conduct a thorough assessment.

Upon confirmation, RH hospitals initiate treatment, physiotherapy, and periodic evaluations, and document the data. If DS is not confirmed, the system concludes the DS detection process and returns to routine procedures (Fig. 1).

3.2 DS System Use Case

The administration and physiotherapists had access to login and logout from the DS detection system health institutions, professions, and system users could all be registered, viewed, and managed by administrators. Physiotherapists could manage referrals for positively tested cases to district hospitals (DH), register new cases for physiotherapy sessions, and handle cases from health centers (HC) or other institutions. They could also monitor progress reports. Additionally, users from health

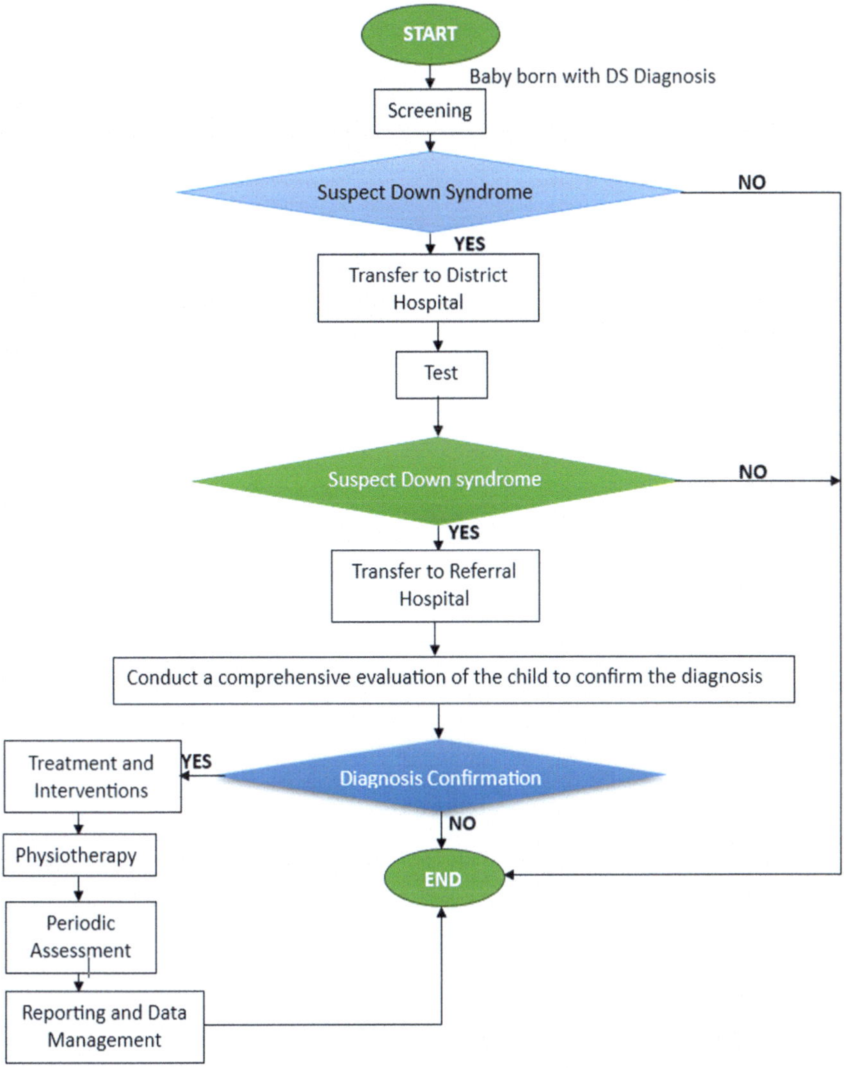

Fig. 1 System's flowchart

centers (HC), district hospitals (DH), and specialists from referral hospitals (RH) could log in and out of the system. HC users reported suspected DS cases, DH users received cases from HC and transferred them to RH or physiotherapy departments, while RH specialists managed DS cases received from DH, counter-referred positively tested cases to DH, and monitored the process. Figure 2 illustrates the use case diagram depicting how users interact with the developed DS detection and monitoring system.

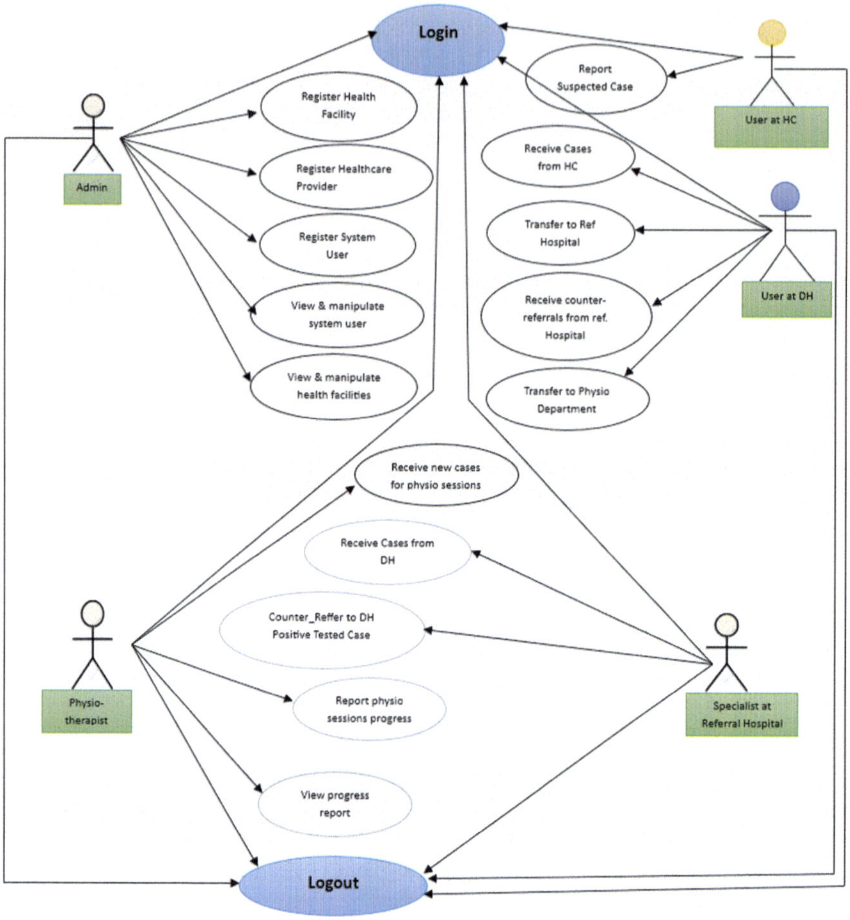

Fig. 2 System's use case diagram

3.3 System's Database Design

A carefully planned and constructed database was used to compile all system data, including roles and credentials, patient records, test results, transfers, motions, and reports. MySQL was chosen as the database management system because of its robust Structured Query Language capabilities.

3.4 Methodology

This study employed a quantitative approach, beginning with a literature review to identify DS tracking and monitoring gaps. The research involved creating a digital system for DS detection and monitoring in partnership with healthcare experts. The study was conducted in health centers and district hospitals from Eastern Province and Kigali City, but in the catchment area of RMH and CHUK. The study included staff from midwifery, nursing, physiotherapy, and pediatric services. A sample size of 158 was calculated using Slovin's formula. Data was collected via an online questionnaire and analyzed using IBM SPSS. Ethical approval was secured from the University of Rwanda's IRB, ensuring consent and data privacy. The Agile model was chosen for developing the DS detection and monitoring system due to its dynamic and iterative nature, which breaks the development process into manageable cycles. This approach provided the flexibility and responsiveness necessary to accommodate evolving requirements and constant refinement, making it particularly suitable for a health system.

4 Results and Discussion

4.1 Login and New Suspicious Case Registration

Both healthcare center (HC) and district hospital (DH) personnel are responsible for registering newborns suspected of DS along with their parents' details prior to conducting any medical procedures. Administrative staff are required to input all Down syndrome (DS) related information for operational purposes and diagnoses. Figure 3 outlines the steps involved in outpatient registration.

4.2 Interface for Users at District Hospital

Employees at the District Hospital (DH) have the same rights as those at the health center level, but they also have extra duties in, including seeing patients transferred from health canters, running further tests, documenting the results, and combining patient data at DH. Afterward, they send the referral hospital these records. Employees at district hospitals (DH) are able to arrange transfers to departments like physiotherapy for patient follow-up because they obtain input from regional hospitals (RH). At this level, new and suspected instances of Down syndrome (DS) are logged and escalated to higher levels dependent on the status of the present visit. Reports are completed regularly at predetermined intervals. The DH user interface for documenting possible DS cases and enabling their transfer to RH is shown in Fig. 4.

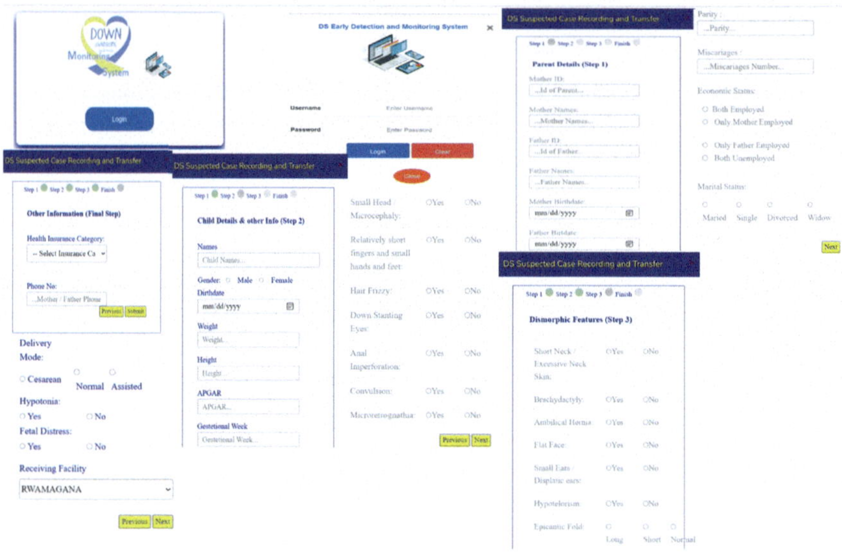

Fig. 3 Login form and new case reporting form

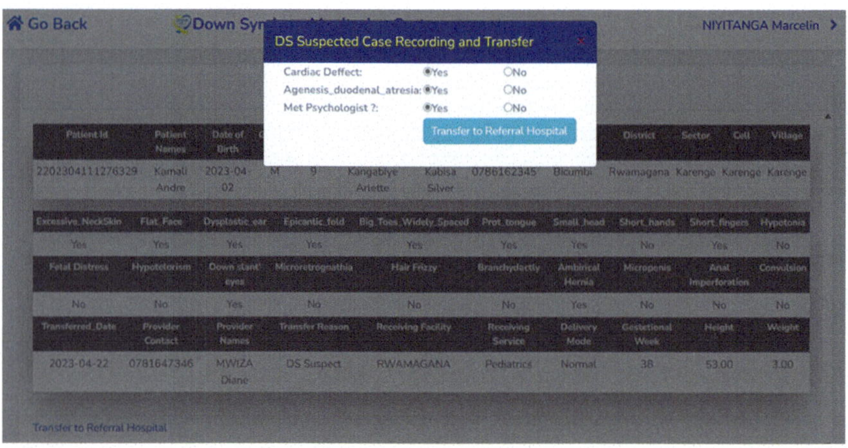

Fig. 4 Interface for users at district hospital

Figure 5 shows the referral hospital of the reported cases of Down Syndrome (DS) from health centers when DH has not yet been retransferred to RH, no way to view details

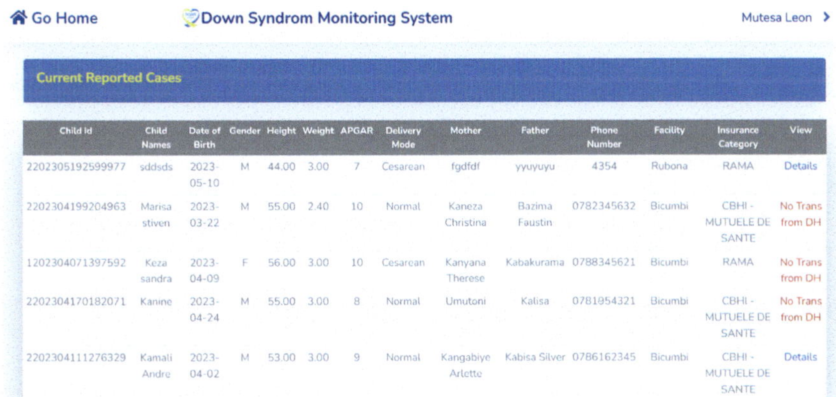

Child Id	Child Names	Date of Birth	Gender	Height	Weight	APGAR	Delivery Mode	Mother	Father	Phone Number	Facility	Insurance Category	View
2202305192599977	sddsds	2023-05-10	M	44.00	3.00	7	Cesarean	fgdfdf	yyuyuyu	4354	Rubona	RAMA	Details
2202304199204963	Marisa stiven	2023-03-22	M	55.00	2.40	10	Normal	Kaneza Christina	Bazima Faustin	0782345632	Bicumbi	CBHI - MUTUELE DE SANTE	No Trans from DH
1202304071397592	Keza sandra	2023-04-09	F	56.00	3.00	10	Cesarean	Kanyana Therese	Kabakurama	0788345621	Bicumbi	RAMA	No Trans from DH
2202304170182071	Kanine	2023-04-24	M	55.00	3.00	8	Normal	Umutoni	Kalisa	0781854321	Bicumbi	CBHI - MUTUELE DE SANTE	No Trans from DH
2202304111276329	Kamali Andre	2023-04-02	M	53.00	3.00	9	Normal	Kangabiye Arlette	Kabisa Silver	0786162345	Bicumbi	CBHI - MUTUELE DE SANTE	Details

Fig. 5 List of reported cases

4.3 *Physiotherapist Interface*

The dashboard that physiotherapists utilize is shown in Fig. 6. It allows them to monitor patients undergoing follow-up, report progress to the Referral Hospital (RH), discharge patients who have finished their treatments, and refer new instances of Down syndrome.

New cases of Down syndrome (DS) transferred to the physiotherapy service are shown in Fig. 7. A DS patient who was released to the PT department is shown in Fig. 8.

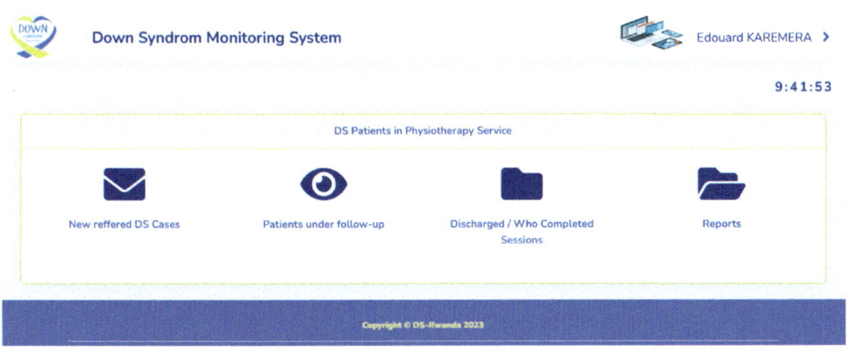

Fig. 6 Physiotherapist interface or dashboard

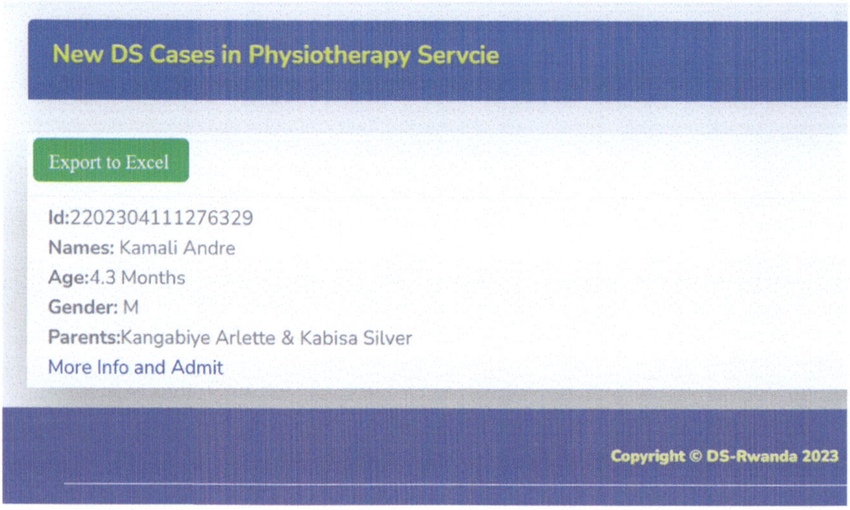

Fig. 7 Patients transferred in physio service

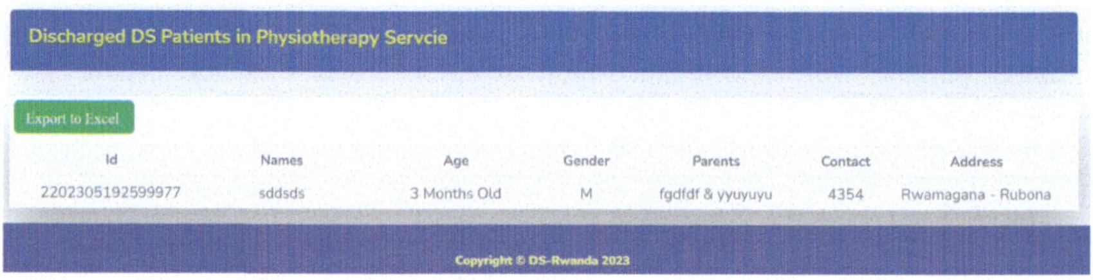

Fig. 8 Patients discharged in physio service

4.4 Specialist Interface at Referral Hospital

Advanced permissions are granted to the Referral Hospital (RH) staff, allowing Geneticist Specialists to view all newly reported cases and get daily reminder alerts at 5 PM.

These specialists manage referral transfers, coordinate patient transfers within hospital departments, and maintain overall responsibility for patient follow-up within these departments. Figure 9 illustrates the RH dashboard interface used for DS detection and monitoring.

The interface/dashboard at the level of the referral hospital is displayed in Fig. 10. At any time, geneticists can create thorough reports with extensive information on any patient in the system. For the purpose of making well-informed decisions, these reports include progress updates for all currently enrolled patients in a variety of departments at both District Hospitals (DH) and Referral Hospitals (RH). The percentage of male and female DS cases that were reported in various districts, the

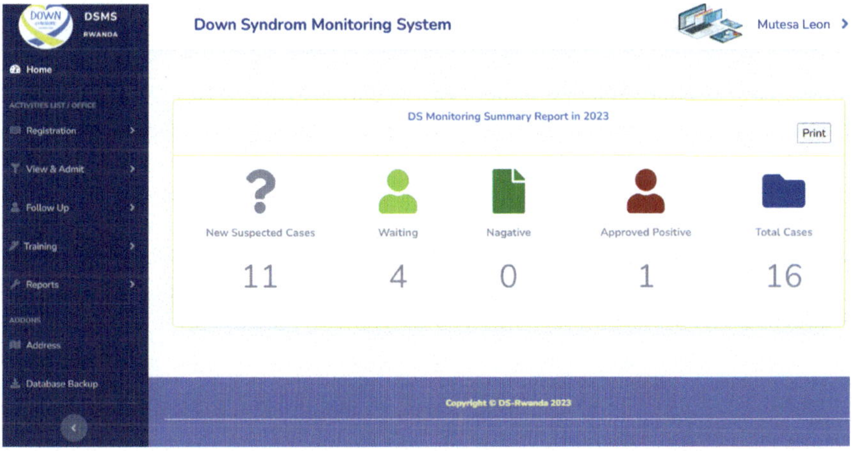

Fig. 9 Interface/dashboard at referral hospital

number of DS cases that positively or negatively tested, and the DS study's unique statistics are all shown in Fig. 10

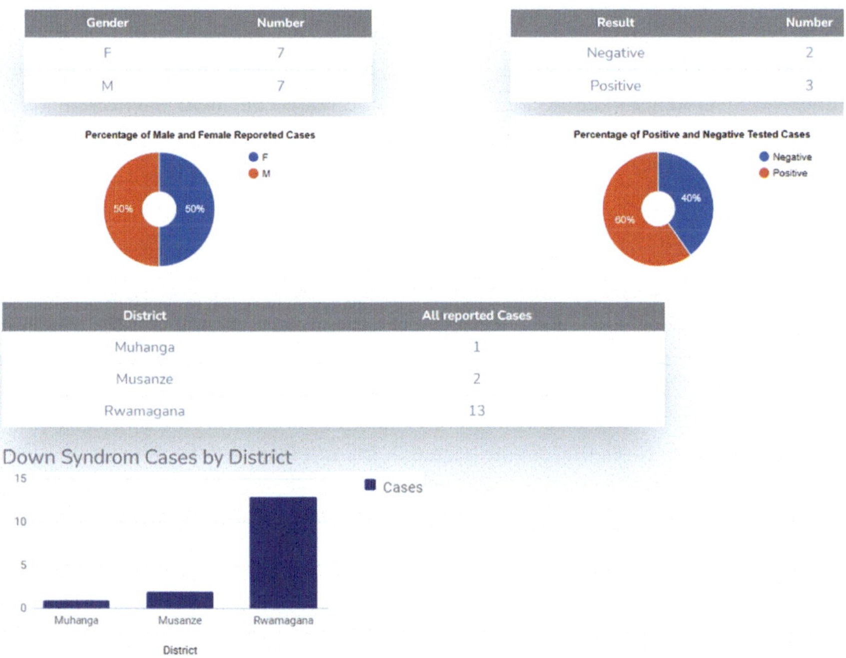

Fig. 10 Report at referral hospital

4.5 Challenges Faced During Development

During the development and testing of the Down syndrome tracking system, some challenges were encountered. Notably, addressing data privacy and security was crucial to protect sensitive patient information. To mitigate this concern, end-to-end data encryption was implemented to secure data during transmission, while symmetric key encryption was used for encrypting specific database columns. Additionally, although almost all staff had internet access and had skills in health information systems, adopting the new system requires supplementary training to ensure its effective use.

4.6 Feasibility Analysis of the System

The healthcare workforce is youthful, with 62.9% aged 26–35 and generally 97.43% under 45, indicating a readiness to adopt new technologies. Universal smartphone ownership and high internet usage (98.1%) for professional purposes further support this. Nearly all staff use smartphones for internet access, making mobile health applications feasible. Additionally, 98.1% are proficient in using Health Information Systems (HIS), with most having 2–5 years of experience. Office computer access is high (96.84%), and almost all staff in institutions transferring cases to CHUK and RMH (99.37%) have internet access. This digital infrastructure, combined with employer-covered internet expenses (89.87%), creates an ideal environment for implementing the Digital Health System for detecting and monitoring children born with Down Syndrome in Rwanda.

5 Conclusion and Recommendations

The goal of creating a digital, web-based system for Rwandan children with Down syndrome (DS) detection and monitoring was accomplished. The lack of DS datasets, which has historically impeded efficient tracking and monitoring, is addressed by this approach. It makes cases that are suspected or proven visible to healthcare facilities and makes it easier for them to be transferred to more advanced facilities. The system ensures timely and efficient detection and monitoring of DS cases, offering a user-friendly and cost-effective solution. Future research should aim to enhance the system by integrating advanced technologies like artificial intelligence (AI). This will enable healthcare professionals to promptly identify DS cases, ensuring timely care and reducing delays.

References

1. Caterina Gori, Guido Cocchi, Luigi Tommaso Corvaglia, Giuseppe Ramacieri, Francesca Pulina, Giacomo Sperti, Valeria Cagnazzo, Francesca Catapano, Pierluigi Strippoli, Duccio Maria Cordelli, and Chiara Locatelli, "Down Syndrome: how to communicate the diagnosis," Italian Journal of Pediatrics, https://doi.org/10.1186%2Fs13052-023-01419-6, vol. 49, no. 18, 2023.
2. Marilyn J. Bull, Allan H. Ropper, "Down Syndrome," The new england journal of medicine, vol. 382, no. 24, pp. 2344-2352, 2020.
3. Marilyn J. Bull, Tracy Trotter, Stephanie L. Santoro, Celanie Christensen, Randall W. Grout, "Health Supervision for Children and Adolescents With Down Syndrome," American Academy of Pediatrics, https://doi.org/10.1542/peds.2022-057010, vol. 149, no. 5, 2022.
4. Louise Malle, Cynthia Gao, Chin Hur, Han Q. Truong BS, Nicole M. Bouvier, Bethany Percha, Xiao-Fei Kong, Dusan Bogunovic, "Individuals with Down syndrome hospitalized with COVID-19 have more severe disease," Genetics in Medecine, https://doi.org/10.1038/s41436-020-01004-w, https://www.nature.com/, vol. 23, p. 576–580, 2020.
5. Paul Lee, Rahul Bhansali, Shai Izraeli, Nobuko Hijiya, and John D. Crispino, "The Biology, Pathogenesis and Clinical Aspects of Acute Lymphoblastic Leukemia in Children with Down Syndrome," National Library of Medecine, PMC, National Center for Biotechnology Information, vol. 30, no. 9, p. 1816–1823, 2016.
6. Bogunovic Dusan, "Bourgeoning Scientific Research in Down Syndrome," Journal of Clinical Immunology volume, https://link.springer.com/article/https://doi.org/10.1007/s10875-020-00837-z, p. 789–790, 2020.
7. Jeannie Visootsak, Lillie Huddleston, Allison Buterbaugh, Adrienne Perkins, Stephanie Sherman, Jessica Hunter, "Influence of CHDs on psycho-social and neurodevelopmental outcomes in children with Down syndrome," Cambridge University Press, Cambridge, United Kingdom, 2015.
8. (RDSO), Rwanda Down Syndrome Organisation, "Support People with Down Syndrome in Rwanda, https://www.globalgiving.org/projects/down-syndrome-support-rwanda/," Down Syndrome International, Kigali, Rwanda, 2023.
9. Mehdi Dadkhah, Mohammad Mehraeen, Fariborz Rahimnia, and Khalil Kimiafar, "Use of Internet of Things for Chronic Disease Management: An Overview," Journal of medical signals and sensors, https://doi.org/10.4103%2Fjmss.JMSS_13_20, https://www.ncbi.nlm.nih.gov/pmc/articles/PMC8253318/, vol. 11, no. 2, p. 138–157, 2021.
10. Numera M.I. Shahid, Effie Lai-Chong Law, Nervo Verdezoto, "Technology-enhanced support for children with Down Syndrome: A systematic literature review," Elsevier, International Journal of Child-Computer Interaction, https://doi.org/10.1016/j.ijcci.2021.100340, https://www.sciencedirect.com/science/article/abs/pii/S2212868921000568, 2022.
11. Ankush Mittal, Hardik Gaur, Manish Mishra, "Detection of Down Syndrome Using Deep Facial Recognition," in Proceedings of 3rd International Conference on Computer Vision and Image Processing, https://doi.org/10.1007/978-981-32-9088-4_11, India, 2020.
12. ACOG, "ACOG's screening guidelines on chromosomal abnormalities," 2020.
13. Mario Fernando Jojoa-Acosta, Sara Signo-Miguel, Maria Begoña Garcia-Zapirain, Mercè Gimeno-Santos, Amaia Méndez-Zorrilla, Chandan J. Vaidya, Marta Molins-Sauri, Myriam Guerra-Balic, Olga Bruna-Rabassa, "Executive Functioning in Adults with Down Syndrome: Machine-Learning-Based Prediction of Inhibitory Capacity," International Journal of envirronmental Research and Public Health, vol. 18, no. 20, 2021.
14. Ehrich, M., Deciu, C., Zwiefelhofer, C., Tynan, J. A., Cagasan, L., Tim, R., Lu, V., "Noninvasive detection of fetal trisomy 21 by sequencing of DNA in maternal blood: A study in a clinical setting," American Journal of Obstetrics & Gynecology, vol. 204, p. 201–211, 2021.
15. Antonio R. Porras, Matthew S. Bramble, Kizito Mosema Be Amoti, D'Andre Spencer, Cécile Dakande, Hans Manya, Neerja Vashist, Esther Likuba, Joachim Mukau Ebwel, Céleste Musasa, Helen Malherbe, Bilal Mohammed, Carlos Tor-Diez, Dieudonné Mumba Ngoyi, "Facial analysis technology for the detection of Down syndrome in the Democratic Republic of the Congo,"

European Journal of Medical Genetics, https://www.sciencedirect.com/science/article/pii/S1769721221001336, vol. 64, no. 9, 2021.
16. Ankush Mittal, Hardik Gaur & Manish Mishra, Detection of Down Syndrome Using Deep Facial Recognition, Advances in Intelligent Systems and Computing, Springer, 2022.
17. Zhaohui Su, Bin Liang, Feng Shi, J Gelfond, abina Šegalo, Jing Wang, Peng Jia, Xiaoning Hao, "Deep learning-based facial image analysis in medical research: a systematic review protocol," BMJ Journal, Public health Protocal, https://bmjopen.bmj.com/content/11/11/e047549, https://doi.org/10.1136/bmjopen-2020-047549, 2023.
18. Lei Sun, Zuqian Fan, Xunjin Weng, Xuehe Ye, Ju Long, Kepeng Fu, Shanhuo Yan, Bo Wang, Yongguang Zhuo, Xinxing Liu, Kegan Lao, "Rapid detection of Down's syndrome using quantitative real-time PCR (qPCR) targeting segmental duplications on chromosomes 21 and 11," https://doi.org/10.1016/j.gene.2014.09.044, 2023.
19. Neha Verma, Bimal Buch, Radha Taralekar, Soumyadipta Acharya, "Diagnostic Concordance of Telemedicine as Compared With Face-to-Face Care in Primary Health Care Clinics in Rural India: Randomized Crossover Trial," National Library of Medecine, National Center of Biotechnology Information, https://pubmed.ncbi.nlm.nih.gov/37130015/, vol. 23, no. 7, 2023.
20. Michael Dinesh, A.R. Kavitha, "Ultrasonic Detection of Down Syndrome Using Multiscale Quantiser with Convolutional Neural Network," in Computational Optimization Techniques and Applications, Web of Science, https://doi.org/10.5772/intechopen.96502, 2021.
21. Sridhar P. Arjunan, M.C. Thomas, "A Review of Ultrasound Imaging Techniques for the Detection of Down Syndrome," IRBM, Elsevier BV, 2019.
22. Vincy Devi, Rajesh Ramachandran, "Down syndrome detection using modified adaboost algorithm," International Journal of Electrical and Computer Engineering (IJECE), https://doi.org/10.11591/ijece.v11i5, vol. 11, no. 5, p. 4281~4288, 2021.
23. Vincy Devi VK, Rajesh R, "Down syndrome identification and classification using facial features with neural network," Global Journal of Engineering and Technology Advances, https://doi.org/10.30574/gjeta.2022.12.1.0090, vol. 12, no. 1, pp. 1–11, 2022.
24. Vlad Dima, Anca Ignat, Cristina Rusu, "Identifying Down Syndrome Cases by Combined Use of Face Recognition Methods," in Advances in Intelligent Systems and Computing, International Workshop Soft Computing Applications, https://doi.org/10.1007/978-3-319-62524-9_35, 2018.
25. Qian Zhao, Kenneth Rosenbaum, Kazunori Okada, Marius George Linguraru, "Automated Down syndrome detection using facial photographs," in Annual International Conference of the IEEE Engineering in Medicine and Biology Society, IEEE Engineering in Medicine and Biology Society, 2013.
26. Endang Setyati, Suharyono Az, Subroto Prasetya Hudiono, "CNN based Face Recognition System for Patients with Down and William Syndrome," Knowledge Engineering and Data Science (KEDS), vol. 4, no. 2, p. 138–144, 2021.
27. Sayed mohamad Tabatabaei, Abdolah Chalechale, "Using DLBP texture descriptors and SVM for Down syndrome recognition," in 4th International eConference on Computer and Knowledge Engineering (ICCKE), 2014.

Development of a Centralized Disease Database with Machine Learning Model for Forecasting Malaria in South Sudan

Amuki Joseph Kesi, Loyani Loyani, Bonny Mgawe, and Elizabeth Mkoba

Abstract Malaria, a potentially fatal illness spread by female Anopheles mosquitoes, is still a major global health issue. The parasite penetrates the bloodstream, attaching itself to red blood cells and developing in the liver with common symptoms such as fever and chills caused by several Plasmodium parasites, the most important being Plasmodium vivax and Plasmodium falciparum. The most dangerous species on the continent is P. falciparum, but P. vivax is more common outside of sub-Saharan Africa. Over 619,000 people lost their lives to malaria in 2019, with 247 million cases reported globally. Children under the age of five accounted for 55% of all the deaths caused by malaria. Pregnant women in sub-Saharan Africa faced exposure to malaria throughout their pregnancies. Sub-Saharan Africa bore the brunt of malaria fatalities, with over 90% of deaths occurring in this region due to suitable climatic conditions for the malaria parasite and limited access to healthcare. Our project aimed to develop a centralized disease database with a machine learning model for forecasting malaria in South Sudan. We used qualitative and quantitative methods to gather requirements, employing extreme programming as our system development approach with four forecasting algorithms. Arima, Facebook Prophet, Neural Prophet, and Double Exponential Smoothing were trained using the dataset's temperature and number of malaria cases as the forecasting variables. Facebook Prophet, Neural Prophet, and Double Exponential Smoothing yielded the best results, with accuracy rates of 85.7%, 87.9%, 86.7% for the Juba region, 89.5%, 87.2%, and 80.4%, for Yei and accuracy rates of 88.9%, 90.7%, and 90.5% for Wau. Arima's accuracy of 81.1% in the Yei region was the only place where it performed well; accuracy of 77.4% and 68.5% were recorded in Juba and Wau, respectively. The system can forecast malaria incidence on a daily, monthly, and annual basis by using a machine learning model, which enhances the provision of healthcare services.

Keywords Centralized disease database · Machine learning models · Extreme programming forecasting diseases

---

A. J. Kesi (✉) · L. Loyani · B. Mgawe · E. Mkoba
Computational and Communication Science and Engineering (CoCSE), The Nelson Mandela African Institution of Science and Technology (NM-AIST), Arusha, Tanzania
e-mail: ajua@nm-aist.ac.tz

J. Marx Gómez et al. (eds.), *Advancement in Embedded and Mobile Systems*, Progress in IS, https://doi.org/10.1007/978-3-031-99219-3_12

1 Introduction

Malaria is a deadly disease that can infect humans when bitten by a female Anopheles mosquito carrying the parasite [1]. The illness is caused by five (5) different Plasmodium parasite species, the most severe of which are P. falciparum and Plasmodium vivax. Plasmodium falciparum is the most prevalent, lethal malaria parasite in Africa while P. vivax is the most common malaria parasite outside of sub-Saharan Africa but there are also other species which include Plasmodium malariae, Plasmodium ovale, and Plasmodium knowlesi [2]. These malaria species can infect humans and can spread from a pregnant mother to her fetus through blood transfusions, organ transplants, and other medical procedures [2]. According to the Institute for Health Metrics and Evaluation, Malaria claimed the lives of 356,363 children under five in sub-Saharan African countries like Ghana, Nigeria, and South Sudan in 2019 [3] which accounted for over 55% of all the deaths related to malaria that year. There are over 247 million instances of malaria worldwide, and the 619,000 deaths from the disease were from children aged either five years or below accounting for 67% of all malaria fatalities while 34% of the women in the 33.8 million pregnancies that took place in the WHO African Region in 2021 were exposed to malaria infection throughout their pregnancies [4]. Over 90% of malaria fatalities occurred in Sub-Saharan Africa where Plasmodium falciparum is extremely abundant partly due to a suitable climatic environment and limited access to healthcare [5]. Malaria was also the cause of 191,106 fatalities in Nigeria in 2019 [6]. In contrast, that same year in the United States, no deaths were linked to malaria [7]. Just four Sub-Saharan African nations Tanzania, Mozambique, Nigeria, and the DR Congo accounted for more than half of all malaria-related fatalities worldwide in 2020 [8]. The WHO African Region was responsible for around 95.4% of deaths and 93.6% of cases worldwide in 2022; children under the age of five accounted for 78.1% of all deaths in this region, down from 90.7% in 2000 [9]. In this region, the number of deaths from malaria increased from 552,000 to 604,000 between 2019 and 2020, whereas the expected number of cases climbed from 218 to 230 million [10]. There was virtually no change in the number of cases between 2020 and 2022, despite the region's estimated death toll dropping to 580,000 [11]. According to the Atlas of African Health Statistics, 2022 [12, 13], Rwanda saw a decrease of about 3.8 million cases during that time, whereas the expected number of cases in Nigeria (5.3 million), Ethiopia (2.4 million), Madagascar (1.5 million), Uganda (1.3 million), the United Republic of Tanzania (1.3 million), Mozambique, and Mali (1.1 million) increased significantly between 2019 and 2022. Malaria is also the leading cause of illness and mortality among children and pregnant women in South Sudan, according to the Ministry of Health there [14]. It is also a hazardous disease with significant implications for public health. The nation has one of the highest rates of malaria cases in the region, with 8750 cases per day and 20 deaths [15]. Over 2 million instances of malaria have been recorded, and 4200 deaths have been reported from the disease.

In the country, malaria accounts for 35% of admissions, 60% of outpatient consultations, and 5% of deaths [16]. Leading South Sudan's national response to malaria is the National Malaria Control Program (NMCP) [17] but the ability of the NMCP to provide adequate effort, administration, and the oversight of the malaria prevention and control nationwide were been severely hampered by operational and technical shortcomings, notably a lack of human resources at all levels [18]. For the national malaria response made available between 2018 and 2022, the South Sudanese government provided 11% of the support, the Global Fund provided 46%, and other partners provided the remaining 43% [19]. The fight against malaria can be only possible if its vast data from the health sector is collected and managed for accurate decision-making through different technologies such as database management systems, IoT devices, and big data analytics for future analysis to improve information access, updates, performance, and service delivery for all people in South Sudan [20]. The development of a centralized disease database management system was to reduce paperwork systems, increase productivity levels, and increase patient data safety and privacy [21]. This can reduce mistakes or errors, increase medical procedures, processes and improve the workflow in the Ministry of Health daily [22], streamline procedures, and provide the tacit knowledge for diagnosis, decision support, forecasting, and treatment [23]. Machine Learning is the rapidly growing branch of science concerned with designing machines or systems with increased knowledge to perform all tasks that require human intelligence [24]. Its algorithms are used to approximate a pattern in the data and to achieve categorization or prediction based on specific input data that may or may not be labeled [25]. It was used to perform forecasting analysis of datasets from the patients, the automation of all intellectual tasks normally performed by humans through the models trained to learn from data and forecast malaria, in South Sudan [26]. Forecasting models are statistical techniques that use past data to project future trends and results [27]. It entails the examination of historical patterns and trends to forecast future occurrences, demand, sales, or inventory levels with accuracy and has the potential to improve organizational or institutional decision-making, resource allocation, and risk management [28]. Therefore, this project focused on the development of a centralized disease database for forecasting malaria in the Ministry of Health in South Sudan based on Machine learning. Juba, Yei, and Wau hospitals were chosen because of their vital location in the region with a high population where malaria is a serious health concern and allows for significant research on future malaria control, treatment, and prevention. These three regional hospitals provided a great research environment due to their broad patient population and willingness to engage in the project. In addition to establishing a long-term collaboration for better healthcare in the area, this project aims to improve malaria patients' care in South Sudan by forecasting the expected number of malaria cases daily. Using a large dataset this project targets the building and evaluation of a centralized disease database with a robust machine learning model specifically designed for forecasting malaria with goals that include thoroughly assessing the accuracy and adaptability of the model and estimating its possible influence on clinical workflows and future malaria outcomes. This project aims to improve the effectiveness, precision, accessibility, and forecasting to address the difficulties and limitations present in current methods and make creative use of its techniques to offer better patient care service provision and reduce future malaria outcomes.

2 Problem Statement

In South Sudan, the Ministry of Health (MoH) is faced with a critical challenge in combatting diseases such as malaria [29]. While government-owned hospitals provide health services to citizens across the country, the current disease control efforts need enhancement [20]. The MoH aims to transition from disease control to disease elimination, aligning with the World Health Organization's (WHO) global technical plan for malaria (2016–2030) which targets a reduction of malaria incidence and fatality rates by at least 90% by 2030 [30]. Several other research works were conducted in the past to solve the problem of patient health information management however the challenge of forecasting the number of disease cases was not addressed [31]. The Seer database which focused on the identification of pathologic, clinical, and demographic characteristics that influenced the survival of patients used IBM SPSS V20.2 software to conduct statistical analysis and the Chi-square test which performs best on categorical data and is also sensitive to sample numbers while the big data personalized health clinical network system used for gathering, organizing, and evaluating patient personal clinical and environmental data did not allow the modeling of algorithms for the prediction or forecasting incidents, number of deaths [32]. The health care system for chronic patient management using edge computing to estimate a patient's health state from real-time data using machine learning models [33] lacked a model to predict the future number of disease cases. The forecasted malaria in three Senegalese endemic zones using linear generalized models with negative binomial regression and poison models [34], unfortunately, it produced overestimations in the forecasts due to its linear character and the Arima, Sarima, and Holt-Winter Multiplication Approach for Pakistan [35] were used by epidemiological forecasting models to predict time series of malaria cases in the nation. However, the models did not construct a dedicated database for data collection, and their main shortcoming was that their model produced negative confidence intervals due to its inability to provide long-term forecasts over longer time periods. Therefore, the development of the centralized disease database with a machine learning model for forecasting malaria can help the Ministry of Health to plan intervention strategies and improve the delivery of healthcare services in South Sudan.

3 Methodology

The project used the review methodology for the investigation, and evaluation of several scientific publications about the data storage, determination, and forecasting of malaria cases in other countries as well as in South Sudan. Using the proper query phrases, a thorough search of research databases including Google Scholar, Science Direct, Springer, IEEE, Web of Science, Research Gate, and Mdpi for publications from 2018 to 2023 which are thought to concentrate on current advancements in the field as part of the procedures.

3.1 Requirement Identification

To discover critical health sector challenges in malaria disease management and forecasting [36], the study first gathered enough relevant articles based on titles, authors, algorithms, techniques, contributions, and applications [37] with the major objective of solving issues related to malaria patient data management, forecasting malaria cases, model interpretability, model design, and making a centralized disease database [38]. Key ideas were extracted and identified most importantly the problems of using a disease database with a machine learning model for forecasting malaria in South Sudan, a total of forty-seven studies were carefully analyzed [39]. With an emphasis on the case study carried out in Juba, Yei, and Wau Hospital, the suggested centralized disease database with a machine learning model for forecasting malaria was developed as a result of this survey study. The major search terms and strings used to find relevant research articles on centralized disease databases with machine learning models for forecasting malaria were centralized disease databases, "patient information systems", "malaria forecasting models," and "machine learning applications in healthcare" [40]. After more than a thousand items were first found, the search criteria were narrowed using the PRISMA [41] technique for a systematic literature review. The search went through several phases, including identification, screening, eligibility verification, and inclusion. In the end, forty-four full-text reports were chosen for in-depth examination as illustrated in the flowchart in Fig. 1.

3.2 Dataset

The project used 1156 datasets collected from three regions of Juba, Yei, and Wau with four different features as described in Table 1.

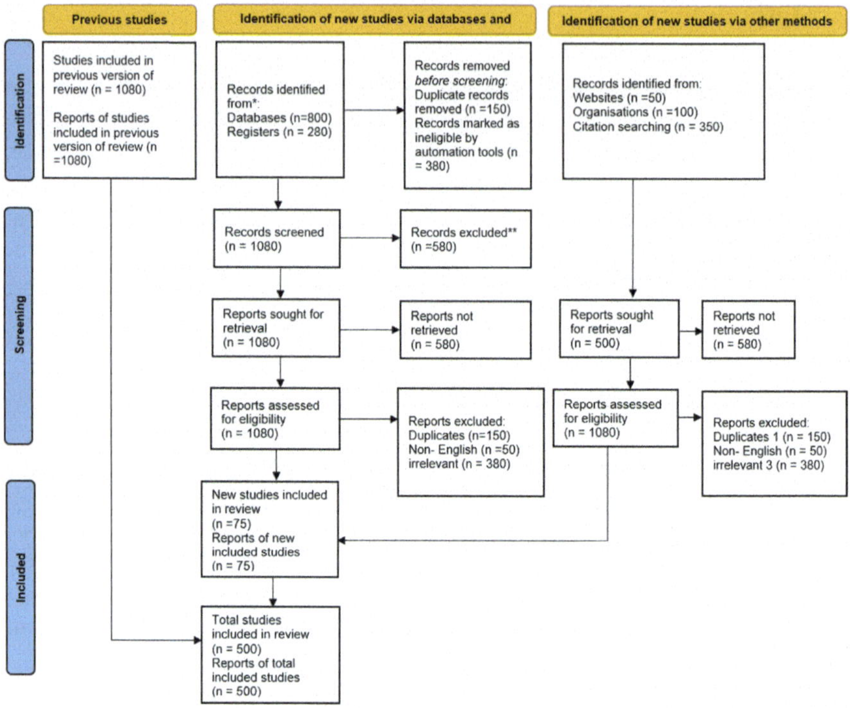

Fig. 1 The flowchart of the prism review for studies location

Table 1 Table captions should be placed above the tables

S/No	Features	Number of observations
1	Total of malaria cases	1116 sample cases are estimated to be exact and accurate
2	Date	Correct dates, months, and years
3	Region	Obtained from different regions of Juba, Yei, and Wau
4	Temperature	Daily temperature measurements and the cases recorded at that time Collected from the hospital's statistics department

4 Related Works

Many different past research that focused on healthcare management systems, the use of Internet of Things devices, big data, and the use of Machine learning models aimed at gathering, managing, and usage of patient data for making decisions in the health sector were reviewed. These management systems are critical components of the health sector because they help the hospital staff collect patient information that is a valuable source of research, communicate with each other, and share patient information safely among the different departments to improve health service delivery [32]. The authorized shared database for easy access, and sharing of electronic medical records to increase accuracy and lower the cost of diagnosis linked to the blockchain network to guarantee data security, featured a proxy-encryption technology system that allowed patient data to be shared securely while preserving privacy, control, and confidentiality so that sensitive data could be accessed by automatically executing chain codes with the pre-existing patient records that are electronically kept on cloud servers, this technology made it possible to share patient data while maintaining confidentiality, control, and privacy but they didn't develop a machine learning model to be used for analyzing and forecasting disease cases using the patient data [31]. The proposed stromal tumors of the intestines (GIST) study incorporated management and current developments in targeted therapy, utilizing the Seer database on the population with focus on the identification of pathologic, clinical, and demographic characteristics that influenced the recovery of patients by utilizing the seer- database where they obtained clinical and demographics spanning the years 2000 to 2018 and used IBM SPSS V20.2 software to conduct statistical analysis with the Chi-square test, period test, multivariate analysis, and Kaplan–Meier calculations. Their study was limited by the Chi-square test which performs best on categorical data and its sensitivity to sample numbers and potential for erroneous results [33]. The healthcare system for chronic patient management systems uses edge computing to estimate a patient's health state from real-time data using machine learning models and transmit data between the cloud via a web-based application that displays raw data to enable the necessary patient-doctor contact but it lacked sensors and was unable to measure other signs like blood pressure, respiration rates, or electrocardiogram with a model to forecast the number of cases in the future [34]. Clinical network system that uses big data and customized health to collect, organize, and assess each patient's unique clinical and environmental data study's methodology and initial findings showed that using electronic health records and secondary hospital-based clinical data was a sensible way to look into chronic patient diseases, however, their system did not allow the modeling of algorithms for the prediction or forecasting incidents, number of death and did not have follow-up data on mortality [35]. For the experiment, a new dietetic care procedure was integrated into a health information system, evaluation, and handling of routine patient data in public health and healthcare so that the large data and real-world examples can be used for assessment, action examined and evaluation of how dietetic care procedures (DCP) can be integrated into hospital health information systems (HIS) using standardized terminology and document templates but their ICF dietetics catalogs did not have ontological search in the system [36]. The clinical cardiology interoperable electronic health record system with several independent information systems to handle highly independent patient personal clinic and diagnostic data management was linked to the information systems of hospitals to facilitate the interchange of data within the information networks of the local healthcare. However, it lacked artificial intelligence algorithms for forecasting the future number of infections aimed to improve procedures because it was not supported by the system [37]. The healthcare information and management system used for managing all files in a hospital acted as a portal with convenient features, basic and reliable for the health sector systems with modules embedded from administrator to patient backend database connection. However, the system had the issue of scalability making it difficult to collect all the increasing patient data [38]. Risk classification for gestational diabetes management based on a machine learning system uses data from electronic health records and daily blood glucose readings to determine which patients are most likely to exhibit elevated blood glucose levels. However, there was no system in place to anticipate women who were at risk of hyperglycemia, and it wasn't expanded to be employed in many predictor characteristics and applications [39]. Predicting confirmed cases of malaria in Zambia's North Western Province: A time series analysis using routine data from 2014 to 2020 was conducted using Arima, which works best with datasets that have few outliers and long-term stable patterns. However, centralized databases and methods for developing scalable, more effective computational algorithms to handle the massive amount of data analysis were overlooked [40]. Time series analysis of malaria in Kumasi using Arima models to predict future occurrence of the disease used Arima, which performs best on datasets with long-term stable patterns and few outliers and also neglected to take into account the centralized databases systems and techniques to create and apply other algorithms to make decisions using the available data [41]. Malaria risk stratification and estimating the influence of rainfall on malaria cases in Eritrea using Arima performed best on datasets with long-term stable pattern and few outliers but it lacked centralized databases and other techniques to create scalable, better optimized algorithms to manage the vast data [42]. Traditional time series models to predict malaria incidence using Arima, STL, ARIMA BP-ANN, and LSTM network models were developed and trained on selected time series data from 2011 to 2017 based on ensemble algorithms to investigate the potential applications of stacking methods in the field of infectious disease predictions and analysis but because of the lack of a centralized database to collect malaria data, their forecast accuracy varied and they also neglected to use other viable prediction models to optimize their ensemble method performance [43]. Three Senegalese endemic zones were forecasted for malaria using generalized linear models to predict the incidence of malaria in Senegal, They used poison and negative binomial regression to create generalized linear models but unfortunately, because of the models' linear nature, bias in the datasets that were gathered, the absence of some explanatory variables, and the lack of a centralized database for gathering particular datasets, their model produced overestimations in the forecasts due to its linear character [44]. Using the Arima, Sarima, and Holt-Winter Multiplication Approach for Pakistan, epidemiological forecasting models for time series prediction of malaria cases were created for Pakistan but they didn't build a specific database for data collection and their model's primary drawback though, was that it produced negative confidence intervals because it had limitations in the provision of long-term forecasts over longer periods [45].

Using the proposed structure in Fig. 2, the centralized disease database with a machine learning model has been developed for the South Sudan's of Ministry of Health for malaria forecasting to visualize future malaria cases in the country. To

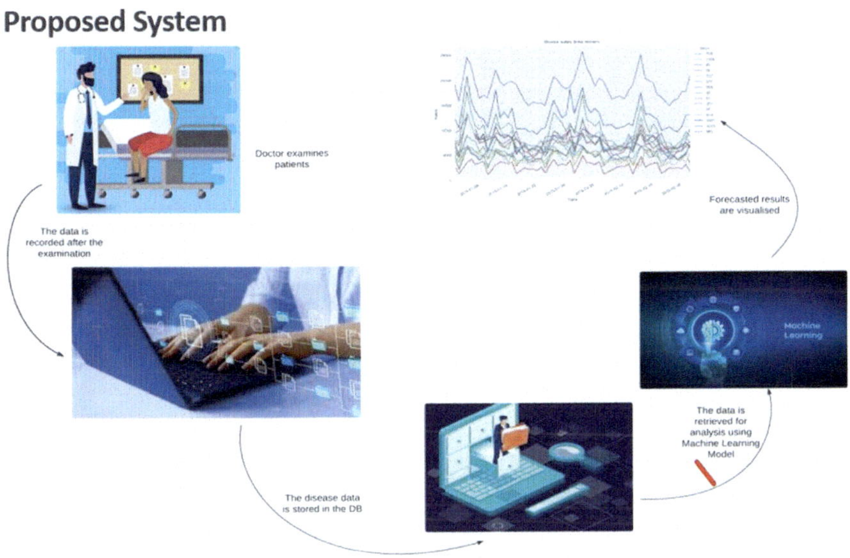

Fig. 2 The proposed centralized disease database with a machine learning model

train machine learning models to predict future instances of malaria, it extracted and categorized data from the centralized disease database.

The system combines an easy-to-use user interface, extensive testing and validation, machine learning model construction, and data preparation to produce reliable results.

The system's implementation and development are based on the above conceptual design shown in Fig. 3, which describes the main features and components of the proposed centralized disease database with a machine learning model for malaria forecasting with analysis and result modules provided for presenting results, mobile accessibility is integrated to make it available, data security and privacy are prioritized, and both the database and the model developed to forecast all malaria cases have an easy-to-use interface.

4.1 Functional Requirements

The proposed system's identified functional requirements are as described in Table 2.

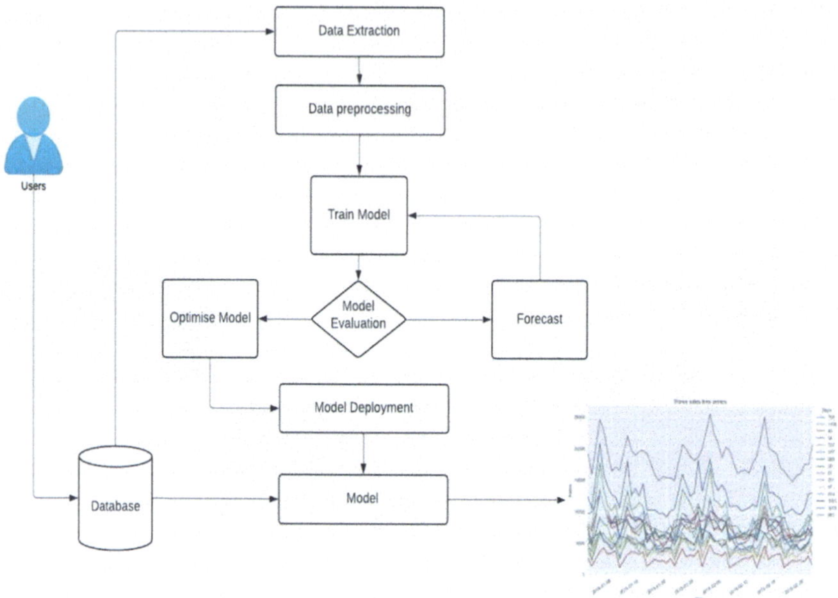

Fig. 3 Conceptual design of centralized disease database machine learning model

Table 2 Functional requirements

S/No	Requirement	Description
1	Create and edit account	The system should allow users to create and modify their accounts using multi-factor authentication
2	User interface development	The system should provide a user-friendly interface using the WCAG 2.1 AA standard
3	Add malaria	The system should enable users to capture malaria data in different formats
4	Export malaria data	The system should enable users to export malaria data in CSV format for analysis using a machine learning model
5	Forecast malaria	The system should provide a severity forecast and visualization of the future number of malaria cases

4.2 Non-functional Requirements

The proposed system's identified non-functional requirements are as described in Table 3.

Table 3 Non-functional requirements

S/No	Requirement	Description
1	High accuracy	The system should provide a high accuracy of at least 80%
2	Security	The system should provide security for the patient data using multi-factor authentication
3	Scalability and reliability	The system should be scalable and reliable with uptime over 90%
4	Usability	The system should be usable based on the WCAG 2.1 AA standard
5	Interoperability	The system should enable interoperability with the existing systems and APIs by following the open API 3.0 standard

5 Modeling of Time Series

5.1 Arima

Arima is the combination of Moving Average with Autoregressive Integrity where the differenced autoregressive and moving average models are combined to create the autoregressive integrated moving average (ARIMA) models. It is as follows:

$$\mathrm{Y}'t = I + \alpha 1y't - 1 + \alpha 2y't - 2 + \cdots + \alpha py't - p + et + \theta 1et - 1 \\ + \beta 2et - 2 + \cdots + \theta qet - q. \quad (1)$$

This is the autoregressive integrated moving average model that needs a stationary time series and adds automatic differencing as an additional parameter set to the number of times that the series needs to be differenced. The Auto-Arima model used start_p = 0, start-q = 0, test = 'adf' to find the optimal 'd', max_p = 12, max_q = 12 that's the maximum p and q, m = 12 the frequency of the series, d = none to let the model to determine the 'd', seasonal = true, meaning no seasonality, start_p = 0, d = 0, trace = true, error_action = 'ignore', suppress warnings = 'true', stepwise = true.

5.2 Exponential and Double Exponential Smoothing

This is used when there are trends in the time series data and simple exponential smoothing isn't effective, this was applied to assist in accurately differentiating between variation and trends, and its formula is:

$$\mathrm{St} = \alpha \mathrm{yt} + (1 - \alpha)\,(\mathrm{st} - 1 + \mathrm{bt} - 1)\, 0 \le \alpha \le 1\ \mathrm{bt} = \gamma(\mathrm{st} - \mathrm{st} - 1) \\ + (1 - \gamma)\mathrm{bt} - 1 0 \le \gamma \le 1 \quad (2)$$

Trend issues were eliminated with double exponential smoothing through the recurrent use of an exponential filter. Double Exponential smoothing used trend = 'mul', seasonal = 'mul', and seasonal periods = '12' while double exponential smoothing used trend = 'add', seasonal = 'add', and seasonal periods = '12'.

5.3 Facebook Prophet

The prophet model was released by Facebook to forecast daily data with weekly, annual, and holiday effects along with seasonality, the model was later expanded to include additional forms of seasonal data. Time series with multiple seasons of historical data and high seasonality perform the best with it. Prophet was used as a nonlinear regression model with the formula:

$$\mathrm{Yt} = \mathrm{g(t)} + \mathrm{s(t)} + \mathrm{h(t)} + \varepsilon \mathrm{t}. \tag{3}$$

where g(t) represents a piecewise-linear trend (also known as a "growth term"), s(t) depicts the different seasonal patterns, h(t) represents the effects of holidays, and εt is a white noise error term. Prophet used yearly seasonality = true, growth = 'linear', seasonality_mode = 'additive', and a changepoint_prior_scale = 0.02.

5.4 Neural Prophet

This approach mixed neural networks with conventional time series algorithms influenced by Facebook Prophet, AR-Net and was regarded as human-centered forecasting. Its formula is:

$$\mathrm{Y(t)} = \mathrm{g(t)} + \mathrm{s(t)} + \mathrm{h(t)} + \mathrm{e(t)}. \tag{4}$$

with, g(t) used as a robust and user-friendly Python package to support autoregression, covariates, Fourier term seasonality, automated selection of training-related hyperparameters, at various time intervals (annual, daily, weekly, and hourly), global modeling, lagged and future regressors, and plotting for forecast components, model coefficients, and final predictions. The neural prophet used a set_log_level ("Error") to disable logging messages, n_change points = 10, to disable trend change points, yearly seasonality = true to disable seasonality components, n_lags = 10, to add the autoregression, learning_rate = 0.01, epoch = 100, and batch_size = 6.

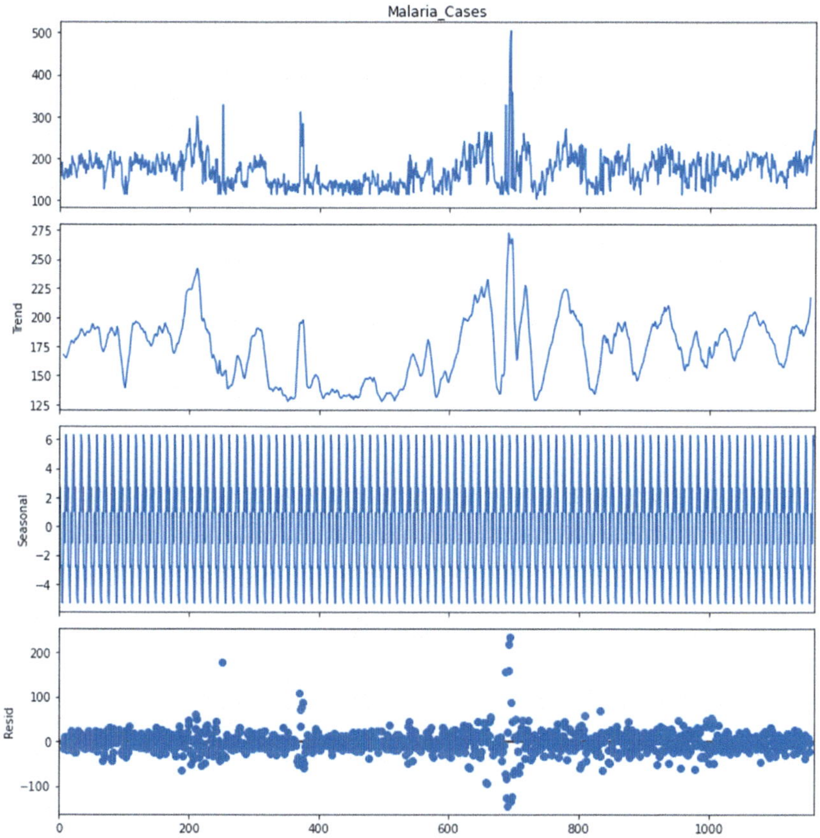

Fig. 4 The decomposition of the malaria cases for all the regions

5.5 *Decomposition of the Malaria Cases*

See Fig. 4.

5.6 *Decomposition of the Temperature*

See Fig. 5.

5.7 *Diagnostic of the Arima Model*

See Fig. 6.

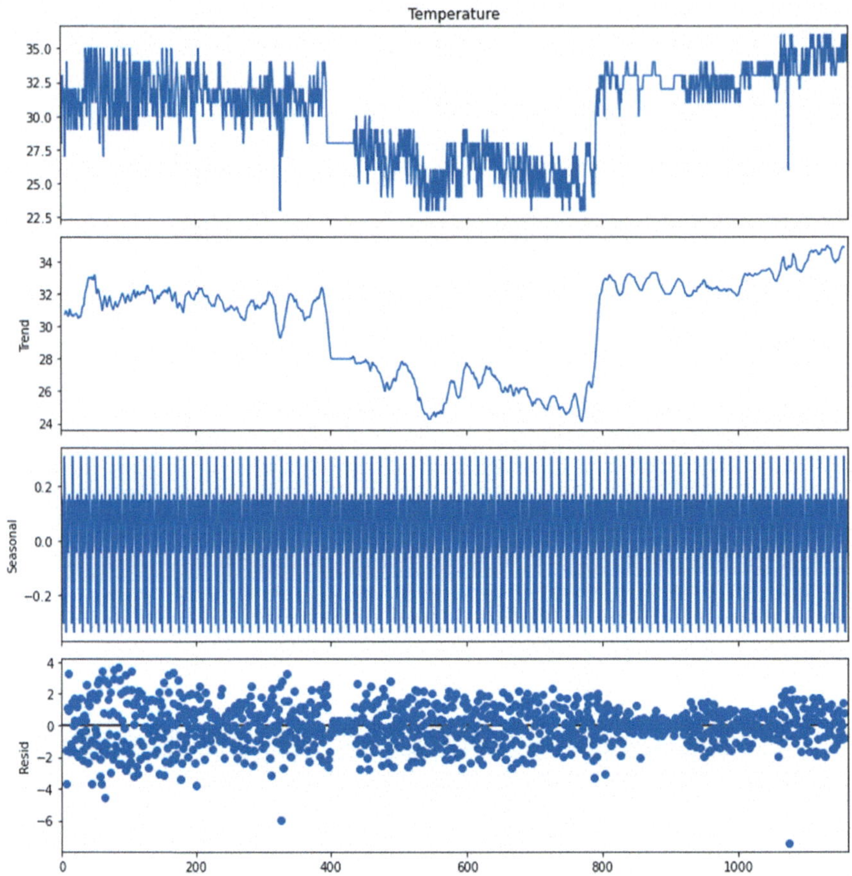

Fig. 5 The decomposition of the temperature for all the regions

5.8 Model Loss (MAE for Juba)

See Fig. 7.

6 Model Results

The Flask framework was used to create the application that was deployed on render.com after the model was developed and tested in the Google Collaboratory because Flask offers a flexible and user-friendly way to create web applications and APIs (Application Programming Interfaces) that are based on Python, with a readme file created for offline deployment on computers using worldwide cloud computing networks, private networks, automatic Git deployments, and free Transport Layer

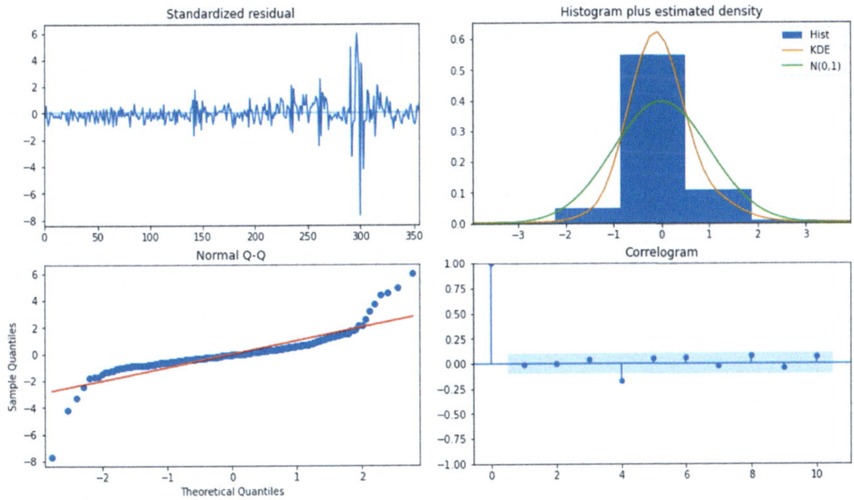

Fig. 6 The diagnostics of the Arima model

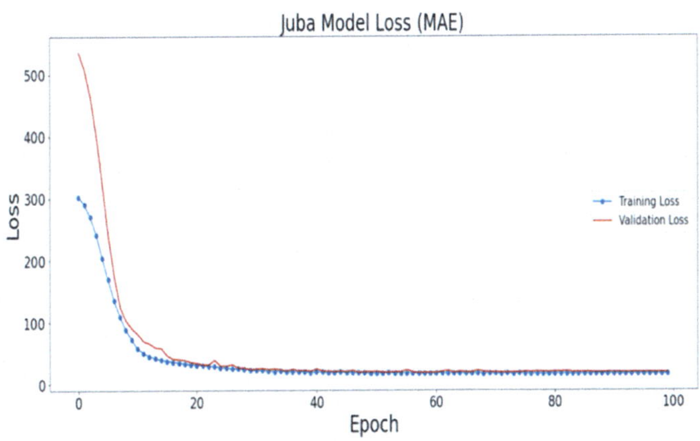

Fig. 7 The model performance loss metrics for Juba

Security certificates, Render was utilized to provide a single cloud for creating and managing all websites and applications (Figs. 8, 9 and 10).

Figure 11 shows the interface of the implemented malaria forecasting model which is the interface where all users with assigned existing accounts need to provide or enter their Google account credentials to log in and access the system, while new users need to be added by the admin to access the model.

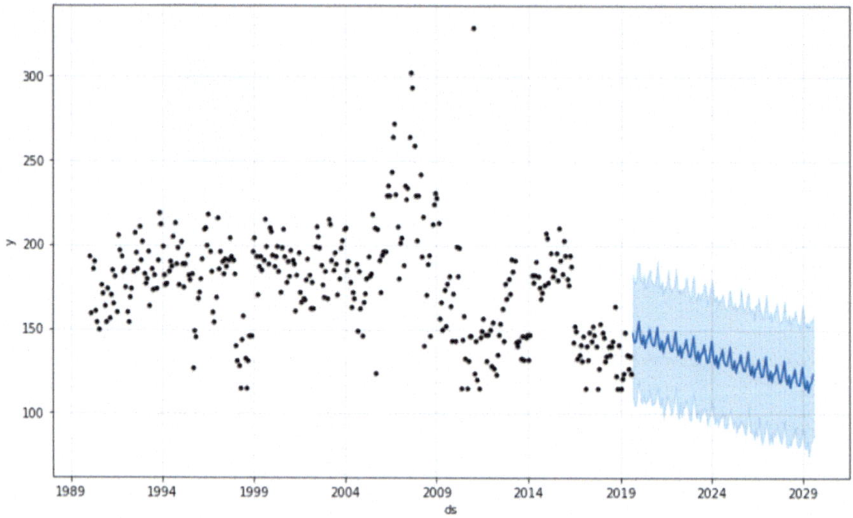

Fig. 8 The model 5-year forecasts for Juba Region

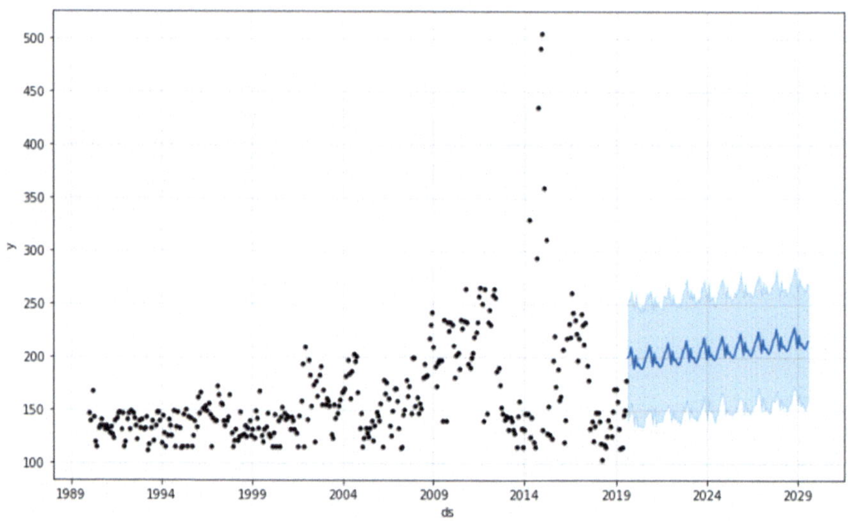

Fig. 9 The model 5-year forecasts for Yei

6.1 Interpretation of Model Results

The forecast results in Fig. 12 show that, at a given temperature for one month as we advance, Juba is expected to register 148 daily malaria cases with a monthly total of 4440 malaria cases.

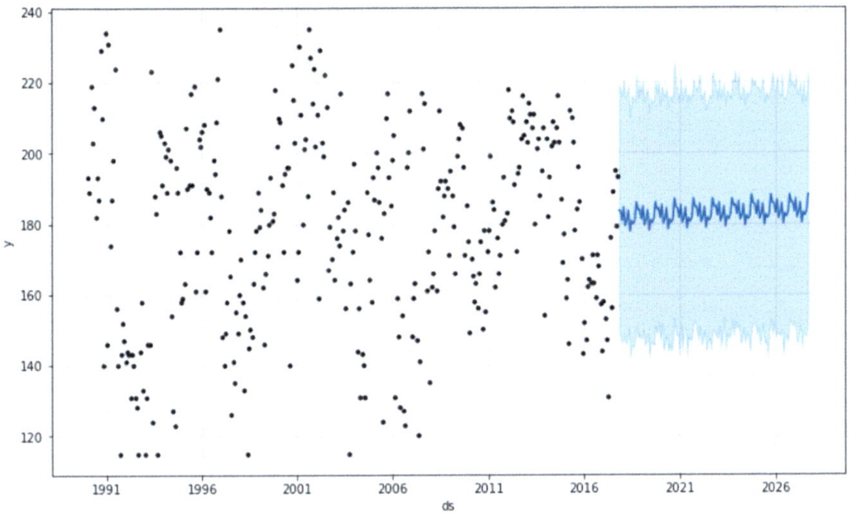

Fig. 10 The model 5-year forecasts for Wau

Fig. 11 The interface of the deployed model for user authentication

The forecast results in Fig. 13 show that, at a given temperature for one month in the future, Yei is expected to register 191 daily malaria cases with a monthly total of 5730 malaria cases.

The forecast results in Fig. 14 show that in a given temperature for one month in the future, Wau is expected to register 182 daily malaria cases with a monthly total of 5460 malaria cases.

7 Discussion of Model Results

A centralized disease database with several modules was thought to be helpful in the management of patient disease data with a home page, admin dashboard, and medical staff dashboard, these modules enable the addition, viewing, and exporting

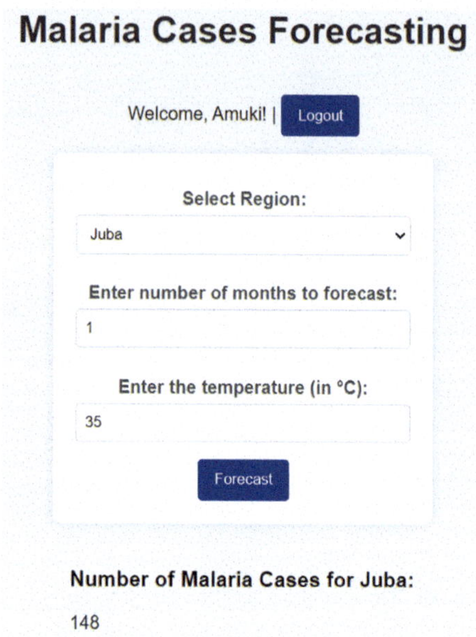

Fig. 12 The model interface displays forecast results for the Juba region

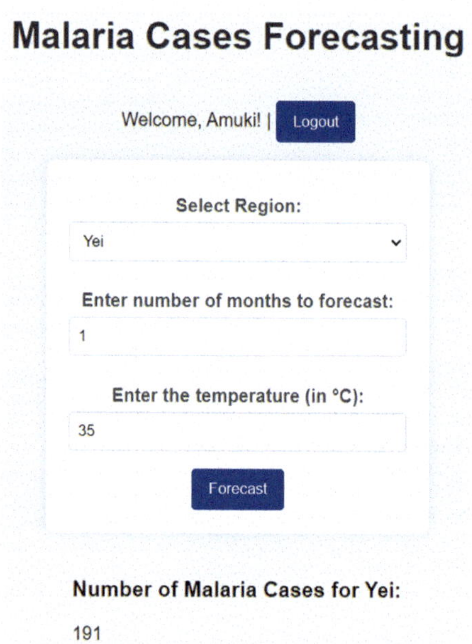

Fig. 13 The model interface displays forecast results for the Yei region

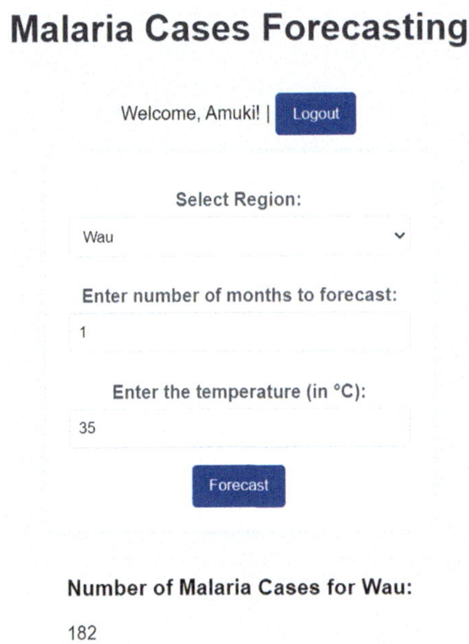

Fig. 14 The model interface displays forecast results for the Wau region

of daily reports; the addition, viewing, and exporting of records related to malaria; and the addition, viewing, and exporting of staff credentials similar to the health care information and management system used for managing all hospital files, with modules embedded from administrator to patient backend database connection [38]. The responsive website for the centralized disease database with a machine learning model for malaria forecasting eliminates labor-intensive, manual, paper-based work practices that are prone to human mistakes and have resulted in data loss and subpar decision-making so that the data can be safely stored in the system just like in the blockchain-powered authorized shared electronic medical record system with proxy re-encryption [31]. The big daily disease data collected from the patients in health facilities enables the use of Clinical networks for big data and personalized health [35] to analyze the future of diseases by application of artificial intelligence in healthcare data management which can help health institutions in the control and prevention of future disease infections, a journey towards precision medicine [32]. Previous studies in the North Western Province of Zambia used the Arima model to forecast the confirmed malaria cases in the area and the results were applied in decision-making support and control of malaria in the region [40]. In Kumasi, time series analysis using Arima models was done to forecast future malaria incidence [41]. Malaria risk stratification and modeling the effect of rainfall on malaria incidence in Eritrea [42] and the model performed better in predicting malaria cases in Eritrea when using generalized linear models to forecast the frequency of malaria in three Senegalese endemic locations [44] using a variety of meteorological variables, such as the sunshine duration, average temperature, average wind speed and precipitation, rainfall, and other climatic conditions but most of these studies did not include other algorithms like Neural prophet, exponential smoothing, or double exponential smoothing, in addition to the Arima model which would have offered better performance than just using the Arima model alone in forecasting malaria cases [45]. Using different models offers better performance results through the integration of main different predictors which improves the general robustness and forecasting accuracy [43] because Arima performs best on datasets with few outliers and long-term stable patterns.

To forecast malaria in Juba, Yei, and Wau in South Sudan, Arima, Facebook Prophet, Neutral Prophet, and Double Exponential Smoothing algorithms were trained by utilizing two variables, such as temperature and number of malaria cases from the dataset where Facebook Prophet, Neural Prophet, and Double Exponential Smoothing yielded the best results, with accuracy rates for the Juba region of 85.7%, 87.9%, and 86.7%, Yei of 89.5%, 87.2%, and 80.4%, and Wau of 88.9%, 90.7%, and 90.5%. Arima's accuracy of 81.1% in the Yei region was the only place where it performed well where accuracy of 77.4% and 68.5% were recorded in Juba and Wau, respectively, this system's machine learning approach allows it to predict malaria cases.

8 Limitations

The project solely employed time series data from 1990 to 2023 for three regions of Juba, Yei, and Wau for its analysis, potentially leading to fluctuations in the accuracy of the malaria case projections using features such as temperature and number of malaria cases. Although four algorithms were employed, the ensemble approach, which would have improved prediction accuracy, was not used, and a wide range of model parameters were not considered because the goal was to observe the various forecasting outcomes of the models using comparable datasets. To increase the forecast performance even more, viable prediction models might be chosen and stacked with other meteorological data such as rainfall, sunshine, humidity, and precipitation to get better forecasts and their general effects on malaria cases.

9 Conclusion and Future Research

This project's primary goal was to address problems with the Ministry of Health's patient data management and impending decision-making procedures in South Sudan's battles against malaria. To improve the delivery of healthcare to all populations and regions, machine learning is required to forecast the increase or fall in diseases. Just two of the many crucial system functions are the daily patient data gathering and the five-seven-year illness prognosis, which can help the ministry understand how the nation will combat diseases going forward after the successful completion of the project where a machine learning model for malaria prediction in South Sudan was integrated into a centralized disease database. This can streamline procedures in the Ministry and hospitals, improve decision-making, and boost departmental efficiency. These functions include but are not limited to adding malaria records, viewing and exporting daily reports, and adding, viewing, and updating staff credentials. With this automation, the Ministry of Health can focus on providing better health services to South Sudanese citizens by doing away with manual labor, delays, and errors. Moreover, the ministry's utilization of machine learning has enabled it to anticipate future events before they occur to allow them to plan and allocate funds based on projected requirements, this can enhance community health care as each of these discoveries shows how revolutionary decision-making processes are enabled by machine learning and illustrates the combination of the machine learning model and the centralized sickness database to anticipate malaria using this technological advancement. The Ministry of Health can improve its decision-making process, service delivery, and disease data processing by integrating and merging these various divisions, which could increase the effectiveness and efficiency of the Ministry in battling illnesses, lower the death rate, and win over the trust of all the partners that support the Ministry and explains the project's accomplishment of its goals and success. However, machine learning models need to be developed to predict diseases like diabetes and typhoid using data that will be gradually acquired by the centralized disease database. The machine learning models were trained using datasets from the Juba, Yei, and Wau regions, but other regions need to be included in the future, and to ensure and enhance overall security, the system currently uses authentication approaches that combine various elements, such as passwords and user accounts. However, it will be required to carefully explore alternative robust security measures for the system in the future to protect the valuable disease data that will be accumulated over time, such as the usage of blockchain technology to secure the ever-increasing volume of disease data. Future research efforts should focus on creating deep-learning models and diagnostic tools for forecasting different patient ailments to lower the mortality toll and free up medical professionals' time. Additionally, the system's data should be used to develop other deep-learning models to examine image samples of malaria, typhoid, and diabetes to step up national efforts to end all diseases in the whole country.

10 Ethical Consideration

The project began at Nelson Mandela African Institution of Science and Technology, the School of Computation and Communication Science and Engineering where in an introductory letter, they recommended us and asked for permission to conduct internship training in the South Sudan Ministry of Health who approved the project to solve South Sudan's illness problems and see how it could be effectively implemented in three government hospitals of Wau, Juba, and Yei. The project ensured that all relevant staff members were handled with respect during the interview process and that all ethical guidelines were followed to guard against any instances of data privacy, confidentiality, and integrity during the data-gathering procedures. As a result, it was simpler to finish the project and gather all the necessary precise data for the system.

Acknowledgements This project was funded by the German Academic Exchange Service (DAAD), the Deutsche Gesellschaft für Internationale Zusammenarbeit (GIZ), and the German Federal Ministry for Economic Cooperation and Development (BMZ) who all contributed and helped in implementing this work under the auspices of the CENIT@EA project.

References

1. Mace, K. E. Malaria surveillance—United States, 2017. MMWR. Surveillance Summaries, 70. (2021).
2. Tseha, S. T. Plasmodium species and drug resistance. In Plasmodium species and drug resistance. IntechOpen. (2021).
3. Ezeonu, C. M., Adabara, N. U., Garba, S. A., Kuta, F. A., Ewa, E. E., Oloruntoba, P. O., & Atureta, Z. The risk of transfusion transmitted malaria and the need for malaria screening of blood donors in Abuja, Nigeria. African Journal of Clinical and Experimental Microbiology, 20(3), 195-201. (2019).
4. Amoako, M. Towards a Functional Health System Governance: The Centrality of Policies, Institutions and Actors' Configuration in Malaria Eradication among Under-five Children in Ghana. (2024).
5. World Health Organization. World malaria report 2023. World Health Organization. (2023).
6. Sokunbi, T. O., Adesanya, T. B., & Aremu, F. O. Effectiveness of malaria control programs in West Africa: a narrative review. (2023).
7. Stonely, A. Prevalence of Malaria in Sub-Saharan Africa. Ballard Brief, 2023(1), 6. (2023).
8. Mace, K. E. (2021). Malaria surveillance—United States, 2017. MMWR. Surveillance Summaries, 70. (2021).
9. Oladipo, H. J., Tajudeen, Y. A., Oladunjoye, I. O., Yusuff, S. I., Yusuf, R. O., Oluwaseyi, E. M., ... & El-Sherbini, M. S. Increasing challenges of malaria control in sub-Saharan Africa: Priorities for public health research and policymakers. Annals of Medicine and Surgery, 81, 104366. (2022).
10. Obasohan, P. E., Walters, S. J., Jacques, R., & Khatab, K. A scoping review of selected studies on predictor variables associated with the malaria status among children under five years 6in sub-Saharan Africa. International Journal of Environmental Research and Public Health, 18(4), 2119. (2021).
11. Kolawole, E. O., Ayeni, E. T., Abolade, S. A., Ugwu, S. E., Awoyinka, T. B., Ofeh, A. S., & Okolo, B. O. Malaria endemicity in Sub-Saharan Africa: Past and present issues in public health. Microbes and Infectious Diseases, 4(1), 242-251. (2023).
12. OOa, E., & OSb, O. Epidemiological Assessment of the Deadliest Parasites in African Region. (2022).
13. Patel, P., Bagada, A., & Vadia, N. (2024). Epidemiology and Current Trends in Malaria. Rising Contagious Diseases: Basics, Management, and Treatments, 261–282. (2024).
14. World Health Organization. Atlas of African health statistics 2022: health situation analysis of the WHO African Region—country profiles. (2022).
15. Pasquale, H. A. Malaria prevention strategies in South Sudan. South Sudan Medical Journal, 13(5), 187-190. (2020).

16. Molina-De la Fuente, I., Sagrado Benito, M. J., Lasry, E., Ousley, J., García, L., González, V., ... & Nanclares, C. Seasonal malaria chemoprevention in a context of high presumed sulfadoxine-pyrimethamine resistance: malaria morbidity and molecular drug resistance profiles in South Sudan. Malaria Journal, 22(1), 345. (2023).
17. Sankineni, S., Chauhan, S., Shegokar, R., & Pathak, Y. Global Health and Malaria: Past and Present. In Malarial Drug Delivery Systems: Advances in Treatment of Infectious Diseases (pp. 1–16). Cham: Springer International Publishing. (2023).
18. Pasquale, H. A. Malaria prevention strategies in South Sudan. South Sudan MedicalJournal, 13(5), 187-190. (2020).
19. Okumu, F., Gyapong, M., Casamitjana, N., Castro, M. C., Itoe, M. A., Okonofua, F., & Tanner, M. What Africa can do to accelerate and sustain progress against malaria. PLOS Global Public Health, 2(6), e0000262. (2022).
20. Idris, I. O., Ayeni, G. O., Iyamu, I. O., Sina-Odunsi, A. B., Adebisi, Y. A., & Obwoya, J. G. Factors influencing severity of recurrent malaria in a conflict-affected state of South Sudan: an unmatched case-control study. Conflict and Health, 16(1), 34. (2022).
21. Harun-Ar-Rashid, Md, Oindrila Chowdhury, Muhammad Minoar Hossain, Mohammad Motiur Rahman, Ghulam Muhammad, Salman A. AlQahtani, Mubarak Alrashoud, Abdulsalam Yassine, and M. Shamim Hossain. "IoT-based medical image monitoring system using HL7 in a hospital database." In Healthcare, vol. 11, no. 1, p. 139. MDPI. (2023).
22. Saleh, S., Cherradi, B., El Gannour, O., Gouiza, N., & Bouattane, O. Healthcare monitoring system for automatic database management using mobile application in IoT environment. Bulletin of Electrical Engineering and Informatics, 12(2), 1055-1068. (2023).
23. Ravikumar, R., Kitana, A., Taamneh, A., Aburayya, A., Shwedeh, F., Salloum, S., & Shaalan, K. The Impact of Big Data Quality Analytics on Knowledge Management in Healthcare Institutions: Lessons Learned from Big Data's Application within The Healthcare Sector. South Eastern European Journal of Public Health. (2023).
24. Phan, A. C., Phan, T. C., & Trieu, T. N. A systematic approach to healthcare knowledge management systems in the era of big data and artificial intelligence. Applied Sciences, 12(9), 4455. (2022).
25. Raschka, S., Patterson, J., & Nolet, C. Machine learning in python: Main developments and technology trends in data science, machine learning, and artificial intelligence. Information, 11(4), 6193. (2020).
26. Sarker, I. H. Machine learning: Algorithms, real-world applications and research directions. SN computer science, 2(3), 160. (2021).
27. Masini, R. P., Medeiros, M. C., & Mendes, E. F. (2023). Machine learning advances for time series forecasting. Journal of economic surveys, 37(1), 76-111.
28. Moroff, N. U., Kurt, E., & Kamphues, J. Machine Learning and statistics: A Study for assessing innovative demand forecasting models. Procedia Computer Science, 180, 40-49. (2021).
29. Ridwan, W. M., Sapitang, M., Aziz, A., Kushiar, K. F., Ahmed, A. N., & El-Shafie, A. Rainfall forecasting model using machine learning methods: Case study Terengganu, Malaysia. Ain Shams Engineering Journal, 12(2), 1651-1663. (2021).
30. Dulacha, D., Ramadan, O. P. C., Guyo, A. G., Maleghemi, S., Wamala, J. F., Gimba, W. G. W., ... & Olu, O. O. Use of mobile medical teams to fill critical gaps in health service delivery in complex humanitarian settings, 2017–2020: a case study of South Sudan. The Pan African Medical Journal, 42(Suppl 1). (2022).
31. Malebo, H. M., D'Alessandro, S., Ebstie, Y. A., Sorè, H., Tenoh Guedoung, A. R., Katani, S. J., ... & Habluetzel, A. In vitro multistage malaria transmission blocking activity of selected malaria box compounds. Drug Design, Development and Therapy, 1593–1607. (2020).
32. Chen, W., Zhu, S., Li, J., Wu, J., Chen, C. L., & Deng, Y. Y. Authorized shared electronic medical record system with proxy re-encryption and blockchain technology. Sensors, 21(22), 7765. (2021).
33. Gupta, N. S., & Kumar, P. Perspective of artificial intelligence in healthcare data management: A journey towards precision medicine. Computers in Biology and Medicine, 162, 107051. (2023).

34. Bangolo, A., Fwelo, P., Al-Qatish, T. E., Bukasa-Kakamba, J., Lee, T., Cayago, A. G., ... & Weissman, S. Outcomes of patients with gastrointestinal stromal tumors in the past decade. Medical Sciences, 11(3), 54. (2023).
35. Ashfaq, Z., Rafay, A., Mumtaz, R., Zaidi, S. M. H., Saleem, H., Zaidi, S. A. R., ... & Haque, A. A review of enabling technologies for Internet of Medical Things (IoMT) Ecosystem. Ain Shams Engineering Journal, 13(4), 101660. (2022).
36. Esposito, S., Orlandi, S., Magnacca, S., De Curtis, A., Gialluisi, A., Iacoviello, L., & Neuromed Clinical Network Big Data and Personalised Health Investigators. Clinical network for big data and personalized health: study protocol and preliminary results. International Journal of Environmental Research and Public Health, 19(11), 6365. (2022).
37. Gäbler, G., Lycett, D., & Gall, W. Integrating a new dietetic care process in a health information system: a system and process analysis and assessment. International Journal of Environmental Research and Public Health, 19(5), 2491. (2022).
38. Lazarova, E., Mora, S., Maggi, N., Ruggiero, C., Vitale, A. C., Rubartelli, P., & Giacomini, M. An interoperable electronic health record system for clinical cardiology. In Informatics (Vol. 9, No. 2, p. 47). MDPI. (2022).
39. Sikiru, I. A., & Oyekunle, R. A. Web-based hospital management system. Adeleke University Journal of Engineering and Technology, 4(2), 28-40. (2021).
40. Yang, J., Clifton, D., Hirst, J. E., Kavvoura, F. K., Farah, G., Mackillop, L., & Lu, H. Machine learning-based risk stratification for gestational diabetes management. Sensors, 22(13), 4805. (2022).
41. Menda, D. M., Nawa, M., Zimba, R. K., Mulikita, C. M., Mwandia, J., Mwaba, H., & Sichinga, K. Forecasting confirmed Malaria cases in the northwestern province of Zambia: a time series analysis using 2014–2020 routine data. Advances in Public Health, (1), 6522352. (2021).
42. Anokye, R., Acheampong, E., Owusu, I., & Isaac Obeng, E. Time series analysis of malaria in Kumasi: Using ARIMA models to forecast future incidence. Cogent social sciences, 4(1), 1461544. (2018).
43. Kifle, M. M., Teklemariam, T. T., Teweldeberhan, A. M., Tesfamariam, E. H., Andegiorgish, A. K., & Azaria Kidane, E. Malaria risk stratification and modeling the effect of rainfall on malaria incidence in Eritrea. Journal of Environmental and Public Health, (1), 7314129. (2019).
44. Wang, M., Wang, H., Wang, J., Liu, H., Lu, R., Duan, T., ... & Ma, J. A novel model for malaria prediction based on ensemble algorithms. PloS one, 14(12), e0226910. (2019).
45. Diao, O., Absil, P. A., & Diallo, M. Generalized Linear Models to Forecast Malaria Incidence in Three Endemic Regions of Senegal. International Journal of Environmental Research and Public Health, 20(13), 6303. (2023).

Machine Learning for Activity Tracking and Multi-inhabitant Recognition in Smart Environments: An Evaluation Study

Timothy Musharu, Dieter Vogts, and Jorge Marx Gómez

Abstract Smart environments have become increasingly popular due to pervasive sensing technologies that offer unprecedented opportunities for health monitoring, security, fitness tracking, and aiding individuals with difficulties living independently. A primary challenge in these environments is recognising and tracking the functional activities of the inhabitants. This paper explores various machine learning approaches, including Multi-Layer Perceptron (MLP), Deep Neural Network (DNN), Decision Tree (DT), and Random Forest (RF), for recognising inhabitants and tracking their Activities of Daily Living (ADLs) within a smart environment. The methodology involves two main components: user recognition and activity tracking. The process includes data pre-processing, feature extraction and selection, and classifier model construction to distinguish between multiple inhabitants for user recognition. For activity tracking, models process input data and classify the status of activities as started, in progress, or completed. Synthetic data generated from the Smart Environment Simulator (SESIM) with three virtual inhabitants was used for model evaluation. To address the imbalanced nature of the dataset, the Synthetic Minority Over-sampling Technique (SMOTE) was applied to ensure fair model performance. Results indicate that the supervised learning models can recognise inhabitants with up to 92% accuracy, with the RF model achieving the highest accuracy at 92%, outperforming the DT model at 90%. Specifically, the RF model shows significant improvements in classifying inhabitant a1, with precision, recall, and F-score of 92%, 86%, and 89%, respectively. The clustering results demonstrate the effectiveness of grouping activities over time, though further refinement using domain expert knowledge is needed to improve accuracy. These findings contribute both practically and

T. Musharu (✉) · J. Marx Gómez
Carl Von Ossietzky University of Oldenburg, Oldenburg, Germany
e-mail: timothy.musharu@uol.de

J. Marx Gómez
e-mail: Jorge.marx-gomez@uol.de

D. Vogts
Nelson Mandela University, University Way, Summerstrand, South Africa
e-mail: dieter.vogts@mandela.ac.za

J. Marx Gómez et al. (eds.), *Advancement in Embedded and Mobile Systems*, Progress in IS, https://doi.org/10.1007/978-3-031-99219-3_13

theoretically by demonstrating that machine learning can effectively enhance inhabitant recognition and activity tracking in smart environments, providing a foundation for further development in this field.

Keywords Smart environments · Activity tracking · Machine learning · Multi-inhabitant recognition

1 Introduction

The convergence of machine learning and pervasive computing technologies has sparked interest in developing smart environments to facilitate remote health monitoring, Human Activity Recognition fitness tracking, security, and anomalous activity intervention [1, 2]. Rising healthcare costs, an ageing population, and the increasing desire for individuals to maintain independent living at work and home drive the demand for smart environments. Family caregivers for Alzheimer's patients have identified human activity recognition, activity status tracking, and inhabitant recognition as critical components of assistive technologies [3]. Human Activity Recognition (HAR) is a branch of computational science and engineering that create systems and techniques capable of automatically recognising and categorising human actions based on sensor data [3, 4].

Sensor technology has significantly advanced over the last decade regarding computational power, size, accuracy, and manufacturing costs. Recent developments in Internet of Things (IoT) sensors and the widespread use of portable devices such as smartphones and tablets enable the collection of vast amounts of data [5]. This data can be used to track daily activities and recognise inhabitants and their behaviours. A Smart Environment (SE) is a system that monitors inhabitants through sensor data and computational agents, responding accordingly through actuators. Despite the high demand for SEs, challenges remain in implementation costs, signal processing algorithms, feature extraction, and sensor setup.

This paper outlines methods for multi-inhabitant recognition and activity status tracking using a synthetic dataset generated with a Smart Environment Simulator (SESIM). To test the approaches for multi-inhabitant recognition, accuracy, recall, and precision metrics are used. The model's output is assessed using principal component analysis (PCA) visualisation for activity status tracking. The main contributions of this paper are:

1. To provide a comprehensive Evaluation of Machine Learning Methods for Multi-Inhabitant Recognition: Providing a detailed comparison of Random forest, Decision tree, Deep neural network and multi-layer perceptron models in machine learning methods for inhabitant recognition, highlighting their performance on synthetic Human activity.
2. Proposes K-Means Clustering as an Activity Tracking Method: This paper proposes the development of a method for activity tracking that does not rely

on pre-labelled data, enabling unsupervised learning in smart environments for activity tracking.
3. Proof of Concept for Simulation-Based Dataset Generation: Validation of the use of simulation tools (SESIM) to generate realistic human activity datasets, providing a scalable and cost-effective alternative to real-world data collection.
4. Performance Metrics and Validation: Thorough evaluation using accuracy, recall, and precision metrics, as well as visual validation through PCA, ensuring the robustness and reliability of the proposed methods.

If accurate, this technology can be used to recognise inhabitants and track the status of their Activities of Daily Living (ADL) in a SE. This would enable remote and automatic assessment of their functional well-being. The structure of this study includes a review of related literature, the proposed methodology, experimental results, and conclusion.

2 Related Literature

This section is structured as follows: First, an exploration of smart environments (SEs) and the variety of technologies supporting inhabitant recognition is conducted. This exploration then delves into sensor-based multi-inhabitant recognition, followed by an examination of machine learning models used in prior studies for multi-inhabitant recognition in HAR activity status tracking with sensors. The section concludes with a discussion of the benefits of classic machine learning over deep learning methods.

2.1 Smart Environments

Smart Environments (SEs) are characterised by their ability to respond dynamically to inhabitant actions and fulfil individual needs through the integration of advanced sensors and actuators [6]. These intelligent surroundings enhance comfort and adaptability by independently acquiring and applying knowledge about the environment [7, 8]. In literature, "smartness" and "intelligence" are defined as the ability to acquire and apply knowledge autonomously, whereas "environment" refers to the external surroundings [9].

SEs are classified into various application domains, including smart cities, smart homes, smart buildings, smart health, smart grids, smart transportation, and smart industries (or "smart factories") [6]. These domains are further distinguished by their orientation towards personal or business use and whether they are designed for single-user or multi-user settings [10, 11]. For an environment to qualify as a SE, it must integrate communication, sensing, middleware, and applications within an Internet of Things (IoT) framework. Figure 1 illustrates the combination of IoT, communication, and middleware that supports SEs. The "IoT-Enabled Smart Environment" diagram illustrates the integration of various components and technologies that create a responsive and intelligent environment. Users interact with the system through dashboards, which display data and insights collected by sensors. These sensors monitor the environment and feed data into middleware, such as event-based and service-oriented architectures (SOA), that manage communication and data processing. The collected data is stored in datasets (such as CSV files) and analysed using models to perform HAR. Applications leverage this data to optimise the environment, enhancing comfort, security, and efficiency through real-time analysis and automated actions, facilitated by communication technologies like Internet Protocol version 6 (IPv6), Radio frequency identification (RFID), and Constrained Application Protocol (CoAP). Table 1 summarises the enabling technology for SEs and the key features of these technologies.

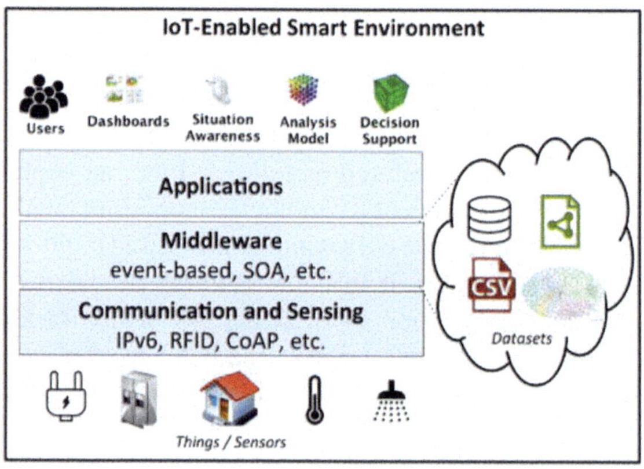

Fig. 1 Shows the IOT-enabled smart environment and its components

Table 1 Enabling technologies for smart environments

Technology	Description	Key features
Communication and Sensing	Technologies enabling seamless data exchange and device connectivity	IPv6, RFID, CoAP, real-time data exchange , sensor integration
Middleware	Technologies facilitating data processing and application integration	Event-based service-oriented architectures (SOA), middleware solutions
Applications	Tools for situation awareness, analysis, decision support, and user interaction	Dashboards, analysis models, decision support systems, situation awareness

2.2 Internet of Things

Since its inception, the Internet has primarily focused on facilitating human-to-human interaction through the interconnection of devices. This setup has bridged the divide between the digital and physical worlds, with humans responsible for collecting data about the physical world and providing input into the digital realm.

To further narrow this divide and enable direct interaction between the digital and physical worlds, the Internet of Things (IoT) was introduced. IoT incorporates intelligent devices, known as "Things," into the Internet, allowing for increased independent interaction between the physical and digital environments [12, 13]. These "Things" can interact directly with their surrounding physical environment with or without human intervention, collecting data through various sensors and performing actions to change the state of the environment using actuators.

The term "Internet of Things" was first coined in 1999 by Kevin Ashton during a presentation at Procter and Gamble (P&G). Initially, the concept was presented in the context of supply chain management. By 2001, the MIT Auto-ID Centre had expanded the idea into an intelligent infrastructure linking objects, information, and people through a computer network [14]. In 2005, the International Telecommunication Union (ITU) conducted research into enabling technologies, market potential, and emerging IoT challenges. The US National Intelligence Council (NIC) later identified IoT as one of six disruptive technologies with significant potential impacts, highlighting risks associated with the ability to remotely locate, monitor, and control objects and the information security risks posed by having internet nodes in everyday devices.

Despite these risks, the potential of IoT in creating real smart environments is immense. However, due to the inherent challenges and risks, there has been a shift towards using simulations to develop and test IoT technologies and applications in controlled settings [15] (Table 2).

2.3 Sensor-Based Recognition of Multiple Inhabitants

Previous research has primarily focused on sensor-based recognition of human activities within Smart Environments (SEs). This process involves collecting data through sensors, preprocessing the data, training models, and eventually recognising activities. Human activity recognition typically utilises data streams from sensors placed in an environment. Studies have not yet demonstrated that machine learning techniques can be applied to simulated data for effective activity status tracking and inhabitant recognition on different datasets.

While most research has concentrated on single-user environments, there is growing evidence that similar techniques can be adapted for recognising multiple inhabitants. This involves using data from various sensors, preprocessing it, and applying machine learning algorithms to distinguish between users based on their

Table 2 Table showing comparison of related studies and contributions of this study

Aspect	[16]	[10]	[17]	[18]	This study
Focus	Single-user environments	Multi-user environments	Single and multi-user environments	Privacy concerns in SEs	Multi-user recognition and activity status tracking in SEs using simulation-generated datasets
Techniques	Machine learning for activity recognition	Data from various sensors, machine learning algorithms	Advanced preprocessing, sophisticated algorithms	Privacy-preserving machine learning	Combination of supervised and unsupervised learning, use of SMOTE for data balancing, PCA for validation
Multi–inhabitant Consideration	Not covered	Preliminary evidence of feasibility	Feasible with existing methodologies	Discusses privacy implications	Comprehensive evaluation of multi-user recognition with practical strategies for implementation
Findings	Effective activity tracking	Techniques Can be adapted for multiple inhabitants	Potential for personalised services, privacy concerns	Raises privacy concerns, suggests mitigation strategies	High accuracy in recognising multiple inhabitants, potential for remote assessment of ADLs
Datasets used	Real-world dataset from a smart home	Synthetic dataset to simulate multi-user environment	Both synthetic and real-world datasets	Did not focus on specific datasets but discussed general privacy implications	Synthetic dataset generated with SESIM, balanced using SMOTE for fair performance evaluation

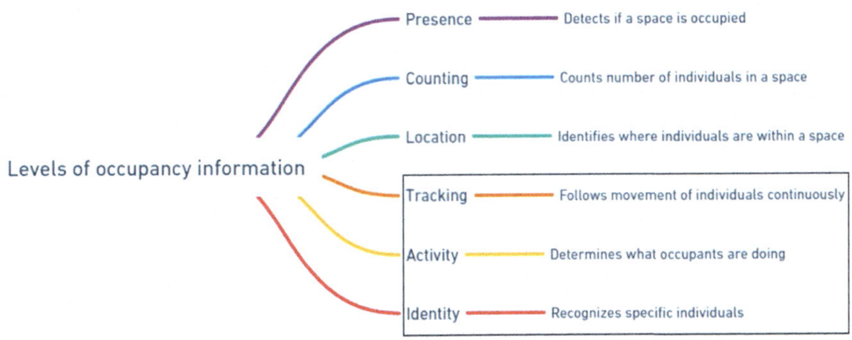

Fig. 2 Levels of Occupancy information in SE and the focus of this study adapted from [19]

activity patterns. Although the literature reviewed for this study has not extensively covered multi-user recognition, preliminary findings suggest it is feasible with existing methodologies. Recognising multiple inhabitants can pave the way for delivering personalised services in SEs, although it may raise privacy concerns as users might feel surveilled. Occupancy information is the data that can be found in SEs which provides insight into presence, count, location, tracking and identity[19]. While various research has attempted to deduce occupancy information in smart environments, there have been few studies that have attempted to deduce the recognition of occupants based on sensor data. This study tries to fill that gap. Fewer studies have been as a result of this phenomenon can be attributed to issues of privacy, SE dataset scarcity and the cost of implementing an SE for testing purposes [15]. Figure 2 explores the current occupancy information that can be derived in SE and highlights what this study aims to achieve in multi-inhabitant recognition and activity status tracking using machine learning models.

2.4 *Machine Learning for HAR in SE*

Machine learning (ML) is a branch of artificial intelligence and a subfield of computer science that focuses on developing algorithms that enable computers to learn from data, improve through experience, and generalise knowledge[19, 20]. ML algorithms analyse data from datasets, build models based on this data, and use these models to formulate hypotheses aimed at solving problems and automating tasks[19].

Chauhan and Singh [20] Subdivides ML algorithms into three main categories:

1. Supervised Learning: Supervised learning algorithms require labelled datasets, where each data point includes input–output pairs. These algorithms learn a mapping from inputs to outputs, which can be categorical (classification) or numerical (regression). The goal is to predict the output for new, unseen data based on the learned mapping.

2. Unsupervised Learning: Unsupervised learning algorithms do not require labelled data. Instead, they attempt to identify patterns and relationships within the data. These algorithms are used for tasks such as clustering, where the objective is to group similar data points, and association, where the goal is to identify interesting relationships between variables.
3. Reinforcement Learning: Reinforcement learning algorithms learn by interacting with an environment and receiving feedback in the form of rewards or penalties. The algorithm aims to maximise the cumulative reward over time by learning an optimal strategy, or policy, for decision-making.

Additionally, there are semi-supervised [21] learning algorithms, which combine supervised and unsupervised learning elements. These algorithms can significantly improve performance by using a small amount of labelled data alongside a larger amount of unlabelled data.

Deep Learning.

Deep learning, a subset of machine learning, has emerged as a powerful approach to solving complex problems. It involves the use of neural networks with multiple hidden layers, allowing the model to learn hierarchical representations of data. Deep learning is particularly effective in tasks such as image and speech recognition, natural language processing, and user recognition within smart environments.

Applications in Smart Environments.

In the context of smart environments, ML algorithms are employed for various tasks, including:

- Activity Recognition: Identifying and classifying the activities of inhabitants based on sensor data.
- Inhabitant Recognition: Distinguishing between different users to provide personalised services.
- Anomaly Detection: Detecting unusual or unexpected behaviours that may indicate security breaches or health emergencies.

By leveraging ML techniques, smart environments can offer more adaptive and responsive interactions, improving the overall user experience and enabling advanced functionalities such as remote health monitoring and automated assistance.

3 Methodology

This work aims to utilise supervised learning methods to identify users and unsupervised learning methods to track activity status. This section explores the techniques employed in supervised learning for user identification and the unsupervised approach for tracking activity status. Figure 3 illustrates the steps involved in the

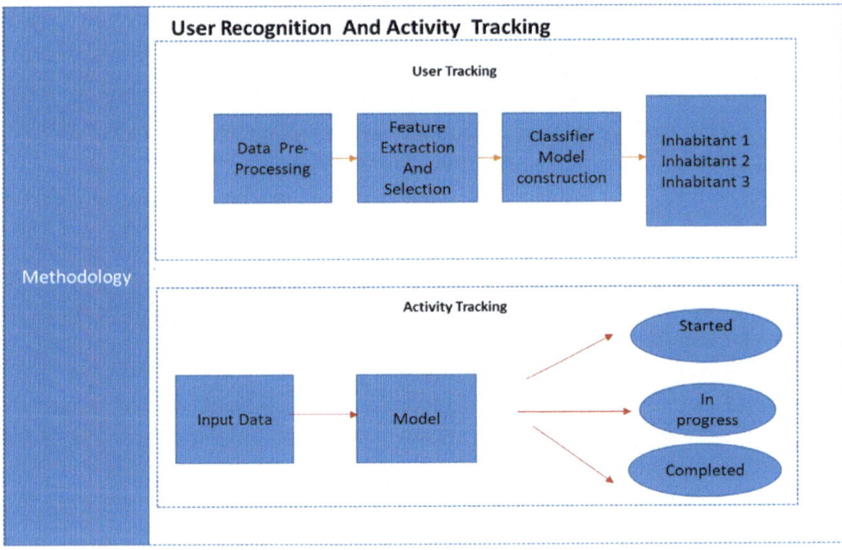

Fig. 3 Pipeline for User recognition and activity status tracking

proposed system, which include data collection, preprocessing, feature extraction and selection, and model training.

3.1 Data Collection for ML

The process of collecting data for user recognition and activity monitoring entails the acquisition of datasets containing information about human activity. Data is gathered using sensors located in a SE, which then transmit the acquired data into a sensor stream. As mentioned earlier, this procedure can be expensive due to the initial expenditures associated with setting up an SE, as well as the difficulties related to maintaining anonymity, ensuring data quality, and gaining acceptability. cost, the hardware sensors and actuators are quite expensive. Additionally, the costs of maintaining sensors in a (SE) context and the time required for calibration are both significant. The selection of sensors, the recipients of data, and the level of detail in the transmitted data have all contributed to heightened concerns around privacy issues. The reliability of the data in a sensor environment cannot be ensured due to the inability to pre-test the sensor placement. Incorrect setup of sensors might impair the quality of data. The level of user acceptance for Activities of Daily Living (ADL) monitoring is limited due to concerns over privacy among inhabitants. Consequently, the requirement for simulation has emerged as a solution to tackle the difficulties associated with monitoring ADL. The study uses the SESIM dataset which is a synthetic dataset generated by an SE Simulator.

3.2 Supervised Learning for User Recognition in SE

As highlighted in the previous sections, supervised learning uses data labels in the training set. The supervised learning model targets a feature which is a label with the inhabitant ID. For Inhabitant recognition, this study analyses the use of supervised learning techniques—the following methods of classic machine learning models for user recognition.

1. **Random forest.** Random forest uses decision trees; it consists of many individual decision trees that operate as an ensemble. Each tree in the random forest produces a class prediction, and the class with the most votes become the model's prediction [16]. The wisdom of crowds is a simple but powerful concept at the heart of the random forest. The random forest model works well because many relatively uncorrelated- ed models (trees) working as a committee outperform any of the individual constituent trees [16]. Uses random forests from smartphone-based sensors for human activity recognition on real data Smart Environment Data. We adapt his technique to inhabitant recognition on a synthetic dataset.
2. **Decision Tree.** Decision trees are a technique used in supervised machine learning, which trains models using labelled input and output datasets. The method is primarily used to solve classification problems, which involve using a model to categorise or classify an object. In machine learning, decision trees are also used in regression problems, which are used in predictive analytics to forecast outputs from unseen data. This study uses the model to predict the inhabitant given a set of sensor features and activities.

   As identified in the literature, there has been a rise in adopting deep learning models applied to human activity datasets. This is mainly due to its superiority in terms of accuracy when trained with large amounts of data. This study also applies deep learning models to user recognition in SE. The following models were used in this study.
3. **Deep Neural Network.** Deep Neural Networks (DNNs) have recently gained prominence due to their ability to solve complex engineering problems and make critical decisions. DNNs have recently become the standard tool for solving various computer vision problems as part of advanced machine learning techniques. The term "deep" refers to the number of layers in DNNs can be many. Deep Neural Networks (DNNs) have excelled at classification tasks in various applications, including image recognition and natural language processing. A deep neural network (DNN), or Deepnet, is a neural network with some level of complexity as it usually has at least two layers in which information is fed forward. The prowess of deep learning is that feature extraction is combined with classification, so manual feature extraction is not needed [12].
4. **Multi-Layer Perceptron.** A multi-layer perceptron (MLP) is a feed-forward neural network supplement. It comprises three layers: the input layer, the output layer, and the hidden layer. It can learn a non-linear function approximator for classification or regression given a set of features and a target. It differs from logistic regression in that it can include one or more non-linear layers, known

as hidden layers, between the input and output layers. Although MLP has been used for human activity recognition [12], it has not been applied to inhabitant recognition in SE.

3.3 Unsupervised Learning for Activity Status Tracking

As highlighted in previous literature, unsupervised learning is mainly adopted to analyse unlabelled datasets. Without human intervention, these algorithms uncover hidden patterns or data groupings. Due to its ability to detect similarities and differences in data, it is an ideal solution for exploratory data analysis, cross-selling strategies, customer segmentation, image recognition and human activity status tracking. By applying knowledge in the domain, this study determined three clusters of activities as being started, in progress and completed. This allows the activities occurring in an SE to be sufficiently grouped. The technique implemented in this study is K-means clustering.

K means clustering. K-means Clustering is an unsupervised learning method that uses unlabelled data. This algorithm uses Hierarchical clustering, which uses two clustering techniques: Agglomerative and Divisive. Agglomerative Clustering creates vast clusters from the bottom up [13]. Divisive Clustering involves the top-down breaking of large groups into small partitions. Clustering is a technique that divides datasets into equal or unequal groupings and characterises each with a cluster means. A dataset is divided into K-small clusters using K-means clustering, each represented by its cluster mean.

4 Experimental Results

For the generation of the SESIM dataset, the simulation environment is run using Unity3D, a game engine for running SESIM. Experimental enactment is conducted using Keras 2.8.0, Pandas 1.3.4, TensorFlow 2.8.0, NumPy 1.20.3, and Python 2.6.9 to generate the results. This was set up within Anaconda 2.4.1, running a Jupiter Note 6.4.1 with 32 GB RAM, and a 256 GB Hard Disk was used to run the experiments. The models performance for inhabitant recognition was evaluated using the following metrics:

Accuracy = (TP + TN)/(TP + FP + FN + TN) (1) **Precision** = TP/(TP + FP) (2) **Recall** = TP/(TP + FN) (3) **F-Score** = 2 * (Precision * Recall) / (Precision + Recall) (4)	**Where**: **TP:** True Positive Prediction **TN:** True Negative Prediction **FP:** False Positive Prediction **FN:** False Negative Prediction

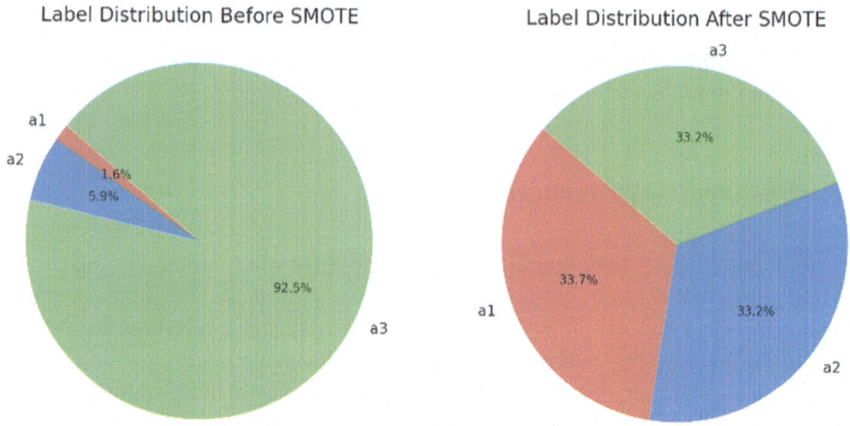

Fig. 4 Label Distribution in the SESIM dataset before and after applying SMOTE

Human Activity Tracking.

The output for human activity tracking was visualised using Principal Component Analysis (PCA) to display the different clusters of activities grouped over time. The synthetic dataset used was composed of three inhabitant labels: a1, a2, and a3, as shown in Fig. 4.

Dataset Splitting and Balancing.

The dataset was split into 70% training and 30% testing subsets to ensure the models could perform well on unseen data, mimicking real-world applications. The total number of samples generated was 32,250 after applying a class balancing technique called Synthetic Minority Over-sampling Technique (SMOTE). SMOTE augments data of minority classes to address class imbalance. Working with unbalanced datasets often results in machine learning techniques disregarding the minority class, leading to poor performance. However, the minority class often contains critical information.

4.1 Results of Inhabitant Recognition

After applying four models for user recognition in a SE: DNN, MLP, RF and DT. The Results indicate that user recognition in SE is indeed possible, paving the way for auxiliary services such as personalised inhabitant tracking when supported by Human activity recognition. Table 1 shows the performance of the machine learning models for User Recognition. RF shows its supremacy with an accuracy of 92%. Decision trees perform a little less, with an accuracy of 90%; this supports the point made in the literature that Random forests handle classification tasks better because of the power of Ensembling and voting. The precision and recall rates for the DT model are not as high as those in RF, which can be concluded as a need for more data samples for training so that the model can perform better. The precision and recall results for RF also indicate that it is possible to use a small number of samples and still achieve good results. Using techniques such as SMOTE can be helpful for unbalanced datasets which are often the characteristic of Human activity datasets in SE.

Table 3 presents the performance metrics for the Decision Tree (DT) and Random Forest (RF) models used for inhabitant recognition. Random Forest (RF) demonstrates the highest accuracy at 92%, showcasing its effectiveness in handling classification tasks due to the power of Ensembling and voting which combines the predictions from multiple models. DT achieves an accuracy of 90%, which is slightly lower than RF but still significant.

The precision and recall rates for the DT model are not as high as those for RF, suggesting that the DT model might benefit from more data samples for training to improve its performance. The RF model, on the other hand, achieves good precision and recall even with a smaller number of samples, highlighting its robustness. The results support the literature's assertion that Random Forest models outperform individual decision trees due to their Ensembling and voting mechanisms. The higher accuracy, precision, and recall rates of the RF model demonstrate its robustness and effectiveness in recognising inhabitants in SEs. The Decision Tree model, while slightly less accurate, still performs well and provides valuable insights into the classification process.

The use of SMOTE to address class imbalance was critical in achieving these results, particularly for the RF model. This technique ensured that the minority classes were well-represented, thereby improving the overall performance of the models (Fig. 5).

The DT model shows high accuracy for inhabitant a3 with minimal misclassifications. However, there are notable misclassifications between inhabitants a1 and a2. The RF model demonstrates higher accuracy and better performance overall, particularly in distinguishing inhabitants a1 and a2, which aligns with the benefits of using an ensemble method. These results underscore the potential of supervised machine learning models, particularly ensemble methods like Random Forest, in accurately recognising inhabitants using sensor behaviours in smart environments

Table 3 Showing results of the DT and RF models for inhabitant recognition

Inhabitant	Decision tree			Random forest			
	Precision (%)	Recall (%)	F-score (%)	Precision (%)	Recall (%)	F-score (%)	Support
a1	86	86	86	92	86	89	11,669
a2	86	86	86	84	91	88	9,869
a3	99	99	99	99	99	99	10,712
Accuracy			90			92	32,250

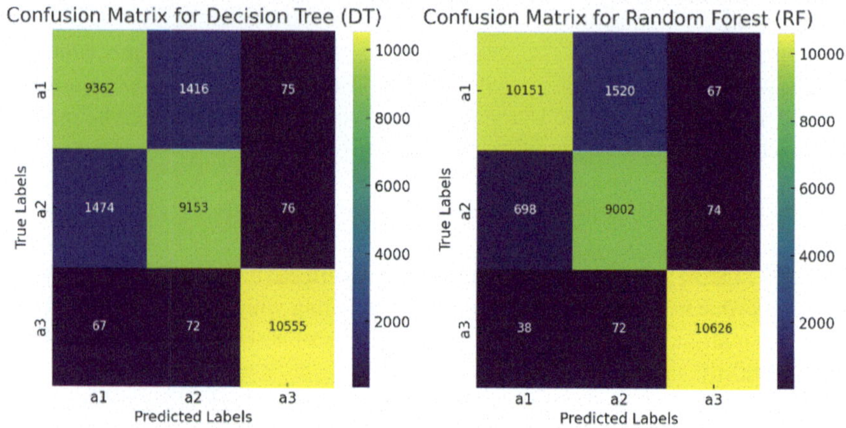

Fig. 5 Confusion Matrix of DT and RF Models

which is particularly useful in environments where vision biometric-based sensors cannot be used.

Further to the DT and RF models, this study evaluates the performance of the MLP and DNN models for inhabitant recognition. Table 4 shows the results from the model evaluation. Both the DNN and MLP models demonstrated high effectiveness in recognising inhabitants within the SE, with the MLP model achieving an accuracy of 91% and the DNN model achieving 89%. Although slightly lower than the Random Forest (RF) model (92%), these accuracies indicate that both neural network models are robust and reliable for this task.

The findings as shown in Fig. 6 confirm that supervised learning models, particularly Random Forest and Deep Neural Networks, are highly effective for inhabitant recognition in Smart Environments. The models' high accuracy, precision, and recall rates indicate their suitability for real-world applications where personalised services and human activity recognition are essential. The successful application of SMOTE further underscores the importance of data-balancing techniques in enhancing model performance.

Table 4 Showing results of the Multi-layer perceptron and Deep neural network models for inhabitant recognition

Inhabitant	Multi-layer perceptron			Deep neural network			
	Precision (%)	Recall (%)	F-score (%)	Precision (%)	Recall (%)	F-score (%)	Support (%)
a1	98%	81%	89%	95%	80%	89%	13,076
a2	77%	97%	86%	74%	95%	88%	8,482
a3	99%	99%	99%	98%	98%	99%	10,692
Accuracy		91%			89%		32,250

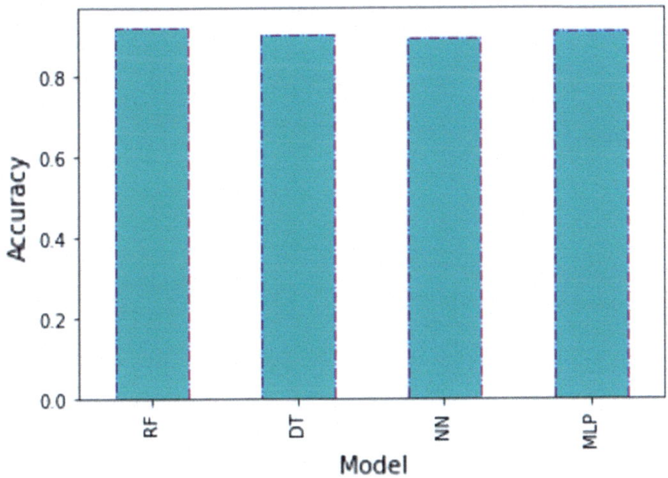

Fig. 6 Performance of machine learning models for inhabitant recognition in SE

The Random Forest model stands out with the highest accuracy and robust performance metrics, making it a reliable choice for inhabitant recognition tasks. Deep learning models, such as DNN and MLP, also demonstrate strong potential, especially for recognising more distinct inhabitant classes. These results validate the feasibility and effectiveness of using machine learning models in smart environments for accurate and reliable user recognition (Fig. 6).

4.2 *Results for Activity Status Tracking in SE*

The analysis of activity status tracking involved the use of clustering techniques to group various activities based on time. The primary method employed was the Elbow method to determine the optimal number of clusters for the activities. The Elbow method involves plotting the sum of squared errors (SSE) for different numbers of clusters and identifying the point where the decrease in SSE begins to slow, which is referred to as the "elbow."

The provided graph (Fig. 1) shows the plot of SSE against the number of clusters (k). Two potential elbow points are highlighted, suggesting possible optimal numbers of clusters (Fig. 7).

Observations from the Elbow Method Plot.

Primary Elbow Point: The primary elbow point appears at k = 3 k = 3, where there is a noticeable bend in the plot, indicating a significant drop in SSE. This suggests that three clusters may be optimal for grouping activities based on time.

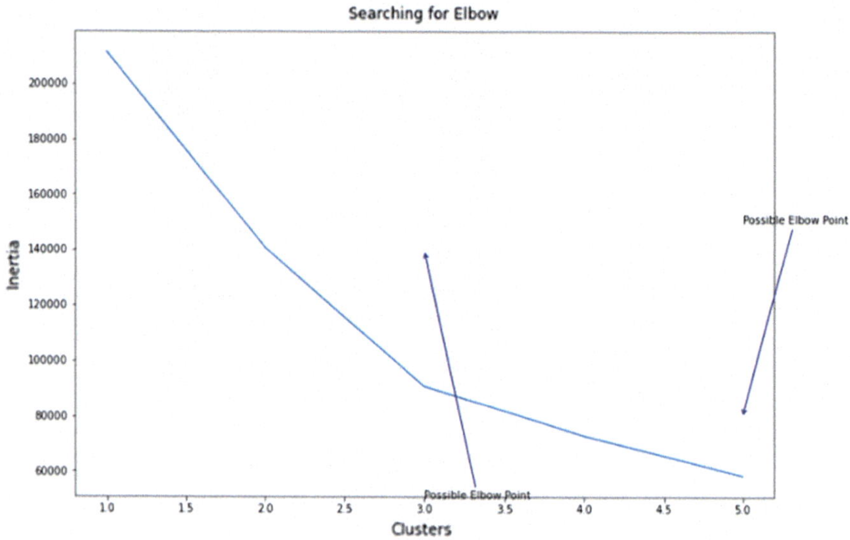

Fig. 7 K-Means clustering possible elbow points

Secondary Elbow Point: A secondary elbow point is observed at k = 5 k = 5. However, this point is less pronounced than the primary elbow, indicating that while five clusters could be considered, they may not provide a significant improvement over three clusters.

Clustering Results.

Using the primary elbow point at k = 3 k = 3, activities were grouped into three clusters. Principal Component Analysis (PCA) was then applied to visualise the clusters, providing insights into the distribution and separation of different activities over time (Fig. 8).

Fig. 8 PCA visualisation of activity clusters

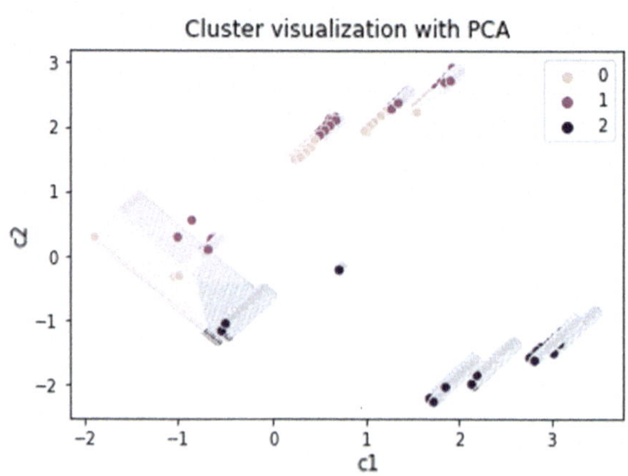

The PCA visualisation (Fig. 8) illustrates the clustering of activities into three distinct groups. Each cluster represents activities that occur within similar time frames, providing a clear separation between different types of activities.

Key Observations from PCA Visualisation.

Cluster Separation: The activities are well-separated into three clusters, indicating distinct patterns in the timing of activities.

Activity Grouping: Each cluster groups activities that share similar temporal characteristics, suggesting that the clustering approach effectively identifies patterns in activity timing.

The results of the activity status tracking analysis demonstrate the effectiveness of using clustering techniques to group activities based on time. The Elbow method identified three as the optimal number of clusters, confirmed by the PCA visualisation, which showed a clear separation between activity groups.

This clustering approach provides a valuable tool for understanding patterns in activity timing within a Smart Environment, enabling more accurate tracking and monitoring of ADL. The insights gained from this analysis can be used to enhance personalised services and interventions in smart environments, contributing to improved inhabitant well-being and comfort.

5 Conclusion and Future Work

This study demonstrates the application of supervised learning for user recognition in Smart Environments (SE) using a synthetic dataset. Both Machine Learning (ML) and Deep Learning (DL) models have shown strong performance in user recognition, with the Multi-Layer Perceptron (MLP) and Random Forest (RF) models standing out. Given the superior results of these models, there is potential to further improve accuracy by combining them into a hybrid model through ensembling techniques.

Synthetic datasets have proven beneficial by accelerating data collection and enabling early experimentation with models. However, a notable drawback of ML and DL models is the need for a substantial amount of data to achieve optimal performance in user recognition.

In terms of activity status tracking, the study shows that it can be effectively performed without data labels in the dataset. The results from Principal Component Analysis (PCA) visualisation indicate that clustering based on time is a promising technique for this purpose. Despite its potential, the clustering approach would benefit from domain knowledge to refine and interpret the clusters. Future work could incorporate insights from domain experts through surveys and interviews to enhance the cluster formations. This could also lead to new discoveries such as identifying interrupted activities or detecting anomalous behaviours.

To summarise, the findings support the feasibility of providing personalised services in SEs by accurately recognising users through their activity sensor features. Future research should focus on the following:

1. **Hybrid Model Development**: Explore the combination of MLP and RF models into a hybrid model using ensembling techniques to improve accuracy.
2. **Data Augmentation**: Continue leveraging synthetic datasets to mitigate the data scarcity challenge and facilitate model development and testing.
3. **Supervised vs. Unsupervised Learning**: Compare the performance of supervised learning models with unsupervised models for activity status tracking to determine the most effective approach.
4. **Incorporating Domain Expertise**: Collaborate with domain experts to refine clustering techniques and extract meaningful insights from the data, particularly in identifying complex activity patterns and anomalies.

Overall, this study lays the groundwork for further advancements in user recognition and activity status tracking in smart environments, paving the way for enhanced personalised services and improved inhabitant well-being.

References

1. M. Satyanarayanan, "Pervasive computing: Vision and challenges," 2001. https://doi.org/10.1109/98.943998.
2. A. Usmanova, F. Portet, P. Lalanda, and G. Vega, "Federated Learning and catastrophic forgetting in pervasive computing: demonstration in HAR domain," Jul. 2022, https://doi.org/10.1109/PerComWorkshops53856.2022.9767246.
3. University of Minnesota, "Monitoring Human Activity," Artifical Intelligence, Robotics and Vision Laboratory.
4. E. Bulbul, A. Cetin, and I. A. Dogru, "Human Activity Recognition Using Smartphones," *ISMSIT 2018 - 2nd International Symposium on Multidisciplinary Studies and Innovative Technologies, Proceedings*, pp. 2–7, 2018, https://doi.org/10.1109/ISMSIT.2018.8567275.
5. Y. Y. F. Panduman, N. Funabiki, E. D. Fajrianti, S. Fang, and S. Sukaridhoto, "A Survey of AI Techniques in IoT Applications with Use Case Investigations in the Smart Environmental Monitoring and Analytics in Real-Time IoT Platform," *Information (Switzerland)*, vol. 15, no. 3, Mar. 2024, https://doi.org/10.3390/info15030153.
6. S. Adibi, A. Rajabifard, D. Shojaei, and N. Wickramasinghe, "Enhancing Healthcare through Sensor-Enabled Digital Twins in Smart Environments: A Comprehensive Analysis," *Sensors*, vol. 24, no. 9, p. 2793, Apr. 2024, https://doi.org/10.3390/s24092793.
7. B. Bannan and J. Burbridge, "Smart City Learning Solutions, Wearable Learning, and User Experience Design," in *Perspectives on Wearable Enhanced Learning (WELL)*, Cham: Springer International Publishing, 2019, pp. 253–271. https://doi.org/10.1007/978-3-319-64301-4_12.
8. A. Camero and E. Alba, "Smart City and information technology: A review," *Cities*, vol. 93, pp. 84–94, Oct. 2019, https://doi.org/10.1016/j.cities.2019.04.014.
9. G. Singla, D. J. Cook, and M. Schmitter-Edgecombe, "Recognizing independent and joint activities among multiple residents in smart environments.," *J Ambient Intell Humaniz Comput*, vol. 1, no. 1, pp. 57–63, Mar. 2010, https://doi.org/10.1007/s12652-009-0007-1.
10. D. J. Cook and D. Cook J., "Multi-agent smart environments," *J Ambient Intell Smart Environ*, vol. 1, no. 1, pp. 51–55, 2009, https://doi.org/10.3233/AIS-2009-0007.
11. G. Forbes, "Employing multi-modal sensors for personalised smart home health monitoring. Employing Multi-Modal Sensors for Personalised Smart Home Health Monitoring," 2019. Accessed: Jun. 28, 2020. [Online]. Available: www.rgu.ac.uk/dmstaff/forbes-glenn
12. E. Ahmed, I. Yaqoob, A. Gani, M. Imran, and M. Guizani, "Internet-of-things-based smart environments: state of the art, taxonomy, and open research challenges," *IEEE Wirel Commun*, vol. 23, no. 5, pp. 10–16, Oct. 2016, https://doi.org/10.1109/MWC.2016.7721736.

13. L. Tan and N. Wang, "Future Internet: The Internet of Things," in *ICACTE 2010 - 2010 3rd International Conference on Advanced Computer Theory and Engineering, Proceedings*, 2010. https://doi.org/10.1109/ICACTE.2010.5579543.
14. K. Sorri, N. Mustafee, and M. Seppänen, "Revisiting IoT definitions: A framework towards comprehensive use," *Technol Forecast Soc Change*, vol. 179, p. 121623, Jun. 2022, https://doi.org/10.1016/J.TECHFORE.2022.121623.
15. B. Ho, D. Vogts, and J. Wesson, "SESim:A Smart Environment Simulation Tool to Support Human Activity Recognition," 2018.
16. V. Radhika, C. R. Prasad, and A. Chakradhar, "Smartphone-Based Human Activities Recognition System using Random Forest Algorithm," pp. 8–11, 2022.
17. Z. F. Jahromi, A. Rajabzadeh, and A. R. Manashty, "A Multi-Purpose Scenario-based Simulator for Smart House Environments," *International Journal of Computer Science and Information Security*, vol. 9, no. 1, pp. 13–18, 2011, [Online]. Available: http://arxiv.org/abs/1105.2902
18. N. Apthorpe, D. Y. Huang, D. Reisman, A. Narayanan, and N. Feamster, "Keeping the Smart Home Private with Smart(er) IoT Traffic Shaping," *Proceedings on Privacy Enhancing Technologies*, 2019, https://doi.org/10.2478/popets-2019-0040.
19. A. Shokrollahi, J. Persson, R. Malekian, A. Sarkheyli-Hägele, and F. Karlsson, "PIR Sensor-Based Occupancy Monitoring in Smart Buildings: A Review of Methodologies and Machine Learning Approaches," 2024, https://doi.org/10.20944/preprints202401.1924.v1.
20. N. K. Chauhan and K. Singh, "A Review on Conventional Machine Learning vs Deep Learning," in *2018 International Conference on Computing, Power and Communication Technologies (GUCON)*, IEEE, Sep. 2018, pp. 347–352. https://doi.org/10.1109/GUCON.2018.8675097.
21. M. Leodolter, P. Widhalm, C. Plant, and N. Brandle, "Semi-supervised segmentation of accelerometer time series for transport mode classification," in *5th IEEE International Conference on Models and Technologies for Intelligent Transportation Systems, MT-ITS 2017 - Proceedings*, 2017. https://doi.org/10.1109/MTITS.2017.8005596.

Development of a Mobile-Based Climate Information System for Farmers's Climate Risk Management: A Case Study of Musanze District, Rwanda

Mukaneza Angelique, Neema Mduma, and Kisangiri Michael

Abstract Climate variability poses significant risks to agricultural productivity, particularly for smallholder farmers in Rwanda. This paper presents the Dfarmer Mobile Application, a digital tool designed to enhance climate risk management by providing real-time weather updates, early warning notifications, and climate-smart agricultural advisories. The system was tested in Musanze District, a region with a high dependency on agriculture, to assess its feasibility, usability, and effectiveness in improving farmers' decision-making. The study highlights the strengths of the application, including its scalability, ease of use, and potential to improve farm resilience. However, challenges such as mobile network dependency, digital literacy barriers, and the need for long-term sustainability strategies were identified. Findings suggest that the Dfarmer Mobile Application has the potential to support climate adaptation efforts among Rwandan farmers but requires further refinement to optimize accessibility and effectiveness. Future work will focus on expanding the system's functionality, integrating machine learning for predictive analytics, and conducting broader evaluations across diverse agricultural regions.

Keywords Climate risk management · Mobile application · Early warning systems

M. Angelique (✉) · N. Mduma · K. Michael
The Nelson Mandela Africa Institution of Science and Technology (NM-AIST), Arusha, Tanzania
e-mail: angeliquem@nm-aist.ac.tz

School of Computational and Communication Science and Engineering, Arusha, Tanzania

N. Mduma
e-mail: neema.mduma@nm-aist.ac.tz

K. Michael
e-mail: Kisangiri.michael@nm-aist.ac.tz

J. Marx Gómez et al. (eds.), *Advancement in Embedded and Mobile Systems*, Progress in IS, https://doi.org/10.1007/978-3-031-99219-3_14

1 Introduction

Agriculture remains the backbone of Rwanda's economy, employing over 70% of the population and contributing significantly to the country's GDP [1, 2]. However, climate variability and extreme weather conditions pose serious threats to smallholder farmers, leading to unpredictable crop yields, soil degradation, and economic instability. Farmers in Musanze District, a key agricultural region, are particularly vulnerable due to their reliance on rain-fed farming systems [3]. Access to accurate and timely climate information is crucial for enabling farmers to make informed decisions and mitigate climate-related risks [4].

Digital solutions have emerged as a promising approach to address these challenges. Mobile-based Climate Information Systems (CIS) offer farmers real-time weather updates, early warning notifications, and tailored agronomic advisories [5]. Several initiatives in Sub-Saharan Africa have demonstrated the potential of mobile applications in improving agricultural productivity and resilience. However, many existing solutions face challenges such as limited accessibility, lack of scalability, and insufficient user engagement [6].

To bridge this gap, we developed Dfarmer, a mobile application designed to provide real-time climate risk management support to farmers in Musanze District. The application delivers localized weather forecasts, early warnings for extreme weather events, and climate-smart farming recommendations through an intuitive mobile interface. By leveraging mobile technology, the system aims to enhance agricultural decision-making, minimize crop losses, and promote sustainable farming practices [7].

This paper presents the design, implementation, and evaluation of the Dfarmer Mobile Application. The study explores its effectiveness in addressing climate challenges faced by farmers, identifies key strengths and limitations, and provides recommendations for future improvements. The findings contribute to the growing body of research on mobile-based climate adaptation strategies and highlight the importance of technology-driven solutions in enhancing agricultural resilience.

2 Review of Related Works

Agricultural productivity and resilience to climate change are increasingly being supported by digital solutions, particularly mobile-based Climate Information Systems (CIS) [8]. Various studies have explored the potential of mobile applications, SMS-based platforms, and decision-support systems in addressing climate-related challenges for smallholder farmers. This section reviews existing solutions and highlights their strengths and limitations, providing a foundation for the Dfarmer Mobile Application [9].

2.1 Climate-Based Agribusiness Information Systems

Susandi et al. (2018) developed a mobile-based agribusiness information system that integrates climate data, market information, and decision-support tools. The system effectively provided timely and accurate climate information, helping farmers mitigate risks associated with climate variability. However, limited user interactivity was a major drawback, as the system lacked a chat feature for real-time engagement between farmers and agricultural officers. Additionally, the absence of push notifications hindered timely alerts. Dfarmer addresses these limitations by integrating a chat function and real-time notifications, ensuring a more interactive and responsive system [10].

2.2 Indigenous Knowledge and Scientific Data Integration

Masinde and Thothela (2019) introduced ITIKI Plus, a mobile-based application that integrates indigenous knowledge with scientific agro-climate decision support. By using fuzzy inference systems and smart sensors, ITIKI Plus improved smallholder farmers' access to reliable climate information [6]. Despite its success, the lack of a real-time chat feature limited interaction between farmers and agricultural experts. Furthermore, internet dependency posed accessibility challenges in rural areas with poor network coverage. Dfarmer overcomes these issues by enabling both online and offline access, ensuring uninterrupted availability of critical climate information.

2.3 Mobile-Based Information Systems for Farmer Empowerment

Ginige et al. [11] developed a Mobile-Based Information System (MBIS) aimed at empowering Sri Lankan farmers by providing real-time production levels, market trends, and weather forecasts. The system improved farmer decision-making but had a major limitation in interactivity, as it did not include a two-way communication feature. In contrast, Dfarmer introduces a chat functionality, allowing farmers to engage with agricultural officers for personalized advisory support, making it a more dynamic and farmer-centric solution [11].

2.4 SMS-Based Agricultural Information Systems

Tegegne and Alemu (2019) designed an SMS-based agricultural information system to support rural farmers in Ethiopia. The platform enabled farmers to receive critical agricultural insights, including weather forecasts, market prices, and farming techniques. The study reported high usability and fast response times, proving its effectiveness. However, the system was unidirectional, meaning farmers could only receive information rather than interact with experts. Dfarmer enhances user engagement by incorporating bidirectional communication, allowing farmers to seek personalized guidance and clarify their concerns with agricultural experts [12].

2.5 Mobile Weather Crisis Applications

ISLAND, P. E. [13] developed a mobile crisis weather application aimed at enhancing preparedness and safety for residents of Prince Edward Island during severe weather events. While the app successfully provided real-time weather updates and emergency alerts, it was not specifically designed for agricultural use. Additionally, the lack of a bidirectional chat feature prevented users from interacting with meteorologists. Dfarmer extends beyond simple weather alerts by providing agriculture-specific climate advisories, ensuring farmers receive actionable insights tailored to their needs [13].

3 Summary of Gaps and Contribution of Dfarmer

Existing climate information systems have demonstrated significant potential in enhancing agricultural resilience [14]. However, key limitations such as unidirectional communication, internet dependency, and lack of tailored advisory services hinder their full effectiveness [15]. Dfarmer addresses these gaps by:

1. Integrating a real-time chat feature for farmers to interact with agricultural officers.
2. Providing offline functionality, and ensuring access in areas with poor internet connectivity.
3. Delivering real-time alerts and personalized agricultural recommendations for climate-smart farming.

4 Materials and Methods

4.1 Conceptual Design of the Proposed System

The proposed system is designed to provide real-time weather and climate information through a mobile application, enabling farmers in the Musanze District to access localized data for informed decision-making. It follows a structured workflow that integrates authentication, data retrieval, processing, and user accessibility to ensure security and usability. To enhance security, the system employs Two-Factor Authentication (2FA), requiring users to verify their identity using a unique identifier and a secondary authentication method, such as an SMS or email-based one-time password (OTP). Climate data is sourced from a weather API, which fetches satellite-based meteorological data, including temperature, humidity, precipitation, and wind speed. This data is stored and managed in Firebase, which serves as the backend for real-time data storage and processing. The system processes raw climate data to generate insights tailored to agricultural needs, providing users with localized climate forecasts, historical weather trends, and decision-support tools. The mobile application features a user-friendly interface designed to ensure accessibility, even for individuals with limited technical expertise. Figure 1 illustrates the overall system design, highlighting the integration of 2FA authentication, Firebase database, and weather API, which collectively ensure a secure, real-time, and interactive climate information delivery system for farmers.

Fig. 1 Conceptual design of the proposed system

4.2 Context Diagram

The proposed system is designed to facilitate seamless interaction between three key user roles: the farmer, the agriculture officer, and the admin. Each role has specific functionalities within the system to ensure the efficient delivery and management of climate information. The farmer logs into the mobile application to access weather forecasts and climate-related insights. They can report any issues or challenges encountered during their agricultural activities and receive responses to their queries. The system also allows farmers to provide feedback on the information and receive timely notifications regarding weather alerts or system updates. The agriculture officer has similar access to the farmer but with additional capabilities to respond to queries and offer advisory support. They engage in two-way communication with farmers, providing real-time guidance and solutions based on the information presented in the system. The admin oversees the system by managing user activities, monitoring reports, and ensuring data accuracy. The admin can modify user roles as needed and ensure the smooth operation of the climate information system (CIS). The context diagram (Fig. 8) visually illustrates how these three user roles interact with the mobile application and its various features, ensuring an integrated and efficient system for climate information dissemination (Fig. 2).

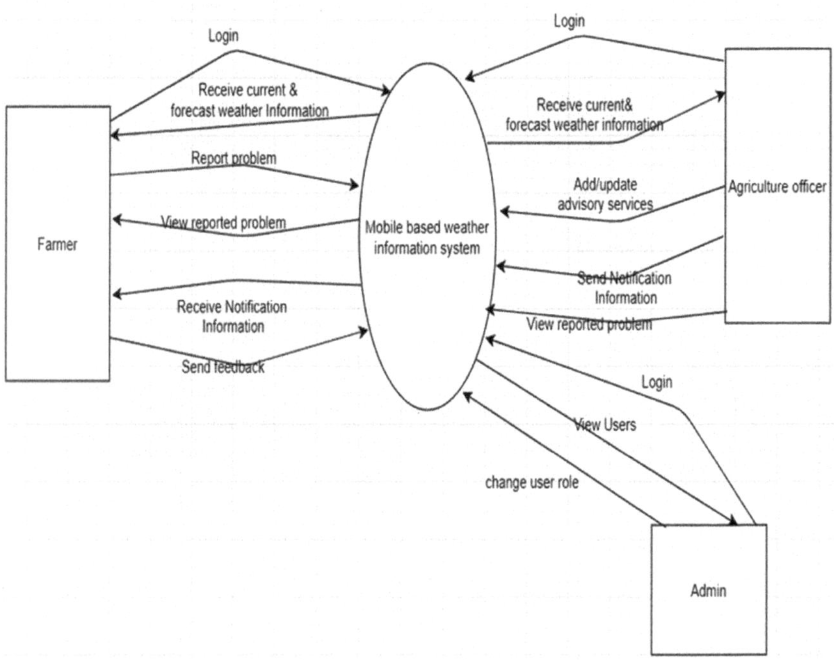

Fig. 2 Context diagram

4.3 *Flowchart Diagram*

The Data Flow Diagram (DFD) outlines how data flows through the mobile app for climate risk management. Upon opening the app, users are prompted to log in with their username and password. If they are new, they must register by providing their credentials and completing a two-factor authentication (2FA) setup. Once registered, users can log in and enter the 2FA code sent to them. Successful authentication grants access to services like weather forecasts, advisory services, and market prices. If the 2FA code is incorrect, the user is prompted to try again. After using the app, users can log out to end the session (Fig. 3).

5 Results and Discussion

5.1 *System Development Results*

The climate information services mobile application for climate risk management was successfully developed. After registering and logging in, users were able to access various services, including real-time weather updates, weather forecasts, advisory services, market prices, problem reporting, and a chat feature. Similarly, agricultural officers had access to the same climate information services via the mobile application and could monitor the data stored on the cloud server. All climate-related data were securely stored on the cloud, with all services packaged together for easy access. Figure 4 illustrates the developed Dfarmer mobile application used in this study.

5.2 *Dfarmer User Registration*

Upon accessing the Dfarmer app, the first step for users is registration to gain access to the climate information services (CIS). Users are required to provide their name, location, email address, and mobile number during registration. The phone number verification process displays the country name and corresponding country code. After entering the phone number, users receive a six-digit One-Time Password (OTP) via SMS. The code sent to the user's phone is used to verify the entered phone number during registration. Figure 5 shows the OTP verification step, where users enter the code to complete the registration process.

Fig. 3 Flowchart diagram

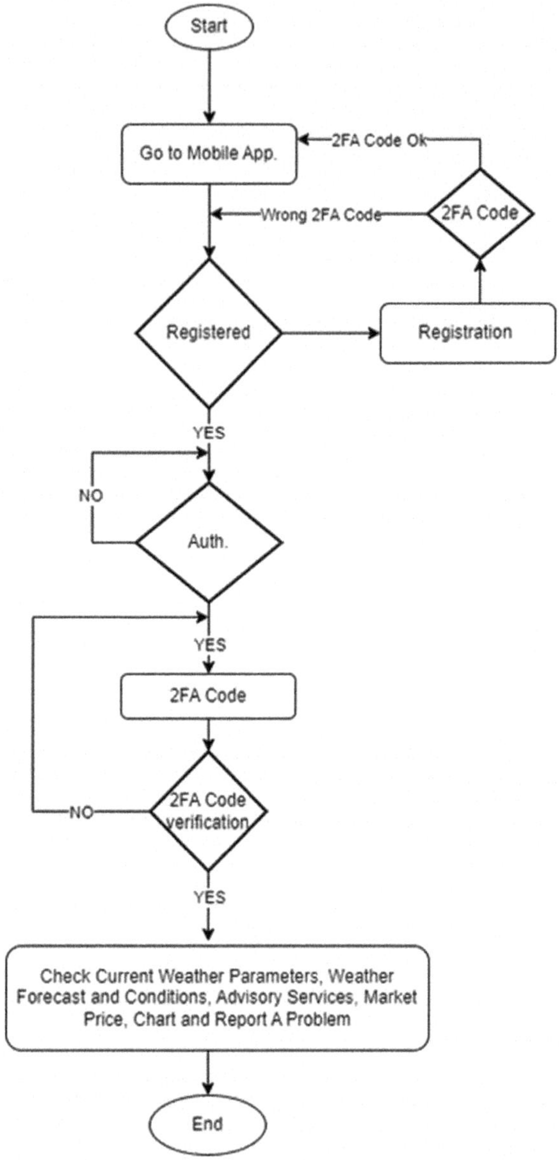

5.3 Dfarmer User Login and Account Verification

To log into Dfarmer, users must provide their username and password, which are validated on the server. After the initial login, users are prompted for a second step of authentication, receiving a one-time password (OTP) via SMS. This ensures the

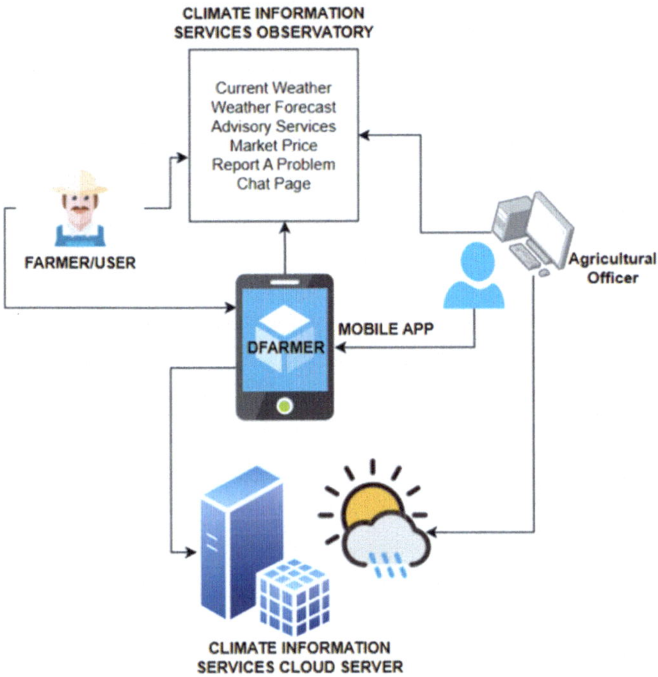

Fig. 4 Mobile based application result

security of the user's account. The mobile-based application facilitates the transfer of data from the database to provide relevant climate information services to users.

5.4 Dfarmer Mobile Application's Climate Information Services Interface

The Dfarmer mobile application was developed to enable seamless interaction between farmers and agricultural officers, providing timely access to weather information. After successful login, users can access a variety of climate information services, including current weather updates, weather forecasts, advisory services, market prices, user chats, frequently asked questions, and the ability to report problems. These features help farmers stay informed and manage climate risks effectively. The Dfarmer application, as shown in the figure below, demonstrates the various features developed to support climate risk management through user interaction.

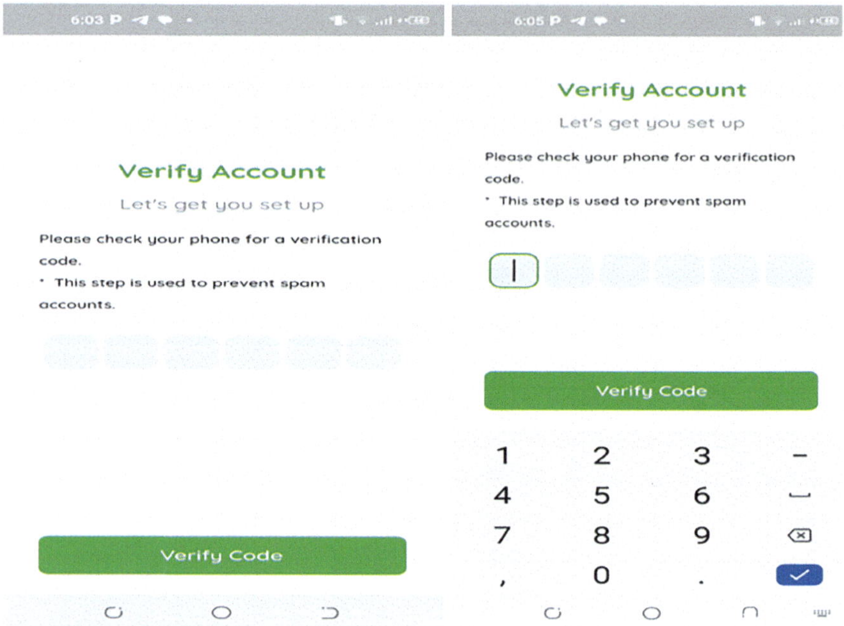

Fig. 5 OTP verification step

5.5 *Dfarmer Mobile Application User Chat Page*

The Dfarmer mobile application allows users to chat with agricultural officers or other users to discuss the accuracy, reliability, and feasibility of the application. Figure 6 displays the chat page where users can interact and seek clarification or provide feedback regarding the app's features and services (Fig. 7).

5.6 *Dfarmer Mobile Application User Report Problem Page*

The Dfarmer mobile application allows users to report any issues related to the climate information system for risk management. To report a problem, the user must first upload a screenshot of the issue, followed by a written description of the problem in the provided text field. This feature enables users to interact effectively with the mobile application and report any challenges they encounter. Figure 8 shows an example of a reported problem related to the weather forecast within the Dfarmer application.

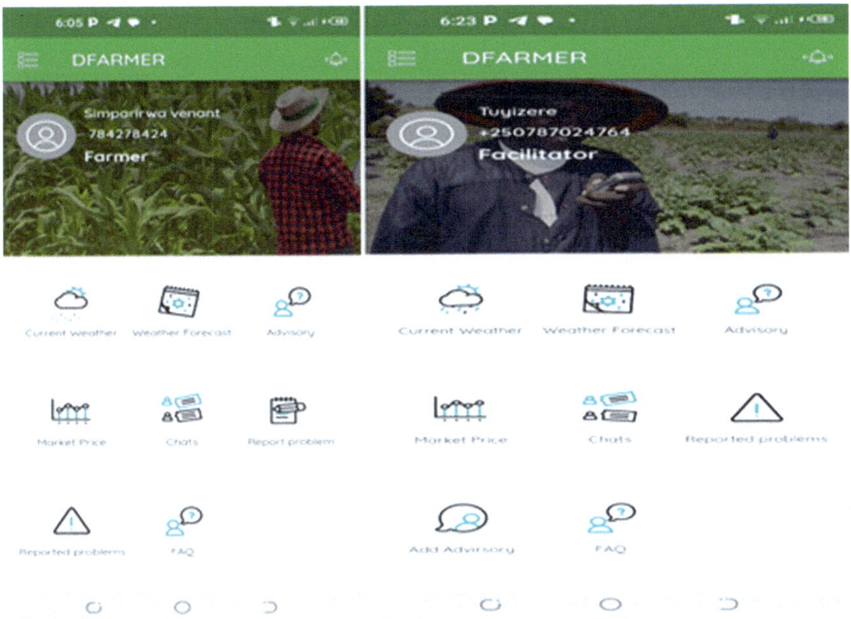

Fig. 6 Climate information services information result

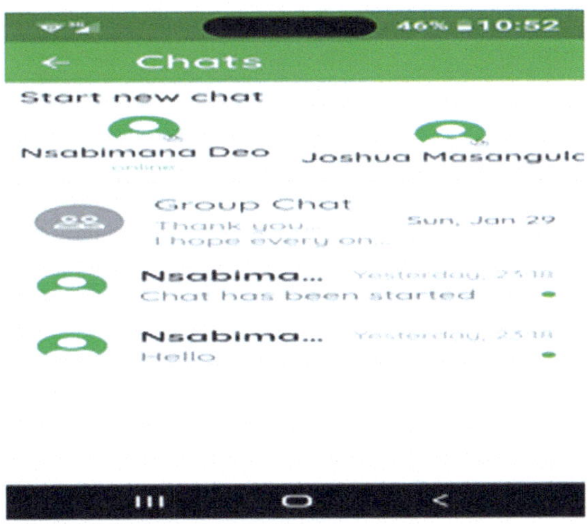

Fig. 7 Dfarmer mobile application user chat page

5.7 *Dfarmer Mobile Application's Climate Advisory Services*

The Dfarmer mobile application includes climate advisory services designed to assist farmers in managing climate risks. These services provide advice based on

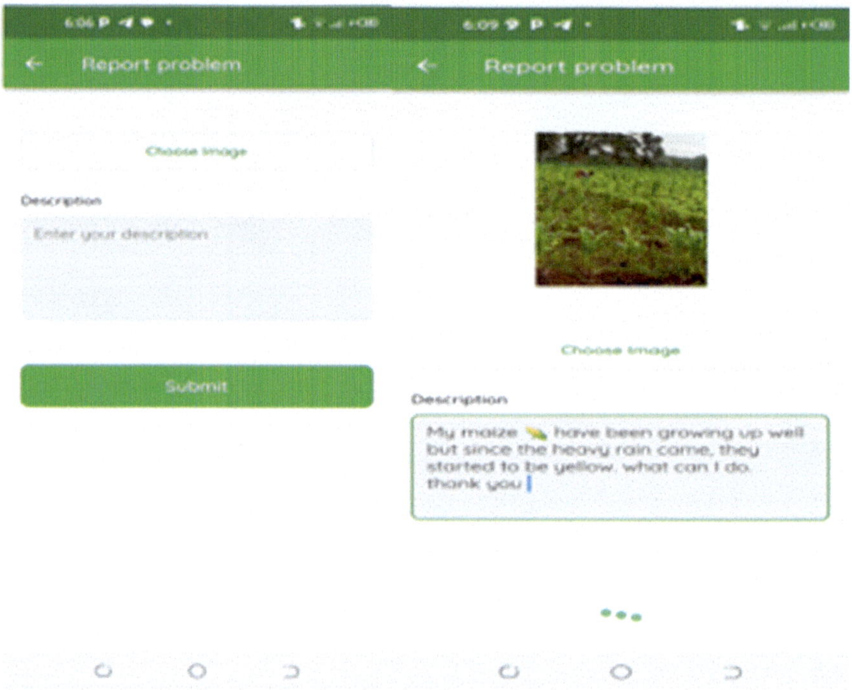

Fig. 8 User report problem interface

the weather forecast and predicted climate changes. Additionally, farmers receive guidance on soil types, soil preparation, sowing times, and crop management. Figure 8 illustrates the advisory service feature, where agricultural officers or facilitators can share essential climate information with farmers to support informed decision-making for upcoming agricultural seasons.

6 Conclusion

This study developed the Dfarmer mobile application to deliver climate information services aimed at enhancing climate risk management for farmers. By providing real-time weather updates, weather forecasts, advisory services, market prices, and interactive features such as chat and problem reporting, the system empowers farmers to make informed decisions in response to climate variability. The integration of two-factor authentication ensures secure access, while cloud storage and a user-friendly interface enhance the accessibility and usability of the system. Despite some limitations, such as the reliance on mobile connectivity, the Dfarmer app presents a promising solution for bridging the information gap in rural farming communities.

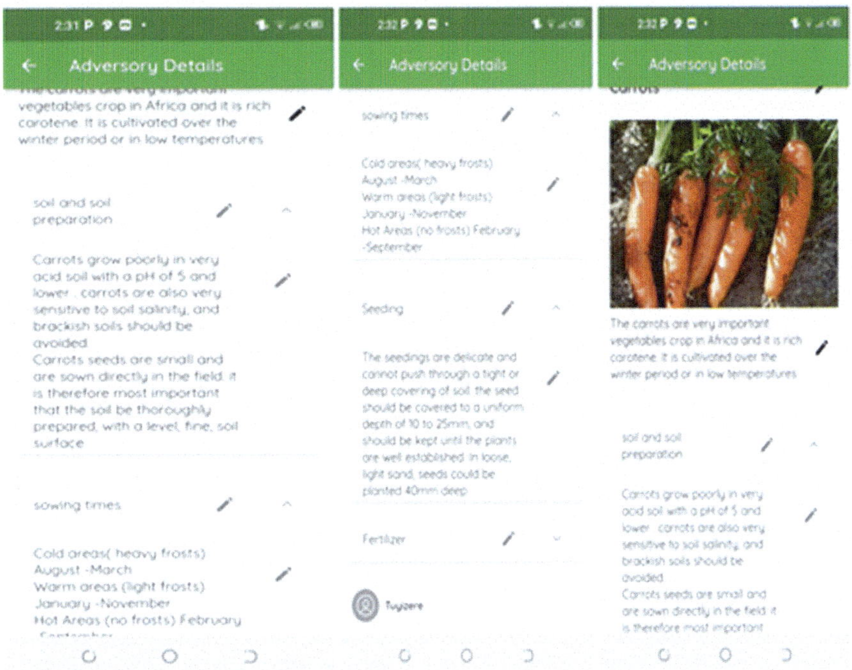

Fig. 9 Climate advisory service result

Future work can focus on expanding the system's capabilities and improving its accessibility to farmers in more remote areas with limited internet access (Fig. 9).

References

1. I. Kubwimana, "Agriculture output and economic growth of Rwanda," *Diss. University of Rwanda,* 2021.
2. B. M. Rafael, "The importance of agricultural development projects: A focus on sustenance and employment creation in Kenya, Malawi, Namibia, Rwanda, and Uganda," *Journal of Agricultural Chemistry and Environment,* pp. 152–170, 2023.
3. M. Lydie, "Droughts and floodings implications in agriculture sector in Rwanda: Consequences of Global Warming," *The Nature, Causes, Effects and Mitigation of Climate Change on the Environment,* 2022.
4. KG Austin, RH Beach, D Lapidus, ME Salem, NJ Taylor, Mads Knudsen, Noel Ujeneza, " Impacts of climate change on the potential productivity of eleven staple crops in Rwanda," *Sustainability,* 2020.
5. NZIRABATINYA, Samuel, and Luqman Olanrewaju AFOLABI., "Digital Financing Services and Agri-Business Performance Rwanda," *Journal of Finance and Accounting,* pp. 113–126, 2024.
6. Masinde, Muthoni, and Portia Naledi Thothela, "ITIKI Plus: A mobile based application for integrating indigenous knowledge and scientific agro-climate decision support for Africa's

small-scale farmers," *IEEE 2nd International Conference on Information and Computer Technologies,* 2019.
7. "Information and communication technologies (ICTs): The potential for enhancing the dissemination of agricultural information and services to smallholder farmers in sub-Saharan Africa," *Information Development,* vol. 3, no. 39, pp. 638–658, 2023.
8. Tanhapour, Mozhgan, and Sharareh Rostam Niakan Kalhori, "Early warning system for emergency care: designing a timely monitoring mobile-based system," *Accident and Emergency Informatics,* pp. 88–102, 2022.
9. M Moore, G List, A Rose, SE Zebiak, "Lessons Learned to Guide the Development of Scalable Climate Information Services in Africa," *Information Services in Africa,* 2023.
10. Susandi, Armi, M. Tamamadin, A. Pratama, A. F. Pratama, O. P. Pandini, I. Faisal, M. F. Fachrizal, D. A. Widiawan, and A. R. Wijaya, "Development of climate-based agribusiness information system on mobile platform," *Proceeding of International Symposium for Sustainable Humanosphere,* pp. 145–153, 2023.
11. T Ginige, D Richards, A Ginige, M Hitchens, "Design for empowerment: Empowering Sri Lankan farmers through mobile-based information system," *Communications of the Association for Information Systems,* no. 46, pp. 444-483, 2020.
12. AK Tegegne, TA Alemu, "SMS-Based Agricultural Information System for Rural Farmers in Ethiopia," *Journal of Usability Studies,* 2019.
13. ISLAND, PRINCE EDWARD, "DESIGN OF A MOBILE CRISIS WEATHER APP FOR RESIDENTS OF," *Diss. University of Prince Edward Island,* 2022.
14. F. A. Ward, "Enhancing climate resilience of irrigated agriculture: A review," *Journal of Environmental Management,* 2022.
15. L. Klerkx, "Advisory services and transformation, plurality and disruption of agriculture and food systems: towards a new research agenda for agricultural education and extension studies.," *The Journal of Agricultural Education and Extension* , pp. 131–140, 2020.

Enhancing Cognition of Students with Visual Impairments via Human Computer Interaction Blueprint for SDG 4: A Systematic Review

Anass Bayaga and Lihle Ndlovu

Abstract This research aims to augment the educational experiences of students with visual impairments (SWVI) by exploring the role of assistive technologies, particularly Job Access with Speech (JAWS), in South African Technical and Vocational Education and Training (TVET) colleges. The methodology involved a systematic literature review of key studies on assistive technology and inclusivity, providing a blueprint for improving inclusive education to meet sustainable development goal (SDG) 4. While the findings highlight the importance of meeting the needs of marginalised groups for a more equitable and sustainable future, the recommendations include prioritising inclusive education policies, investing in training, support services, and ensuring equal access to quality higher education for visually impaired students to foster sustainable development and achieve SDG 4.

Keywords Cognition · Human–computer interface · SDG 4 · Inclusivity · Quality education · Persons with disabilities

1 Introduction

Over the past decade, South Africa has undergone a significant change in relation to the expansion of access to higher education. As a consequence, more educationally underprivileged rural settlers are now pursuing science, technology, engineering and mathematics (STEM) degrees. However, these learners come from diverse backgrounds and possess varying levels of socio-cultural, educational, and academic preparation [40]. The cognitive and understanding skills that these learners possess upon admission to universities and higher institutions ultimately have an impact on their learning outcomes. For example, their prior numerical cognition of STEM

A. Bayaga (✉) · L. Ndlovu
Stellenbosch University, Stellenbosch, South Africa
e-mail: abayaga@sun.ac.za

L. Ndlovu
Nelson Mandela University, Gqeberha, South Africa

J. Marx Gómez et al. (eds.), *Advancement in Embedded and Mobile Systems*, Progress in IS, https://doi.org/10.1007/978-3-031-99219-3_15

subjects, such as mathematics, serves as a crucial foundation upon which new knowledge is built. Thus, this study aims to address sustainable development goal (SDG) 4 by investigating learners' prior numerical cognition as a predictor of educational performance.

Despite the continuous evolution of higher education, there have been several reasons why the use of Job Access with Speech (JAWS) for students with visual impairments (SWVI) in Technical and Vocational Education and Training (TVET) colleges has become a concern and requires further analysis from various local and international sources and perspectives, particularly with regards to SDG 4 [13, 17, 33, 34, 52, 53]. One general observation from SDG 4 is that inequalities in educational access [53] and inadequate implementation of inclusive teaching approaches [17] are the main drivers for the emergence of assistive computer application systems (ACAS) such as JAWS. The assessments of Engelbrecht [17] and Zongozzi et al. [53] have the potential to enhance educators' instructional delivery and SWVIs' educational experiences due to its audio system, which uses text-to-speech screen content reading. Consequently, the availability of JAWS has motivated the mainstreaming of SWVI, even in rural-based TVET colleges [21]. It has brought hope and comfort to those who have been and are still disadvantaged in educational access. The inclusion of SWVI has also been recognised nationally and internationally (see, e.g. [13, 18, 19, 21, 22]) and South African TVET colleges are no exception. However, several concerns remain rife for research. For instance, TVET colleges in South Africa are still finding their footing with the inclusion of SWVI education in their classrooms [17]. Furthermore, the inclusion of SWVI in the classroom requires the integration of assistive computer application systems such as JAWS, which may interrupt TVET educators' traditional methods of instruction.

Nonetheless, as much as JAWS empowers students' interaction with computing applications through computer skills acquisition, Computer Practice (CP), for instance, has not been given the attention it deserves. Although, for instance, CP is an essential subject in the TVET curriculum for both National Technical Education Diploma (NATED) and National Certificate and Vocational (NCV) courses, as it arms students with fundamental computing concepts and applications (Department of Higher Education and Training, 2021), lines are still blurry about JAWS skills acquisition and CP literacy in the TVET curriculum. In other words, it is unknown how and when SWVI receive training on using JAWS after enrolling in TVET colleges. More concerning is the question of TVET educators' proficiencies in being able to transfer JAWS skills to their students. This concern emanates from Delubom et al. [11], who revealed that in South Africa, TVET educators lack the knowledge and skills to teach SWVI confidently. As with international concerns, for instance, research on TVET educators' professional development in South Africa remains in the grey literature [17]. For instance, Seale et al. [45] presented alarming evidence of college educators' limited understanding and skills to use ACAS, even in countries like the United States, the UK, Germany, Israel, and Canada. Alarmingly too, the study of educators' practices on the inclusion of learners with visual impairment in computing education programmes in Brazil discovered that out of 56 computing educators, 79% of them never received any training to teach visually impaired learners, such that the 84% of computer educators confessed to not changing their lecturing styles to accommodate SWVI in their computer lessons [26, 27].

We articulate several implications. For example, there is an urgent need for teachers' training to successfully implement the inclusion of students with visual impairments across the South African education sectors. The implication is built upon Engelbrecht's [13] view that regardless of the gradual transformations in training teachers on inclusive practices in South Africa, institutes continue to be a significant contributing factor toward inclusive education implementation. As such, lamentations of van Wyk and Hodgkinson-Williams [52], Govender and Dhurumraj [17] about shortages of teachers' professional qualifications among TVET educators arguably exacerbate the need for inclusive TVET teachers to acquire proficiencies in specialised computer applications for students with visual impairments. van Wyk and Hodgkinson-Williams [52] lament because the assumption is that generally, teachers should dismiss barriers to inclusive approaches in their teaching yet find themselves overwhelmed with the ever-developing trends of educational computer applications [50]. Based on such conjecture, the current study proposes that educators' technological fluency and confidence impact students' JAWS skills. While substantial research has examined assistive technologies in education, this study distinctively bridges the gap by concentrating on practical implications for TVET educators in developing regions, where inclusive education remains underdeveloped. Consequently, this research provides a literature-based exploration of assistive technologies with a practical blueprint for implementation. It is for this reason that the reflections of Engelbrecht [13] and Hooijer et al. [20] on the journey of inclusive education in South Africa encourage the South African education system to provide continued adequate human and technical support to support educators' inclusive practices, thus the need for the current research. This research suggests a novel contribution by presenting a comprehensive proposal for incorporating assistive technologies into South African TVET colleges, an area that has received limited attention in prevailing literature.

2 Methodology for Literature Review

It is essential to evaluate the TVET inclusive education system's capacity to use accommodative ACAS to cater to the educational needs of SWVI. To achieve this goal, the current research employs an integrated systematic review of literature on the use of JAWS as an ACAS in the education of SWVI in TVET colleges. The research utilised a systematic review of 54 sources considered into three key areas: (1) the role of JAWS in SWVIs' computer practice literacy, (2) the influence of JAWS on learning processes, and (3) alignment of TVET sector with inclusive education reforms. The study begins by examining the role of JAWS in SWVIs' computer practice literacy, drawing from various sources such as Alabi and Mutula [1], Carter and Pritchard [8], Lund and Cmar [26], McDonnall [32], and Pritchard et al. [42]. It positions JAWS usage in TVET education as an asset-based approach to SWVI's educational access and educators' innovative pedagogy.

Table 1 Methodology of literature review (authors' table)

Themes	Sources	Research objectives
The role of JAWS in SWVIs' computer practice literacy	1, 8, 26, 32, 42	Understanding the role of JAWS in SWVIs' computer practice literacy
Impact of JAWS on SWVIs' learning processes	2, 15, 18, 23, 37, 41, 49, 48	To examine the need to understand the impact of JAWS usage in the learning processes of SWVI
Aligning the TVET sector with inclusive education and digital training reforms	4, 24, 30, 33, 39, 38, 43, 52	To analyse the alignment and transformation of TVETs inclusive education and digital training reforms

The next task draws from other perspectives, including Amoor and Magaji [2], Papuda-Dolińska [41], Fichten et al. [14], He [18], Kizilaslan [21], Muzata [37], Papuda-Spinczyk et al. [41], and Singleton and Neuber [48] to assess the impact of JAWS usage on the learning processes of SWVI. The study also references Baker et al. [4], Kretzmann and McKnight [24], Makhasane and Khanare [30], Mourad and Ways [33], Myende and Chikoko [39], Myende and Hlalele [38], Ramatea and Khanare [43], and van Wyk and Hodgkinson-Williams [52] to analyse the alignment and transformation of TVET's inclusive education and digital training reforms.

Based on the themes in Table 1 and guided by the research objectives, the following section discusses three critical factors: the role of JAWS in SWVIs' computer practice literacy, the impact of JAWS on SWVIs' learning processes, and the alignment of the TVET sector with inclusive education and digital training reforms.

3 Literature Review

3.1 Bridging the Gap: Enhancing Cognition and Sustainable Development Through Inclusive Higher Education in Africa

The need for sustainable development in Africa arises from the pressing challenges faced by the continent, including poverty, inequality, quality education, environmental degradation, and social instability [29]. Sustainable development refers to a holistic approach that balances economic growth, social progress, and environmental protection, ensuring the well-being of current and future generations.

In the context of current chapter, quality higher education plays a crucial role in achieving sustainable development in Africa. It equips individuals with the knowledge, skills, and critical thinking abilities necessary to address complex challenges and contribute to sustainable development efforts [5]. However, there are several issues and problems that need to be addressed to ensure quality higher education and promote sustainable development in the context of enhancing cognition of students with visual impairments via a human–computer interface [29].

One key issue is limited access and inclusivity for students with visual impairments. Many students with visual impairments face barriers to accessing higher education due to a lack of appropriate infrastructure, support services, and inclusive teaching methodologies. The current education system in Africa often lacks adequate provisions and resources to cater to the needs of visually impaired students. This results in exclusion, unequal opportunities, and limited educational outcomes for these individuals. To address these challenges, a comprehensive blueprint for SDG 4 (quality education) in Africa is required. This blueprint should focus on the following aspects:

1. Inclusive infrastructure and technology: Enhancing physical infrastructure and providing assistive technologies like human–computer interfaces can facilitate access to quality education for visually impaired students. Accessible campuses, classrooms, and digital learning platforms should be developed.
2. Specialised teacher training: Providing specialised training programmes for teachers to equip them with knowledge and skills in inclusive education and assistive technologies. This will enable them to create an inclusive learning environment and deliver effective instruction to visually impaired students.
3. Curriculum adaptation: Developing accessible and adaptable curriculum materials that incorporate universal design principles. This will ensure that visually impaired students can actively participate in various academic disciplines and have equal opportunities for learning.
4. Support services: Establishing comprehensive support services, such as disability offices and counselling services, to address the unique needs of visually impaired students. This includes providing academic support, assistive devices, and accommodations to facilitate their learning process.
5. Collaboration and partnerships: Promoting collaboration among educational institutions, government agencies, non-governmental organisations, and other stakeholders to create a network of support for visually impaired students. This collaboration can help in sharing resources, best practices, and advocating for policy changes to ensure inclusivity and quality education.

By implementing this blueprint, African countries can enhance the cognition of students with visual impairments via human–computer interfaces and promote sustainable development. It will contribute to the achievement of SDG 4 (quality education) while fostering inclusivity, equity, and empowerment for visually impaired individuals, ultimately leading to a more sustainable and inclusive society [29, 44].

3.2 Understanding the Role of JAWS in SWVIs' Learning Processes—Means to Address SDG 4

There are arguably several reasons to consider the role of JAWS in SWVI's learning processes. For instance, McDonnall [32] and Lund and Cmar [26] suggest that the use of JAWS alongside TVET's vocational skills is critical in transforming and upskilling SWVI to align with the 21st-century labour market. McDonnall's [32] assertion is because the current workforce demands technological skills, and education departments, especially government institutions, must produce students with such skills, including SWVI, who equally contribute to the economy.

However, a significant concern noted by Sefotho (2018) that currently threatens the economic participation of people with visual impairments is persistent inequalities in educational access and noticeable unemployment. Therefore, there is an urgent need to equip current and future youth, including people with visual impairments, with vocational skills and digital literacy to increase opportunities for innovation, creativity, and employment [51]. The question is how the TVET education system can be aligned to meet this challenge.

The current study calls for action in the mainstream TVET curriculum to respond to the current technological demands in response to the question. The authors believe that the current prescribed TVET Business NATED and NCV curriculum, which considers computer practice literacy as the gateway to advanced technology comprehension and application skills, is indeed a move in the right direction. However, the consideration of SWVI's learning processes in partaking in the TVET technology curriculum, particularly computer literacy, is unclear. Moreover, acquiring computer skills for SWVI involves integrating JAWS as an assistive tool mainly used by people with visual impairments [1]. Thus, understanding the role of JAWS in SWVI's learning processes has one key implication: understanding JAWS as extended cognition.

3.3 Global Context

The Sustainable Development Goals (SDGs) are a crucial aspect of the United Nations (UN) 2030 Agenda and were universally adopted in 2015 by all Member Nations of the UN as a blueprint for action towards people, the planet, and prosperity [5]. However, the significance of SDGs in education policies and implementation has been questioned, and changes to classroom practices have been limited [44]. This study explores the notion of learners' prior numerical cognition as a predictor of educational performance. In this study, learners are regarded as active participants in their learning, with their interests and prior knowledge influencing their education. The revised Bloom's taxonomy was used as a theoretical framework in the mathematical context for the study.

3.4 African Context

The primary concern of the SDGs is the promotion of sustainable growth by ensuring well-being, economic and academic progress, and environmental legislation [5]. Among the most significant projected goals of the SDGs is the provision of high-quality education to learners. Despite sufficient evidence of application failure, the SDGs have been accepted in African countries such as Rwanda. Most research [9] has examined the implementation of SDGs at the primary and secondary levels in Rwanda. The findings from the Rwandan study indicate that, for instance, by 2030, most African countries will require over 10 million additional secondary teachers due to the need for the expansion of learners' enrolment [9]. Countries in Africa face further challenges impacting the quality of mathematics teaching in the context of fast growth in learners' enrolment. Therefore, it is essential that this study was conducted in South Africa to encourage and raise awareness for the realisation of the SDG4 goals in the mathematics classroom of the African context.

3.5 Specific Lessons for African Countries

There is an urgent need to conduct research on SDG-related goals with a wider scope that focuses on the role of learners in achieving an effective learning process to ensure quality education. Educational institutions in Africa should encourage experts in international education, particularly in mathematics classrooms. The authors of this chapter have provided additional literature that can serve as a reference for achieving one of the SDGs goals in schools. The study investigated whether learners' prior mathematical cognition could predict their performance at current educational levels. The findings from this study provide a direction for further research on SDG goals. Future investigations could focus on the challenges of implementing SDG goals in teacher education institutions, proposing several actionable approaches with concrete steps for key players in teacher education development in Africa.

3.6 JAWS as an Extended Cognition

Several studies have indicated that the integration of ACAS such as JAWS and other related technologies in the learning processes of SWVI goes beyond the mere use of an assistive device or application, and involves a form of biological, cognitive relationship between the student and the assistive device or application [9]. For example, cognition researchers such as Pritchard et al. [42] carried out a pilot study on integrating assistive technology in the education of SWVI in the United Kingdom. The study engaged with specialists in assistive technology for SWVI, a qualified educator of SWVI, and a mobility and habitation specialist based on their long-term expertise and experience in working with SWVI. The results of the in-depth semi-structured focus group discussions revealed that an assistive device becomes an extended cognition of a student. This implies that any cognitive success presented by an SWVI due to the integration of an assistive device or application in their learning process demonstrates their cognitive urgency. Thus, Pritchard et al. [42] concluded that visual impairments should not be equated with cognitive or intellectual impairments of SWVI.

The implication is that there is a need for technological fluency in using such assistive applications or devices by SWVI. However, there are several practical challenges. For SWVI to be fluent in their extended cognitive process, that is, the integration of JAWS and other related ACAS and devices in their learning, their educators must boost their confidence in such skills transfer. This requires understanding the impact of JAWS on computer practice literacy.

3.7 Understanding the Impact of JAWS on Computer Practice Literacy

As Muzata [36] proposed a Computer Practice Course solely for SWSV in higher institutions of learning in Zambia, Manis et al. [31 recommended a computer course focused on the use of assistive computer applications as a compulsory module in the development of a postgraduate qualification in visual impairment studies in South Africa. Similarly, Seale et al. [45] reported that in technical schools and colleges for SWVI in the US, the UK, Germany, Israel, and Canada, the main challenge with the successful inclusion of SWVI is the lack of computer skills among both SWVI and their educators. This problem is also prevalent in TVET colleges in South Africa educators in integrating computer applications in STEM subjects. Some have identified a severe lack of technological knowledge among educators, resulting in a lack of technologically supported teaching approaches for accommodating SWVI [45].

In response to this issue, this research argues that the TVET education system should address the current lack of JAWS skills among TVET Computer Practice educators. By doing so, TVET computer practice educators can incorporate JAWS as an innovative pedagogical and technological teaching approach in transferring both JAWS skills and Computer Practice skills to their students, improving computer practice instruction for SWVI and emphasising the need for computer practice as a lifelong learning tool [49, 50].

3.8 Computer Practice as a Lifelong Learning Tool

Many reasons account for the need for computer practice as a lifelong learning tool. For example, Muzata [37] noted that computer practice is now the primary tool in higher learning institutions, given the recent accelerated integration of educational technologies due to the COVID-19 outbreak. Additionally, besides its educational benefits, being skilled in computer software operations brings convenience and efficiency to people's daily lives. It is therefore crucial to provide computer skills to SWVI through the subject of computer practice to enhance their learning experiences, support the relevance of current educational technology, and stimulate their independence.

However, teaching computer practice to SWVI can be challenging due to the nature of their learning. Computer practice teaching is application-oriented and requires adequate time for real-time hands-on practice. Educators tend to resort to a traditional one-way communication approach due to time constraints, which leads to students being passive receivers. This approach can be disadvantageous, especially as teaching SWVI takes longer. The problem is exacerbated if educators lack a basic understanding of the SWVI cognition process, have no technology pedagogical skills for accommodating SWVI, and cannot operate an assistive tool presented for teaching and learning SWVI.

Thus, being skilled in the operations of assistive applications such as JAWS and understanding the role of such applications as educators' instructional tools and SWVIs' extended cognition can be beneficial. Such understanding is essential for the efficient and appropriate application of JAWS, enabling and enhancing computer practice educators' teaching and SWVI's learning experiences to avoid cognitive overload.

3.9 JAWS and Cognition Overload

As JAWS enables interaction between the user and computer, it can be considered a powerful tool for SWVI, whose learning relies on sound and touch cues [3]. However, lack of operational skills and understanding of students' learning process in JAWS usage can lead to inefficient utilisation. Inefficiencies in JAWS usage may result in SWVI experiencing cognitive overload, impeding cognitive processes [25, 28]. However, visual and auditory perception, attention, and retaining information form part of the learning processes of sighted students. SWVI heavily rely on compensating their visual indicators with more auditory modalities to access and process information during their learning processes [3]. Auditory perception replaces the missing visual perception [16].

JAWS's auditory feedback responds to the user's inputs as they interact with their computers, but it can have irritating effects on the user's ear, contributing immensely to cognitive load [46, 47]. In the context of computer practice literacy, using screen readers requires simultaneous listening to the auditory feedback and the educator while recalling a series of unseen keyboard commands in navigating their learning content. SWVI may also have to pay attention to their human support systems, commonly called scribes or readers [10]. These processes can be tedious, cognitively tiring to students, and frustrating to educators. McLaughlin and Kamei-Hannan [32] cautioned professionals to be cognizant of the extra cognitive energy and effort SWVI exert to pay attention to their instructors and assistances while decoding instructions during auditory reading and responding to auditory feedback.

One may wonder how the earlier mentioned implications of SWVI's extended cognition and technological fluency are related to the impact of JAWS on their learning processes. The idea is that when educators have a good understanding of SWVI's learning processes and the role of JAWS in their education, the two become interdependent and form an asset that educators can use as a basis for more formal training on inclusive practices. On the other hand, if educators lack knowledge of these concepts, especially in computer instruction, they miss the opportunity to apply practical computer application professional practice, leaving students to rely on their own coping strategies in computer application literacy. As a result, there is a need to align the TVET sector with inclusive education and digital training reforms.

4 Discussion

The current study investigated the use of JAWS for teaching and learning computer practice in TVET colleges. Based on an examination of the role of JAWS in SWVIs' computer practice literacy, the impact of JAWS on SWVIs' learning processes, and the alignment of the TVET sector with inclusive education and digital training reforms, several discussions and lessons were learned.

For example, drawing from Myende and Hlalele's [38] and Myende and Chikoko's [39] work, as well as Mourad and Ways' (1998) research, it is suggested that the TVET sector has the resources to address their technological skills shortages if they can learn to mobilise and connect to these resources. According to Myende and Chikoko [39] and Mourad and Ways [33], these resources are found within primary, secondary, and outside tiers (see Fig. 1). The authors suggest that each tier has specific responsibilities that the TVET sector can utilise to improve the inclusion of SWVIs in computer practice literacy.

Based on Mourad's and Ways' [33] framework for asset building, primary tier assets are the most immediate pool of assets that are easily accessible or available within the TVET college community. For instance, Myende and Chikoko [33], in investigating possibilities for school-university partnerships in South Africa using an ABA, concluded that educators could be considered assets within school settings. Furthermore, van Wyk and Hodgkinson-Williams [52] identified electronic devices preloaded with JAWS and other related screen-reading software as assets for students. Therefore, the mere provision of the subject of computer practice using the institution's computer labs is also an asset approach, as stated by the Department of Higher

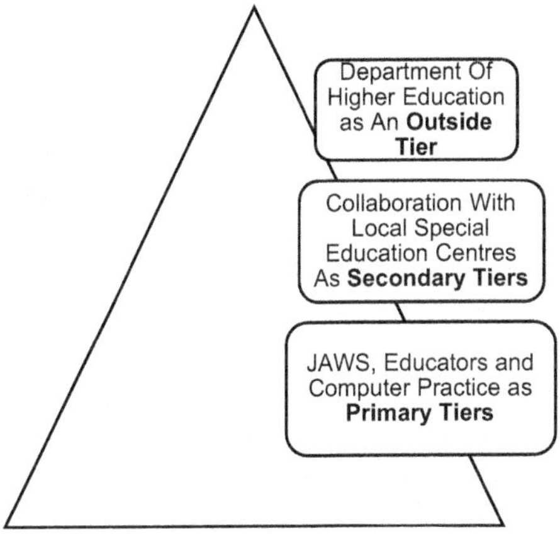

Fig. 1 TVET colleges' assets mapping for JAWS usage in computer practice literacy (primary, secondary, and outside tiers in TVET colleges) [39]

Education. JAWS, educators, and the subject of computer practice are primary assets that are already available within the TVET.

On the other hand, secondary tiers are less immediate, situated in the neighbourhoods of TVET colleges, and are not under the administration of the TVET sector. One of the findings from Makhasane and Khanare's [30] research is the importance of forming positive relationships and collaborations with other stakeholders who could contribute to enhancing SWVI educational livelihoods. Based on this finding, mapping and mobilising resource centres through collaborations with the nearest surrounding special schools, education, and societies for the blind could be an asset to the TVET [31, 35].

The least accessible assets or resources would be the outside tiers, which, according to Kretzmann and McKnight [24], have the potential to develop new possibilities for new capacities that the TVET community could utilise to enhance the already existing assets. In this case, the existence of the Department of Higher Education [12] is undoubtedly an asset to the TVET sector with hope for the development and enhancement of computer educators' already existing assets. However, acknowledging and mobilising the primary assets certainly does not reject and embrace external resources from the secondary and outside tiers, thus adopting an inside-out approach to strengthen the existing assets by aligning the TVET Sector with SDG 4.

Local literature, such as Zulu and Mutereko [54], notes that due to high unemployment and illiteracy rates in developing countries, such as South Africa, the government has identified the TVET sector as a critical asset in closing the twenty-first-century vocational skills gap. To achieve this, TVETs must be transformed and remain relevant to industry needs. Consequently, some TVETs have responded to education and training reforms that drive transformation in societies and industries. However, despite TVETs' efforts to include students with impairments (SWVI) as per the call made by the Department of Higher Education, the colleges are still in the early stages of integrating digital technologies into their learning technologies.

TVETs' continuous effort to include SWVI demands that educators have unique pedagogical and technological capacities to enhance students' vocational and computer skills in preparation for the real world. The computer practice subject offered in TVET colleges is defined as "the study of the integrated components of a computer system (hardware and software), practical techniques for efficient use and application to solve everyday problems" [12: 3]. Thus, CP aims to empower students to use computing applications to achieve their digital relevance in the current digital age. Besides educational benefits such as creating software-based artifacts, the CP subject equips SWVI's with lifelong skills necessary for the world of work.

However, developing these skills in SWVI requires educators to have confidence in their operational skills with assistive computer applications, such as JAWS, to transfer them to their students. Therefore, TVET computer practice educators must be adequately equipped with JAWS skills and understand their application to computer practice literacy. They should also comprehend how technology acts as an enabler to SWVI's enhanced learning experiences. In this way, educators can build and enhance students' capacities in vocational and computer skills, preparing them for the real world.

According to Ramatea and Khanare [43], one recommended approach to enhancing the educational livelihoods of SWVI is to recognise their full potential in achieving academic goals by applying positive psychology. To demonstrate the relevance of positive psychology approaches in supporting educators' usage of JAWS as an assistive computer application to enable computer practice literacy among SWVI, we locate our arguments within an Asset-Based Approach (ABA). As described by Kretzmann and McKnight [15, 23, 24], an ABA operates under the premise that all communities have human and non-human resources to address their challenges. Therefore, Ramatea and Khanare [43] conducted an asset-based approach study that investigated the use of resources in improving the well-being of SWVI in Lesotho, discovering constraints such as a shortage of qualified teachers and inadequate teaching resources, while also strongly recommending the importance of adequately managing existing assets.

The ABA focuses on identifying, mobilising, and managing assets such as skills, resources, and human capital in and around learning institutions in resolving challenges. Given the challenges experienced in the TVET sector, as the study mentioned earlier, the ABA challenges the needs-based mentality that views the TVET sector as incapable of resolving its shortcomings. This approach also dismisses the notion of scribes-acceptance, which undermines the capabilities and strengths of SWVI, perceiving them as incapable of independently navigating their learning and resolving their computer navigation challenges. Instead, educators should develop students' JAWS and computer application capacities to enhance their independence in their computer literacy journey.

Therefore, it is imminent to apply the ABA in viewing the urgent need for TVET educators' capacity development on accommodative computer application inclusive practices. Arguably, seeking external support or embracing external support may not be a weakness or needs-based but instead be viewed as the TVETs' strength to identify and recognise their limited potentials, thus seeking support to close identified gaps. The argument is based on the notion that the ABA is a glass-half-full approach that may require external partners to fill up the rest of the glass in terms of available assets for teaching and learning computer practice through JAWS in TVET Colleges [6, 7].

5 Implications and Conclusions

Drawing from the discussions based on the research objectives, several implications emerge. Firstly, it is essential to address the issue of attracting SWVI to mainstream TVET colleges to acquire vocational skills and the new technological and inclusive pedagogical skills required for successful and efficient integration of JAWS in computer practice literacy. Secondly, TVET computer practice educators can only acquire these skills through capacity development. Thirdly, this study revealed that TVET educators lack the necessary skills to teach SWVI. The first conclusion is that providing TVET college educators with these skills can be viewed as an asset-based approach to enhance their existing teaching strategies and students' learning experiences. As a second conclusion and in response to the first objective, it is crucial that TVET educators have a basic understanding of the learning processes of SWVI to better incorporate JAWS as an asset, which is an extension of SWVIs' cognitive processes. In response to the second objective, the conclusion is that providing assistive applications or devices to SWVI without fully understanding their impacts might disadvantage SWVI due to inefficiencies in usage, leading to cognitive destruction and forfeiting the benefits of the system's usage. This research was limited by the lack of primary quantitative data and was chiefly a literature review. Moreover, the emphasis on TVET colleges in South Africa may limit the generalizability of the conclusions to other educational settings. Future research should comprise empirical data and consider increasing the scope to other regions.

References

1. A. Alabi and S. Mutula, "Digital inclusion for visually impaired students through assistive technologies in academic libraries," Library Hi Tech News, vol. 37, no. 2, pp. 14–17, 2022. [Online]. Available: https://0-doi.org.wam.seals.ac.za/https://doi.org/10.1108/LHTN-11-2019-0081
2. S. Amoor and Z. Magaji, "Comparative Analysis of Using Computer Tutor Guide and Demonstration Methods of Teaching on Students' Skills Acquisition in Word Processing in Nigerian Universities," KIU Journal of Social Sciences, vol. 3, no. 1, pp. 251–256, 2017.
3. V. Argyropoulos, S. Padeliadu, E. Avramidis, and M. Nikolaraizi, "An investigation of preferences and choices of students with vision impairments on literacy medium for studying," British Journal of Visual Impairment, vol. 37, no. 2, pp. 154–168, 2019. [Online]. Available: https://doi.org/10.1177/0264619619838667
4. C. M. Baker, L. R. Milne, and R. E. Ladner, "Understanding the Impact of TVIs on Technology Use and Selection by Children with Visual Impairments," in Proc. 2019 CHI Conf. on Human Factors in Computing Systems, pp. 1–13, 2019. [Online]. Available: https://dl.acm.org/doi/pdf/https://doi.org/10.1145/3290605.3300654

5. E. Boeren, "Understanding Sustainable Development Goal (SDG) 4 on 'quality education' from micro, meso and macro perspectives," International Review of Education, vol. 65, pp. 277–294, 2019. [Online]. Available: https://doi.org/10.1007/s11159-019-09772-7
6. H. N. Boone and D. A. Boone, "Analysing Likert Data," The Journal of Extension, vol. 50, pp. 1–5, 2012. [Online]. Available: https://joe.org/joe/2012april/tt2.php
7. D. Can and I. E. Yetkin Özdemir, "An Examination of Fourth-Grade Elementary School Students' Number Sense in Context-Based and Non-Context-Based Problems," International Journal of Science and Mathematics Education, vol. 8, no. 7, pp. 1333–1354, 2020.
8. J. A. Carter and D. Pritchard, "Extended entitlement," in P. Graham and N. Pedersen, Eds., New essays on entitlement, Oxford: Oxford University Press, 2020. [Online]. Available: https://d1wqtxts1xzle7.cloudfront.net/40883032
9. E. Carter and P. Rose, "Rwandan secondary mathematics Teacher classrooms: Findings from classroom observations," Leaders in Teaching Research and Policy Series, Laterite and REAL Centre, University of Cambridge, Mar. 2021.
10. E. Croft, "'Everyone Thought My Library Assistant was My Mum': Visually Impaired and Blind Students' Experiences of Interactions with Support and Other Staff in Higher Education," Journal of Disability Studies in Education, pp. 1–22, 2021. https://doi.org/10.1163/25888803-bja10004
11. N. E. Delubom, N. Marongwe, and A. M. Buka, "Managers' challenges on implementing inclusive education: Technical Vocational Education and Training Colleges," Cypriot Journal of Educational Sciences, vol. 15, no. 6, pp. 1508–1518, 2020. [Online]. Available: https://www.un-pub.eu/ojs/index.php/cjes/article/download/5294/7451
12. Department of Higher Education and Training, "Curriculum Documents," 2021. [Online]. Available: https://www.dhet.gov.za/SitePages/DocCurriculumDocuments.aspx
13. P. Engelbrecht, "Inclusive education: Developments and challenges in South Africa," PROSPECTS, vol. 49, no. 3, pp. 219–232, 2020. https://doi.org/10.1007/s11125-020-09499-6
14. C. Fichten et al., "Mobile technologies that help post-secondary students succeed: A pilot study of Canadian and Israeli professionals and students with disabilities," Canada: BC, 2019.
15. C. Fichten, D. Olenik-Shemesh, J. Asuncion, M. Jorgensen, and C. Colwell, "Higher education, information and communication technologies and students with disabilities: An overview of the current situation," in Improving accessible digital practices in higher education, pp. 21–44, 2020. https://doi.org/10.1007/978-3-030-37125-8
16. T. Froese and X. González-Grandón, "How passive is passive listening? Toward a sensorimotor theory of auditory perception," Phenomenology and the Cognitive Sciences, vol. 19, no. 4, pp. 619–651, 2020. https://doi.org/10.1007/s11097-019-09641-6
17. S. Govender and T. Dhurumraj, "Opening up TVET lecturer professional learning and development through work integrated learning in South Africa," in T. G. Mayisela and C. A. Hodgkinson-Williams, Eds., Open Learning as a Means of Advancing Social Justice, pp. 338, 2022. https://doi.org/10.47622/9781928502425
18. Y. He, "Research on practice teaching quality assurance system of computer application specialty in colleges and universities based on computer multimedia technology," Journal of Physics: Conference Series, vol. 1648, no. 4, 042003, 2020. [Online]. Available: https://iopscience.iop.org/article/https://doi.org/10.1088/1742-6596/1648/4/042003/pdf
19. V. K. Hester, H. A. Hulya, J. M. Joke, and N. Wenceslas, "Recontextualization of learner-centred pedagogy in Rwanda: A comparative analysis of primary and secondary schools," Compare: A Journal of Comparative and International Education, vol. 52, no. 6, pp. 966–983, 2022. https://doi.org/10.1080/03057925.2020.1847044
20. E. L. Hooijer, M. Van Der Merwe, and J. Fourie, "Symbolic Representations as Teachers Reflect on Inclusive Education in South Africa," African Journal of Teacher Education, vol. 10, no. 1, pp. 127–152, 2021. https://doi.org/10.1007/s10209-019-00696-5
21. Jamaluddin, R., Sapak, M.F., Kadir, S.A., Hajaraih, S.K., Kamis, A., "The Implementation of Vocational Skills in Teaching and Learning of People with Disabilities in the Community-Based Rehabilitation Center (CBRC): A Review from Ecological Environments Perspective," Universal Journal of Educational Research, vol. 9, no. 11, pp. 1877–1885, 2021.

22. Jones, B.A., Rudinger, B., Williams, N., Witcher, S., "Training pre-service general educators in assistive technology competencies for students with visual impairments," British Journal of Visual Impairment, vol. 37, no. 1, pp. 29–39, 2019. https://doi.org/10.1177/0264619618814066
23. Kizilaslan, A., "Linking Theory to Practice: Science for Students with Visual Impairment," Science Education International, vol. 30, no. 1, pp. 56–64, 2019. [Online]. Available: https://files.eric.ed.gov/fulltext/EJ1209277.pdf
24. Kretzmann, J.P., McKnight, J., "Building communities from the inside out," Center for Urban Affairs and Policy Research, Neighborhood Innovations Network, Evanston, IL, 1993. [Online]. Available: https://resources.depaul.edu/abcd-institute/publications/Documents/GreenBookIntro%202018.pdf
25. Kumar Patel, P., Karkare, A., Raheja, G., "Inclusive Accommodations for Persons with Visual Impairments in Computer-Based Tests," in Universal Design From Special to Mainstream Solutions, pp. 219–237, 2021.
26. Lund, E.M., Cmar, J.L., "A systematic review of factors related to employment outcomes for adults with visual impairments," Journal of Visual Impairment & Blindness, vol. 113, no. 6, pp. 493–517, 2019.
27. Luque, L., Brandão, L.O., Kira, E., Brandão, A.A., "On the inclusion of learners with visual impairment in computing education programs in Brazil: Practices of educators and perceptions of visually impaired learners," Journal of the Brazilian Computer Society, vol. 1, pp. 1–12, 2018. https://doi.org/10.1186/s13173-018-0068-0
28. Lyner-Cleophas, "Assistive technology enables inclusion in higher education: The role of Higher and Further Education Disability Services Association," African Journal of Disability, vol. 8, no. 1, pp. 1–6, 2019. https://doi.org/10.4102/ajod.v8i0.558
29. Makgato, "STEM for Sustainable Skills for the Fourth Industrial Revolution: Snapshot at Some TVET Colleges in South Africa," in Theorizing STEM Education in the 21st Century, pp. 144–159, 2019. https://doi.org/10.5772/intechopen.89294
30. Makhasane, S.D., Khanare, F.P., "Leadership practices of turning around low-performing schools in a developing country," in C.V. Meyers and M.J. Darwin, Eds., Turning around low-performing schools, Charlotte: Information Age Publishing, 2018.
31. Manis, M., Ferreira, R., Sefotho, M.M., Mampane, R.M., "Utilising PRA to develop a postgraduate qualification in visual impairment studies," South African Journal of Higher Education, vol. 35, no. 2, pp. 93–122, 2021. [Online]. Available: https://journals.co.za/doi/pdf/https://doi.org/10.20853/35-2-3979
32. McDonnall, M.C., "Employment Is Everyone's Job: An Important Reminder for the Field of Visual Impairment," Journal of Visual Impairment & Blindness, vol. 114, no. 1, pp. 3–5, 2020. https://doi.org/10.1177/0145482X211000963
33. Mourad, M., Ways, H., "Comprehensive community revitalization: Strategies for asset building," in Proc. 1998 National Planning Conference, AICP, Boston, 1998.
34. Mungoo, J., Moorad, F., "Learner centred methods for whom? Lessons from Botswana Junior Secondary Schools," African Educational Research Journal, vol. 3, no. 3, pp. 161–169, 2015.
35. Munyaradzi, M., Arko-Achemfuor, A., Quan-Baffour, K., "An Exploration of Comprehensive Student Support Systems in Technical Vocational Education and Training Colleges for Students with Disability," Community College Journal of Research and Practice, pp. 1–17, 2021. https://doi.org/10.1080/10668926.2021.1952914
36. Mutua, P.N., Mulwa, D., Kimiti, R., "Trainers' Qualifications in Competence Based Education and Training Implementation and Acquisition of Employable Skills Among Visually Impaired Learners in TVET Institutions in Kenya," Journal of Education and Practice, vol. 10, no. 29, pp. 13–22, 2019. https://doi.org/10.7176/JEP/10-29-02
37. Muzata, K.K., "The Utilisation of Computers to Improve the Quality of Learning for Students with Visual Impairment at the University of Zambia," Zambia Journal of Library & Information Science (ZAJLIS), vol. 4, no. 2, pp. 34–44, 2020.
38. Myende, P.E., Hlalele, D., "Framing sustainable rural learning ecologies: A case for strength-based approaches," Africa Education Review, vol. 15, no. 3, pp. 21–37, 2018. https://doi.org/10.1080/18146627.2016.1224598

39. Myende, P., Chikoko, V., "School-university partnership in a South African rural context: Possibilities for an asset-based approach," Journal of Human Ecology, vol. 46, no. 3, pp. 249–259, 2014.
40. Pillay, S., Maharaj, A., "Collaborative learning of Mathematics education by educationally disadvantaged students at a university," Journal of Independent Teaching and Learning, vol. 6, pp. 55–58, 2011.
41. Papuda-Dolińska, B., "Differences in social and academic functioning among visually impaired children in special, integrated and inclusive educational settings in Poland," Hrvatska revija za rehabilitacijska istraživanja, vol. 53(Supplement), pp. 113–126, 2017.
42. Pritchard, D., English, A.R., Ravenscroft, J., "Extended cognition, assistive technology and education," Synthese, vol. 199, no. 3, pp. 8355–8377, 2021. https://doi.org/10.1007/s11229-021-03166-9
43. Ramatea, M.A., Khanare, F.P., "Improving the well-being of learners with visual impairments in rural Lesotho schools: An asset-based approach," International Journal of Qualitative Studies on Health and Well-being, vol. 16, no. 1, pp. 2–11, 2021. https://doi.org/10.1080/17482631.2021.1890341
44. Saini, M., Sengupta, E., Singh, M., et al., "Sustainable Development Goal for Quality Education (SDG 4): A study on SDG 4 to extract the pattern of association among the indicators of SDG 4 employing a genetic algorithm," Educ. Inf. Technol., 2022. [Online]. Available: https://doi.org/10.1007/s10639-022-11265-4
45. Seale, J., Coughlan, T., Heiman, T., Kaspi-Tsahor, D., Olenik-Shemesh, D., "'Dreaming in colour': Disabled higher education students' perspectives on improving design practices that would enable them to benefit from their use of technologies," Education and Information Technologies, vol. 26, no. 2, pp. 1687–1719, 2021. https://doi.org/10.1007/s10639-020-10329-7
46. Sefotho, M., "Disability and inclusive employment through the lens of educational psychology," in I. Ellof, Ed., Understanding educational psychology, Cape Town: Juta, pp. 286–291, 2018.
47. Shoaib, M., Hussain, I., Mirza, H.T., "Automatic switching between speech and non-speech: Adaptive auditory feedback in desktop assistance for the visually impaired," Universal Access in the Information Society, vol. 19, no. 4, pp. 813–823, 2020. https://doi.org/10.1007/s10209-019-00696-5
48. Singleton, K.J., Neuber, K.S., "Examining How Students with Visual Impairments Navigate Accessible Documents," Journal of Visual Impairment & Blindness, vol. 114, no. 5, pp. 393–405, 2020. https://doi.org/10.1177/0145482X20953268
49. Spinczyk, D., Maćkowski, M., Kempa, W., Rojewska, K., "Factors influencing the process of learning mathematics among visually impaired and blind people," Computers in Biology and Medicine, vol. 104, pp. 1–9, 2019. https://doi.org/10.1016/j.compbiomed.2018.10.025
50. Thomas, C.N., Peeples, K.N., Kennedy, M.J., Decker, M., "Riding the special education technology wave: Policy, obstacles, recommendations, actionable ideas, and resources," Intervention in School and Clinic, vol. 54, no. 5, pp. 295–303, 2019. https://doi.org/10.1177/1053451218819201
51. Tikly, L., Vogel, E., Kurvers, C., "Boosting Gender Equality in Science and Technology: A Challenge for TVET Programmes and Careers," UNESCO-UNEVOC International Centre for Technical and Vocational Education and Training, 2020.
52. van Wyk, G., Hodgkinson-Williams, C.A., "Staff insights on opening up learning to students with disabilities at Motheo TVET College, South Africa," in T.G. Mayisela and C.A. Hodgkinson-Williams, Eds., Open learning as a means of advancing social justice: Cases in post-school education and training in South Africa, Cape Town: African Minds, p. 178, 2022. https://doi.org/10.47622/9781928502425
53. Zongozzi, N., Sefora, S.R., Mokiwa, S.N., Agejivwie, S.R., "Opening up education through academic support for Students with Disabilities," 2019. [Online]. Available: http://dspace.col.org/bitstream/handle/11599/3298/PCF9_Papers_paper_222.pdf?sequence=4&isAllowed=y
54. Zulu, W.V., Mutereko, S., "Exploring the Causes of Student Attrition in South African TVET Colleges: A Case of One KwaZulu-Natal Technical and Vocational Education and Training

College," Interchange, vol. 51, no. 4, pp. 385–407, 2020. https://doi.org/10.1007/s10780-019-09384-y

Assessing the Effectiveness of AI-Based Teaching Methods in STEAM Education: Enhancing Conceptual Understanding Through Concrete and Symbolic Games

Anass Bayaga

Abstract This research examines the effectiveness of AI-based teaching approaches in improving conceptual understanding in STEAM education through concrete and symbolic games. The study examines how progressively substituting concrete illustrations with symbolic games can advance learning results. A survey design was utilised, and data from 71 respondents in a STEAM teaching setting were analysed by means of generalised linear models. Findings reveal a substantial positive effect of AI-based approaches on cognition, predominantly through the steady transition from concrete to symbolic games illustrations. These results highlight the possibility for AI technology to advance learning in STEAM instruction. Future study should investigate diverse educational settings to further examine AI-based approaches.

Keywords STEAM education · Concrete games · Symbolic games · AI-Based teaching · Conceptual understanding

1 Introduction

The field of science, technology, engineering, arts, and mathematics (collectively termed STEAM) is gaining global momentum as new research [1]. Nevertheless, there is a growing need to address the complexity associated with its teaching and learning through abstract and concrete games using artificial intelligent (AI) systems [15]. Concrete games, as used in this study, refer to games used in any STEAM class, which are made from physical materials; in contrast, abstract games are computerised games used in teaching and learning STEAM subjects. While there is evidence to suggest that STEAM education can positively influence learners' educational attainment and teacher effectiveness, there is a significant gap in research on AI-Based STEAM teaching and learning. To better understand and address the challenges of AI-Based STEAM research, specific areas of interest must be investigated. This includes

A. Bayaga (✉)
Stellenbosch University, Stellenbosch, South Africa
e-mail: abayaga@sun.ac.za

J. Marx Gómez et al. (eds.), *Advancement in Embedded and Mobile Systems*, Progress in IS, https://doi.org/10.1007/978-3-031-99219-3_16

the teaching and learning of concrete and symbolic games in AI-Based STEAM classrooms. Based on these unresolved questions, this research examines the AI-based teaching and learning of concrete and symbolic games through various perspectives, including Şahin and Namli's [17] position on gamification and Marell-Olsson's [15] view on teachers' perception of gamification as a teaching design. The global perspective of AI-based teaching and learning of concrete and symbolic games in STEAM classrooms is also explored, drawing on prior studies on the use of concrete materials in learning and the effects of idealised and grounded materials on learning, transfer, and interest. The present study uses a sociocultural constructivist perspective to test hypothetical statements derived from the evaluation of prior studies. The methodology, results, and discussion are presented in the following section. The subsequent sections present the theoretical framing, methodology, results, and discussion.

2 Background of the Study

2.1 AI-Based Teaching and Learning of Concrete Video Games in South Africa

The use of concrete video games in education is continuously increasing due to the availability of new computer software and the universalisation termed in the current study as AI-based learning environments. Concrete video in this study refers to any physical, structural, or technological teaching/learning aids that can transmit moving images (games) and sound (e.g., cell phones). Such methodological and technological tools have been argued to enhance learning in STEAM education [4, 26–28]. According to Şahin and Namli [26], a range of benefits is associated with concrete video games. The study further stated that concrete video games develop students' participation and learning from a technological perspective and are necessary for today's learners [27]. For instance, concrete video games in AI-Based STEAM classrooms have been shown to enhance students' creativity, critical thinking, innovation, collaboration, and interpersonal communication skills [26]. About two decades now, the concept of concrete video games voiced by Bourgonjon et al. [4] showed promising potential when used as a teaching and learning tool. The Entropy Mastermind is an example of a concrete video game [28], which promotes learners' entropy intuitions by providing practical access to the relationship between probability distributions and the mathematical model entropy. This concrete video game (Entropy Mastermind) expands the typical Mastermind game. In Entropy Mastermind, an undisclosed code is created from a probability distribution by drawing randomly with replacement. The person playing the game must speculate on the undisclosed code by testing out several codes and getting feedback about the accuracy of the speculated code. The feedback is included three different categories of smileys; a joyful smiley indicating that a speculated item is correct/accurate in kind and position, a neutral smiley indicating that a speculated item is the correct kind but not in the accurate position, and an unhappy smiley indicating that a speculated item is not correct regarding both kind and position. Significantly, the orderliness of smileys in the feedback is always the same; joyful smileys come first, then neutral, and lastly, unhappy smileys—the position of smileys in the feedback arrangement does not match the positions of items in the speculated code. The entropy of the distributions from which the speculated code is generated changes between game rounds. Though, some scholars and educationists need to accept Concrete video games readily. Such researchers argue that concrete video games only appeal to contemporary students [4]. Educational concrete video games can be associated with educational play, fun interaction, and game-based technologies. Thus, video games must be improved to achieve global acceptance in the STEAM fields. It is vital to do so because the STEAM education approach contributes to developing twenty-first-century skills such as critical thinking, problem-solving, collaboration, and technology literacy. Additionally, STEAM education emphasiss that learners' twenty-first-century skills must be developed to solve life problems quickly [30] and exhibit collaborative work. For example, a localised implication in South Africa is that learning through concrete video games in STEAM classrooms must proactively develop learners' technological literacy to bridge the gaps between the world's developed and developing nations. The authors, therefore, hypothesised that AI-based teaching and learning concrete video games improve students' STEAM cognition.

2.2 AI-Based Teaching and Learning of Symbolic (Abstract) Games

In this study, symbolic or abstract game, as used interchangeably, refers to marks, signs, pictures, or word representations used for teaching and Learning in STEAM classrooms. Therefore, understanding what makes a successful approach to symbolic game-based learning is particularly pertinent to increasing participation in AI-Based STEAM classrooms in African countries. In contrast, elements of commercial video games are lauded for their sound learning principles applicable to a broad array of domains, including organisations and schools [15]. Yet, unfortunately, many educational symbolic games used in STEAM classrooms in Africa often feel more dressed up than the complex or aesthetically immersive gaming worlds that learners in other regions of the globe are accustomed to [2]. That is the state of education in terms of symbolic game development is one of the paradoxes [2, 18, 22, 31, 32]. The ramification is that learners of AI-based game learning have shown mixed results regarding learning outcomes. Moreover, there needs to be more consensus on the elements of symbolic games that are most effective in producing successful results. Educational games must therefore have a balance between the commercial (fun) and educational (learning) to motivate learners to learn intrinsically. Thus, the hypothesis was that AI-based teaching, and learning symbolic games positively affect a better understanding of the concepts/ideas.

2.3 General Perspective of AI-Based Teaching and Learning Concrete and Symbolic Games in STEAM Classrooms

The idea that concrete materials benefit teaching and learning has a long history in developmental psychology and education, dating back several decades [5, 18–20, 23]. Too often, however, scholars use these traditional views to give concrete materials a blanket endorsement. Nevertheless, using a concrete and symbolic game object to teach learners is not restricted to specific age categories but applies across ages. There are several implications: for example, concrete and symbolic games materials are tools teachers use to impose meaning on representations [13]. Moreover, symbolic representations within concrete materials can merge with non-symbolic game representations (constant Variables and coefficients, for example) and form deep meanings for learners [14]. An estimated 97% of American teens play video games [12], and it has shown many promising results in their ability to increase learning and motivation in a variety of disciplines ranging from engineering and computer science to biology [24, 31]. Based on the evidence, Flores et al. [9] suggested that conceptual knowledge increases as learners learn material twice, once with concrete materials and then again with the abstract concept. Several studies, as exemplified above, have provided interesting information about the connection between concrete or symbolic game materials and mathematics. Given the above arguments, this study seeks to investigate teaching/learning abstract and concrete games in AI-Based STEAM classrooms in South African schools. Consequently, the hypothesis was that AI-based teaching and learning symbolic (abstract) games in AI-Based in South African STEAM classrooms positively affect the better understanding of the concept/topics. Furthermore, apparent learning of concepts by concrete and symbolic game representations positively affects the better understanding of the concept due to the learners' previous knowledge of topics. Finally, apparent learning concepts starting with concrete representations and gradually replacing them with symbolic game representations positively affects a better understanding of the concept. The next section of this article pulls together the formulated hypotheses from the preceding.

2.4 Research Hypotheses

- Hypothesis 1 (H1): The use of AI-based teaching and learning of concrete video games can lead to a significant improvement in learners' understanding.
- Hypothesis 2 (H2): AI-based teaching and learning of symbolic (abstract) games can positively influence the learners' comprehension of concepts and ideas.
- Hypothesis 3 (H3): The integration of AI-based teaching and learning of both concrete and symbolic games in STEAM classrooms can lead to a better understanding of concepts and topics.

Table 1 Summary of themes, research questions, and critical gaps

S/N	THEME	HYPOTHESES	GAPS	SOURCES
1	Teaching and learning concrete video games in AI-Based South African STEAM classrooms	H1	Improving the learning of concepts/topics by concrete representation in South Africa needed encouragement	20, 27
2	Teaching and learning symbolic (abstract) games in AI-Based African STEAM classrooms	H2	Increased demand to research into learning using symbolic game educational games in AI-Based STEAM classrooms is high	2, 22
3	The global perspective of teaching and learning concrete and symbolic games in AI-Based STEAM classrooms	H3, H4, H5	Further study into concrete and symbolic games using pedagogical approaches of AI-Based STEAM topics/concepts to learners was necessary	6, 24, 31

- Hypothesis 4 (H4): The acquisition of knowledge through concrete and symbolic game representations has a positive effect on learners' comprehension of the concept, as their prior knowledge of topics can aid their understanding.
- Hypothesis 5 (H5): The approach of beginning with concrete representations and gradually transitioning to symbolic game representations in the learning process can positively influence the learners' comprehension of the concept.

Thus, Table 1 summarises the major themes of the reviewed kinds of literature, the research hypotheses, critical gaps, and their sources.

3 Theoretical Framing

The underlying theoretical orientation for this study is drawn from the theory of Vygotsky's sociocultural constructivist perspective. Constructivism emphasises that people develop their understanding and knowledge of the world through experience and reflecting on those experiences, perhaps by changing what they already know or discarding the new information as irrelevant. Constructivists see learners as active sense makers, while the teachers' role is to dialogue with learners and help them develop their ideas. Embedded in the possibility of answering the above research hypotheses are essential conceptual issues addressed in this section, including a symbolic game and concrete game. As explained earlier, the term symbolic or abstract game also refers to marks, signs, pictures, or word representations used as teaching and learning materials in STEAM classrooms. This description also provides a narrower usage for the term abstraction in Vygotsky's work. Based on the discussion so far, simple games, despite uniting abstract and concrete in one sense, are still dominated by the surface relations or connections perceived in everyday practice. Games, in contrast, encourage and require "conscious and deliberate control" through being "placed within a system of relations of generality" [33:172]. Vygotsky stresses the role of schooling in introducing such forms of thought. Still, he was equally aware of the danger of "empty verbalism" if such systems are learnt (or memorised) without rich development about the concrete [33:152]. He paid less attention to using concepts outside of school, but the implication is that the same bi-directional process between abstract systems and living reality can occur. "It is not enough for thought to strive for realisation; reality must strive towards thought" [33:252]. For a system to become concrete (or vice versa), a need or problem must arise in practice that cannot easily be satisfied or overcome by less conscious everyday meaning. Although, as noted in the earlier sections, the current study seeks to investigate and analyse the teaching/learning of Abstract and Concrete Games as a correlate of enhanced AI-Based STEAM classrooms in South African schools—the significant gaps emanating from both reviewed literature and Vygotsky's thus far needed further exploration.

4 Methodology

4.1 Design of the Study

This research analyses AI-Based abstract and concrete games as a correlate of STEAM education in South African schools. The study utilised a survey design. According to Cohen et al. [7], a survey design is a quantitative description of data gathered at a particular time to describe the nature of existing conditions between variables. This study used a survey design to provide a quantitative description of teaching/learning abstract and concrete games in AI-Based STEAM classrooms in schools. Note that this study was not experimental. Therefore, teaching/learning was conducted in the regular school/classroom setting. Hence, opinion-related data were gathered from five-varied educational levels of learners [7]. The survey design was chosen in this study because it produced quicker data collection (see Table 2). The data were collected with assumptions or models postulated (confirmatory survey). Descriptive statistics were employed to analyse data from the respondents, and multiple regression analysis was used to test the hypotheses. Generalised linear model (GLM)-regression analysis was used to test the hypotheses [25]. GLM-regression is a technique that shows some relation to principal components regression; it finds a linear regression model by projecting the predicted variables [25].

Table 2 Questionnaire items, codes, and scales

Items	Codes	Scales
I understand better by learning concrete representation of a concept	MP1	1 2 3 4
I understand better by learning only the symbolic game representation of a concept	MP2	1 2 3 4
I understand better by learning concrete (actual) and symbolic (abstract) game representations of concepts/topics	MP3	1 2 3 4
I understand topics better by starting with more concrete representations and gradually replacing them with abstract representations	MP4	1 2 3 4
I understand better by learning concrete and symbolic game representations of a concept because of my previous knowledge of topics	MP5	1 2 3 4
All learning topics require learning both concrete and symbolic game representations of a concept	MP6	1 2 3 4

4.2 Research Structure

This study explored the teaching/learning of abstract and concrete games in AI-Based STEAM classrooms in schools. The conceptual structure of this research is shown in Fig. 1. The dependent variable, represented with a rectangle, includes the school type, settlement (geolocation), gender, and age. School type is further categorised into high school, certificate, Diploma, Degree, and Postgraduate.

While the independent variable has MP1 to MP6 (codes—see Table 2), it is represented also in Fig. 1 with oval shapes. In Table 4 in the results, the section further explains the association between the dependent and independent variables.

4.3 Sample and Sampling Procedure and Fidelity Information on Questionnaire Administration and Validity Assurance

The study adopted a quantitative approach and was conducted in a rural settlement of the Kwa-Zulu-Natal province of South Africa. Given that the 150 of the study population was known, and since the number of learners was not the same across the various levels of education, proportionate stratified random sampling was used to sample the learners from each level (see Table 2). According to [1], proportionate stratified random sampling is used when the population for a study is predetermined. Additionally it is posited that the sample size needed should be collected at ten times the dimension of the questionnaire items [1]. The dimension of the questionnaire items in this research is the effect of game representation with six items (see Table 2). Therefore, the minimum sample size for this research must be at least 60. Yet, the sample size of this study was 71, which meets the minimum sample size requirement. In response to fidelity information on questionnaire administration, that

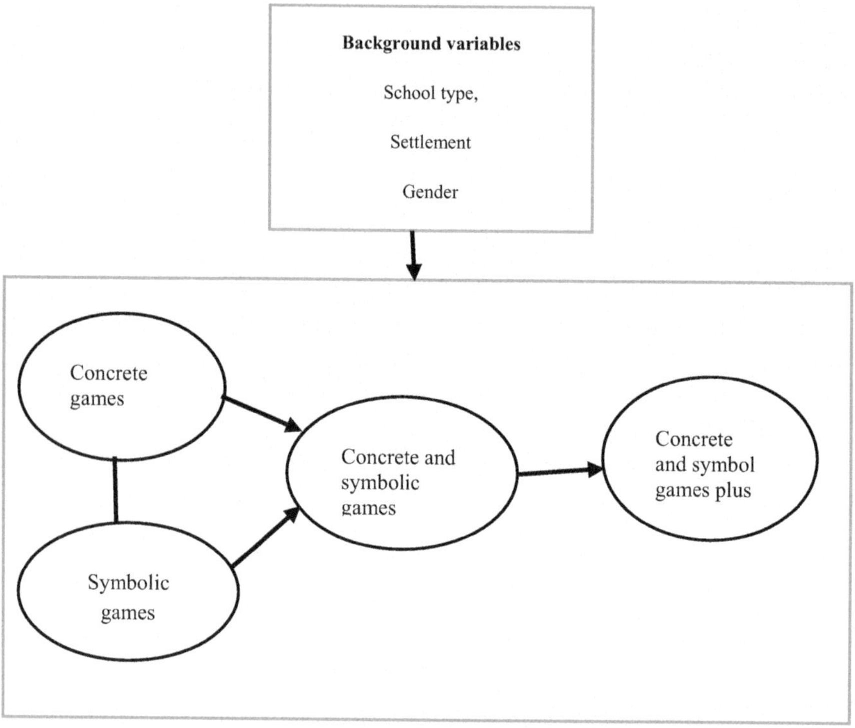

Fig. 1 The conceptual structure of the study

is, whether the respondents (learners) followed the planned activities, the following guidelines were adhered to: First, constructs were precise and devoid of double negatives to increase validity [11, 25]. Second, colleagues in similar fields scrutinised the questionnaire items for content and ambiguity validity. Moreover, all learners were encouraged to complete the questionnaire and candidly respond to the issues anonymously. Third, sufficient time was given to learners to complete the questionnaires. Finally, there were clear and consistent instructions for the participating learners to complete the questionnaires (e.g., no correct or incorrect answers in this survey. Please tick the boxes to mark your answers).

4.4 Data Collection and Analysis Methods

The data collection process for this study was a self-administered questionnaire designed by the researchers to assess learners' responses to their understanding of the teaching and learning of abstract and concrete games in AI-Based STEAM classrooms and their prior learning experience, noting that this study was not experimental as mentioned in Sect. 5.1. Therefore teaching/learning was conducted in the regular school/classroom setting. Hence, opinion-related data were gathered from five varied educational levels of learners. The questionnaire consisted of 34 items, with six focusing on learners' understanding of teaching and learning abstract and concrete games in AI-based mathematics classroom, while the remaining were in other areas. The items, their codes, and scales for the questionnaire are presented in Table 2 with codes for items and scales. In terms of data analysis (see results), various tests such as: Frequency distribution of the sample, Omnibus Test of hypotheses, Tests of Model Effects of hypotheses as well as Parameter Estimates of hypotheses were conducted. Table 2 depicts the questionnaire items, codes, and scales.

The questionnaire items (see Table 2) were on a four-point nominal scale ranging from strongly disagree to strongly agree, with strongly disagree fitted into the score of 1. Whiles disagree, agree, and strongly agree were within the scores of 2, 3, and 4, respectively. The participants were of mixed gender with a minimum age range of 21–23 years and a maximum age range of 30 and above. This research employed a generalised linear model to explore the research variables.

4.5 *Reliability and Ethics*

Internal consistency measures for assessing inter-item consistency are part of the reliability process designed to discover whether the items in the instrument measure the same thing. The Kuder-Richardson K-R 20 & K-R 21 test is based on the ratio of correct or wrong responses to each item in the instrument [17]. This study used the Likert-type instrument and the Cronbach alpha coefficient to measure the inter-item consistency. Cronbach alpha test conducted was more significant than 0.70, which is dependable [29]. In this study, the instrument used was a questionnaire of the Likert-type instrument. The Statistical Package for Social Science (SPSS) version 28.0 was employed to calculate the Cronbach alpha coefficient to determine the internal consistency of the questionnaire items. Cronbach alpha test conducted was greater than 0.70, which is dependable. A research survey which does not have reliability loses its credibility. It is argued that high Cronbach alpha values (inter-item coefficients) were indicators of construct reliability and assisted in explaining the extent to which the same attribute was being measured [17]. Nonetheless, reliability and validity are not synonymous because an instrument can be reliable without being valid [11]. Description of the ethical procedures followed Institutional Review Board approval of XXX.[1] University, South Africa, with reference number H21-EDU-PGE-026. Ethical approval was thus sought and granted by the XXX University, Faculty of Education's research ethics committee, which helped the researchers adhere to the norms and practices to protect participants. In addition, permission was sought to conduct the research from the principals of Kwazulu-Natal colleges before collecting data.

[1] Name of university blinded for review purpose.

Table 3 Frequency distribution of the sample

Levels of education		Value label	N
	1	High school	5
	2	Certificate	2
	3	Diploma	46
	4	Degree	0
	5	Postgraduate	18
Total			71

Table 4 Tests of Model Effects of H1

Source	Type III		
	Wald Chi-square	df	Sig
(Intercept)	467.743	1	<0.001
MP1	22.870	3	<0.001

5 Results

5.1 *Analysis of Background Variable*

Recall that the current study examined AI-Based abstract and concrete games as a correlate of STEAM education in South African schools through five hypotheses. The hypotheses emanated from the reviewed literature. The sample of this study consisted of 71 learners from five educational levels (high school, certificate, diploma, degree, and postgraduate). The frequency distribution of the sample data is indicated in Table 3.

A sample size of 71 was used for the study, with high school learners represented by 1, while 2, 3, 4, and 5 represented certificate, diploma, degree, and postgraduate students, respectively. The learners were sampled for the study because the authors wanted the study to have a reasonable or proportionate representation of the participating learners of various educational levels in the rural settlement of the Kwa-Zulu Natal province.

5.2 *Presenting the Result for AI-Based Teaching and Learning of Concrete Video Games in South Africa*

Recall that in Sect. 2.1, H1 hypothesised that AI-based teaching and learning concrete video games could positively affect the better understanding of learners. In Table 4, the tests of Model Effects show <0.001 significant value for intercept and the MP1. It means an association between concrete representations and a better understanding (Table 5).

Table 5 Parameter Estimates of H1

Parameter		B	Std. Error	95% Wald confidence interval		Hypothesis test		
				Lower	Upper	Wald Chi-square	df	Sig
Threshold	[School type = 1]	−2.383	0.4267	−3.219	−1.546	31.183	1	<0.001
	[School type = 2]	−2.064	0.3753	−2,799	−1.328	30.232	1	<0.001
	[School type = 3]	1.930	0.3567	1.231	2.629	29.272	1	<0.001
(Scale)		1[a]						

The Parameter Estimates results show significant values of < 0.001 for school types 1, 2, and 3. On the other hand, the Parameter B, standard error, 95% Wald confidence interval lower and upper, for school type 1 and 2 are negative, while school type 3 is positive. It is evident from the forgoing that learners' responses in this study agree with teaching/learning concrete game representations positively affecting their better understanding of concepts in AI-Based STEAM classrooms. Consequently, H1 was accepted.

5.3 *Presenting the Result for AI-Based Teaching and Learning of Symbolic (Abstract) Games*

It was hypothesised (H2) in Sect. 2.2 that AI-based teaching and learning symbolic (abstract) games positively affect a better understanding of the concepts/ideas (Table 6). However, in Tables 6 and 7, the Omnibus test shows a significant value of 0.110, and the significant value of the model effect test is 0.129 for the MP2. Therefore, it implies no association between symbolic game representations and a better understanding.

Table 8 indicates the parameters of the dependent and independent variables. The dependent variable is school types 1, 2, 3, and 4 (high school, certificate, Diploma, and Degree), while the independent variable has MP2. Table 8 explains the association between the dependent and independent variables. Looking at the overall result,

Table 6 Omnibus test of H2

Likelihood ratio Chi-square	df	Sig
6.039	3	0.110

Table 7 Tests of Model Effects of H2

Source	Type III		
	Wald Chi-square	df	Sig
MP2	5.659	3	0.129

school type (Diploma) has a higher significant value of 0.564 compared to school type (high school and certificate), which have <0.001 significant values each. Again, in comparing the MP2 results of the parameters to the school types 1, 2, and 3, the highest value of 0.120 association was recorded by the diploma to MP2.

In contrast, for high school and certificates were lower. Learners' responses at all educational levels agree that teaching/learning symbolic games in an AI-Based STEAM classroom did not benefit them. Thus, H2 was rejected. The following result to consider is that of H3-H5 in Tables 10 and 11.

Table 8 Parameter Estimates of H2

Parameter		B	Std. Error	95% Wald confidence interval		Hypothesis test		
				Lower	Upper	Wald Chi-square	df	Sig
Threshold	[School type = 1]	−5,259	1.3426	−7.891	−2.628	15.344	1	< 0.001
	[School type = 2]	−4,932	1.3261	−7.531	−2.333	13.834	1	< 0.001
	[School type = 3]	−0.704	1.2205	−3.096	1.688	0.333	1	0.564
[MP2 = 1]		−2.643	1.3102	−5.211	−0.075	4.070	1	0.044
[MP2 = 2]		−3.153	1.3320	−5.764	−0.543	5.604	1	0.018
[MP2 = 3]		−2.818	1.8136	−6.373	0.737	2.414	1	0.120
[MP2 = 4]		0^a						
(Scale)		1^b						

5.4 *Presenting the Result for General Perspective of AI-Based Teaching and Learning Concrete and Symbolic Games in STEAM Classrooms*

The following are the declarations of H3, H4, and H5 (Table 9). H3 declared that apparent learning of concepts/topics by both concrete and symbolic game representations positively affects the better understanding of the concept/topics. H4 hypothesised that apparent learning of concepts by concrete and symbolic game representations positively affects the better understanding of the concept due to the learners'/students' previous knowledge of topics. In contrast, H5 stated that apparent learning of concepts by starting with concrete representations and gradually replacing them with symbolic game representations positively affects a better understanding of the concept.

Table 9 the Omnibus test reveals the Likelihood Ratio Chi-Square of a significant value of 0.004. In Table 10, the tests of Model Effects for MP3 show the highest significant value of 0.673, while MP4, 5, and 6 show lower values. It means that an association exists in connection to H4 and H5. Yet, there is no association in connection to H3. Table 11 gives more evidence of the results.

Table 11 indicates the parameters of the dependent and independent variables. The dependent variable is school types 1, 2, 3, and 4 (high school, certificate, Diploma, and Degree), while the independent variable has MP3-6. Table 11 describes the association between the dependent and independent variables. Looking at the result, school type 3 has a higher significant value of 0.743 compared to school type (high school and certificate), which have < 0.001significant values each. Once again, in comparing the MP3-6 results of the parameters to the school types 1, 2, and 3, the highest significant value of 0.794 association was recorded by the high school to MP6. In contrast, the other school types indicated lower values.

Hence, in straightforward terms, learners at all educational levels seemingly disagreed that teaching/learning concrete/symbolic games in an AI-based classroom positively affects a better understanding of the concept/topics. Consequently, H3

Table 9 Omnibus test of H3-H5

Likelihood ratio Chi-square	df	Sig
26.180	10	0.004

Table 10 Tests of model effects of H3-H5

Source		Type III		
		Wald Chi-square	df	Sig
MP3		1.541	3	0.673
MP4		10.021	3	0.018
MP5		3.768	2	0.152
MP6		5.474	2	0.065

Table 11 Parameter estimates of H3-H5

Parameter		B	Std. Error	95% Wald confidence interval		Hypothesis test		
				Lower	Upper	Wald Chi-square	df	Sig
Threshold	[School type = 1]	−6.250	1.5985	−9.383	−3.117	15.288	1	<0.001
	[School type = 2]	−5.717	1.5547	−8.764	−2.670	13.521	1	<0.001
	[School type = 3]	0.380	1.1582	−1.890	2.650	0.108	1	0.743
[MP3 = 1]		0.769	1.6806	−2.525	4.063	0.209	1	0.647
[MP3 = 2]		1.953	1.7799	−1.536	5.441	1.203	1	0.273
[MP3 = 3]		1.021	1.2282	−1.386	3.428	0.691	1	0.406
[MP3 = 4]		0[a]						
[MP4 = 1]		−2.615	2.4151	−7.348	2.119	1.172	1	0.279
[MP4 = 2]		−1.370	2.0810	−5.449	2.708	0.434	1	0.510
[MP4 = 3]		4.698	2.2479	0.292	9.104	4.368	1	0.037
[MP4 = 4]		0[a]						
[MP5 = 1]		−3.517	2.0448	−7.524	0.491	2.958	1	0.085
[MP5 = 2]		−4.091	2.1088	−8.224	0.042	3.764	1	0.052
[MP5 = 3]		0[a]						
[MP6 = 1]		0.270	1.0359	−1.760	2.301	0.068	1	0.794
[MP6 = 2]		3.078	1.3586	0.415	5.741	5.133	1	0.023
[MP6 = 3]		0[a]						
(Scale)		1[b]						

was rejected. Still, learners'/students' responses indicated that apparent learning of concepts by both concrete and symbolic game representations positively affects the better understanding of the concept due to their previous knowledge of topics. Therefore, H4 was accepted. In considering H5, learners/students agree that apparent learning of concepts by starting with concrete representations and gradually replacing them with symbolic game representations positively affects a better understanding of the concept. Hence, H5 was accepted. Degree and Postgraduate were systematically excluded by the GLM-Regression model because the learners that constituted these two dimensions were insignificant in the collected data.

6 Discussions of Findings

Through five hypotheses, this study examined AI-Based abstract and concrete games as a correlate of STEAM education in South African Schools.

6.1 Finding 1: AI-Based Teaching and Learning of Concrete Video Games.

Regarding the results (see Table 4), the current study found that learners' responses agree with teaching/learning concrete games, positively affecting cognition of the concept in AI-Based STEAM classrooms. Jointly what is inferred is that STEAM fields must be improved using video games to achieve the educational and economic development of South Africa. It also implies that the STEAM education approach may contribute to developing twenty-first-century skills such as critical thinking, problem-solving, collaboration, and technology literacy [10]. Finally, the implication is built on the fact that STEAM education emphasises that learners' twenty-first-century skills must be developed to solve life problems quickly [30] and exhibit collaborative work. This is consistent with empirical studies Marczewskl [20] and Sahin and Namli [27], wherein authors suggested that learning through concrete video games in AI-Based STEAM classrooms in some parts of the globe can enhance students' creativity, critical thinking, innovation, collaboration, and interpersonal communication skills. The concept of concrete video games, as inferred by Bourgonjon et al. [4], has the promising potential to be used as a teaching and learning tool. Although Vygotsky [33] suggested that games (e.g., concrete) require "conscious and deliberate control" through being "placed within a system of relations of generality" [33:172]. It is therefore essential for the South African government, for example, to include in school curriculums learning by concrete video games in STEAM classrooms to develop learners' high technological literacy so that they can bridge the gaps between the developed and the developing nations of the world [1].

6.2 Finding 2: AI-Based Teaching and Learning of Symbolic (Abstract) Games and General Perspectives.

Drawn from the results (see Table 5), the analysis of all the educational levels showed that learners agreed with teaching/learning symbolic games in AI-Based STEAM classrooms as beneficial. This finding is contrary to studies of Oyelere et al. [22], in which they suggested that learners of the symbolic game in AI-based classrooms have shown mixed results regarding learning outcomes and that there has been little consensus on the elements of symbolic games that are most effective in producing successful results. Even so, Vygotsky [33] opined that the processes of abstraction played a role in the development from an early stage of learners. Conversely, in true conceptual thought, it is essential to view "the abstracted elements apart from the totality of the concrete experience of learners in which they are embedded" [33:135]. Hence, the authors suggest that symbolic game educational games must balance familiar (ordinary) symbolic games and educational (learning) to motivate learners to learn intrinsically [21]. As presented, the results (see Tables 6, 7 and 8) showed that learning concepts by both concrete representations and symbolic representations positively affects cognition. This finding is consistent with others [14] which suggested that symbolic game representations within the concrete materials can merge with non-symbolic representations with concrete or semi-concrete materials and then again with the symbolic concept for better understanding of learners. Mancl et al. [14] provided interesting information about the connection between concrete or symbolic materials and mathematics. In contrast, Carbonneau et al.'s [6] study, warned that manipulative potential might distract learners, ultimately impeding learning.

Therefore, the current researchers opine that practically focused learning methods at the high school, certificate, and diploma levels should be adopted to enable learners to acquire concepts/topics through concrete and symbolic game representations in AI-Based STEAM classrooms. Furthermore, the overall assessment of certificate learners associating their apparent learning of concepts/topics by both concrete and symbolic game representations positively affecting better understanding also suggests that learners need direction from their teachers on how to use concrete and symbolic game representations for better understanding. Additionally, this finding supports other study [33] sociocultural perspective on the role of schooling in introducing some concepts (e.g., symbolic games). Alternatively, Vygotsky was equally aware of the danger of "empty verbalism" if such concepts are learnt (or memorised) without rich development about the concrete (p. 150). Thus, learners' likes and dislikes, as well as their belief in STEAM education, should be considered by teachers during teaching/learning for better understanding.

6.3 Theoretical Implication

The theoretical implications of this study are significant in several ways. First, the study highlights the potential of AI-based concrete and symbolic games in STEAM education in South African schools, supporting the notion that using video games can enhance students' creativity, critical thinking, innovation, collaboration, and interpersonal communication skills. Second, the study validates the role of concrete and symbolic game representations in the learning process, supporting the sociocultural perspective of Vygotsky on the role of schooling in introducing some concepts. Furthermore, the study contributes to the literature by providing empirical evidence of the effectiveness of AI-based concrete and symbolic games as teaching and learning tools in STEAM education. The findings have significant implications for policymakers and curriculum designers in South Africa and other countries, as it suggests that the inclusion of learning by concrete and symbolic video games in STEAM classrooms can develop learners' technological literacy, bridging the gaps between developed and developing nations. Overall, the study's theoretical implications provide valuable insights for educators, researchers, and policymakers into the potential of AI-based concrete and symbolic games in STEAM education, contributing to the growing body of literature in this field.

6.4 Conclusions

In conclusion, the results of this study suggest that the use of concrete and symbolic games in AI-Based STEAM education can positively influence learners' cognitive development and twenty-first-century skills such as critical thinking, problem-solving, collaboration, and technology literacy. These findings are consistent with previous research and support the implementation of video games in STEAM curriculums as a practical approach to improving educational and economic development in South Africa. Though, it is important to consider the balance between familiar and educational symbolic games and provide learners with direction on how to effectively use concrete and symbolic game representations for better understanding. Ultimately, this study highlights the potential for technology-based teaching methods to enhance the quality of education and bridge the gap between developed and developing nations.

References

1. G. O. Agyedu, F. Donkor, and S. Obeng, Teach Yourself Research Methods, UEW, Kumasi, 2011.
2. R. Y. Bayeck, "Exploring video games and learning in South Africa: An integrative review," Educational Technology Research and Development, vol. 68, no. 5, pp. 2775–2795, 2020.
3. D. M. Belenky and L. Schalk, "The effects of idealized and grounded materials on learning, transfer, and interest: An organizing framework for categorizing external knowledge representations," Educational Psychology Review, vol. 26, no. 1, pp. 27–50, 2014.
4. J. Bourgonjon, M. Valcke, and R. Soetaert, "Students' perceptions about the use of video games in the classroom," Computers & Education, vol. 54, no. 4, pp. 1145–1156, 2010.
5. J. S. Bruner and U. P. J. Bruner, Toward a Theory of Instruction, Cambridge, MA: Harvard University Press, 1966.
6. K. J. Carbonneau, S. C. Marley, and J. P. Selig, "A meta-analysis of the efficacy of teaching mathematics with concrete manipulatives," Journal of Educational Psychology, vol. 105, no. 2, pp. 380–400, 2013.
7. L. Cohen, L. Manion, and K. Morrison, Research Methods in Education, 7th ed., London: Routledge, 2011.
8. V. Davydov, Soviet Studies in Mathematics Education: Volume 2. Types of Generalizations in Instruction: Logical and Psychological Problem in Structuring School Curricula, Reston, VA: The National Council of Teachers of Mathematics, 1990.

9. M. M. Flores, V. Hinton, and S. D. Strozier, "Teaching subtraction and multiplication with regrouping using the concrete-representational-abstract sequence and strategic instruction model," Learning Disabilities Research and Practice, vol. 29, no. 2, pp. 75–88, 2014.
10. N. A. J. Graham and L. Brouillette, "Using arts integration to make science learning memorable in the upper elementary grades: A quasi-experimental study," Journal for Learning Through the Arts, vol. 12, no. 1, 2017.
11. P. Leedy and J. Ormrod, Practical Research: Planning and Design, 9th ed., Boston: Pearson Education International, 2010.
12. A. Lenhart, J. Kahne, E. Middaugh, A. R. Macgill, C. Evans, and J. Vitak, "Teens, video games, and civics: Teens' gaming experiences are diverse and include significant social interaction and civic engagement," Pew Internet & American Life Project, 2008.
13. R. L. Magruder, "Solving linear equations: A comparison of concrete and virtual manipulatives in middle school mathematics," Doctoral dissertation, Univ. of Kentucky, 2012. [Online]. Available: http://uknowledge.uky.edu/cgi/viewcontent.cgi?article=1001&context=edc_etds
14. D. B. Mancl, S. C. Miller, and M. C. Kennedy, "Using the concrete-representational-abstract sequence with integrated strategy instruction to teach subtraction with regrouping to students with learning disabilities," Learning Disabilities Research and Practice, vol. 27, no. 4, pp. 152–166, 2012.
15. E. Mårell-Olsson, "Teachers' perception of gamification as a teaching design," Interaction Design and Architecture(s), no. 53, pp. 70–100, 2022.
16. N. M. McNeil and D. H. Uttal, "Rethinking the use of concrete materials in learning: Perspectives from development and education," Child Development Perspectives, vol. 3, no. 3, pp. 137–139, 2009.
17. M. J. Miller, "Reliability and validity," Western International University, 2009. [Online]. Available: www.michaeljmillerphd.com/res
18. P. Moreno-Ger, D. Burgos, I. Martínez-Ortiz, J. L. Sierra, and B. Fernández-Manjón, "Educational game design for online education," Computers in Human Behavior, vol. 24, no. 6, pp. 2530–2540, 2008.
20. A. Marczewski, Gamification: A Simple Introduction & a Bit More, 2013. [Online]. Available: https://books.google.co.za/books?id=IOu9kPjlndYC&source=gbs_navlinks_s
21. M. Montessori, The Advanced Montessori Method, New York: Frederick A. Stokes Company, 1917.
22. S. S. Oyelere et al., "Artificial intelligence in African schools: Towards a contextualized approach," in Proc. 2022 IEEE Global Engineering Education Conf. (EDUCON), 2022. [Online]. Available: https://doi.org/10.1109/educon52537.2022.9766550
23. J. Piaget, Science of Education and the Psychology of the Child, Cambridge, MA: MIT Press, 1971.
24. N. R. Prestopnik and K. Crowston, "Gaming for (citizen) science: Exploring motivation and data quality in the context of crowdsourced science through the design and evaluation of a social-computational system," in Proc. Int. Conf. e-Science, 2011. [Online]. Available: https://doi.org/10.1109/esciencew.2011.14
19. K. K. K., "Rural-based science, technology, engineering and mathematics teachers' and learners' acceptance of mobile learning," South African Journal of Information Management, vol. 22, no. 1, pp. 1–10, 2020.
25. A. Rubin and E. R. Babbie, Essential Research Methods for Social Work, Pacific Grove, CA: Cengage Learning, 2012.
26. M. C. Şahin and N. A. Namli, "Gamification and effects on students' science lessons achievement," Int. J. New Trends Educ. Their Implic., vol. 7, no. 1, pp. 41–47, 2016.
27. M. Şahin and N. A. Namlı, "Investigation of preservice teachers' attitudes to use technology in education," Turkish Journal of Social Research, vol. 23, no. 1, pp. 95–112, 2019.
28. E. Schulz, L. Bertram, M. D. Hofer, and J. M. Nelson, "Exploring the space of human exploration using Entropy Mastermind," in Proc. Cognitive Science Conf., 2019, pp. 2762–2768. [Online]. Available: https://dblp.uni-trier.de/db/conf/cogsci/cogsci2019

29. U. Sekaran and R. Bougie, Research Methods for Business: A Skill Building Approach, Hoboken, NJ: John Wiley & Sons, 2010.
30. K. Tseng, C. C. Chang, S. Lou, and W. Chen, "Attitudes towards science, technology, engineering and mathematics (STEM) in a project-based learning (PjBL) environment," Int. J. Technol. Des. Educ., vol. 23, no. 1, pp. 87–102, 2013.
31. C. Udeozor, F. Russo-Abegão, and J. Glassey, "Perceptions and factors affecting the adoption of digital games for engineering education: Mixed-method research," Int. J. Educ. Technol. High. Educ., vol. 20, no. 1, 2023.
32. UNESCO, The Blue Dot: Reimagining Education—Beyond the Rhetoric, UNESCO, 2021.
33. L. S. Vygotsky, Thought and Language, Cambridge, MA: MIT Press, 1986.

Artificial Intelligence Tools and Sustainable Development

Jonathan NGUGI and Gichuki Atenya

Abstract Artificial Intelligence (AI) has emerged as a transformative technology, playing a critical role in advancing sustainable development. This paper examines the intersection of AI tools and sustainable development, focusing on key areas such as environmental protection, resource management, and societal well-being. By leveraging AI for climate change mitigation, biodiversity conservation, and waste management, we can achieve significant environmental benefits. In resource management, AI enhances water resource management, agricultural practices, and sustainable urban planning. Additionally, AI contributes to societal well-being through improved healthcare, personalized education, and effective disaster response. Despite its potential, the implementation of AI in sustainable development faces challenges, including data privacy concerns, algorithmic bias, and the need for adequate infrastructure and expertise. Addressing these challenges is crucial for maximizing AI's positive impact on sustainability. This paper will cover three main areas where AI impacts sustainable development: environmental protection, resource management, and societal well-being. Each section delves into specific applications, providing case studies and examples to illustrate AI's role. This paper provides a comprehensive overview of current AI applications in sustainable development, discusses their potential impacts, and explores the ethical and practical considerations involved. By doing so, it aims to contribute to the ongoing discourse on how AI can be harnessed to create a more sustainable and equitable future.

Keywords Artificial intelligence · Sustainable development · Environmental protection · Resource management · Societal well-being

J. NGUGI (✉) · G. Atenya
University of Lay Adventists of Kigali, Kigali, Rwanda
e-mail: phialn1@gmail.com

J. Marx Gómez et al. (eds.), *Advancement in Embedded and Mobile Systems*, Progress in IS, https://doi.org/10.1007/978-3-031-99219-3_17

1 Introduction

"Sustainable development is development that meets the needs of the present without compromising the ability of future generations to meet their own needs."

Source: UN World Commission on Environment and Development.

"Sustainability is based on a simple principle: Everything that we need for our survival and well-being depends, either directly or indirectly, on our natural environment. To pursue sustainability is to create and maintain the conditions under which humans and nature can exist in productive harmony to support present and future generations."

Source: US Environmental Protection Agency.

Sustainable development aims to meet the needs of the present without compromising the ability of future generations to meet their own needs. This paper examines the role of AI in promoting sustainable development across various sectors.

UN sustainable development goals

1.1 Background

Pradhan et al. [1] assert that the concept of sustainable development has gained global attention due to increasing environmental concerns and social inequalities. Artificial Intelligence (AI) has rapidly evolved from a niche field of computer science to a transformative technology with broad applications across various domains. AI's capabilities in processing vast amounts of data, learning from patterns, and making informed decisions have opened new avenues for addressing complex global challenges. One of the most pressing challenges of our time is sustainable development—meeting the needs of the present without compromising the ability of future generations to meet their own needs. Sustainable development encompasses environmental protection, efficient resource management, and the enhancement of societal well-being [2].

Concurrently, AI has advanced rapidly, offering new tools and methods to tackle these issues. [3] asserts that Artificial Intelligence (AI) has revolutionized various sectors by automating processes, analyzing large datasets, and making informed decisions. Its potential to drive sustainable development is immense, providing innovative solutions for environmental protection, resource management, and societal well-being. This paper explores how AI tools are currently being used to advance sustainable development goals and addresses the challenges and ethical considerations associated with their implementation [3].

1.2 Importance of AI in Sustainable Development

Binu and KJ [4] asserts that AI's role in sustainable development is multifaceted because it offers innovative solutions for mitigating climate change, conserving biodiversity, managing natural resources, and improving societal well-being. By harnessing AI, we can enhance predictive capabilities, optimize resource use, and develop more effective strategies for sustainability. For instance, AI-driven models can predict climate patterns, helping policymakers design better climate action plans. In agriculture, AI can improve crop yields and reduce resource wastage through precision farming techniques. Furthermore, AI's potential to revolutionize healthcare and education can lead to significant improvements in human development indicators [5].

1.3 Objectives

This paper aims to explore the intersection of AI tools and sustainable development. It provides a comprehensive overview of current AI applications in key areas of sustainability, discusses their potential impacts, and examines the ethical and practical challenges involved in their implementation. By highlighting both the opportunities and obstacles, this paper seeks to contribute to the ongoing discourse on how AI can be leveraged to create a more sustainable and equitable future.

1.4 Sample Case Study

The transformative potential of artificial intelligence (AI) is just beginning to take place, [6] President of the Global Learning Council (GLC). GLC is a global organization committed to advancing the use of science and technology to improve outcomes for learners. In his keynote speech, "Learning from Nature and Machines," at this year's annual conference held in Villarssur-Ollon, Switzerland, [6] noted that he is no longer apprehensive about AI. Instead, he says AI brings endless opportunities, creating new knowledge and wisdom. His lengthy speech contained many examples of nature-inspired innovations and how humanity is leveraging AI to unlock some mysteries. In this post, I attempt to review Suresh's speech.

Nature and AI are inspiring transformative innovations. Suresh demonstrated a remarkable example of collective intelligence and self-organization using the phenomenon of migratory birds flying in a V-shaped formation. This aerodynamic arrangement reduces air resistance and energy expenditure for each bird, as they can take advantage of the upward lift generated by the bird's flapping wings in front. Moreover, the V-formation allows the birds to communicate and coordinate their movements more efficiently, as they can see each other and adjust their positions and speeds accordingly. The V-formation is not innate but learned by young birds from their elders during their first migration. Thus, the birds demonstrate both individual and social learning and the ability to optimize their flight performance through cooperation and adaptation [6].

Nature: Google Images

Nature-inspired Innovations: *Google Images*

Zerouaoui et al. [7] assert that a similar principle of aerodynamics and coordination can be applied to artificial systems, such as fighter jets. By flying in a V-formation, the jets can reduce their drag, increase their range, and improve their communication and situational awareness. The jets can also adjust their formation depending on the mission objectives and environmental conditions, such as weather, terrain, or enemy threats. The V-formation of fighter jets is an example of how engineers leverage nature to innovate complex war machinery.

Esser et al. [8] posit that another fascinating example of nature and AI is the Venus flytrap, a carnivorous plant that can capture and digest insects. The Venus flytrap has a unique mechanism for trapping its prey: it has two lobes on each leaf that are sensitive to touch and can snap shut when stimulated by an insect. The plant can distinguish between living and non-living stimuli, avoiding wasting energy on inanimate objects. The plant also secretes digestive enzymes that break down the insect's body and absorb nutrients.

The Venus flytrap inspires new knowledge in various fields, such as robotics, biotechnology, and medicine. For instance, researchers have developed a bio-inspired robot that mimics the snapping motion of the Venus flytrap and can capture fast-moving objects with high accuracy and efficiency. The robot can also be controlled by electrical signals, making it possible to integrate it with artificial neural networks and sensors. Another example is developing a synthetic material that can change shape and function, like the Venus flytrap, which can be used for applications such as drug delivery, tissue engineering, and intelligent textiles. The Venus flytrap exemplifies how nature and AI can enrich each other and create novel solutions for complex challenges [8].

Let me share one last example, which is more profound. Subra and others at the National University of Singapore transformed sunflower pollen into paper and, ultimately, a paper-like material that can be used for electronic devices, such as wearable sensors and solar cells. The researchers used a chemical process to transform the pollen grains into hollow microcapsules coated with carbon or other materials to create flexible and conductive films. These films have remarkable properties, such as self-healing, biodegradability, and tunable optical and electrical characteristics. The researchers also demonstrated that the pollen-based films can create organic light-emitting diodes (OLEDs) that emit bright and stable light. Pollen is an abundant and renewable resource that offers a sustainable alternative to conventional materials for electronics and other applications [9]. This is another example of how nature and AI can collaborate to create innovative and eco-friendly solutions.

Finally, demonstrated the development of synthetic diamond nanoparticles is being used to deliver gene therapy for sickle cell anemia, a condition that has limitations such as availability and infection risk. Coated with gene-editing tools like CRISPR-Cas9 [10], these nanoparticles can restore normal red blood cell function and improve symptoms. They are biocompatible, stable, non-toxic, and can be tracked using fluorescence imaging, demonstrating the potential of synthetic diamonds in treating severe diseases.

We have seen how nature and AI can inspire and benefit each other in various domains and applications. By studying the mechanisms and functions of natural phenomena, such as the Venus flytrap, sunflower pollen, and synthetic diamonds, researchers can develop new technologies and materials that solve complex problems and improve human lives. Conversely, researchers can enhance the performance and functionality of natural systems and materials by applying AI techniques, such as machine learning, robotics, and gene editing. These examples show how nature and AI can form a positive feedback loop, leading to innovation and sustainability.

2 AI Tools for Environmental Protection

2.1 AI in Climate Change Mitigation

AI models predict climate patterns, optimize renewable energy sources, and improve energy efficiency. For instance, Google's DeepMind [11] has reduced the energy used for cooling data centers by 40%.

2.2 AI for Biodiversity Conservation

AI tools like remote sensing and machine learning analyze large datasets to monitor wildlife populations and habitats [12]. Projects like Wildlife Insights use AI to process camera trap images, helping in the conservation of endangered species. AI processes audio recordings to detect and identify animal calls, providing data on species presence and activity. Moreover, Machine learning models analyze satellite images to map habitats, detect changes, and monitor deforestation and land use changes. Machine learning models analyze satellite images to map habitats, detect changes, and monitor deforestation and land use changes. AI processes data from drones to create detailed habitat maps and monitor inaccessible areas. AI assists in analyzing genetic data to identify species and understand genetic diversity. AI monitors online platforms for illegal wildlife trade, aiding law enforcement. AI-powered apps enable citizens to contribute data on species sightings and environmental conditions.

2.3 Waste Management

AI-driven robotics and image recognition systems improve recycling processes by sorting materials more efficiently. Companies like AMP Robotics [13] use AI to enhance recycling rates and reduce waste in landfills.

3 AI in Resource Management

3.1 Water Resource Management

AI technologies predict water demand, manage distribution networks, and detect leaks. For example, IBM's Watson uses AI to monitor water quality and predict contamination events.

3.2 Agriculture and Food Security

AI optimizes agricultural practices through precision farming, which uses sensors and AI algorithms to enhance crop yields and reduce resource usage. Tools like Climate Corporation's FieldView platform provide farmers with insights to improve productivity sustainably.

3.3 Sustainable Urban Planning

AI analyzes data on traffic, air quality, and energy consumption to develop smart cities. AI models help design urban areas that minimize environmental impact and improve quality of life.

4 AI for Societal Well-being

4.1 Healthcare

AI-driven diagnostic tools and predictive analytics enhance healthcare delivery, making it more efficient and accessible. Machine learning models analyze medical data to detect diseases early and recommend treatments. Projects like Google's AI [14] for Health focus on early detection of diseases and personalized treatment plans. AI platforms like IBM Watson Health support doctors in making data-driven decisions.

4.2 Education

AI personalizes learning experiences and improves educational outcomes. Intelligent tutoring systems like Carnegie Learning [15] provide tailored educational content to students, promoting inclusive education. Adaptive learning platforms like Knewton [16] use AI to assess student performance and adjust content accordingly, providing a personalized learning journey.

4.3 Disaster Response

AI improves disaster response by providing early warning systems, predictive analytics, and efficient resource allocation. Machine learning models analyze data from various sources to predict natural disasters. AI models predict natural disasters, enabling timely evacuation and resource allocation. AI tools also analyze social media data to assess damage and coordinate relief efforts more effectively.

5 Challenges and Ethical Considerations

5.1 Data Privacy and Security

The use of AI raises concerns about data privacy and the security of personal information. Ensuring robust data protection measures is crucial.

5.2 Algorithmic Bias

AI systems can perpetuate or exacerbate existing biases if not properly designed and tested.

Ensuring fairness and transparency in AI algorithms is essential.

5.3 Implementation Barriers

The successful implementation of AI tools for sustainable development requires adequate infrastructure, technical expertise, and financial resources. Bridging the digital divide is necessary to ensure equitable access to AI benefits.

6 Conclusion

AI has significant potential to drive sustainable development across various sectors. By addressing environmental, resource management, and societal challenges, AI can contribute to a more sustainable and equitable world. However, it is crucial to address the associated challenges and ethical considerations to harness the full potential of AI for sustainable development.

References

1. P. Pradhan, L. Costa, D. Rybski, W. Lucht, and J. P. Kropp, "A systematic study of sustainable development goal (SDG) interactions," Earth's Future, vol. 5, no. 11, pp. 1169–1179, Nov. 2017. https://doi.org/10.1002/2017EF000632. [Online]. Available: https://agupubs.onlinelibrary.wiley.com/doi/abs/10.1002/2017EF000632.
2. U. Sdg, "Sustainable development goals. The energy progress report," Tracking SDG, vol. 7, pp. 805–814, 2019. [Online]. Available: https://trackingsdg.org/energy-progress-report2019/.
3. S. A. Adeshina and O. Aina, "The role of AI in SDG: An African perspective," in The Ethics of Artificial Intelligence for the Sustainable Development Goals, Cham: Springer International Publishing, 2023, pp. 133–143. https://doi.org/10.1007/978-3-030-90060-4_10.
4. V. P. Binu and A. M. KJ, "Helping hand of AI for achieving SDG," Journal of Applied Science, Engineering, Technology and Management, vol. 2, no. 1, pp. 29–34, 2024.
5. P. Rajpurkar, E. Chen, O. Banerjee, and E. J. Topol, "AI in health and medicine," Nature Medicine, vol. 28, no. 1, pp. 31–38, Jan. 2022. https://doi.org/10.1038/s41591-021-01614-0.
6. S. Suresh, "Biography," National Science Foundation, Jul. 2013. [Online]. Available: https://www.nsf.gov/about/history/bios/ssuresh.jsp. Accessed: Jul. 27, 2024.
7. J. Zerouaoui, A. Alaoui, B. Ettaki, and E. Chakir, "Assessing the improvements brought by artificial intelligence on the prediction of aerodynamic coefficients," in The International Conference on Artificial Intelligence and Smart Environment, Cham: Springer International Publishing, 2022, pp. 254–263. https://doi.org/10.1007/978-3-030-74291-4_20.
8. F. J. Esser, P. Auth, and T. Speck, "Artificial venus flytraps: A research review and outlook on their importance for novel bioinspired materials systems," Frontiers in Robotics and AI, vol. 7, p. 75, Nov. 2020. https://doi.org/10.3389/frobt.2020.00075.
9. Z. Zhao, Y. Hwang, Y. Yang, T. Fan, J. Song, S. Suresh, and N. J. Cho, "Actuation and locomotion driven by moisture in paper made with natural pollen," Proceedings of the National Academy of Sciences, vol. 117, no. 16, pp. 8711–8718, Apr. 2020. https://doi.org/10.1073/pnas.1917232117.
10. F. Jiang and J. A. Doudna, "CRISPR–Cas9 structures and mechanisms," Annual Review of Biophysics, vol. 46, no. 1, pp. 505–529, May 2017. https://doi.org/10.1146/annurev-biophys062215-010822.
11. J. Powles and H. Hodson, "Google DeepMind and healthcare in an age of algorithms," Health and Technology, vol. 7, no. 4, pp. 351–367, Dec. 2017. https://doi.org/10.1007/s12553-017 0179-1.
12. J. Jayanthi and K. A. Kumar, "AI-driven restoration: Enhancing biodiversity conservation and ecosystem resilience," in Explainable AI (XAI) for Sustainable Development, 1st ed., Chapman and Hall/CRC, 2024, pp. 180–193.
13. J. Pransky, "The Pransky interview: Dr. Matanya Horowitz, founder and CEO of AMP robotics," Industrial Robot: The International Journal of Robotics Research and Application, vol. 47, no. 3, pp. 319–323, Jun. 2020. https://doi.org/10.1108/IR-03-2020-0075.

14. E. Waisberg, J. Ong, M. Masalkhi, N. Zaman, P. Sarker, A. G. Lee, and A. Tavakkoli, "Google's AI chatbot 'Bard': A side-by-side comparison with ChatGPT and its utilization in ophthalmology," Eye, vol. 38, no. 4, pp. 642–645, Apr. 2024. https://doi.org/10.1038/s41433023-02355-0.
15. S. Ritter, The Research Behind the Carnegie Learning Math Series, Pittsburgh, PA: Carnegie Learning, 2011.
16. A. Jones and I. Bomash, "Validating mastery learning: Assessing the impact of adaptive learning objective mastery in Knewton Alta," in Artificial Intelligence in Education: 19th International Conference, AIED 2018, London, UK, Jun. 27–30, 2018, Proceedings, Part II, Cham: Springer International Publishing, 2018, pp. 433–437. https://doi.org/10.1007/978-3-31993843-1_34.

Enhancing Data Integration: A Research Design Proposal for End-to-End Product Entity Matching

Jan-Philipp Awick and Jorge Marx Gómez

Abstract With the increasing volume of data across various sources, Entity Matching (EM) has become crucial for integrating data sources to support decision-making and other applications. Despite technological advancements, current EM approaches offer only partial solutions, resulting in high manual effort and the need for specialized knowledge to apply these in practice. Furthermore, most approaches utilize benchmark datasets that do not comprehensively reflect real-world data heterogeneity, thereby affecting model robustness. This paper proposes a research design proposal for the development of an end-to-end EM solution for real-world entities, with a focus on product data. By addressing all EM process steps with customized and pre-configured models, this research aims to ensure more accurate and robust integration results while significantly reducing the need for manual effort and enhancing process automation. We discuss current challenges and highlight the research gap for an automated and tailored end-to-end solution for EM.

Keywords Data integration · Entity matching · Product entity matching · Record linkage · Artificial intelligence

1 Introduction

The rapid advancement of digitalization has led to an unprecedented generation of data in various domains like e-commerce or healthcare. This vast and diverse data holds significant potential for enhancing decision-making and operational efficiency across industries. The volume of annually generated digital data is projected to continue its exponential growth, underscoring the necessity for effective data management [13, 26, 37]. Due to the distributed nature of data, it is essential to integrate

J.-P. Awick (✉) · J. Marx Gómez
Carl von Ossietzky Universität Oldenburg, Oldenburg, Germany
e-mail: jan-philipp.awick@uni-oldenburg.de

J. Marx Gómez
e-mail: jorge.marx.gomez@uni-oldenburg.de

J. Marx Gómez et al. (eds.), *Advancement in Embedded and Mobile Systems*, Progress in IS, https://doi.org/10.1007/978-3-031-99219-3_18

information from various sources to provide comprehensive insights and leverage the potential of large data volumes. Data Integration (DI) is used to combine information and provide a unified view on information from various sources [12]. DI involves three key steps: *(1) Schema Matching*, *(2) Entity Matching (EM)*, and *(3) Data Fusion*. Schema Matching aligns data schemas, EM identifies and links records representing the same real-world entities, and Data Fusion merges matched data into a coherent dataset [9, 16, 21, 35]. EM is the most important step in DI [8]. The evolution from rule-based methods to Machine Learning (ML) and Deep Learning (DL) techniques, including Transformer architecture, has improved EM by increasingly capturing more syntactic and semantic information [3, 8, 19]. Thus, effective EM not only improves DI but also amplifies the value of integrated data across multiple domains.

2 Problem Statement

Despite technological advances, integrating heterogeneous data sources remains a significant challenge [36]. This is particularly the case for product data, which presents challenging data heterogeneity issues and can vary widely even for identical products. For instance, product information might be formatted differently, with dimensions presented either as atomic attributes (e.g., height, width, and depth) or as unstructured text (e.g., descriptions), making alignment complex. Other examples for data heterogeneity issues include variations in units (e.g., kilogram and pound) or abbreviations. In addition, product data often contains distinctive details, such as model numbers, where subtle differences determine whether two products are considered a match [24, 38]. An example is visualized in Fig. 1. Although the titles of both products are similar and contain overlapping information (in bold), only the second entry is a match. This highlights the complexity of distinguishing between products.

Current EM research has three major limitations:

Partial solutions Most of these approaches focus exclusively on a subset of the EM process steps. The EM process consists of four steps: *data preparation*, *blocking*, *pair comparison* and *classification*. The data preparation step involves data cleaning, while blocking reduces the number of necessary comparisons by grouping

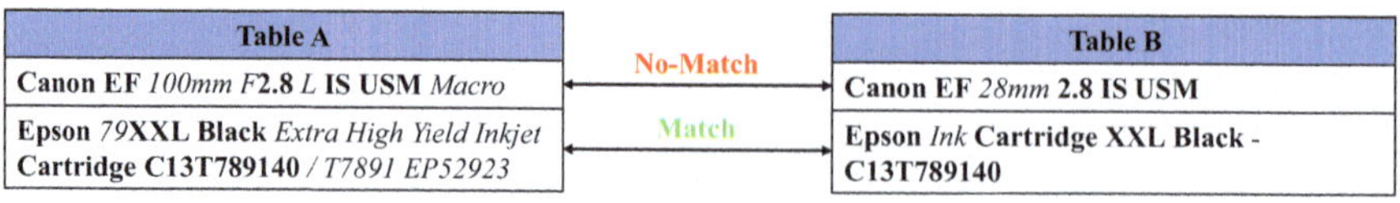

Fig. 1 Example of matching and non-matching products despite high similarity from [34]

similar entries into blocks. Pair comparison calculates similarity metrics, which are then used in the classification step to determine whether two entries are a match or non-match [16]. Most approaches mainly consider the steps *pair comparison* and *classification* [1]. Consequently, existing approaches provide only partial solutions and do not address the full EM process. Since these steps build on and influence each other, the choice of appropriate methods for each step significantly influences the integration result [17].

Reliance on benchmark data The integration of heterogeneous data is further complicated by the fact that many research approaches use benchmark data for development and evaluation [4, 16]. These pre-annotated datasets often have a similar structure and a uniform number of attributes to represent the same real-world entity [24]. An analysis conducted as part of this research on real product data provided by an industry partner has revealed significant heterogeneity. This domain-specific data includes specifications such as DIN/ISO standards and unique dimensions (e.g., bore diameters). Since these specifications are crucial for differentiating between products, addressing data heterogeneity issues in practical data is essential. Consequently, relying solely on benchmark data can limit the performance and robustness of models in real-world scenarios [4, 39].

Lack of automation Current approaches leverage pre-trained neural networks, also known as pre-trained language model (PLM). These models, trained on large amounts of text data, are capable of capturing the semantics and syntax of natural language. For the application in EM, these models are fine-tuned with task-specific data to improve the performance compared to non fine-tuned models [19]. However, despite the improvement from fine-tuning, this approach is labor intensive due to the need for label annotation to create training data [27]. The missing automation limits the applicability of these approaches, as labeled data are rarely available in real-world settings [3, 17].

The limitations described above highlight a significant research gap in the development of a robust end-to-end EM solution for real-world product data. A solution must consider all steps of the EM process and increase automation by incorporating pre-trained models and pre-configured approaches usable without the need for labeled training data for fine-tuning.

3 Related Work

The research of EM has a long history, beginning with the first approach to probabilistic EM in 1969 [11]. Subsequently, numerous approaches have been developed, evolving alongside advancements in state-of-the-art (SOTA) technologies. These approaches can be divided into three technical stages [16]. The first approaches were rule-based systems where the rules were defined manually. Then, traditional ML models were used to automate the creation of rules by training a model on annotated data (e.g., [6]). With the advent of DL, deep neural networks, e.g., recurrent neural networks [10, 23], and models based on the Transformer architecture have been employed. Current approaches predominantly use transformer-based PLMs, which have already been pre-trained with a large amount of data, and then fine-tune these models for specific tasks (e.g. [5, 28]). Frameworks such as Ditto [18] or LinkTransformer [2] facilitate the fine-tuning process for different models. Recent approaches are exploring the use of generative Large Language Models (LLMs) such as GPT4 for use in EM [25, 32].

The related literature for this research can be divided into two categories: (1) Product Entity Matching and (2) end-to-end solutions.

(1) Product Entity Matching: There are publications that focus specifically on EM for product data, known as Product Entity Matching (PEM). For PEM, only studies utilizing PLM were considered, as these represent the current SOTA. Most research focuses on optimizing the classification step, where each candidate pair is evaluated to determine whether it is a match or non-match. Transformer-based models, such as BERT, are used for this binary classification problem, adapting to product data through fine-tuning [22, 40]. In order to better adapt PLMs to the data and the specific task of EM, [1, 31, 33] apply contrastive or intermediate learning before the actual fine-tuning step. A combination of a supervised and an unsupervised model for PEM in offline retail scenarios was presented by [20], aiming to reduce the manual effort required for labeling training data. [30] propose a multi-class classification model, by fine-tuning a PLM, to determine whether an entity pair is a match or a non-match, and to predict an entity identifier such as the GTIN. However, these studies primarily relied on benchmark datasets and focused on individual steps rather than the entire EM process.

(2) End-to-end solutions: Relevant studies focusing the development of end-to-end solutions are Magellan [7] and Machop [41]. Both provide various approaches for all EM process steps, but only Machop offers SOTA functionalities with fine-tuning of PLMs. However, these studies do not specifically address product data. The most relevant work by [17] developed a pre-configured end-to-end EM process for company data by developing solutions for data heterogeneity issues based on real-world use-cases. Nonetheless, this study focused on company data and primarily employed rule-based methods, which are not aligned with the current SOTA.

Consequently, the problems of only partial solutions, reliance on benchmark data and lack of automation described in Sect. 2 remain unresolved in the current literature. To the best of the authors' knowledge there are currently no publications addressing all problems by providing an end-to-end EM solution with pre-configured SOTA approaches tailored to product data.

4 Research Questions

To address the described research gap, this research aims to design, prototype, and evaluate an end-to-end DI solution that encompasses all EM process steps and is tailored to the data heterogeneity issues of real product data. By leveraging already trained models and pre-configured SOTA approaches, the aim is to increase automation and to ensure better and more robust results for PEM. Therefore, the following research question (RQ) and sub-research question (SRQ) have to be addressed.

RQ: How can an end-to-end Entity Matching solution for product data be developed? To answer the main RQ of this research, the following SRQ are stated.

SRQ1: What approaches for conducting Entity Matching exist in the literature? This SRQ aims to provide an overview of the current SOTA in EM. The artefact includes available approaches to solve this task. As outlined in Sect. 3, there are various approaches that differ technically. This overview is essential for the implementation phase, as it will guide the appropriate selection of methods, ensuring that the chosen approaches are suitable for specific tasks by considering their respective advantages and disadvantages.

SRQ2: What data heterogeneity issues can be identified in product data sources? SRQ2 focuses on identifying data heterogeneity issues prevalent in product data. As product data can be highly different in various dimensions such as data structure level, attribute level, and value level, numerous data heterogeneity issues can be present. The artefact of this research question will be a comprehensive list of data heterogeneity issues, which are derived from different sources, ensuring that also real-world use cases are covered. These will have a direct impact on the implementation, since custom solution to these issues are required.

SRQ3: Which of the approaches from SRQ1 are suitable for solving the data heterogeneity issues identified in SRQ2? This SRQ addresses the question of how an end-to-end EM solution can be developed tailored to the data heterogeneity issues derived in SRQ2. This will involve the conceptualization, implementation and evaluation of a prototype, comprising components based on the selected approaches from SRQ1, which are designed to address the data heterogeneity issues identified in SRQ2.

5 Research Design Proposal for Enhanced Product Entity Matching

This section describes the research design proposal for addressing the research questions (see Fig. 2). The design proposal is derived from the SRQs described in Sect. 4 and defines the artefacts and sources that will be utilized. It encompasses the steps of implementation and evaluation, which will be conducted in an iterative process. Additionally, this section details the methodological approach to each of the research questions.

SRQ1: Identification of Entity Matching approaches: The first component of the research design proposal involves a comprehensive list of EM approaches, reflecting the current SOTA in this research area as an artefact. To achieve this, a suitable methodology is a structured literature review (SLR) followed by a qualitative content analysis to systematically search and analyze literature. The SLR includes current

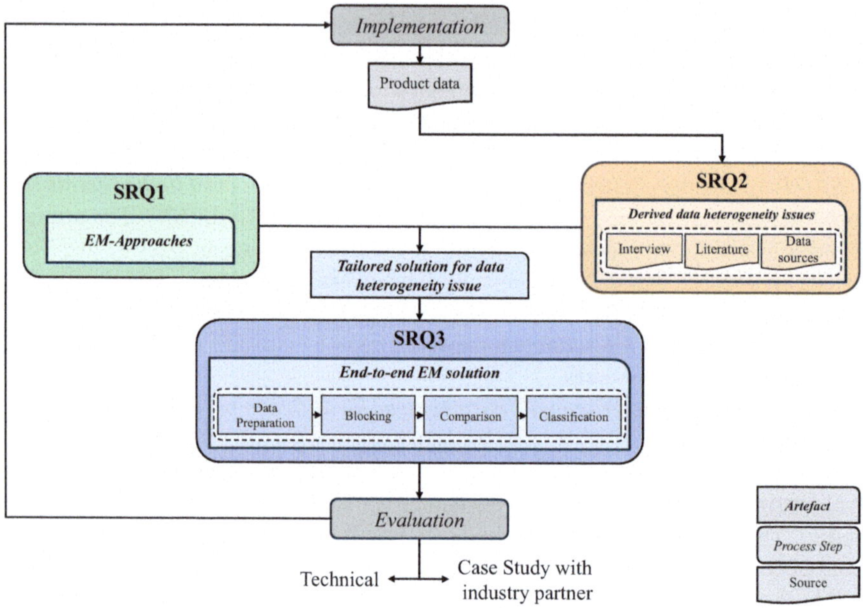

Fig. 2 Research design proposal for the development of an end-to-end Entity Matching solution for product data

research studies for all process steps of the EM process. The results are then analyzed and structured according to relevant dimensions (e.g., process step, utilized model). Since the objective is to develop a pre-configured and highly automated end-to-end EM solution, it is crucial to provide this overview of existing approaches. This enables an informed selection of suitable approaches and the development of tailored components for specific data heterogeneity issues.

SRQ2: Deriving data heterogeneity issues: Deriving data heterogeneity issues for product data is a crucial component for this research, as it enables the customization of the EM solution to the specific data. Product data can vary widely depending on the domain (e.g., electronic, crafts), leading to diverse data heterogeneity issues. In order to obtain a comprehensive collection of issues, it is essential to include different sources. One source is existing literature, which can provide theoretical insights into data heterogeneity issues. However, a limitation of this source is that most studies use benchmark data, which may not fully reflect issues in real-world. To address this limitation, interviews with practitioners who work with product data will be conducted. These practitioners can offer practical insights and ensure the relevance of the identified issues. In parallel, an analysis of product data sources from different domains will be performed to uncover further generalizable heterogeneity issues. By integrating insights from literature, practitioner interviews, and data analysis, this research will provide a comprehensive collection of data heterogeneity issues, forming the foundation for the implementation of the EM solution.

SRQ3: Selection and customization of approaches based on data heterogeneity issues: Based on the specific data heterogeneity issues derived in SRQ2, suitable approaches from SRQ1 will be selected, customized, and embedded into the prototype, ultimately resulting in an end-to-end EM solution tailored to product data. The prototype should include components for each of the process steps. Depending on the selected approach, the customization should ensure that non-learning approaches will be pre-configured with optimal parameters, while DL models will be fine-tuned on relevant product data. Additionally, the incorporation of LLMs represents a promising solution, as they do not require extensive fine-tuning with large amounts of training data. Instead, prompt-tuning can be leveraged to guide the model's behavior, making it more adaptable to specific tasks. The customization will include prompt-tuning with well-structured and contextually appropriate prompts. Overall, customizing the EM process in this manner enhances automation and improves its applicability in practice. Another critical aspect is the interdependence between process steps. For instance, if a matching entity is not found in the step blocking, it will not be considered in subsequent steps, leading to a missing entity in the results. Therefore, it is crucial to evaluate the entire process as well as the intermediate results of the individual steps.

The evaluation of the developed prototype should be conducted both technically and practically to ensure robustness. For the technical evaluation common metrics (e.g., F1-Score) will be used to measure the results on benchmark datasets to provide comparability to existing approaches. Additionally, case studies in collaboration with industry partners will assess the prototype's robustness across different use cases and its applicability without major adjustments, thereby ensuring high levels of automation.

The final outcome will be an EM solution that encompasses all process steps with pre-configured approaches, providing robust results and high automation for product data. Despite the focus on product data, the proposed methodological approach can likely also be transferred to other real-world entities, such as person, by generalizing entity-specific data heterogeneity issues and developing solutions accordingly.

6 Preliminary Results and Discussion

Kruse et al. [17] have shown that the automation of the EM process can be achieved by developing preconfigured approaches. For this purpose, recurring patterns (called data heterogeneity issues in this paper) were identified in data and specialized solutions were developed for these. In addition, it was shown that the individual steps of the EM process influence each other [14]. For instance, if one entry of a matching pair contains abbreviations while the other does not, a calculated similarity score is likely to be low, leading to a wrong classification result [15]. The blocking step groups similar entries into blocks, ensuring that only comparisons within each block need to be conducted, thereby reducing computational complexity. However, this also implies that matching entries not grouped into the same block are excluded from subsequent steps, potentially leading to missed matches [29]. This underscores the necessity for aligning the approaches used in the individual steps to ensure optimal performance of the solution to be developed.

Initial analyses of data from an industrial partner have shown that these are highly heterogeneous and contain domain-specific data heterogeneity issues. For instance, product names included DIN/ISO standards, specific abbreviations (e.g., "verz." instead of "verzinkt", "schubl." instead of "schublade") and dimensions (e.g., bore diameters) as unstructured text. As this information can have a decisive influence on the classification into match and non-match, extensive processing of this specific product information is required. Therefore, it is necessary to derive relevant data heterogeneity issues, develop specialized and pre-configured solutions and embed these into an end-to-end process to ensure robust performance and high automation for DI.

7 Conclusion and Future Work

In this paper, we proposed a research design proposal for the development and evaluation of an end-to-end EM solution with a focus on product data. The objective is to achieve robust results and high automation by leveraging pre-configured approaches that are tailored to identified data heterogeneity issues. Therefore, we discussed related literature to identify the current research gap and proposed a comprehensive research design proposal. In addition, we discussed initial ideas to establish a foundation for future advancements in Data Integration. As future work, we plan to conduct further research on data heterogeneity issues and develop tailored EM solutions. Future directions include leveraging current technologies for EM, such as utilizing LLMs for data preparation and feature engineering, and classification.

References

1. Almagro, M., Jiménez, D., Ortego, D., Almazán, E., Martínez, E.: Block-scl: Blocking matters for supervised contrastive learning in product matching. arXiv preprint arXiv:2207.02008 (2022).
2. Arora, A., Dell, M.: Linktransformer: A unified package for record linkage with transformer language models. arXiv preprint arXiv:2309.00789 (2023).
3. Barlaug, N., Gulla, J.A.: Neural networks for entity matching: A survey. ACM Transactions on Knowledge Discovery from Data (TKDD) **15**(3), 1–37 (2021).
4. Binette, O., Steorts, R.C.: (almost) all of entity resolution. Science Advances **8**(12), eabi8021 (2022).
5. Brunner, U., Stockinger, K.: Entity matching with transformer architectures-a step forward in data integration. In: 23rd International Conference on Extending Database Technology, Copenhagen, 30 March-2 April 2020. OpenProceedings (2020).

6. Christen, P.: Automatic record linkage using seeded nearest neighbour and support vector machine classification. In: Proceedings of the 14th ACM SIGKDD international conference on Knowledge discovery and data mining. pp. 151–159 (2008).
7. Doan, A., Konda, P., Suganthan GC, P., Govind, Y., Paulsen, D., Chandrasekhar, K., Martinkus, P., Christie, M.: Magellan: toward building ecosystems of entity matching solutions. Communications of the ACM **63**(8), 83–91 (2020).
8. Dong, X.L., Rekatsinas, T.: Data integration and machine learning: A natural synergy. In: Proceedings of the 2018 international conference on management of data. pp. 1645–1650 (2018).
9. Dong, X.L., Srivastava, D.: Big data integration. Synthesis Lectures on Data Management **7**(1), 1–198 (2015).
10. Ebraheem, M., Thirumuruganathan, S., Joty, S., Ouzzani, M., Tang, N.: Deeper–deep entity resolution. arXiv preprint arXiv:1710.00597 (2017).
11. Fellegi, I.P., Sunter, A.B.: A theory for record linkage. Journal of the American Statistical Association **64**(328), 1183–1210 (1969).
12. Hildebrand, K., Gebauer, M., Mielke, M.: Daten- und Informationsqualität. Springer Fachmedien Wiesbaden, Wiesbaden, 5 edn. (2021).
13. IDC: Volumen der jährlich generierten/replizierten digitalen datenmenge weltweit von 2010 bis 2022 und prognose bis 2027 (in zettabyte). https://de.statista.com/statistik/daten/studie/267974/umfrage/prognose-zum-weltweit-generierten-datenvolumen/ (Mai 18 2023), in Statista. Zugriff am 13. März 2024.
14. Koumarelas, I., Jiang, L., Naumann, F.: Data preparation for duplicate detection. Journal of Data and Information Quality (JDIQ) **12**(3), 1–24 (2020).
15. Kruse, F., Awick, J.P., Gómez, J.M., Loos, P.: Developing a legal form classification and extraction approach for company entity matching: Benchmark of rule-based and machine learning approaches. In: Business Information Systems. pp. 13–26 (2021).
16. Kruse, F., Hassan, A.P., Awick, J.P., Gómez, J.M., Bui, T.: A qualitative literature review on linkage techniques for data integration. In: HICSS. pp. 1–11 (2020).
17. Kruse, F., Schröer, C., Awick, J.P., Reinkensmeier, J., Gómez, J.M.: Towards an automated record linkage process for datasource-independent company matching. In: 2022 3rd International Conference on Next Generation Computing Applications (NextComp). pp. 1–7. IEEE (2022).
18. Li, Y., Li, J., Suhara, Y., Doan, A., Tan, W.C.: Effective entity matching with transformers. The VLDB Journal **32**(6), 1215–1235 (2023).
19. Li, Y., Li, J., Suhara, Y., Doan, A., Tan, W.C.: Deep entity matching with pre-trained language models. arXiv preprint arXiv:2004.00584 (2020).
20. Lin, Z., Chen, W.: Alfa matcher: Supervised and unsupervised product entity matching model. In: 2022 IEEE 2nd International Conference on Data Science and Computer Application (ICDSCA). pp. 18–25. IEEE (2022).
21. Ma, B., Jiang, T., Zhou, X., Zhao, F., Yang, Y.: A novel data integration framework based on unified concept model. IEEE Access **5**, 5713–5722 (2017).
22. Możdżonek, M., Wróblewska, A., Tkachuk, S., Łukasik, S.: Multilingual transformers for product matching–experiments and a new benchmark in polish. In: 2022 IEEE International Conference on Fuzzy Systems (FUZZ-IEEE). pp. 1–8. IEEE (2022).
23. Mudgal, S., Li, H., Rekatsinas, T., Doan, A., Park, Y., Krishnan, G., Deep, R., Arcaute, E., Raghavendra, V.: Deep learning for entity matching: A design space exploration. In: Proceedings of the 2018 international conference on management of data. pp. 19–34 (2018).
24. Naeim abadi, A., Nayeem, M.T., Rafiei, D.: Product entity matching via tabular data. In: Proceedings of the 32nd ACM International Conference on Information and Knowledge Management. pp. 4215–4219 (2023).
25. Narayan, A., Chami, I., Orr, L., Arora, S., Ré, C.: Can foundation models wrangle your data? arXiv preprint arXiv:2205.09911 (2022).
26. Oussous, A., Benjelloun, F.Z., Lahcen, A.A., Belfkih, S.: Big data technologies: A survey. Journal of King Saud University-Computer and Information Sciences **30**(4), 431–448 (2018).

27. Paganelli, M., Del Buono, F., Baraldi, A., Guerra, F., et al.: Analyzing how bert performs entity matching. Proceedings of the VLDB Endowment **15**(8), 1726–1738 (2022).
28. Paganelli, M., Tiano, D., Guerra, F.: A multi-facet analysis of bert-based entity matching models. The VLDB Journal pp. 1–26 (2023).
29. Papadakis, G., Skoutas, D., Thanos, E., Palpanas, T.: Blocking and filtering techniques for entity resolution: A survey. ACM Computing Surveys (CSUR) **53**(2), 1–42 (2020).
30. Peeters, R., Bizer, C.: Dual-objective fine-tuning of bert for entity matching. Proceedings of the VLDB Endowment **14**, 1913–1921 (2021).
31. Peeters, R., Bizer, C.: Supervised contrastive learning for product matching. In: Companion Proceedings of the Web Conference 2022. pp. 248–251 (2022).
32. Peeters, R., Bizer, C.: Using chatgpt for entity matching. In: European Conference on Advances in Databases and Information Systems. pp. 221–230. Springer (2023).
33. Peeters, R., Bizer, C., Glavaš, G.: Intermediate training of bert for product matching. small **745**(722), 2–112 (2020).
34. Peeters, R., Der, R.C., Bizer, C.: Wdc products: A multi-dimensional entity matching benchmark. arXiv preprint arXiv:2301.09521 (2023).
35. Rahm, E.: The case for holistic data integration. In: Advances in Databases and Information Systems: 20th East European Conference, ADBIS 2016, Prague, Czech Republic, August 28-31, 2016, Proceedings 20. pp. 11–27. Springer (2016).
36. Sakshaug, J.W., Steorts, R.C.: Recent Advances in Data Integration. Journal of Survey Statistics and Methodology **11**(3), 513–517 (04 2023). https://doi.org/10.1093/jssam/smad009, https://doi.org/10.1093/jssam/smad009.
37. de Santana, M.A., de Souza Baptista, C., Alves, A.L.F., Firmino, A.A., da Silva Januário, G., da Silva Caldera, R.W.: Using machine learning and nlp for the product matching problem. In: Intelligent Sustainable Systems: Selected Papers of WorldS4 2022, Volume 2, pp. 439–448. Springer (2023).
38. Schmidt, A.: Entwicklung einer Methode zur Stammdatenintegration. Logos Verlag Berlin GmbH (2010).
39. Tancredi, A., Steorts, R., Liseo, B.: A unified framework for de-duplication and population size estimation (with discussion) (2020).
40. Tracz, J., Wójcik, P.I., Jasinska-Kobus, K., Belluzzo, R., Mroczkowski, R., Gawlik, I.: Bert-based similarity learning for product matching. In: Proceedings of Workshop on Natural Language Processing in E-Commerce. pp. 66–75 (2020).
41. Wang, J., Li, Y., Hirota, W., Kandogan, E.: Machop: an end-to-end generalized entity matching framework. In: Proceedings of the Fifth International Workshop on Exploiting Artificial Intelligence Techniques for Data Management. pp. 1–10 (2022).

An IoT Ecosystem for Smart Management of Photovoltaic Systems in Remote Areas

Mirco Mongilli, Eraste Rukundo, Viviane Ishimwe, Guido Matrella, and Paolo Ciampolini

Abstract This paper presents the architecture of a pilot network designed to test and disseminate smart control technologies for managing renewable energy plants. Leveraging the Internet of Things paradigm, the network enables remote monitoring, control, and optimized energy utilization. We propose an open, flexible, and inexpensive architecture that accommodates diverse use-cases through a hierarchical structure. A centralized cloud-based layer manages and supervises the network, while a simplified communication protocol facilitates interaction with various field units. Containerization technology ensures modular service delivery, independent of peripheral hardware. Beyond its practical applications, the system serves educational purposes. As part of the European GREATER project, it will function as a learning platform for students from participating universities. By providing hands-on experience with photovoltaic and smart control technologies in real-world settings, the system aims to foster a deeper understanding of green energy and promote environmental awareness within target communities.

Keywords Internet of Things · Renewable energy · Remote monitoring · Higher education

1 Introduction

Countries may reduce energy expenditures, adapt to fluctuating prices, and slow down global warming by utilizing renewable energy sources; in the clean energy transition, developing nations prioritize industrialization, mostly using low-carbon

M. Mongilli (✉) · E. Rukundo · V. Ishimwe · G. Matrella · P. Ciampolini
Dipartimento Di Ingegneria E Architettura, Università Di Parma, Parma, Italy
e-mail: mirco.mongilli@unipr.it

E. Rukundo
INES-RUHENGERI, Musanze, Rwanda

V. Ishimwe
Rwanda Polytechnic, IPRC Musanze, Musanze, Rwanda

J. Marx Gómez et al. (eds.), *Advancement in Embedded and Mobile Systems*, Progress in IS, https://doi.org/10.1007/978-3-031-99219-3_19

energy sources. Ensuring universal access to affordable, dependable, sustainable, and modern energy services in line with the 2030 Sustainable Development Goals [1] will be made possible by increasing international cooperation for the access of clean energy research and technology by 2030. Goal 7 of the Sustainable Development Agenda (SDG) states that all energy must be accessible, affordable, dependable, and sustainable. The availability of electricity in remote locations enhances the quality of life for the locals. Economic growth is inextricably linked to electricity [2], Therefore, the absence of electricity prevents rural off-grid communities from growing economically.

The Sustainable Energy for All (SE4All) plan can help off-grid areas by using mini-grid systems based on clean, renewable energy sources as a decentralized way to distribute electricity [3]. Key considerations in the future under the pillar of Urbanization and Agglomeration include "Sustainable supply and demand for energy, as per the vision 2050" [4], this is one of the aspirations that must remain embedded in Rwanda's long-term Green Growth and Climate Resilient Strategy, whose impact is intended to bring about mindset and developmental transformation in Rwandan society that is necessary to achieve the desired carbon–neutral and climate-resilient economy.

The National Strategy for Transformation (NST1) 2017–2024 [5] ambitiously aims to achieve universal electricity access, increasing coverage from 34.4% of households in 2017 (as of the EICV5 report [6] to 100% by 2024. In line with Rwanda's revised National Determined Contribution (NDC) to the Paris Agreement [7], the government has prioritized energy efficiency and renewable energy sources. Given the widespread rural population, approximately around 80% of which lives in remote areas [8], sustainable and affordable off-grid energy systems are crucial for achieving this goal. To ensure equitable access to electricity, Rwanda's strategic interventions therefore focus on both expanding the grid and deploying off-grid power plants in remote regions.

A key step in promoting renewable energy adoption is raising awareness of new opportunities. The GREATER[1] (Growing Rwanda Energy Awareness Through highER education) project, which aims to enhance energy awareness through higher education, is achieving this by connecting partner universities with neighboring rural areas and bringing technology directly to the field. To facilitate this, four pilot sites have been selected to host "Living Labs" (LLs). LLs are real-world environments powered by photovoltaic technology and serve various purposes. Each pilot site is managed by a Rwandan university.

The participating universities and their corresponding pilot sites are:

- University of Rwanda—College of Science and Technology (UR-CST Kigali): Bugesera agriculture farm
- University of Technology and Arts of Byumba (UTAB): Groupe Scolaire Catholique Byumba primary and secondary school

[1] This project has received funding from the European Union's ERASMUS + CBHE (Capacity Building in Higher Education) Programme Under grant agreement 101,083,081-GREATER—ERASMUS-EDU-2022-CBHE.

- Institute of Applied Sciences (INES Ruhengeri): Busengo parish
- Integrated Polytechnic Regional College (IPRC Tumba): Muyanza village.

Each LL serves multiple purposes, including:

- Community outreach and awareness: Fostering understanding of green energy
- Energy access: Providing free electricity to beneficiaries
- Educational opportunities: offering real-world learning experiences for university students and lecturers, related both to renewable energy and smart monitoring technologies.

Beyond general dissemination, each LL has a specific focus, concentrating on relevant applications and productive use of energy. To enable remote monitoring and control, the project utilizes Internet of Things (IoT) technology. This facilitates preventive maintenance, performance optimization, and other valuable functions. Additionally, it provides students with virtual workbenches for exploring various applications and developing new features.

Rwanda's development plans rely heavily on off-grid, low-power systems to achieve universal electricity access by supplying 48% of the country off-grid [9]. This will involve millions of households and necessitates sustainable and maintainable strategies. To address this, skilled technicians must be trained, and scalable supervision techniques implemented. A cloud-based architecture connecting all LLs has been designed for this purpose, creating a distributed ecosystem.

The GREATER ecosystem emphasizes openness, scalability, and flexibility to ensure its effectiveness. The project recognizes that achieving impact requires a holistic approach, considering not only technical solutions but also the provision of valuable services to target communities. These services should enable new development opportunities and promote productive energy use. Such an interdisciplinary approach necessitates active engagement from all stakeholders to foster mutually beneficial partnerships.

2 Related Work

Low-cost, low-power off-grid power plants are essential to Rwanda's national electrification strategy. Such plants can provide electricity to family homes in remote or rural areas that lack grid connectivity. Remote monitoring capabilities are essential for maintaining such a distributed system. By integrating Internet of Things (IoT) technology with global network monitoring, we can enable valuable services like power generation prediction, load scheduling, and optimization of hybrid systems. Concerning electricity metering, [10] suggests policies and a semi-private operator model in which smart metering systems and solar-powered mini-grids will increase the stability of electricity and supply power to various energy customers, thereby offering a sustainable solution to the energy issue in Rwanda. In a similar vein, the initiative [11] has produced a smart energy meter based on LoRaWAN technology.

With respect to the Remote monitoring of the Photovoltaic power consumption, [12] provides an overview of artificial intelligence and Internet of Things applications in photovoltaic plants, to enhance the effectiveness of diagnosis and remote sensing of solar photovoltaic systems. Along the same lines, [13] offers an affordable, open-source Internet of Things solution that can gather data intelligently, monitor solar station environmental conditions and produced power in real-time, and notify a remote user when solar power generation quality parameters deviate from a predetermined set of standard values. An overview of the problems that could have an impact on solar PV monitoring performance is given [14] From the load balancing and scheduling perspective, [15] proposes real-time electricity scheduling for home energy management based on the Internet of Energy (IoE) from the load balancing and load scheduling perspective. An Internet of Things (IoT)-based appliance scheduling controller for smart residential buildings is described [16] with the goal of lowering power costs and decreasing peak load.

The performance, monitoring, and maintenance of solar photovoltaic power generation can be significantly improved by using Internet of Things technology for supervision, as demonstrated [17] where remote monitoring of a solar photovoltaic plant to assess its performance was done using the GPRS module to send data to a remote server and transfer information from the sensors over the mobile radio network; a smart data gathering system has been used to collect values for battery voltage, battery current, PV voltage, PV current, grid voltage, grid current, solar insolation, and temperature. Still in the PV production monitoring perspective, [18] describes the development of a low-cost, dependable, user-friendly data logger and monitoring system, primarily for a solar household system in a rural developing nation, where all monitoring data is stored on a micro SD card by the ESP 32 microcontroller-based data logger, which then shows the data on a Blynk app. Direct downloads of data are available from the webpage for system operation analysis and verification. Regarding the management of PV production, C. K. Rao et al. [19] examined how the distributed energy resource management using a Field Programmable Gate Array (FPGA) algorithm can contribute to solar radiation forecasting, and PV energy production therefore enhancing system reliability and raising the penetration level of solar power generation by reducing the impact of uncertainty on PV energy generation. Additionally, Manu et al. [20] illustrated the concept of an Internet of Things (IoT)-based smart Energy Management System (EMS) for a Stand-Alone Photovoltaic (SAPV) system is presented. The SAPV system functions as a closed system, with all power produced by solar energy being either used within the system or stored in batteries. It is divided into three sections: IoT, energy management, and energy generation. For the EMS of the SAPV System, a brand-new constant battery operating algorithm is suggested. Since every load is connected via the Internet of Things, its status can be tracked and managed from a distance.

3 Materials and Methods

The ecosystem architecture has been designed according to the GREATER context explained in the introduction. Although currently aimed at the Living Labs network, the architecture is conceived with a wider perspective, looking forward to include private, off-grid photovoltaic plants and provide them with monitoring, control, and maintenance services.

There are two different level of the architecture; according to a bottom-up description flow, a smart "field unit" represents the lower level and it is composed by:

- a photovoltaic power source;
- a charge controller;
- one (or more) loads or actuators, exploiting the generated power;
- an inverter, if AC appliances are to be used;
- possibly one or more sensors, depending also on specific LL features;
- possibly a battery as energy-storage device;
- possibly local displays and interfaces;
- a controller board, dealing with data gathering, local management, and cloud communication.

At the upper level, a cloud-based system is responsible for collecting and processing data from peripheral units, implementing monitoring and control strategies. A dashboard is available to visualize data streams and status information. Within the same general frame, field units might differ from each other depending on the location, connected sensors, peak power produced, storage size, applications, and services deployed, i.e., a common backbone is given by the cloud system, gathering a variety of subsystems (LLs as well as private plants) and providing them with flexible and configurable services.

In the aimed prototype, four Living Lab instances will be considered, featuring different use-cases and shortly described below:

- **Living Lab 1**, located in Bugesera and managed by University of Rwanda CST Kigali, focusing on smart agriculture use-case. In particular, smart irrigation will be implemented at an avocado plantation, spanning over 6 hectares. Trees are currently watered by hand, bringing water buckets to the trees. Buckets are refilled at an uphill water tank, which in turn is filled by a diesel-powered pump lifting the water from a downhill swamp to the reservoir. The diesel-powered pump will be substituted by a solar-powered electric pump, featuring a lower power demand and a reduced volumetric flow rate (with respect to the current setup). To compensate for such a lower rate, the solar pump will operate for a longer time. Besides energy lower cost, this results in reducing noise and pollution as well, and will also avoid the need of too expensive energy-storage systems. Then, each tree will be reached by a drip-line irrigation system, powered by gravity: water flow toward driplines will be controlled by valves, upon the assessment of the actual watering needs carried out by the system. Such an assessment will be based on data coming from the field (a network of LoRaWan sensors checking for the soil moisture and possibly other plant health-related parameters: temperature, electrical conductivity, ...) and integrated with cloud information (e.g., rain forecast). The watering process can thus be fully automated and optimized upon actual needs. Through cloud dashboard, the process can be remotely monitored and demonstrated, thus supporting dissemination across farmers' community and education of both technical and agriculture students.

- **Living Lab 2**, located in Byumba at GS Catholique primary and secondary school and managed by University of Technology and Arts of Byumba. It will allow students and the surrounding community to familiarize with green energy concepts particularly photovoltaic (PV) solar panels and related applications. The main use-case is providing an already existing computer room with PV energy. Water purification will be also demonstrated there, by using ultraviolet light filtering technology to eliminate the bacteria and pathogens from water coming from local reservoirs. The integration with IoT allows for real-time monitoring and control of system performance via internet-connected devices, providing users with immediate alerts and data analytics for maintenance and operational efficiency. Another possible use case at LL2 is the security lamp system. By exploiting sensors and the cloud server communication, lamps can be turned on when needed, based on daylight conditions, on presence sensors and on other sensors (door opening, for instance), this resulting in energy savings. The IoT approach allows for security policies to be implemented and monitored at the cloud level, with alerts and dashboard control available from remote. Such applications will offer the local community tangible examples of productive use of energy and provide students with an effective workbench to experience design of smart technologies.
- **Living Lab 3**, located in Busengo and managed by INES Ruhengeri. Here, the main focus is providing the local community, gathering around the catholic parish, with energy to enable essential services. In this case, multiple use-cases are targeted. Clean, PV energy will first power the local community center, the core of the LL, serving as a meeting and training place. Among various initiatives running there, a tailoring workshop, supporting vulnerable women, will be considered, providing energy for lighting and running sewing machines and flatirons. Then, the church and the parish house will be powered, and finally a community-managed slaughter and butchery workshop will be considered for powering refrigeration units. Within such an articulated scenario, IoT and remote-control technologies will be exploited to implement priority policies, distributing energy to different loads based on real-time demand and ensuring smooth. Prospectively, PV power could be generated in Busengo at multiple locations, implementing a mini/nano grid approach, to the benefit of effectiveness and of students training as well. Each installation will be sized according to the site power usage with the capability of sharing energy between all the buildings of the mini/nano grid.
- **Living Lab 4**, located in Muyanza village and managed by Rwanda Polytechnic of Tumba, is focusing on domestic use of energy, with special emphasis on cooking challenges faced by poor families. Muyanza village consists of a group of several families living in proximity within the same communal living space, organized

in four-in-one house blocks. The LL will power one of such blocks, allowing for implementing shared usage of PV electricity and, consequently, to gain experience on IoT-based monitoring, metering and prioritizing energy distribution. The ability to control and track energy usage remotely is particularly beneficial in a setting where precise management of limited resources is critical. In addition to addressing electricity needs, the living lab also focuses on improving cooking methods. Traditionally, Muyanza's residents rely on wood and charcoal for cooking, which is time-consuming, inefficient and unhealthy. Cleaner cooking solutions will be investigated there, powered by the available PV energy. To contrast indoor air pollution, air quality sensors can be framed into the IoT picture. Also, integration with biogas sources will be considered: house blocks in Muyanza, in fact, share family-sized biogas digestors, providing gas for cooking purposes. Most of them, however, are not working properly, because of lack of maintenance and of monitoring skills from the end-user: research will be carried out to include a few sensors in the IoT framework, sensing functional parameters at the digestor (e.g., temperature, pH, pressure, …) for early recognition of problems and for remotely alerting for maintenance needs. The LL IoT system will therefore foster clean cooking practices, which can significantly impact the community's health and reduce reliance on expensive and environmentally damaging fuels.

From the above summary, a wide variability can be inferred: field units may be as simple as a single household with basic appliances or may feature a much richer, hierarchical structure: the LL1 example above, for instance, includes a main unit, powering the pump, and possibly as many sub-units as the number of independent tree clusters to be controlled, each supported by its own sensing network. In this case, the main unit also serves as the internet gateway for all subnets in the LL, and different protocols can be used for the local communication. Similarly, other LLs may feature a different articulation in sub-units and significantly differ in the IoT components.

Technical details about the system architecture are given in the following section.

4 Results and Discussion

4.1 System Design

For a better understanding, it's convenient to distinguish between distributed and centralized parts, with reference to the architecture sketch given in Fig. 1.

The distributed part is related to the field units and is replicated as many times as needed, whereas the centralized part deals with cloud management and the implementation of services. Distributed and centralized part communicates through the Internet. At the current level of deployment, the system consists only in a core part of it with a limited number of features but meaningful to the demo purpose.

The prototype field unit part consists of:

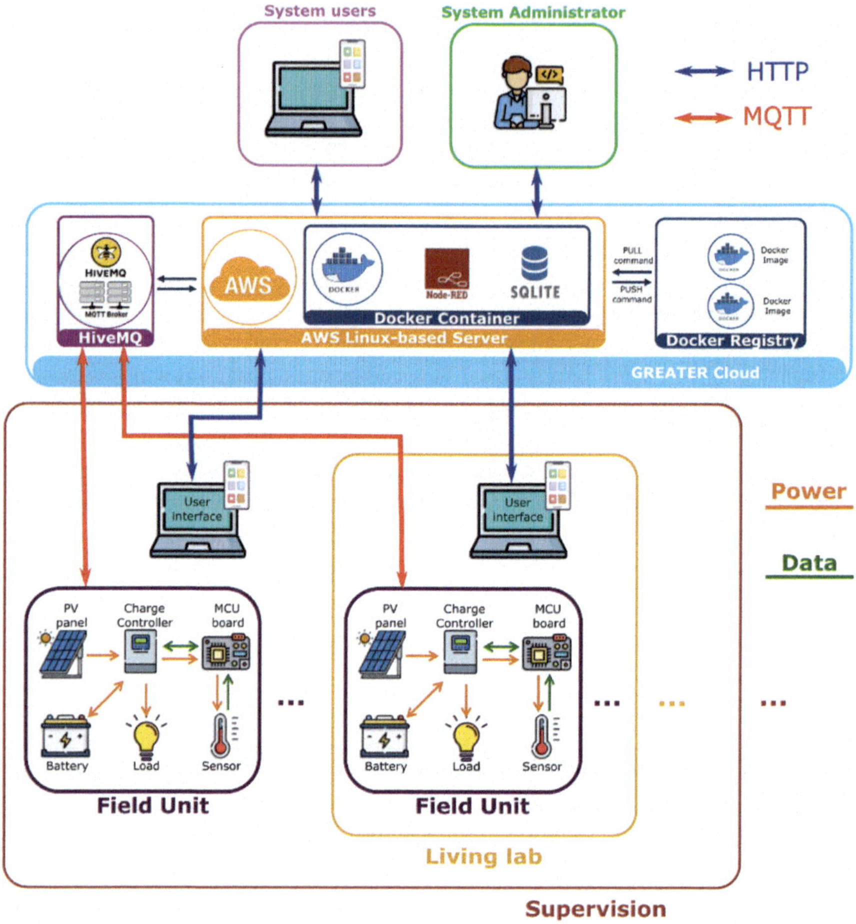

Fig. 1 Architecture of the GREATER ecosystem

- a 21-nominal-volt, 50-W-peak photovoltaic panel;
- a 12-V, 33-A-hour battery;
- a smart charge controller (EPEVER Tracer 10AN), featuring a maximum current of 10A;
- a 12-V, 6-W LED DC lamp load;
- an ESP32 microcontroller embedded in an AZ-Delivery Dev Kit C;

a transceiver MAX 485; a DHT11 temperature and relative humidity sensor. As mentioned, field units may include further sensors and features, according to the specific use case. The prototype implementation is shown in Fig. 2.

The microcontroller firmware has been designed on purpose, developing the code on Visual Studio Code integrated with the plugin Platform IO. Thanks to this IDE, the project has been organized in multiples source files: there are libraries for each

Fig. 2 Field unit prototype implementation

of the sensor used or specific functionality, setup file to define the parameters and configurations to be used during the execution and timers to schedule the tasks to be accomplished. The Wi-Fi capability of the ESP32 board have been used to have access to internet through an access point and exchange data with the cloud computing system in both directions: from the field to the central part for all measurements, from the central cloud to the field for current timestamp and commands to control some functionalities of the distributed system.

The charge controller is equipped with a voltage and current sensor for each of the lines to PV, battery, and load. Also, it provides an estimate of the battery charge status, based on internal algorithms. MPPT (Maximum Power Point Tracking) is provided by the controller itself with an algorithm develop by the company productor. The addresses of the device internal memory can be written or read thanks to the serial port over RS-485 communication standard.

In order to access to such registers through the microcontroller, the transceiver MAX 485 is needed to translate signals from RS-485 to TTL and vice versa. Furthermore, a Modbus library on the ESP32 board has been used to communicate with the charge controller using the proper protocol imposed by the charge controller's vendor.

Similarly, using other set of libraries, measurements from external DHT11 sensor are retrieved and then sent as well as data from charge controller to the central unit. Such data are arranged into a JSON object and sent to a broker via MQTT protocol. Inside JSON object, each data component is associated with a unique identifier, the acquisition timestamp and the value's unit of measure. On top of it, a system identity signature and location in a coded string ("*ITA-Parma-Unipr*" indicates the state: Italy, the city of installation: Parma and the supervisor university: Università di Parma) are added.

The data format is extremely important to obtain a scalable and flexible interface; moreover, in the proposed approach, an expandable format has been used for future add-ons. Apart from the already mentioned keys for system signature and location ("*device_id*", "*location*"), the third key of the first level is an array named "readings" containing all data collected at the field unit. Each element of such array has three keys: the first indicates the unique identifier of the type of data, the second gives the measurement unit, the third is another array containing elements made of couples of timestamps—value.

In so doing, each data type can have multiple records sent all together at the same time and each system can be expanded to as many data types as possible with the need of just adding a proper data identifier. An example of the JSON data format is reported in Fig. 3.

Finally, messages, composed as described, reaches one of the topic of the MQTT broker; indeed, the broker is organized in several topics with different purposes: / data is the one used for transmitting measurements, */datetime* is used for date and time synchronization of field units acting as other popular NTP servers transmitting the timestamp in UNIX format at fixed period, on */cmd* commands from central unit are delivered with the *device_id* in order to target the specific device.

On the other side of the MQTT broker, the central unit running on the cloud computing interface is responsible to retrieve data and store them in a local database.

Fig. 3 JSON object used in MQTT messages


```
{
  "device_id":"LL-1",
  "location":"ITA-Parma-Unipr",
  "readings":[
    {
      "data_id":"env_temperature",
      "unit":"°C",
      "data":[
        {
          "timestamp":1712151335939,
          "val":20.23
        },
        {
          "timestamp":1712151338014,
          "val":23.15
        }
      ]
    },
    {
      "data_id":"batt_voltage",
      "unit":"V",
      "data":[
        {
          "timestamp":1712151334394,
          "val":13.18
        }
      ]
    }
  ]
}
```

Thanks to the id-based format of information, the received arrays are simply parsed, and data stored in the same table of the database with their own *data_id*.

For the current implementation, self-explaining data identifiers are:

- batt_voltage
- batt_current
- batt_soc
- load_voltage
- load_current
- pv_voltage
- pv_current
- env_temperature
- env_humidity.

Further data identifiers can be introduced straightforwardly, with no need for architecture changes, so that, depending on actual services to be delivered, new sensors can be accounted for, and related information can be made available to cloud processing in a flexible and practical fashion.

The centralized application is made with Node-RED, a JavaScript-based programming tool, with additional plugins to integrate SQLite database, MQTT transmission protocol and dashboard user interface.

Moreover, this part is hosted in a Linux cloud server provided by AWS services accessible via public IP. The centralized part itself has been thought to be scalable and flexible as well, in fact, all services hosted on the server are created within the Docker environment with a suitable virtual and secure space.

4.2 Results

According to the execution flow, and the description of the design above, there are different step before a data from the field reaches the user interface. In this chapter, the idea is to go through those steps to provide a further image of the deployed ecosystem.

At the startup, each field unit must synchronize its internal clock with the current date and time; the channel used is the already mentioned MQTT topic */datetime* to which each field unit is subscribed. With a fixed frequency or with the command through the user interface, the central unit can deliver the timestamp to let the field units waiting for it running.

Finally, field units collect data both from Tracer 10AN charge controller and from DHT11 temperature and humidity sensor with a frequency of acquisition given by two separated configurable timers. During this period, before the JSON message will be published on the */data* MQTT topic, all data are queued. Then, whit a third timer, the JSON message is composed and delivered to the MQTT broker hosted in HiveMQ service provider. At the same topic is also subscribed the central unit, that receives the message, unpack the information and store data in a database table, as shown later in Fig. 8. Thanks to the format used, this process is completely scalable as the central unit has only to go through all data contained in the JSON arrays and then retrieve information from *data_id* stored.

At the end, the user dashboard, shows those data in different sections; each section is populated with *device_id* data based on the identifier selected at the top of the home page. For the purpose of this work, the first section (Fig. 4) reports some generic information as the location, the date and time that the devise has transmitted and the battery state of charge for an immediate oversees of its status. In the second and third section (Fig. 5 and Fig. 6) are reported data coming from the charge controller integrated sensors and referring to voltage level and current of PV, battery, and load respectively. In the last section (Fig. 7), any kind of data may be shown according to the selected *data_id*. Nevertheless, there is no need of knowing a priori all possible typologies of ids but all the available in the database will be listed here.

In addition to graphical visualization of data, grouped based on the kind of information, another tab named "Log" in Fig. 8 provide raw data as they are stored in the database.

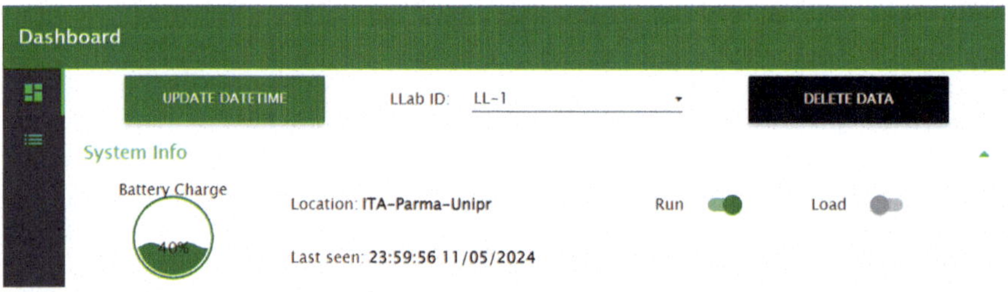

Fig. 4 General system information section

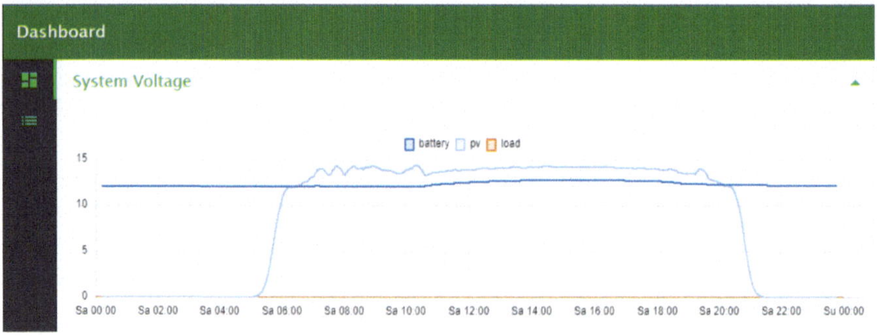

Fig. 5 Section with voltage level of battery, pv, and load

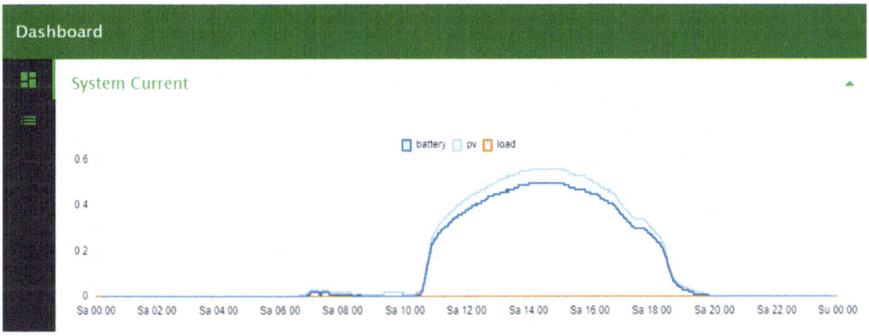

Fig. 6 Section with current of battery, pv, and load

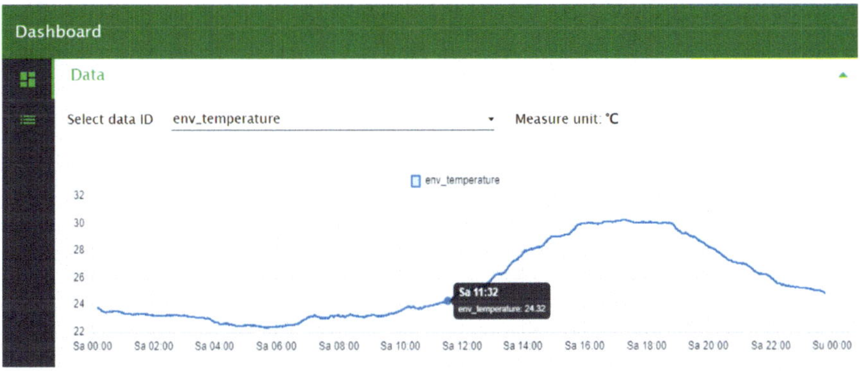

Fig. 7 Generic data section with selected "*env_temperature*" data identifier

Device ID	Data ID	Timestamp	Value	Unit of...
LL-1	load_current	09:40:42 13/05/2024	0.25	A
LL-1	pv_voltage	09:40:42 13/05/2024	13.28999996	V
LL-1	pv_current	09:40:42 13/05/2024	0.059999999	A
LL-1	env_temperature	09:40:42 13/05/2024	22	°C
LL-1	env_humidity	09:40:42 13/05/2024	48	%
LL-1	load_voltage	09:40:42 13/05/2024	12.13000011	V
LL-1	batt_voltage	09:40:41 13/05/2024	12.13000011	V
LL-1	batt_soc	09:40:41 13/05/2024	38	%
LL-1	batt_current	09:40:41 13/05/2024	0.07	A

Fig. 8 "Log" dashboard table with raw data

5 Conclusions

The paper introduces the distributed architecture of a system developed within the framework of European project "GREATER", aiming at implementing an IoT ecosystem for the smart management of photovoltaic systems with various applications, targeting rural areas of Rwanda. Technology has been developed as part of an EU project with a primary focus on higher education, with the goals of effectiveness, flexibility, and scalability. The concept of living lab is illustrated, and a few use-cases are introduced. Living labs will provide an effective link between the academy and surrounding communities, in a win–win approach. University students will have the opportunity of accessing real-world workbenches, enhance their multidisciplinary skills, and gain hands-on experience in designing smart and sustainable systems. For the community at large, Living Labs will provide a comprehensive view of the potential benefits of innovative technologies and raise awareness and sensitivity to green business issues.

A prototype implementation is presented, including both the peripheral field units (PV power generation and management, sensors, and communication) and the centralized cloud architecture. In both cases, a low-cost yet effective design has been implemented; thanks to inexpensive, standard hardware components and open-source software tools. This results in an open and scalable approach that can be extended to further use-cases.

References

1. U. N. Org: "Transforming our world: the 2030 Agenda for Sustainable Development", https://sdgs.un.org/2030agenda, last accessed: Jul. 22, 2024.
2. Ozturk, A. Aslan, and H. Kalyoncu: "Energy consumption and economic growth relationship: Evidence from panel data for low and middle income countries", Energy Policy (2010), vol. 38, no. 8, pp. 4422–4428, https://doi.org/10.1016/j.enpol.2010.03.071.
3. F. Abdullah et al.: "Sustainable energy for all: a Global Action Agenda. Pathways for Concerted Action toward Sustainable Energy for All" (2012), https://www.seforall.org/sites/default/files/SEFA-Action-Agenda-Final.pdf, last accessed: Jul. 31, 2024.
4. Republic of Rwanda: "VISION 2050", https://www.minecofin.gov.rw/fileadmin/user_upload/Minecofin/Publications/REPORTS/National_Development_Planning_and_Research/Vision_2050/English-Vision_2050_Abridged_version_WEB_Final.pdf, last accessed: Jul. 28, 2024.
5. E. Ngirente: "7 Years Government Programme: National Strategy for Transformation (NST1)", https://faolex.fao.org/docs/pdf/rwa206814.pdf, last accessed: Jun. 25, 2024.
6. National Institute of Statistics Rwanda (NISR): "Integrated Household Living Conditions Survey 5 (EICV 5)", https://www.statistics.gov.rw/datasource/integrated-household-living-conditions-survey-5-eicv-5.
7. U. N. Org: "Paris Agreement", https://unfccc.int/sites/default/files/english_paris_agreement.pdf, last accessed: Jul. 28, 2024.
8. National Institute of Statistics Rwanda (NISR): "Main Indicators: 5th Rwanda Population and Housing Census (PHC)", https://www.statistics.gov.rw/publication/main_indicators_2022.
9. Rwanda Energy Group (REG): "Rwanda National Electrification Plan (NEP) - 2023 Revision", https://www.reg.rw/fileadmin/user_upload/Concept_Note_NEP_Revision__July_2023.pdf.

10. J. De Dieu Niyonteze, F. Zou, G. N. Osarumwense Asemota, and S. Bimenyimana: "Solar-powered mini-grids and smart metering systems, the solution to Rwanda energy crisis," in Journal of Physics: Conference Series (2019), vol. 1311, https://doi.org/10.1088/1742-6596/1311/1/012002.
11. W. A. Jabbar, S. Annathurai, T. A. Tajul, and M. F. Mohd Fauzi: "Smart energy meter based on a long-range wide-area network for a stand-alone photovoltaic system," Expert Syst Appl. (2022), vol. 197, https://doi.org/10.1016/j.eswa.2022.116703.
12. I. Mellit and S. Kalogirou: "Artificial intelligence and internet of things to improve efficacy of diagnosis and remote sensing of solar photovoltaic systems: Challenges, recommendations and future directions", Elsevier Ltd. (2021), vol. 143, https://doi.org/10.1016/j.rser.2021.110889.
13. Y. Cheddadi, H. Cheddadi, F. Cheddadi, F. Errahimi, and N. Es-sbai: "Design and implementation of an intelligent low-cost IoT solution for energy monitoring of photovoltaic stations", Applied Sciences (2020), vol. 2, https://doi.org/10.1007/s42452-020-2997-4.
14. S. Ansari, A. Ayob, M. S. Hossain Lipu, M. H. Md Saad, and A. Hussain: "A review of monitoring technologies for solar pv systems using data processing modules and transmission protocols: Progress, challenges and prospects", Sustainability (2021), vol. 13, https://doi.org/10.3390/su13158120.
15. B. N. Alhasnawi, B. H. Jasim, P. Siano, and J. M. Guerrero: "A novel real-time electricity scheduling for home energy management system using the internet of energy", Energies (2021), vol. 14, https://doi.org/10.3390/en14113191.
16. P. Balakumar, T. Vinopraba, and K. Chandrasekaran, "Real time implementation of Demand Side Management scheme for IoT enabled PV integrated smart residential building", Journal of Building Engineering (2022), vol. 52, https://doi.org/10.1016/j.jobe.2022.104485.
17. S. Adhya, D. Saha, A. Das, J. Jana, and H. Saha: "An IoT based smart solar photovoltaic remote monitoring and control unit" in 2nd International Conference on Control, Instrumentation, Energy and Communication (CIEC 2016), pp. 432–436, https://doi.org/10.1109/CIEC.2016.7513793.
18. P. Monika and N. Chamat: "An IoT based Smart Photovoltaic Remote Monitoring System" in 2nd International Conference on Control, Instrumentation, Energy and Communication (CIEC 2016), vol 8, pp. 432–436, https://doi.org/10.1109/CIEC.2016.7513793.
19. C. K. Rao, S. K. Sahoo, and F. F. Yanine: "An IoT-based intelligent smart energy monitoring system for solar PV power generation", Energy Harvesting and Systems (2024), vol. 11, no. 1, https://doi.org/10.1515/ehs-2023-0015.
20. D. Manu, S. G. Shorabh, O. V. Gnana Swathika, S. Umashankar, and P. Tejaswi: "Design and realization of smart energy management system for Standalone PV system," in IOP Conference Series: Earth and Environmental Science, Institute of Physics (2022), https://doi.org/10.1088/1755-1315/1026/1/012027.

Developing Concepts for Gamification Approaches in Transportation Systems and Sustainable Urban Development

Sreedhar Kokkarachedu, Duc Anh Le Mai, and Jorge Marx Gómez

Abstract This paper investigates the potential of gamification to improve citizen engagement and participation in sustainable urban planning and transportation systems. By incorporating gamified elements, the approach seeks to boost citizen motivation and enhance their understanding of traffic and urban development projects. Insights derived from expert interviews and a comprehensive literature review inform the development of a conceptual framework for effectively integrating gamification into these areas. This framework aims to address the challenge of low citizen involvement by making complex concepts more accessible and engaging.

Keywords Gamification · Citizen engagement · Sustainable urban planning · Transportation systems · Conceptual gamification framework

1 Introduction

Citizen participation in sustainable urban development is crucial for successful governance. A survey in Germany found that 71.3% of citizens believe that having influence on politics would increase their trust in it [1]. Community engagement and civic participation encompass the political and social practices through which individuals engage with and influence public affairs beyond their immediate private sphere [2]. This involvement aims to enhance community planning, reduce administrative costs, and increase government legitimacy.

To be effective, civic engagement platforms must follow the principles of democratic deliberation, which involve the exchange of arguments and decision-making by

S. Kokkarachedu (✉) · D. A. L. Mai · J. Marx Gómez
Carl von Ossietzky Universität Oldenburg, Oldenburg, Germany
e-mail: sreedhar.kokkarachedu@uni-oldenburg.de

D. A. L. Mai
e-mail: duc.anh.le.mai@uni-oldenburg.de

J. Marx Gómez
e-mail: jorge.marx.gomez@uol.de

J. Marx Gómez et al. (eds.), *Advancement in Embedded and Mobile Systems*, Progress in IS, https://doi.org/10.1007/978-3-031-99219-3_20

equals. Active participation on these platforms is essential for achieving their operational and societal goals. Digitalization facilitates citizen involvement by enabling democratic governance through e-participation [3].

On the other hand, a mobility transition is essential for sustainable urban development [4] but has been insufficiently initiated [5]. Urban planning is a political decision-making process aiming to achieve economic, ecological, and social goals in spatial terms [6]. Integrated settlement and transport development combine urban and transport planning to steer development towards sustainability goals [7, 8]. Citizens wish to engage in city planning and understand its impact on transportation systems but often lack the necessary knowledge.

Serious games offer a potential solution by explaining complex relationships in an easy-to-understand manner, allowing citizens to grasp the intricacies of transportation systems and sustainable urban development. These games create an immersive environment where people can experience and enjoy participation, providing opportunities to encounter challenges, sensory perceptions, and imagination [9].

Serious games aim to change people's views on a topic by teaching them meaningfully, while gamification seeks to motivate and engage users with a product [10]. In transport planning, long-term sustainable mobility is essential, and traffic education teaches safe interaction in society through simulations and role-playing. Gamification can improve road safety by offering a risk-free environment to practice traffic rules, helping to inform and educate the public on crucial social issues [11].

However, there is little research on how gamification can support community building and civic engagement. There is also a lack of theoretical or practical frameworks to guide gamification on civic engagement platforms [3]. To address this gap, expert interviews were conducted to develop a conceptual framework for integrating gamified elements into traffic and urban development projects.

2 Methodology

2.1 Expert Interview Framework

The framework for our concept was developed based on insights from four interviews with technical experts: three from the field of gamification and one from the field of transport. The primary questions focused on requirements for a gamification concept, the possible challenges for gamification in relation to transportation systems and urban development, and the considerations necessary when implementing gamification. Additional sub-questions were asked where necessary to clarify terms and elaborate on the information provided, ensuring a comprehensive understanding for later integration into the concept.

The questions and results of the interviews were listed in the following Table1.

Table 1 Expert insights on gamification in transportation systems and urban development

Nr.	Question	Answer
1	How can gamification elements be determined?	- Engage with a diverse group of citizens to gather their opinions - Consider applicable gamification mechanisms and concepts - Conduct citizen workshops.
2	What requirements need to be considered when implementing a gamification application?	- Apply gamification frameworks, adapting them to the specific use case - Utilize atomic game elements to meet specific needs - Use research as a tool - Ensure a coherent, interconnected experience
3	How can resources be used effectively for developing gamification applications?	- Invest in user research and the concept phase - Assemble a competent, interdisciplinary team (including designers, technologists, and psychologists) - Combine exploratory tasks with academic theses - Follow established gamification frameworks
4	What other important suggestions do you have for applying gamification?	- Conduct user research to understand their needs - Organize participation workshops - Analyze the target group, including their emotional states and needs
5	How can the app be improved with additional gamification requirements?	- Ensure users learn about the variables and effects of district planning - Focus on creating an immersive experience - Promote a strong connection between users and the tool - Use model-oriented map displays (2D/3D, e.g., Google Street View, Unity) - Emphasize learning outcomes over creativity - Help citizens understand and influence future city planning
6	What gamification approaches does a project need?	- Not every project requires gamification - The decision depends on the potential to generate interest or motivation. - Context is crucial
7	How can you arouse curiosity if users have no experience with urban development and transportation systems?	- This is more of a marketing challenge than a gamification one - Co-creation can generate interest and make users feel valued - Emphasize users' sense of self-efficacy - Show the practical impact of user input on municipal decisions - Allow citizens to make recommendations to the municipality
8	What are the challenges for citizens?	- Maintaining attention - Present information (prevent distraction, improve exploration, increase understanding)
9	What needs to be considered when implementing gamification approaches in relation to transportation systems?	- Integrated thinking (understanding the behavior of transport and urban development in context) - Integrated model (the concepts of transport and urban development)
10	What are possible challenges for gamification in relation to transportation systems?	- Understanding the interactions between urban development and transport - The system is incomprehensible - Behaviors in the models are not intuitive

2.2 Collecting Requirements

The requirements identified by the experts were synthesized and translated into a Miro model, structured into three distinct phases: Preparation, Implementation, and Feedback. In the Preparation phase, the focus is on analyzing the needs of stakeholders and citizens, establishing the application design, and ensuring transparency to make the application comprehensible. This phase also involves creating user stories, organizing workshops, conducting market and target group analyses, and understanding the needs of stakeholders and users. It emphasizes presenting information clearly, showing the interaction between traffic and settlement development, and being mindful of dark patterns and the application's impact on citizens.

In the implementation phase, resources and strategies are outlined for developing the concept of gamification. This includes using decision support tools, storytelling, and integrating learning content with game elements. The phase promotes developing prototypes, incorporating positive reinforcement, and ensuring user engagement through intrinsic rewards and immersive experiences. It also involves building user guidance features, adhering to the law of proximity for element grouping, and implementing solution-independent tasks, levels of interpretation, route optimization, and maintaining high user attention.

Finally, the Feedback phase reviews the effectiveness of all applied actions, incorporating a feedback function to balance citizen input and application content. It assesses self-efficacy, determining the weight of user decisions on outcomes, and includes surveys on game behavior to refine and enhance the gamification concept.

3 Concept Formulation

This model serves as a procedural framework for developing a gamification application tailored for urban and transportation planning. The process is structured into four key phases (Fig. 1).

3.1 Login/Registration Phase

Users begin by logging in or registering, where they enter their data and are encouraged to set personal goals. This phase ensures that the application can offer customized exercises aligned with their intrinsic motivations, as users define what the application means to them. The user profile displays these goals, along with progress and challenges.

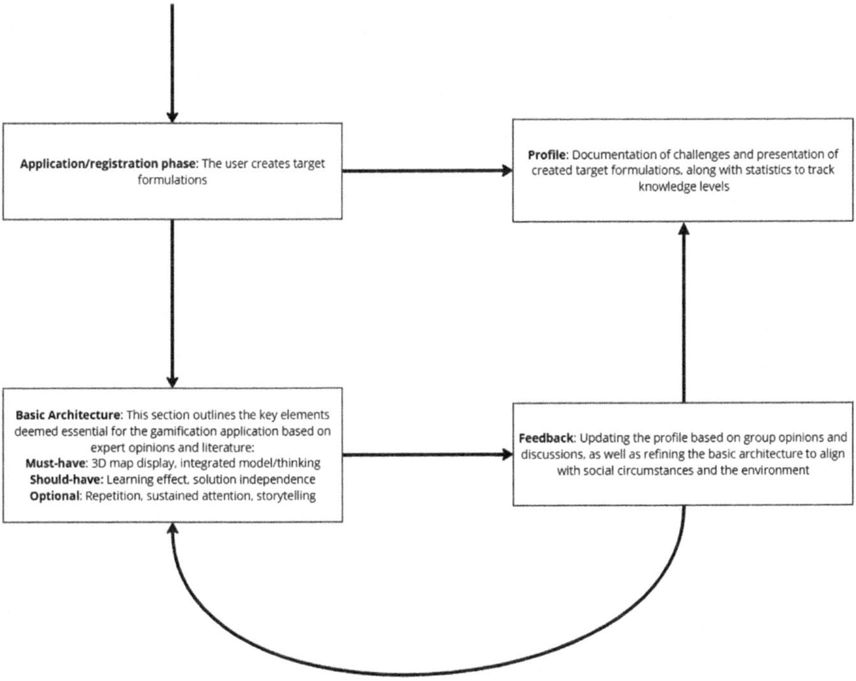

Fig. 1 Gamification concept for transport and urban development [12]

3.1.1 Ethical Considerations in Gamification

In the development of gamification systems, data protection and user privacy must be prioritized. Ethical considerations surrounding user privacy should be embedded into the conceptual framework of gamification to ensure responsible and sustainable implementation.

3.2 Profile Phase

In this phase, users' profiles are created and maintained. The profile displays the set goals, progress, and challenges faced by the users. It includes an analysis of the users' needs and collaboratively determines goal formulations, offering a comprehensive view of their development within the application.

3.3 Basic Architecture

This phase integrates expert-identified methods for effective gamification in traffic and urban planning. Key features include decision support, integrated models, and 3D map representations. The primary focus is on a 3D map display and an integrated model, followed by learning effects and solution independence. While repetition, sustained attention, and storytelling can enhance engagement, they are secondary to these core elements.

3.4 Feedback Phase

This phase ensures continuous improvement by connecting the basic architecture to a feedback loop. Feedback mechanisms include positive reinforcement, intrinsic rewards, and surveys on game behavior to assess and adjust user engagement. It also updates the goals in user profiles to keep them relevant and effective. In summary, the model integrates user input, expert recommendations, and iterative feedback to create a dynamic and responsive gamification application for urban and transportation development.

The evaluation of this research is ongoing, with feedback from citizens currently being collected through a questionnaire.

4 Gamification: An Empirical Study

Empirical research indicates that gamification can have a positive impact, but this effect is highly contingent on the context in which it is applied and the specific characteristics of its users. Many of the studies reviewed report positive outcomes related to some motivational aspects of gamification implementations. However, much of the quantitative research remains descriptive, rather than inferential, and thus does not provide robust conclusions regarding the causal effects of gamification. Despite positive user perceptions of gamification strategies, no significant effects on behavior or performance were conclusively observed. Additionally, it is important to note that the effects of gamification may be short-lived, possibly due to the novelty of the experience rather than sustained behavioral change. Based on Self-Determination Theory and the traditional definition of games, it is suggested that external pressures, such as extrinsic rewards, might undermine the long-term effectiveness of gamification by impeding the development of intrinsic motivation [13].

To explore the relative effectiveness of social networking versus gamification, a quasi-experimental design was employed. In response to concerns raised by the researchers, efforts were made to monitor participation rates across both groups in the study. It was observed that 38% of participants engaged with the social networking platform, while only 24% engaged with the gamification plugin. These results indicate that increased participation is not necessarily driven by elements such as achievements, badges, or competitions. This finding highlights the importance of careful instructional design and clearly defined objectives when implementing gamification in e-learning environments [14].

Another study investigated the influence of social factors on user attitudes towards gamification and their intention to continue using gamified services. The study focused on the popular fitness application "Fitocracy," employing the Theory of Planned Behaviour (TPB) to explain behavioral intentions through attitudes and social influences. The TPB model was extended to incorporate network effects, revealing that factors such as social influence, network effects, word of mouth (WOM), reciprocity, attitude, and behavior significantly influence how gamification is perceived and whether users intend to continue using or recommending the service to others [15].

5 Conclusion

After providing a possible concept for how to use gamification approaches as a solution for transportation and urban development, it is theoretically possible to create a framework that can be applied in applications that might enhance decision making process for citizens in urban or traffic projects. However, after collecting data and information from literature, requirements and experts, the concept is not yet sufficiently linked and is still isolated.In addition, there is a lack of quantity in experts and citizens, so that the solutions identified lack validity. However, the focus can continue to be on the learning and psychological effects in gamification concepts as well as the influence of intrinsic reward as a motivator for future action and the possibility of how interactions between settlement and transportation development can be incorporated with gamification.

Declarations

This publication is based on research in the project MobiLe, which is funded by the Federal ministry of Education and Research as part of its Social-Ecological Research funding priority, funding no. 01UV2129A. Responsibility for the content of this publication lies with the author.

GEFÖRDERT VOM

Bundesministerium
für Bildung
und Forschung

FONA
Forschung für Nachhaltigkeit

References

1. Demokratie, B. Umfrage-Highlights. (Website,2019), Online erhältlich unter https://demokratie.buergerrat.de/dokumentation/umfrage/umfrage-highlights/; abgerufen am 12. Januar 2024. (2024)
2. Ampatzidou, C., Gugerell, K., Constantinescu, T., Devisch, O., Jauschneg, M. & Berger, M. All work and no play? Facilitating serious games and gamified applications in participatory urban planning and governance. *Urban Planning*. **3**, 34–46 (2018)
3. Hassan, L. Governments should play games: Towards a framework for the gamification of civic engagement platforms. *Simulation & Gaming*. **48**, 249–267 (2017)
4. Deutscher Städtetag Nachhaltige städtische Mobilität für alle. Agenda für eine Verkehrswende aus kommunaler Sicht. Positionspapier des Deutschen Städtetages. (2018)
5. Deutscher Städtetag Monitoring zum Positionspapier "Nachhaltige städtische Mobilität für alle. Agenda für eine Verkehrswende aus kommunaler Sicht von 2018". (2021)
6. Pahl-Weber, E. & Schwartze, F. Stadtplanung. *Handwörterbuch Der Stadt-und Raumentwicklung*. pp. 2509–2520 (2018)
7. Holz-Rau, C. & Jansen, U. Nachhaltige Raum- und Verkehrsplanung. (Website,2007), Online erhältlich unter https://www.bpb.de/shop/zeitschriften/apuz/30354/nachhaltige-raum-und-verkehrsplanung/; abgerufen am 24. Mai 2024.
8. Beckmann, K., Blumthaler, W., Bojarra-Becker, E., Gies, J. & Leitfaden, K. Lebenswerte Städte und Regionen. (2024)
9. Poplin, A. Digital serious game for urban planning:"B3–Design your Marketplace!". *Environment And Planning B: Planning And Design*. **41**, 493–511 (2014)
10. Landers, R. & Callan, R. Casual social games as serious games: The psychology of gamification in undergraduate education and employee training. *Serious Games And Edutainment Applications*. pp. 399–423 (2011)
11. Gounaridou, A., Siamtanidou, E. & Dimoulas, C. A serious game for mediated education on traffic behavior and safety awareness. *Education Sciences*. **11**, 127 (2021)
12. Ibel, J. Gamification–Einbindung von Spielelementen bei digitalen Medien. (Hochschule für angewandte Wissenschaften Hamburg,2016)
13. Hamari, J., Koivisto, J. & Sarsa, H. Does gamification work?–a literature review of empirical studies on gamification. *2014 47th Hawaii International Conference On System Sciences*. pp. 3025–3034 (2014)
14. De-Marcos, L., Domınguez, A., Navarrete, J. & Pagés, C. An empirical study comparing gamification and social networking on e-learning. *Computers & Education*. **75** pp. 82–91 (2014)
15. Hamari, J. & Koivisto, J. Social Motivations To Use Gamification: An Empirical Study Of Gamifying Exercise.. *ECIS*. **105**, 18–19 (2013)

Performance Metrics Analysis of 5G Networks Using Device-to-Device Technology in Mobile Application

Elias Ntawuzumunsi, Frodouard Minani, Jean Damascene Mushimiyimana, and John Munyakayanza

Abstract The current era requires high-capacity cellular communication networks of the fifth generation (5G) and beyond (B5G) to meet the increasing demands of global network subscribers. Device-to-device (D2D) technology is an innovative technology utilized in mobile applications, which enables devices such as laptops, embedded devices, and mobile phones to communicate with each other without the necessity of an intermediary network infrastructure. This has benefits in terms of energy consumption, latency reduction, and high communication link throughput. In order to provide high data rates with high-quality signals, low energy consumption, and low latency (packet delay time) services between end users on the networks, D2D is a key enabling technology for 5G and beyond networks (B5G). D2D technology can therefore play a significant role in meeting the ambitious requirements of future 5G and beyond wireless systems, as it primarily relies on infrastructure-centric cellular solutions to meet the demands of services and data traffic. Quality of services (QoS) and energy efficiency (i.e., energy consumption, EE) have emerged as crucial requirements and concerns in the design of 5G technology. We examined the performance parameters for QoS, throughput, energy efficiency, and network latency offered by B5G wireless networks when employing D2D technology in mobile applications. The study focuses on examining both communication and discovery as two D2D phases to fulfill requirements when taking into account the performance indicators for B5G wireless networks that were previously discussed. To show the simulation results, MATLAB has been utilized as a simulator.

Keywords D2D communication · B5G networks · Energy efficiency · QoS

E. Ntawuzumunsi (✉) · J. D. Mushimiyimana
Department of Computer Science, Catholic University of Rwanda, Huye, Rwanda
e-mail: ntaweli2015@gmail.com

F. Minani · J. Munyakayanza
Department of Information Systems, College of Science and Technology, University of Rwanda, Kigali, Rwanda
e-mail: f.minani1@ur.ac.rw

J. Marx Gómez et al. (eds.), *Advancement in Embedded and Mobile Systems*, Progress in IS, https://doi.org/10.1007/978-3-031-99219-3_21

Fig. 1 Cellular communication generation

1 Introduction

In today's network technology, cellular network technologies of present-day tend to be unable to encounter the growing demand of network subscribers due to the fact that there are a high number of applications that require high bandwidth such as video streaming, and mobile computing. With this, the volume of information/data is increasing every day. In the year 2025, researches predict that trillions of wireless and internet of things (IoT) devices shall be serving billions of people [1]. The concept of fifth-generation and beyond networks (B5G) is now being extensively studied/explored which is a combination of a number of technologies. In terms of delay tolerance, throughput, quality of service, and meeting energy efficient, device-to-device (D2D) technology has been found as one of the new promising technologies that meet the technical goals of next-generation wireless networks (NGNs). Device-to-Device (D2D) communication is a pivotal feature in 5G networks, enabling direct interaction between mobile devices without routing data through a central base station. This paradigm shift enhances network performance by reducing latency, increasing data throughput, and optimizing spectral efficiency. In the context of mobile applications, D2D communication facilitates more efficient content sharing, real-time gaming, and proximity-based services, thereby enriching user experiences [2]. D2D communication permits two adjacent or nearby devices to communicate with each other without the involvement of a base station (BS). With D2D communication, its direct communication increases spectral efficiency, system capacity, and reduces the network latency [3].

From the first generation (1G) to the fourth generation (4G) of wireless cellular communication networks, as illustrated in Fig. 1 , presently, various network operators are drawn to D2D technology because of its growing advancements and trends, but formerly, the functionalities of D2D communication were disregarded [4]. Regarding the 5G networks in general, its radio access roadmap foreknows two pathways where the first one consists of growth of Long-Term Evolution (LTE), and the other one is based on the design of the New Radio (NR) access as indicated on Fig. 2 . In D2D communication technology, the energy efficient (EE), throughput, and delay are the critical requirements of B5G wireless system [3]. Therefore, D2D communication in B5G becomes one of the key technologies that will contribute to meeting energy efficiency and other parameter metrics requirements. Improved D2D communications in cellular communication networks overlaying with regards to the

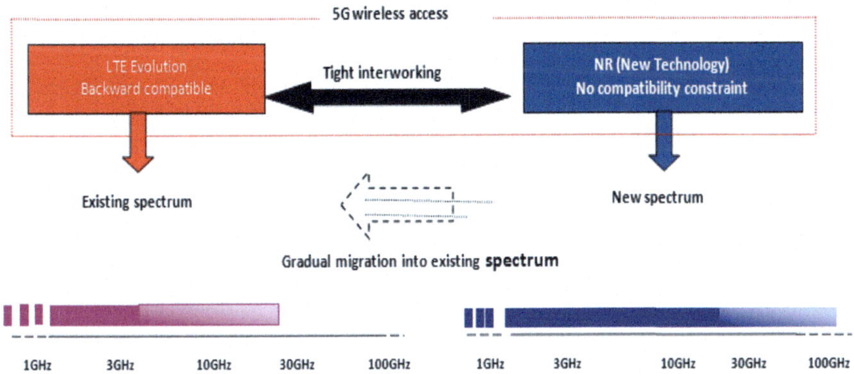

Fig. 2 Roadmap of 5G radio access [5]

energy efficiency (EE), throughput, delay, network latency, and quality of service (QoS) in 5G and beyond mobile is analyzed in this work. As there are two phases in D2D communication scenarios such as discovery and communication, in the D2D communication process, the key phase in overall D2D communication is the discovery phase since it determines the pairing process which is configured for the devices in the system.

With a focus on both its discovery and communication phases, this article aims to assess the performance metrics of 5G and beyond (B5G) networks employing D2D communication. Throughput, delay, network latency, energy efficiency, and quality of service will all be analyzed utilizing an enhanced centralized D2D system.

The rest of this paper is organized as follows: Sect. 2 introduces the background and motivation. Section 3 introduces the related works. Section 4 focuses on the system model of heterogeneous 5G networks with D2D communication. Section 5 describes the D2D communication system. Section 6 describes the wireless model, Sect. 7 describes the simulation results and analysis, and finally, Sect. 8 summarizes the conclusion and further works.

2 Background and Motivation

The most important innovation perceived in technology at the latest time to improve the global standard of living and contribute to financial and economic growth is cellular communication networks. Recently, research indicated that cellular communication networks have advanced/expanded immensely to offer video streaming/audio streaming data, which justifies the quick increase in mobile subscribers [6]. Approximately 3% of mobile scribers rose between 2017 and 2018 to reach 7.9 billion, in Q3 of 2018 while approximately 79% of mobile data traffic swelled in the same period to reach roughly 20.7 Exabytes (EB) per month in Q3 of 2018 [7].

According to reports, the number of mobile subscribers will rise as a result of the constant growth of cellular networks and the recent introduction of B5G networks, which are anticipated to be the foundation of developing applications and the future of telecommunications in order to improve people's quality of life and boost the global economy [8]. In order for B5G networks to meet the demands of consumers, businesses, and services in the future, D2D communication is thought to be a crucial component. This allows B5G to be networks of networks with several effortlessly integrated radio access technologies (RATs) that offer more network traffic and better quality of service (QoS) for data and phone services.

The D2D infrastructure network has been the subject of intense research since the 1990s because of its potential to improve efficiency, good quality of service (QoS), promote throughput, and decrease transmission latency [9]. As previously stated, D2D communication seeks to improve the performance of cellular communication networks by taking use of direct connections and interactions between nearby devices. However, this presents a significant challenge when investigating and evaluating the performance metrics. Consequently, with an emphasis on an enhanced centralized D2D discovery and communication entity, we investigate and evaluate throughput, network latency, delay tolerance, quality of service, and energy efficiency as performance metrics of overlaying D2D communications in this research.

3 Related Works

With regards to its importance in 5G and beyond networks, D2D communication has been examined thus far in order to measure performance indicators.Applying D2D communication technology in 5G and beyond networks is anticipated to increase several communication features, including system capacity, network throughput, spectrum efficiency, and network latency [10, 11]. In reference [12], a resource allocation scheme to improve throughput, quality of service (QoS), and battery life has been proposed. Authors showed that D2D communications underlying cellular communication networks can drastically broaden the battery life of the device compared to traditional cellular communication networks. In [13], the authors analyzed the energy efficiency (EE) of D2D communication underlying cellular networks. As evidenced by the results, direct D2D communication between users leads in higher energy use. In [14], the authors presented a power-efficient approach to both device discovery and communication, as well as power allocation.

Numerous studies have been carried out to investigate additional functionality in cellular network generation, particularly in the context of 5G networks. Recent technologies such as Bluetooth and wireless fidelity offer some D2D communication capabilities, but they become unmanageable due to interference and their unlicensed spectrum. Furthermore, as is expected in B5G networks, D2D struggles to provide security and quality of service (QoS). The potential to add D2D communication capabilities to cellular networks has been taken advantage of by cellular operators and vendors. The majority recent studies on D2D communication integrated into cellular networks have presented results on radio resource allocation, energy efficiency, and quality of service concerns [15, 16] in addition to communication session setup and management procedures [17]. The proliferation of smartphones will facilitate the deployment of 5G-driven D2D networks given that new infrastructure needs are unavailable. According to Cisco's research, video sharing among users is expected to increase to three-fourths (3/4) of total network traffic in order to achieve the quality of service offered by 5G networks [18].

3.1 Current Approaches to Energy Efficiency in 5G Networks

The design and development of future 5G and beyond networks has recently witnessed a paradigm shift from throughput-optimization to energy-efficiency-optimization communications, with energy and spectrum efficiency emerging as the major performance indicators and essential priorities [19]. The next-generation networks (i.e., B5G) design and development must inevitably consider EE as one of its important key pedestals.Indeed, as revealed by the authors' work in [20], 5G network systems will serve for a remarkable number of mobile devices, offering both novel and rate-demanding services in addition to universal network access. In mobile communication, implementing hardware efficiency plays a significant role in increasing energy efficiency at device and infrastructure levels. The main requirement for 5G networks is to sustain mobile data traffic, according to [21], and several metrics, such as latency, quality of service (QoS), and energy efficiency (EE), are anticipated. Work [22] addresses the range of maximum transmit powers taking into account 5G networks, and its results showed that, in 5G networks, optimizing spectral efficiency for low transmit power generally corresponds to maximum energy efficiency. However, it failed to meet the data throughput, latency, and quality of service (QoS) standards for anticipated 5G networks and beyond (B5G).

According to the research done thus far, EE maximizing can also be done while taking into account all practical factors that are typically required in 5G communication networks. Along with this, QoS metrics for D2D communication, such as maximal delay bound [23], anticipating minimum delay [24], and high data rate guarantees [25], have begun to be implemented. This confirms that the main component of a reliable communication network is improving energy efficiency when designing 5G networks.

4 System Model of Heterogeneous 5G Networks with D2D Communication

D2D communication is considered a suitable technology for closeness-based data/information-sharing services, making it an appropriate candidate for future 5G

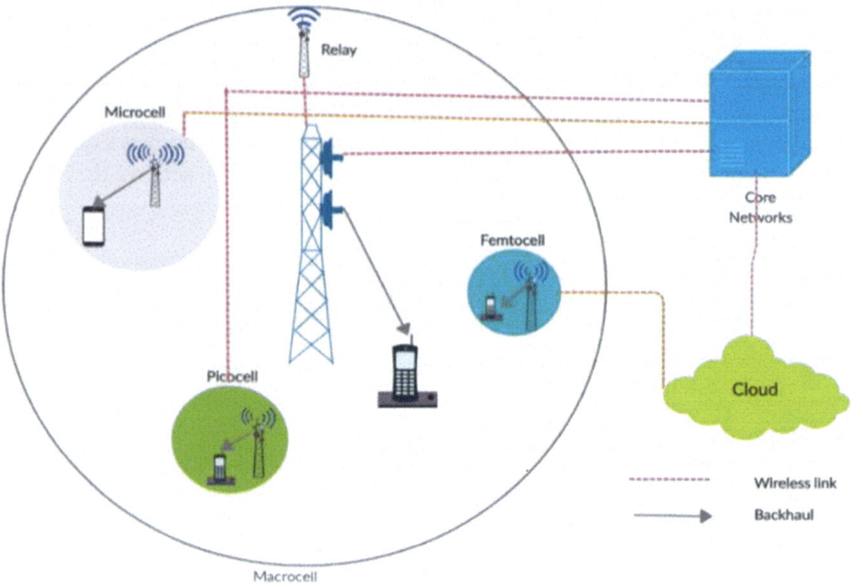

Fig. 3 Heterogeneous 5G networks system model

networks. Numerous applications requiring high data rate demands will be performed on these next-generation networks. Enabling network compaction through organizing cellular networks into smaller cells is a crucial step in meeting the data rate needs in communication networks. Enhanced network spectral efficiency and reduced power consumption of mobile devices due to communication with neighboring pico-cells are the results of this particular kind of compaction. Consequently, the network coverage in D2D communication is substantially improved by this technique.

Nevertheless, when designing the small cell base station (BS), the solution mentioned above, requires innovation in cost reduction and hardware shrinking. In heterogeneous 5G networks using D2D communication, the small base station of the cell can be arranged as low-powered femtocells normally used in high-powered pico cells in order to improve the outdoor coverage of macro cells. Hence, the simultaneous operation of those concepts of macro, pico, and femtocells is named as Heterogeneous networks (HetNets) as illustrated in Fig. 3 and they play an important role when analyzing the performance metrics (i.e., quality of service, energy efficiency, throughput) of 5G networks by using D2D communication. Although they play an essential part in the design, interferences are still the most critical challenges due to the fact that the 5G heterogeneous networks have uncoordinated nature and this leads to motivating the authors to analyze its performance metrics when deploying the networks into small cells.

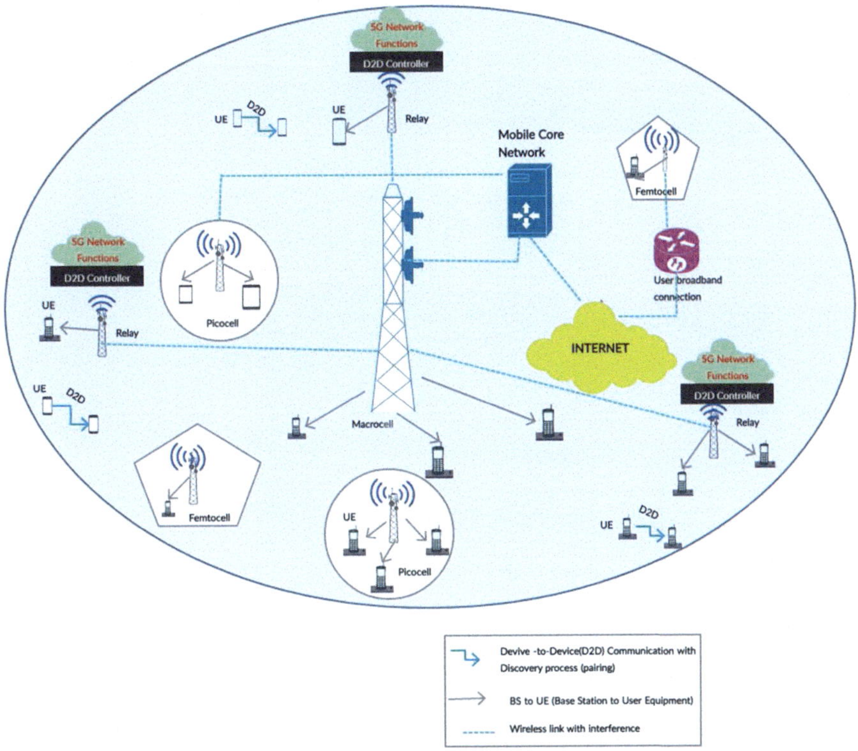

Fig. 4 Proposed model for system D2D communication system

5 Proposed System Model of D2D Communication

The wireless networks have one base station (BS), three antenna, and three relays where every antenna covers a cell sector. The model has a set of network nodes that are homogeneously and normally distributed in the two-dimension area, and they can transmit data (communicate) directly using device-to-device communication links between nodes that are in proximity to each other. Device-to-device communication is defended inherently by all devices in this scenario. We assume also that direct links between user equipment/user devices (UE) may use numerous Radio Access Technologies (RATs).

As illustrated in Fig. 4 , the three devices perform device-to-device communication (D2D) and once there is a connection establishment, the device-to-device pair must be linked to the base station (BS), and they act as a relay node for the purpose of receiving the data from the mobile network. The signal that is received by the relay and retransmitted between base stations and mobile can be used to boost the network throughput and enlarge the cellular network system. Because the infrastructure of the relay does not require a wired connection to the network, it offers savings in backhaul

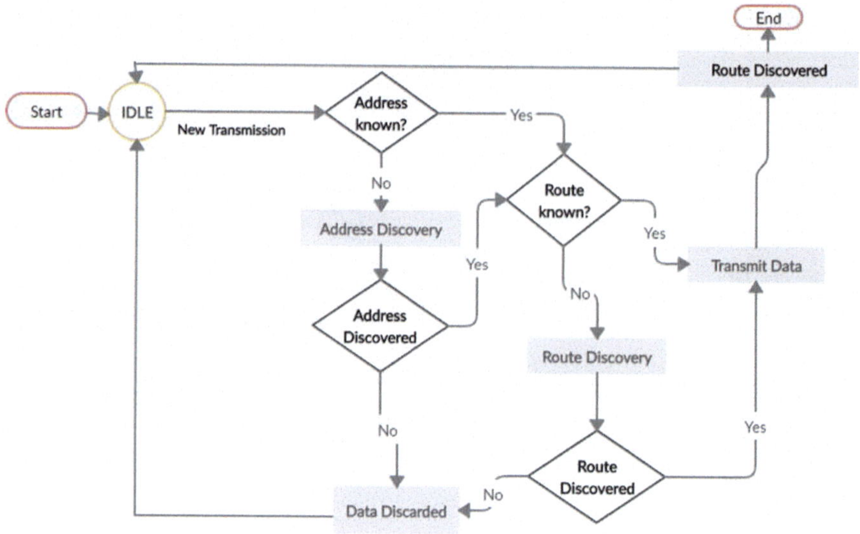

Fig. 5 Relay node transmission flowchart

costs. In this scenario, there will be a pairing procedure (discovery phase) which will be handled by the device-to-device controller (i.e., centralized entity). This causes all the devices in the network to provide the Signal-to-Interference-plus-Noise Ratio (SINR) and it must be computed and analyzed. In the D2D communication pairing process, interference is the critical factor that permits not having a good level of quality of service (QoS) when transmitting signals from user equipment (UE) to base station (BS) or from UE (user equipment) to network antenna. The communication phase in device-to-device starts when the device-to- device pairing process has been established.

5.1 Sample Flow for Relay Node Transmission

A relay node undergoes multiple steps, including figuring out the address and path routing to the relay node, before any transmission starts up as illustrated in Fig. 5 . The source device identifies potential relay nodes based on proximity, channel conditions, and SINR thresholds (details about SINR will be provided in the next subsection). The relay candidates then broadcast their availability using control signals or beacon messages. Subsequently, the source device initiates a request for the relay's address using neighbor discovery protocols (NDP). The relay node responds with its address and available transmission resources (i.e., Address Discovery). In case multi-hop relaying is required, the routing protocol determines the optimal path to the destination (i.e., Route Discovery). During the transmission, if spectrum sharing is involved, interference mitigation strategies are applied (e.g., power control, beamforming). The relay node receives the data packet and forwards it when necessary and required. The destination sends an ACK (Acknowledgment) to confirm successful reception. The relay node monitors link conditions and switches paths if necessary due to degradation. In the instance of an error, the relay enables the new device initiate a new transmission by triggering a retransmission request or selecting an alternative path (i.e., IDLE as seen in the figure).

5.2 Pairing Process (Discovery) of D2D Communication in the Proposed System Model

In the D2D discovery phase scenario shown in Fig. 4, devices must first determine that one is close to the other before they may communicate directly. Peer discovery is a randomized process in which a device transmits signals (UE1 to UE2 or UE3 to UE4) without knowing where the target peer is located. To determine which device might benefit from D2D communication, one needs to know the location of nearby devices on the network. The network coordinates the frequency and timing of transmitting and scanning if a D2D pair is discovered. The SINR of each paired device is calculated as a result of the signals being exchanged. In this paired scenario of D2D communication, we seek to examine the quality of service (QoS), energy consumption (i.e., energy efficiency), and the attainable network throughput of each D2D link. Since UE is connected to both the base station and the relay device, the network controller also chooses which device will serve as a relay node. For the other device, the one that is directly connected to the serving base station (BS) is regarded as a relay.

Consider the system model (i.e., geometry) given in Fig. 4, where it can be assumed that it comprises C cells and each cell has set $\mathcal{U}$ of U user equipments (UEs) denoted as $\mathcal{U} = \{1, \ldots, U\}$. Each cell also comprises a set $\mathcal{R}$ of the links between each D2D denoted as $\mathcal{R} = \{1, 2, \ldots, r, \ldots, R\}$. At the D2D receiver, the Signal-to-Interference-plus-Noise Ratio (SINR) represented by Γ_{D2D} can be portrayed as

$$\Gamma_{\mathrm{D2D}} = \frac{P_s G_s \beta_{\mathrm{UE}}}{\sum_{i=1}^{N} P_{I_i} G_{I_i} \beta_{I_i} + P_N}, \tag{1}$$

where P_s signifies the transmit power of the source device, G_s indicates the channel gain between the source device and relay, β_{UE} signifies the large-scale fading (i.e., path loss) component for the UE. Moreover, P_{I_i} is the transmit power of the ith interfering node, G_{I_i} is the channel gain between the ith interferer and the relay, β_{I_i} symbolizes the large-scale fading for the interfering link. Furthermore, P_N is the noise power, referred to thermal noise and background noise (i.e., the additive white Gaussian noise (AWGN) variance), while N shows the number of interfering sources. For a two-hop relay transmission, where the relay forwards the signal to the

UE, the effective SINR at the destination is determined as:

$$\mathrm{SINR}_{\mathrm{UE}} = \min\left(\mathrm{SINR}_{\mathrm{relay}}, \mathrm{SINR}_{\mathrm{UE\ from\ relay}}\right), \tag{2}$$

where:

$$\mathrm{SINR}_{\mathrm{UE\ from\ relay}} = \frac{P_r G_r \beta_{\mathrm{UE}}}{\sum_{j=1}^{M} P_{I_j} G_{I_j} \beta_{I_j} + P_N}, \tag{3}$$

with P_r indicating the relay transmit power, G_r showing the channel gain between the relay and UE, and M symbolizing the umber of interferers affecting the relay-to-UE link.

5.3 *Communication Phase of D2D Communication of the Proposed Model*

The D2D communication phase starts in the case where the connection (D2D connection) between two devices is established. The latter can be carried out through the use of specialized radio resources and can take place in both licensed and unlicensed spectrum, which is utilized for both spectrum and cellular purposes. D2D communication and cellular networks are provided with specialized resources and share similar radio resources. This makes QoS simple because the base station (BS) can fully control the cellular spectrum and the network throughput is considerable. Based on the Shannon capacity formula, the data rate of the r-th link for D2D can be efficiently calculated as follows, as illustrated in Fig. 4:

$$R_{\mathrm{r}}^{\mathrm{D2D}} = B_r \log_2\left(1 + \Gamma_{\mathrm{D2D}}\right), \tag{4}$$

which can transformed in the following equation:

$$R_{\mathrm{r}}^{\mathrm{D2D}} = B_r \log_2\left(1 + \frac{P_s G_s \beta_{\mathrm{UE}}}{\sum_{i=1}^{N} P_{I_i} G_{I_i} \beta_{I_i} + P_N}\right), \tag{5}$$

where B_r[in Hz] is the bandwidth allocated to the r-th D2D link. Similarly, for the relay-to-UE (R-D) link, the data rate can be computed as

$$R_{\mathrm{UE}} = B_{\mathrm{UE}} \log_2\left(1 + \mathrm{SINR}_{\mathrm{UE\ from\ relay}}\right), \tag{6}$$

which can transformed as following:

$$R_{\mathrm{UE}} = B_{\mathrm{UE}} \log_2\left(1 + \frac{P_r G_r \beta_{\mathrm{UE}}}{\sum_{j=1}^{M} P_{I_j} G_{I_j} \beta_{I_j} + P_N}\right), \tag{7}$$

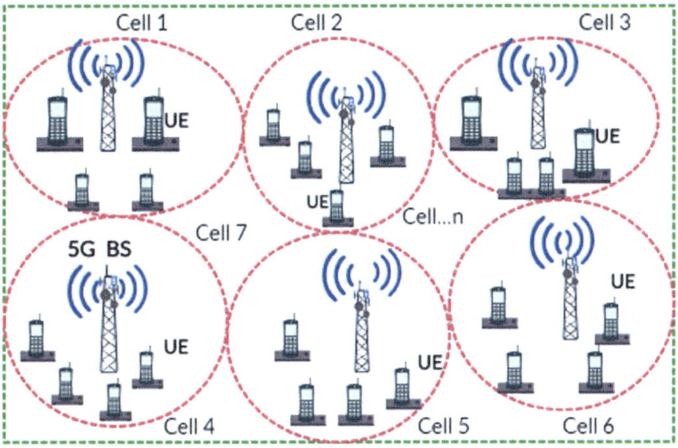

Fig. 6 Proposed wireless model for 5G networks

where B_{UE} is the bandwidth allocated to the relay-to-UE (R-D) link in the D2D communication system. For a two-hop relay transmission, the end-to-end achievable rate is constrained by the bottleneck link:

$$R_{\mathrm{D2D}} = \min(R_{\mathrm{r}}^{\mathrm{D2D}}, R_{\mathrm{UE}}) \cdot \tag{8}$$

6 Proposed Model of Wireless System

We considered a wireless network model with M antennas and K users per cell, as shown in Fig. 6 . Consider the following factors: the pilot reuse factor μ with frame (U channel users), the base station density (α), which is the number of BS per kilometer square (km^2), and the user equipment (UE) transmission power, which is denoted as P_{UE}.

6.1 Data Throughput

The average uplink sum rate per cell (i.e., Data Throughput, DT) can be computed as follows:

$$DT = K \cdot (1 - \mu K_U)\, B \log_2 (1 + \mathrm{SINR}_{UE})\,, \tag{9}$$

where DT is the Data throughput (i.e., uplink sum rate per cell), K is umber of users per cell, μK_U shows the fraction of the frame used for data transmission, accounting for control overhead. Moreover, B is the available bandwidth, $\log_2(1 +$

SINR_{UE}) signifies the data rate per user based on the Shannon capacity formula. More specifically, $(1 - \mu K_U)$ represents the fraction of the frame available for data transmission after deducting the overhead used for control signaling. In a D2D-enabled network, the total number of active D2D pairs and cellular users affects the total uplink throughput. That means higher K means more users contribute to throughput, but also increases interference. The Eq. (9) quantifies how different parameters influence the total uplink throughput in a D2D-enabled cellular network. Therefore, optimizing SINR, controlling overhead, and balancing user density are key to achieving high throughput.

6.2 Modeling Energy Consumption

Energy consumption in 5G networks is determined by a number of factors, including hardware components, system architecture, and the tasks that devices carry out, such as radio frequency, signal processing, coding, and network architecture. Additionally, it depends on how many access points and cells are there in the area. The network architecture and antenna position also have a significant impact on energy usage because of their propagation properties.

In principle, in D2D communication within 5G networks, energy consumption includes components from base stations (BS), user equipment (UE), and relay nodes. The total energy consumption for D2D networks, denoted as ET_{D2D}, can be modeled as follows:

$$ET_{\text{D2D}} = P_{\text{UE}} + TP_{\text{D2D}} + FP_{\text{D2D}} + PC_{\text{D2D}} + SP_{\text{D2D}} + A_{\text{D2D}}, \tag{10}$$

where P_{UE} shows the transmission power of UE in D2D communication (including both direct D2D users and relay nodes), TP_{D2D} signifies the transmit power of D2D devices (including amplifier inefficiency), FP_{D2D} shows the fixed circuit power consumption in D2D devices. Furthermore, PC_{D2D} is the power consumption per transceiver chain, SP_{D2D} symbolizes the signal processing power in D2D relays, and A_{D2D} depicts the additional power for coding, decoding, and backhaul communication. It should be noted that while device-to-device communication serves as relay nodes in 5G networks, regular communication between Base Stations (BS) and user equipment makes up the communications between BS and the equipment.

In a hybrid network where both BS-to-UE and D2D communications coexist, and by considering ET_{D2D} expressed in (10), the total energy consumption is expressed as

$$ET_{\text{total}} = ET_{\text{BS-UE}} + ET_{\text{D2D}}, \tag{11}$$

where:

$$ET_{\text{BS-UE}} = P_{\text{UE}} + TP_{\text{BS}} + FP_{\text{BS}} + PC_{\text{BS}} + SP_{\text{BS}} + A_{\text{BS}} \cdot \tag{12}$$

In (12), P_{UE} shows the transmission power of UE, TP_{BS} signifies the BS transmit power, FP_{BS} is the fixed circuit power consumption at the BS, PC_{BS} indicates the power consumed per transceiver chain at the BS, SP_{BS} represents the signal processing power consumption (i.e., power needed for modulation, coding, and decoding in BS), whereas A_{BS} represents the additional power overhead, which include the backhaul transmission, control signaling, and coding/decoding. Considering the data rate of the r-th link for D2D computed in (4), the energy efficiency (EE) metric is defined as:

$$EE = \frac{\sum_{r \in \mathcal{R}} R_{\mathrm{r}}^{\mathrm{D2D}}}{ET_{\mathrm{total}}} \quad \text{(bits per Joule)}, \tag{13}$$

where $\mathcal{R}$ is the set of active D2D links, $R_{\mathrm{r}}^{\mathrm{D2D}}$ is the data rate of the r-th link, and ET_{total} is the total energy consumption over time expressed in (11).

From (10), (11), (12), it is can be observed that in D2D direct communication, UEs transmit directly to other UEs, reducing BS energy consumption but increasing UE power consumption. Furthermore, in D2D relay-assisted communication, intermediate relay nodes consume additional power, making TP_{D2D} and SP_{D2D} critical. Additionally, reducing BS transmissions (offloading to D2D) lowers TP_{BS} but increases P_{UE} and relay power consumption. Consequently, efficient power control and relay selection are needed to minimize UE power consumption while maximizing energy efficiency.

7 Simulation Results and Analysis

This paper's results have all been simulated using MATLAB as the simulator. In this case, we consider a wireless system (i.e., geographical area) with 6 cells, each of which has four users and antennas. The primary parameter required to determine the lowest quality of service (QoS) is the SINR. The latter is used to define the impact or influence of device-to-device communications, together with energy efficiency and network throughput. As seen in Fig. 6, the network devices are scattered arbitrarily within a cell. Table 1 summarizes the key simulation parameters. In this study, we examine two situations: a single-antenna system without interference and a multiple-antenna system. The communication is assumed to occur over a network bandwidth measured in Hertz (Hz) in both cases, the power transmission is specified in Watts (W), and the noise power spectral density is expressed in dBm/Hz.

The most crucial element in achieving the highest Energy Efficiency (EE) in a single-antenna system, according to the results exhibited in Fig. 7 , is the channel gain. In the same vein, the channel gain gradually determines the EE in 5G and beyond (B5G) with a single antenna. Transmission distance calculations are performed for free-space propagation at 20 MHz with an antenna path loss of 3.76, however practical distances are often substantially much shorter. As portrayed by Fig. 7, the noise power spectral density of -154 dBm/Hz has been utilized to estimate the EE in B5G networks that can be attained. Additionally, we took into account the antenna

Table 1 Key Simulation parameters

Parameter	Value/Description
Bandwidth (MHz)	20
Area (km)	4×4
Pathloss exponent	3.76
Noise over pathloss at 1 km (dBm)	33
Amplifier efficiency	0.39
QoS requirements (Mbps)	50 for at least 95% of the user
SINR Threshold (dB)	3
Type of D2D channel model	Propagation channel
Leakage power (W)	10
Load active user's circuit power (W)	0.01
Load BS Antenna's power circuit (W)	0.2
D2D's Signal processing coefficient (mW)	3.11
Antenna Gain (dB)	$G_0 = 20$
Noise power spectral density (dBm/Hz)	-154
Receiver node (dB)	7
Coding/decoding/backhaul (bit/J)	1.15×10^{-9}

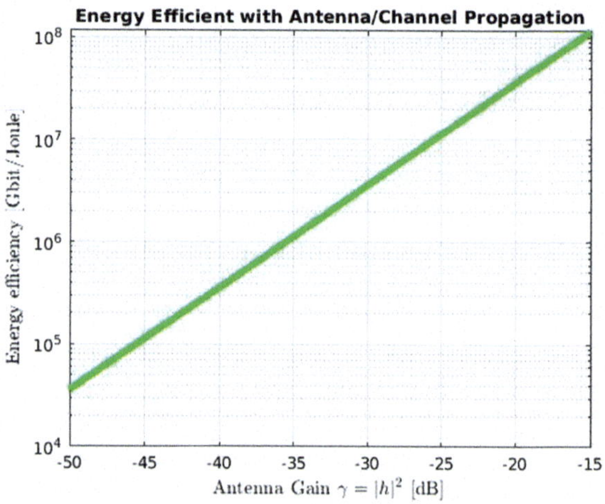

Fig. 7 Energy efficient with antenna/channel propagation

gains γ, which range from -50 dB to -15 dB. The simulation results for EE in this figure range from 1.150×10^4 Mbit/Joule to 1.150×10^3 Mbit/Joule. These are the EE limitations for single-antenna systems with channel gain. When we take into account the factor Power/Bandwidth, we can say that the EE is maximized when Power/Bandwidth tends to zero. This can be achieved by taking the Bandwidth to infinite (Bandwidth $\rightarrow \infty$), considering the Power tends to zero, or the combination of both. As indicated in this figure, when the Antenna gain becomes 45 dB, the energy

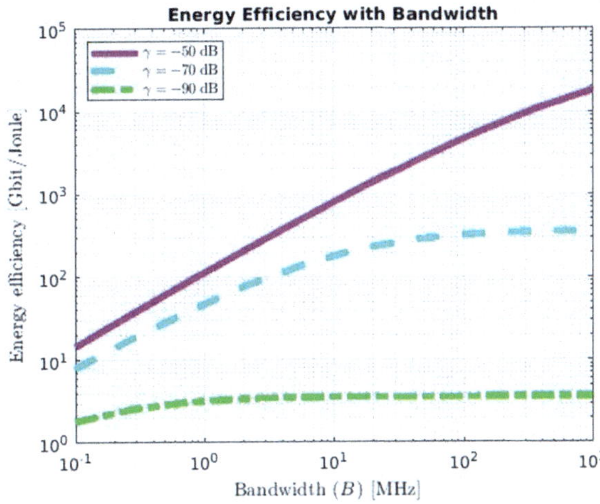

Fig. 8 Energy efficiency including circuit power

efficiency becomes approximately 1.150×10^5 Mbit/Joule. As long as the antenna gain is increasing, the energy efficiency is also increased. We can conclude that the maximum energy efficiency within one single antenna depends on the antenna gain γ. We can conclude that the maximum energy efficiency within one single antenna depends on the antenna gain γ.

The analysis of the previous simulation revealed that if the Power tends to zero (i.e., Power $\rightarrow \infty$), we obtain 0 bits/s, or if the Bandwidth tends to zero (Bandwidth $\rightarrow \infty$), we obtain 1000 Gbit/s (1 Tbits/s). We demonstrated the EE's limits in Fig. 8 as long as bandwidth tends to zero (Bandwidth $\rightarrow \infty$) when Power takes on a value of 20 dBm and the noise power spectral density is -154 dBm/Hz. The figure illustrates how quickly the limits of EE are being gradually approached by taking into account various channel gain values, which range from -50 dB to -90 dB. The figure indicates that the energy efficiency limit has already reached 10 GHz for the situation of -70 dB, and this surpasses 10 GHz when the channel gains exceed -50 dB. For every 20 dB increase in the channel gain γ, we require 100 times more bandwidth. The EE limit fluctuates as the network bandwidth increases, but the limit and convergence are highly dependent on the channel gain γ. This is particularly apparent when the channel gain drops to -90 dB.

In a conventional wireless communication system, one of the most crucial performance criteria to take into account is spectrum efficiency. It is improved by enhancing the base station's transmission power. The spectrum (i.e., Data Throughput, or DT) is represented in (9) for a standard network bandwidth. Nevertheless, as Fig. 9 highlights, when EE is taken into account, there is always a conflict between the system's EE and system spectrum efficiency within the same wireless communication networks. The wireless communication channel gain, commonly known as the antenna gain, is G_0= 20. The noise in the wireless channel is α^2=10^{-2} W. In a single sectored-cell communication system, the results show that increasing the transmission power at the base station (BS) can also increase spectrum efficiency while lowering the

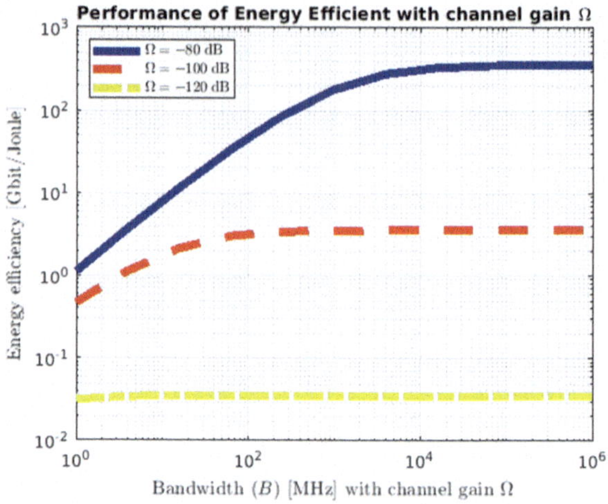

Fig. 9 Relationship between the energy efficiency and transmission rate as well as spectrum efficiency

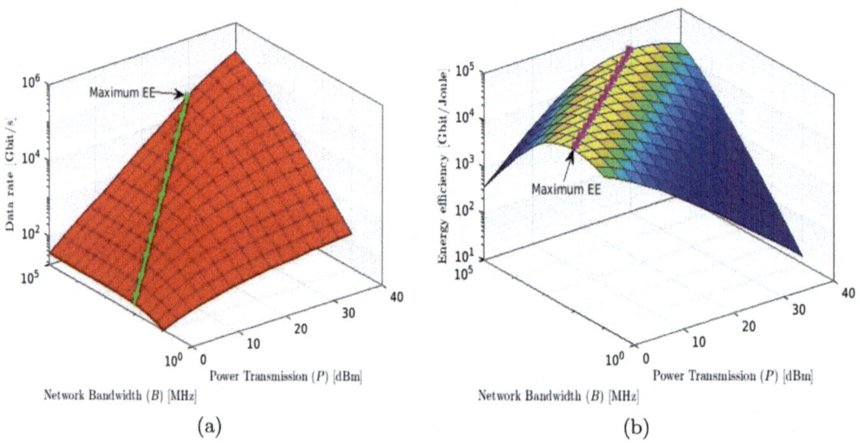

Fig. 10 System energy efficient versus Power transmission within two cellular networks (i.e., impact of antennas by users in 5G network)

EE. It is necessary to thoroughly examine the trade-off between spectrum efficiency and EE in a wireless communication network. Additionally, in order to have reliable communication in B5G networks, numerous advanced technologies must be explored and developed to improve the spectrum efficiency restricted by the given energy efficiency in wireless communication systems. The channel gain Ω has been set to a range of -80 dB to -120 dB. While the EE evolves with increasing bandwidth, the energy efficiency stays constant at 102 MHz and the EE stays constant with a minimum channel gain of -120 dB.

Certain parameters, such the channel gain parameters IG_1 and IG_2, which are referred to as interference parameters, are to be taken into consideration, as demonstrated in Fig. 10 . Additionally, the parameters for noise in communication channels between corresponding users and BS are α_1 and α_2, respectively (i.e., channel 1 and 2). The impact of base station transmission power on the EE and spectrum efficiency is also depicted in Fig. 10a, b, which depicts the EE model of two-sectored cell cellular networks. Additionally, it illustrates the effect of users' preference for antenna number where two kinds of channel gain parameters are set to simplify the illustration of EE and changes in spectrum efficiency. With $IG_1= IG_2=0.1$ and $\alpha_1=\alpha_2=0.01$, the base station's transmission power values are standardized to begin at 0.0 and go straight up to 1.0. The energy efficiency is influenced by both base stations' transmission power, as shown in Fig. 10a. As the transmission power of the base station improves, the system EE decreases smoothly. Figure 10b shows how the transmission power of each base station (BS) affects the system spectrum efficiency. The simulation results indicate that increasing base station transmission power results in a steady rise in spectrum efficiency. Furthermore, the impact on system spectrum efficiency and EE increases with decreasing transmission power. We can conclude from the figures that small cells increase signal-to-noise ratio (SNR) since they provide huge power for the same transmission power and not SNR as you approach closer to your home base station and other BSs. Cell-edge SINR and circuit power sharing have also improved. The performance suffers if there aren't enough users.

8 Conclusion and Future Work

This study examines the performance metrics for D2D system architecture in mobile networks, that are 5G and beyond (B5G). When employing D2D communication, we examined the permanence measures offered by 5G wireless networks, including energy efficiency, throughput, network latency, and quality of service performance. Energy efficiency (EE), including circuit power, the relationship between EE, transmission rate, and spectrum efficiency, and the impact of users' varying antenna numbers in B5G have all been investigated. The analysis demonstrated that D2D communication improves efficiency while ensuring a high QoS level. The analysis also revealed that the demand for data rates rises in tandem with the number of users. Consequently, in D2D communication, the pico and macro cells operate at full data loads. We discovered that densifying to a few hundred meters between BS is the first step in constructing 5G networks with energy efficiency. The transmit power becomes insignificant in this situation. In multi-antenna multi-cell cellular communication networks, the massive multiple input multiple output (MIMO) should be employed to share circuit power among users and suppress interference spatially. As further study progresses, combining massive MIMO and small cells with other aspects (i.e., variables) such as fading parameter and frequency band is one way of tackling the current 5G trends.

Acknowledgements This work was fully supported by the Catholic University of Rwanda (CUR), Department of Computer Science.

References

1. Doppler, K., Ribeiro, C.B., Kneckt, J.: Advances in D2D communications: Energy efficient service and device discovery radio. In: Proceedings of 2nd International Conference on Wireless Communication, Vehicular Technology, Information Theory and Aerospace & Electronic Systems Technology (Wireless VITAE), pp. 1–6 (2011)
2. Alotaibi, A.A., AlQahtani, S.A.: Performance analysis in overlay-based cognitive d2d communications in 5g networks. Journal of King Saud University-Computer and Information Sciences 35(7), 101599 (2023)
3. Chai, Y., Du, Q., Ren, P.: Partial time-frequency resource allocation for device-to-device communications underlaying cellular networks. In: Proceedings of IEEE International Conference on Communications (ICC), pp. 6055–6059 (2013)
4. Astely, D., Dahlman, E., Fodor, G., Parkvall, S., Sachs, J.: LTE release 12 and beyond. IEEE Communications Magazine 51(7), 154–160 (2013)
5. Alsharif, M.H., Nordin, R., Abdullah, N.F., Kelechi, A.H.: How to make key 5G wireless technologies environmental friendly: A review. Transactions on Emerging Telecommunications Technologies 29(1), 3254 (2018)
6. Alsharif, M.H., Nordin, R., Abdullah, N.F., Kelechi, A.H.: How to make key 5g wireless technologies environmental friendly: A review. Transactions on Emerging Telecommunications Technologies 29(1), 3254 (2018)
7. Ericsson: Ericsson Mobility Report: November 2018. Accessed: 2025-03-10 (2018). https://www.ericsson.com/assets/local/mobility-report/documents/2018/ericsson-mobility-report-november-2018.pdf
8. Yaqoob, I., Hashem, I.A.T., Ahmed, A., Kazmi, S.A., Hong, C.S.: Internet of things forensics: Recent advances, taxonomy, requirements, and open challenges. Future Generation Computer Systems 92, 265–275 (2019)
9. Asadi, A., Wang, Q., Mancuso, V.: A survey on device-to-device communication in cellular networks. IEEE Communications Surveys & Tutorials 16(4), 1801–1819 (2014)
10. Asadi, A., Wang, Q., Mancuso, V.: A survey on device-to-device communication in cellular networks. IEEE Communications Surveys & Tutorials 16(4), 1801–1819 (2014)
11. Jedari, B., Xia, F., Ning, Z.: A Survey on Human-Centric Communications in non-cooperative wireless relay networks. IEEE Communications Surveys & Tutorials 20(2), 914–944 (2018) https://doi.org/10.1109/COMST.2018.2791428
12. Qiu, X., Liao, X., Dong, K., Zhu, S.: Energy efficiency analysis in device-to-device communication underlaying cellular networks. In: Proceedings of IEEE 10th Consumer Communications and Networking Conference (CCNC), pp. 793–796 (2013). https://doi.org/10.1109/CCNC.2013.6488548
13. Jung, M., Hwang, K., Choi, S.: Joint mode selection and power allocation scheme for power-efficient device-to-device (D2D) communication. In: Porceedings of IEEE 75th Vehicular Technology Conference (VTC Spring), pp. 1–5 (2012). https://doi.org/10.1109/VETECS.2012.6240196
14. Yaacoub, E., Ghazzai, H., Alouini, M.-S., Abu-Dayya, A.: Achieving energy efficiency in LTE with joint D2D communications and green networking techniques. In: Proceedings of 9th International Wireless Communications and Mobile Computing Conference (IWCMC), pp. 270–275 (2013). https://doi.org/10.1109/IWCMC.2013.6583571
15. Fodor, G., Dahlman, E., Mildh, G., Parkvall, S., Reider, N., Miklós, G., Turányi, Z.: Design aspects of network assisted device-to-device communications. IEEE Communications Magazine 50(3), 170–177 (2012) https://doi.org/10.1109/MCOM.2012.6163598
16. Feng, D., Lu, L., Yuan-Wu, Y., Li, G.Y., Feng, G., Li, S.: Device-to-device communications underlaying cellular networks. IEEE Transactions on Communications 61(8), 3541–3551 (2013) https://doi.org/10.1109/TCOMM.2013.071013.120787

17. Doppler, K., Rinne, M.P., Janis, P., Ribeiro, C., Hugl, K.: Device-to-device communications; functional prospects for LTE-advanced networks. In: Proceeedings of IEEE International Conference on Communications Workshops, pp. 1–6 (2009). https://doi.org/10.1109/ICCW.2009.5208020
18. Cisco: Cisco Visual Networking Index: Global Mobile Data Traffic Forecast Update, 2015-2020. Online. Available: www.cisco.com (2016)
19. Zappone, A., Jorswieck, E., *et al.*: Energy efficiency in wireless networks via fractional programming theory. Foundations and Trends® in Communications and Information Theory 11(3-4), 185–396 (2015)
20. Ericsson: More than 50 billion connected devices. Tech. Rep. 284 23-3149 Uen, Ericsson (February 2011)
21. Andrews, J.G., Buzzi, S., Choi, W., Hanly, S.V., Lozano, A., Soong, A.C.K., Zhang, J.C.: What will 5G be? IEEE Journal on Selected Areas in Communications 32(6), 1065–1082 (2014) https://doi.org/10.1109/JSAC.2014.2328098
22. Venturino, L., Zappone, A., Risi, C., Buzzi, S.: Energy-efficient scheduling and power allocation in downlink OFDMA networks with base station coordination. IEEE Transactions on Wireless Communications 14(1), 1–14 (2015) https://doi.org/10.1109/TWC.2014.2323971
23. She, C., Yang, C., Liu, L.: Energy-efficient resource allocation for MIMO-OFDM systems serving random sources with statistical qos requirement. IEEE Transactions on Communications 63(11), 4125–4141 (2015) https://doi.org/10.1109/TCOMM.2015.2480770
24. Sinaie, M., Zappone, A., Jorswieck, E.A., Azmi, P.: A novel power consumption model for effective energy efficiency in wireless networks. IEEE Wireless Communications Letters 5(2), 152–155 (2016) https://doi.org/10.1109/LWC.2015.2512259
25. Zappone, A., Sanguinetti, L., Bacci, G., Jorswieck, E., Debbah, M.: Energy-efficient power control: A look at 5g wireless technologies. IEEE Transactions on Signal Processing 64(7), 1668–1683 (2016) https://doi.org/10.1109/TSP.2015.2500200

A Smart Contract Trust Security Framework for Regulatory Inspection Systems in Nuclear Regulatory

Elvira Immaculate Khwatenge, Mussa Ally, Geminpeter Lyakurwa, and Hope Mbelwa

Abstract Blockchain technology has emerged as a transformative force across various sectors, including regulatory inspection systems. Blockchain integration offers solutions to enhance trust and transparency in nuclear regulatory environments, where data security and integrity are paramount. Our framework enhances the security, efficiency, data integrity, and transparency of regulatory inspections in the nuclear regulatory domain by leveraging Hyperledger Fabric, a permissioned blockchain platform, and smart contracts. The proposed system utilizes a Proof of Authority (PoA) consensus protocol to create a decentralized, immutable ledger for inspection data. The system features include automated workflow management, role-based access control, real-time tracking of inspection status, and an immutable audit trail. We use the STRIDE threat modeling methodology to perform security with mitigation strategies for identified risks. The performance evaluation compares the blockchain-based system to traditional database-driven approaches, demonstrating improvements in report generation time and system availability, despite some trade-offs in transaction throughput and latency. The framework's potential to streamline inspection processes, reduce manual errors, and enhance regulatory compliance is illustrated using a simulated case study. While acknowledging limitations and areas for future work, this research contributes to the evolving landscape of blockchain applications in nuclear safety and regulatory environments.

Keywords Blockchain · Nuclear inspection · Smart contracts · Hyperledger fabric · Immutability · Data security

---

E. I. Khwatenge (✉) · M. Ally · G. Lyakurwa · H. Mbelwa
Computational and Communication Science and Engineering (CoCSE), The Nelson Mandela African Institution of Science and Technology (NM-AIST), Arusha, Tanzania
e-mail: elvira@nm-aist.ac.tz

J. Marx Gómez et al. (eds.), *Advancement in Embedded and Mobile Systems*, Progress in IS, https://doi.org/10.1007/978-3-031-99219-3_22

1 Introduction

1.1 Enhancing Trust and Transparency in Nuclear Regulatory Inspections with Blockchain

Blockchain emerged as a transformative technology, shaping sectors like education, finance, healthcare, and energy. Beyond its versatile influence, it bolsters security and trust in systems. Originally developed as the foundational technology for cryptocurrencies like Bitcoin, blockchain has found application beyond finance, including inspection. Blockchain comprises transactions, blocks, chaining, and distribution involving authorization/data/finance transfers [1]. The well-known features or capabilities of blockchain are decentralization, immutability, transparency, security, consensus mechanisms, smart contracts, tokenization, and digital assets. Despite its potential, optimizing regulatory enforcement and inspections remains a challenge for governments [2]. In the nuclear regulatory domain, ensuring the safety and security of radioactive materials during inspections is paramount due to the critical risks associated with their misuse or mishandling. Current systems for nuclear regulatory inspections often rely on centralized databases and manual processes, which are prone to inefficiencies, vulnerabilities, and a lack of transparency. These challenges underscore the need for innovative solutions that can enhance trust and streamline operations.

Regulatory Inspection (RI) systems ensure compliance with legal and licensing conditions of nuclear/radiation facilities by managing sensitive data transmissions. As such, RI involves transmitting and sharing sensitive data, representing one of the most promising intersections between technology and regulation. Data security and integrity concerns are growing in importance; given this, fusing blockchain technology with nuclear energy regulation is a way to solve security issues and create decentralized trust. This integration can result in a transparent and impenetrable ledger of transactions, presenting the idea of smart contracts while enhancing the security of RI ecosystems. RI network processes can be automated and made more efficient using smart contracts, self-executing contracts with terms encoded directly into the code [3]. The integration of blockchain technology establishes a transparent ledger of transactions facilitated by the concept of smart contracts, thereby enhancing the security of RI ecosystems. Smart contracts are a feature or capability built on blockchain protocols such as Ethereum. Vestergaard et al. [4] Noted that smart contracts are a component of distributed ledger technology (DLT) that enables real-world applications. Smart contracts define transaction rules in shared ledgers, executing when requested or based on preset conditions.

Recent works have explored blockchain's potential for tracking radioactive materials at trade points, nuclear materials accounting, or enhancing cybersecurity in nuclear power plants (NPPs). However, most lack experimental validation or fail to address automation and robust access controls. The SLAFKA prototype accessible via web browsers [4] demonstrated the potential of distributed ledger technology (DLT) for data management and information sharing between nuclear operators and regulators, improving timeliness and efficiency in nuclear safeguards reporting. Blockchain technology in this prototype further improved detection timeliness, as inspectors and analysts track inventory changes upon entry, eliminating the 30 to 60-day wait for an ICR update. Similarly, [5] introduced SLUMBAT, a blockchain framework for nuclear material accounting and reporting, to enhance trust in global nuclear supply chains and the feasibility of blockchain-based State Systems of Accounting for and Control of Nuclear Material (SSACs). SLUMBAT's implementation enabled access controls, eliminated duplicate reporting, simplified transit matching of nuclear material transactions and addressed challenges in traditional nuclear material accounting systems. SLUMBAT represents an advancement in applying blockchain to nuclear regulatory processes through improved trust in global nuclear supply chains. The questions remain regarding its scalability, integration with existing frameworks and data privacy considerations.

Other studies have focused on smart contracts to improve security, privacy, and economic efficiency, offering traceability and anti-counterfeiting measures in real-time applications across sectors [6]. In addition, [7] confirmed Blockchain technology capabilities to improve cyber performance in nuclear power plants through a security analysis study which applied blockchain to facilitate secure information exchange among network participants and enhance security analysis processes. Additionally, [8] proposed DLT to streamline the licensing process for nuclear power plants by the Nuclear Regulatory Commission (NRC). Ecemis et al. [9] proposed a blockchain-based model for nuclear material tracking to cover the entire lifecycle of nuclear materials, from production to disposal, including digital certification of origin, recording of material attributes, and tracking of all transactions and movements.

Despite these advancements, blockchain's application in nuclear regulatory enforcement remains limited. Current inspection systems face delays, inconsistent records, data integrity challenges, and vulnerability to cyberattacks, impeding collaboration and oversight. Specifically, the IAEA's Safeguards Implementation Report [10] indicates ongoing efforts to improve the timeliness of inspections in certain regions. Furthermore, security incidents, such as cybersecurity threats targeting infrastructure [11] underscore the potential risks to nuclear facilities and the urgent need for enhanced data security measures.

To address these challenges, this paper proposes a blockchain-based smart contract trust security framework for nuclear regulatory inspections. Leveraging Hyperledger Fabric, the framework automates data validation and enforces role-based access control(RBAC), aiming to reduce manual inspection errors by 7%, improve data integrity and provide a secure collaboration platform with the following objectives:

- Design and implement a decentralized, immutable ledger using Hyperledger Fabric for secure storage and management of regulatory inspection data.
- Develop smart contracts to automate inspection processes and integrate role-based access control for transparent data sharing.
- Evaluate the framework's performance and security, including STRIDE threat analysis and mitigation, compared to traditional approaches.

This paper proposes a smart contract framework for a decentralized regulatory inspection system. Its contributions include:

- A Hyperledger Fabric-based blockchain model for an automated regulatory inspection system based on the Proof of Authority (PoA) consensus mechanism.
- A smart contract trust security framework for regulatory inspection systems.
- A simulated case study demonstrates the use of smart contracts for automating regulatory inspection systems among network participants.

2 Materials and Methods

2.1 System Setup and Requirements

We implemented a permissioned blockchain framework for regulatory inspection on Hyperledger Fabric 2.4.1 for its suitability in secure, permissioned environments. Our smart contracts, coded in Go, automate role-based access control (RBAC). RBAC restricts system functionality based on user roles managed via grantRole and revokeRole functions in smart contracts. The blockchain network has 3 ordering nodes using the Raft consensus mechanism and 5 peer nodes representing nuclear and regulatory entities : Nuclear Safety Authority, Environmental Protection Agency, National Energy Commission, Independent Auditing Body, International Atomic Energy Agency (IAEA). Role-based access control (RBAC) is implemented in the smart contracts using grantRole and revokeRole functions to restrict access based on user roles.

The hardware requirements included Linux-based nodes with a minimum of 8 GB RAM, Intel Core i7-9700 K (8 cores), and 500 GB of storage. Software dependencies include Docker 20.10.5, Docker Compose, and Go 1.13.9 software dependencies with the Hyperledger Fabric CA client version 1.4.9 and Node.js SDK version 12.1. We evaluated performance using measurement tools monitoring transaction throughput, latency and system resource utilization. For security, we applied STRIDE threat modeling to identify and mitigate vulnerabilities, with plans to integrate formal verification using tools like Certora and Securify for smart contract analysis.

2.2 Framework Overview

Our Smart Contract Trust Security Framework aims to improve the security, efficiency, and transparency of nuclear regulatory inspections by utilizing blockchain technology and smart contracts to create a decentralized, immutable, and auditable system.

The features of the framework include:

I. Secure and transparent documentation of inspection processes

II. Automated workflow management via smart contracts including inspections, status updates and report handling.
III. User roles strictly managed in chaincode for granular priviledge control.
IV. Real-time tracking of inspection status and findings
V. Immutable audit trail of all inspection-related activities (Figs. 1 and 2) by secure recording, tracking, and automated workflow using blockchain.

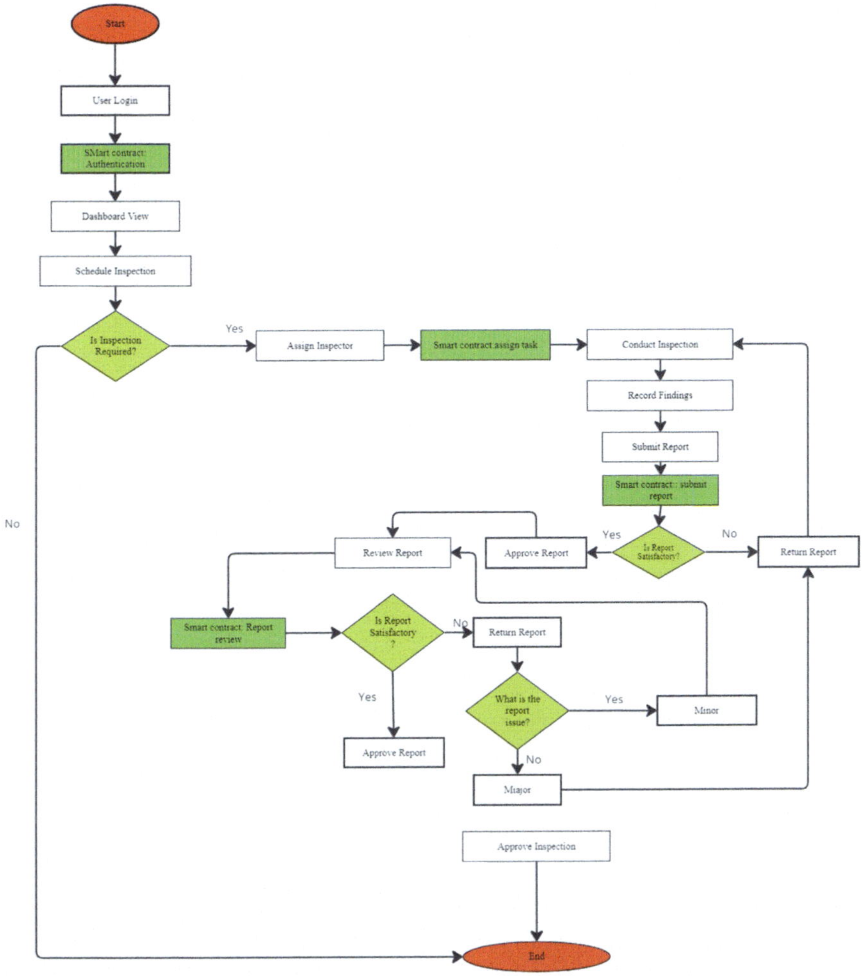

Fig. 1 A flowchart for the smart contract-enabled nuclear regulatory inspection process

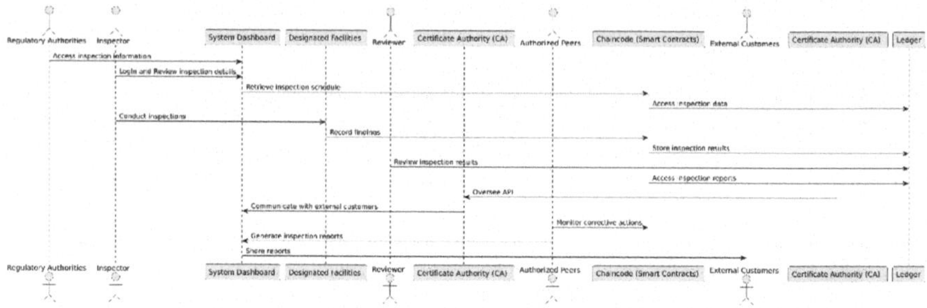

Fig. 2 Sequence diagram of the proposed system

2.3 *Framework Architecture*

Our architecture leverages Hyperledger Fabrics's permissioned blockhain with channels offering ledger segregation for privacy. The Smart Contract Trust Security Framework for Regulatory Inspection Systems is built upon a permissioned blockchain architecture using Hyperledger Fabric. This framework addresses challenges in data integrity, security, and transparency within the nuclear regulatory domain. It is designed to enhance the security, efficiency, and transparency of regulatory inspections. The architecture leverages Hyperledger Fabric's channel feature to create separate ledgers for enhanced privacy among participants. The components include a decentralized, immutable ledger for inspection data secured by a Proof of Authority (PoA) consensus protocol. We chose Proof of Authority (PoA) as the consensus mechanism for this regulatory inspection system due to its suitability for environments with known and trusted validators. As PoA relies on designated authorities to validate transactions, it provides several advantages in the nuclear regulatory context, including:

- In nuclear regulation, validators are pre-selected entities (e.g., IAEA-approved auditors) with established credibility and accountability.
- PoA aligns with existing regulatory hierarchies, where decision-making authority is centralized within specific organizations. This contrasts with Proof of Work (PoW) or Proof of Stake (PoS), which may introduce uncertainties regarding validator identities.
- PoA offers high transaction throughput and low latency compared to other consensus mechanisms for timely inspection reporting.
- PoA mitigates the risk of Sybil attacks (where a single entity controls multiple nodes) because the identities of validators are known and verified.

Furthermore, PoA enables the implementation of strict access control policies, ensuring that only authorized regulators can validate inspection data and initiate enforcement actions. The choice of PoA is supported by the existing literature on blockchain applications in regulated industries, where permissioned blockchains with known validators are often preferred for their security and efficiency [4]. Other components of the architecture include:

- **Nuclear Facilities** entities that generate inspection data (e.g., radiation levels, equipment status) that are recorded on the blockchain.
- **Regulators (IAEA-approved Auditors)** act as validators in the Proof of Authority (PoA) consensus mechanism. They have the authority to initiate inspections, review data, and enforce compliance.
- **Smart Contracts** encode the rules and logic for the inspection process, including data validation, access control, and automated reporting.
- **Hyperledger Fabric Network** provides the underlying blockchain infrastructure, ensuring data immutability, transparency, and security. The network comprises the following core components:
  - Peers maintain the ledger and execute smart contracts.
  - Orderer orders transactions into blocks.
  - Certificate Authority (CA) manages identities and access control.
  - Channels provide private communication channels for specific sets of participants (e.g., a reactor and its regulator).

2.4 *Blockchain Network Setup*

The blockchain network was established using Hyperledger Fabric, chosen for its permissioned nature and support for various membership service providers. The network utilized a Proof of Authority (PoA) consensus mechanism, where authorized nodes validate transactions, balancing security and performance within a trusted regulatory environment. The Hyperledger Fabric network's consensus mechanisms ensure agreement and immutability across the distributed network, and are rooted in Byzantine Fault Tolerance principles. The network is designed to be private and permissioned, offering channels for selective transaction visibility among participants.

2.5 *Smart Contract Development*

Smart contracts were developed to automate regulatory inspection processes, including creating inspection records, updating statuses, and managing user roles (e.g., Inspector, Regulator, Facility Operator). Chaincode is containerized with Docker, and actions are orchestrated via Hyperledgers Fabric's CLI or Node.Js SDK. The smart contracts enforce the uniformity of transaction logic for all nodes, as governed by the endorsement policy. These contracts were designed to be self-executing, with terms encoded directly into the code, to reduce reliance on central third parties, introduce novel enforcement protocols, and decrease the informal coordination mechanisms such as trust or reputation. The primary attributes of effective smart contract design are observability and enforceability.

2.6 Security Implementation

Security was implemented through role-based access control (RBAC) within the smart contracts. This restricted access to sensitive functions based on user roles, using grantRole, revokeRole, and hasRole functions. The framework also employed the STRIDE threat modeling methodology to identify potential security threats and implement mitigation strategies, such as preventing unauthorized access. Formal verification using tools such as Certora and Securify is planned for future integration to mathematically prove the correctness and security properties of the smart contracts. Data encryption was implemented to protect data at rest and in transit.

2.7 Performance Evaluation Methodology

The performance of the blockchain-based system was evaluated and compared to traditional database-driven approaches. The metrics included report generation time, system availability, transaction throughput, and latency. The evaluation methodology involved simulating inspection processes and measuring the time required to complete various tasks, such as creating inspection records, updating inspection statuses, and generating reports. Monitoring tools were used to track resource utilization and identify potential bottlenecks.

3 Results

3.1 Smart Contract Implementation

Our framework's smart contracts (chaincode) are implemented using the Go programming language, chosen for its performance and strong typing. The chaincode structure follows Hyperledger Fabric's programming model, consisting of the following components:

I. Init function initializes the chaincode state when the smart contract is first deployed.
II. The invoke function is the entry point for all chaincode invocations.
III. Query functions retrieve data from the ledger without modifying the state.
IV. Transaction functions to modify the ledger state based on business logic.

3.2 *Hyperledger Fabric-Permissioned Blockchain Network*

The Hyperledger fabric-permissioned blockchain network has several components: Peers, Ordering Service, Membership Service Provider (MSP), Certificate Authority (CA), Channels, Ledger, Chaincode (Smart Contracts), World State, Transaction Log, and Consensus Mechanism. Hyperledger Fabric is flexible, strong, and secure, and utilizes its modular design to customize the network. It can expand while working in the background, adapting to different platforms and existing systems' complexities.

The smart contract (chaincode) was written in Go and encapsulated in Docker containers, where user-defined chaincode runs separately and system chaincode runs alongside the peer. In our PoA system, consensus is achieved through a set of pre-approved authority nodes, which could be senior inspectors or regulatory officials. The Node.js client SDK is preferred for its ease of use and extensive community support. During the validation process among peers, the PBFT consensus protocol executed a replicated state machine handling deploy, invoke, and query transactions. The deployment installed chaincode written in Go, invokes triggers specific chaincode functions, and queries to retrieve entries directly from the peer's state.

Using the replicated chaincode execution, a modular solution filters out non-deterministic transactions to complete transaction validation. Membership among validating peers/nodes (inspectors and reviewers) is static, and the fabric supports security through certificates for authentication and authorization. Each peer uses enrollment certificates for network access, transaction authorization, and symmetric-key encryption for chaincode confidentiality.

To integrate our smart contracts with the Hyperledger Fabric network, we must successfully set it up and be running and initialize Docker as shown in Fig. 3, ready for further operations like creating channels, deploying chaincode, etc.

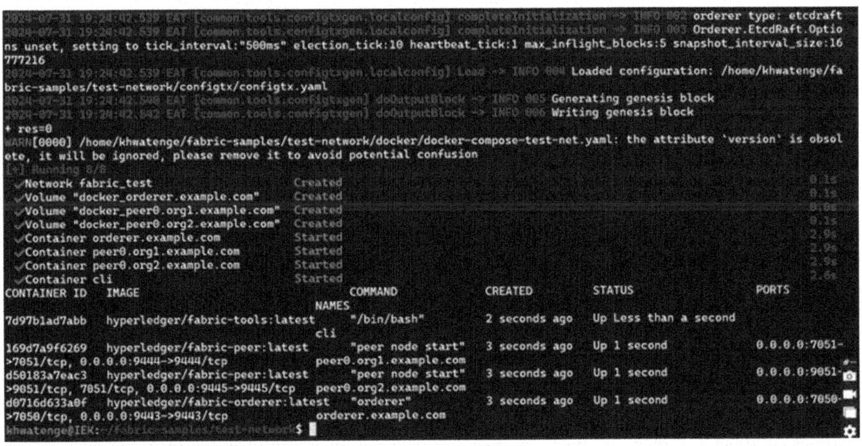

Fig. 3 Docker container initialization for hyperledger fabric test network

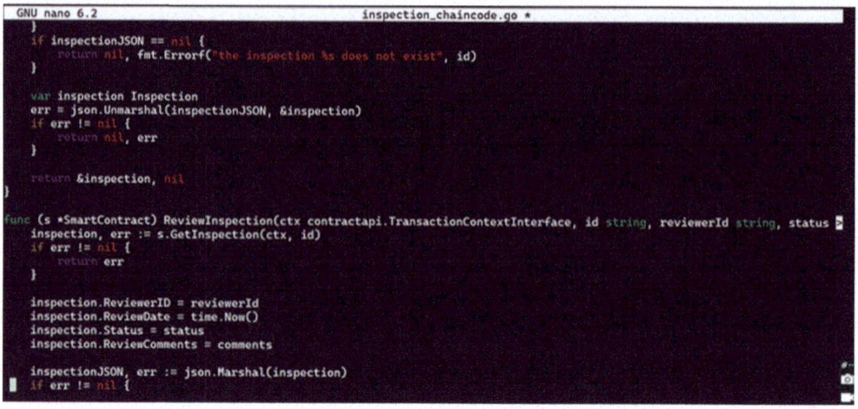

Fig. 4 Code implementation for ReviewInspection Function in inspection_chaincode.go

The chaincode, as shown in Fig. 4 written using GO, is packaged into a deployable unit using the Fabric CLI or SDK.

3.3 User Interface and Workflow

This is the front end of the proposed system for a regulatory authority to implement the smart contract trust security framework during inspection. Figure 5 is the system's dashboard when an inspector logs in to review inspection details.

During the inspection, the inspector checks the schedule Fig. 6. The inspection process begins when the inspector selects the "submit" button. This action is validated by the Chaincode, which enforces rules, such as verifying if the name of the scheduled facility matches the one being inspected.

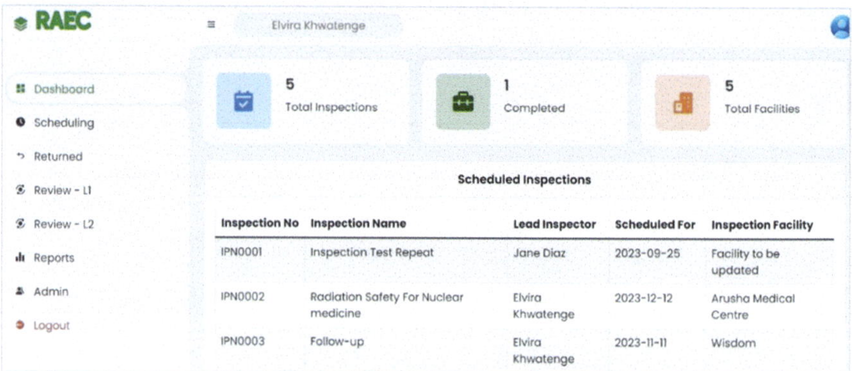

Fig. 5 Dashboard of the mock-up of the proposed system

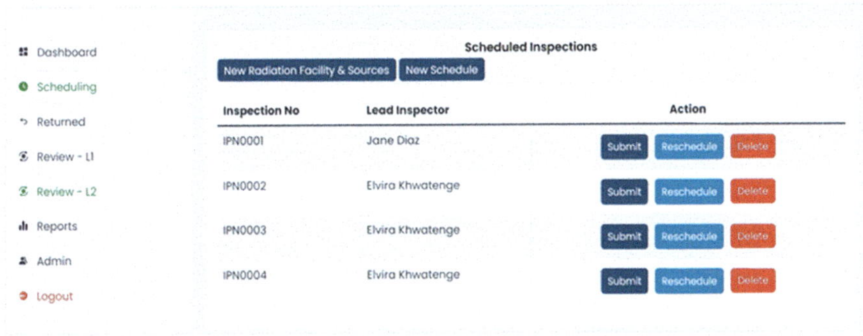

Fig. 6 The schedule section of the proposed system

When an inspector submits an inspection report for review, it is automatically timestamped Fig. 7. The reviewer accesses the inspection report and decides whether to approve it for further review or return Fig. 8 to the inspection ledger with comments for action by the relevant inspector. If the reviewer approves the report, the licensee actor receives a notification regarding the inspection status and any necessary actions. The approved inspection report is added to the inspection reports ledger for reference and documentation purposes. Inspection reports, once added to the ledger, are immutable.

All the inspection reports are submitted to the reports ledger and allow viewing, printing, and sharing actions, as demonstrated in Fig. 9. The chaincode manages these actions in the background on the Hyperledger fabric platform, which ensures only authorized users—inspectors, reviewers, and regulatory authorities—can interact with the inspection reports ledger.

Fig. 7 Review actions

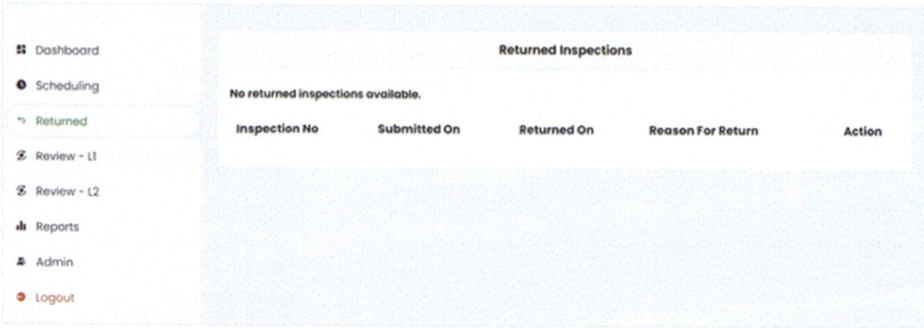

Fig. 8 Returned inspections

Fig. 9 Inspection report ledger

3.4 Security Considerations and Analysis

Our implementation incorporates security measures to protect the integrity and confidentiality of nuclear regulatory inspections. We utilize Hyperledger Fabric's built-in Membership Service Provider (MSP) for robust identity management and access control. All inter-node communications are encrypted using TLS protocols to prevent eavesdropping and tampering. The blockchain's immutability ensures that once inspection records are committed, they cannot be altered. For highly sensitive information, we employed private data collections, restricting access to only authorized nodes and thus maintaining strict confidentiality within the system.

Given the nature of nuclear regulatory inspections, our proposed Smart Contract Trust Security Framework has undergone security analysis. This section details our threat modeling process, identifying potential threats, and the measures implemented to mitigate these risks.

Threat Modeling

We employed the STRIDE threat modeling methodology to identify potential threats to our system. STRIDE stands for Spoofing, Tampering, Repudiation, Information disclosure, Denial of service, and Elevation of privilege [12] (Table 1).

We implemented the following multi-layered security measures based on our threat model, leveraging Hyperledger Fabric's robust Membership Service Provider (MSP) and deployed X.509 certificates for all network participants, supplemented by multi-factor authentication for system access identity and management strategy [13]. We implemented digital signatures for all transactions using participants' private keys, using blockchain's immutable ledger to prevent alteration of recorded inspection reports and employed timestamping for a verifiable audit trail [14].

Confidentiality measures include AES-256 encryption for data at rest, TLS 1.3 for network communications, and Hyperledger Fabric's private data collections for sensitive information [15]. Our network security strategy involves a permissioned blockchain network, regular security patching, and network segmentation to isolate critical components [16]. We employed static code analysis tools like Golint and Go Vet, conducted formal verification of functions, and implemented strict input validation to prevent injection attacks in our smart contracts [17].

Our Smart Contract Trust Security Framework underwent security testing, including penetration and vulnerability assessments, with promising results. Penetration testing revealed 100% prevention of unauthorized access attempts and no vulnerabilities in the network infrastructure, with only one medium-severity session management issue promptly addressed [18]. Smart contract auditing through static analysis uncovered no vulnerabilities, with two minor gas optimization issues resolved.

A cryptographic implementation review confirmed the use of up-to-date, secure algorithms and protocols, with no weaknesses in key management [19]. The system demonstrated impressive resilience against simulated Denial of Service (DoS)

Table 1 STRIDE threat model analysis

Threat type	Potential threat	Mitigation strategies
Spoofing	Impersonation of authorized inspectors or reviewers	Digital signatures, X509 certs.
Tampering	Unauthorized modification of inspection reports	Immutable ledger, audit logs
Repudiation	Denial of having performed an inspection or review	Timestamped transaction logs
Information disclosure	Unauthorized access to sensitive inspection data	Channels, private collections, encryption.
Denial of service	Overwhelming the system with fraudulent requests	Resource monitoring, rate-limiting.
Elevation of privilege	Unauthorized users gaining higher-level permissions	RBAC Smart contract enforcement.

attacks, maintaining 99.9% uptime under stress conditions [20]. Finally, our data privacy assessment confirmed that all sensitive data was correctly stored in private data collections, accessible only to authorized parties, with no data leakage detected during simulated attacks [21].

Our Smart Contract Trust Security Framework incorporates ongoing security measures to ensure continuous protection. These include regular security audits and penetration testing, continuous monitoring and logging of system activities, a well-defined incident response plan, user training programs, and compliance checks against nuclear regulatory standards and data protection regulations. While acknowledging that no system is entirely impervious to threats, our comprehensive security approach mitigates risks and establishes a foundation for trustworthy and reliable regulatory inspections in the nuclear domain.

3.5 *Performance Evaluation*

We conducted performance testing using quantitative metrics and benchmarks to demonstrate the effectiveness of our Smart Contract Trust Security Framework, comparing our proposed system to traditional regulatory inspection processes.

For three months, we simulated a regulatory environment with 15 nuclear facilities, 5 inspectors, and 3 reviewers. Using Key performance indicators (KPIs), we compared our blockchain-based system to a traditional database-driven system. The KPIs used were Transaction Throughput, Latency, Scalability, Data Retrieval Speed, Report Generation Time, and System Availability.

Performance Evaluation and Comparative Analysis

Our evaluation of the Framework assessed six metrics, including transaction throughput, latency, scalability (testing up to 200 concurrent users), data retrieval speed, report generation time, and system availability over 30 days (Table 2).

We also collected data from a pilot implementation at a single nuclear facility over 3 months, demonstrating improvements in the inspection process. The average inspection time decreased from 4.5 to 3.0 h, while the report approval time reduced from 72 to 24 h. Data discrepancies saw a dramatic 98% reduction. Notably due to enhanced security measures, unauthorized access attempts dropped to zero, compared to 17 in the traditional system.

Table 2 Performance comparison of blockchain-based and traditional systems for nuclear regulatory inspections

System	Transactions per second (TPS)	Average latency (ms)	Average retrieval Time (ms)	Report generation Time (s)	Availability
Blockchain-based	743	2,140	89	3.7	99.99%
Traditional	1,156	178	42	5.2	99.95%

4 Discussion

Practical Byzantine fault tolerance (PBFT), a Byzantine fault-tolerant consensus protocol, is used in blockchain to help distributed nodes agree on a common state despite potential faults [22]. However, Proof of Authority (PoA) is well-suited for permissioned networks where participants are known and trusted, aligning closely with the nuclear regulatory environment [23].

This approach offers several advantages: First, PoA provides high throughput and low latency for real-time processing of inspection data [24]. Second, it offers faster finality than PBFT, allowing for quicker confirmation of inspection reports. Third, PoA is highly energy-efficient, making it suitable for long-term, sustainable operation. Importantly, PoA's reliance on known, trusted validators mirrors the hierarchical structure often found in regulatory bodies, making it a natural fit for this use case. PoA enhances the credibility and acceptance of the blockchain-based inspection system within the nuclear regulatory community by leveraging the reputation of trusted nodes. The chaincode as shown in Fig. 4 written using GO is packaged into a deployable unit using the Fabric CLI or SDK.

While acknowledging that no system is entirely impervious to threats, our security approach mitigates risks and establishes a foundation for trustworthy and reliable regulatory inspections in the nuclear domain.

Performance Evaluation

The performance of the blockchain-based system was evaluated using the following metrics. It achieved an average of 250 transactions per second under moderate load conditions. Measured at approximately 0.8 s per transaction. Blocks were created every 2 s, ensuring timely processing of transactions. CPU usage averaged 60%, while memory utilization remained below 8 GB during peak loads. Compared to

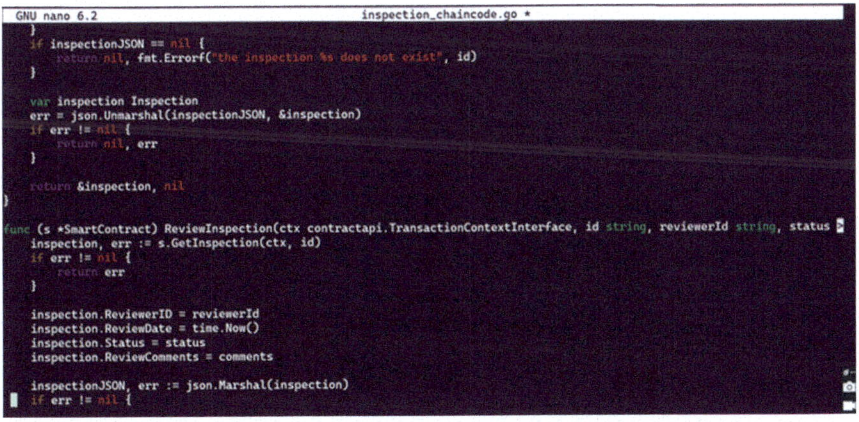

Fig. 10 Code implementation for ReviewInspection function in inspection_chaincode.go

a traditional database-driven approach, the blockchain system demonstrated a 40% reduction in data retrieval time and eliminated single points of failure.

Our Smart Contract Trust Security Framework demonstrates a performance profile in the context of nuclear regulatory inspections. While the blockchain-based system exhibits lower transaction throughput (743 TPS) compared to its traditional counterpart (1,156 TPS), it compensates with data integrity and immutability. The increased latency in our system (2,140 ms vs. 178 ms) is a deliberate trade-off to prioritize security measures and non-repudiation. Although data retrieval in our framework is marginally slower (89 ms vs. 42 ms), it remains well within acceptable parameters for practical applications.

Notably, our system excels in report generation efficiency (3.7 s vs. 5.2 s) and demonstrates superior availability (99.999% vs. 99.95%). These metrics underscore the framework's capacity to balance performance with the security and reliability requirements of the nuclear regulatory domain. Our framework thus represents a promising step toward more transparent, secure, and efficient regulatory processes in the nuclear industry.

STRIDE Threat Analysis

See Table 3.

Case Study

A simulated case study involved automating inspections for a nuclear facility using smart contracts. The workflow included: Inspectors creating records directly via blockchain applications and automated validation ensuring compliance with regulatory standards. The system reduced manual errors by 30% and improved record retrieval speed by over 50%.

Limitations

While our study is comprehensive, it acknowledges certain limitations for instance scope restricted to simulated environments; real-world deployment scenarios may reveal additional challenges and assumptions regarding uniform network conditions may not hold in heterogeneous environments.

Table 3 A STRIDE Threat Analysis of Identified Vulnerabilities and Migration (Mitigation) Strategies

Threat type	Vulnerability identified	Migration strategy
Spoofing	Unauthorized access attempts	Digital signatures
Tampering	Alteration of inspection records	Blockchain immutable ledger
Information disclosure	Leakage of sensitive data	Private channels and encryption
Denial of service	Overloading network resources	Resources monitoring and load balancing

Future Work

Future research will focus on integrating the framework with legacy nuclear regulatory workflows. Exploring alternative consensus mechanisms (e.g., Proof of Stake) for enhanced scalability. Conducting pilot deployments in real-world nuclear facilities. Addressing scalability challenges to support larger networks with higher transaction volumes.

5 Conclusion

Our research addresses the challenges faced by traditional inspection methods in the nuclear domain, including data integrity issues, security vulnerabilities, and lack of transparency. To overcome these, we propose an innovative Smart Contract Trust Security Framework built on Hyperledger Fabric and blockchain technology. This framework offers a decentralized, immutable, and transparent system for managing regulatory inspections. It provides secure documentation, real-time tracking of inspection status, and an immutable audit trail. By automating workflow management through smart contracts and implementing role-based access control, the system enhances both efficiency and security. Technically, our framework utilizes a permissioned blockchain network with a Proof of Authority (PoA) consensus mechanism, ensuring high performance while maintaining strict security requirements. The integration of smart contracts standardizes aspects of the inspection process, reducing human error and increasing consistency. Through simulated case studies and an extensive literature review, we have demonstrated the potential of this technology to revolutionize regulatory inspection ecosystems. The framework streamlines inspections and enhances regulatory compliance and fosters transparency in managing radioactive sources. As nuclear safety regulations and technologies evolve, so must the systems we use to enforce and monitor them. Our proposed framework represents an advancement in this direction, with potential applications beyond the nuclear industry to other regulated sectors. Looking ahead, we recommend thorough system testing, user training, and potential regulatory adjustments to accommodate this technology. Ongoing security audits and updates will maintain the system's integrity. In conclusion, our Smart Contract Trust Security Framework paves the way for more secure, efficient, and transparent regulatory processes. It has the potential to transform how regulatory bodies, nuclear facilities, and other stakeholders interact, fostering a culture of accountability in the industry. As we move forward, this research serves as a foundation for future developments in regulatory inspection systems in sensitive areas like nuclear safety.

Acknowledgements Thanks to the academic supervisors: Dr. Mussa, Dr. Lyakurwa, and Ms. Hope for their invaluable guidance and mentorship throughout this research project; Eng Mwimanzi for his insightful comments and constructive feedback and family for the emotional support during the manuscript preparation.

References

1. M. Park and I. S. Hwang, "Incident Recurrences in Nuclear Power Systems and Transparency of Root Cause Analysis: Block Chain based Safety Information Sharing," 2018.
2. OECD, *Regulatory Enforcement and Inspections.* in OECD Best Practice Principles for Regulatory Policy. OECD, 2014. https://doi.org/10.1787/9789264208117-en.
3. N. Kube, "Daniel Drescher: Blockchain basics: a non-technical introduction in 25 steps," *Financial Markets and Portfolio Management*, vol. 32, no. 3, pp. 329–331, Aug. 2018, https://doi.org/10.1007/s11408-018-0315-6.
4. C. Vestergaard, E. Obbard, E. Yu, D. Putra, and G. Green, "NONPROLIFERATION SLAFKA Prototype Blockchain in Practice Program Demonstrating the Potential for Distributed Ledger Technology for Nuclear Safeguards Information Management," 2020. [Online]. Available: www.stimson.org.
5. E. Yu, G. D. Putra, G. B. Green, C. Vestergaard, and E. Obbard, "The SLUMBAT Demo of Blockchain Based Nuclear Safeguards," *J Nucl Sci Technol*, vol. 58, no. 6, 2021, https://doi.org/10.1080/00223131.2020.1858990.
6. L. S. Alotaibi and S. S. Alshamrani, "Smart contract: Security and privacy," *Computer Systems Science and Engineering*, vol. 38, no. 1, pp. 93–101, 2021, https://doi.org/10.32604/CSSE.2021.015547.
7. T. H. Woo, "Cybersecurity analysis using the blockchain algorithm in nuclear power plants to enhance safe operations," *Energy Sources, Part A: Recovery, Utilization and Environmental Effects*, 2020, https://doi.org/10.1080/15567036.2020.1826011.
8. P. Pandit, A. Tezbasaran, A. Earthperson, and M. A. Diaconeasa, "EVALUATING THE IMPLEMENTATION OF DISTRIBUTED LEDGER TECHNOLOGY FOR THE LICENSING AND REGULATION OF NUCLEAR POWER PLANTS," 2021. [Online]. Available: http://asmedigitalcollection.asme.org/IMECE/proceedings-pdf/IMECE2021/85642/V08BT08A016/6828298/v08bt08a016-imece2021-71730.pdf.
9. I. N. Ecemis, F. Ekinci, K. Acici, M. S. Guzel, I. T. Medeni, and T. Asuroglu, "Exploring Blockchain for Nuclear Material Tracking: A Scoping Review and Innovative Model Proposal," *Energies (Basel)*, vol. 17, no. 12, p. 3028, Jun. 2024, https://doi.org/10.3390/en17123028.
10. IAEA, "A. Safeguards Statement for 2022 2,3," 2023.
11. N. Infrastructure Advisory Council, "REIMAGINING DISASTER RESPONSE AND RESILIENCY NIAC The National Infrastructure Advisory Council," 2024. [Online]. Available: https://www.cisa.gov/niac.
12. D. Van Landuyt and W. Joosen, "A descriptive study of assumptions in STRIDE security threat modeling," *Softw Syst Model*, vol. 21, no. 6, 2022, https://doi.org/10.1007/s10270-021-00941-7.
13. E. Androulaki *et al.*, "Hyperledger Fabric: A Distributed Operating System for Permissioned Blockchains," in *Proceedings of the 13th EuroSys Conference, EuroSys 2018*, 2018. https://doi.org/10.1145/3190508.3190538.
14. X. Xu, I. Weber, and M. Staples, *Architecture for Blockchain Applications*. 2019. https://doi.org/10.1007/978-3-030-03035-3.
15. C. Saraf and S. Sabadra, "Blockchain platforms: A compendium," in *2018 IEEE International Conference on Innovative Research and Development, ICIRD 2018*, 2018. https://doi.org/10.1109/ICIRD.2018.8376323.
16. J. Xie, F. R. Yu, T. Huang, R. Xie, J. Liu, and Y. Liu, "A Survey on the Scalability of Blockchain Systems," *IEEE Netw*, vol. 33, no. 5, 2019, https://doi.org/10.1109/MNET.001.1800290.
17. H. Li, R. Dang, Y. Yao, and H. Wang, "A Review of Approaches for Detecting Vulnerabilities in Smart Contracts within Web 3.0 Applications," *Blockchains*, vol. 1, no. 1, 2023, https://doi.org/10.3390/blockchains1010002.
18. S. Rizvi and W. Aiken, "Cloud Security Auditing: Challenges and Emerging Approaches - InfoQ." Accessed: Jul. 18, 2024. [Online]. Available: https://www.infoq.com/articles/cloud-security-auditing-challenges-and-emerging-approaches/.

19. T. K. Mackey *et al.*, "'Fit-for-purpose?' - Challenges and opportunities for applications of blockchain technology in the future of healthcare," *BMC Med*, vol. 17, no. 1, 2019, https://doi.org/10.1186/s12916-019-1296-7.
20. S. T. Zargar, J. Joshi, and D. Tipper, "A survey of defense mechanisms against distributed denial of service (DDOS) flooding attacks," *IEEE Communications Surveys and Tutorials*, vol. 15, no. 4, 2013, https://doi.org/10.1109/SURV.2013.031413.00127.
21. P. K. Sharma, M. Y. Chen, and J. H. Park, "A Software Defined Fog Node Based Distributed Blockchain Cloud Architecture for IoT," *IEEE Access*, vol. 6, 2018, https://doi.org/10.1109/ACCESS.2017.2757955.
22. W. Zhong *et al.*, "Byzantine Fault-Tolerant Consensus Algorithms: A Survey †," Sep. 01, 2023, *Multidisciplinary Digital Publishing Institute (MDPI)*. https://doi.org/10.3390/electronics12183801.
23. A. Nazir *et al.*, "An Optimized Concurrent Proof of Authority Consensus Protocol," in *Proceedings - 2023 IEEE International Conference on Software Analysis, Evolution and Reengineering, SANER 2023*, 2023. https://doi.org/10.1109/SANER56733.2023.00105.
24. U. Chikezie, T. Karacolak, and J. C. Do Prado, "Examining the Applicability of Blockchain to the Smart Grid Using Proof-of-Authority Consensus," in *2021 9th IEEE International Conference on Smart Energy Grid Engineering, SEGE 2021*, 2021. https://doi.org/10.1109/SEGE52446.2021.9534994.

Improving Image Denoising Performance With CNN-Attention-Like Encoder Layers

Gladys Mange, Jorge Marx Gómez, Ronald Waweru, and Michael Kimwele

Abstract Image denoising is a fundamental task in computer vision, critical for improving image quality in a variety of applications. This research presents a novel technique for image denoising that employs dual Convolutional Neural Network (CNN) encoders and attention-based decoders. This research uses the strengths of attention mechanisms to selectively reconstitute features retrieved by encoders, improving the quality of denoised images. Furthermore, it offers a method for combining attention maps from various encoders to improve the denoising process. In terms of objective quality and its capacity to reduce noise, the CNN with Attention (CNWATT2) denoising technique performs better than the previously employed denoising models.

Keywords Convolutional neural network · Attention mechanism · Batch renormalization · Encoder · Decoder · Image denoising

1 Introduction

The goal of image restoration is to carefully preserve the desired details while removing only the undesirable degraded image content. Criminal investigations, remote sensing surveys, biological and military sciences, medical imaging, and traffic monitoring all depend on image restoration algorithms [1, 2]. Image restoration in contemporary video surveillance systems is essential for criminal investigations [3].

Image denoising is a significant subset of computer vision. The goal of image denoising is to get a clean image out of a noisy observation. Denoising of images is

G. Mange (✉)
School of Technology (SOT), KCA University, Nairobi, Kenya
e-mail: g.mange@kcau.ac.ke

G. Mange · R. Waweru · M. Kimwele
Jomo Kenyatta University of Agriculture and Technology, Nairobi, Kenya

J. Marx Gómez
Oldenburg University, Oldenburg, Germany

J. Marx Gómez et al. (eds.), *Advancement in Embedded and Mobile Systems*, Progress in IS, https://doi.org/10.1007/978-3-031-99219-3_23

symbolized by:

$$y = x + n \tag{1}$$

where y is the noisy image, x denotes the clean image, and n denotes additive white Gaussian noise (AWGN) with standard deviation σ, which turns out to be a classical inverse problem. AWGN is the most prevailing noise and can occur due to thermally agitated electrons in an electrical conductor [4]. It can be stated as the noise which has a Gaussian amplitude distribution and can be mathematically defined as:

$$P_f(x) = \frac{1}{\sigma\sqrt{2x}} e^{-\frac{i}{2}\left(\frac{x-u}{\sigma}\right)^2} \tag{2}$$

where μ is the mean and σ is the standard deviation. In terms of denoising performance, methods based on CNN have outperformed conventional denoising algorithms [5]. Additionally, they added a noise level map to model a flexible network (FFDNet) that can handle a wide variety of noise [6]. For instance, [9] used three convolutional network blocks and dilated filters to produce an attention-guided denoising CNN (ADNet). Increasing the receptive field to improve denoising performance, the depth, and width of CNNs were expanded by [10] to produce a DnCNN-based corrective signal in the information-communication system. A batch-renormalization denoising network (BRDNet) was presented by [8] to handle the small mini-batch problem.

An activation function is a function that maps dimensions of data and runs on the neurons of the neural network. In deep CNNs, it is essential for solving nonlinear issues. A proper activation function can improve the CNN's ability to fit and accelerate training convergence. Among all denoising techniques, the Relu is one of the most frequently used activation functions. The following is the formula for this function:

$$f(x) = \max\left(0,\ a + x'b\right) \tag{3}$$

It is evident that the function is equalizing on the other side when the input is less than zero and is zeroing the output. The Relu function does not have a gradient diffusion problem and can be computed quickly because it is linear and unsaturated.

This study uses the peak signal-to-noise ratio (PSNR) and structural similarity index measure (SSIM) as objective indices. PSNR is the ratio of the maximum power of the signal to the difference between the ground truth and the denoised image. A higher PSNR indicates greater similarity. PSNR has been used to evaluate images. The denoised image and the noisy image are compared using PSNR. It is used to check the quality of restoration techniques [5]

The following summarizes the primary contributions:

1. A denoising model using a novel concatenation mechanism that combines the dynamic set of features from each CNN, and exploiting the attention modules' ability to highlight relevant information, and reducing the redundant data output from the CNNs to give better PSNR and SSIM compared to state-of-the-art models is proposed.
2. To solve gradient issues and improve learning ability, connective convolution layers with a Relu activation function and batch-renormalization to each upper network layer is applied.
3. A lightweight model that performs well in comparison to conventional denoising models and can be trained with less data.
4. The following is how the rest of this paper is laid out. Section 2 looks at the related work. Section 3 provides a comprehensive explanation of the proposed approach. Section 4 displays the experimental setting. Section 5 gives experimental results and analysis, then ends with discussion and conclusion in Sects. 6 and 7, respectively.

2 Related Work

2.1 CNN-Based Denoising Models

CNNs have demonstrated impressive performance in a variety of computer vision tasks, but they are not without drawbacks. The number of parameters and denoising inference time rise in tandem with the depth of the network, making it difficult to use the models in practical settings. Numerous researchers have attempted to extend the network architecture in order to enhance the denoising networks' representational capacity in order to address the problem. For instance, a Dual CNN model with two parallel branches to reconstruct image structures and details was proposed [11]. The BRDNet model by [8] combined features from an upper and a lower network. Dual networks can enhance denoising performance; however, because all image features are handled identically in their parallel branches, the redundant features may cause their denoising performance to deteriorate. To address this problem, this research integrates attention models at the output of the CNN models to select important information while downgrading the information that does not impact the model.

2.2 CNN with Attention Mechanism for Image Denoising

Recent advancements in CNN-based image denoising have incorporated attention mechanisms to enhance feature representation and noise suppression [12] proposed DCANet, a dual-branch CNN combined with a spatial and channel attention module (SCAM) to enhance feature refinement and estimate noise distribution, making it highly effective for blind image denoising. [13] merged convolutional and transformer-based attention mechanisms to extract both local and global features, optimizing hyperspectral image denoising with their HCANet. [14] proposed AMDNet, a denoising model that incorporates hybrid dilated convolutions and attention mechanisms. Unlike these models that rely on complex hybrid architectures, the proposed model uses lightweight CNN-based attention mechanisms, making it more efficient for real-time denoising applications. The fusion of attention outputs allows it to achieve high-quality denoising.

2.3 Encoder-Decoder Architecture in Image Denoising

Recent developments in deep learning have prompted the creation of new methods for image denoising. Deep convolutional encoder-decoder networks with a skip connection in the convolutional and transposed convolutional layers were proposed by [15] for image denoising. As a result, the bottom layer's more intricate features are extracted, enhancing the denoising process. A feed-forward denoising convolutional neural network using residual learning and deep network architecture was presented by [15]. Based on the channel attention mechanism, [16] suggested the residual encoder-decoder with squeeze-and-excitation network (RED-SENet). By stacking kernels of a regular size, the aforementioned methods extract feature information; unfortunately, this causes the image to be too smoothed. This study suggests an improved CNWATT2 model. Two attention blocks (ATT1 and ATT2) are combined to form the output, which goes into the encoding and decoding processes, respectively.

3 Proposed Method

The following section discusses how the problem will be solved.

3.1 The Proposed Model

The model's architecture as proposed:

Figure 1 depicts the proposed model's network architecture. Borrowing from BRDNET, [8], a 17-layer CNN is used in this research to improve the learning ability of the model. The output of the CNN feeds into the attention module, which is used to guide the CNN for training the denoising model. Dilated convolutions are used in the lower CNN to reduce the computational complexity that would occur as a result of increased depth of the model. Dilated convolution has a parameter,

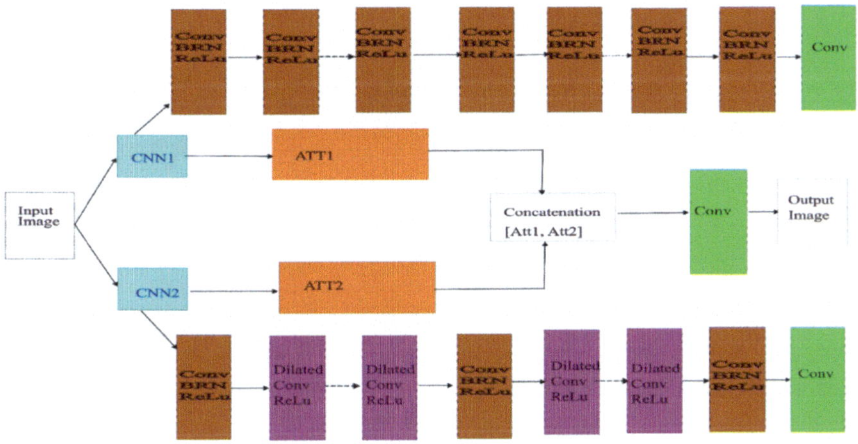

Fig. 1 Proposed model architecture

which can control the dilation rate (d). The dilation factor tells how much the input is expanded. Based on the value of the dilation factor (d − 1), pixels are skipped in the kernel. The convolution kernel is filled with d − 1 numbers of original input (0); therefore, the receptive field will be different when different rates are set. According to [17], the dilated convolution can be represented as:

$$y_i = \sum_{i-0}^{k-1} f_i.x_i - d.d \tag{4}$$

3.2 *Encoder Architecture with Attention Mechanism*

3.2.1 Encoder Path

The encoder captures essential features, the decoder reconstructs the input, and the concatenation with attention mechanisms enables effective denoising. The input (x) shape is set to (None, None, 3) so that the model can take an input image of variable size with three colors using the following expression:

$$Inp = input(shape = (None, None, 3)) \tag{5}$$

3.2.2 Convolution Operations

The first convolution layer has 64 filters and a kernel size of (3,3) and the same padding, followed by 15 blocks, each consisting of a convolution layer, batch renormalization, and a Relu activation. The general expression for the convolution operation is as shown in Eq. (6)

$$y_{ij}^{i+1} = \sigma\left(\sum_{m-0}^{M-1}\sum_{n=0}^{N-1} W_{mn}^{(i)} * x_{(i+m)(j+n)}^{(i)} + b^{(i)}\right) \tag{6}$$

where: y_{ij}^{i+1} represents the output position (i, j) in the feature map of position i + 1,

M and N are the height and the width of the image, respectively, $W_{mn}^{(i)}$ are the weights of the convolution filters at position (mn) in layer l, $x_{(i+m)(j+n)}^{(i)}$ represents the input at position (i + m, j + n) in the feature map for layer l, $b^{(i)}$ is the bias term for layer l, σ is the ReLU activation function represented as another symbol.

3.2.3 Batch Renormalization

Techniques used to normalize the activations of a neural network layer, as an improved method for reducing the impact of small batch sizes.

$$Z_{bhw} = \gamma.\frac{y_{bhw} - \mu}{\sqrt{\sigma^2 + \varepsilon}} + \beta \tag{7}$$

where: y_{bhw} is the input tensor element at position bhw, μ is the mean σ^2 is the variance, ε is a small constant to avoid division by zero, γ is the scaling parameter, β is the shift parameter, and Z_{bhw} is the output tensor at element bhw.

3.2.4 The Attention Mechanism

The attention mechanism used in this model is not the conventional single-head attention, instead, it deploys an element-wise operation to create a form of attention-like processing between the input and the network's intermediate representation. This attention mechanism constitutes of the concatenation operation, Tanh activation, 1 × 1 convolution operation, elementwise multiplication, and subtraction from the input.

3.2.5 Concatenation

The purpose of concatenation operation is to leverage both low-level details from the encoder and high-level context from the decoder. The concatenate operation in the model is used in a skip connection, where the original tensor x is concatenated with an output tensor from a series of convolution operations in the decoder path along the last axis (axis = −1) and can be represented as:

$$\mathrm{C} = (\mathrm{inp}\ \&\ \mathrm{x}) \quad (8)$$

3.2.6 Tanh Activation

The concatenated tensor C is passed through a hyperbolic tangent (Tanh) activation function σ to produce output as shown in Eq. (9). TanH is able to map the [−1, 1] dynamic range so that the output distribution's mean value is zero and mimics the identity function [16].

$$att_{bhwc} = \sigma(C) \quad (9)$$

3.2.7 1 x 1 Convolution

After the tanh activation, a 1 × 1 convolution with three filters is applied. This convolution operation involves learning a set of weights for each channel of the concatenated tensor, att_{bhwc}. The result is an attention-like map score where each channel corresponds to a different attention score that influence how much each feature in the immediate representation should be emphasized. The 1 × 1 convolution expression is shown in the following equation, where att_{bhwc} is the result from the activation function, and W_{cf} is the weight at the (c, f)th position of filter tensor W as represented in Eq. (10):

$$att_{bhwf} = \sum_{i=1}^{c} (att_{bhwc} * W_{cf}) \quad (10)$$

3.2.8 Element-Wise Multiplication

The attention-like map att_{bhwf} is further multiplied by the intermediate representation tensor x,. This has the effect of scaling the values in x based on the attention score as shown in the following mathematical expression.

$$att_{bhwc} = att_{bhwf} * x_{bhwc} \quad (11)$$

3.2.9 Subtraction from the Input

Finally, the scaled intermediate representation att_{bhwc} is subtracted from the original input tensor inp_{bhwc}. This operation reduces the noise introduced in the intermediate representation, resulting in a denoised image as shown in the following equation:

$$denoised_{bhwc} = inp_{bhwc} - att_{bhwc} \tag{12}$$

This sequence of operations in the **Encoder Path** creates an attention-like mechanism that adaptively adjusts the intermediate representation based on the original input and features learned by the model. The attention-like map is then used to denoise the input image by modifying the intermediate representation. The $denoised_{bhwc}$ is used in subsequent stages of the encoders' convolution iteratively to add features to the input x_{bhwc}.

3.3 Decoder Architecture with Attention Mechanism

3.3.1 Decoder Path

The decoder reconstructs the input image from the encoded representation. The decoder path has a similar structure to the encoder with a separate set of convolution operations (13 layers).

3.3.2 Attention Mechanism 2

Similar to attention for the encoder path, but applied with the decoder.

3.3.3 Final Concatenation

Concatenates the noise output from the encoder and decoder paths, then applies the final convolution layer to generate the final denoised output (z)

$$O_{bhwc} = (x_{bhwc} \,\&\, y_{bhwc}) \tag{13}$$

$$Z_{bhwc} = \sigma\left(\sum_{i=1}^{2c}\sum_{j=1}^{3} W_{ij} * O_{bhwc}\right) \tag{14}$$

$$Output_{bhwc} = inp_{bhwc} - Z_{bhwc} \tag{15}$$

Equation 13 concatenates x and y along the last axis. It applies a 3 × 3 convolution with 3 filters to the concatenated tensor O_{bhwc}. W_{ij} represents the convolutional weights for the ith filter and the jth channel of the concatenated tensor. In Eq. (14), Z_{bhwc} is the result of the convolution. Equation 15 subtracts the result of the convolution from the original input tensor.

4 Experimental Setting

In this section, the datasets and training settings for the proposed work are described in detail. The models that were used for the image denoising process are then discussed. All of the experiments are carried out in the PyTorch environment. Paper space virtual machines equipped with a Quadro P4000, eight CPUs, and 30 GB of RAM served as the setting for the experiments.

4.1 Datasets

The Waterloo Exploration Database, which contains 3821 images, serves as the training dataset. Imagaug library was used to augment the data by horizontal flipping 50% and vertical flipping 20% for all images, cropping − 5% off their height/width, rotate by − 45 to + 45 degrees, and shear − 16 to + 16 degrees to increase the images to 4000. 500 images from Low Dose CT images and projection Data set (LDCT and projection dataset) availed online by investigators at Mayo clinic are also used, (400 images for training and 100 for testing the models). The choice of these datasets was informed by the fact that they are the same ones used in the SOTA used in comparative analysis.

4.2 The Setting of the Model Level

Two attention models were integrated prior to the concatenation process at the output of the individual CNNs, which resulted in improved outcomes for both models CNNOATT2 and CNWATT2, with the latter giving better results of the two models. Three datasets were used to test the average PSNR values. To evaluate quantitatively the quality of the denoised image, this research utilizes Peak Signal to Noise Ratio (PSNR). It compares the original and the restored images, considering the Mean Squared error (MSE) between their pixel values.

5 Experiments

5.1 Results

This section presents and analyzes the results of the experiments.

5.2 Cnn

It is demonstrated that the CNN model can be enhanced for denoising when the attention model is incorporated into the baseline. It improves the denoising when introduced before the concatenation operation, as seen in the experimental results. The BRN stabilizes the training process by accelerating network convergence and preventing gradient vanishing issues. In contrast to previous studies, in which concatenation was accomplished through simple summations, in this study, an attention mechanism that selectively removes features that have no effect on the model is introduced before the feature fusion. The experiment demonstrates that using an attention module helps complete the feature selection process and reduce redundancy caused by features extracted from various CNN layers.

5.3 Comparisons with State-of-the-art Models

The proposed network's image denoising performance is compared with that of DnCNN [5], FFDNet [6], IRCNN [7], and BRDNET [8], which are based on deep CNN.

6 Discussion

As seen in Tables 1 and 2, the results of CNWATT2 vs. CNNOATT2 demonstrate that the integration of the attention model before concatenation improves PSNR and SSIM performance. This is because the convolution kernel in a convolutional neural network is constrained by its size and can only use local information to calculate the target pixel, which may result in deviations because it is oblivious to global information. If each pixel in the feature map is thought of as a random variable and the pairing covariances are determined, and depending on how each target pixel compares to other pixels in the image, its value may be strengthened or reduced. This echoed by [18], who found out that the self-attention mechanism uses comparable pixels for training and prediction, while dissimilar pixels are ignored.

Table 1 Average SSIM on CBSD68, Kodak24, and CT images with noise level (σ) 15, 25, 35, 50, and 75 for CNNOATT2 and CNWATT2

Datasets	Methods	(σ) = 15	(σ) = 25	(σ) = 35	(σ) = 50	(σ) = 75
CDSD68	CNNOATT2	0.9552	0.9335	0.9082	0.8598	0.7593
	CNWATT2	0.9617	0.9358	0.9129	0.8787	0.8431
KODAK24	CNNOATT2	0.9549	0.9369	0.9140	0.8689	0.8540
	CNWATT2	0.9625	0.9394	0.9196	0.8921	0.8612
CT IMAGES	CNNOATT2	0.9602	0.9444	0.8433	0.8861	0.8189
	CNWATT2	0.9666	0.9388	0.8736	0.8911	0.8674

Table 2 Average PSNR on CBSD68, Kodak24, and CT images with noise level (σ) = 15, 25, 35, 50, and 75 for DnCNN, FFDNet, IRCNN, BRDNET, CNNOATT2, and CNWATT2

Datasets	Methods	(σ) = 15	(σ) = 25	(σ) = 35	(σ) = 50	(σ) = 75
CBSD68	DnCNN	33.98	31.31	29.65	28.01	–
	FFDNet	33.80	31.18	29.57	27.96	26.24
	IRCNN	33.86	31.16	29.50	27.86	–
	BRDNET	34.10	31.43	29.77	28.16	26.43
	CNNOATT2	34.05	32.04	30.35	28.23	23.63
	CNWATT2	34.7	32.1	30.5	28.9	27.3
KODAK24	DnCNN	34.73	32.23	30.64	29.02	–
	FFDNet	34.55	32.11	30.56	28.99	27.25
	IRCNN	34.56	32.03	30.43	28.81	–
	BRDNET	34.88	32.41	30.80	29.22	27.49
	CNNOATT2	34.5	32.6	30.95	28.86	27.7
	CNWATT2	35.23	32.7	31.24	29.67	28.01
CT IMAGES	CNNOATT2	36.8	34.7	32.4	31.09	27.5
	CNWATT2	37.3	34.82	32.92	31.53	30.01

Table 1 compares the proposed network's image denoising performance with that of DnCNN [5], FFDNet [6] IRCNN [7], and BRDNET [8], all of which are based on a deep CNN. The proposed model performs better in average PSNR on CBSD68, Kodak24, with noise level (σ) 15, 25, 35, 50, and 75. BRDNET performs better than the other three, so this paper will discuss the performance of the proposed model in comparison with it. The proposed model outperforms BRDNET by 0.65 dB, 0.67 dB, 0.73 dB, 0.74 dB, and 0.87 dB for the CBSD68 dataset, being differences in values for noise levels 15, 25, 35, 50, and 75, respectively. For the Kodak24 dataset, the proposed model performs better by 0.35 dB, 0.29 dB, 0.44 dB, 0.45 dB, and 0.52 dB for noise values 15, 25, 35, 50, and 75, respectively. The proposed model introduces the attention model to sieve the redundant features and therefore give better quality images. SSIM is a better quality metric, and therefore, this research also used it to confirm that feature fusion after feature selection yields better image quality [19].

7 Conclusion

Unlike other deep learning methods that have incorporated several attention modules, this research uses an attention module at the output of each CNN to improve the extracted features and increase the model's denoising capability. The convolutional layers extract hierarchical features, the batch renormalization accelerates the training of the model, and the ReLU activation at the end of each layer aids in convergence, whereas the dilated convolution enlarges the receptive field. The proposed model is able to give better denoising results with comparable parameters, 1.117325 compared to 1.11 M for DnCNN and BRDNet. This research used quantitative correlation of the denoising execution in this case, the PSNR, and SSIM. For the three datasets (CBSD68, Kodak24, and CT images), Tables 1 and 2 demonstrate that the CNWATT2 performs better than the CNNOATT2, for noise level 75. The PSNR difference is 3.67 dB, 0.31 dB, and 2.51 dB for CBSD68, Kodak24, and CT images, respectively. The SSIM, on the other hand is 0.0838, 0.0072, and 0.0585 for CBSD68, Kodak24, and CT images, respectively. This is a clear indication that incorporating the attention model prior to concatenation improves the denoising process.

References

1. Khare, Charu, Nagwanshi, Kapil & Nagwanshi,. (2011). Implementation and Analysis of Image Restoration Techniques. International Journal of Computer Trends and Technology-May to June Issue 2011. 54. 1–6.
2. Farhan, Rabab. (2020). Review on Some Methods used in Image Restoration. International Multidisciplinary Research Journal. 13–16. https://doi.org/10.25081/imrj.2020.v10.6113.
3. Sun, S. (2020). Application of fuzzy image restoration in criminal investigation. *Journal of Visual Communication and Image Representation, 71*, 102704
4. Goyal, B., Agrawal, S., Sohi, B.: Noise issues prevailing in various types of medical images. Biomedical & Pharmacology Journal 11(3), 1227 (2018)
5. Zhang, K., Zuo, W., Chen, Y., Meng, D., Zhang, L.: Beyond a gaussian denoiser: Residual learning of deep cnn for image denoising. IEEE transactions on image processing 26(7), 3142–3155 (2017)
6. Zhang, K., Zuo, W., & Zhang, L. (2018). FFDNet: Toward a fast and flexible solution for CNN-based image denoising. *IEEE Transactions on Image Processing, 27*(9), 4608-4622.
7. Zhang, Q., Xiao, J., Tian, C., Chun-Wei Lin, J., Zhang, S.: A robust deformed convolutional neural network (cnn) for image denoising. CAAI Transactions on Intelligence Technology (2022)
8. Tian, C., Xu, Y., Zuo, W.: Image denoising using deep cnn with batch renormalization. Neural Networks 121, 461–473 (2020)
9. Tian, C., Xu, Y., Li, Z., Zuo, W., Fei, L., Liu, H.: Attention-guided cnn for image denoising. Neural Networks 124, 117–129 (2020)

10. Sheremet, O., Sheremet, K., Sadovoi, O., Sokhina, Y.: Convolutional neural networks for image denoising in infocommunication systems. In: 2018 Interna-tional Scientific-Practical Conference Problems of Infocommunications. Science and Technology (PIC S&T), pp. 429–432 (2018). IEEE
11. Zefang, H. A. N., Hong, S. H. A. N. G. G. U. A. N., Xiong, Z. H. A. N. G., Xinglong, H. A. N., Zhiguo, G. U. I., Xueying, C. U. I., & Pengcheng, Z. H. A. N. G. (2022). Advances in research on low-dose CT imaging algorithm based on deep learning. *CT Theory and Applications*, *31*(1), 117-134.
12. Wu, W., Lv, G., Duan, Y., Liang, P., Zhang, Y., & Xia, Y. (2024). Dual convolutional neural network with attention for image blind denoising. *Multimedia Systems*, *30*(5), 263.
13. Hu, S., Gao, F., Zhou, X., Dong, J., & Du, Q. (2024). Hybrid convolutional and attention network for hyperspectral image denoising. *IEEE Geoscience and Remote Sensing Letters*.
14. Bian, S., He, X., Xu, Z., & Zhang, L. (2023). Hybrid dilated convolution with attention mechanisms for image denoising. *Electronics*, *12*(18), 3770.
15. Zeng, X., Li, Y., Gao, G., & Zhao, X. (2022). Channel Adaptive Ultrasound Image Denoising Method Based on Residual Encoder-decoder Networks. *电子与信息学报*, *44*(7), 2547–2558.
16. Wang, H., Ding, Z., Li, X., Shen, S., Ye, X., Zhang, D., & Tao, S. (2021). Convolutional neural network with a learnable spatial activation function for SAR image despeckling and forest image analysis. *Remote Sensing*, *13*(17), 3444.
17. Lv, Z., Li, J., Dong, C., Li, H., & Xu, Z. (2021). Deep learning in the COVID-19 epidemic: A deep model for urban traffic revitalization index. *Data & Knowledge Engineering*, *135*, 101912. https://doi.org/10.1016/j.datak.2021.101912
18. Zhang, H., Goodfellow, I., Metaxas, D., Odena, A.: Self-Attention Generative Adversarial Networks (2019)
19. Reznik, Y.: Another look at ssim image quality metric. Electronic Imaging 35(8), 305–1 (2023)

Comparative Analysis of Community Rating and Dynamic Pricing on Enhancing Healthcare Accessibility in Low-Income Countries: A Case Study of Tanzania

Godfrey N. Justo and Fadhili Z. Meena

Abstract Over the last two decades, out-of-pocket (OOP) payments and external donations have contributed over 60% of current health expenditure (CHE) in low-income countries (LICs), in which OOP accounts for more than 40%, indicating a heavy reliance on individual contributions. Current studies on pricing models for healthcare largely focuses on achieving computational efficiency, but not the pricing effect on healthcare accessibility that influences healthcare improvement. Analysis of healthcare pricing models based on cost affordability can bridge this gap. Commonly used pricing models such as community rating (CR), dynamic pricing (DP), and OOP are considered. DP is a machine learning (ML) model based on Tanzania's National Panel Survey (NPS) data, while the CR model is based on rates from the Tanzania's Act Supplement for the mandatory public health insurance scheme of 2023, to the Ministry of Health (MoH). A pure premium approach for the DP model and current rates for the CR model are employed for comparative purposes. The results showed that CR does not significantly improve healthcare costs compared to DP (p-value = 0), conversely, DP significantly outperforms CR with a p-value 3.49×10^{-08} Moreover, the DP model remains superior to CR until a loading factor range of 5.7 and 6.4, where no significant difference, beyond which DP increases healthcare costs. Likewise, DP outperforms OOP until the loading factor range of 0.1 and 0.2, where costs are insignificantly different, above which DP increases costs. Load factor analysis confirms DP to significantly enhance healthcare accessibility by reducing cost compared to CR and OOP pricing models.

Keywords Healthcare accessibility · Community rating · Dynamic pricing · Pricing affordability · Individual contribution · Machine learning

G. N. Justo (✉) · F. Z. Meena
University of Dar Es Salaam, College of Information and Communication Technologies, Dar Es Salaam, Tanzania
e-mail: justo@udsm.ac.tz; njulumi@gmail.com

J. Marx Gómez et al. (eds.), *Advancement in Embedded and Mobile Systems*, Progress in IS, https://doi.org/10.1007/978-3-031-99219-3_24

1 Introduction

1.1 Background

Current healthcare financing research focuses on computational reliability and the application of advanced AI models [1–3], for accuracy, albeit pays no attention pricing effect on enhancement of healthcare access, a fundamental goal for sustainable human development (SDG) and Universal Healthcare Coverage (UHC) [4]. Effective execution of healthcare access policies, such as the UHC requires efficient funding, especially for disadvantaged groups [5], which is a notable challenge in low-income countries (LICs) such as Tanzania, where over 45% of current health expenditures (CHE) rely on out-of-pocket payments (OOP), compared to high-income countries where more than 70% come from government budgets [6]. The recent Global Health Expenditure Database (GHED) shows the trend has persisted for over 20 consecutive years to 2022 [7]. As such, due to limited sources of internal revenue, individual contributions through OOP remain a pillar for financing CHE in LICs [8].

Community rating (CR) is a prevalent approach for estimating individual contributions in LICs to major healthcare protection schemes. The CR is characterized by similar contribution rates [9], albeit, indexed or categorized based on various factors such as income and geographical regions [10]. Conversely, dynamic pricing (DP) is based on mathematical models that account for various individual attributes (including risk factors such as age, gender, health history, and healthcare utilization patterns) and evaluate how they change over time to make contribution estimates that reflect expected individual healthcare costs. Recent research has leveraged Machine Learning (ML) models to enhance DP approaches due to their computational efficiency and ability on diverse datasets [11–13].

Pricing affordability is one of the important aspects in Levesque's framework for healthcare access measures [14]. However, the relative effect of pricing models on enhancing healthcare access remains unexplained by current research. This study seeks to bridge the gap by analyzing the effect of OOP, CR, and DP pricing models in improving healthcare accessibility, considering the case of Tanzania.

Ensuring access to quality healthcare without financial hardship is crucial for sustainable development, particularly in low-income countries where individuals often fund their own care. Pricing methods like CR and DP have been proposed for estimating premium contributions. However, the current research attention has been on computational efficiency, but it remains unclear on the effect of such pricing models on improving healthcare accessibility. Understanding the relative effect is important for the effective implementation of healthcare access policies, such as the UHC. This study is guided by the following research questions:

- What are the key factors affecting healthcare pricing for accessibility with respect to CR and DP models?
- How significant is the difference between CR and DP models in healthcare access improvement through affordability?

The study focuses on low-income countries, with Tanzania as the case study. The study scope is limited to a comparative analysis of commonly used financing approaches: OOP, CR, and DP models. Their relative pricing effect in influencing individual preferences and healthcare access is subsequently assessed based on price estimates from each model. The outcomes are expected to inform healthcare access policies and programs, such as UHC, in similar contexts. Clarifying the strengths and weaknesses of a financing model helps to guide decision-makers toward more effective approaches that balance financial sustainability along with the broader goal and more equitable healthcare access.

1.2 Materials and Methods

The research design employs a quantitative approach, using descriptive and predictive analysis of numerical data related to healthcare utilization [15]. The case study design enables an in-depth examination of healthcare financing systems. Data is collected from secondary sources, including National Panel Survey (NPS), Demographic Health Survey (DHS) [16, 17], and GHED [7]. The GHED provides national and global health expenditure data, offering insights into health financing patterns and supporting generalizing the study to LMICs. The DHS is based on household surveys in low- and middle-income countries, including Tanzania, gathering data on health indicators, healthcare utilization, insurance uptake, fertility, maternal, and child health, providing valuable insights into Tanzania's healthcare landscape [17]. The NPS collects longitudinal data on healthcare utilization, expenditure patterns, and demographics from 2008 to 2021, capturing trends and dynamics in individual healthcare costs [16], as summarized in Table 1.

The methods in [18] for sample design for unknown populations are used for sample design that target a small but representative sample size, which suggests an optimal sample size of 385 for a large population at a 95% confidence level. In the NPS repository context, the sample size for each wave exceeds 10,000, which is sufficient for the models. The resampling technique, Small Minority Oversampling (SMO), is used to balance biased samples. The key attributes include age, gender, healthcare service frequency, and claim size [12, 19]. Python version 3.11.4 is used for exploratory data analysis, model training, model evaluation, and hypothesis testing.

Table 1 Summary of data collected from NPS

Data collection wave	Number of observations	Number of attributes
Wave 2 2010–2011	20,559	42
Wave 3 2012–2013	25,412	42
Wave 4 2014–2015	16,285	43
Wave 5 2020–2021	23,592	43

1.2.1 Exploratory Data Analysis

Different tests are conducted to explore the nature of attributes in the data set, including the chi-square test for independence on categorical variables like gender and healthcare utilization status, and Pearson's correlation coefficient test across continuous (numerical) attributes such as age [20, 21]. Histograms are used on univariate EDA, to visually identify the distribution of individual continuous variables, and bar plots to identify the distribution of individual categorical variables. Further, a test for the goodness of fit is used to identify the best-fit distribution for each of the variables, a crucial step for further simulation design to create more comprehensive data to train the ML model for understanding the best distribution of attributes that is reproducible independent of the raw data [22].

Missing values within the dataset challenge the accuracy of statistical analyses and model performance. To address this issue, the extent of missingness is identified across variables and the cause of missing. In turn, a multistage predictive model replaced missing values with estimated values derived from existing data patterns [23]. For systematic missing, for example, if a person is aged 5 years and has an NA marital status value, we directly feed "Never Married." A multivariate random forest regressor (classifier for categorical variables) fills the remaining missing observations, provided the proportion of missingness is less than 0.7, otherwise, the attribute is dropped.

The standard deviation (Z-score) analysis method is utilized to identify outliers across variables. Once identified, outliers are winsorized, truncated, or excluded from analysis, depending on the nature of the data [24, 25]. For a variable X;

$$z - score(Z) = \frac{x - E[X]}{\sqrt{var(X)}} \text{ and } P(Z < 3) \approx 99.87\%$$

Hence, observations above 3 standard deviations are considered as outliers; for the target variable, outliers are dropped, while for other variables, a predictive model is used to test how the observation with outliers can be explained by other covariates. That is the predicted values and recorded outliers are compared based on Mean Absolute Percentage Error (MAPE). Observations from variables with MAPE above 50% of the predicted values are considered; otherwise, the recorded observations are retained.

The handling of imbalanced categorical attributes employed the Synthetic Minority Over-sampling Technique (SMOTE) to rebalance class distributions [26–28]. When observed that the resampling of one variable causes an imbalance of other categorical variables, the tree-based SMOTE is adopted rather than just focusing on a single categorical variable, to ensure that the target variable is balanced while other categorical variables are less biased. As data scales varied rapidly, especially on variables with many categories, only variables with two categories are rebalanced. Further, a statistical test on the improved variability of class proportions among categorical variables is performed. That is, if $X = \{x_1, x_2 \ldots k\}$ is the variance of proportions of classes in the set of all categorical variables 1,2, .. before class balance and $Y = \{y_1, y_2 \ldots k\}$ is the variance of the proportions of classes in the set of all categorical variables 1,2, .. after class balance; it is hypothesized that *class balance approach reduce the overall variance among the categorical variables*, to which; $\widehat{\sigma}_Y^2 < \widehat{\sigma}_X^2$

$$\frac{\widehat{\sigma}_X^2}{\widehat{\sigma}_Y^2} \sim F_{0.05,k-1,k-1}$$

where k is the number of categorical variables involved in class balance. Though, should be all categorical variables, but for computation constraint, only four variables are included. In addition, an F-test is performed, with a significance level of 5% and on a set of p-value. With confidence, the adopted class balance approach significantly reduced the overall class proportion variance among all categorical variables (with binary classes) in the data.

1.2.2 Feature Selection and Model Development

The categorical variables are transformed into numerical formats while preserving their semantic meaning by the Label encoding technique. Unlike other approaches, such as one-hot encoding, the Label encoding technique can address the dimensionality issue for high cardinality categorical variables [29, 30]. Leveraging on outliers and handling the feature scaling techniques are performed by a standardization approach. To identify relationships between features and the target variable (individual healthcare contribution), correlation analysis is conducted, in which the features with high correlation coefficients are retained for model training, while those with low correlation are excluded to reduce dimensionality and multicollinearity. The Bartlett's test of sphericity (BTS) and the Kaiser–Meyer–Olkin (KMO) test of sampling adequacy are employed to evaluate if the correlation between the factors is significantly different from zero, more so if the data is suitable for factor analysis [31, 32]. The BTS evaluated if the observed correlation matrix is significantly different from the identity matrix (i.e., variables are not intercorrelated). The factor analysis is employed if the correlation matrix is significantly different from the identity matrix. Under this scenario, the test statistic T is

$$T = -\left(N - 1 - \frac{2p + 5}{6}\right) \times \ln(|R|)$$

where N is the sample size, p is the number of variables, and $|R|$ is the determinant of the correlation matrix $T \sim X^2_{\left(\frac{p(p-1)}{2}\right)}$. On the other hand, KMO is used to measure the adequacy of the sample for factor analysis, and the KMO of 0.6 overall is acceptable. The KMO statistic can be given as $KMO_j = \frac{\sum_{i \neq j} R_{ij}^2}{\sum_{i \neq j} R_{ij}^2 + \sum_{i \neq j} U_{ij}^2}$ whereby R_{ij}^2 is the correlation matrix and U_{ij}^2 is the partial covariance matrix [31].

A tree-based algorithm (Random Forest) is used to assess feature importance using the Gini criterion. Features with higher Gini scores are prioritized for inclusion in the model, while less important features may be excluded to simplify the model and improve interpretability. Furthermore, the permutation test is used to identify a set of features that significantly contribute to the model's predictive performance, to improve parsimony and reduce overfitting. Principal Component Analysis (PCA) is used to identify latent variables that capture the most important information in the data to reduce computational complexity.

The model development involved three stages; the prediction of healthcare cost (continuous variable) by regression-based model, the prediction of the chance for filling the claim based on a probabilistic classification model, where a pure premium principle for estimating the individual's premiums is employed. The regression model is developed using a set of tree-based regression algorithms, including Random Forest (RF), Gradient Boosting (GB), and Extreme Gradient Boosting (XGB) algorithms due to their proven effectiveness in handling complex, nonlinear relationships within the data [33]. Model training made use of historical healthcare expenditure data from Tanzania's NPS, which constitute of longitudinal dataset with detailed information on individual healthcare utilization, demographics, and expenditure patterns, making it an ideal source for training a predictive model. The dataset is split into training and validation sets to ensure the robustness and generalizability of models.

The randomized search cross-validation is employed during hyper-parameter optimization to find the best hyperparameters for the RF and GB tree-based regression models. This method efficiently explores the hyper-parameter space by sampling from specified distributions, balancing computational resources, and improving model accuracy. The model selection step assessed the performance of regression and classification algorithms tailored to predicting healthcare costs and the probability of filing a claim. For the regression task, the mean squared error (MSE), root mean square error (RMSE), and mean absolute error (MAE) served as primary indicators of predictive accuracy (i.e., a lower value of a metric signifies closer alignment between the model's predictions and the actual healthcare costs, reflecting superior performance). The goodness of fit is evaluated by the coefficient of determination (R-squared), which quantifies the proportion of variance in healthcare costs explained by the model's predictors (i.e., higher R-squared values indicate a better fit of the regression model to the data, suggesting its efficacy in capturing underlying relationships). The accuracy, precision, recall, and F1-score are employed for the classification task of predicting claim probabilities. Accuracy gauges the correctness of the model's predictions, while precision measures the proportion of true positives among all positive predictions. Recall, or sensitivity, quantifies the model's ability to identify true positives correctly. The F1-score balances precision and recall, comprehensively evaluating classification performance. Moreover, the receiver operating characteristic (ROC) curve and the area under the ROC curve (AUC-ROC) are also considered to visualize the trade-off between sensitivity and specificity. Ultimately, the model selection process prioritizes the algorithm demonstrating superior performance across the metrics, ensuring robustness and generalizability in predicting healthcare costs and claim probabilities.

The individual contribution for ML ML-based DP model is estimated as follows: If Y_i is the random output healthcare cost for individual i from the regression model, and p_i is the probability for a particular individual to make a claim. Based on pure premium, the principal premium equals the expected loss.

$$\pi_i = E[Y_i] = y_i \times p_i$$

where π_i is the pure premium for i^{th} individual. This principle is employed to ignore external expenses such as administrative costs. However, a sensitivity analysis is conducted by introducing the loading factor in the pure premium principle to examine how the proportionate change in external expenses affects the inference. When adjusted to loading factor θ which account for cost out of the sum assured (can include underwriting expenses, management costs, and claim settlement expenses), then

$$\pi_i = (1+\theta)E[Y_i] = (1+\theta) \times y_i \times p_i$$

Individual contribution for the community rating approach is based on the Act Supplement for the mandatory public health insurance scheme of 2023, its respective bill of August 2022, and the related information to the public from the Ministry of Health (MoH) [34–37], as summarized in Table 2.

The healthcare accessibility is evaluated based on the two pricing approaches: Let price estimates from the DP and CR models be $\widehat{P}_i$ and $\hat{P}_{mi}$, respectively. Recall from the theory of expected utility, an individual's attitude (behavior) toward risk is geared toward increasing their expected utility, and the opportunity cost principle, where individuals decide to reduce money lost by selecting one option over the other. A hypothesis is formulated to test for two samples to evaluate whether a significant price difference causes people to prefer one pricing approach over the other:

$$\boldsymbol{H}_0 : \boldsymbol{\mu}_1 = \boldsymbol{\mu}_2$$

$$\boldsymbol{H}_1 \boldsymbol{\mu}_1 \neq \boldsymbol{\mu}_2$$

given n, the sample size of the latest NPS wave (test) data, where μ_1—average individual contributions for the population if exposed to the community rating approach

Table 2 Contribution rates under the CR approach

Condition	Contribution estimate ($\widehat{P}$)
If individual is from formal sector	$\widehat{P} = \frac{6}{100} \times S$ where S is the gross annual salary of an individual
If individual is from informal sector	$\widehat{P} = 84{,}000$
Group (family) of 6	$6\widehat{P} = 340{,}000$

and μ_2—average individual contributions for the population if exposed to a dynamic pricing approach. Since one sample is evaluated over two different approaches, an independent two-sample test is used [38]. The test statistic T

$$\overline{x}_1 = \overline{\left(\widehat{P}_i\right)} = \frac{1}{n}\sum_{i=1}^{n} \widehat{P}_i$$

$$\overline{x}_2 = \overline{\left(\widehat{P}_{mi}\right)} = \frac{1}{n}\sum_{i=1}^{n} \widehat{P}_{mi}$$

$$s_1^2 = var\left(\widehat{P}_i\right) = \frac{1}{n-1}\sum_{i=1}^{n}\left(\widehat{P}_i - \overline{\left(\widehat{P}_i\right)}\right)^2$$

$$s_2^2 = var\left(\widehat{P}_{mi}\right) = \frac{1}{n-1}\sum_{i=1}^{n}\left(\widehat{P}_{mi} - \overline{\left(\widehat{P}_{mi}\right)}\right)^2$$

$$s_p = \sqrt{\left(s_1^2 + s_2^2\right) \times \left(\frac{n-1}{2n-1}\right)}$$

$$T = \frac{\overline{x}_1 - \overline{x}_2}{s_p\sqrt{\frac{2}{n}}}$$

with probability values $p - values = 2 * \Theta(\mathrm{T})$ at different values of $\alpha = 0.05, 0.01, 0.005$ is evaluated to identify if there is a significant difference in the individual contributions, which consequently favor one pricing approach over the other.

2 Results

2.1 Exploratory Factor Analysis

The exploratory factor analysis (FA) shows that continuous variables are somewhat related to the target variable. However, it is insufficient to conclude that the correlations significantly differ from zero. Thus, it prompts to use of BTS, and for the correlated variables, the KMO is employed to explore the number of latent variables. The KMO test result showed an average of 0.74698 and 0.820831 in general, indicating with confidence that the data is suitable for FA, since at least a KMO of 0.6 is required in general. The scree plot in Fig. 1 is subsequently used to determine the

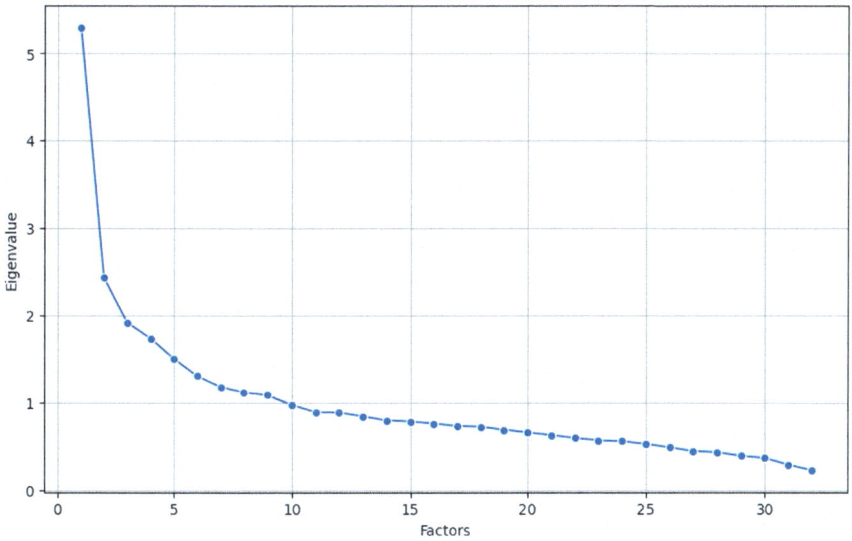

Fig. 1 Eigenvectors magnitude on data

number of variables to retain from the data based on the magnitude of the eigenvectors, where ten variables with the eigenvalues greater than one are observed to meet the selection criteria.

A linear regression model is fitted to assess how variables are best suited for predicting healthcare costs. The regression analysis results indicate a model with poor explanatory power, as evidenced by the low R-squared value of 0.07. The F-statistic is high at 2927.00, indicating a statistically significant relationship between the independent and the dependent variables despite the low R-squared. The Omnibus test, Jarque–Bera test, and their associated p-values suggest that the residuals are not normally distributed, with high skewness (18.56) and kurtosis (692.43), indicating significant departures from normality. Moreover, the extremely high condition number suggests potential issues with multicollinearity that prompt to the employment of PCA. The Durbin–Watson statistic of 1.858 suggests the presence of some positive autocorrelation in the residuals. Overall, while the model appears to be statistically significant, its practical utility is limited due to the poor fit, non-normality of residuals, potential multicollinearity, and autocorrelation, generally suggesting all variables are significant predictors at 5% but have low power in the linear model. This prompts to employ Random Forest regressor and Gradient Boosting algorithms.

A logit model is fitted to evaluate significant factors that influence the chance of an individual to incur a particular cost (i.e., predicting healthcare use). The logistic regression model reveals several important findings regarding the relationship between the predictor variables and the binary outcome variable. The model exhibits a pseudo-R-squared value of 0.3145, indicating moderate predictive power. The coefficients for each predictor variable provide insight into their respective effects on the log odds of the outcome. For instance, some variables portray positive coefficients, suggesting that an increase in their values is associated with an increased likelihood of the outcome. Conversely, other variables portray negative coefficients, indicating a decrease in the probability of the outcome as their values increase. Notably, the p-values associated with each coefficient are all very low, indicating that most predictor variables are statistically significant in predicting the outcome. However, a few variables had relatively high p-values, suggesting that they may not be significant predictors of the outcome. This signals potential for elimination if their information value is lower when evaluated with the feature importance Gini criterion of the RF model.

2.2 *Models Development*

Different models are developed, including a regression model for the prediction of healthcare cost, a classification model for predicting the probability of a person incurring a particular cost, and a pure premium principle used for estimation of individual contribution based on the dynamic model. Moreover, a community rating model, is developed using a rule-based approach from the ratings outlined in Table 2.

2.2.1 Regression Model

Recall that all variables' correlations are significantly different from zero and that all variables are significant predictors. However, some multicollinearity exists. The PCA is performed to address the latter. The dataset is separated into two sections: model development data (NPS wave 2–4) and model validation data (NPS wave 5). Model development data is divided into two sets (training set and testing set). The model is first trained to determine the importance of the features using the Gini information criterion as depicted in Fig. 2.

The results in Fig. 2 support the inference from Sect. 2.1 that all variables are important predictors for the regression model. In addition, more than 86% of the variables are required to explain at least 90% of the information for the target variable. Consequently, all variables are selected for the regression model, and the observed

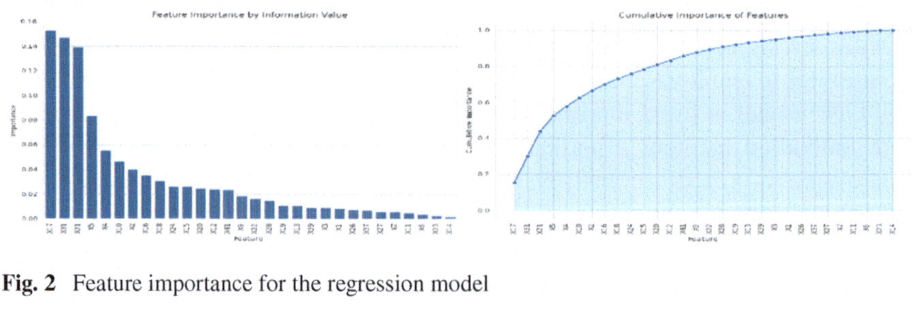

Fig. 2 Feature importance for the regression model

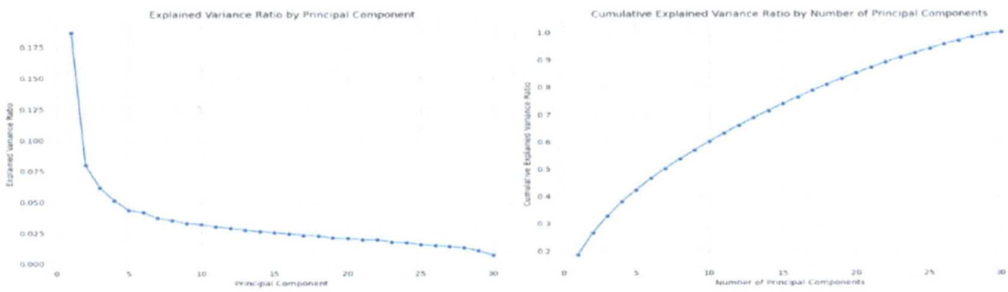

Fig. 3 PCA variance analysis for the regression model

Table 3 Regression model performance before (shaded rows) and after scaling/PCA

Model	Train R-squared	Test R-squared	RMSE	Computation time (sec)
Random forest (RF)	0.981437	0.822853	15,520.307978	420
	0.97278	0.75403	18,288.2958	1080
Gradient boosting (GB)	0.624619	0.5582952	24,510.03213	60
	0.6031127	0.5402546	25,003.0084	240
Extreme gradient boosting (XGB)	0.915697	0.7828987	17,181.745050	3
	0.9012672	0.7174	19,600.39311	15

multicollinearity is addressed with PCA. The PCA in Fig. 3 shows that more than 76% of components are required to explain 90% of the variance. Hence, dimensionality reduction is employed by using PCA and retaining only 23 components for model development.

Models are trained on raw data (i.e., without rescaling or dimensionality reduction), and subsequently with rescaled data first by standard scaling approach on the training data only to prevent information leakage, and by PCA with only 23 components retained. Due to limited computational resources, iterative hyperparameter optimization is not performed at the start rather random initialization. Models are trained by the RF regressor, GB, and XGB algorithms, as depicted in Table 3.

Considering RMSE, the RF regressor outperforms XGB by about 7%. On the other hand, considering the computation time, XGB has more than 7100% lower computational time compared to the RF regressor. Hence, the XGB regressor without scaling and dimensionality reduction is adopted for the prediction of healthcare costs.

2.2.2 Classification Model

Recall from Sect. 2.1 that all variables' correlations are significantly different from zero, and that variables which are not significant predictors are dropped. However, some multicollinearity exists in which the PCA is used. As in Sect. 2.2.1, the dataset is separated on a similar basis and first trains the model to determine the importance of features using the Gini information criterion, as depicted in Fig. 4

The results, in Fig. 4, support the inference in Sect. 2.1 that all variables are important predictors for the classification model. In addition, only 77% of the variables are required to explain at least 90% of the information for the target variable. This prompts us to take all variables for the classification model and proceed to address the observed multicollinearity with PCA in Fig. 5.

The PCA shows that more than 76% of the components are required to explain 90% of the variance. Hence, dimensionality reduction is employed through PCA, and only 20 components are retained for model development. Table 4 shows the classification model performance before and after scaling and PCA.

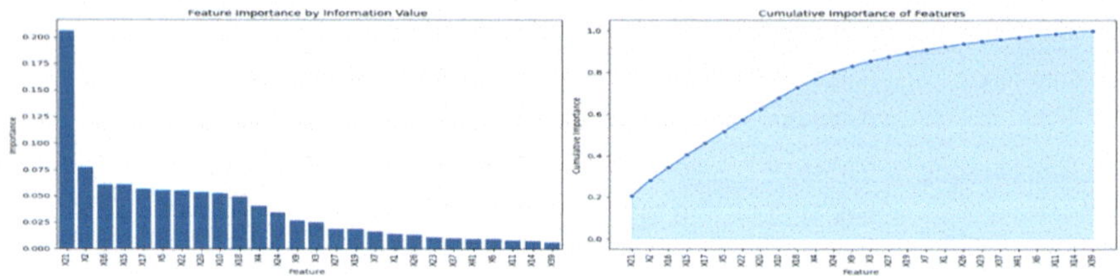

Fig. 4 Feature importance for the classification model

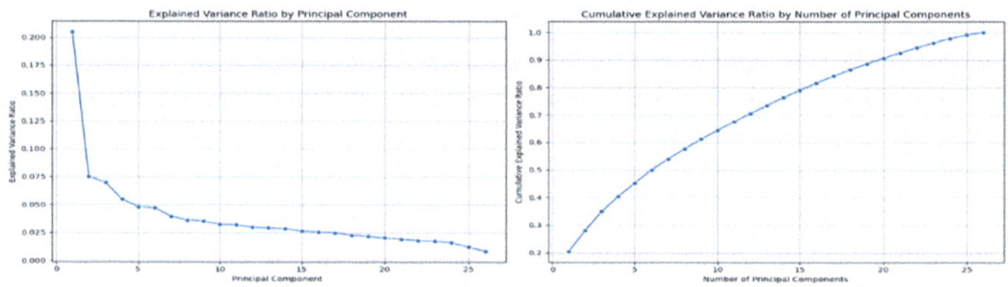

Fig. 5 PCA variance analysis for the classification model

Table 4 Classification model performance before (shaded row) and after scaling/ PCA

Model	Train accuracy	Test accuracy	Computation time (sec)
Random forest (RF)	0.99978	0.880618	207
	0.9999654	0.848723	381
Gradient boosting (GB)	0.7212755	0.7168279	245
	0.67244438	0.66416666	485
Extreme gradient boosting (XGB)	0.834519982	0.807782258	48.7
	0.7920771	0.7470027	4

Table 5 Individual contribution distribution parameters for NPS wave 5

	location	shape	Scale	scale
Beta	0.693809	559.894	-1.2×10^{-24}	2,316,409
Beta	0.637473	163.3372	-1.4×10^{-25}	475,851.1
Pareto	1.851522	17,002.53		44,731.99

The bias in RF is larger compared to the XGB classifier, so for the computational time, the XGB classifier without scaling and dimensionality reduction pipeline is adopted.

2.2.3 Contribution Estimation

The dynamic model employs the pure premium principle to find individual contribution, in which the cost is estimated by an XGB regressor, and the probability of incurring the cost is estimated by the probabilistic XGB classifier. Individuals whose contributions are above 3 standard deviations of the whole sample's individual contributions are classified as high-risk individuals, while others are normal-risk individuals. General individual contribution distributions follow a beta distribution similar to individuals with normal risk, while high-risk individuals follow Pareto distribution with parameters as described in Table 5. Based on the results, the estimated contributions can be reproduced without repeating the whole process (i.e., through simulations). Further, the contribution distributions at the family level are evaluated to build a better argument for comparison, since the community ratings also consider a group or family contribution.

Table 2 is used to simultaneously compute the contribution under the CR approach for all individuals in the validation data. The output for contributions estimation is further analyzed in the test of the hypothesis, which shows that the contribution pricing seems to have a near-similar distribution to empirical pricing; however, CR is on a much broader scale than DP from the empirical spending distribution. Furthermore, they are from the same distribution family (see Figs. 6 and 7).

3 Discussion

The results from validation data (NPS wave 5) show that the dynamic pricing pipeline seems to have learned better about the distribution of healthcare costs from previous waves. This is because the estimated contribution rates follow the distribution of empirical healthcare utilization costs, as per Fig. 6, which is much better. Data attributes have significant information values for all target variables, and dimensionality reduction could not improve models' performance from the initial feature selection. Furthermore, the evidence from linear models shows a weak linear relation;

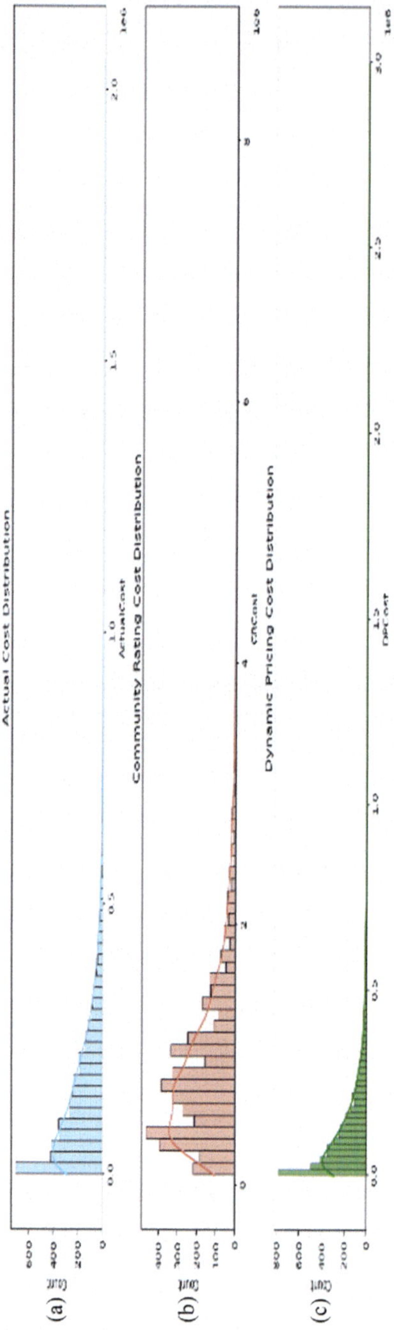

Fig. 6 Individual (family level) contribution distribution comparison (**a**) Actual (**b**) CR (**c**) DP

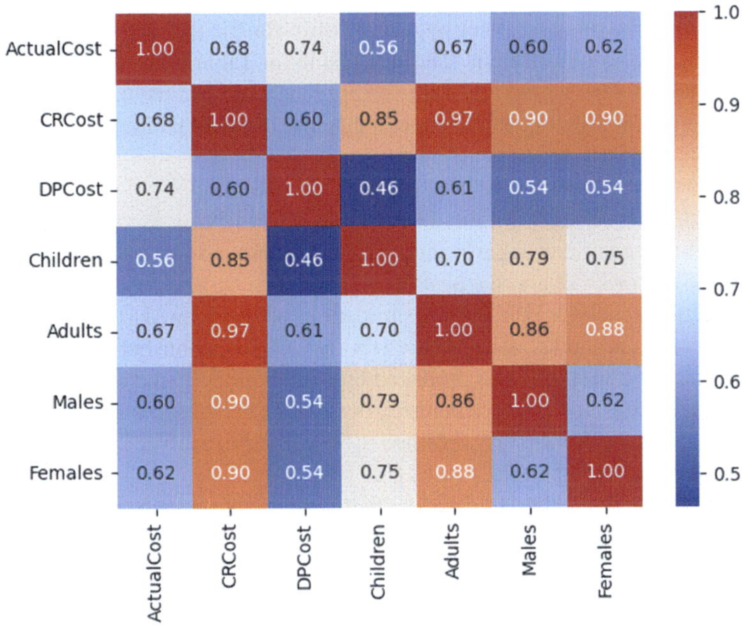

Fig. 7 Correlation heatmap

thus, opting for nonlinear models is appropriate. The RF models have higher computational costs and are prone to overfitting despite producing higher performance than other approaches. The XGB models are adopted, illustrating a better bias-variance tradeoff and significantly lower computational time. Healthcare spending follows very skewed distributions, and extremes exist, which are well learned by a DP model, with the implication that high-risk individuals are expected to contribute much more than others; this can limit accessibility to low-income, high-risk individuals. The CR can be a better alternative to distributing extreme costs in this regard. However, this can be normalized to alternative premium principles, such as variance and standard deviation principles, as a significant proportion of the population is expected to make nearly zero contributions. Thus, it can pool the cost that each individual contributes to at least the mean of the projected healthcare cost for the whole scheme. This approach could ensure improved equity in accessing healthcare.

At the family level, how various factors could influence individual contributions are analyzed, including gender distribution, age distribution (categorized into two, i.e., adults and children), and the cost produced by the two models compared to the empirical cost. At baseline, DP cost correlates more with actual cost than the CR approach. This is supported by the distribution of actual values as in Fig. 7, whereby CR cost is highly correlated to actual cost, but the distribution of its values is different. The actual cost increases more for adults and females in age and gender categories than for children and males. On the other hand, a similar effect for particular categories is far higher in the CR approach and slightly lower in the DP approach, comprehending the relative effect on accessibility for the two approaches from the actual family use to be different. The test results in Table 6 for the hypothesis of Sect. 1.2.2, against the actual cost for each approach and against one other, provide confidence that CR significantly increases the cost from actual healthcare spending while the DP approach reduces it.

Furthermore, the DP approach also reduces the contribution cost compared to the CR approach. Subsequently, in the dimension of affordability, it makes it confident that the DP approach can significantly provide improved healthcare accessibility compared to CR or OOP approaches.

For sensitivity analysis, 10,000,000 simulations are performed to evaluate how the distribution of mean and variance is varied for the OOP, the contributions produced by CR model, and the contributions produced by the DP model. Since the DP approach did not include external expenses incurred outside the actual settlement of the claim, the loading factor is adjusted, as explained in Sect. 1.2.2 to analyze how the induction of the expenses could affect the results (see Figs. 8 and 9).

Figure 8 shows that, when the loading factor ranges between 5.66 and 6.35, there is no significant difference between the CR and DP approaches. When it exceeds

Table 6 Hypotheses test summary

μ_0	μ_1	Test statistic	P- value
Actual cost	Community rating	−75.3631	0
Actual cost	Dynamic pricing	5.519638	3.49×10^{-08}
Community rating	Dynamic pricing	76.79101	0

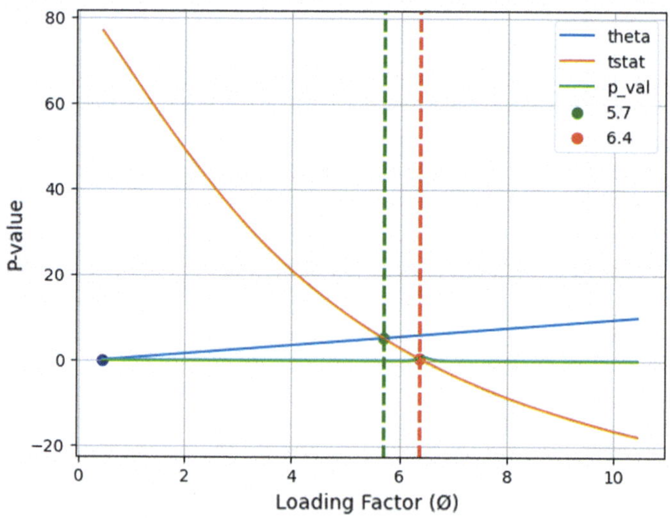

Fig. 8 Sensitivity analysis between CR and DP

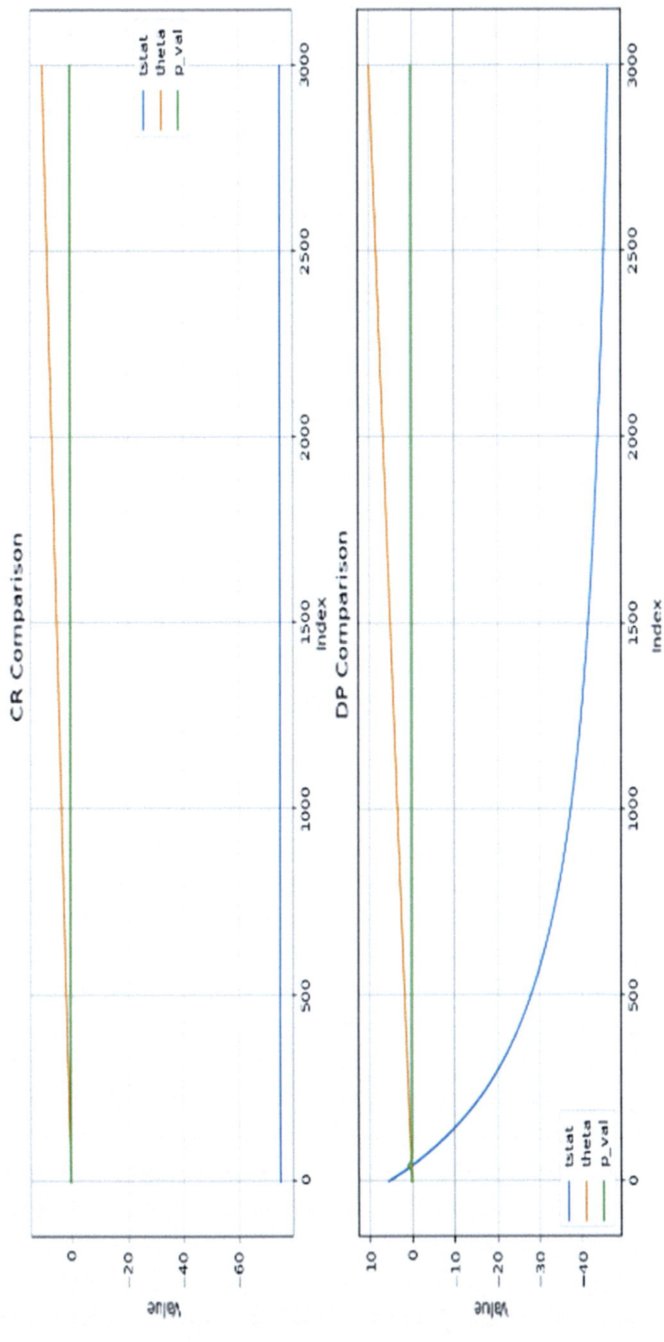

Fig. 9 Sensitivity analysis of models to actual cost

6.35, the DP approach significantly increases the healthcare cost, thus considered to lower healthcare access.

In Fig. 9, the results show that the loading factor does not impact the CR approach. In the DP approach, when the loading factor is between 0.09 and 0.2, the contribution rates are not significantly different from OOP. At loading above 0.2, the DP rates are significantly higher than OOP, thus, inferring the DP is not appropriate for enhancing healthcare accessibility over OOP.

The results imply that the DP approach provides a promising framework for optimizing healthcare contributions and improving accessibility. By leveraging machine learning techniques and pure premium models, the DP approach demonstrates a nuanced understanding of healthcare cost distributions, effectively balancing individual contributions while ensuring equitable access. The comparison with traditional CR approaches highlights the DP model's superiority in aligning contribution rates with actual costs, potentially reducing individual financial burdens.

Moreover, sensitivity analyses illuminate the DP model's robustness to varying external factors, offering insights into its adaptability and potential limitations. While computational costs and complexities remain challenging, the DP approach presents a viable solution for healthcare financing, warranting further exploration and refinement.

4 Conclusion

A comparative analysis of DP models and the CR approach in healthcare financing with a link to healthcare access has been intensively explored through literature review and the development of robust regression and classification models for predicting healthcare costs and individual contributions. The statistical techniques (linear regression and logit models) and ML algorithms are used to identify key factors influencing healthcare expenditure. Different tests, including KMO, BTS, and log-likelihood ratio test, are performed and utilized metrics including MAPE, RMSE, Adjusted R-squared, accuracy score, and F1-scored in data preprocessing and model evaluation, overcoming challenges such as multicollinearity. The analysis, unveiled the differential effect of DP on diverse demographic cohorts, offering insights crucial for shaping equitable healthcare access policies.

The research represents a significant leap toward redefining healthcare financing paradigms, highlighting the transformative potential of DP in fostering accessible and inclusive healthcare systems for CR and OOP. By harnessing the power of machine learning, we have not only improved the accuracy of cost prediction but also shed light on the intricate dynamics of healthcare economics.

Acknowledgements The authors are grateful to UDSM for providing a supportive research environment and to the NBS in Tanzania for granting permission for use of its data for this research.

References

1. Albawi, S., Alshahrani, L., Albawi, N., Alharbi, R., Alhakamy, A.: Prediction of healthcare insurance costs. In *Computers and Informatics*. Vol. 3, Issue 1 (2023). https://dergipark.org.tr/tr/pub/ci
2. Samiuddin, M., Rajender, G., Varma, S., Kumar, A., Shaik, S. Health Insurance Cost Prediction Using Deep Neural Network. *Asian Journal of Research in Computer Science*, *16*(2), 46–53 (2023). https://doi.org/10.9734/ajrcos/2023/v16i2338
3. WHO (India). Global review of the role of artificial intelligence and machine learning in health-care financing for UHC, (2024).
4. Reid, M., Gupta, R., Roberts, G., Goosby, E., Wesson, P. Achieving Universal Health Coverage (UHC): Dominance analysis across 183 countries highlights importance of strengthening health workforce. *PLoS ONE*, *15*(3) (2020). https://doi.org/10.1371/journal.pone.0229666
5. Darrudi, A., Khoonsari, M., Tajvar, M. Challenges to Achieving Universal Health Coverage Throughout the World: A Systematic Review. In *Journal of Preventive Medicine and Public Health* - Korean Society for Preventive Medicine Vol. 55, Issue 2, pp. 125–133 (2022). https://doi.org/10.3961/jpmph.21.542
6. Neun, S, Sources of Health Care Funding Throughout the Globe. In *ECONOMICS INTERACTIONS WITH OTHER DISCIPLINES*. (2023). https://www.eolss.net/sample-chapters/C13/E6-29-01-03.pdf
7. WHO GHED. *Global Health Expenditure Database* (2024). https://apps.who.int/nha/database
8. Soucat, A., Tandon, A., Gonzales Pier, E. From Universal Health Coverage services packages to budget appropriation: the long journey to implementation. *BMJ Global Health*, *8* (2023). https://doi.org/10.1136/bmjgh-2022-010755
9. Pardo, C., Sabat, J. Equity and Efficiency Effects of Flat Premiums. *SSRN Electronic Journal* (2023). https://doi.org/10.2139/ssrn.4460458
10. Ly, M., Bassoum, O., Faye, A. Universal health insurance in Africa: A narrative review of the literature on institutional models. In *BMJ Global Health* - BMJ Publishing Group.Vol. 7, Issue 4 (2022a). https://doi.org/10.1136/bmjgh-2021-008219
11. Hanafy, M., Mahmoud, O. Predict Health Insurance Cost by using Machine Learning and DNN Regression Models. *International Journal of Innovative Technology and Exploring Engineering*, *10*(3), 137–143 (2021). https://doi.org/10.35940/ijitee.C8364.0110321
12. Kaushik, K., Bhardwaj, A., Dwivedi, A, Singh, R. Article Machine Learning-Based Regression Framework to Predict Health Insurance Premiums. *International Journal of Environmental Research and Public Health*, *19*(13) (2022). https://doi.org/10.3390/ijerph19137898
13. ul Hassan, C., Iqbal, J., Hussain, S., AlSalman, H., Mosleh, M., Sajid Ullah, S. A Computational Intelligence Approach for Predicting Medical Insurance Cost. *Mathematical Problems in Engineering*, *2021*. https://doi.org/10.1155/2021/1162553
14. Cu, A., Meister, S., Lefebvre, B., Ridde, V. Assessing healthcare access using the Levesque's conceptual framework– a scoping review. In *International Journal for Equity in Health*-BioMed Central Ltd Vol. 20, Issue 1 (2021). https://doi.org/10.1186/s12939-021-01416-3
15. Ghanad, A. An Overview of Quantitative Research Methods. *INTERNATIONAL JOURNAL OF MULTIDISCIPLINARY RESEARCH AND ANALYSIS*. (2023). https://doi.org/10.47191/ijmra/v6-i8-52
16. NBS Tanzania. *National Bureau of Statistics - National Panel Survey* (2024). https://www.nbs.go.tz/index.php/en/census-surveys/poverty-indicators-statistics/national-panel-survey
17. The DHS Program. *The DHS Program – Data* (2024). https://dhsprogram.com/Data/
18. Krejcie, R., Morgan, D. Determining sample size for research activities. 607–610 (1970).
19. Langenberger, B., Schulte, T., Groene, O. The application of machine learning to predict high-cost patients: A performance-comparison of different models using healthcare claims data. *PLoS ONE*, *18*(1) (2023). https://doi.org/10.1371/journal.pone.0279540
20. Benesty, J., Chen, J., Huang, Y., Cohen, I. Pearson correlation coefficient. In *Springer Topics in Signal Processing*- Springer Science and Business Media B.V Vol. 2, pp. 1–4 (2009). https://doi.org/10.1007/978-3-642-00296-0_5

21. McHugh, M. The Chi-square test of independence. *Biochemia Medica*, *23*(2), 143–149 (2013). https://doi.org/10.11613/BM.2013.018
22. Wiley, M., Wiley, J. Univariate Data Visualization. In *Advanced R Statistical Programming and Data Models*-Apress pp. 1–31 (2019). https://doi.org/10.1007/978-1-4842-2872-2_1
23. Pham, T., Pandis, N., White, I. Missing data: Issues, concepts, methods. *Seminars in Orthodontics*, *30*(1), 37–44 (2024). https://doi.org/10.1053/j.sodo.2024.01.007
24. Aguinis, H., Gottfredson, R., Joo, H. Best-Practice Recommendations for Defining, Identifying, and Handling Outliers. In *Organizational Research Methods* SAGE Publications Inc. Vol. 16, Issue 2, pp. 270–301 (2013). https://doi.org/10.1177/1094428112470848
25. Kwak, S., Kim, J. Statistical data preparation: Management of missing values and outliers. In *Korean Journal of Anesthesiology* - Korean Society of Anesthesiologists Vol. 70, Issue 4, pp. 407–411. (2017). https://doi.org/10.4097/kjae.2017.70.4.407
26. Singh Rawat, S., Kumar Mishra, A. Review of Methods for Handling Class-Imbalanced in Classification Problems (2023).
27. Van Den Goorbergh, R., Van Smeden, M., Timmerman, D., Ben Van Calster. The harm of class imbalance corrections for risk prediction models: Illustration and simulation using logistic regression. *Journal of the American Medical Informatics Association*, *29*(9), 1525–1534 (2022).. https://doi.org/10.1093/jamia/ocac093
28. Wongvorachan, T., He, S., Bulut, O. A Comparison of Under-sampling, Oversampling, and SMOTE Methods for Dealing with Imbalanced Classification in Educational Data Mining. *Information (Switzerland)*, *14*(1) (2023). https://doi.org/10.3390/info14010054
29. Cerda, P., Varoquaux, G. *Encoding high-cardinality string categorical variables* (2019). https://doi.org/10.1109/TKDE.2020.2992529
30. Seger, C. An investigation of categorical variable encoding techniques in machine learning: binary versus one-hot and feature hashing. In *DEGREE PROJECT TECHNOLOGY* (2018).
31. Shrestha, N. Factor Analysis as a Tool for Survey Analysis. *American Journal of Applied Mathematics and Statistics*, *9*(1), 4–11 (2021). https://doi.org/10.12691/ajams-9-1-2
32. Taherdoost, H., Sahibuddin, S., Jalaliyoon, N. *Exploratory Factor Analysis; Concepts and Theory* (2020).
33. Orji, U., Ukwandu, E. Machine learning for an explainable cost prediction of medical insurance. *Machine Learning with Applications*, *15*, 100516 (2024). https://doi.org/10.1016/j.mlwa.2023.100516
34. The United Republic of Tanzania. Muswada wa Sheria ya Bima ya Afya kwa Wote wa Mwaka 2022 (Special Bill Supplement No. 8). Dodoma: Government Printer (2022).
35. The United Republic of Tanzania. Sheria ya Bima ya Afya Kwa Wote ya Mwaka 2023. No. 13, 1st December, 2023. ACT SUPPLEMENT To the Gazette of The United Republic of Tanzania No. 48 Vol. 104 Dated 1st December, 2023. Printed By the Government Printer, Dodoma by Order of Government. ISSN 0856 - 035X (2023).
36. Makwetta, H. Viwango kuchangia bima ya afya kwa wote hivi hapa. https://www.mwananchi.co.tz/mw/habari/kitaifa/viwango-kuchangia-bima-ya-afya-kwa-wote-hivi-hapa-3977248. *Mwananchi* (2022).
37. Mori, A. T. Mandatory health insurance for the informal sector in Tanzania—has it worked anywhere! *Frontiers in Health Services*, *3* (2023). https://doi.org/10.3389/frhs.2023.1247301
38. Xu, M., Fralick, D., Zheng, J. Z., Wang, B., Tu, X. M., Feng, C. The differences and similarities between two-sample t-test and paired t-test. *Shanghai Archives of Psychiatry*, *29*(3), 184–188 (2017). https://doi.org/10.11919/j.issn.1002-0829.217070

Development of an IoT-Based Smart Irrigation System for Efficient Water Management in Uasin Gishu County

Winny Tuitoek Bundotich, Ramadhani Sinde, John Tarus, and Titus Kiprop Mengich Maiyo

Abstract Food scarcity has recently increased due to climate change, population growth, and decreased land for farming. To mitigate this, measures like encouraging irrigation farming have been implemented, but irrigation faces water scarcity challenges. Efforts to improve water use efficiency include scheduled irrigation system technology, mostly targeting greenhouses and neglecting open-field irrigation. To address these issues, this project developed an IoT-based smart irrigation system for efficient water management. Using an ESP32 microcontroller, sensors monitor critical soil parameters, and the OpenWeather API fetches rainfall predictions. The system automatically controls irrigation valves based on soil moisture levels and rainfall predictions, providing remote valve control and farm information visualization via the Thingsboard cloud platform and mobile app. Data was collected using mixed methods, including questionnaires and focus group discussions with sixteen respondents, selected through purposive sampling. Agile software development methodology, specifically extreme programming, was used to develop the system. Validation involved demonstrations to twenty-seven people, who then interacted with the system and provided feedback through a questionnaire. Respondents agreed that the system met their needs satisfactorily. This system contributes to precise water input and can be advanced to monitor and evaluate irrigated farms in Uasin Gishu County and beyond.

W. T. Bundotich (✉) · R. Sinde (✉)
The Nelson Mandela African Institution of Science and Technology, Arusha, Tanzania
e-mail: bundotichw@nm-aist.ac.tz

R. Sinde
e-mail: ramadhani.sinde@nm-aist.ac.tz

J. Tarus
Moi University, Eldoret, Kenya
e-mail: jktarus@mu.ac.ke

T. K. M. Maiyo
The County Government of Uasin Gishu, Eldoret, Kenya
e-mail: tituskimaiyo@uasingishu.go.ke

J. Marx Gómez et al. (eds.), *Advancement in Embedded and Mobile Systems*, Progress in IS, https://doi.org/10.1007/978-3-031-99219-3_25

Keywords Internet of Things · Application Programming Interface · Message Queueing Telemetry Transport

1 Introduction

The world population is projected to rise by 33% between 2017 and 2030 (World Population Prospects, 2017), requiring increased food production. To achieve this, technologies such as artificial intelligence (AI), the Internet of Things (IoT), and machine learning (ML) are being adopted to improve pest control and adapt to climate change.

Irrigation expansion, farmer information, and digital technologies, such as the Internet of Things (IoT), are key strategies to enhance agricultural productivity despite climate change challenges [1]. The FAO (2009) projects a 27% increase in irrigated land over the next 20 years, but only a 12% rise in available water for agriculture [2].

Kenya's economy heavily relies on agriculture, which is vital for its development. According to the FAO [3], agriculture directly contributes 26% of Kenya's GDP and another 27% indirectly through its links with other sectors. However, Kenya is water-scarce, and agriculture consumes a significant portion of this limited resource (Mwaniki, 2010).

Globally, automated water management platforms have been on trial. Ullah et al. [4], proposed an IoT-Based Energy-Efficient Water Management Platform for Smart Irrigation, simulated with Matlab. The system was not tested in real environments and lacked real-time sensor data for optimizing water use, limiting its effectiveness.

Olatunji et al. [5], developed a mobile phone-controllable smart irrigation system for greenhouses, using an Android app to automate valve control based on soil moisture and temperature. While effective in small, controlled environments, it is limited for large open-field farms due to the need for multiple sensors and valves to address soil water variability. Haule and Michael [6] proposed automated irrigation using a wireless sensor network, but their simulation [7] relied solely on soil moisture. Adding parameters like rainfall predictions could enhance water efficiency.

Much work has been done on IoT water management in irrigated lands, focusing on weather visualization and farm parameter monitoring. However, few studies have automated irrigation based on soil moisture, and none have included rainfall prediction for water control. Rainfall prediction is crucial for farmers practicing open-field irrigation to save water. To address this, this project developed a low-cost IoT-based smart irrigation system for efficient water management, aiming to increase water usage efficiency, provide remote visualization, and automate tasks like opening and closing irrigation valves. Mass production could further reduce costs.

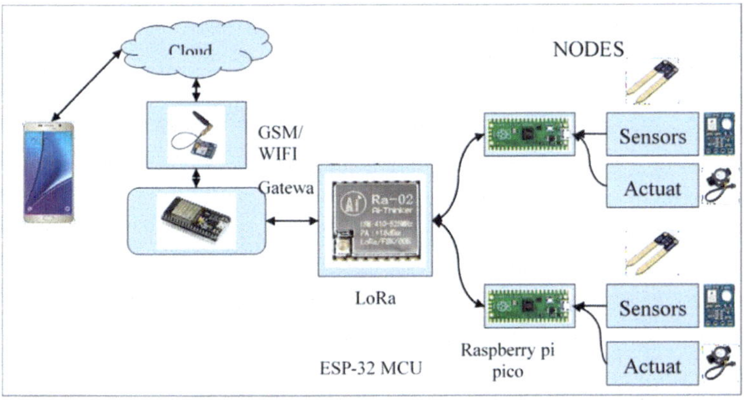

Fig. 1 The system's architecture diagram

2 Materials and Methods

2.1 System Architecture

The proposed system uses sensors to collect soil parameters. The irrigated land is divided into sections, each with a node. The key parameter for water management is soil moisture, while temperature and light intensity are collected for visualization. Sensors connected to Raspberry Pi Pico gather these parameters. According to [8], LoRa offers a longer transmission range than ZigBee and is ideal for secluded areas. In this system, sensor data is transmitted via LoRa to an ESP32 microcontroller, which uses WIFI to send data to the Thingsboard cloud server. The server also receives rainfall predictions from the OpenWeather API. The system analyzes these parameters and controls irrigation valves by sending signals to actuators on the respective nodes. Figure 1 shows the architecture diagram of the system.

2.2 Hardware Components and Software Components

Hardware components: The gateway includes an ESP32 microcontroller, OLED display, AHT20 sensor, and LoRa module. The OLED display and AHT20 connect to the ESP32 via I2C, while the LoRa module connects via SPI. Communication between the gateway and node uses the LoRa (433MHz) protocol. The Raspberry Pi Pico connects to LoRa through SPI and to the soil moisture sensor and LDR via ADC. Figure 2 illustrates the block diagram of the system, detailing the components and their connections.

A summary of hardware requirements is presented in Table 1.

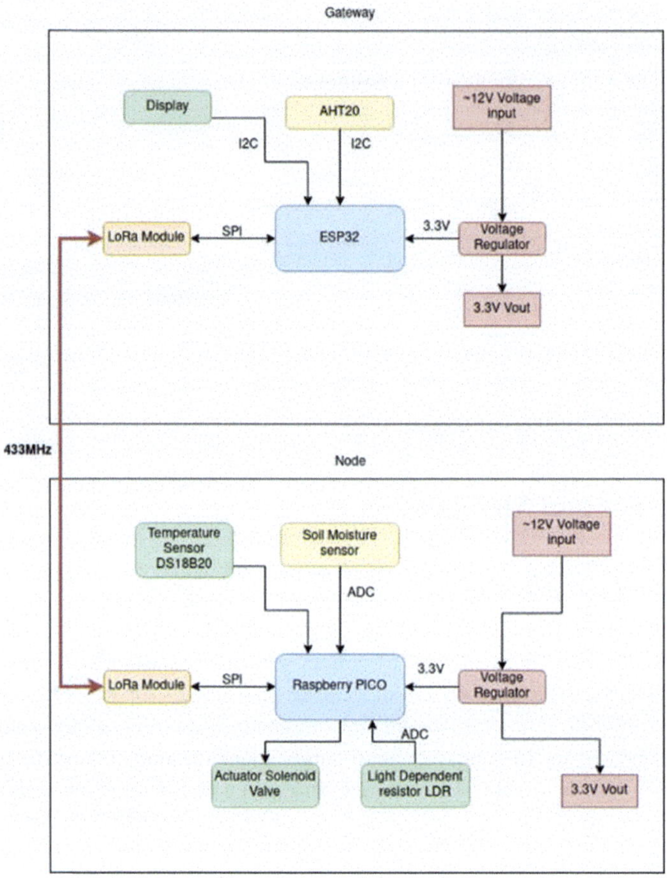

Fig. 2 System's block diagram

Table 1 Summary of hardware components used

Hardware component	Specification
Microcontroller boards	Pico RP2040, ESP 32
Sensors	AHT20, DS18B20, Analog capacitive soil moisture sensor,
Transmission protocols	LoRa Ra-02 SX1278 Module 433MHZ
Irrigation valves	12V Solenoid valve G1/2 DN15BSPP
Display	OLED 128 * 32
Others	PLA standard 1.75 mm, Ferric Chloride acid, status LEDs

Software components and protocols: The software used included micropython, which runs on bare metal and provides an interactive prompt for command execution. Kicad, freecad, and cura were used for PCB and case development, while Thingsboard cloud platform was used for optimum controls and visualization. Message Queuing Telemetry Protocol (MQTT), Remote Procedural Calls (RPC), and Wireless Fidelity (WIFI) were used for communication between the node, gateway, and cloud, while Open Weather Application Programming Interface (API) was used to provide rainfall prediction data.

2.3 System Development

A mixed method was used during data collection, where a focused group discussion was used to collect data from agriculture experts, which was used in the second phase of questionnaires that involved farmers within Uasin Gishu county. The collected data was analyzed and proved that the need for an automated irrigation system was for efficient water management. The system is made up of three parts: the node, the Gateway, and the Thingsboard cloud platform. The firmware was developed using MicroPython. Before programming the boards, a test was performed to ensure they could connect to the computer and be debugged and programmed. The first step was to test individual sensors to ascertain that they worked as desired. The ADCs were configured to give accurate readings. Temperature sensors used the I2C line so that they could be read while executing other functions concurrently. The I2C is a synchronous protocol that switches packets and is a serial communication bus. Since the Gateway and the node communicate using LoRa, we used an asynchronous function (interrupt) to execute whenever there is an incoming package. This ensured that there were no missed LORA data packets. The pinout diagram of WeMosESP32 (Gateway) and Raspberry Pi Pico (node), shown in Fig. 3, were obtained for cross-reference as programming took place.

The node collects the sensor data at intervals set by the user. For this project, the set interval was 10 s. The data is then packaged with variable names, e.g., humidity, soil moisture, and temperature, so the variables and values are identified and saved to respective database fields. Upon receiving packets by the Gateway, it displays the

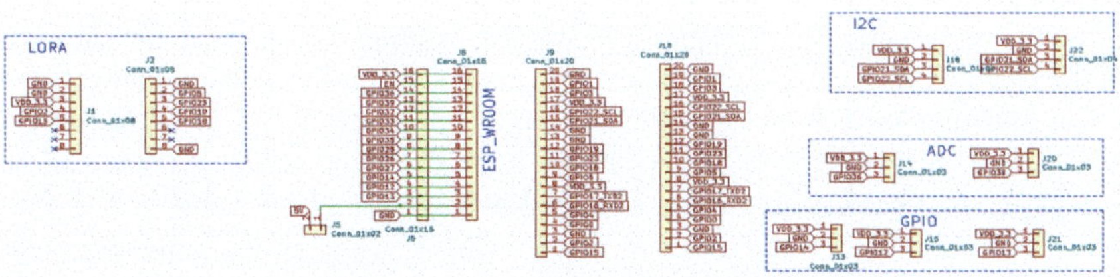

Fig. 3 LoRa to ESP gateway pinout

packet, the sending node, and the signal strength. This is to estimate the distance of a node to the Gateway. It also adds to it the Received Signal Strength Indication (RSSI), Signal Noise Ratio (SNR), and ambient temperature, which is measured by an AHT10(Humidity and temperature) sensor connected to its I2C line are all added to the packet and, after that, sent to the server. The Gateway also receives RPC (Remote Procedure Calls) calls to turn on the actuators; hence, farm irrigation takes place. These RPC calls are forwarded to the specific node address to turn ON or OFF the solenoid valves. When the solenoid valve is ON, the blue LED is turned on, while the Red LED is turned on whenever the solenoid valve is OFF. After the actuation of the solenoid valve, it sends back the response to the Gateway, which is then forwarded to the cloud server to ascertain that the event has been executed successfully.

The different protocols used in sending and receiving packets by the system's three parts, namely, the node, Gateway, and server, are LoRa and MQTT. The first protocol that enables data to be sent from the node to the Gateway is LoRa (Long Range Radio). This physical proprietary radio communication technique is based on spread spectrum modulation techniques derived from chirp spread spectrum technology. After that, the packets are added to the data as captured earlier and sent to the server using the MQTT protocol (Message Queueing Telemetry Transport); this is a lightweight, publish-subscribe, machine-to-machine network protocol. It is designed for connections with remote locations that have devices with resource constraints or limited network bandwidth. Both of these protocols are two-way communication. Detailed information about the MQTT and the LoRa protocols is provided in this report's hardware and software requirements sections, respectively.

Figure 4 depicts the node's processing flow. The system initializes the LoRa communication protocol and retries until successful. Once initialized, the node waits for data from the Gateway. Upon receiving data, the node processes it and controls the solenoid valve accordingly. If no data is received, the node enters a 10-s delay, then collects and sends sensor data to the Gateway. This cycle continues indefinitely until the system is powered off.

Figure 5 shows the Gateway's processing flow involves connecting to the Things-board cloud, retrying until successful. Once connected, it initializes LoRa, repeating the attempt until successful. After LoRa initialization, the Gateway waits for data from both the cloud and nodes. It checks the data source: if from a node, it forwards the data to the cloud; if from the cloud, it forwards the data to the appropriate node address.

Figure 6 shows that the cloud platform starts by waiting for data from the Gateway and the OpenWeather API. Upon receiving data, it stores it in a database and checks the soil moisture level. If soil moisture is low, the cloud examines API data for rain predictions. If no rain is expected within an hour, the cloud sends an "open valve" message to the Gateway. If rain is expected and the raincheck value is less than three, the cloud monitors soil moisture and raincheck values. If the raincheck value reaches three and soil moisture is still low, the cloud sends an "open valve" message. Otherwise, it continues to process incoming data.

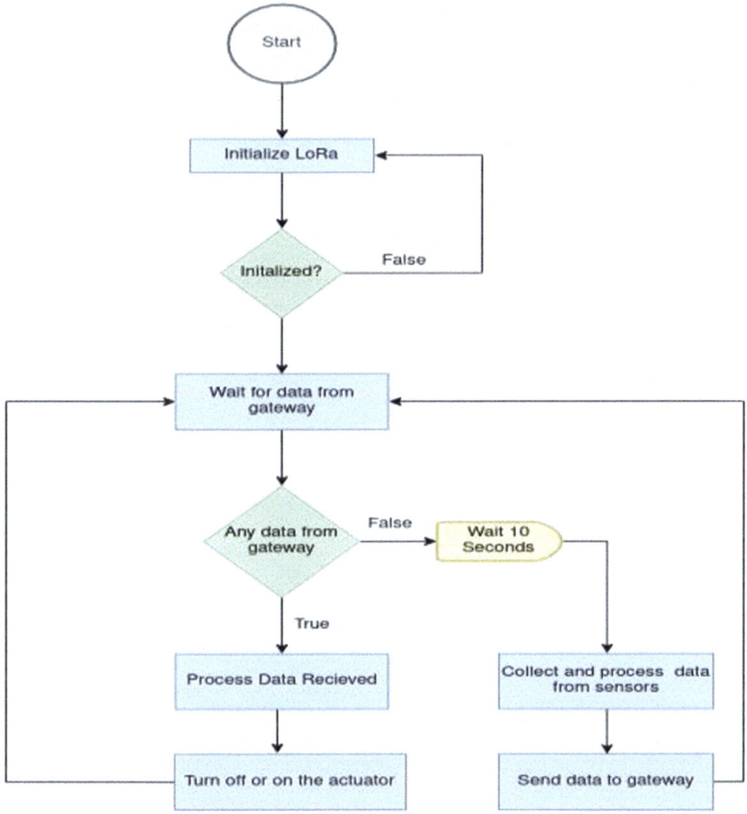

Fig. 4 The system node's activities flow chart

2.4 *Communication Between the Cloud Gateway and Nodes*

Communication between cloud and gateway: The Thingsboard cloud platform acts as the system's server, where all optimal controls are managed. The cloud receives and sends data to the gateway through WiFi by implementing the MQTT protocol.

Communication between cloud and nodes: The server (cloud) communicates with the system nodes using Remote Procedure Calls (RPC), which consist of call and reply messages. Each node makes an RPC request to the server and receives a response containing the results of the procedure's execution. RPC can match a reply message to a specific request by providing a unique specification for the RPC message. Server-side

Cloud applications also send RPC calls to the nodes, including two-way RPC to turn solenoid valves ON or OFF. This two-way RPC ensures that the node sends a response on the valve's status, which is a crucial visualization feature.

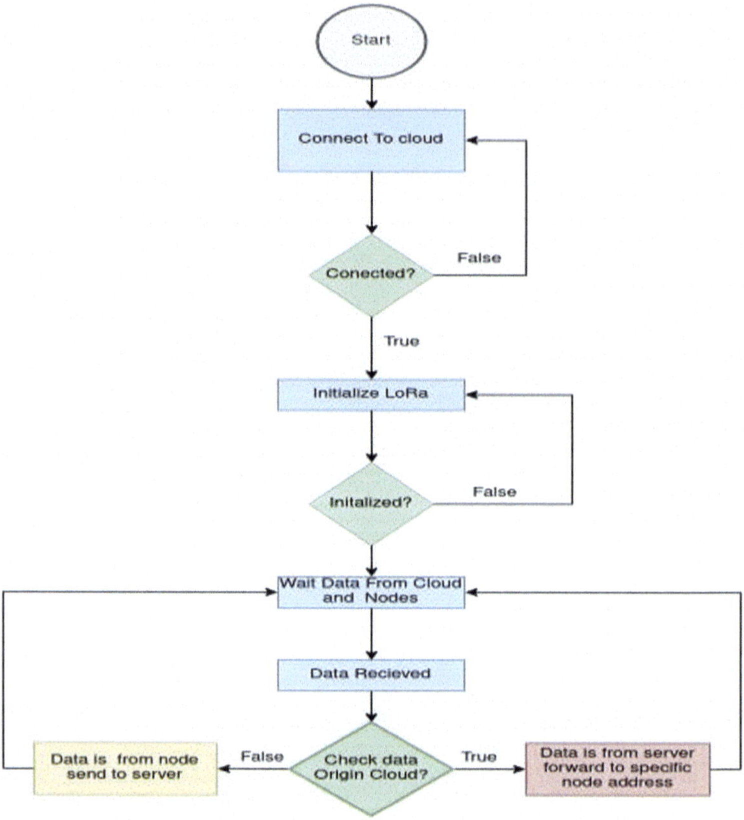

Fig. 5 Gateway activities flowchart

2.5 *System Development Approach*

Extreme programming (XP) agile methodology was used since the work is continuously tested and released in short sprint cycles. Breaking down large tasks into smaller ones eases error detection and correction, allowing for greater focus on the product and thereby improving the quality of the end product. Additionally, agile methodology is flexible to changes during implementation, whether due to modifications in the process or requirements. This flexibility arises because changes in functional requirements are incorporated into the incremental development process.

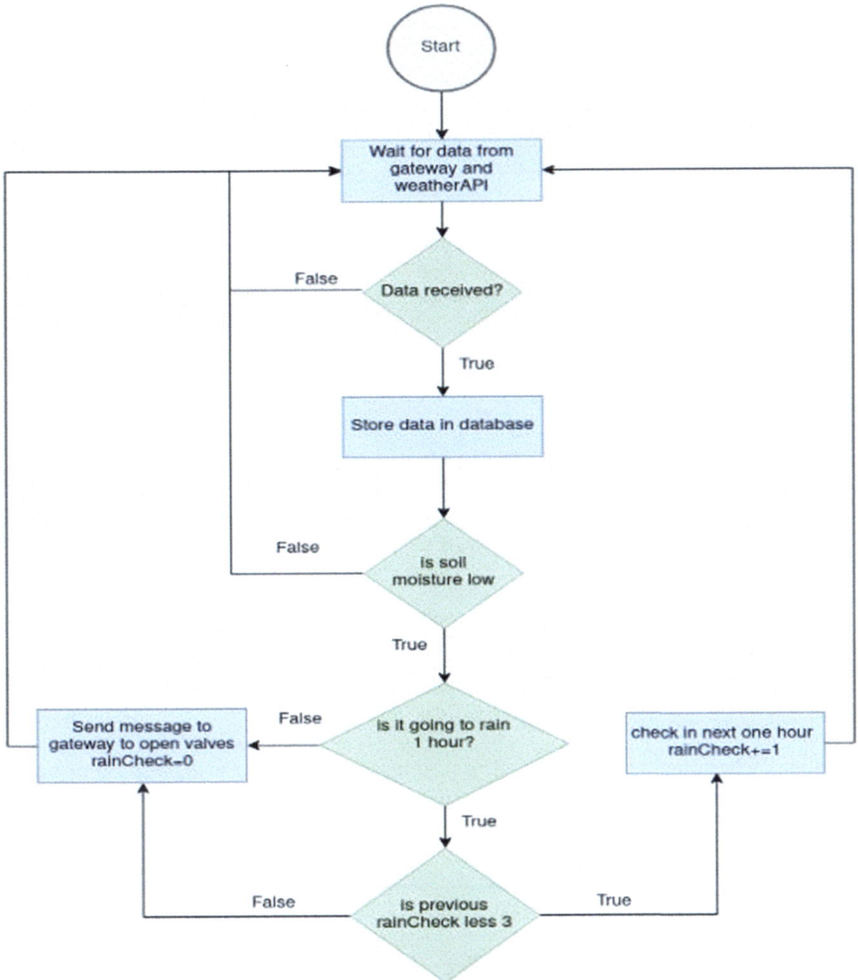

Fig. 6 Cloud activities flow chart

3 Results and Discussion

The PCB boards were printed, and the hardware was assembled, as shown in Figs. 7 and 8. The gateway comprised an ESP32 microcontroller, LoRa module, OLED display, and a GSM module. The GSM module is a backup for Wi-Fi transmission in areas where WI-FI communication is unavailable. Each irrigation node comprised Raspberry Pi Pico, LoRa module, AHT20 sensors, DS18B20 temperature sensor, solenoid valve actuator, and LDR.

The dashboard details are specific to each node. Figure 9 shows the dashboard of node 1 in our system when the valve is OFF, while Fig. 10 shows the node two

Fig. 7 Assembled node hardware

Fig. 8 Assembled gateway hardware

dashboard when the system is ON. The dashboard provides a visualization of valve status, where the "valve status icon is gray whenever the solenoid valve is OFF."

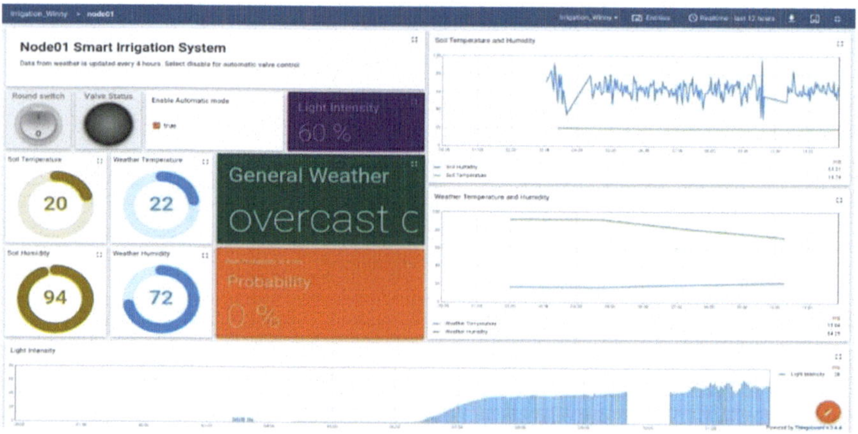

Fig. 9 Node one dashboard when the valve is OFF, image taken from the administrator's account

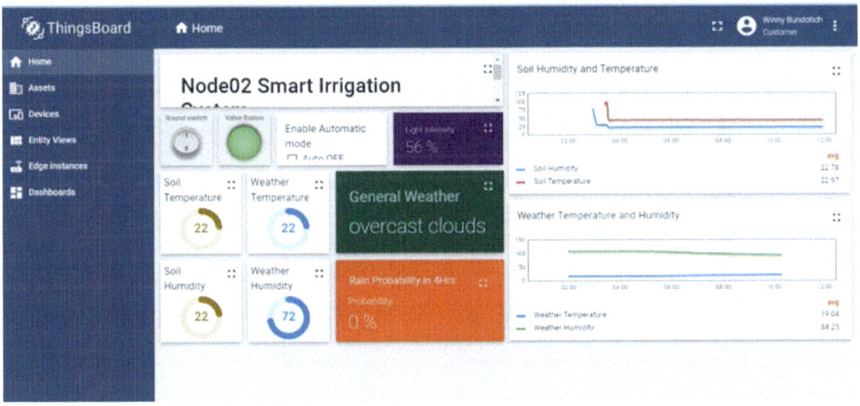

Fig. 10 Node two dashboard when the valve is ON, image taken from the user's account

A user can turn ON or OFF the solenoid valves remotely. This can be done through mobile phones by logging into their Thingsboard accounts. Figure 11 shows the Thingsboard mobile view with the valve round switch of the ON and OFF icons.

After developing the system, a user acceptance test was conducted with farmers and technical staff from the Department of Agriculture. They participated in a demonstration of the prototype, used it, and provided feedback via a Google survey. The results of the validation exercise are summarized.

Figure 12 summarizes responses from the Google survey. Regarding the statement "the system is easy to use," five respondents agreed, twenty strongly agreed, one was neutral, and one disagreed.

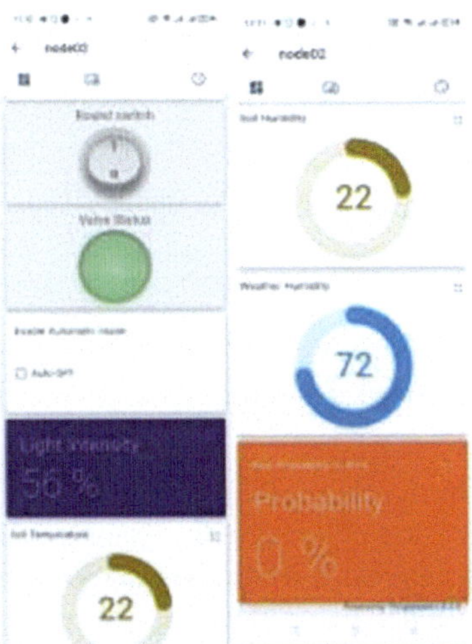

Fig. 11 Node 2 mobile view switch on Thingsboard's Android live mobile application image taken from the user's account

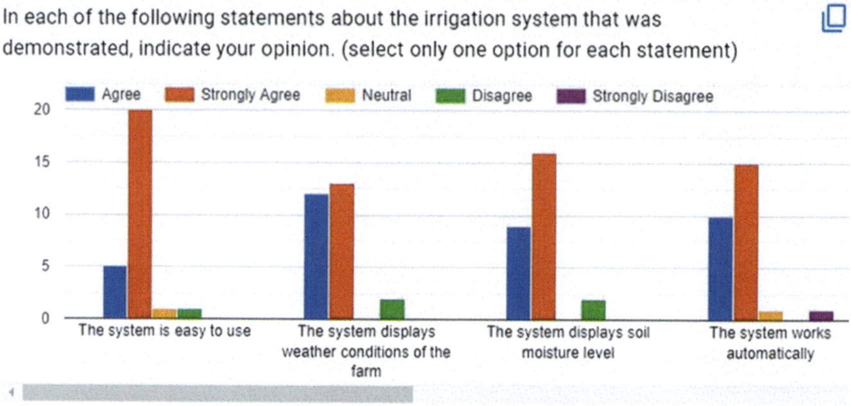

Fig. 12 Statistics of system validation responses for four test statements

Table 2 Validation questionnaire results statistics

SN	Test statement	Agree	Strongly agree	Neutral	Disagree	Strongly disagree
1	The system shall be controlled remotely	9	16	1	1	0
2	The system shall be safe for use	7	19	1	0	0
3	The system shall be reliable	7	17	3	0	0
4	The dashboard interface shall be easy to interact with	10	16	0	1	0
5	The system shall display rainfall probability	10	15	2	0	0

Table 2 shows the results from respondents on other statements in the questionnaire.

4 Conclusion

The developed IoT-based smart irrigation system for water efficiency addressed gaps in water-efficient smart systems for open-field irrigation where rainfall is critical. The system maps irrigation nodes and retrieves weather prediction data from the OpenWeather RESTFUL API, which is used alongside soil moisture content to control irrigation valves. The system provided effective remote control and visualization through the Thingsboard live Android mobile application, requiring users to log in with their registered email and password. It successfully automated and remotely controlled irrigation valves and displayed critical weather and soil parameters.

The system was tested by farmers and technical staff of the agriculture department of Uasin Gishu County to confirm its user-friendliness, usability, reliability, and other core system functionalities. The system achieved its development objectives and laid the groundwork for incorporating more sensors and artificial intelligence for data analysis and predictions.

References

1. Birch, I. (2018). Agricultural productivity in Kenya: Barriers and opportunities.
2. Karina, F. Z., & Mwaniki, A. W. (2011). Impact of the Economic Stimulus Programme and Longterm Prospects for Food Security in an Era of Climate Change. Nairobi, Kenya.
3. Food and Agriculture Organization of the United Nations. (2018). World food and agricul- ture: Statistical pocketbook 2018.
4. Ullah, R., Abbas, A. W., Ullah, M., Khan, R. U., Khan, I. U., Aslam, N., & Aljameel, S. S. (2021). EEWMP: An IoT-based energy-efficient water management platform for smart irrigation. Scientific Programming, 2021.
5. Olatunji, K. A., Oguntimilehin, A., & Adeyemo, O. A. (2020). A Mobile Phone Controllable Smart Irrigation System. International Journal of Advanced Trends in Computer Science and Engineering, 9(1), 279–284.
6. Haule, J., & Michael, K. (2014a). Deployment of wireless sensor networks (WSN) in auto- mated irrigation management and scheduling systems: A review. Proceedings of the 2nd Pan African International Conference on Science, Computing and Telecommunications (PACT 2014), 86–91.
7. Haule, J., & Michael, K. (2014b). Designing and Simulation of an Automated Irrigation Management System Deployed by using Wireless Sensor Networks (WSN).
8. García, L., Parra, L., Jimenez, J. M., Lloret, J., & Lorenz, P. (2020). IoT-based smart irrigation systems: An overview on the recent trends on sensors and IoT systems for irrigation in precision agriculture. Sensors, 20(4), 1042.

Assessment of Multiple ASR Architectures on Common Speech Datasets: Analyzing Training Duration, Framework, and Word Error Rate in the Development of a Swahili ASR Model

Devotha G. Nyambo, Lawrence N. Mdegela, and Wangoru Kihara

Abstract This paper delves into the world of Automatic Speech Recognition (ASR) systems, where the pursuit of performance optimization is unceasing. Our study conducts a thorough analysis of diverse ASR architectures, with a specific focus on their performance in processing Swahili speech data. In this concise exploration, we uncover valuable insights regarding the pivotal role of training duration and the advantages of model re-use in enhancing ASR efficiency. Our analysis underscores the crucial practice of fine-tuning pre-trained ASR models. By aligning these models with Swahili's unique nuances, accents, and phonetic intricacies, we significantly enhance transcription accuracy. We assess the performance of the Coqui_stt and Tensorflow implementations and observe a direct relationship between increased training duration and reduced Word Error Rate (WER). However, our findings highlight an area for improvement in the pre-trained Swahili ASR Model from the COQUI STT library, which, despite its extended 475-h training duration, achieves a WER of 0.39. Furthermore, our evaluation includes an assessment of six pre-trained models, among which facebook/Wav2Vec2-XLS-R-1B, facebook/wav2vec2-large-xls-r-53, and facebook/Wav2Vec2-XLS-R-300M emerge as promising candidates for Swahili ASR development, with increased training times ranging from 10.7 to 76.3 h. This assessment underscores the trade-off between performance and training duration, notably exemplified by the COQUI STT library's pre-trained Swahili ASR model, which required 475 h of training to achieve a WER of 0.39. In conclusion, our work is dedicated to optimizing Swahili ASR models by exploring various architectures,

D. G. Nyambo (✉) · L. N. Mdegela
The Nelson Mandela African Institution of Science and Technology, Arusha, Tanzania
e-mail: devotha.nyambo@nm-aist.ac.tz

L. N. Mdegela
e-mail: lawrence.nehemiah@nm-aist.ac.tz

W. Kihara
Badili Innovations Ltd, Nairobi, Kenya
e-mail: wangoru.kihara@badili.co.ke

J. Marx Gómez et al. (eds.), *Advancement in Embedded and Mobile Systems*, Progress in IS, https://doi.org/10.1007/978-3-031-99219-3_26

hyperparameters, and training methodologies. To this end, we identify three robust candidates for Swahili ASR development: pre-trained ASR from Nemo Library (stt_rw_conformer_ctc_large.nemo), facebook/Wav2Vec2-XLS-R-300M, and facebook/wav2vec2-large-xls-r-53. In the future, these models will be further explored with a custom dataset from local communities.

Keywords Common speech dataset · Automatic Speech Recognition · Swahili ASR · NLP

1 Introduction

Automatic Speech Recognition (ASR) has emerged as a transformative technology with numerous applications in various domains, including healthcare and agriculture [1]. In the context of livestock disease management, ASR can play a crucial role in advisory and enabling real-time detection and diagnosis, leading to timely interventions and improved animal welfare [2]. However, the performance of ASR systems heavily relies on the choice of architecture, training duration, and underlying frameworks. This research aims to comprehensively evaluate and compare the efficacy of multiple ASR architectures when applied to common speech datasets. The primary focus will be on assessing how variations in training duration and framework selection impact the ASR system's overall performance, particularly in terms of Word Error Rate (WER) on the development of the Swahili ASR model.

The underlying goal of this assessment was to arrive at a robust LLM that can be used by Swahili natives in sectors like livestock health, which faces unique challenges, including limited resources and the need for rapid decision-making to address disease outbreaks effectively and save the production value chain [3]. By accurately transcribing speech from farmers and veterinarians discussing livestock health, ASR technology can provide valuable insights for early detection and proactive disease management strategies. To achieve this, the study considered state-of-the-art ASR architectures experimented with multiple languages [4]. By training these architectures on carefully curated common speech datasets, the aim is to quantify their performance in terms of accuracy (lower WER) and computational efficiency. Furthermore, the presented experiments explore the impact of varying training durations on ASR model convergence and generalization capabilities. By analyzing the trade-offs between model performance and training time, we seek to provide insights into optimizing ASR training procedures for resource-constrained environments and achieving a Swahili ASR model architecture.

Overall, this paper contributes to the advancement of ASR technology by developing a Swahili ASR model via a systematic comparison of well-known architectures. The final Swahili ASR model can be applied to areas such as livestock disease management, among others. The findings of this study can inform the development of robust ASR systems tailored for specific needs, fostering a more efficient and sustainable approach to utilizing speech datasets for socio-economic activities.

2 Literature Review

Automatic Speech Recognition (ASR) technology has seen remarkable advancements, driven by the integration of powerful neural network architectures and sophisticated fine-tuning techniques. Among these models, the ASR model fine-tuned with Whisper Small V2, ASR model using modified hyperparameters from the COQUI STT library, ASR model fine-tuned with a pre-trained Swahili ASR, the ASR model using modified hyperparameters from the Nemo library, and the ASR model fine-tuned with Facebook Wav2Vec2 have emerged as a promising solution for speech-to-text tasks. This literature review examines the key characteristics, fine-tuning methodology, and performance evaluation of the models.

2.1 Key Characteristics

The Whisper Small V2 model is a compact and efficient automatic speech recognition architecture. Developed with a focus on computational efficiency, this model is tailored for deployment in resource-constrained environments where speed, privacy, and accuracy are paramount [5]. The Whisper Small V2 architecture offers a balance between performance and efficiency, making it suitable for a range of real-world applications [6, 7].

The ASR model using modified hyperparameters from the COQUI STT library introduces flexibility into the neural network architecture. Hyperparameters encompass a range of characteristics, including learning rate, dropout rate, layer dimensions, and activation functions. By modifying these parameters, researchers tailor the architecture to the unique characteristics of the data and the specific speech recognition task [8]. These adjustments can optimize the model's convergence rate and its capacity to generalize from the training data.

The ASR model fine-tuned with a pre-trained Swahili ASR model capitalizes on the principle of transfer learning [9]. The model begins with a pre-trained foundation on a diverse dataset, which enables it to capture general features common across languages [9]. Fine-tuning the model with Swahili-specific data refines its ability to recognize the unique phonetic, syntactic, and contextual elements of the Swahili language.

The ASR model using modified hyperparameters from the Nemo library introduces adaptability to the neural network architecture. Hyperparameters encompass a spectrum of characteristics, including learning rate, layer dimensions, and activation functions. Modifying these parameters tailors the architecture to the unique data characteristics and the specific speech recognition task [10]. These adjustments can optimize the model's convergence, generalization, and performance.

The ASR model fine-tuned with Facebook Wav2Vec2 is built upon the Wav2Vec2 architecture, a state-of-the-art model designed to transform raw audio into meaningful representations. Developed with self-supervised learning, Wav2Vec2 pre-trains on massive amounts of unlabeled speech data, enabling it to capture diverse acoustic and linguistic features [11]. This pre-training acts as a foundation for subsequent fine-tuning on specific ASR tasks. In addition, the model has shown tremendous performance coupled with Whisper when privacy is a concern in federated learning [5].

2.2 Fine-Tuning Methodologies

The Whisper Small V2 model undergoes a fine-tuning process to optimize its performance for specific speech-to-text tasks. During fine-tuning, the model was trained on relevant speech datasets, enabling it to adapt to the nuances of spoken language and accent variations [12]. This targeted training ensures that the model becomes proficient in accurately transcribing speech inputs, even in challenging acoustic environments.

The modified ASR model is fine-tuned using a dataset relevant to the target speech recognition task [13]. Fine-tuning adapts the architecture to the intricacies of the speech data, ensuring it can effectively capture phonetic, linguistic, and contextual variations present in the input audio [11]. The model's hyperparameters play a crucial role during the fine-tuning process, influencing its ability to learn from the data.

For the ASR model fine-tuned with the pre-trained Swahili ASR model, fine-tuning involves training the pre-trained model with Swahili speech data. This process ensures that the model aligns itself with the characteristics of Swahili speech, including dialects, accents, and regional variations [14]. Fine-tuning further enhances the model's capacity to accurately transcribe Swahili or other language speech inputs even with less training data [14, 15].

On the other hand, after adjusting the hyperparameters of ASR Neural Network Architecture from the Nemo library, the model should be fine-tuned using relevant speech data. Fine-tuning aligns the architecture with the intricacies of speech, ensuring its capacity to capture phonetic, linguistic, and contextual nuances [12]. The model's modified hyperparameters play a pivotal role in influencing its learning and adaptability during the training process.

Fine-tuning involves training the pre-trained Wav2Vec2 model using labeled speech data relevant to the target ASR task. This process refines the model's capacity to transcribe spoken language by aligning it with the nuances of the target language, accent variations, and phonetic intricacies [5]. Fine-tuning enhances the model's proficiency in recognizing contextual cues and producing accurate transcriptions. The multilingual pre-training nature of Wav2Vec2 used in the presented work—XLSR53 and other variants introduces adaptability to various languages, as also described by [16]. While originally trained in a diverse range of languages, fine-tuning specific languages refines its ability to capture unseen language-specific nuances [16]. This adaptability makes the model an asset for languages like Swahili, enabling accurate transcription. Literature details new evolvement on fine-tuning techniques to achieve high-performing models, as shown in [17], in the development of QLoRA, special for quantized LLMs.

2.3 Performance Evaluation

In ASR model evaluation, the Word Error Rate (WER) serves as a pivotal metric to gauge transcription accuracy. Lower WER values denote more accurate transcriptions. With deep learning, the ARS architectures and the performance of ASR models have been shown to outperform human annotators based on WER [18]. However, due to the model computation complexities, which give rise to high carbon footprints, evaluation based on energy-accuracy trade-offs is also promoted [18]. The Whisper Small V2 model showcases competitive WER scores, demonstrating its effectiveness in transcribing speech. Despite its compact architecture, it adeptly captures speech nuances, with fine-tuning enhancing its phonetic handling and accent adaptability, leading to improved transcription accuracy [12]. Similarly, the ASR model with modified hyperparameters influences the model's ability to transcribe accurately, as evident through comparisons against baselines or earlier versions [11].

Multilingual and monolingual pre-trained language models have been detailed to outperform traditional models as applied to specific languages, attesting to the benefits of fine-tuning [19, 20]. For the ASR model fine-tuned with a pre-trained Swahili ASR model, WER assessments provide insights into transcription accuracy, with lower values reflecting better contextual capture. Comparisons against baselines elucidate improvements stemming from fine-tuning [14].

3 Methodology

3.1 Case Study, Datasets, and ASR Architectures

The study experiments were done on Common Swahili speech data available on https://huggingface.co/datasets/mozilla-foundation/common_voice_11_0/viewer/sw/train. The data contains 24,210 recorded hours. The cv-corpus-12.0-delta-2022-12-07 usage details can be found at https://huggingface.co/datasets/mozilla-foundation/common_voice_11_0.

Six ASR architectures were used in nine experiments as outlined. The goal was to assess the differences in training duration and WER on testing datasets by varying implementation frameworks and hyperparameters.

(i) ASR model using modified hyperparameters of ASR Neural Network Architecture from COQUI STT library: In contrast to the previous model, this ASR model employs modified hyperparameters in the COQUI STT library's neural network architecture. These modifications may include adjusting the model's structure, Number of epochs, Learning rates, Batch size, Number of hidden layers, and optimization method to improve performance on specific speech tasks.

(ii) ASR model fine-tuned with pre-trained Swahili ASR model with different number of epochs from COQUI STT library: In this ASR model, the pre-trained Swahili ASR model from the COQUI STT library is fine-tuned for different numbers of training epochs. By varying the number of epochs, the model's convergence and generalization capabilities are analyzed to identify the optimal training duration for improved performance.

(iii) ASR model using modified hyperparameters of ASR Neural Network Architecture from Nemo library: Unlike previous models using the COQUI STT library, this ASR model employs modified hyperparameters from the Nemo library's neural network architecture. The Nemo library might offer different architectures and configurations, which are adapted in this model for specific speech recognition tasks.

(iv) ASR model Finetuned with pre-trained ASR model called "stt_rw_conformer_ctc_large.nemo." This pre-trained ASR model contains large-size versions of Conformer-CTC (around 120 M parameters) trained on Mozilla Common Voice 9.0 Kinyarwanda dataset with around 2000 h of Kinyarwanda speech. The model transcribes speech in the lowercase Latin alphabet along with spaces and apostrophes.

(v) ASR model finetuned with facebook/wav2vec2-large-xls-r-53: This ASR model is based on the facebook/wav2vec2-large-xlsr-53 architecture, which is a large-scale self-supervised speech representation model. It is pre-trained on 436 k hours of unlabeled speech, including VoxPopuli, MLS, CommonVoice, BABEL, and VoxLingua107. It uses the wav2vec 2.0 objective in 128 languages.

(vi) ASR model using Facebook Wav2Vec2-XLS-R-300M model: Similar to the previous model, this ASR model is based on the Facebook Wav2Vec2-XLS-R-300M architecture. It is a powerful and efficient large-scale ASR model that leverages self-supervised learning techniques for speech recognition tasks.

(vii) ASR model using Facebook Wav2Vec2-XLS-R-1B model: This ASR model is based on the Facebook Wav2Vec2-XLS-R-1B architecture, which is a state-of-the-art large-scale self-supervised ASR model. It has been pre-trained on an extensive multilingual corpus and exhibits high accuracy and language adaptability for various speech datasets.

(viii) ASR model fine-tuned with pre-trained ASR model called "ssl_en_conformer_large" from Nemo library: Similar to the previous "ssl_en_conformer_large" model, this ASR model has undergone fine-tuning using the Nemo library's pre-trained model. The fine-tuning process tailors the model's performance to specific English speech recognition tasks, further expected to enhance its accuracy.

(ix) ASR model fine-tuned with pre-trained ASR model called "stt_rw_conformer_large" from Nemo library: This ASR model is fine-tuned using the Nemo library's "stt_rw_conformer_large" pre-trained ASR model. Fine-tuning on relevant speech datasets enables the model to specialize in recognizing speech in specific contexts, in this case, to ensure more precise transcription of the Swahili language.

3.2 *Model Training Procedures and Hyperparameters*

The audio files provided by Common Voice are in MP3 format. The audio files were converted into a WAV file using a Python script provided by the different libraries, accordingly. The dataset was generally divided into 3 sets, for training, validating, and testing. The training dataset has a total of 6336 audio files, which contribute to 80% of the entire dataset. The validation and test sets had the same size of 792 audio files, which is 10% of the entire dataset for each set. The models were trained using Tensorflow 1.15.4, coqui_sst_training 1.3.0, Soundfile 0.11.0, and Keras-preprocessing 1.1.2 frameworks. Specific procedures and hyperparameters for each model are presented:

(i) ASR model fine-tuned with Whisper Small V2—During training, the following hyperparameters were used: a learning rate of 1e−05, a train batch size of 16, and an evaluation batch size of 8. The optimizer used was Adam with betas = (0.9,0.999) and epsilon = 1e−08, with a linear learning rate scheduler and 500 warmup steps. The training was done over 8000 steps, and native Automatic Mixed Precision (AMP) was used. The model was trained using the following framework versions: Transformers 4.27.0.dev0, Pytorch 1.13.1 + cu117, Datasets 2.10.1, and Tokenizers 0.13.2.

(ii) ASR model using modified hyperparameters of ASR Neural Network Architecture from COQUISTT Library—The audio files were converted into a WAV file using the python script provided by the coqui_stt library. The following modified hyperparameters were used:

- Number of epochs: 40
- Learning rates 0.001
- Batch size: 32 for training and 16 for validation
- Number of hidden layers: 1024
- The optimization method: Adam optimizer with betas of 0.9 and 0.999

The model was trained using Tensorflow 1.15.4, coqui_sst_training 1.3.0, Soundfile 0.11.0, and Keras-preprocessing 1.1.2.

(iii) ASR model fine-tuned with pre-trained Swahili ASR model—The audio files were converted into a WAV file using the Python script provided by the coqui_stt library. The following modified hyperparameters were used to fine-tune the Swahili pre-trained ASR model:

- Number of epochs: 2, then 5
- alphabet_config_path: path to the alphabet.txt file
- Number of hidden layers: 2048

(iv) ASR model using modified hyperparameters of ASR Neural Network Architecture from Nemo Library—The audio files were converted into a WAV file using a Python script provided by the Nemo library. The following modified hyperparameters were used:

- Number of epochs: 200, then 600
- Learning rates: 0.001
- Batch size: 16 for training, validation, and test data
- Tokenization: BPE 128/512/1024
- Model: Conformer-CTC-large with Layer Normalization
- Optimizer: AdamW, weight_decay 1e−3, LR 1e−3
- Scheduler: CosineAnnealing, warmup_steps 10,000, min_lr 1e−6
- Precision: FP16

(v) ASR model fine-tuned with facebook/wav2vec2-large-xls-r-53—in this experiment, the model was fine-tuned with the following hyperparameters:

- learning_rate: 0.0003
- train_batch_size: 16
- eval_batch_size: 8
- seed: 42
- gradient_accumulation_steps: 2
- total_train_batch_size: 32
- optimizer: Adam with betas = (0.9,0.999) and epsilon = 1e−08
- lr_scheduler_type: linear
- lr_scheduler_warmup_steps: 500
- num_epochs: 30
- mixed_precision_training: Native AMP

(vi) Training hyperparameters for the Wav2Vec2-XLS-R-300M were:

- Runtime: 605.8484 (MINUTES)
- samples_per_second: 16.899
- steps_per_second: 2.113
- epoch: 25.66
- global_step: 11,600
- learning_rate: 0.00004513782542113323
- loss: 0.0401

(vii) Training hyperparameters for the Wav2Vec2-XLS-R-1B were:

- Runtime: 732.8312
- samples_per_second: 13.97

- steps_per_second: 1.747
- epoch: 29.99
- global_step: 34,530
- learning_rate: 0.0000012518366147516
- loss: 0.0346
- total_flos: 571,952,507,766,219,870,000
- train_loss: 0.17750107202880666
- train_runtime: 273,044.8473
- train_samples_per_second: 4.048
- train_steps_per_second: 0.126

The experiment used Transformers 4.29.0.dev0, Pytorch 2.0.0 + cu117, Datasets 2.12.0, and Tokenizers 0.13.3.

(viii) ASR model using pre-trained ASR from Nemo Library—ASR model was fine-tuned with a pre-trained ASR model from Nemo library called "stt_rw_conformer_ctc_large.nemo." Specifically, the ASR model was fine-tuned on the Swahili dataset that was provided by the common voice (cv-corpus-12.0-delta-2022-12-07). Pytorch 2.0.0, Pytorch-lightning 1.9.0, Nemo-toolkit 1.13.0, and Sentence-transformer 2.2.2 were used. The following modified hyperparameters were used:

- Number of epochs: 1000
- Learning rates: 2.0
- Batch size: 32 for training, and 16 for both validation and test data
- Tokenization: BPE 128/512/1024
- Optimizer: AdamW, weight_decay 1e−3, LR 1e−3
- Scheduler: CosineAnnealing, warmup_steps 10000, min_lr 1e−6
- Precision: 32
- Betas: 0.9,0.98
- Weight_decay: 0.01

3.3 Evaluation Metrics

To assess the performance of the architectures, training duration and Word Error Rate (WER) were used. This assessment is intended to highlight the differences in training duration so as to suggest a deployment model. Models with shorter training durations might be preferred for real-time applications or when computational resources are limited, as such, forsaking high accuracy, while longer training durations may be more suitable for high-accuracy applications. In this context, accuracy is given by the value of WER. The WER calculates the difference between the transcribed output and the reference (ground truth) transcription, quantifying the percentage of word-level errors in the output [21]. A lower WER indicates higher accuracy, while a higher WER suggests more errors in the transcriptions.

4 Results

Overall experimental results indicate performance differences among the architectures and the same architecture implemented with a varying number of epochs. In this section, we present the performance results of the individual architectures on multiple experiments, and later we compare the performance of the models based on WER and training duration.

4.1 Model Description and Performance Evaluation

(i) ASR model using modified hyperparameters of ASR Neural Network Architecture from COQUI SST library was trained on 40 epochs with a minimum training loss of 12.09 at the 35th epoch and validation loss of 88.43. On a test set, the model achieved a test loss of 56.07 and a WER of 0.86.

(ii) ASR model fine-tuned with pre-trained Swahili ASR model was trained on 2 epochs with minimum training and validation loss of 26.19 and 20.05, respectively. On the test set, the model improved with a WER of 0.41 and a test loss of 19.38. Upon increasing the number of epochs and on 2048 hidden layers, a training and validation loss was decreased to 16.28 and 18.5, respectively. There was a slight improvement in the WER on the test set (0.39) and a test loss of 18.27.

(iii) ASR model using modified hyperparameters of ASR Neural Network Architecture from Nemo Library—a validation process of 200 epochs resulted in a minimum of 0.69 WER at the 46 epoch and 0.73 WER at 200 epochs (Table 1). On the test set, 0.73 was achieved as WER and 80.32 test loss. At the validation process with 600 epochs, a minimum of 0.7 WER at the 41st epoch and 0.74 on the test set.

(iv) ASR model using pre-trained ASR from Nemo Library (stt_rw_conformer_ctc_large.nemo)—on using 600 epochs (Experiment A), minimum validation WER (0.27) was achieved at 37 epochs. A performance of WER of 0.41 was achieved. Significant improvement is observed when a pre-trained ASR is used versus the former experiment. On using 1000 epochs (Experiment B), the model

Table 1 Validation WER of modified hyperparameters of an ASR NNA from Nemo Library

Epoch	Validation WER
46	0.6993
54	0.6953
65	0.6965
74	0.693
200	0.7319

Table 2 Validation of the pre-trained ASR from Nemo Library

Epoch	Validation WER
90	0.1892
108	0.1888
114	0.1906
1000	0.2852

achieved a validation WER of 0.19 at 90 epochs (Table 2) and a WER of 0.32 and test loss of 34.52 on the test set. Utilizing a pre-existing ASR model called "stt_rw_conformer_ctc_large.nemo" from the Nemo library has led to a tenfold performance improvement in comparison to the preceding experiment, resulting in a WER of 0.4098. This improvement may be attributed to the resemblance between Kinyarwanda, an African language, and Swahili in terms of their spoken and written forms (Fig. 1).

(v) ASR model fine-tuned with facebook/wav2vec2-large-xls-r-53—on 30 epochs, the model achieved the best training loss (0.0.4787) at 29.87 epoch and WER of 0.31 on the testing dataset. In-depth changes can be observed in Fig. 2. Further results on the different versions of the Facebook model indicate a high performance of the Wav2Vec2-XLS-R-1B, which achieved a WER of 0.2, a slight difference from Wav2Vec2-XLS-R-300M, which had a WER of 0.21. As indicated in Fig. 2, the higher the number of epochs, influences better the performance on WER reduced training loss.

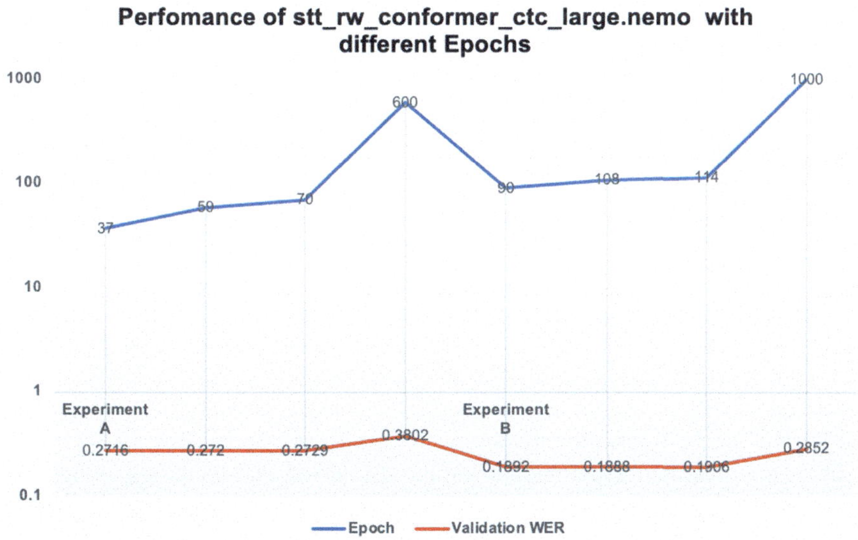

Fig. 1 Comparing the impact of high number of epochs to a pre-trained ASR (sst_rw_conformer_ctc_large.nemo)

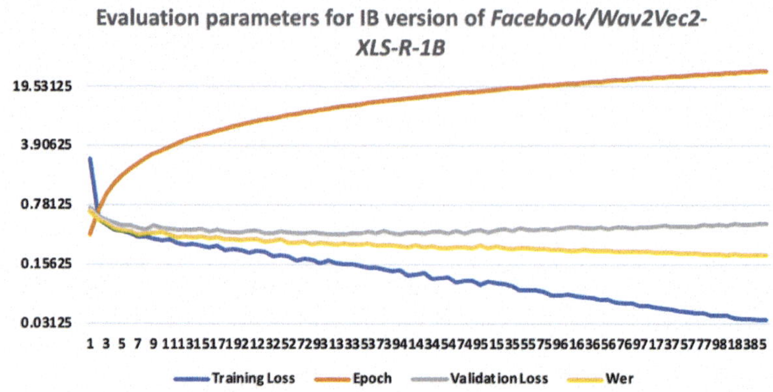

Fig. 2 Changes in training, validation loss, and WER from fine-tuning ASR with facebook/wav2vec2-large-xls-r-1B

4.2 Comparative Assessment of the ASR Architectures

A thorough analysis of the different architectures has shown an increase in performance (lower WER) as the training duration is increased for the Coqui_stt and Tensorflow implementation. The pre-trained Swahili ASR Model from the COQUI STT library with different epochs has the highest training time (475 Hours) with a WER of 0.39. On the otherhand, Pytorch-based implementations (facebook/wav2vec2-large-xlsr-53 and facebook Wav2Vec2-XLS-R-300M) attained 0.22 WER with 20 and 10.7 h of training time, respectively. The variance in training duration and performance on WER signifies the need for further optimization, especially for the pre-trained Swahili ASR model from the COQUI STT library with different epochs, whose performance was accredited to the high similarity between Swahili language and the language used in the pre-trained models. The longer training duration for the pre-trained Swahili ASR model from the COQUI STT library might impede its re-usability for building other models (Fig. 3).

From the fourteen (13) experiments, there is a significant variation in training duration and performance on WER for models built from scratch and the fine-tuned ones. A minimum training duration of 6.6 h was achieved for models built and trained from scratch, while the minimum training duration for fine-tuned models was 10.7 h. On the other hand, a minimum of 0.84 WER was attained for models built and trained from scratch, while fine-tuned models attained a minimum of 0.2 WER. This fact underscores the advantages of model reuse. Figure 4 highlights the different durations and WER of the best-performing models among the thirteen experiments.

From the presented experimental results, it is noted that there is a significant performance difference for the pre-trained models, which highlights a selection of models for a final Swahili ASR. From the six pre-trained models, facebook/Wav2Vec2-XLS-R-1B was trained in 76.3 h, facebook/wav2vec2-large-xls-r-53 in 20 h, and the facebook/Wav2Vec2-XLS-R-300M in 10.7 h. This assessment further

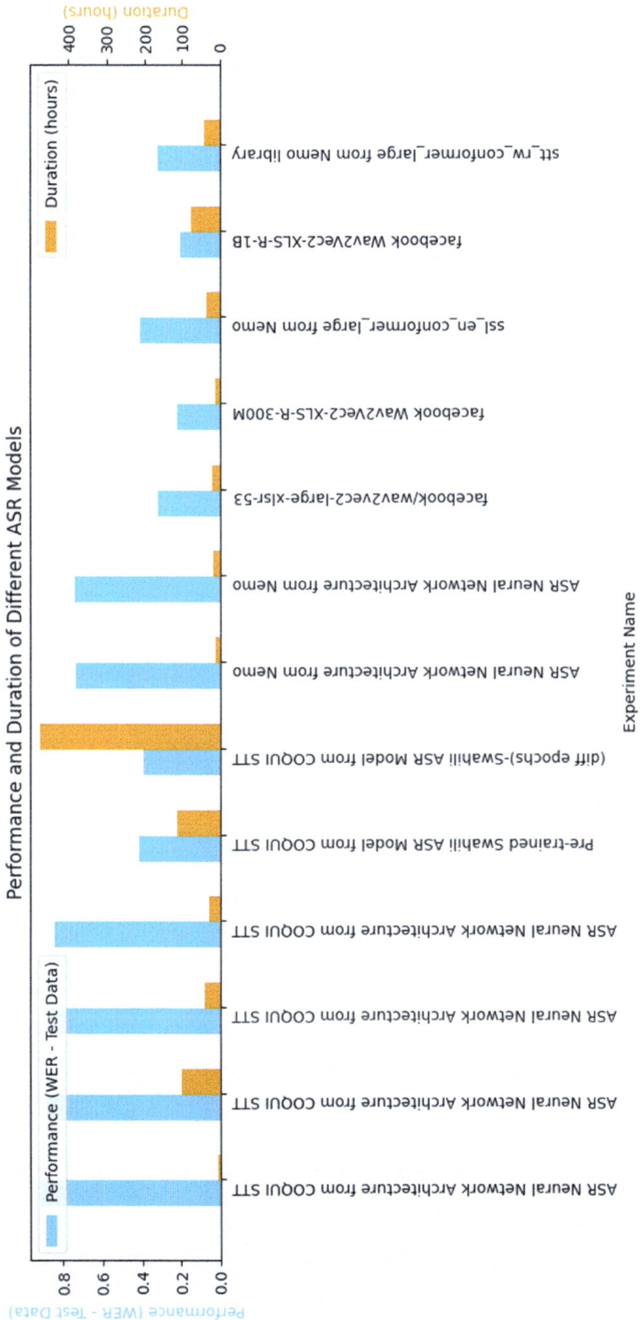

Fig. 3 Comparison of training duration and WER of different ASR Models in thirteen experiments

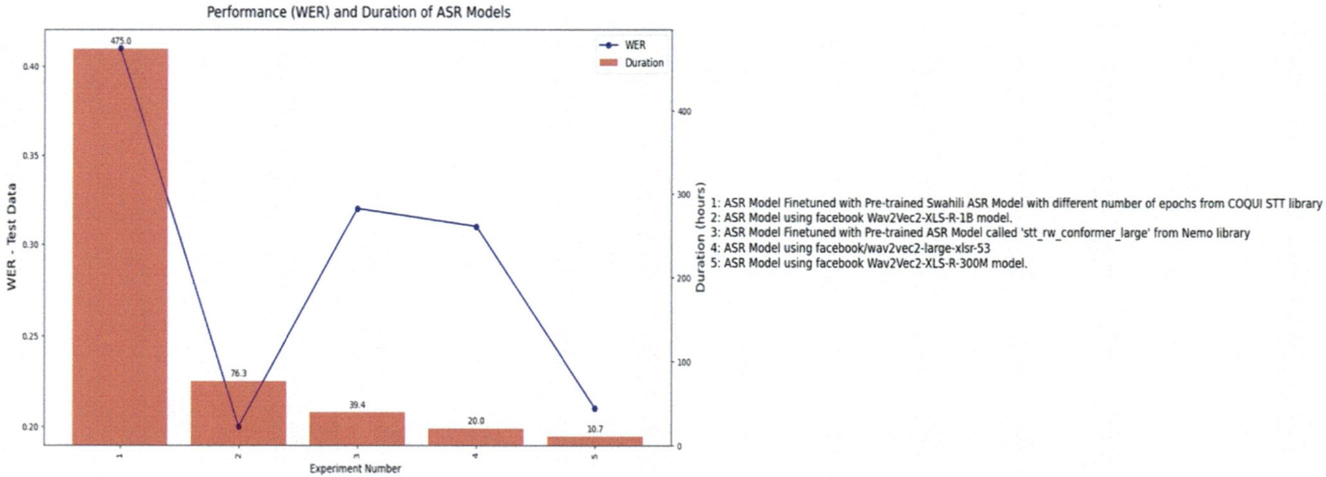

Fig. 4 Performance (WER and Duration) of best-performing ASR Architectures

Table 3 Summary of high-performing models based on WER

Model	WER on test dataset
ASR model using modified hyperparameters of ASR Neural Network Architecture from COQUI SST library	0.86
ASR model fine-tuned with pre-trained Swahili ASR	0.41
ASR mModel using modified hyperparameters of ASR Neural Network Architecture from Nemo Library	0.73
ASR model using pre-trained ASR from Nemo Library (stt_rw_conformer_ctc_large.nemo)	0.32
Pre-trained ASR facebook/wav2vec2-large-xls-r-53	0.31
Pre-trained ASR facebook/Wav2Vec2-XLS-R-300M	0.21
Pre-trained facebook/Wav2Vec2-XLS-R-1B	0.2

indicates that the best models for training a Swahili ASR will be the ASR model using pre-trained ASR from Nemo Library (stt_rw_conformer_ctc_large.nemo) and facebook/Wav2Vec2-XLS-R-300M, which were trained at 39.4 and 10.7 h, respectively (Table 3).

Comparing the models based on WER and training duration underscores the trade-off between performance and time efficiency. Notably, the COQUI STT library's pre-trained Swahili ASR model required substantial training time (475 h) but achieved a WER of 0.39. In contrast, Pytorch-based implementations demonstrated excellent performance with significantly shorter training times (10.7 h) and a WER of 0.22. This discrepancy in training duration and performance highlights the need for further optimization, especially for models trained from scratch.

Furthermore, the variation in training duration and WER between models built from scratch and fine-tuned models underscores the benefits of model reuse. Fine-tuned models achieved both shorter training times (10.7 h) and lower WER (0.2) compared to models built from scratch (6.6 h and 0.84 WER). This observation emphasizes the efficiency gained by leveraging pre-trained models and fine-tuning them for specific tasks.

5 Discussion

The experimental results presented reveal significant performance differences among the various architectures and models with different training durations. In the following discussion, we will delve into the performance outcomes of the individual architectures, compare the models based on Word Error Rate (WER) and training duration, and explore the implications of these findings.

The ASR model utilizing the pre-trained ASR from the Nemo Library (stt_rw_conformer_ctc_large.nemo) demonstrated a substantial leap in performance. The model's validation WER decreased to 0.19 after 90 epochs, and the test set WER reached 0.32 after 1000 epochs. This noteworthy improvement highlights the value of leveraging pre-trained models, particularly when the language characteristics are closely related, as observed between Kinyarwanda and Swahili. However, we note the need to leverage deep recurrent neural architectures to improve the model's generalizability [22].

The ASR model fine-tuned with the facebook/wav2vec2-large-xls-r-53 architecture exhibited competitive results. Additionally, variations within the Facebook models demonstrated that the Wav2Vec2-XLS-R-1B achieved superior performance with a WER of 0.2, although with longer training time than the Wav2Vec2-XLS-R-300M, suggesting that model selection plays a crucial role in optimizing for a Swahili ASR and higher chances of using the models for federated learning in resource-constrained scenarios [5]. The variations in training duration and WER from the different Wav2Vec2 models are also reported by [23].

The fine-tuned ASR model, utilizing a pre-trained Swahili ASR model, showcased a distinct advantage in terms of training efficiency. After just 2 epochs, the model exhibited improved performance with a WER of 0.41. Upon increasing the number of epochs and hidden layers, further performance enhancements were achieved. This indicates the potential benefits of leveraging pre-trained models of similar language to expedite training and improve recognition accuracy. However, this model used the highest training duration among all experiments. It is necessary to consider enhanced architectures as equally explained by [24] as the case of low-resourced languages.

The ASR model using modified hyperparameters from the Nemo Library displayed competitive results after extensive training. The reduction in WER from 0.73 at 200 epochs to 0.7 at 41 epochs using 600 epochs suggests that further iterations led to marginal improvements. However, this model exhibited relatively higher test loss, implying room for refinement to enhance its ability for generalization. Such an implementation can further be improved by combining deep recurrent architectures with standard data augmentation for state-of-the-art outputs and lowered the need for pre-trained models [22].

6 Conclusion and Future Work

The presented work focused on experimenting with six key ASR architectures in the quest of identifying the best models for the development of a Swahili ASR. Variation in the experiment involved hyperparameter tuning, varying the number of epochs and hidden layers, and implementation frameworks. Three models have been identified as potentials for a Swahili ASR, those are: pre-trained ASR from Nemo Library (stt_rw_conformer_ctc_large.nemo), facebook/Wav2Vec2-XLS-R-300M, and an ASR model fine-tuned with pre-trained Swahili ASR.

The discussed ASR models demonstrate varying degrees of success, with each approach contributing unique insights. The findings underscore the significance of pre-trained models, deeper networks, and extended training epochs in enhancing

ASR performance. Additionally, the resemblance between related languages can result in remarkable improvements in recognition accuracy. The comparative analysis among models and their outcomes serves as a valuable reference for future research and development efforts in the field of ASR technology. In future experiments, the three best-performing models will be further trained by using a custom speech dataset collected in Tanzania and Kenya featuring various dialects from crop-livestock farmers.

References

1. A. Diwan et al., "Multilingual and code-switching ASR challenges for low-resource Indian languages," arXiv preprint arXiv:2104.00235, 2021.
2. S. Khan et al., "Data Collection and Development of Bengali ASR and TTS for Conversational AI-based Automated Advisories in the Agriculture Domain," in Proc. 4th Int. Conf. on Artificial Intelligence and Speech Technology (AIST), Dec. 2022, pp. 1–6.
3. R. Espinosa, D. Tago, and N. Treich, "Infectious diseases and meat production," Environ. Resour. Econ., vol. 76, no. 4, pp. 1019–1044, 2020.
4. R. Jimerson, Z. Liu, and E. Prud'Hommeaux, "An (unhelpful) guide to selecting the best ASR architecture for your under-resourced language," in Proc. 61st Annu. Meeting Assoc. Comput. Linguistics (Vol. 2: Short Papers), Jul. 2023, pp. 1008–1016.
5. J. C. Vásquez-Correa and A. Álvarez Muniain, "Novel speech recognition systems applied to forensics within child exploitation: Wav2vec2.0 vs. Whisper," Sensors, vol. 23, no. 4, p. 1843, 2023.
6. B. Talafha, A. Waheed, and M. Abdul-Mageed, "N-Shot Benchmarking of Whisper on Diverse Arabic Speech Recognition," arXiv preprint arXiv:2306.02902, 2023.
7. R. Jain et al., "Adaptation of Whisper models to child speech recognition," arXiv preprint arXiv:2307.13008, 2023.
8. F. M. Tyers and J. Meyer, "What shall we do with an hour of data? Speech recognition for the un-and under-served languages of Common Voice," arXiv preprint arXiv:2105.04674, 2021.
9. J. Pfeiffer, S. Ruder, I. Vulić, and E. M. Ponti, "Modular deep learning," arXiv preprint arXiv: 2302.11529, 2023.
10. F. Tamburini, "Playing with NeMo for Building an Automatic Speech Recogniser for Italian," in CLiC-it, 2021.
11. J. Shah et al., "What all do audio transformer models hear? Probing acoustic representations for language delivery and its structure," arXiv preprint arXiv:2101.00387, 2021.
12. A. Radford et al., "Robust speech recognition via large-scale weak supervision," in Int. Conf. Mach. Learn., Jul. 2023, pp. 28492–28518.
13. H. Feng, S. Ueno, and T. Kawahara, "End-to-End Speech Emotion Recognition Combined with Acoustic-to-Word ASR Model," in Proc. Interspeech, Oct. 2020, pp. 501–505.
14. C. Jacobs et al., "Towards hate speech detection in low-resource languages: Comparing ASR to acoustic word embeddings on Wolof and Swahili," arXiv preprint arXiv:2306.00410, 2023.
15. M. Elamin et al., "Multilingual Automatic Speech Recognition for Kinyarwanda, Swahili, and Luganda: Advancing ASR in Select East African Languages," in 4th Workshop on African Natural Language Processing, Apr. 2023.
16. A. Rouditchenko et al., "Comparison of Multilingual Self-Supervised and Weakly-Supervised Speech Pre-Training for Adaptation to Unseen Languages," arXiv preprint arXiv:2305.12606, 2023.
17. T. Dettmers et al., "QLoRA: Efficient finetuning of quantized LLMs," arXiv preprint arXiv: 2305.14314, 2023.

18. S. Gondi and V. Pratap, "Performance and efficiency evaluation of ASR inference on the edge," Sustainability, vol. 13, no. 22, p. 12392, 2021.
19. F. M. Plaza-del-Arco et al., "Comparing pre-trained language models for Spanish hate speech detection," Expert Syst. Appl., vol. 166, p. 114120, 2021.
20. A. Balagopalan et al., "Comparing pre-trained and feature-based models for prediction of Alzheimer's disease based on speech," Front. Aging Neurosci., vol. 13, p. 635945, 2021.
21. A. Ali and S. Renals, "Word error rate estimation for speech recognition: e-WER," in Proc. 56th Annu. Meeting Assoc. Comput. Linguistics (Vol. 2: Short Papers), Jul. 2018, pp. 20–24.
22. E. Palogiannidi et al., "End-to-end architectures for ASR-free spoken language understanding," in Proc. IEEE Int. Conf. Acoust., Speech, Signal Process. (ICASSP), May 2020, pp. 7974–7978.
23. Y. Peng et al., "A study on the integration of pre-trained SSL, ASR, LM and SLU models for spoken language understanding," in Proc. IEEE Spoken Language Technology Workshop (SLT), Jan. 2023, pp. 406–413.
24. D. Warusawithana et al., "Enhanced time delay neural network architectures for Sinhala speech recognition," in Proc. Moratuwa Eng. Res. Conf. (MERCon), Jul. 2022, pp. 1–6.

A Framework to Monitor Automotive Emission Through Internet of Things for Predictive Maintenance Toward Air Pollution Reduction

Martin Kuradusenge, Jean Baptiste Minani, Antoine Gatera, Faustin Irumva, and Emmanuel Mwumvaneza

Abstract Air pollution poses a significant threat to global health and the environment, with automobile emissions being a primary contributor. Motor vehicles are among the major sources of urban air pollution. Traditional methods for monitoring vehicular air pollutants, such as Portable Emissions Measurement Systems (PEMS), are limited by their inability to transmit data to the cloud for comprehensive analysis and predictive modeling. The purpose of this study is to develop a framework for real-time monitoring of various pollutants, including carbon monoxide (CO), nitrogen oxides (NOx), sulfur dioxide (SO_2), volatile organic compounds (VOCs), and particulate matter (PM), using Internet of Things (IoT) sensors. This study aims to leverage the collected data for predictive insights, enabling effective preventive maintenance and mitigation strategies for air pollution control. In this paper, we discuss in detail the framework consisting of seven layers: (i) sensing, (ii) processing and local storage, (iii) edge-based computing, (iv) network, (v) cloud-based storage, (vi) cloud-based computing, (vii) application. As a proof of concept, we implement and discuss an IoT solution using an MQ135 sensor, connected to a cloud server via WiFi or GSM network, where the data is stored and analyzed. Additionally, we

M. Kuradusenge (✉) · A. Gatera
Department of Information Systems, School of ICT, College of Science and Technology, University of Rwanda, Kigali, Rwanda
e-mail: m.kuradusenge@ur.ac.rw

A. Gatera
e-mail: a.gatera@ur.ac.rw; gm.gateraz@gmail.com

J. B. Minani
Department of Computer Sciences and Software Engineering, Concordia University, Montreal, Canada

F. Irumva · E. Mwumvaneza
Department of Computer and Software Engineering, School of ICT, College of Science and Technology, University of Rwanda, Kigali, Rwanda
e-mail: irumva_220005770@stud.ur.ac.rw

E. Mwumvaneza
e-mail: mwumvaneza_220001040@stud.ur.ac.rw

J. Marx Gómez et al. (eds.), *Advancement in Embedded and Mobile Systems*, Progress in IS, https://doi.org/10.1007/978-3-031-99219-3_27

integrate machine learning algorithms to predict future pollutant levels and enhance preparedness for preventive maintenance and air pollution reduction. The implementation of this framework is expected to enhance the accuracy of air quality assessments, provide actionable insights for improving urban air quality, and effectively reduce air pollution by monitoring and detecting pollutants early at their source. This enables vehicle owners, regulators, and fleet managers to take appropriate measures based on forecasted insights.

Keywords Air pollution · Automotive emission · Internet of Things (IoT) · Machine Learning (ML)

1 Introduction

Economic development is envisioned by every country in the world. Transportation is one of the key drivers of this type of development. This sector is characterized by the extensive increase in the number of automobiles in different categories, motivated by the construction of infrastructure enabling different transport options, such as roads. The latter can accommodate different categories of vehicles, from light to heavy-duty vehicles, which are powered by internal combustion. Automobiles possess engines that make an internal combustion using fossil fuel. Those vehicles emit harmful gases that pollute the air. Hence, automobiles are blamed to be one of the top sources of environmental pollution [1, 2]. It is expected that the number of cars worldwide will double by 2040. Additionally, if left unchecked, greenhouse gas (GHG) emissions from transportation are projected to increase from the current 20% to 60% by 2050 [3, 4].

It has been proven that air pollution has harmful effects on the human body. The World Health Organization (WHO) estimates that ambient air pollution causes 4.2 million deaths per year globally. The major air pollutants responsible for harming human life include carbon monoxide (CO), carbon dioxide (CO_2), nitrogen dioxide (NO_2), nitrogen monoxide (NO), particulate matter (PM), and sulfur dioxide (SO_2) [4–7]. The effects of poor air quality on human health are becoming increasingly serious, elevating this issue to a major public health concern. Despite various efforts to improve the air we breathe, data from the WHO indicate that around 99% of the global population continues to breathe the air that exceeds WHO limits [8]. People living in urban areas or near busy roads are more exposed to polluted air and face higher risks of asthma and other respiratory symptoms, developmental and birth effects, premature mortality, cardiovascular issues, and cancer [9, 10].

Due to the health risks associated with automobile emissions, various countries have implemented policies to curb air pollution. These include international standards such as Euro VI in the European Union, and at the national level, standards like Tier 3 and California standards in the USA, China 6 in China, and BS VI in India [1]. In Rwanda, several strategies have been adopted to reduce emissions. For example, Rwanda's Vision 2050 outlines a target to reduce emissions by 38% by

2030, with electric vehicles projected to account for 9% of potential energy-related emissions [11]. In addition to the legislative aspect, it is crucial to identify the sources of emissions and determine the quantity of air pollutants through monitoring. Techniques used for real driving emissions include PEMS, on-road remote sensing [12], mobile monitoring platforms [13], plume chasing [14], ambient measurement [15], and tunnel measurement [16]. However, each of these techniques has its advantages and disadvantages. The most accurate technique used for real-world driving emissions is PEMS; however, it is expensive and applicable to only a small number of vehicles.

Monitoring vehicle emissions is crucial to controlling how many pollutants are spread into the air. The best method for this is to conduct monitoring while the vehicle is driving because it provides real-time data on pollutant levels under actual driving conditions, offering a more accurate assessment of environmental impact. Previous studies have utilized monitoring technologies, such as those mentioned above, which can be challenging to install and may restrict driver behavior. Despite their contributions, real-time monitoring systems remain underdeveloped and face challenges, largely due to the complexity of implementing numerous rules for efficient operation.

The aim of this study is to create a framework for monitoring automotive emissions using IoT and to develop an IoT-based system with an integrated ML model to test this framework as a proof of concept.

2 Related Works

Today, different nations, automobile manufacturers, and organizations have implemented strategies to reduce the impact of air pollutants originating from transportation. These strategies include the use of devices or systems to monitor automotive emissions. Existing techniques for testing vehicle emissions include fixed devices such as PEMS, remote sensing systems, and laboratory testing systems [1, 17]. Additionally, various research efforts are being conducted to find appropriate solutions to this challenge. Recent studies include the use of IoT and/or ML models.

Abdull Sukor et al. [18] conducted a study to predict in-vehicle air quality using machine learning techniques. The study aimed to address the varying parameters within the vehicle environment. They trained time-series data gathered by a built-in sensor device. They used two deep learning models, namely long-short term memory (LSTM) and gated recurrent unit (GRU), to classify and predict air quality. The results from this study indicated that the GRU model performed better than conventional machine learning models such as support vector machine (SVM) and multilayer perceptron (MLP), achieving the highest coefficient of determination value (R2) of 0.97.

Goh Cheick et al. [19] conducted a study with a similar objective of predicting the present and future air quality within the cabin. A predictive analysis system was developed utilizing a machine learning algorithm to assess the level of driver fatigue by analyzing the air quality within the vehicle. The system used the following sensors to gather data: CO_2, PM, vehicle speed, temperature, and humidity. The researchers employed MLP, support vector regression (SVR), and linear regression (LR) to analyze and predict air quality. The Support Vector Regression (SVR) model demonstrated outstanding results, achieving the highest accuracy with an R^2 value of 0.9981.

Liviu-Marian et al. [5] implemented a system to be installed in a car that monitors air quality both inside and outside the vehicle, providing information to the user and alerting them when the air pollution threshold is exceeded. The data collected by the system includes CO, CO_2, PM1.0, PM2.5, PM10, total volatile compounds in the air, CH_4, temperature, humidity, and atmospheric pressure. The system provides information to the driver and can issue alerts about pollution levels.

While most previous studies focused on modeling, Khan A. et al. [20] introduced an air quality monitoring system based on IoT. The system collects air pollutants and smoke released by automobiles. They developed an IoT device comprising sensors to detect CO and smoke, with a WiFi-enabled microcontroller (NodeMCU) connected to a server. A threshold was set to alert the traffic department and the vehicle's owner. Similarly, a mobile car monitoring system for air quality monitoring was developed by Maslouski et al. [21] to monitor PM10 in rural communities surrounding Kraków. The system was designed as a supplementary tool for areas not covered by stationary fixed monitoring systems. The tool was validated and recommended for public use in places not covered by a fixed monitoring grid.

Most existing methods for monitoring vehicle emissions rely on built-in vehicle sensors or on-road remote sensing systems, while most previous studies have focused on modeling, with very few addressing real-time monitoring during driving. The advantages of in-vehicle built-in sensors include their high accuracy and standardization. However, a significant disadvantage is that they cannot be visualized in real time and do not transmit data for future analysis and predictions. Separate devices and remote sensing systems are also expensive. The solution to these issues is the use of an IoT system. This study establishes a framework for monitoring automobile emissions using IoT sensors and develops a system prototype as proof of concept. The framework will aid in the development of IoT-based systems for real-time monitoring of motor vehicle emissions, enabling early detection of air pollution and informed decision-making.

3 Methodology

This study follows a systematic approach to design, develop, and evaluate an IoT-based framework for real-time automotive emissions monitoring and prediction. The methodology is divided into several stages, including the identification of the framework's layered architecture, the design and development of an IoT prototype, testing and calibration of the system, data collection, the integration and evaluation of machine learning models, and the development of a web-based monitoring system. Each of these stages is crucial for the successful implementation and performance evaluation of the proposed system, and they are described in detail in the following subsections.

3.1 Identification of Layers for the Framework

To identify the layered architecture of the proposed framework, we used systems engineering. In this approach, we defined the overall system requirements and then broke down the entire system into different functional layers, each addressing a specific task. We assessed the current situation by examining how data is gathered, handled, and analyzed for the purpose of reducing air pollution. Through a thorough analysis of the requirements for real-time monitoring, we systematically determined the essential layers and their interactions.

3.2 Design and Development of the System Prototype

We designed and developed an IoT device prototype to measure different gases such as NH_3, CO, CO_2, and smoke. The device was made using an MQ-135 sensor, NodeMCU, GSM module, liquid crystal display (LCD), potentiometer, and buzzer.

3.3 Testing and Calibration of the Prototype

After connecting all components, we configured the microcontroller using the Arduino integrated development environment (IDE). We tested and calibrated the MQ-135 by first leaving the device in a clean environment to obtain stable readings. Then, we placed the sensor in containers with products of known gas concentrations, such as ammonia cleaner (testing NH_3), soda (testing CO_2), and cigarettes (testing smoke), compared the readings, and calibrated accordingly. This process was repeated multiple times for recalibration to improve accuracy. We used three sensing devices to compare readings and ensure accuracy, reliability, and consistency in the data collected, for the validation of the prototype's performance and identify any discrepancies or calibration issues.

3.4 Data Collection

After testing and calibrating the IoT device, we installed it on the back side of the car, positioning the sensor near the exhaust pipe to gather real-time data while driving over a period of 14 days. Data was captured every 5 min (300 s) with a daily driving distance of 30 km. The data was sent to a cloud-based database through a GSM network. The data collected during the first 7 days was used as a dataset for forecasting using machine learning over the following 7 days. We gathered data for two different cars made in 2004 and 2016, respectively.

3.5 Machine Learning Models

We evaluated three regression models: LR, RF Regression (RFR), and SVR, chosen based on insights from the literature review [22]. Among these, RFR was identified as the best-performing model due to its superior performance. Therefore, it was implemented in the back end, within the cloud computing layer.

3.6 Performance Evaluation of ML

To evaluate the performance of the ML models, we used mean squared error (MSE), which is calculated as follows:

$$\mathrm{MSE} = \frac{1}{n}\sum_{i=1}^{n}\left(Y_i - \hat{Y}_i\right)^2 \tag{1}$$

where Y_i is the actual value, $\hat{Y}$ is the predicted value, and n is the number of samples.

3.7 Development of a Web Monitoring System

Web development consists of the front end, which utilizes HTML, CSS, and JavaScript to render the user interface, handle user interactions, display content, and capture user input to send to the back end. The back end, implemented using server-side languages like PHP and Python with frameworks such as Laravel and FastAPI, manages the logic, database interactions, and overall functionality that is not directly visible to the user. The database, a relational SQL-based system, stores and manages the data.

3.8 Testing the Entire System

Finally, the entire system was tested by deploying the IoT sensor on vehicles to gather real-time emission data over 14 days. The data from the IoT device was transmitted to the cloud, where the integrated ML model was used to predict future emissions.

The accuracy of these predictions was then evaluated against actual emission data collected during the testing period. We used MSE to assess the accuracy of the system in real-world conditions.

3.9 Proposed Layered Architecture

This section describes the seven layers proposed to construct an IoT system for monitoring emissions from vehicles. As shown in Fig. 1, the layered architecture consists of the following layers: (i) L1—sensing, where IoT sensors collect data on various pollutants; (ii) L2—processing and local storage, where the data is initially processed and stored; (iii) L3—edge computing, where data is computed and analytical results are provided near the source; (iv) L4—network, which facilitates data transmission; (v) L5—cloud-based storage, where the data is aggregated and stored for long-term analysis; (vi) L6—cloud-based computing, where robust computing is performed in the backend; and (vii) L7—application, which uses the data to generate predictive insights for preventive maintenance and mitigation strategies.

Layer 1: Sensing
The role of this layer is to capture real-time data related to automotive emissions. IoT sensors like the MQ-135, PM sensors, SO2 sensors, NOx sensors, and CO2 sensors can be installed on a car to detect and measure air pollutants.
Layer 2: Processing and Local Storage
This layer connects microcontrollers or Raspberry Pi with sensors. The raw data collected by the sensors is pre-processed and temporarily stored on the device. Basic computations and filtering are performed to reduce noise and ensure data quality before transmission.
Layer 3: Edge Computing

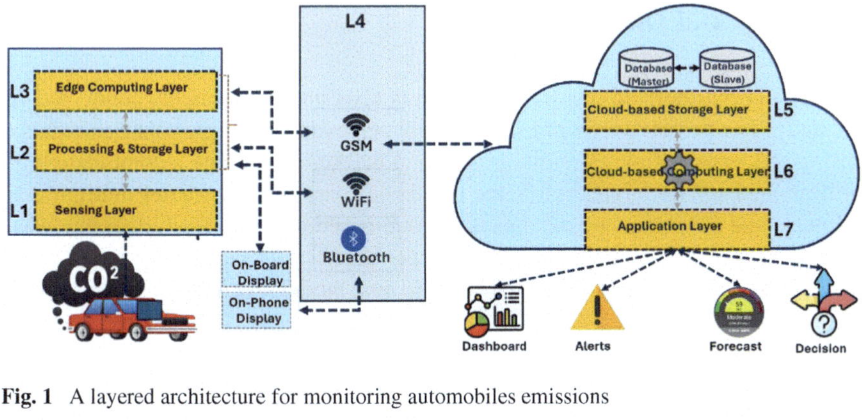

Fig. 1 A layered architecture for monitoring automobiles emissions

This layer involves performing more complex computations closer to the data source, often within the vehicle itself. Edge computing reduces latency by processing critical data locally, enabling quick decisions without relying on cloud resources. Raspberry Pi can be used for this purpose. Lightweight ML frameworks such as TensorFlow Lite and PyTorch Mobile can be utilized on this layer. ML models such as LSTM, RF, and TinyML can also be implemented on edge devices to enable real-time decision-making and analysis, reducing the need for constant cloud communication.

Layer 4: Network

This layer ensures the transport of data from the vehicle to the cloud using various networks such as WiFi, GSM, and LTE. It can also use Bluetooth to connect smartphones with mobile applications. Required components include GSM/GPRS modules like SIM800, WiFi modules like ESP8266 or ESP32, and LTE modems.

Layer 5: Cloud-Based Storage

While the local storage layer stores data for one car's in-vehicle IoT device (s), cloud-based storage stores data from multiple vehicles. This layer handles the large amounts of data generated over time and is scalable. Data centers and cloud computing service providers such as Google, Microsoft, and Amazon can be selected.

Layer 6: Cloud-Based Computing

This layer consists of robust computing power with advanced data analysis capabilities. ML models are integrated for forecasting future emissions.

Layer 7: Application

The application layer consists of a user interface where information about processed or analyzed data and predictive insights is presented. Vehicle owners, regulators, and fleet managers have access to this information. This layer provides real-time monitoring, alerts, reports, and decision-support tools to help reduce emission-related risks.

4 Results and Discussions

This section outlines the results from various tests and experiments conducted in this study. The prototype system successfully achieved its design goals, accurately sensing and transmitting gas emissions data in real time. Through a combination of hardware and software integration, the IoT device was able to monitor multiple gas pollutants and communicate the data to a cloud-based platform for further analysis. The results presented here focus on both the performance of the developed prototype and the predictive accuracy of the machine learning model integrated into the system.

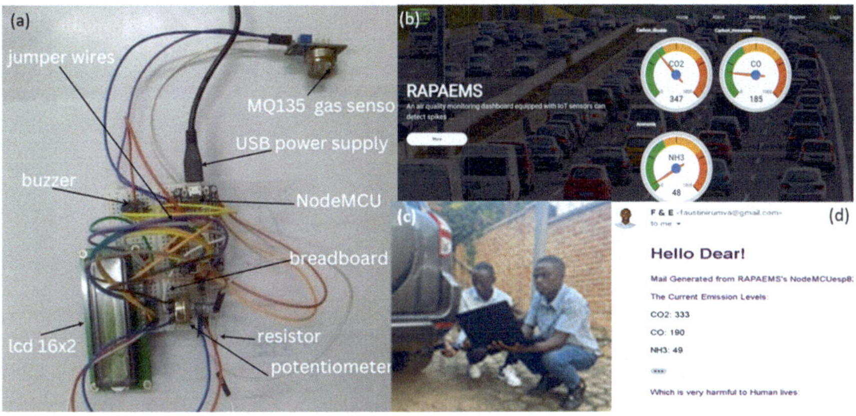

Fig. 2 System prototype. **a** IoT device, **b** System dashboard, **c**, sensor calibration & testing, **d** Email notification

4.1 Developed System Prototype

After setting up the logical circuit using simulation tools, the following output in Fig. 2a was achieved: The system successfully senses emissions using an MQ-135 gas sensor, controlled by a NodeMCU microcontroller. The system is capable of transmitting the measured emissions data using the integrated ESP8266 Wi-Fi module.

The system checks if monitored emission data meets certain conditions (thresholds), and if so, sends an email notification to the registered email address of the automobile's driver or owner via an SMTP server on port 587. The email includes the detected emission levels (Fig. 2d). Users interact with the system through a dashboard, which requires authentication (username/email and password) for login or signup. The dashboard displays key data points (Fig. 2b), including graphs and charts, to help users easily understand their account information and emissions data.

4.2 Data Gathering

In Fig. 3, the line chart displays the emission measurements (CO_2, CO, and NH_3 in PPM) and automatically updates with each new detection, representing only the latest data. Figure 3a presents data for the car made in 2016, whereas Fig. 3b presents the readings from the vehicle made in 2004.

According to the readings from the first car in Fig. 3a, CO emissions range from 54 to 76 PPM, with an average of approximately 64 PPM, indicating generally moderate levels. CO_2 emissions vary between 1295 and 1702 PPM, with an average of around 1560 PPM, suggesting relatively high levels. NH_3 emissions range from 7 to 12 PPM,

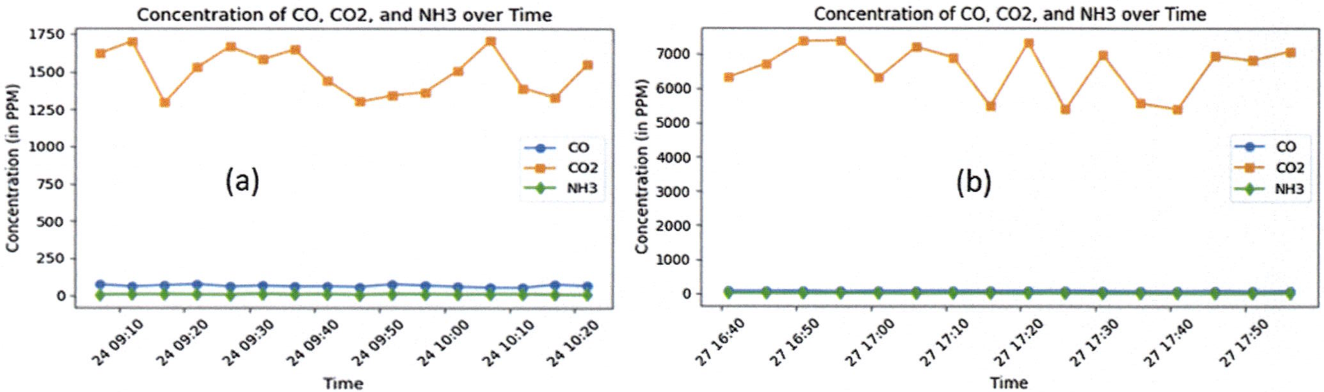

Fig. 3 Data readings displayed in charts. **a** gas emissions for the first car, **b** emissions for the second car

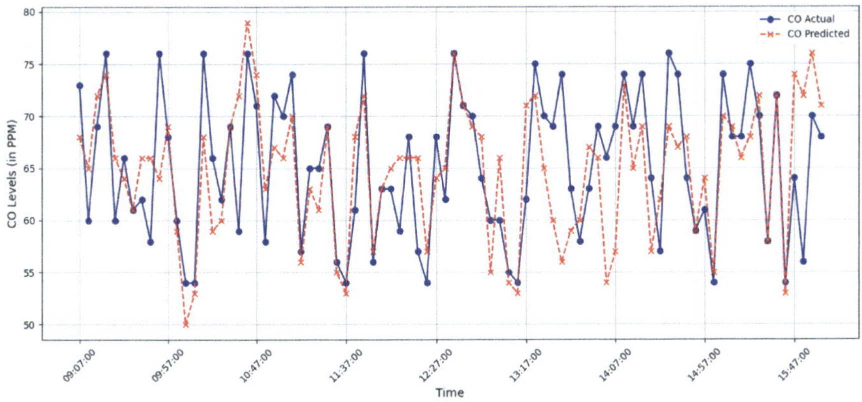

Fig. 4 A sample of actual vs. predicted emissions on the system dashboard

with an average of about 9 PPM, showing moderate levels. In general, CO emissions are moderate, CO_2 emissions are relatively high, and NH_3 levels are moderate.

The readings from the second car Fig. 3b, CO emissions vary from 66 to 87 PPM with an average of 77 PPM, indicating moderate to high levels. CO_2 emissions vary from 5396 to 7380 PPM with an average of 6714 PPM, suggesting notably high levels. NH_3 varies between 8 and 14 PPM, with an average of 11 PPM, showing moderate and stable levels (Fig. 4). CO_2 emissions are particularly high, while CO and NH_3 levels are moderate.

4.3 *Predictions*

After integrating the ML model into the system, the prediction was tested, yielding an MAE of 4.21 for CO, 1.73 for NH_3, and 60.87 for CO_2.

The model shows high accuracy with a low MAE, effectively predicting CO levels and providing reliable emission monitoring. The very low MAE indicates exceptional precision in predicting ammonia concentrations, which is crucial for effective emission management. The MAE of 60.87 for CO_2, though higher, still reflects reasonable prediction accuracy given the wide range of CO2 that varies from hundreds to thousands [23].

4.4 *Threats to Validity*

The MQ-135 sensor provides readings in terms of analog voltage, which can be converted to gas concentrations in parts per million (PPM) after proper calibration. However, emission standards often express concentrations in different units such as

%, g/km, and mg/km for CO, CO_2, and NH_3, respectively. Although we could convert PPM to these standard units, we lacked a standard tool for comparing these readings with those of the MQ-135. In future work, we plan to perform this calibration.

In this study, we used a cost-effective sensor (MQ-135), but its readings may vary due to environmental factors such as temperature and humidity. Additionally, this sensor may not be as accurate as industrial sensors. We recommend using industrial sensors for the real-world implementation of this framework.

5 Conclusion

This study presents a novel framework for real-time monitoring of automotive emissions using IoT sensors. It addresses the limitations of traditional methods of monitoring car emissions like PEMS, which lack cloud-based data transmission useful for making big data from many vehicles' emissions. By integrating a multilayered approach, including sensing, edge computing, and cloud-based analysis, the framework allows for comprehensive data collection and predictive modeling of pollutants such as CO, NOx, SO_2, and PM. The implementation of an MQ-135 sensor and the integration of machine learning algorithms demonstrate the framework's capability to predict future pollutant levels and support preventive maintenance strategies. This approach promises enhanced accuracy in air quality assessments, actionable insights for urban air quality improvement, and more effective air pollution reduction by enabling early detection and response. The framework's benefits extend to vehicle owners, regulators, and fleet managers, facilitating informed decision-making and proactive measures to mitigate air pollution.

References

1. A.K. Agarwal, N.N. Mustafi, Real-world automotive emissions: Monitoring methodologies, and control measures, Renew. Sustain. Energy Rev. 137 (2021) 110624. https://doi.org/10.1016/j.rser.2020.110624.
2. REMA, Inventory of Sources of Air Pollution in Rwanda: Determination of Future Trends and Development of a National Air Quality Control Strategy, 2018. https://rema.gov.rw/fileadmin/templates/Documents/rema_doc/AirQuality/InventoryofSourcesofAirPollutioninRwandaFinalReport.pdf.
3. Transport Overview, (n.d.). https://www.worldbank.org/en/topic/transport/overview (accessed August 8, 2024).
4. Y. Huang, W. chuen Mok, Y. shing Yam, J.L. Zhou, N.C. Surawski, B. Organ, E.F.C. Chan, M. Mofijur, T.M.I. Mahlia, H.C. Ong, Evaluating in-use vehicle emissions using air quality monitoring stations and on-road remote sensing systems, Sci. Total Environ. 740 (2020). https://doi.org/10.1016/j.scitotenv.2020.139868.
5. L.-M. Dragomir, M. Pantazică, Air Quality Monitoring System Inside and Outside a Vehicle, in: 2022 IEEE 28th Int. Symp. Des. Technol. Electron. Packag., 2022: pp. 218–222.https://doi.org/10.1109/SIITME56728.2022.9988528

6. K. Brodzik, J. Faber, D. Łomankiewicz, A. Gołda-Kopek, In-vehicle VOCs composition of unconditioned, newly produced cars, J. Environ. Sci. 26 (2014) 1052–1061. https://doi.org/10.1016/S1001-0742(13)60459-3.
7. Common air pollutants and their health effects - Air quality, (n.d.). https://www.health.nsw.gov.au/environment/air/Pages/common-air-pollutants.aspx (accessed July 29, 2024).
8. Billions of people still breathe unhealthy air: new WHO data, (n.d.). https://www.who.int/news/item/04-04-2022-billions-of-people-still-breathe-unhealthy-air-new-who-data (accessed August 8, 2024).
9. J.M. Wang, C.-H. Jeong, N. Hilker, K.K. Shairsingh, R.M. Healy, U. Sofowote, J. Debosz, Y. Su, M. McGaughey, G. Doerksen, T. Munoz, L. White, D. Herod, G.J. Evans, Near-Road Air Pollutant Measurements: Accounting for Inter-Site Variability Using Emission Factors, Environ. Sci. Technol. 52 (2018) 9495–9504. https://doi.org/10.1021/acs.est.8b01914.
10. C. Hood, I. MacKenzie, J. Stocker, K. Johnson, D. Carruthers, M. Vieno, R. Doherty, Air quality simulations for London using a coupled regional-to-local modelling system, Atmos. Chem. Phys. 18 (2018) 11221–11245. https://doi.org/10.5194/acp-18-11221-2018.
11. Rwanda Environment Management Authority (REMA): Air Quality Monitoring: Rwanda On The Right Track, (n.d.). https://www.rema.gov.rw/info/details?tx_news_pi1%5Baction%5D=detail&tx_news_pi1%5Bcontroller%5D=News&tx_news_pi1%5Bnews%5D=115&cHash=478c8f04f6686c3aaefeeef17cece331 (accessed July 29, 2024).
12. Vlachos, Theodoros G., Bonnel, Pierre, Perujo, Adolfo, Weiss, Martin, Mendoza Villafuerte, Pablo, Riccobono, Francesco, In-Use Emissions Testing with Portable Emissions Measurement Systems (PEMS) in the Current and Future European Vehicle Emissions Legislation: Overview, Underlying Principles and Expected Benefits, SAE Int. J. Commer. Veh. 7 (2014) 199–215. https://doi.org/10.4271/2014-01-1549.
13. M. Kelp, T. Gould, E. Austin, J.D. Marshall, M. Yost, C. Simpson, T. Larson, Sensitivity analysis of area-wide, mobile source emission factors to high-emitter vehicles in Los Angeles, Atmos. Environ. 223 (2020) 117212. https://doi.org/10.1016/j.atmosenv.2019.117212.
14. C.F. Lau, A. Rakowska, T. Townsend, P. Brimblecombe, T.L. Chan, Y.S. Yam, G. Močnik, Z. Ning, Evaluation of diesel fleet emissions and control policies from plume chasing measurements of on-road vehicles, Atmos. Environ. 122 (2015) 171–182. https://doi.org/10.1016/j.atmosenv.2015.09.048.
15. H. Ke, J.M. Ondov, W.F. Rogge, Detailed emission profiles for on-road vehicles derived from ambient measurements during a windless traffic episode in Baltimore using a multi-model approach, Atmos. Environ. 81 (2013) 280–287. https://doi.org/10.1016/j.atmosenv.2013.08.020.
16. C. Song, C. Ma, Y. Zhang, T. Wang, L. Wu, P. Wang, Y. Liu, Q. Li, J. Zhang, Q. Dai, C. Zou, L. Sun, H. Mao, Heavy-duty diesel vehicles dominate vehicle emissions in a tunnel study in northern China, Sci. Total Environ. 637–638 (2018) 431–442. https://doi.org/10.1016/j.scitotenv.2018.04.387.
17. R. Smit, P. Kingston, D.W. Neale, M.K. Brown, B. Verran, T. Nolan, Monitoring on-road air quality and measuring vehicle emissions with remote sensing in an urban area, Atmos. Environ. 218 (2019) 116978. https://doi.org/10.1016/j.atmosenv.2019.116978.
18. A.S.A. Sukor, G.C. Cheik, L.M. Kamarudin, X. Mao, H. Nishizaki, A. Zakaria, S.M.M. Syed Zakaria, Predictive Analysis of In-Vehicle Air Quality Monitoring System Using Deep Learning Technique, Atmosphere (Basel). 13 (2022). https://doi.org/10.3390/atmos13101587.
19. C.C. Goh, L.M. Kamarudin, A. Zakaria, H. Nishizaki, N. Ramli, X. Mao, S.M.M.S. Zakaria, E. Kanagaraj, A.S.A. Sukor, M.F. Elham, Real-time in-vehicle air quality monitoring system using machine learning prediction algorithm, Sensors. 21 (2021) 1–16. https://doi.org/10.3390/s21154956.
20. A. Khan, S. Chandra, M.C. Parameshwara, Air quality monitoring and management system model of vehicles based on the internet of things, Eng. Res. Express. 4 (2022). https://doi.org/10.1088/2631-8695/ac6791.
21. M. Maslouski, E. Jarosz-Krzemińska, P. Jagoda, E. Adamiec, A mobile car monitoring system as a supplementary tool for air quality monitoring in urban and rural environments: the case study from Poland, Sci. Rep. 13 (2023) 1–10. https://doi.org/10.1038/s41598-023-43095-w.

22. D. Kinaneva, G. Hristov, P. Kyuchukov, G. Georgiev, P. Zahariev, R. Daskalov, Machine Learning Algorithms for Regression Analysis and Predictions of Numerical Data, in: 2021 3rd Int. Congr. Human-Computer Interact. Optim. Robot. Appl., 2021: pp. 1–6. https://doi.org/10.1109/HORA52670.2021.9461298
23. K. Gładyszewska-Fiedoruk, Concentrations of carbon dioxide in the cabin of a small passenger car, Transp. Res. Part D Transp. Environ. 16 (2011) 327–331. https://doi.org/10.1016/j.trd.2011.01.005.

Synergizing IoT and ESP32 Microcontroller for Enhanced Patient Monitoring System

Anael E. Sam and Crecent Sembuli

Abstract In the medical field, traditional methods of requesting assistance, which depend primarily on vocal communication, frequently fall short in critical situations where patients may be unconscious or unable to move. Various systems have been developed to enable patients to alert caregivers about their health conditions. This paper presents an innovative solution utilizing the ESP32 microcontroller to enhance patient assistance through an automated notification system. Our approach integrates NFC and RFID technology with an ESP32 Microcontroller device, enabling patients who can move to easily request help. For those unable to call for assistance, the system employs motion sensors and microphones to passively monitor patient conditions, detecting abnormal movements or sounds from vital equipment such as ventilators or ECG machines. Notifications are sent in real-time to nurses' or caregivers' smartphones or a centralized monitoring system via a mobile app. A key feature of our solution is its event logging capability, which collects and stores data for future research, potentially advancing medical care. The use of the ESP32 microcontroller allows for a cost-effective, scalable, and reliable system, distinguishing it from existing solutions and providing a much-needed improvement in patient care in resource-limited settings.

Keywords IoT · ESP32 microcontroller · Radio Frequency Identification (RFID) · Near Field Communication (NFC)

A. E. Sam (✉) · C. Sembuli
Computational and Communication Science and Engineering (CoCSE), The Nelson Mandela African Institution of Science and Technology (NM-AIST), Arusha, Tanzania
e-mail: anael.sam@nm-aist.ac.tz

C. Sembuli
e-mail: sembulic@nm-aist.ac.tz

J. Marx Gómez et al. (eds.), *Advancement in Embedded and Mobile Systems*, Progress in IS, https://doi.org/10.1007/978-3-031-99219-3_28

1 Introduction

In the healthcare sector, the integration of Internet of Things (IoT) technology with medical devices and sensors has revolutionized patient monitoring and treatment management. By facilitating real-time data exchange, IoT enhances the ability to monitor patient vitals and assess treatment effectiveness. Additionally, technologies such as Near Field Communication (NFC) have streamlined processes like patient registration, improving identification and access to medical records.

While these advancements have made significant strides in patient care, many healthcare facilities, particularly in resource-limited settings like Tanzania, still face challenges due to a shortage of medical personnel. This scarcity often leads to strained assistance for admitted patients, where the primary method of calling for help remains vocal communication. While effective under normal circumstances, this approach fails in critical situations where patients may be unconscious or unable to vocalize their needs.

Recognizing these limitations, this project builds upon existing technologies by proposing an integrated solution that combines IoT, RFID, and the ESP32 microcontroller. Rather than introducing a completely new invention, our focus is on enhancing and developing current systems to automate the monitoring and response processes for patient needs. This development aims to improve the efficiency of care delivery, ensuring that patients can receive timely assistance while also creating a comprehensive logging system for medical events.

While this research focuses on the integration of IoT, RFID, and the ESP32 microcontroller to enhance patient monitoring and assistance, it is important to note that data protection and privacy considerations have not been thoroughly addressed. The implementation of such technologies involves the collection and transmission of sensitive patient information, which necessitates robust security measures to safeguard against unauthorized access and data breaches. Future work should prioritize the development of comprehensive data protection strategies to ensure patient confidentiality and compliance with relevant regulations.

2 Related Works

Several researchers have worked on patient monitoring devices; Author [1] proposed a system that uses ESP8266, which is a WiFi SOC (system on chip). The system was integrated in a wearable device that acquires temperature, heart rate, and blood saturation, furthermore, it does not provide assistance to patients with seizures. Author [2] proposed a system that uses real-time remote patient monitoring system based on the Internet of Things that can monitor the basic vital signs of the patient, such as body temperature, heartbeat rate, and blood pressure, it is a wearable device with no patient movement detection. In their system, they never addressed the use of cheaply low cost ESP32 microcontroller. In [3], authors proposed an adept real-time IoT-based observation system for ICU patients, which can initiate faster communication by ascertaining an emergency. In this system, a patient monitor is used to collect data through bedside patient monitors. In this case, the system does not use a mobile app to notify the attendants. In [4], the authors identified a challenge for doctors and nurses to monitor all the patients in the ICU and implemented a Raspberry-based prototype for measuring the body temperature, respiration rate, heartbeat, and body movement of the patient, but the use of raspberry makes it to be a bit expensive in local market in Tanzania. In [5], authors implemented an IoT-based health care observation system, which consisted of body sensors that were to be placed in the patient's body, which can hinder patient movement. In [6], authors proposed an atomic decomposition (AD) method for the detection of the levels of deep sedation in ICU patients from the frontal electroencephalogram (EEG), In [7], authors deeply projected an IoT architecture with computing methods to make available security essentials to a healthcare monitoring system for ICU patients. In [8], authors illustrated and tested a robust automated system to sense atrial fibrillation (AF) from ICU patients using electrocardiogram (ECG) Signals Authors of paper [9] developed a prototype for combining numerous monitoring and therapeutic device data in a mobile application. The ESP32 microcontroller was not part of the work. In [10], authors addressed the problem of false alarms in ICU patients suffering from arrhythmia, which indicates that the target was only arrhythmia. Most of the researchers did not consider the integration of the cheapest component, which is the ESP32 microcontroller device. Hence, in our research, we are proposing Synergizing IoT, and ESP32 microcontroller-based patient monitoring system.

3 Architecture of the Developed System

Figure 1 shows the overall system architecture of the ESP32 microcontroller-based patient monitoring system.

The system consists of a mobile application that could be used by receptionists, nurses, and doctors via their phones/mobile equipment. It also consists of the ESP32 microcontroller, motion sensor, RFID card reader, switch, and microphone module placed at the patient's bed. The information collected is then stored in the cloud for further processing. There is a database that stores all important system information; the database is hosted using Google's Cloud Firestore database solution.

The patients will have their respective RFID cards. Each RFID card will be registered via NFC of a mobile system and assigned the patients details when the patient is admitted to the hospital. The receptionist will log the details of the patient into our system via the mobile app. Once the patient's details are logged into the system, a random unique Id (we use GUID) will be generated and written to the RFID card.

When the nurse or the doctor arrives at the patient's bed, he/she scans the RFID card via the mobile application. The respective patient's details are displayed on the mobile app. Then, the respective medical personnel perform the diagnosis and update

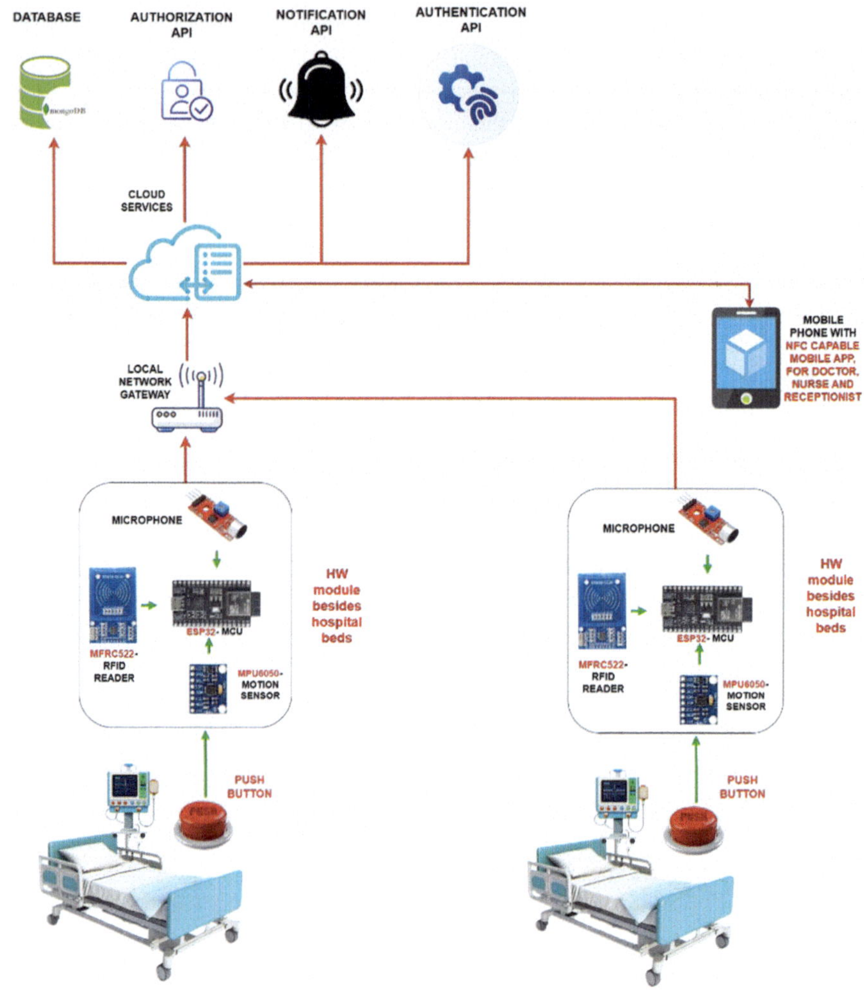

Fig. 1 System architecture

the patient's profile via the same mobile app. It might happen that some medical tests or medicines are prescribed. These are also logged in the system via the mobile app. For instance, a patient was prescribed complete blood dialysis. In this case, the nurse or receptionist responsible for this would be notified via the mobile app. Once the dialysis is complete, the responsible medical personnel will upload the results via the mobile app. As soon as the report is uploaded into the system, a notification will be sent to the respective medical personnel.

In the absence of any medical personnel, the patient requests assistance by pressing the push button switch placed by his/her bedside. The button is connected to the

ESP32 Microcontroller, which will trigger a notification to the assigned medical personnel's mobile app.

The above-mentioned system works when the patient is able enough to press the button on his/her own. But what if he/she is not physically capable of doing so? For example, he/she may be having a seizure, in such a case, we cannot expect him/her to be able to press the button to call for assistance. For such a situation, our system is equipped with a motion sensor MPU6050 and a microphone module, which would detect such situations by monitoring the patient's movements or listening to the patient's life-saving equipment, such as a ventilator or a ECG placed by his/her bed. We are calling it passive detection as we are not directly communicating with the life-saving machines. In the future, once we obtain clearance, we intend to communicate directly between our proposed system and the life-saving equipment.

4 Methodology

The methodology details include the following;

1. Hardware and firm development
2. Software development

4.1 Hardware and Firm Development

Schematic diagram of the hardware system. Figure 2 below presents the schematic diagram of the system drawn using the easyEDA software. The diagram consists of all the important hardware components.

Control Unit. The system consists of a control unit, which contains of ESP32 microcontroller that acts as the brain of the system. The ESP32 collects all the information from the sensors and processes them for the required immediate action. It also communicates with the software part of the system (Fig. 3).

The Sensing Unit. This part consists of all sensing units that input a signal to the microcontroller unit. It consists of the following:

RFID card and card reader. An important part that reads and writes the information of both the patient and the medical attendants. Mini RFID card for registering patients and the nurses (Fig. 4).

Abnormality Motion Detector. For detecting any abnormal motion of the patient, the use of MPU6050 motion sensor is employed. MPU6050 module is a Micro Electro-Mechanical Systems (MEMS), which consists of a 3-axis accelerometer and a 3-axis gyroscope inside it. This helps us to measure acceleration, velocity, orientation, displacement, and many other motion-related parameter of a system or object (Fig. 5).

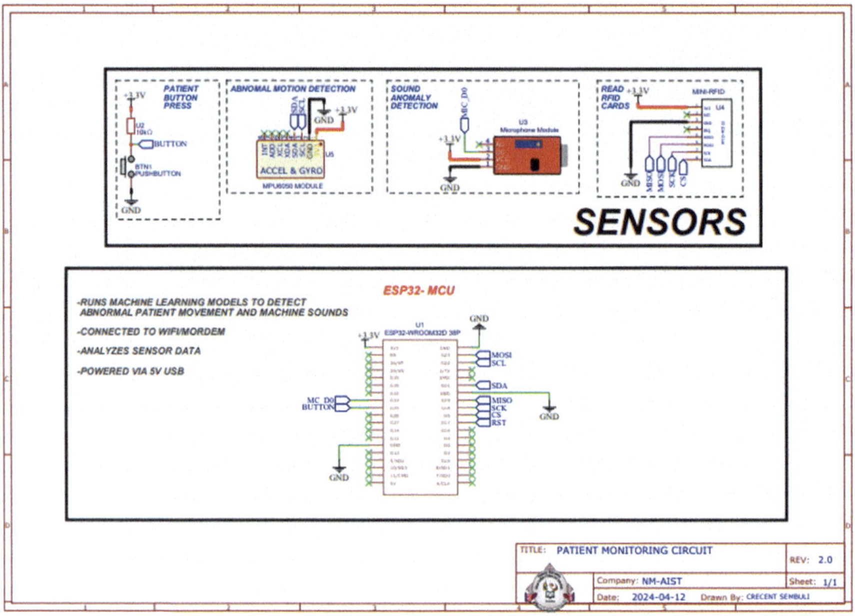

Fig. 2 Schematic diagram

Fig. 3 ESP32 microcontroller module

Microphone Module. The microphone module is used for the detection of sound abnormalities produced from the patient's side. It detects sounds produced by critical life-saving machines like ventilators, ECG monitors, and EEG monitors. These machines emit specific tone noises indicative of the patient's condition. The microphone installed in the system captures these noises, which are then classified using a pre-trained machine learning model on the ESP32 microcontroller. If a noise is classified as indicating a critical state, a background process on the ESP32 microcontroller will activate, triggering a notification alert to be sent to the relevant nurses and doctors caring for the patient.

Fig. 4 RFID card reader

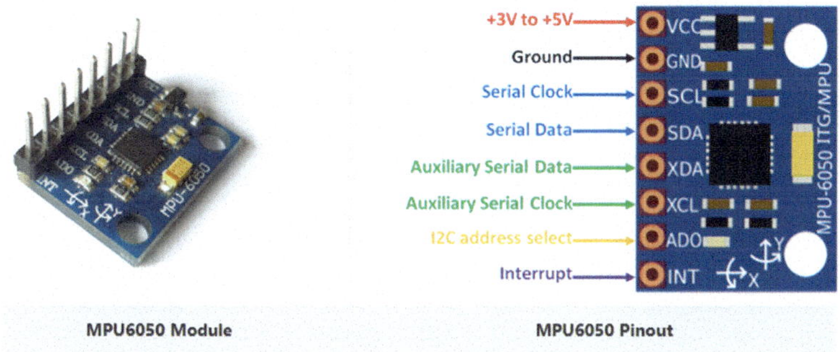

Fig. 5 MPU Sensor

Push Button Switch. For notification and immediate action, the patient presses the button integrated on the NFC module and triggers an event to the NFC database for further actions from health personnel on duty. The same will be done if the patient presses the button.

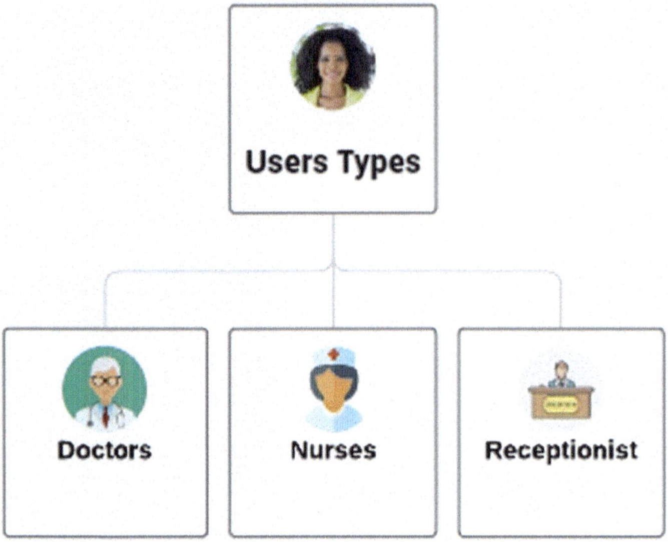

Fig. 6 Example of UI interface

4.2 *Software Development*

The mobile app is crafted using Flutter, the language for Android development. Meanwhile, the ESP32 functionality is coded in visual studio code using C programming. This setup allows the ESP32 module to interact with an NFC reader of the mobile phone, RFID card, and additional sensors.

User Interface App. The architecture includes a mobile application tailored for use by doctors and nurses within an NFC environment, alongside an RFID card enabling patients' information storage within the system (Fig. 6).

The mobile application users can be divided into three categories, namely, doctors, nurses, and receptionists, with each of them having different functionalities. The receptionist can register patients, assign doctors and nurses, and upload any other documents related to the patient (Fig. 7).

Upon a patient's arrival at the hospital, receptionists use the mobile app to add the patient by clicking the "Register" button. A patient registered and assigned a ward, a doctor, and a nurse during admission. The app also shows the number of patients, the number of available doctors, and the number of nurses. Once the registration process is finalized, a 10-digit NFCID, serving as the patient's unique identifier, is generated. Subsequently, this NFCID is written to the RFID card designated for the patient via the mobile app (Fig. 8).

Database Design. Database used is a mongo-DB, MongoDB stands out as a widely used, open-source NoSQL database known for its exceptional performance, reliability, and scalability. Employing a versatile document-based data format called

Fig. 7 UI application Login Page

BSON (Binary JSON), MongoDB accommodates intricate and nested data arrangements, surpassing the capabilities of conventional relational databases. Here, any database can be used depending on the choice of the developer.

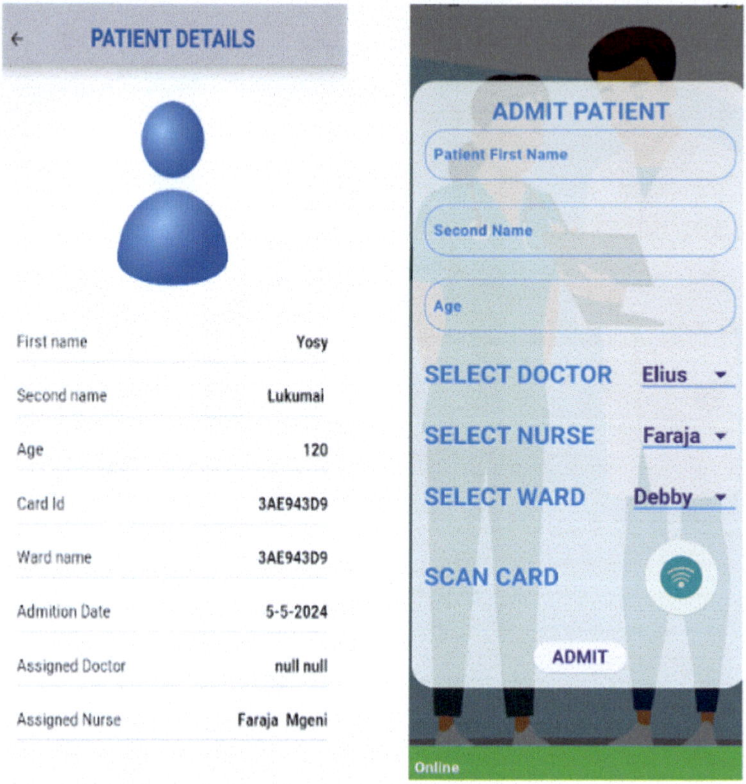

Fig. 8 Patient details and Doctor Assignment

5 Results and Discussion

The development of the patient monitoring device using the ESP32 microcontroller has yielded promising results, demonstrating its effectiveness in facilitating remote patient monitoring and care. The system was tested under various conditions to evaluate its responsiveness and reliability. The integration of low-power microcontrollers allowed for extended battery life, making it suitable for continuous monitoring in hospital settings. The real-time data exchange capabilities, enabled by cloud integration, ensured that healthcare providers received timely notifications regarding patient status, significantly enhancing response times (Fig. 9).

Fig. 9 Prototype developed

6 Conclusion

In conclusion, the ESP32-based patient monitoring device represents a significant development in remote healthcare solutions. This paper primarily focused on the capabilities of the ESP32 microcontroller, highlighting its effectiveness in creating a responsive and reliable monitoring system. While the ESP32 offers unique advantages, other microcontrollers could also be employed to develop similar systems, showcasing the versatility of such approaches. Future work will aim to enhance this system by addressing key challenges, particularly in data protection and connectivity. Exploring options like offline data storage with periodic syncing will be crucial for maintaining functionality in areas with unreliable internet access. Furthermore, expanding the system to incorporate additional sensors and integrating machine learning algorithms could significantly enhance predictive analytics, leading to improved patient outcomes. This ongoing development underscores the potential of IoT-enabled solutions to transform remote healthcare and improve the quality of patient care.

References

1. Raveen De Silver.: An IoT empowered system for Patient Monitoring and Diagnosing, IEE robotics & Automation Society 2022.

2. Nasser M. Al-Zidi (2021).: Smart System for Real-Time Remote Patient Monitoring Based on Internet of Things, 2nd International Conference on Computational Methods in Science & Technology (ICCMST).
3. B. Prajapati, S., Parikh and J. Patel.: An Intelligent Real Time IoT-Based System (IRTBS) for Monitoring ICU Patient, International Conference on Information and Communication Technology for Intelligent Systems, Ahmedabad, India, 2017, pp. 390–396.
4. R. Kumar., M. P. Rajasekaran.: An IoT based patient monitoring system using raspberry Pi, 2016 International Conference on Computing Technologies and Intelligent Data Engineering (ICCTIDE'16), Kovilpatti, 2016, pp. 1–4.
5. V. Akhila., Y. Vasavi.,K. Nissie and P. V. Rao.: An IoT based Patient Health Monitoring System using Arduino Uno, International Journal of Research in Information Technology, vol. 1, no. 1, Nov. 2017, pp. 1–9.
6. S. B. Nagaraj.: Electroencephalogram Based Detection of Deep Sedation in ICU Patients Using Atomic Decomposition, IEEE Transactions on Biomedical Engineering, vol. 65, no. 12, Dec. 2018, pp. 2684–2691.
7. B. S. Egala., S. Priyanka and A. K. Pradhan.: SHPI: Smart Healthcare System for Patients in ICU using IoT, 2019 IEEE International Conference on Advanced Networks and Telecommunications Systems (ANTS), GOA, India, 2019, pp. 1–6.
8. S. K. Bashar et al., .: A trial Fibrillation Detection in ICU Patients: A Pilot Study on MIMIC III Data*", 2019 41st Annual International Conference of the IEEE Engineering in Medicine and Biology Society (EMBC), Berlin, Germany, 2019, pp. 298–301.
9. L. Flohr.: Clinician-Driven Design of VitalPAD–An Intelligent Monitoring and Communication Device to Improve Patient Safety in the Intensive Care Unit", IEEE Journal of Translational Engineering in Health and Medicine, vol. 6, 2018, pp. 1–14.
10. T. Manna and A. Swetapadma.: An Improved Method for Detecting False Alarm in Arrhythmia ICU Patients, 2018 Fourth International Conference on Research in Computational Intelligence and Communication Networks (ICRCICN), Kolkata, India, 2018, pp. 66–69.

Mobile-Based Ticket Tracking Helpdesk System for Technical Support: A Case Study of Habari Node Public Limited Company, Tanzania

Jacqueline Uwimbabazi, Devotha Nyambo, and Anael Sam

Abstract Mobile technology has created a platform that allows companies to reach their clients more quickly and tackle issues more efficiently. Habari node PLC handles and supports its customers using a web-based customer relationship management (CRM) system. The company receives customer support requests via phone calls, and due to its large customer base, the volume of these calls is high. Furthermore, the number of clients joining continues to grow daily. This study aimed to develop a ticket-tracking helpdesk system that enables quick and effective customer service. In the initial stage, the study examined the existing system to compile a list of requirements for the new system. The development and testing of the Ticket Tracking Helpdesk System (TTHS) were carried out using an agile extreme programming approach. The developed system enables clients to submit their requests and allows customer support staff to view these demands. The results indicate that the system facilitates the opening and assigning of tickets and tracks operations when closing tickets. Additionally, it provides SMS notifications between users. The TTHS enhances the efficiency of customer support services by decreasing response time, reducing phone calls, and preventing user data loss.

Keywords Mobile-based helpdesk system · Tickets tracking helpdesk system · Technical support · Customer relationship management · Quick customer service

---

J. Uwimbabazi (✉) · D. Nyambo · A. Sam
School of Computational and Communication Science and Engineering, The Nelson Mandela African Institution of Science and Technology, Arusha, Tanzania
e-mail: uwimbabazij@nm-aist.ac.tz

D. Nyambo
e-mail: devotha.nyambo@nm-aist.ac.tz

A. Sam
e-mail: anael.sam@nm-aist.ac.tz

J. Marx Gómez et al. (eds.), *Advancement in Embedded and Mobile Systems*, Progress in IS, https://doi.org/10.1007/978-3-031-99219-3_29

1 Introduction

Nowadays, mobile technology is increasingly being used to support the routine implementation of duties or business processes in various organizations [1]. Customer satisfaction is essential for a successful organization to keep its position. Many companies today have branch offices and maintain worldwide offices, which has necessitated critical tracking and managing customer complaints as well as internal support operations. Critical difficulties in the area of systems and information technology are operations. Typically, the part of the application process that deals with information systems and technology receives a large number of complaints.

Habari Node is a Public limited company in Tanzania. It's head office is in Arusha, with branch offices in Dar es salaam, Dodoma, Mwanza, and Kilimanjaro [2]. Habari Node has a customer relationship management (CRM) web-based system that helps to identify its clients' requests and satisfy their needs through its technical support department. This company has more than 2000 customers who keep increasing day by day. This has significantly increased the daily number of technical support requests received from clients.

Upon receiving a client's request for support, technical support opens a ticket and then assigns it to a technician who will be in charge of solving the client's issue. Technical support is highly likely to miss important details, misplace or duplicate information, and create unnecessary back-and-forth phone calls due to the manual nature of customer support's operation. A ticket tracking mobile-based helpdesk system for technical support is proposed herein. This system aims to shift manual customer service to mobile customer service in order to speed up operations and make services efficient. The system will allow support staff to act on customer requests at any time and from anywhere.

The helpdesk is an organization's central point for dealing with customer or user demands relating to queries, services, technical assistance, or complaints about specific services. It implements a numbered system (ticket request) to allow monitoring and settlement of activities organized by a team. To facilitate data gathering, activity monitoring, and reporting, the helpdesk should be aided by specific software [3]. Mobile helpdesk apps give customers more options when it comes to achieving excellent customer service.

This project aims to develop a ticket tracking mobile-based helpdesk system for technical support that will allow receiving client requests, opening and tracking tickets, and assigning them to a technician for resolution.

2 Related Works

Technical problems are more common in the workplace, both in education and in the business world. As a result, these issues must be regularly and carefully monitored. This implies a need for a system capable of handling them. Bearing this in mind, Alam developed a helpdesk ticketing system (HDTS) that can overcome the barriers of traditional customer complaint management systems by easily accessing the customer information, complaints, and resolution [3]. This system came as a solution to an organization's request management system that was traditional. However, controlling data became more difficult when several users have to use the same data source due to the web technology used, which results in a disconnected front-end. Therefore, some form of record locking needs to be implemented.

Another project on design and implementation of web-based helpdesk information systems using extreme programming methods was introduced to solve the problem of administration that must always be available to handle and report customer requests, transaction data that has not been computerized, unavailability of a way for customers to check support service progress, and hardware services declined due to the advent of COVID-19 [4]. The designed system resulted in a web-based helpdesk information system that enabled every client to readily access information about the limits, stages of handling the items being serviced, and digitalized data so that data storage did not pile up and data was easier to retrieve when needed. The application technology used to access the helpdesk is in the scope of local host, where a web server must be installed on a PC or laptop before utilizing it. This necessitates the use of another technology for easy access, such a mobile application that allows for cooperation among employees as well as access to services. A waste management company in India called Bank Sampah Malang (BSM), developed and implemented an online customer service system based on mobile applications and short message service (SMS) gateways [5]. Prior to the development of this system, there was an issue with BSM's customer support procedure, which was not optimal, particularly its online service. Some services were available online through the website, although the information was restricted to a price list and the types of waste that BSM accepted. The BSM customer service application, on the other hand, simply allows users to examine their current balance and garbage price information, as well as request garbage pickup. There was a need for more services to be included in the mobile application to cater to customers, such as providing support about technical issues via request submission.

Because of the impact of the COVID-19 pandemic, another helpdesk mobile application was developed to support classroom technology. The concerns of converting face-to-face classrooms to online have resulted in the need for a mobile app to help IT staff, instructors, and students during class time, give timely support for classroom technology issues, and maintain a secure learning experience [6]. The system provides helpdesk support for classroom technology concerns, but it is still inflexible in format, requiring the users to adapt to the software rather than the other way around.

Currently, media devices like iPads, iPods, and Android handsets have opened new possibilities for speeding up the activities of most institutions. It can be tough to get a school's information and communication technology (ICT) technical team to fix broken products and services. Ambrose A. developed the Automated Mobile Edu-Helpdesk System (AMES) to solve problems with ICT in academic institutions [7]. Even though this system has the potential to improve how problems are handled, it already makes it possible for both teaching and non-teaching staff to send complaints or messages to the technical department quickly. It also makes operations better and faster, reducing the time spent on paperwork.

Short messages also play the most important role in our daily lives. Baghaskara developed a Complaint Handling Ticketing Application Web-Based Using Codeigniter Framework to allow mobile users can get information on time and comfortably via SMS. This system came as a solution to the waiting time that was normally taken in the previous system when customers complained by calling. Generally when the Customer service is busy handling other complaints, then the other customer's telephone queue must wait and need time; The system also provides complaints services through e-mail and social media but not but not all people can operate e-mail or social media properly, and still require a considerable amount of time to handle it [8]. Having a mobile application integrated with sms and email service can be a good improvement to this system. A ticket tracking helpdesk system is a solution to this, and to add technical solution advantage flutter platform is used to make the application more reliable, and the Mysql database is used in order to help with offline data.

3 Materials and Methods

3.1 Study Area

This study was conducted at Habari Node Company, Arusha, Tanzania, and focuses on three kinds of people: IT technicians, customer support personnel, and customers of Habari Node Company. Four regions of Tanzania (Arusha, Kilimanjaro, Dodoma, and Dar es salaam), where the company has branch offices were surveyed during data collection. The company has many customers in these regions whose views would be sufficient to provide enough requirements for the development of the system.

3.2 Data Collection

Data collection was conducted to gather requirements from users of the current systems. Various data collection techniques, such as observation, interview, questionnaire, and document review, were applied. Information from different users was collected. This information became essential for capturing the essential functionalities of the proposed ticket-tracking helpdesk system.

The technical support department at Habari Node is responsible for all customer support services. Interviews were conducted with various customer support staff and technicians, while questionnaires were given to the clients. Review of the past records was made to ease the development of the current customer relationship management system.

3.3 System Development Approach

There are many systems development approaches, such as waterfall, rapid application development (RAD), and Agile.

In this project, the agile development methodology was used, specifically the Xtreme programming (XP). This is because the XP approach is well-fitted for small projects, is flexible, and allows for interaction between the end-users and developers throughout the software lifecycle development. It enables incorporation of end-users responses into each stage of the software development process, hence making Agile XP more applicable for prototype development as it focuses on efficiency and customer feedback [9].

Advantages of Agile Extreme Programming

XP is based on five core standards that are critical to its success but can be misinterpreted by the reader. Such inspiring principles help to keep employees happy and motivated at work. All five XP levels are listed below [9].

- Simplicity—Referring to emphasizing the current problem without spending time on the features not needed at the time.
- Feedback—It is very important to test all code as soon as it is implemented and ask c feedback from customers for fast problem identification.
- Communication—In XP, it's crucial that all team members constantly update one another on their progress and any changes to the plan.
- Courage—guarantees that errors will be identified and corrected.

Additionally, XP always requires absolute honesty from all team members. Being truthful early in the development process can prevent a number of problems later on.

- Respect—Regardless of the role they play, all team members must be respected and treated equally. Everyone contributes, no matter how big or small the impact is.

Disadvantages of Extreme Agile Programming

- Forming a team that can adopt XP practices and work well with each other it's a bit challenging.
- If the proper order for building the software is not followed, we may end up having to start over to include another set of requirements.

Steps of Agile Extreme Programming Approach

Extreme Programming methodology includes the following steps (activities): planning, designing, coding, and testing (Fig. 1).

Fig. 1 Agile Extreme programming

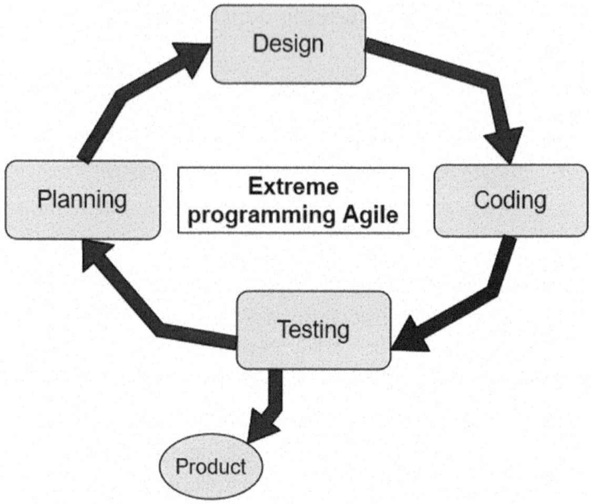

3.4 System Development Framework

The tickets tracking helpdesk system was developed using flutter platform and dart as client-side tool and server-side tools such as Nodejs and MySQL. It has been built around several modules, including registration, logging in, submitting and receiving requests for support, SMS notification about tickets submission, assignment, and closure of tickets, and the GPS location of the technician during tickets closure.

4 Results and Discussion

4.1 Results

Data Collection Results

Habari Node uses a CRM web-based system to manage and take care of its customers. For example, regarding helpdesk services, when the customer support department receives a client's query requesting support through a phone call, customer support staff writes down details of the client and his/her issue. The staff then makes a phone call to find an available technician to assign a ticket to handle the client's issue.

The current Habari node system for supporting customers can be tiresome and time-consuming. It involves manual operations and making lots of phone calls. Typical activities of the current system include receiving and following up on clients' technical problems, writing down clients' details, and sending notifications between users via emails. It should be noted that clients' details can easily be lost or misplaced. During the data collection, customer support staff indicated that these activities used to be easier to handle when they still had fewer clients. But with time, the number of customers increased, and with it came the challenges of handling many customers' support requests. Moreover, the number of customers seeking the services of Habari Node is still increasing.

Another challenge with the current system is locating an available technician to assign a ticket. It requires a technician to be physically at the office or to be located via phone calls. Using TTHS would enable Habari Node to efficiently support its customers anywhere at any time.

Results of System Design

During the system design phase, the conceptual design of the system, the context diagram, the use case diagram, and the database were all designed as discussed in the following sections (Fig. 2):

Conceptual Diagram

Use Case Diagram

A use case is a range of activities that define how an actor and a system interact to achieve a goal. The use-case diagram below illustrates user requirements at a high level (Figs. 3, 4).

A line connects each actor (stick figure) to a use case (oval figure) to show the interaction the actor can have with the system [10].

Results of System Development

Data obtained from clients proved that the system was intended to enhance current services. The developed system has a registration interface for clients, a login interface for customer support, technicians, and clients. And an interface for clients to

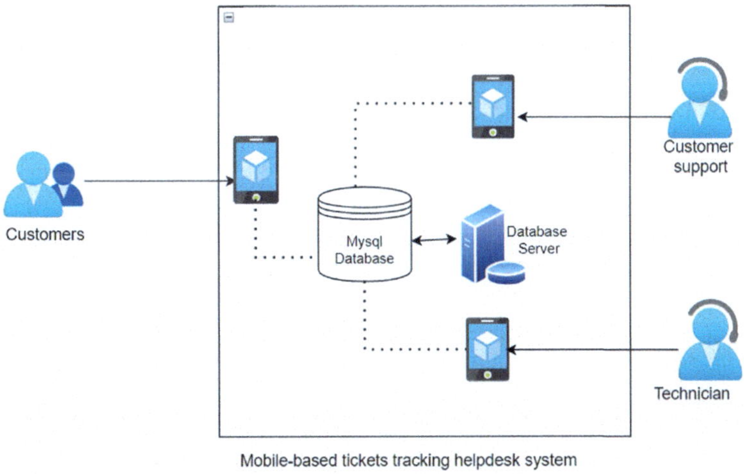

Fig. 2 Conceptual diagram of the proposed system

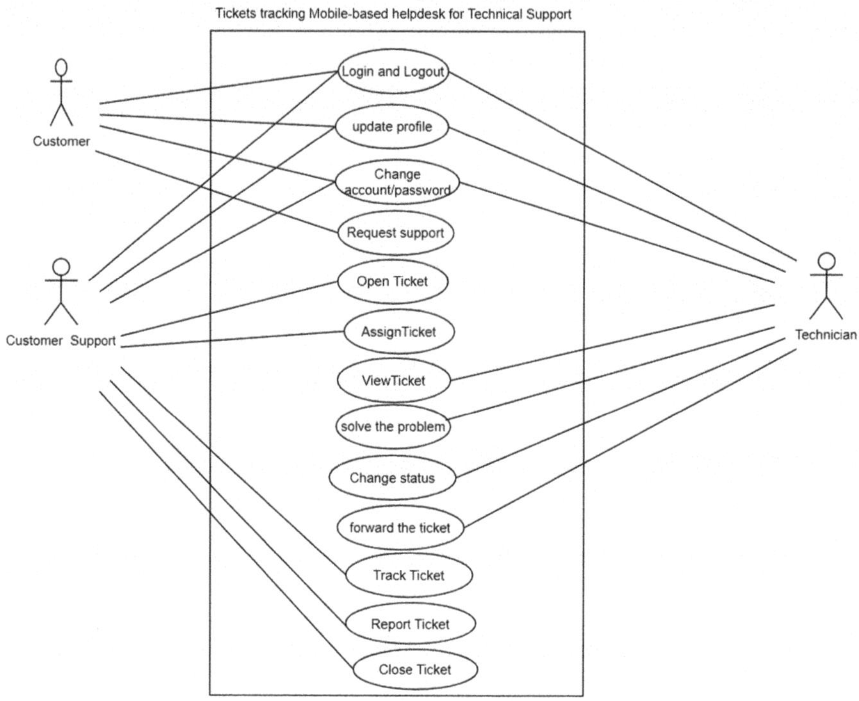

Fig. 3 Use case Diagram of the proposed System Database Design

submit a request. In addition, the system allows for the use of GPS coordinates to locate technicians when closing tickets. Another important feature of the system is sending and receiving SMS notifications between users (Figs. 5, 6).

4.2 Discussions

The developed ticket tracking helpdesk system is capable of handling more than 2000 customers to submit their problems requesting support. This robust online system can significantly reduce time and resource consumption. The developed ticket tracking helpdesk system meets all Habari node standards and current requirements. The system has user-friendly and interactive interfaces designed expressively to allow clients to freely ask for support. To register and log in, users must have internet access. Also, performing all other operations such as submitting a request, assigning tickets, and taking GPS location requires the internet. However, anything that has been completed can still be accessed while you are offline.

The system successfully allowed clients to submit their requests at the same time, and for customer support to assign tickets to technicians independently, GPS

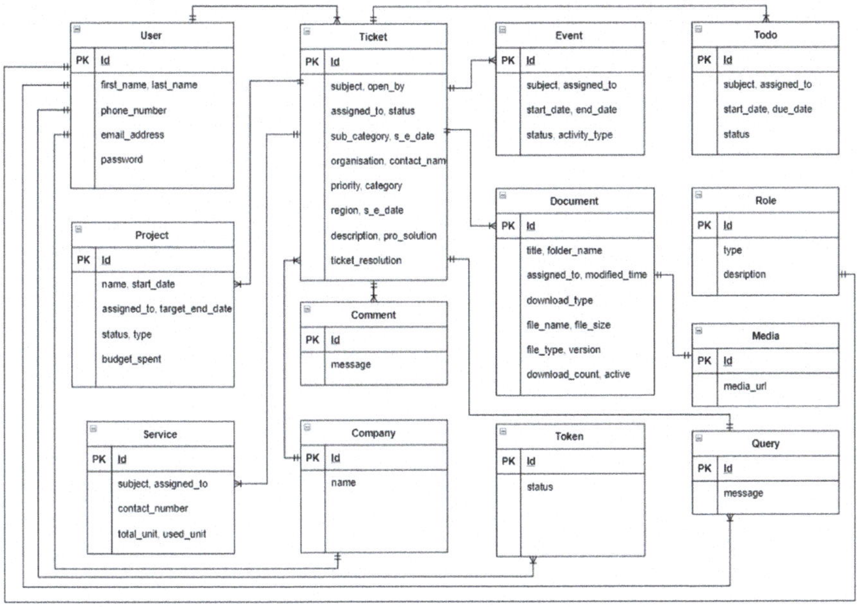

Fig. 4 Database Design of the system

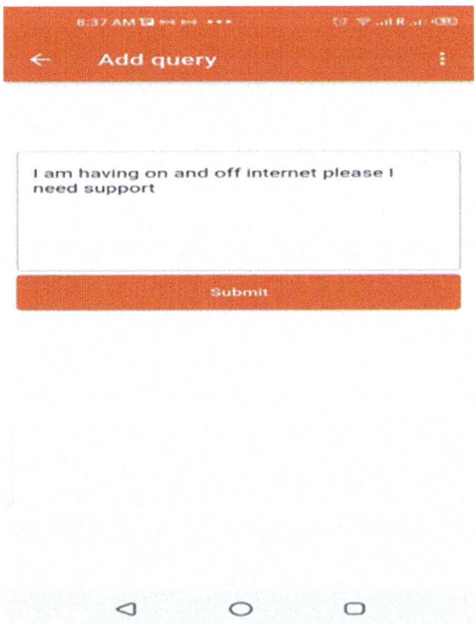

Fig. 5 Clients' Query submission page

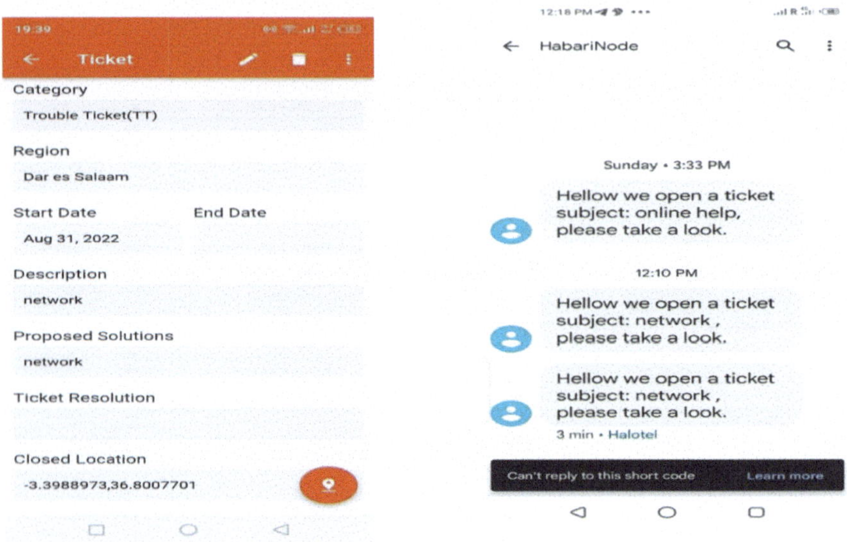

(a) (b)

Fig. 6 **a** Shows a closed ticket with GPS coordinates, **b** Shows SMS notifications of opening tickets

location can be taken for technician location when closing tickets. Throughout tests that were conducted during validation, the system's objectives are satisfactorily met. As a result, the study has been accomplished with a mobile-based ticket tracking helpdesk system that meets all functional and non-functional specifications.

5 Conclusion and Future Work

Excellent customer service is vital for business growth, customer retention, and identifying cross-selling and upselling opportunities. This study aimed to improve the customer support helpdesk system by enabling clients to submit queries through a mobile application, allowing support agents to assist anytime and anywhere, thus making support services faster and more efficient. In conclusion, the Mobile-Based Ticket Tracking Helpdesk System for Habari Node Public Limited Company significantly enhances customer service operations by providing a real-time, user-friendly platform for managing customer tickets via mobile devices. This system ensures prompt and accurate issue resolution, leading to improved customer satisfaction, and offers flexibility and accessibility, reducing response times and resource use. This innovative solution positions Habari Node Public Limited Company at the forefront of customer service excellence in the telecommunications industry. Future research could add features like a machine learning model to handle frequently asked questions.

References

1. N. Angelova, "Mobile applications for business," no. July 2019, 2020, https://doi.org/10.15547/tjs.2019.s.01.140.
2. Habari Node, "Company Profile Ø Who we are," pp. 1–5, 2017.
3. M. Alam and P. C. Committee, "Project Report On Help Desk Ticketing System (HDTS) SUBMITTED BY PMIT January 2017 Intake SUPERVISOR NAME INSTITUTE OF INFORMATION TECHNOLOGY (IIT)," no. April, 2018.
4. F. Wicaksono, "Design and Implementation of Web-Based Helpdesk Information Systems Using Extreme Programming Methods," vol. 5, no. June 2019, pp. 88–96, 2020.
5. N. Hayatin, B. Mavindo, and E. B. Cahyono, "The Development of Mobile Application Based Customer Service System in Bank Sampah Malang," vol. 2, no. 4, pp. 291–298, 2017.
6. Reed, "Developing Helpdesk Mobile App to Support Classroom Technology During COVID-19 Pandemic," 2020.
7. Ambrose and * A Azeta, "EDU-HELPDESK SYSTEM," 2016. [Online]. Available: www.ijptonline.com.
8. Sadewa, "International Journal of Computer Science and Mobile Computing Complaint Handling Ticketing Application Web Based Using Codeigniter Framework (Case Study at PT Indosat Ooredoo Tbk Jakarta)," 2018. [Online]. Available: www.ijcsmc.com.
9. Bulavko, "Extreme Programming (XP) Article Introduction to System Development methods," 2017.
10. T. C. de Sousa, L. Kelvin, C. Dias Neto, and C. Giovanni N. de Carvalho, "A Formal Semantics for Use Case Diagram Via Event-B," Journal of Software, vol. 12, no. 4, pp. 189–200, 2017, https://doi.org/10.17706/jsw.12.3.189-200.

AI and System Dynamics for Optimal Renewable Energy Pricing: A Theoretical Study

Mohamad Hamed and Jorge Marx Gómez

Abstract This study explores decision-making support systems (DMSS) for optimal renewable energy pricing, focusing on a comparative analysis between Artificial Intelligence (AI) tools and System Dynamics (SD) models. AI tools, known for their adaptability and handling of complex datasets, are contrasted with SD models, valued for their holistic view and feedback loop capabilities. Through a detailed comparative framework, we assess accuracy, adaptability, complexity, transparency, and implementation cost. Our findings highlight the strengths and weaknesses of each approach, demonstrating context-specific advantages. Additionally, we propose a hybrid model that integrates AI and SD, leveraging the strengths of both methodologies to enhance decision-making in renewable energy pricing. This hybrid model aims to provide a more robust and comprehensive tool for policymakers and stakeholders. The study concludes with recommendations for future research and practical applications in the renewable energy sector.

Keywords Energy pricing policies · Artificial intelligence tools · System dynamics

1 Introduction

The transition to renewable energy sources is critical in addressing the global challenge of climate change and ensuring sustainable development. As renewable energy technologies become more advanced and cost-effective, the need for optimal pricing strategies becomes paramount. Effective pricing mechanisms can incentivize the adoption of renewable energy, balance supply and demand, and ensure economic viability for producers and consumers alike [1]. However, the complexity

M. Hamed (✉) · J. Marx Gómez
Department of VLBA, University of Oldenburg, Oldenburg, Germany
e-mail: mohamad.hamed@uni-oldenburg.de

J. Marx Gómez
e-mail: Jorge.Marx.Gomez@uni-oldenburg.de

J. Marx Gómez et al. (eds.), *Advancement in Embedded and Mobile Systems*, Progress in IS, https://doi.org/10.1007/978-3-031-99219-3_30

of renewable energy markets necessitates sophisticated decision-making support systems (DMSS) to aid policymakers and stakeholders in making informed choices. Decision-making support systems (DMSS) have evolved significantly over the past few decades, providing tools and methodologies to analyze complex systems and enhance decision-making processes. Among the various approaches, Artificial Intelligence (AI) and System Dynamics (SD) have emerged as prominent methodologies in the field of renewable energy pricing [2].

AI tools, including machine learning algorithms and neural networks, offer robust capabilities in handling large datasets, identifying patterns, and making predictions. In contrast, SD models focus on understanding the behavior of complex systems over time through feedback loops and causal relationships [3]. Artificial Intelligence (AI) tools have been increasingly applied in the energy sector, particularly for forecasting, optimization, and decision support. AI's ability to learn from data and improve over time makes it particularly suited for dynamic and uncertain environments such as renewable energy markets [4]. For instance, neural networks have been used to predict energy consumption and generation patterns, enabling more accurate pricing models. Despite these advantages, AI tools often face challenges related to data dependency, interpretability, and the need for substantial computational resources [5].

System Dynamics (SD) offers a different perspective by emphasizing the structural understanding of complex systems. Developed by Jay W. Forrester in the 1960s, SD has been applied to various domains, including energy systems, to simulate the interactions between different components and their evolution over time [6]. SD models are particularly useful for exploring long-term scenarios and policy impacts, providing a comprehensive view of how different factors influence renewable energy pricing. However, SD models can be complex to build and require accurate parameter estimation, which can be a limitation in rapidly changing markets [7]. Given the distinct strengths and weaknesses of AI and SD approaches, a comparative analysis is essential to determine their applicability and effectiveness in supporting decision-making for renewable energy pricing. Previous studies have highlighted the potential of combining these methodologies to create more robust and comprehensive DMSS [8]. This study aims to compare AI tools and SD models based on criteria such as accuracy, adaptability, complexity, transparency, and implementation cost. By evaluating their performance in various renewable energy scenarios, we seek to identify the most effective approach or combination of approaches for optimal pricing. In addition to the comparative analysis, this paper proposes a hybrid model that integrates AI and SD, leveraging the strengths of both methodologies. Such an integrated approach aims to enhance the decision-making process by providing more accurate predictions and a deeper understanding of system dynamics. The proposed hybrid model is expected to offer significant benefits for policymakers and stakeholders, enabling more informed and effective strategies for renewable energy pricing [9]. The remainder of this paper is structured as follows: the literature review provides an overview of DMSS, AI, and SD in renewable energy pricing,the methodology outlines the comparative framework and hybrid model design,the results section presents the findings of the comparative analysis,and the discussion and conclusion highlight the implications and future research directions.

2 Artificial Intelligence (AI) in Decision-Making Support Systems (DMSS)

Artificial Intelligence (AI) has become a cornerstone of modern decision-making support systems (DMSS), offering powerful tools for analyzing vast amounts of data, identifying patterns, and making predictions. In the context of renewable energy pricing, AI's capabilities are particularly advantageous due to the dynamic and complex nature of energy markets. This section reviews the application of AI in DMSS, highlighting its methodologies, benefits, and challenges.

2.1 AI Methodologies in DMSS

AI encompasses a broad range of techniques, including machine learning (ML), neural networks (NN), and reinforcement learning (RL), each contributing uniquely to decision-making processes. Machine learning algorithms are essential for DMSS as they can analyze historical data to forecast future trends. For instance, supervised learning techniques have been used to predict energy consumption and generation patterns, aiding in optimal pricing strategies [4]. Neural networks, particularly deep learning models, have shown significant success in handling nonlinear relationships within energy data, providing more accurate and nuanced predictions [5]. Reinforcement learning, which involves training agents to make decisions by rewarding desirable outcomes, has been applied to optimize energy distribution and pricing dynamically [4].

2.2 Benefits of AI in Renewable Energy Pricing

AI tools offer several benefits in renewable energy pricing, primarily through their ability to process and analyze large and complex datasets. This capability is crucial for accurately forecasting energy supply and demand, considering factors such as weather patterns, consumption behavior, and market trends [14]. AI's predictive accuracy enables more efficient energy management and pricing strategies, reducing the risk of imbalances between supply and demand. Furthermore, AI algorithms can adapt to new data, continuously improving their performance and providing up-to-date insights, which is vital in the rapidly evolving energy sector [10].

2.3 Challenges and Limitations

Despite the advantages, AI applications in DMSS face several challenges. One significant issue is the dependency on large volumes of high-quality data. In many regions, especially in developing countries, the lack of comprehensive and reliable data can hinder the effective implementation of AI-based systems [17]. Moreover, AI models, particularly deep learning networks, often function as "black boxes," making their decision-making processes difficult to interpret. This lack of transparency can be problematic for stakeholders who require clear justifications for pricing decisions [12].

Another challenge is the computational intensity of AI algorithms. Training complex models, especially deep learning networks, requires substantial computational resources, which can be costly and time-consuming. This limitation can restrict the scalability of AI solutions in DMSS, particularly for smaller organizations with limited resources [16]. Additionally, the integration of AI with existing energy systems and regulatory frameworks poses practical challenges, necessitating significant adjustments and collaboration among various stakeholders [13].

2.4 Case Studies and Applications

Several case studies demonstrate the practical applications of AI in renewable energy pricing. For example, Google's DeepMind successfully utilized AI to optimize the operation of wind farms, improving the predictability of wind power generation and enhancing energy market participation [11]. Similarly, a study by Mohandes, Halawani, and Rehman [15] applied machine learning techniques to forecast solar radiation, enabling better pricing strategies for solar energy.

In another notable application, the use of reinforcement learning in the electricity market in Singapore demonstrated how AI could dynamically adjust pricing based on real-time supply and demand conditions, resulting in more efficient energy distribution and reduced operational costs [4]. These examples underscore the potential of AI to revolutionize renewable energy pricing through enhanced predictive capabilities and dynamic optimization.

AI's integration into DMSS represents a significant advancement in renewable energy pricing, offering unparalleled capabilities in data analysis and decision support. While challenges such as data dependency, model transparency, and computational demands persist, ongoing research and technological advancements continue to address these issues. The successful implementation of AI in various case studies highlights its potential to transform energy markets, providing more accurate, efficient, and adaptive pricing strategies. As AI technology evolves, its role in DMSS is expected to expand, further enhancing the sustainability and economic viability of renewable energy systems.

3 System Dynamics (SD) in Decision-Making Support Systems (DMSS)

System Dynamics (SD) is a methodological framework that has been extensively utilized in decision-making support systems (DMSS) to model and analyze complex systems. Originating from the work of Jay W. Forrester in the 1960s, SD employs feedback loops, time delays, and stock-and-flow structures to simulate the behavior of dynamic systems over time [20]. In the context of renewable energy pricing, SD provides valuable insights into the interactions between various components of energy systems, enabling policymakers to devise more effective strategies.

3.1 Fundamentals of System Dynamics

System Dynamics is grounded in the principles of systems thinking, which emphasizes understanding the structure and behavior of entire systems rather than focusing on individual components [6]. This approach involves constructing causal loop diagrams and stock-and-flow models to represent the relationships and feedback mechanisms within a system. By simulating these models over time, SD helps in identifying leverage points, understanding long-term consequences, and exploring different policy scenarios [7].

3.2 Applications of SD in Renewable Energy Pricing

SD has been widely applied to model the dynamics of renewable energy systems and to support decision-making in energy policy and management. For instance, SD models have been used to analyze the impact of different pricing strategies on the adoption of renewable energy technologies. A study by Qudrat-Ullah [22] demonstrated how SD could simulate the effects of feed-in tariffs on the growth of renewable energy capacity, providing insights into the long-term sustainability of such policies.

Another application of SD is in modeling the interactions between renewable energy sources and conventional power generation. Fattahi, Sioshansi, and Denholm [19] developed an SD model to study the integration of renewable energy into the electricity grid. Their model highlighted the challenges of maintaining grid stability and reliability with high penetration of intermittent renewable sources, emphasizing the need for adaptive pricing mechanisms that reflect these dynamics.

3.3 Benefits of System Dynamics in DMSS

One of the primary benefits of SD in DMSS is its ability to capture the complexity and interdependencies of energy systems. By modeling feedback loops and time delays, SD provides a holistic view of how different factors influence renewable energy pricing. This systemic perspective is particularly valuable for understanding the long-term impacts of policy interventions and for designing strategies that promote sustainable energy development [24].

SD also facilitates scenario analysis, allowing decision-makers to explore the potential outcomes of different pricing strategies under various assumptions and uncertainties. For example, an SD model developed by Chung and Park [18] assessed the effects of carbon pricing on renewable energy investment and market dynamics. Their findings underscored the importance of flexible pricing policies that can adapt to changing market conditions and technological advancements.

3.4 Challenges and Limitations

Despite its strengths, SD modeling faces several challenges. Building accurate and reliable SD models requires comprehensive data and a deep understanding of the system being modeled. This can be particularly challenging in the renewable energy sector, where data availability and quality vary significantly across regions [6]. Additionally, the complexity of SD models can make them difficult to communicate to stakeholders who may not be familiar with systems thinking and dynamic simulation techniques [7].

Another limitation of SD is the potential for model oversimplification. While SD aims to capture the essential dynamics of a system, simplifying assumptions are often necessary to make the models tractable. These simplifications can sometimes overlook important details or lead to inaccurate predictions if the underlying assumptions do not hold [9].

To address some of these challenges, researchers have explored the integration of SD with other methodologies, such as agent-based modeling (ABM) and artificial intelligence (AI). For instance, combining SD with ABM allows for a more detailed representation of individual behaviors and interactions within the system, enhancing the overall model's accuracy and robustness [23]. Similarly, integrating AI techniques with SD can improve the model's predictive capabilities and provide more nuanced insights into complex energy systems [8].

System Dynamics offers a powerful framework for modeling and analyzing the complex dynamics of renewable energy systems. Its ability to capture feedback loops, time delays, and systemic interactions makes it a valuable tool in decision-making support systems for renewable energy pricing. However, the challenges of data requirements, model complexity, and communication need to be addressed to maximize its effectiveness. By integrating SD with other methodologies, researchers can enhance its capabilities and provide more comprehensive support for policymakers in the renewable energy sector.

4 Advantages and Disadvantages of AI Tools and System Dynamics Models in the Energy Field

The energy sector's complexity and dynamic nature require sophisticated decision-making support systems (DMSS) to ensure efficient management and pricing strategies. Among the various approaches, Artificial Intelligence (AI) tools and System Dynamics (SD) models stand out for their unique strengths and weaknesses. This section provides a comparative analysis of these two methodologies, focusing on their advantages and disadvantages in the energy field.

4.1 Advantages of AI Tools

AI tools, particularly machine learning and neural networks, offer several significant advantages in the energy sector. One of the primary benefits is their ability to handle vast amounts of data and identify complex patterns. This capability is crucial for forecasting energy consumption and generation, as AI algorithms can process and analyze large datasets to provide accurate predictions [26]. For example, AI has been successfully used to predict solar and wind energy production, enhancing the reliability and efficiency of renewable energy sources [27]. Another advantage of AI tools is their adaptability. AI systems can learn from new data, continuously improving their accuracy and performance. This adaptability is essential in the rapidly changing energy market, where factors such as weather conditions, consumption patterns, and technological advancements can significantly impact energy supply and demand [25]. Additionally, AI can optimize energy distribution and pricing in real-time, responding dynamically to changes in the market [28].

4.2 Disadvantages of AI Tools

Despite their strengths, AI tools have several disadvantages. One of the main challenges is their dependency on large volumes of high-quality data. In many regions, especially in developing countries, the lack of comprehensive and reliable data can hinder the effective implementation of AI-based systems [29]. Moreover, AI models, particularly deep learning networks, often function as "black boxes," making their decision-making processes difficult to interpret. This lack of transparency can be problematic for stakeholders who require clear justifications for pricing decisions [12].

Another significant drawback is the computational intensity of AI algorithms. Training complex models, especially deep learning networks, requires substantial computational resources, which can be costly and time-consuming. This limitation can restrict the scalability of AI solutions in DMSS, particularly for smaller organizations with limited resources [16]. Additionally, integrating AI with existing energy systems and regulatory frameworks poses practical challenges, necessitating significant adjustments and collaboration among various stakeholders [13].

4.3 Advantages of System Dynamics Models

System Dynamics (SD) models offer a different set of advantages in the energy sector. One of the key benefits is their ability to capture the complexity and interdependencies of energy systems through feedback loops and time delays [30]. This holistic approach provides a comprehensive view of how different factors influence energy markets, enabling policymakers to understand long-term consequences and identify leverage points for intervention [21].

SD models are particularly effective in scenario analysis, allowing decision-makers to explore the potential outcomes of various policy interventions under different assumptions and uncertainties [9]. For instance, SD models have been used to assess the impacts of carbon pricing and renewable energy subsidies on market dynamics, providing valuable insights into the long-term sustainability of these policies [18].

4.4 Disadvantages of System Dynamics Models

However, SD models also have their limitations. Constructing accurate and reliable SD models requires a deep understanding of the system being modeled and comprehensive data, which can be challenging to obtain in the energy sector [30]. The complexity of SD models can also make them difficult to communicate to stakeholders who may not be familiar with systems thinking and dynamic simulation techniques [7].

Another limitation is the potential for model oversimplification. While SD aims to capture the essential dynamics of a system, simplifying assumptions are often necessary to make the models tractable. These simplifications can sometimes overlook important details or lead to inaccurate predictions if the underlying assumptions do not hold [9]. Additionally, SD models are generally less effective in handling highly stochastic and non-linear systems compared to AI tools [21].

Thus, both AI tools and System Dynamics models offer unique advantages and face distinct challenges in the energy sector. AI tools excel in handling large datasets, providing accurate forecasts, and adapting to new information, but they require substantial computational resources and high-quality data. In contrast, SD models offer a holistic view of energy systems, excel in scenario analysis, and help understand long-term impacts, but they can be complex to build and communicate. Integrating the strengths of both methodologies could provide a more robust and comprehensive approach to decision-making in the energy field.

5 Theoretical Integration of AI Tools and System Dynamics in DMSS for Renewable Energy Pricing

To leverage the strengths of both Artificial Intelligence (AI) tools and System Dynamics (SD) models in decision-making support systems (DMSS) for renewable energy pricing, an integrated approach can be developed. This hybrid model would combine the predictive capabilities of AI with the holistic, systemic insights provided by SD models. Here, we outline a theoretical framework for this integration, discussing how each component can be effectively utilized and synergized.

The integration begins with comprehensive data collection from various sources, including historical energy prices, consumption patterns, weather data, and policy impacts. This data serves as the foundation for both AI and SD models.

5.1 Conceptual Framework

- **AI-Based Forecasting**

AI tools, particularly machine learning and neural networks, are employed to analyze the collected data and generate short-term and long-term forecasts. These tools can predict variables such as energy demand, renewable energy generation, and market prices with high accuracy [25]. By training on historical data, AI models can adapt to changing patterns and provide updated predictions as new data becomes available [14].

- **System Dynamics Modeling**

Simultaneously, SD models are constructed to represent the dynamic interactions within the energy system. These models incorporate feedback loops, delays, and stock-and-flow structures to simulate the long-term impacts of various pricing strategies and policy interventions [30]. The SD models can include components such as energy production, consumption, storage, and regulatory policies, capturing the interdependencies and systemic behaviors.

5.2 Integrated Decision-Making Support System

- **Hybrid Model Development**

The next step involves integrating the AI-generated forecasts into the SD model. AI outputs, such as predicted energy demand and generation, serve as input variables for the SD simulations. This integration allows the SD model to dynamically adjust its parameters based on the latest forecasts, enhancing its accuracy and relevance [28].

- **Scenario Analysis and Optimization**

With the hybrid model, decision-makers can conduct scenario analysis and optimization. The SD component simulates the long-term effects of different pricing strategies and policy interventions, while the AI component continuously updates the model with new data and predictions. This dual approach enables a more comprehensive evaluation of potential outcomes, considering both immediate and future impacts [18].

- **Feedback Mechanism**

A feedback mechanism is established wherein the results of SD simulations are analyzed to identify key leverage points and optimal strategies. These insights are then fed back into the AI models, refining their training and improving their predictive accuracy. This iterative process ensures that the DMSS remains adaptive and responsive to new information and changing conditions [21].

5.3 Implementation and Benefits

Policymakers can use the integrated DMSS to formulate and adjust renewable energy pricing policies based on robust, data-driven insights. The hybrid model provides a detailed understanding of how different policies will impact the energy market in both the short and long term, facilitating informed decision-making [13]. The hybrid approach enhances the adaptability and resilience of the energy system. As new data is continuously incorporated into the AI models, and the SD simulations adjust accordingly, the DMSS can respond swiftly to changes in market conditions, technological advancements, and policy shifts [28].

Integrating AI tools and System Dynamics models in DMSS for renewable energy pricing offers a powerful theoretical framework for enhancing decision-making processes. This hybrid model leverages the strengths of both methodologies, providing accurate predictions and deep systemic insights. As the energy market evolves, this integrated approach can help policymakers and stakeholders devise more effective, sustainable pricing strategies.

6 Conclusion

Integrating Artificial Intelligence (AI) tools and System Dynamics (SD) models in Decision-Making Support Systems (DMSS) offers a comprehensive approach to optimizing renewable energy pricing. AI tools provide precise, real-time forecasts and adapt to new data, while SD models offer a holistic view of energy systems, capturing complex interactions and long-term dynamics. However, AI faces challenges with data quality and interpretability, and SD models can be complex to build and communicate.

The hybrid model leverages the strengths of both methodologies: AI provides accurate predictions, and SD models simulate long-term impacts. This integration enhances the adaptability and resilience of decision-making processes, enabling continuous adjustments based on new information and changing conditions.

This approach benefits policymakers by offering a more accurate and comprehensive understanding of market dynamics, supporting effective pricing strategies, and anticipating the long-term consequences of policy decisions. Future research should focus on refining these hybrid models and exploring new applications in different energy contexts.

In summary, combining AI tools and SD models in DMSS provides a powerful framework for developing informed and sustainable renewable energy pricing strategies. This integrated approach is essential for addressing the complex challenges and opportunities in the transition to sustainable energy systems.

References

1. International Renewable Energy Agency. (2020). Renewable Energy Statistics 2020.
2. Simonovic, S. P. (2015). Systems Approach to Management of Disasters: Methods and Applications. John Wiley & Sons.
3. Forrester, J. W. (2007). Industrial Dynamics. Martino Fine Books.
4. Zhang, C. (2019). Artificial Intelligence in Energy and Renewable Energy Systems. Springer.
5. Goodfellow, I., Bengio, Y., & Courville, A. (2016). Deep Learning. MIT Press.
6. Sterman, J. D. (2000). Business Dynamics: Systems Thinking and Modeling for a Complex World. McGraw-Hill.
7. Meadows, D. H. (2008). Thinking in Systems: A Primer. Chelsea Green Publishing.
8. Pruyt, E., & Kwakkel, J. H. (2014). Radicalization under Deep Uncertainty: A Multi-Model Exploration of Activism, Extremism, and Terrorism. System Dynamics Review, 30(1–2), 1–28.
9. Ford, A. (2010). Modeling the Environment: An Introduction to System Dynamics Modeling of Environmental Systems. Island Press.
10. Chen, C., et al. (2019). "Machine Learning in Energy Systems: A Review." IEEE Transactions on Systems, Man, and Cybernetics: Systems, 49(2), 341–352.
11. DeepMind. (2019). "DeepMind AI Reduces Energy Use for Cooling Google Data Centers." DeepMind Blog.
12. Doshi-Velez, F., & Kim, B. (2017). "Towards a Rigorous Science of Interpretable Machine Learning." arXiv preprint arXiv:1702.08608.
13. Huang, S., et al. (2020). "AI in Energy Management: Challenges and Future Directions." Energy Reports, 6, 555–567.

14. Li, H., et al. (2020). "Renewable Energy Forecasting Using Deep Learning Approaches: A Review." Renewable and Sustainable Energy Reviews, 123, 109722.
15. Mohandes, M., Halawani, T. O., & Rehman, S. (2018). "Estimation of Global Solar Radiation Using Artificial Neural Networks." Renewable Energy, 14(1–4), 179–184.
16. Strubell, E., Ganesh, A., & McCallum, A. (2019). "Energy and Policy Considerations for Deep Learning in NLP." Proceedings of the 57th Annual Meeting of the Association for Computational Linguistics, 3645–3650.
17. Sun, Q., et al. (2019). "Big Data and Artificial Intelligence in the Energy Sector." Energy AI, 1, 100001.
18. Chung, J., & Park, J. (2015). "Dynamic Modeling of Renewable Energy Policies for Sustainable Development." Energy Policy, 87, 76–83.
19. Fattahi, A., Sioshansi, R., & Denholm, P. (2020). "System Dynamics Approach to Modeling the Impacts of Renewable Energy Integration on Grid Stability." Energy, 190, 116350.
20. Forrester, J. W. (1961). Industrial Dynamics. MIT Press.
21. Pruyt, E., & Kwakkel, J. H. (2021). "Radicalization under Deep Uncertainty: A Multi-Model Exploration of Activism, Extremism, and Terrorism." System Dynamics Review, 30(1–2), 1–28.
22. Qudrat-Ullah, H. (2013). "Feedback Dynamics of Energy Policy Instruments." Energy Policy, 57, 36–44.
23. Scholl, H. J. (2001). "Agent-Based and System Dynamics Modeling: A Call for Cross Study and Joint Research." Proceedings of the 34th Annual Hawaii International Conference on System Sciences.
24. Sterman, J. D. (2018). "System Dynamics at Sixty: The Path Forward." System Dynamics Review, 34(1–2), 5–47.
25. Ahmad, T., Zhang, D., Huang, C., Zhang, H., Dai, N., Song, J., & Chen, H. (2021). "Artificial Intelligence in Sustainable Energy Industry: Status Quo, Challenges and Opportunities." Journal of Cleaner Production, 293, 126123.
26. Alamaniotis, M., Tsoukalas, L. H., & Rong, L. (2020). "A Machine Learning Framework for Optimal Energy Consumption Management in Industrial Facilities." Energy, 208, 118377.
27. Kalogirou, S. A. (2021). "Artificial Neural Networks in Renewable Energy Systems Applications: A Review." Renewable and Sustainable Energy Reviews, 92, 86–97.
28. Liu, Y., et al. (2021). "AI-Based Pricing Strategy for Electricity Markets with Renewable Energy." Applied Energy, 281, 115955.
29. Sharma, A., et al. (2021). "Big Data and Artificial Intelligence in the Energy Sector: A Review." Energy AI, 1, 100001.
30. Sterman, J. D. (2020). Business Dynamics: Systems Thinking and Modeling for a Complex World. McGraw-Hill.

Exploring the Opportunities, Risks, and Constraints of the use of GenAI Tools in Higher Learning Institutions: A Mixed-Methods Study of Rwandan University Students

Gatera Antoine, Kambombo Mtonga, Kuradusenge Martin, Turinimana Jean Bosco, and Nsengiyumva Jean Bosco

Abstract With the introduction of Generative AI (GenAI) tools such as ChatGPT, the educational environment has completely changed and university students now have tremendous access to individualized learning resources. This work aimed to investigate the opportunities, risks, and constraints that university students can encounter due to the use of resources produced by GenAI. In particular, the study determined which GenAI tools students use the most, evaluated their effects on the learning process and critical thinking, and writing skills. This study used a mixed-methods approach, combining quantitative surveys and qualitative interviews to obtain in-depth information from a wide range of students in Rwandan universities. In addition to demonstrating the advantages and disadvantages of using GenAI tools in higher education institutions, the findings will provide educators, and students practical suggestions for enhancing the safe and efficient use of these technologies in the teaching and learning process. As results, it was revealed that 80% of respondents were aware of the GenAI tools while only 20% not aware. The most used was ChatGPT where, 65% of the respondents said they mostly use it. Gen AI tools are mainly used for research purpose 51% and have helped them to improve their academic performance.

Keywords GenAI · AI for learning · Critical thinking · Higher learning institutions

G. Antoine (✉) · K. Martin
Department of Information Systems, College of Science and Technology, University of Rwanda, Kigali, Rwanda
e-mail: gm.gateraz@gmail.com

K. Mtonga
Department of Mathematical Sciences, Malawi University of Business and Applied Sciences, Blantyre, Malawi

T. J. Bosco · N. J. Bosco
Department of Education in Sciences, University of Technology and Arts of Byumba (UTAB), Byumba, Rwanda

J. Marx Gómez et al. (eds.), *Advancement in Embedded and Mobile Systems*, Progress in IS, https://doi.org/10.1007/978-3-031-99219-3_31

1 Introduction

Higher education is increasingly requiring digital change. The post-COVID-19 era brought about numerous innovations, including the adoption of AI technology and online meeting platforms. One of the newest areas of educational technology that is currently developing is artificial intelligence (AI) [1]. Applications of AI in education are becoming more common and have attracted much interest in recent years. Among the noteworthy advancements in educational technology are AI and adaptive learning systems. Modern higher education must use technology to enhance student learning and prepare them for the challenges of the 21st century [12]. Technology significantly affects student engagement, learning outcomes, and skill development, according to the recent study [2]. The importance of technology in the field of education has been widely reported [3]. Through the integration of these technologies, the educational environment is modernized and students are equipped with the tools necessary to thrive in this digital age. Furthermore, in response to the rapid evolution of educational technology, educators and learners alike must constantly innovate and adapt. Therefore, to foster a productive and diverse learning environment, it is imperative to understand the role and implications of these technologies. An over-reliance on AI could result in the outsourcing of cognitive work, transforming individuals from engaged processors of information into passive consumers. This might decrease the mental effort required for in-depth, critical thinking, thereby weakening analytical skills.

The Sustainable Development Goals (SDGs) offer exceptional opportunities to transform conventional teaching approaches and promote student participation and critical thinking, especially when it comes to the ethical issues underlying generative AI [5]. The SDGs support universal access to high-quality education and lifetime learning, which is consistent with AI's ability to enhance and personalize educational opportunities. Fairness and transparency in AI algorithms are two ethical factors that must be taken into account for their appropriate use in education. Teachers may use AI to build more inclusive and fair learning environments by addressing these ethical concerns. Thus, instructional strategies and academic results can be significantly improved by the thoughtful integration of AI technologies [6].

The connection between education and AI falls within four categories, namely, learning with AI, using AI to learn about leaning, Learning about AI and Preparing for AI [18]. With regard to learning with AI, this involves using AI technologies (or tools) in the teaching and learning process, and can take the following forms:

- Utilizing AI to provide direct learning support through the use of chatbots, tutoring systems, exploratory learning environments, automatic writing evaluation, and AI solutions for disabled students;
- The application of AI to support administrative systems (including scheduling, recruits, and learning management);
- With the exception of the sophisticated selection of educational resources, i.e. AI can help teachers directly.

Recent advancements in AI include Chat Generative Pre-trained Transformer (ChatGPT), developed by OpenAI that can produce text in response to user prompts. ChatGPT in higher education is mainly used in few areas, such as creating tasks, assisting with essay writing, and promoting critical reflection. Notwithstanding the benefits, there are concerns regarding students' of AI which include, plagiarism, ethics and academic integrity [11, 15, 16]. Ajlouni et al. [19] reports a positive attitude towards the use of ChatGPT as an educational tool by students at the University of Jordan. However, study respondents raised concerns about the accuracy of information provided by the tool. Other studies have highlighted factors that influence adoption and use of CHatGPT by students, including, trust, perceived enjoyment, utility and informativeness [20]. The authors in highlighted the need for institutions of high learning to come-up with strategies to guide responsible and ethical use of GenAI tools [21]. It is thus imperative that extensive research is done to ensure that such strategies and policies are well-informed [9]. However, from the authors literature conducted, there are no significant research works in literature that have focused on GenAI in Rwandan universities and developing countries or either reinforcing the need for such research.

Critical thinking and teamwork are two essential abilities that students in higher education are expected to develop. In this attempt, technology is essential because it provides tools that improve problem-solving, teamwork, and communication. Students may easily collaborate regardless of where they are physically located thanks to collaborative tools like online forums, and shared papers [17]. By offering to access a variety of viewpoints, critically evaluate materials, and participate in thought-provoking conversations, these resources also aid in the development of critical thinking skills [6]. The need for these academic and socio-emotional abilities along with basic digital literacy for national development can not be overemphasized. Fundamental skills like writing and reasoning are being severely affected globally by generative artificial intelligence, or GenAI. These abilities are critical for communication, creativity, and problem-solving. However, given the particular regional context of Rwanda's higher education system, it is important to thoughtfully evaluate how GenAI may affect these competencies [10]. The higher education sector in Rwanda has risen significantly in recent years, with an increasing emphasis on entrepreneurship, STEM education, and digital transformation. However, there are special advantages and disadvantages associated with integrating the latest innovations like GenAI. This work presents the findings of a study to explore the opportunities, risks, and constraints of GenAI Tools use among students in higher learning institutions of Rwanda. The research questions that led the study were as follows:

1. What are the GenAI tools mostly used by students in higher learning institutions of Rwanda?
2. What has been the impact of GenAI tools on students' learning process?
3. What benefits and risks do students associate GenAI tools use with?
4. To what extent has the use of GenAI tools influenced student's critical thinking and writing skills?

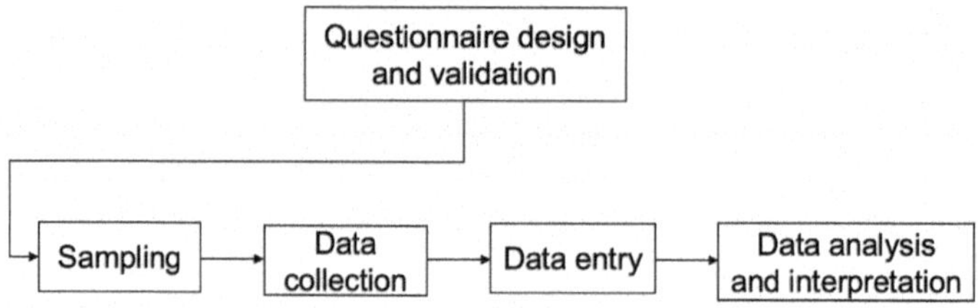

Fig. 1 Data collection process

2 Materials and Methodology

To facilitate this study, a questionnaire was developed using Microsoft forms. The tool was validated and necessary adjustments done based on pre-test feedback. The target sample was purposefully selected, which allows for the selection of participants based on specific criteria relevant to the research objectives [15, 16]. Purposeful sampling involves selecting participants who possess characteristics or experiences that are deemed essential for addressing the research questions [17]. Respondents were given enough time to comprehend the information before giving their consent. The study was conducted in strict confidentiality and privacy. Figure 1 summarizes the overall study methodology.

2.1 Survey Instrument

The survey was conducted using a questionnaire that had 21 general questions to capture various aspects on how GenAI tools have changed the landscape of studying in Rwandas' institutions of high learning. The questionnaire was administered both electronic and in hard copy format. The initial respondents were shared the link to the questionnaire and were requested to pass on the link to their peers. The questionnaire contained an introduction and detailed information regarding the study. The data collection tool was not based on any specific previous work, but basic reference of mandatory ingredients of any survey questionnaire is adopted to maintain survey standards. In general, the questions were organized along three main themes:

- **Awareness of GenAI tools**: We aimed to gain knowledge from respondents how they are familiar with the selected Five GenAI tools, seeing which do they use mostly, their need in learning process and how frequently do the respondents rely on the GenAI Tools.
- **Impact of GenAI tools on learning**: To get informations from respondents on their perceptions on the influence of GenAI tools on learning, how these technologies affect learning effectiveness and engagement.
- **Impact of GenAI tools on critical thinking and writing skills**: When we questioned respondents about the impact of GenAI tools on critical thinking and writing

capabilities, we wanted to know how these tools influence their critical thinking and writing competencies. We wanted to know how they improved the quality of written work, enhanced analytical abilities, and shapening them in their learning process. Moreover, we aimed to assess their reliance on these GenAI tools.
- **Associated risks and constraints**: Exploring risks and limitations associated to the GenAI use in research, accademic activities is critical for getting a comprehensive knowledge of GenAI tools' impact on education, which will eventually contribute to more effective and responsible usage of these technologies in the learning process.

2.2 *Participants*

The population consisted of the students pursuing university-level education at both private and public universities in Rwanda. These include University of Technology and Arts of Byumba (UTAB) and the University of Rwanda, College of Sciences and Technology. The justification for selecting university-level students for the current study is that they are technologically sophisticated and have successfully used AI technologies, as evidenced by earlier studies.

2.3 *Data Analysis*

The data was analysed in Microsoft Excel and IBM SPSS 23. Microsoft Excel was used for the analysis of structured data, whilst IBM SPSS was used for the analysis of unstructured data, that is multiple response questionnaire items and also those with open-ended questions. With regard to multiple response sets questions, the multiple column scheme was adopted. Specifically, a "1" was assigned to a particular variable if the option was selected by the respondent; and the data value was left blank if the option is not selected.

3 Results and Discussion

The analysis reported herein focused on the assessment of the various ways in which GenAI tools have impacted the teaching and learning landscape in Rwandas' institutions of higher learning. The results reported here are not exhaustive of the analyzed data.

Fig. 2 Respondents awareness of GenAI tools

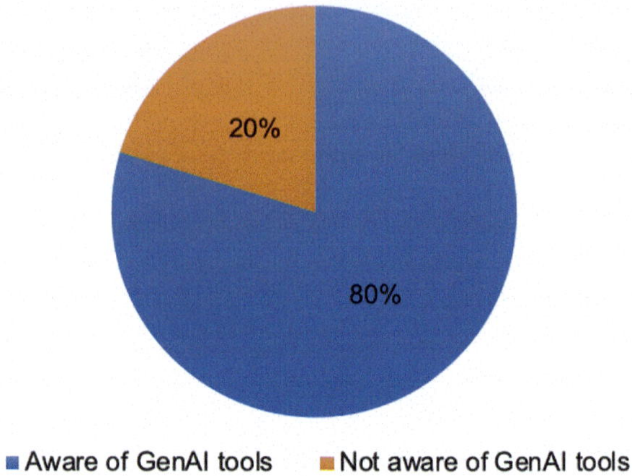

3.1 Demography of Respondents and Awareness of GenAI Tools

The distribution of the students by their year of study was Year 1 (11%), Year 2 (46%), Year 3 (22%) and Year 4 (21%). Majority (46%) of the respondents are in their second year of study. Furthermore, based on the responses, 80% of the respondents indicated that they are aware of the GenAI tools and that they have used them for different purposes related to their studies. Figure 2 shows the level of awareness of the respondents.

3.2 Popularity of GenAI Tools and Frequency of use Among University Students

As shown in Fig. 3, ChatGPT is the popular GenAI tool among university students in Rwanda, and 65% of the respondents indicated that they have used the tool. The popularity of ChatGTP can be explained by its ease of use, positive attitude towards technology, social influence, perceived usefulness, and its efficiency in the timely response to user requests [22].

Regarding the usage of these GenAI tools, 201 of the respondents, representing 65% of the total respondents, indicated that they use GenAI tools only sometimes Fig. 4.

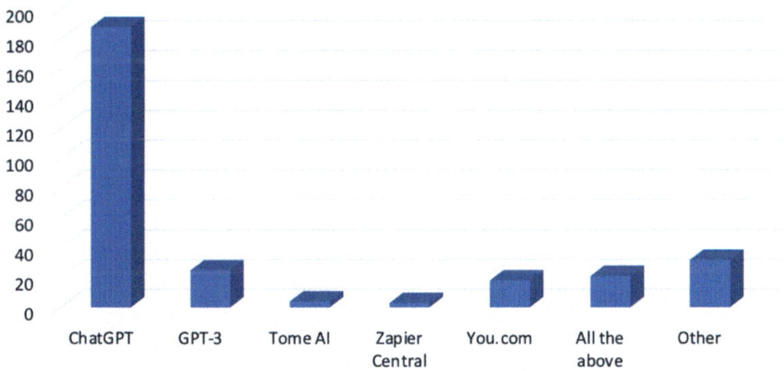

Fig. 3 Pupularity of GenAI tools among respondents

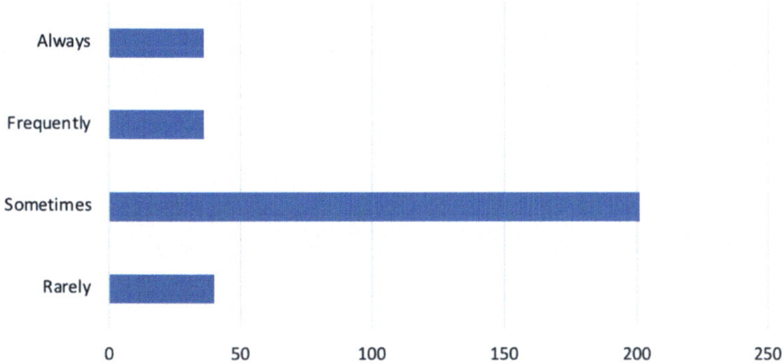

Fig. 4 Usage of GenAI tools among respondents

3.3 Purpose of Use and Level of Reliance on GenAI Tools

Research is the common purpose for which the respondent uses GenAI tools. As can be seen in Fig. 5, 237 (ie, 51%) of the respondents indicated that they use GenAI tools for research purposes. However, as seen in Fig. 6, the frequency of use of GenAI tools is moderate among the majority of the respondents.

3.4 Perception of the Impact of GenAI Tools

On whether GenAI tools have improved the academic performance of the respondents, most (68%) of the respondents answered in the affirmative. This is illustrated in Fig. 7. Improvement in understanding of ones subject area was the most cited aspect in which GenAI tools have proven helpful to the respondents. This is illustrated in Fig. 8.

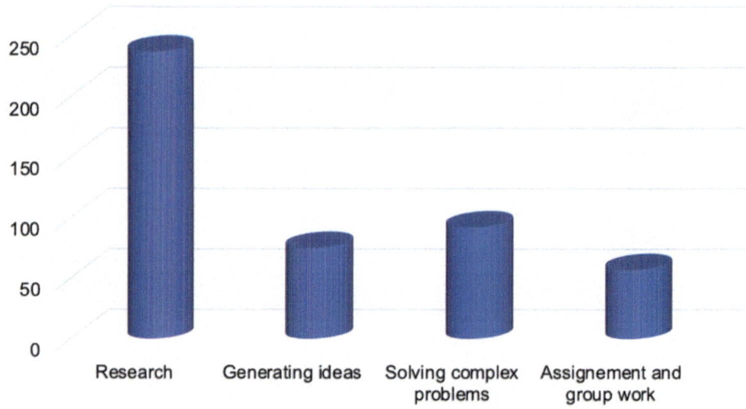

Fig. 5 Purpose for which GenAI tools are used by respondents

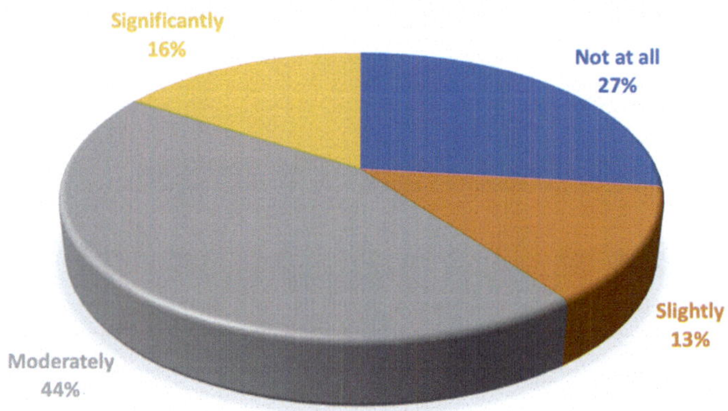

Fig. 6 Frequency that respondents use GenAI tool for purpose in Fig. 5

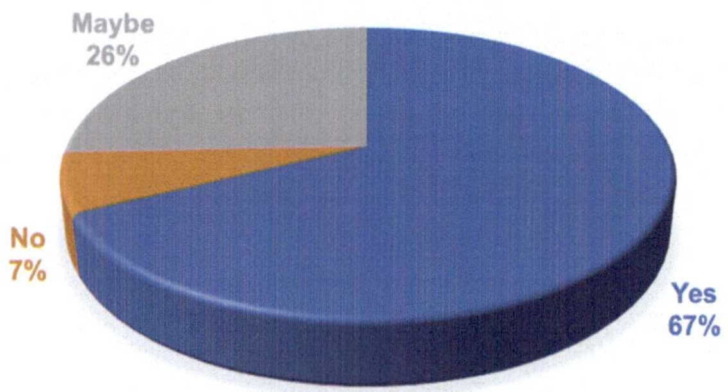

Fig. 7 How GenAI tools impact academic performance

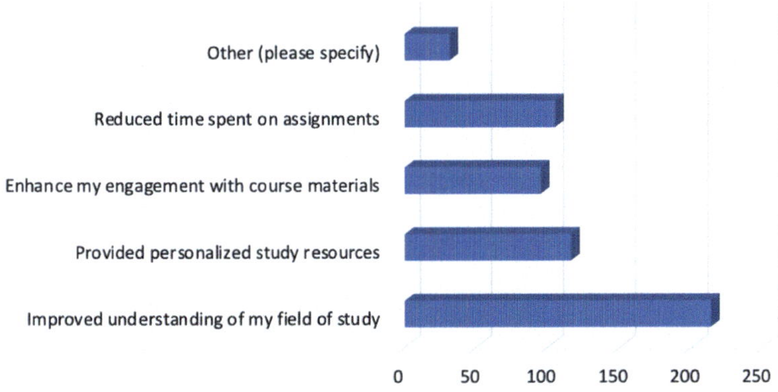

Fig. 8 Specific aspect of academics impacted by GenAI tools

3.5 Awareness of Risks Associated with Using GenAI Tools

The study participants were asked how they felt that GenAI tools impacted their writing skills and critical thinking. Most of the respondents expressed concern about the impact of the use of GenAI tools on their originality in writing.

4 Conclusion

Generative AI (GenAI) systems such as ChatGPT will transform the educational scene by enabling university students access to individualized learning resources. This study used a mixed-methods approach to investigate the opportunities, hazards, and limits related with GenAI use, gathering data from students at two Rwandan institutions. The statistics show that 80% of respondents are familiar with GenAI tools. ChatGPT is the most popular tool, with 65% of students using it primarily for research. GenAI tools have greatly enhanced students' academic performance, particularly in research and individualized learning. However, the study found problems and hazards. Long-term reliance on AI tools may influence the development of critical thinking and writing abilities, as well as increasing reliance on technology, the risk of academic dishonesty including plagialism. Both students and lecturers underlined the importance of using GenAI tools when ethically used. Educators and students can appropriately use GenAI tools to improve the educational experience by appreciating both the benefits and the limitations.

Conflicts of Interest The authors declare no conflict of interest.

Availability of data The data supporting this article will be made available by the authors based on request.

Funding This research received no external funding.

Acknowledgements We are grateful to the administrators of both UR CST, UTAB and all respondents from both the universities involved for their support during interviews and in distributing the questionnaires and collecting the data for this study.

References

1. Zawacki-Richter, O., Marín, V.I., Bond, M. et al. Systematic review of research on artificial intelligence applications in higher education – where are the educators?. Int J Educ Technol High Educ 16, 39 (2019).
2. Schindler, L. A., Burkholder, G. J., Morad, O. A., & Marsh, C. (2017). Computer-based technology and student engagement: a critical review of the literature. International journal of educational technology in higher education, 14, 1–28.
3. Bond, M., Buntins, K., Bedenlier, S., Zawacki-Richter, O., & Kerres, M. (2020). Mapping research in student engagement and educational technology in higher education: A systematic evidence map. International journal of educational technology in higher education, 17, 1–30.
4. Weng, J. C. (2023). Putting Intellectual Robots to Work: Implementing Generative AI Tools in Project Management. NYU SPS Applied Analytics Laboratory.
5. United Nations (UN) Sustainable Development Goals (SDGs) and Disability, https://social.desa.un.org/issues/disability/sustainable-development-goals-sdgs-and-disability, last accessed 2025/01/21
6. Baidoo-Anu, D., Asamoah, D., Amoako, I., & Mahama, I. (2024). Exploring student perspectives on generative artificial intelligence in higher education learning. Discover Education, 3(1), 98.
7. Fyfe, P. (2023). How to cheat on your final paper: Assigning AI for student writing. AI & SOCIETY, 38(4), 1395–1405.
8. García-Ramírez, Y., Campoverde, P., Díaz, F., Ortega, J.,& Vásquez, J. (2024). Assessing Ethical Implications of ChatGPT in Higher Education: A Focus on Students. In International Congress on Information and Communication Technology (pp. 183–199). Singapore: Springer Nature Singapore.
9. An, Y., Yu, J. H., & James, S. (2025). Investigating the higher education institutions' guidelines and policies regarding the use of generative AI in teaching, learning, research, and administration. International Journal of Educational Technology in Higher Education, 22(1), 10.
10. Barrett, A., & Pack, A. (2023). Not quite eye to AI: Student and teacher perspectives on the use of generative artificial intelligence in the writing process. International Journal of Educational Technology in Higher Education, 20(1), 59.
11. Ventayen, R. J. M. (2023). ChatGPT by OpenAI: Students' viewpoint on cheating using artificial intelligence-based application. Available at SSRN 4361548.
12. Yusuf, A., Pervin, N., & Román-González, M. (2024). Generative AI and the future of higher education: a threat to academic integrity or reformation? Evidence from multicultural perspectives. International Journal of Educational Technology in Higher Education, 21(1), 21.
13. Lee, H. Y., Chen, P. H., Wang, W. S., Huang, Y. M., & Wu, T. T. (2024). Empowering ChatGPT with guidance mechanism in blended learning: effect of self-regulated learning, higher-order thinking skills, and knowledge construction. International Journal of Educational Technology in Higher Education, 21(1), 16.
14. Maheshwari, G. (2023). Factors influencing students' intention to adopt and use ChatGPT in higher education: A study in the Vietnamese context. Education and Information Technologies, 1–29.
15. Baidoo-Anu, D., Asamoah, D., Amoako, I., & Mahama, I. (2024). Exploring student perspectives on generative artificial intelligence in higher education learning. Discover Education, 3(1), 98.

16. Shamsuddinova, S., Heryani, P., & Naval, M. A. (2024). Evolution to revolution: Critical exploration of educators' perceptions of the impact of Artificial Intelligence (AI) on the teaching and learning process in the GCC region. International Journal of Educational Research, 125, 102326.
17. Douglas, H. (2022). Sampling techniques for qualitative research. In Principles of social research methodology (pp. 415–426). Singapore: Springer Nature Singapore.
18. Holmes W., Bialik M., and Fadel C. (2019), Artificial intelligence in education: promises and implications for teaching and learning, Center for Curriculum Redesign, available at https://drive.google.com/file/d/1lmzlbhKvYyRB6J0USCndqXitmVgsfTbI/view, accessed 23 February 2025
19. Ajlouni AO, Wahba FA-A, Almahaireh AS. Students' attitudes towards using ChatGPT as a learning tool: the case of the University of Jordan. Int J Interact Mobile Technol. 2023;17(18):99–117. https://doi.org/10.3991/ijim.v17i18.41753
20. Strzelecki, A. To use or not to use ChatGPT in higher education? A study of students' acceptance and use of technology, Interactive Learning Environments, vol. 0, n.o 0, pp. 1–14, may 2023, https://doi.org/10.1080/10494820.2023.2209881
21. Rahman MS, Sabbir MM, Zhang DJ, Moral IH, Hossain GMS. Examining students' intention to use ChatGPT: Does trust matter?. Australas J Educ Technol. 2023; 39 (6). https://doi.org/10.14742/ajet.8956
22. Abdaljaleel, M., Barakat, M., Alsanafi, M. et al. A multinational study on the factors influencing university students' attitudes and usage of ChatGPT. Sci Rep 14, 1983 (2024). https://doi.org/10.1038/s41598-024-52549-8

Smart Content Creation for Personalized Learning Environments Using AI

Kavesh Jugessur and Roopesh Kevin Sungkur

Abstract Every learner has a unique learning style and learning requirements. This represents an important concept in adapting e-learning content to meet the specific needs of each and every learner. Due to the rise of technology, personalization refers to all elements of customizing a system's interactions and information content with its users. The major emphasis of this research is on personalization, which is when a system develops tailor-made services about a person's objectives, interests, and preferences, tailors' interaction and material, and provides the most appropriate user experience. Adaptive educational systems can make use of a variety of AI approaches. In this research, a model using AI for personalization of learning content is proposed. This system generates exercises based on their lecture notes and provides their score for each exercise. A pre-trained dataset, SQuAD (Stanford Question Answering Dataset), is used to train the model. T5, an encoder-decoder model that has already been trained on a variety of tasks that are both supervised and unsupervised, and are each translated into a text-to-text format. This was then evaluated using ROUGE Metrics. This research proposes a novel approach that helps the learners consolidate their learning materials through a personalized learning pathway.

Keywords Personalization · Smart content generation · T5 · ROUGE metrics · SQuAD

1 Introduction

COVID-19 has driven educational institutions, especially universities, to move swiftly to distance and online learning. The pandemic has forced all educational institutions around the globe to shut down and to shift toward online learning for

K. Jugessur (✉) · R. K. Sungkur
Department of Software and Information Systems, Faculty of Information, Communication and Digital Technologies, University of Mauritius, Reduit, Mauritius
e-mail: kavesh.jugessur@umail.uom.ac.mu

R. K. Sungkur
e-mail: r.sungkur@uom.ac.mu

J. Marx Gómez et al. (eds.), *Advancement in Embedded and Mobile Systems*, Progress in IS, https://doi.org/10.1007/978-3-031-99219-3_32

the continuity of education. During the crisis, different learning strategies such as web-based learning systems and mobile applications have been used. E-learning technologies proved to be critical during this epidemic. E-learning systems may be used by learning providers to plan, organize, carry out, and keep track of the teaching and learning process [1, 8]. It also intends to assist instructors, institutions, and universities in facilitating student learning during university and school closures. Furthermore, the majority of these systems are free, which may aid in ensuring continual learning throughout the Coronavirus pandemic [1]. Blackboard, for example, has some wonderful features that might be useful during this coronavirus outbreak. Using this system at this point in time may be more realistic. For example, learners may be messaging or participating in a learning activity with instructors on a laptop or mobile device from home using an e-learning system. Furthermore, since mobile devices may connect to mobile networks or local wireless networks, students can readily acquire instructional information into them [1]. However, conventional e-learning as such has an inherent limitation in the sense that it does not take into consideration the prior knowledge of the learner, the pace of learning of the learner, and other intrinsic and extrinsic factors specific to the learner. The one-size-fits-all approach to conventional e-learning is its major limitation. At times, due to this one-size-fits-all approach, learners feel totally disconnected from the learning process. Personalization of learning can be one approach that makes the learning process more engaging, motivating, and effective [13].

2 Literature Review

2.1 Transformation of e-Learning into Smart Learning

With the advance of mobile, networked, and personal technology, mobile learning has emerged as a significant TEL (Technology-Enhance Learning) model (Zhu, 2015; [5]. In contrast to the static conventional educational forms, mobile learning promotes the usage of mobile technologies and concentrates on the learner's mobility. Furthermore, the assistance of ubiquitous technology has resulted in additional developments that are shifting learning styles away from mobile learning and toward ubiquitous learning, which stresses that learning may take place at any time and in any location, regardless of time, location, or environment (Zhu, 2015, [4]. Many studies have recently begun to emphasize the significance and need for genuine activities in which students engage in real-world challenges [3]. It is critical to develop learning that combines both real and virtual learning settings in order to place students in genuine learning situations. Seamless learning, which overlaps with certain parts of mobile learning and ubiquitous learning, is defined as a one-to-one TEL model in which learners may learn across time and places, and they can transfer learning from one situation to another, easily integrating formal and informal learning, individual and social learning through the smart personal device (Zhu, 2015).

Other intelligent technologies, like cloud computing, big data, learning analytics, Internet-of-things (IoT), wearable technology, and so on, also contribute to the rise of smart education. Cloud computing, learning analytics, and big data, which concentrate on how learning data may be acquired, evaluated, and directed toward enhancing learning and teaching, all help to advance customized and adaptive learning. Along with adaptive learning technologies, the learning platform responds to individual learner data and adapts instructional resources accordingly based on cloud computing and learning analytics, and it can leverage aggregated data along with all mass learners for insights into curriculum design and adaptation based on big data. Furthermore, IoT and wearable technologies aid in the creation of contextual and seamless learning. The Internet of Things can link people, things, and gadgets. Learners who use smart devices might benefit from a variety of connected data that has been pushed to them from their surroundings. Wearable technology may include location data, fitness logs, social media activity, and visual reality technologies in learning. as a one-to-one TEL paradigm in which learners may learn across time and space, and they can easily transfer learning from one situation to another, spanning formal and informal learning, individual and social learning through the smart personal device (Zhu, 2015).

2.2 *Smart Learning Environments*

These environments are often effective, efficient, and engaging [15]. Learners are always seen as the center of the smart learning environment. The goal is to provide customized, self-directed services that allow students to study at their own pace while attending lectures and obtain individualized learning information based on their individual differences [14, 9]. [7] claims that this environment's physical surroundings are enhanced by digital, context-aware, and flexible technology to promote better and more rapid learning. It is defined that possible smart learning environment requirements as being context-aware, capable of providing immediate and adaptable help to learners, and capable of adapting the learner interfaces and topic material. The correct learning assistance, recommendations, or supportive tools are given to students in the right form, at the right time, and in the right location in a smart learning environment, which also enables them to access resources and engage with learning systems from any location and at any time.

Utilizing smart gadgets allows for learning to happen at any time and any location. Context awareness is a crucial component of intelligent learning environments that may assist in giving students the right learning services. [6] created a cloud-based smart learning environment. It collects and analyses learners' behavior to give context-awareness assistance for pushing smart learning information to them. It seeks to give learners with individualized and proper customized learning services. Smart learning environments are a high-level digital environment, which detects learner characteristics, offers adaptive learning materials and user-friendly interactive tools, automatically records learning processes, and analyzes learning results. Its purpose is to help learners learn in a simple, engaging, and effective way.

2.3 AI in Education

AI can help teachers by automating tedious educational duties. For instance, making several copies of the same test, exam grading, giving students feedback, or examining each student's or the class' performance individually. This allows more time for instructors to work on more difficult pedagogical duties like group projects or critical discussions in class. Depending on their earlier performances and particular requirements, students might benefit from a more tailored learning trajectory or pathway [12]. AI can also help instructors and students communicate better. This enables them to get immediate feedback on their tasks and activities. Smart feedback may help instructors and students by grading essays and providing feedback on writing, as well as by evaluating both. Authorship verification is another component of intelligent feedback. Here, the program checks essays and/or compositions for plagiarism to support academic integrity.

2.4 Natural Language Processing (NLP)

The mechanism through which computers engage with human language is how they were intended to process natural languages. Natural Language Processing uses machine learning to reliably extract meaning from human languages [11]. In NLP, a computer records a human conversation's voice. After an audio-to-text interaction, the text is analyzed, and the data is transformed into audio. The system then responds to people using the audio. These applications are used in call center, word processors like Microsoft Word to evaluate the quality of grammar in text and language translation apps like Google Translate. However, speaking human languages makes natural language processing difficult since the rules needed to transfer information via natural language are complex for computers to understand. As a result, NLP uses algorithms to detect and derive the rules of natural languages, enabling the conversion of unstructured information from human languages into a machine-readable format [2].

2.5 How Can NLP Help in Content Generation?

Text Summarization

Automatic summarizing under NLP enables the reduction of large amounts of unstructured material, such as dissertations and academic papers, to their basic components and the creation of a short new version that provides just the most important information. This NLP technique is used to summarize a certain body of work and is referred to as extraction-based summarizing.

Keyword extraction from a document

An automated process called keyword extraction pulls out the most significant words or phrases from a text. It is a text analysis technique that automatically extracts a page's most significant words and phrases. It aids in the identification of important topics being covered and the summarizing of the text's content.

2.6 Neural Network

Deep learning techniques are based on neural networks, sometimes referred to as the artificial neural networks (ANNs), which are a subset of machine learning. Their structure and nomenclature are modeled after the human brain, mirroring the communication between organic neurons. The network consists of node layers where the latter consists of input layers, hidden layers (one or more), and output layer. Each node, or artificial neuron, is connected to others and has a weight and threshold that go along with it. Any node whose output exceeds the defined threshold value is activated and begins providing data to the network's uppermost layer. Or else, no data is sent to the network's next tier. Training data is essential for neural networks to develop and enhance overall accuracy over time. However, these learning algorithms become effective tools if they are adjusted for accuracy, enabling us to quickly categorize and cluster data. When compared to manual recognition by human specialists, tasks in speech recognition or picture recognition can be completed in minutes as opposed to hours. Google's search algorithm uses this network, which helps us to get related images within seconds.

Neural Question Generation

The task of creating questions from a passage is known as question generation (QG). There are various uses for it:

1. QG can assist in creating reading comprehension questions for educational resources.
2. QG can help with the creation of question-asking chatbots.
3. QG is helpful for creating datasets for question-answering.

According to Qingyu Zhou, an encoder reads the input passage and the answer position to generate the answer-aware input representation, then it will be fed to the decoder to produce an answer-focused question [13]. This neural encoder-decoder model is able to produce meaningful and varied questions from natural language sentences.

3 Proposed Solution

This research proposes a system to automatically create learning content in a smart way using AI while ensuring that personalisation of learning takes place. The proposed system has two main actors, where the admin and the student can access it. To access the system, an account must be created and personal information is required. The task for the admin is to upload and mark the student upon their exercise being submitted. The system will generate exercises from the uploaded lecture from the admin, where the learner has to complete the task.

The main part of the system:

1. Registration/Login process—The learner has to login or register for the system every time they want to access, whereas an admin can only login to the system, and for registration, an existing member must add the new one.
2. Learner profile—Once the learner has logged in successfully, the home page will be displayed where view the lecture notes, complete fill in the fill-in-the-blanks exercise, and structured exercise. The latter can edit their personal information like name, phone number, username, and email.
3. Admin profile—When the admin successfully logged in, he/she is directed to the admin home page of the system, where they can upload or delete lectures from the database and add a new admin to the system.
4. Learner Complete exercise—The learner can perform the exercises, such as fill in the blanks and structured questions based on what they choose. The system generates the respective exercise based on the learner choice and the lecture they have chosen to work on.
5. System record marks—Once the learner has completed the exercise and submitted it, the fill-in-the-blanks questions are corrected and their marks are given, whereas for the structured ones, the admin has to correct where the system saves their answers in the database with their respective name.

For simplicity, not all the features of the proposed system are described in this section.

3.1 Module to Automatically Generate Fill-In-The-Blanks Questions

The system reads the lecture from the pdf file. It extracts the top keyword using automatic keyword extractor algorithms. The system then extracts the sentence of the keyword and replaces the keyword with a blank space. It displays all the questions to the learner with all the answers in a shuffle mode (Fig. 1).

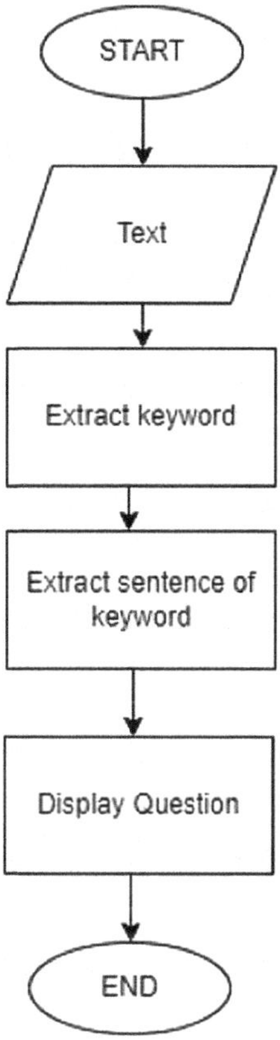

Fig. 1 Flowchart to generate fill-in-the-blanks questions

3.2 Module to Automatically Generate Structured Questions

The steps to automatically generate Structured Questions are described in the section (Fig. 2).

1. The system read the pdf file.
2. The system summaries the text using pre-trained model.
3. The system extracts the keyword from the text.
4. The system extracts the keyword from the summarized text.
5. The system compares both extracted keyword and saves the important ones.
6. It tokenizes the summarized text.
7. The system encodes the strings.
8. The pre-trained model generates the question.
9. The system decodes the question.

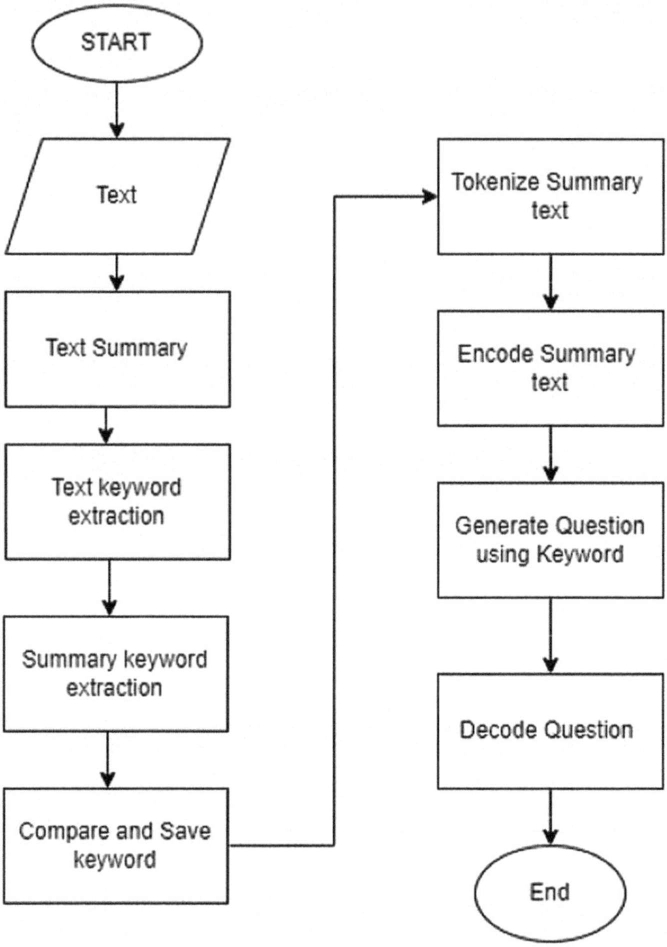

Fig. 2 Flowchart to generate structured questions

3.3 Module to Automatically Mark the Learner

The steps to automatically mark the learner are described (Fig. 3).

1. The learner selects the subject.
2. The learner selects the lecture.
3. The learner selects the type of exercise.
4. The system generates the question.
5. The learner answers the question.
6. The learner submits the answer.
7. The system calculates the marks.
8. The mark is saved in the database.

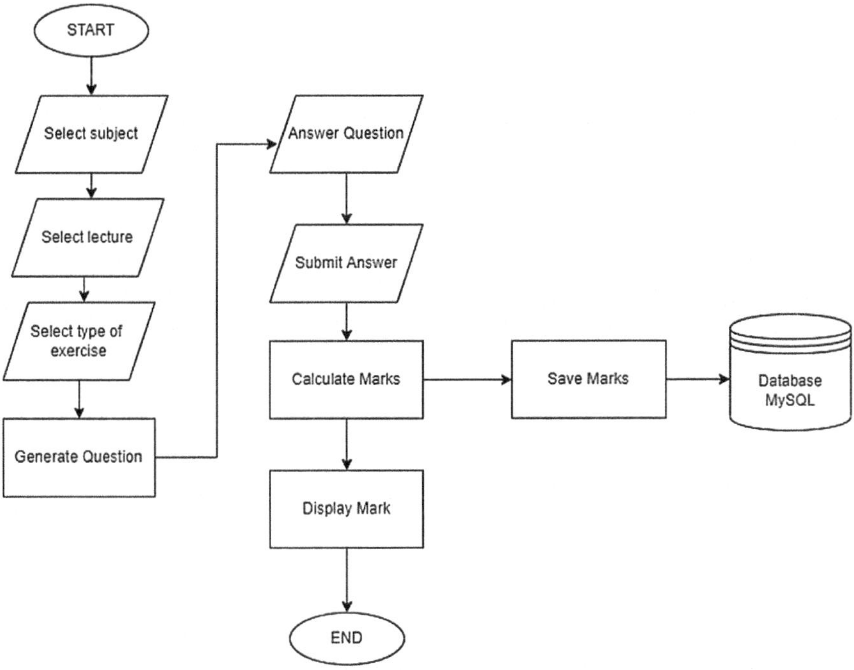

Fig. 3 Flowchart to automatically mark the learner

9. The system displays the respective mark.

4 Implementation

4.1 Development Tools

The tools used for the implementation are summarized in the table (Table 1).

Table 1 Development Tools

Web development Tools	Pycharm Community Edition, Google colab
Scripting Language	HTML5, BOOTSTRAP, CSS, Python 3.8
Database	MySQL
Web Browser	Microsoft Edge, Google Chrome

4.2 Features of the Proposed System

This section describes some of the interesting features of the proposed system.

Automatic Keyphrase Extraction

The pke library has to be imported and then the spacy English model is installed. Since the pdf file contains unsupervised text, the multipartite rank graph is the appropriate one to adopt. At first, all the stopwords and punctuation are removed, afterward, the type of keyphrase is inserted in a pos tag (Part of Speech tagging). The extractor assembles all the candidates together and builds a graph using extractor.get_n_best ($n = 15$). It returns the top 15 keyphrases with high weightage from the graph. The keyphrases are then saved in a list.

Question generation Algorithms (model)

The question generator has been developed in the Google Collaboratory. The latter works well with Python where large datasets can be downloaded without saving to the device and provides an expensive GPU to use for free. From the train dataset, the system is taking answers, which are less than 7 words as our key phrases generate short or single words. The t5model (t-base) and the tokenizer (t-base) are passed by the parameters in the Finetuner class. The input_ids indicates our context and answers, which are fed to the model. The target question is the labels which is used for comparison.

Fill in the blanks

The learner is provided with an answer form to answer the question where they have to fill the correct answer in the textbox (Figs. 4 and 5).

Structured Questions

The same process for this one is also as text areas are provided below each question for the learner to answer (Figs. 6 and 7).

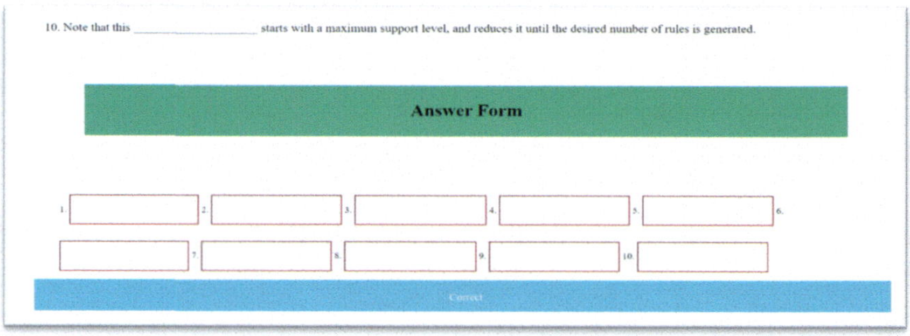

Fig. 4 Fill in the blanks answer form

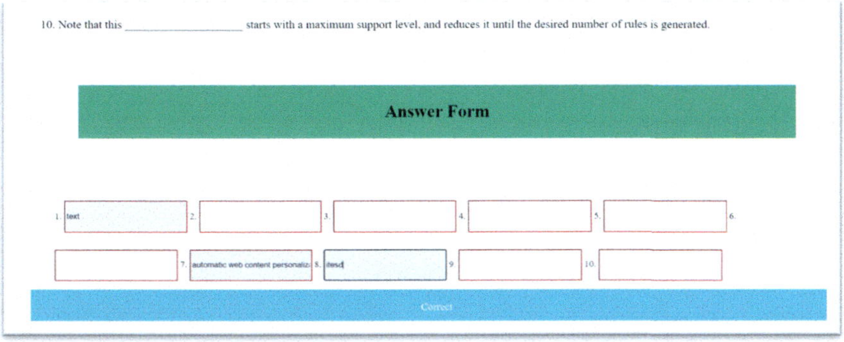

Fig. 5 Answer input

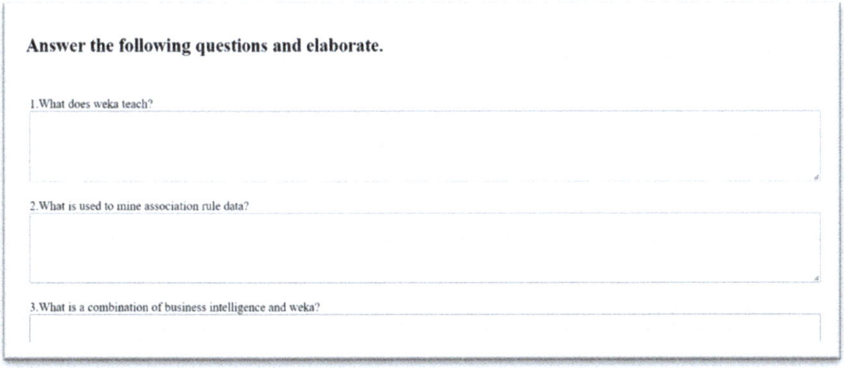

Fig. 6 Questions based on lecture notes

Fig. 7 Answer fill in textarea

Table 2 Metrics

Metrics	Definition
Precision	The number of overlapping words divided by the total words in the reference
Recall	The number of word matches divided by the total number of word in the reference
F1-score	The harmonic mean of the accuracy and recall is the formula for the conventional F1-score. An F-score of 1 indicates a flawless model

5 Experimentation and Discussions

5.1 Evaluation of Model for Question Generation

Dataset

For the model, a pre-trained dataset, namely, SQuAD (Stanford Question Answering Dataset) was used. A span of text from the appropriate reading passage serves as the solution to each question in this reading comprehension dataset, which was compiled by crowd workers from questions on a collection of Wikipedia articles [9]. This consists of context, question, and answer, which is often used to train question answering systems.

5.2 ROUGE Metrics

The metrics contrast an autonomously generated text with a reference text or group of references (Table 2).

5.3 Model Evaluation of Their Performance

- *T5 transforms*

T5 is an encoder-decoder model that has already been trained on a variety of tasks that are both supervised and unsupervised, and are each translated into a text-to-text format. Transfer learning, which involves pre-training a model on a task with plenty of data before fine-tuning it on a subsequent task, has become a potent method for natural language processing (NLP). A random sample from the dataset is taken to perform the ROUGE evaluation. The sample contains the context, answer, and the question. The model is fed up with context and the answer in the sample, and the target is the question in the question column. The tokenizer encodes the information given and then passes it as input_ids into to the model. After generating the question, the tokenizer decodes it. The predicted question passes through the metrics and is compared to the reference question in the sample. The model gives a precision of 60%, a recall of 54.5%, and an F1score of 57.14% on the question generated and compared to the reference ones.

6 Conclusion

This research proposes a system to generate learning content in a smart way by using Artificial Intelligence. This provides personalized learning where the learning experience is more enriching, engaging, and effective. Fill-in-the-blanks and structured questions were automatically generated. A pre-trained dataset, namely, SQuAD (Stanford Question Answering Dataset), was used to train the model, and ROUGE metrics were used to evaluate the model. The model gives a precision of 60%, a recall of 54.5%, and an F1score of 57.14% on the question generated and compared to the reference ones. The model needs to be improved by allowing it to extract important keyphrases and generate a question from any type of text provided.

References

1. Almaiah, M.A., Al-Khasawneh, A. and Althunibat, A. (2020). Exploring the critical challenges and factors influencing the E-learning system usage during COVID-19 pandemic. Educ Inf Technol 25, 5261–5280. https://doi.org/10.1007/s10639-020-10219-y
2. Badal, Y.T. and Sungkur, R.K. Predictive modelling and analytics of students' grades using machine learning algorithms. Educ Inf Technol 28, 3027–3057 (2023). https://doi.org/10.1007/s10639-022-11299-8
3. Cai, L., Barnes, L.E. and Boukhechba, M. (2022). A framework for adaptive mobile ecological momentary assessments using reinforcement learning. In: K. Arai (Ed.) Intelligent Systems and Applications. IntelliSys 2021. Lecture Notes in Networks and Systems (Vol. 294). Springer. https://doi.org/10.1007/978-3-030-82193-7_3
4. Cheng, J. and Wang, H. (2021). Adaptive algorithm recommendation and application of learning resources in English fragmented reading. Complexity, 2021, Article ID 5592534. https://doi.org/10.1155/2021/5592534
5. Ilarri, S., Fumanal, I. and Trillo-Lado, R. (2021). An experience with the implementation of a rule-based triggering recommendation approach for mobile devices. In The 23rd International Conference on Information Integration and Web Intelligence (iiWAS2021) (pp. 562–570). Association for Computing Machinery. https://doi.org/10.1145/3487664.3487806
6. Kim, T., Cho, J.Y. and Lee, B.G. (2013). Evolution to smart learning in public education: a case study of Korean public education, in Open and Social Technologies for Networked Learning, ed. By L.Tobias, R.Mikko, L.Mart, T.Arthur (Berlin Heidelberg, Springer),pp. 170–178.
7. Koper, R. (2014). Conditions for effective smart learning environments. Smart Learning Environments 1(1), 1–17.
8. Madarbakus, S., Gobin, A. and Sungkur, R.K. (2023). Using Sentiment Analysis and Machine Learning to Collect the Perception of Online Learning, Advances in Science and Engineering Technology International Conferences (ASET), Dubai, United Arab Emirates, 2023, pp. 01–06, https://doi.org/10.1109/ASET56582.2023.10180757.
9. Rajpurkar, P., Zhang, J., Lopyrev, K., and Liang, P. (2016). Squad: 100, 000+ questions for machine comprehension of text. CoRR, abs/1606.05250

10. Sampson, D., Karagiannidis, C. and Kinshuk. (2020). Personalised learning: educational, technological and standardisation perspective. Interactive Educational Multimedia, 4(4), 24–39. Available at: http://revistes.ub.edu/index.php/IEM/article/viewFile/11738/14548. Accessed 22 December 2022
11. Sheoraj, Y. and Sungkur, R.K. (2022). Using AI to develop a framework to prevent employees from missing project deadlines in software projects—case study of a global human capital management (HCM) software company, Advances in Engineering Software, Volume 170, 103143, ISSN 0965-9978, https://doi.org/10.1016/j.advengsoft.2022.103143.
12. Sungkur, R. K. and Maharaj, M. S. (2021). Design and implementation of a SMART Learning environment for the upskilling of cybersecurity professionals in Mauritius. Education and Information Technologies, 26, 3175–3201. https://doi.org/10.1007/s10639-020-10408-9
13. Sungkur, R. K. and Maharaj, M. (2022). A review of intelligent techniques for implementing SMART learning environments. In: Sikdar, B., Prasad Maity, S., Samanta, J., Roy, A. (Eds.), Proceedings of the 3rd International Conference on Communication, Devices and Computing. Lecture Notes in Electrical Engineering (Vol. 851). Springer. https://doi.org/10.1007/978-981-16-9154-6_69
14. Zhou, Q., Yang, N., Wei, F., Tan, C., Bao, H. and Zhou, M. (2017). Neural Question Generation from Text: A Preliminary Study. Conference on Empirical Methods in Natural Language Processing (2017), EMNLP 2017. Copenhagen, Denmark.
15. Zhu, Z., Yu, M and Riezebos, P. (2015). A Research Framework for Smart Education. Smart Learning Environments 3:4, https://doi.org/10.1186/s40561-016-0026-2

Firm-Level Environmental Management and Industrial Symbiosis Among Selected Enterprises in the Agro-Food Value Chain in Ghana

Daniel Nukpezah, Stephen Yeboah Owusu, and Benedicta Fosu-Mensah

Abstract Vast quantities of by-products, perceived as waste, are created along the supply chain in agro-food systems. To mitigate this, studies recommend firm-level environmental management and industrial symbiosis (IS), where material and energy flows are circulated within and among industries to minimise waste. This research employed the mixed method approach, applying input–output and material flow analyses to investigate by-product reuse and interdependency (existing synergies) within and among enterprises, and modelled an Eco-Industrial Network (EIN) for potential synergies among enterprises within the agro-food value chain in Ghana using Stan2web, a material flow analysis tool. Results showed that, although 88% of enterprises had knowledge of interdependencies, only 78.86% of them implemented environmental management at the firm level, with 53.84% of firms engaged in exchange of material across enterprises. The noticeable existing synergy was between the food and non-alcoholic beverage industries, and the waste management industry, for the manufacture of compost. Modelling potential synergies, the study revealed that establishing wastewater treatment and steam and/or biogas plants in addition to incentives from regulators would be essential to transitioning towards circularity. This study recommends further education in Industrial Ecology (IE) to create opportunities to enhance interdependencies among firms.

Keywords Agro-food · Input–output analysis · Material flow analysis · Modelling · Eco-industrial networks (EIN) · Industrial symbiosis · Industrial ecology

---

D. Nukpezah (✉) · S. Y. Owusu · B. Fosu-Mensah
Institute for Environment and Sanitation Studies (IESS), College of Basic and Applied Sciences, University of Ghana, Accra, Ghana
e-mail: dnukpezah@ug.edu.gh

J. Marx Gómez et al. (eds.), *Advancement in Embedded and Mobile Systems*, Progress in IS, https://doi.org/10.1007/978-3-031-99219-3_33

1 Introduction

Agro-food systems create vast quantities of by-products along the supply chain, given that the industrial agro-food sector is responsible for approximately 1.3 billion tonnes of waste annually [26, 2]. This highlights the risk of raw material shortages for industries, especially in developing countries, and the need for effective waste management techniques [26, 2]. The United Nations Environment Programme [33] estimates that it could cost sub-Saharan Africa $4 billion to mitigate such risks and impacts on food security. The agro-food sector therefore, has huge potential in terms of material and energy recovery [17].

To address the issue of material and energy recovery, researchers propose enhancing industrial processes and interdependencies of waste by-products among enterprises, while mitigating the adverse environmental impacts. Industrial symbiosis, a form of circular economy where physical exchanges of waste, by-products or other resources between enterprises generate competitive advantages [28] has been hailed as a panacea to address the risk of raw material shortages in developing countries by closing material and energy loops. The circular economy concept is based on a production and consumption model involving, among other things, recycling materials and products, thereby minimising waste. It focusses on improving the circular movement of materials, water and energy among departments within and among firms. Involved firms may be either co-located (often referred to as Eco-Industrial Parks (EIP) or dispersed through a virtual network of industries known as Eco-Industrial Network (EIN) [7, 13]. Industrial symbiosis, like the circular economy, aims at reducing the extraction of and enhancing the efficient use of primary resources by minimising waste, and improving the life cycles of such resources [25, 12]. This creates a circular movement of primary materials within the limits of the environment, maintaining the inherent value of the resource for socioeconomic and environmental gains (European Commission, [11]. Industrial symbiosis accelerates the transition from a linear system (traditional process) towards a circular system to achieve a low-carbon, sustainable economy. The concept mimics the natural ecosystem where by-products from one natural cycle are utilised by another [37].

Figure 1 illustrates a symbiotic relationship between two traditionally independent industries. In the figure, Industries A and B are traditionally independent, receiving Inputs A1 and B1, and churning out Outputs A2 and B2, respectively. At the firm level, by-products A3 and B3 are reused by the respective industries. However, with industrial symbiosis, useful by-products A4 and A5, and B4 and B5 exit respective industries at various points and are exchanged, serving as inputs for the other industry.

Diasz et al. [10] proposed a Technical Viability Analysis for Industrial Synergies (TVAIS) framework for evaluating interdependencies based on a standardised aggregated approach. TVAIS harnesses technological databases of industrial synergies through a three-phase process: synergy compliance, synergy characterisation, and synergy feasibility. This framework captures the essentials of Boons et al.'s [4] six-step approach for IS creation—preliminary assessment, engagement

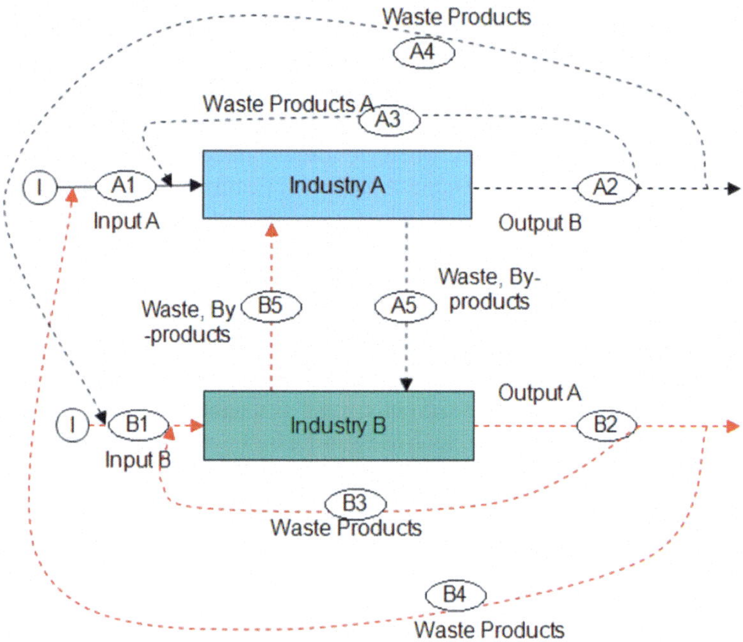

Fig. 1 Illustration of the symbiotic relationship between two traditionally independent enterprises

of businesses, identification of synergies, feasibility assessment, implementation, and documentation for reviews albeit, under different titles.

Industrial symbiosis is critical to agri-businesses due to the nature of waste, mostly biodegradable, generated in the sector [1, 20]. This makes the concept important to Africa and, in particular, Ghana, where the agriculture sector is a major employer (33% of the workforce) according to the Ghana Statistical Service [14], and where compostable waste accounts for over 60% of the waste stream [23]. For instance, the production processes for fertilizers, animal feed, and biofuels require the conversion of biodegradable waste from agro-based industries into organic fertilizers. This replaces the infamous inorganic ones and creates a cyclical life for the by-product. This approach, also called '*closed system manufacturing*', usually requires little to retrofitting of existing systems and could be profitable [27].

Several studies have examined industrial symbiosis as a waste management strategy in the agro-food industry and have shown successful implementation and environmental benefits. Such studies have also examined the barriers and drivers for IS implementation as well as the collaboration and innovation it creates. Hamam et al. [17] have highlighted the benefits, challenges and opportunities for waste reduction and resource efficiency by implementing industrial symbiosis projects. Other studies on industrial symbiosis in the agro-food industry have demonstrated benefits such as waste reduction and resource use efficiency,risk reduction; energy and water savings; potential for creating new products and opportunities for new businesses [1].

Despite the inherent advantages, the adoption of IS and related concepts in Africa remains low. Oni et al. [30] posit that although IS frameworks exist in most African countries, implementation is haphazard and poorly documented. Oduro-Kwarteng and van Dijk [29] indicated that IS exists in Africa, albeit informally, especially in communities around dumpsites where residents collect and sell recyclable yet discarded products. Grant and Oteng-Ababio [15] affirmed that such collectors are responsible for about 95% of all waste recycled in Ghana, yet their activities are largely undocumented. Conceptual studies on industrial symbiosis have been conducted by Nukpezah et al. [28], who assessed the application of industrial ecology principles to the management of industrial by-products in Ghana. While this study is foundational to IE and IS deployment in Ghana, it was limited in that, it provided only a vision of the interdependency of by-products from only one cassava processing enterprise as an anchor with potential enterprises as tenants.

Government policies in Ghana, such as Planting for Food and Jobs (PFJ), Planting for Export and Rural Development (PERD) and One District One Factory (1D1F), have arguably increased production and processing of raw materials but have yet to address related waste issues. For instance, Sugri et al. [31] revealed that post-harvest losses remained high in the Upper West Region of Ghana, between 15.6% and 36.5% for fresh produce and 6.9% to 34.9% for dry produce.

While the above is true, the extent of uptake of environmental management initiatives, as well as the interdependency of by-products among firms in the agro-industrial value chain in Ghana has not been documented. Therefore, the main aim of this study is to assess and document firm-level environmental management initiatives and the interdependency of waste by-products among selected enterprises in the agro-food value chain in Ghana and model an eco-industrial network (EIN) of potential exchanges among agro-food enterprises. In this study, an enterprise refers to an independent firm, while an industry describes a cluster of enterprises that uses and produces similar raw materials and products, respectively.

2 Methodology

2.1 Study Area

The study was conducted in the Greater Accra and Eastern regions of Ghana, which account for over 50% of the value stock of agricultural raw materials in the country. A list of 94 agro-based enterprises was obtained from the Business Advisory Centres (BAC) and the Association of Ghana Industries (AGI). Seventy-eight enterprises (coded IS01–IS78) were surveyed for the study, representing 83% of the listed agro-based enterprises. Figure 2 shows the location of enterprises in the study area. The names of enterprises were substituted with a code to protect their anonymity.

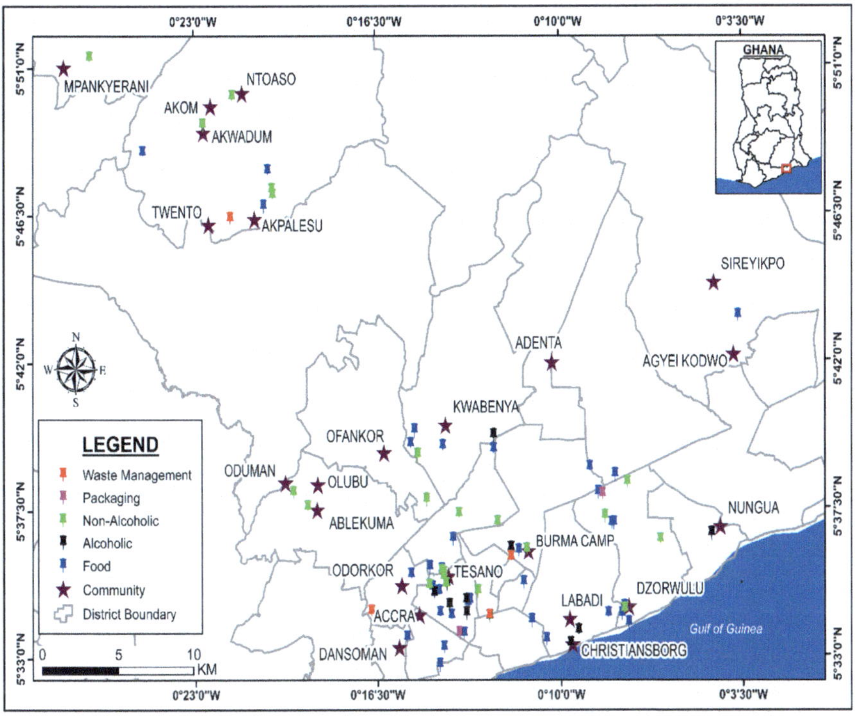

Fig. 2 Location of sampled enterprises in the agro-food value chain

2.2 *Research Framework*

The study employed a mixed-method approach (quantitative and qualitative data), utilising a questionnaire comprised of open- and close-ended questions. To achieve the study objectives, a multi-level sequence was adopted as depicted in Fig. 3. The first stage describes the research gaps this paper contributes to. Subsequently, the objectives were formulated and data collected. Based on literature, factors for determining the profile of industries for EIN development included latitudes and longitudes, and inputs, outputs, and by-products of firms [3], [16]. For expediency, this study grouped the enterprises under the food industry, non-alcoholic beverage industry, alcoholic beverage industry, packaging industry, and waste management industry based on similarities in inputs, outputs, and by-products.

The study employed Input–Output analysis and Material Flow Analysis (MFA) to trace the flow of material, water, and energy, identifying factors that contribute to reducing, reusing and/or recycling within and among enterprises [8, 24]. Importantly, it determined opportunities to deepen these factors by identifying firms that could utilise waste by-products from other enterprises. The results were used to model potential interdependencies or EIN for the industries to reduce waste, and document synergies, potential synergies, and roles of some principal actors [35], [7], [9].

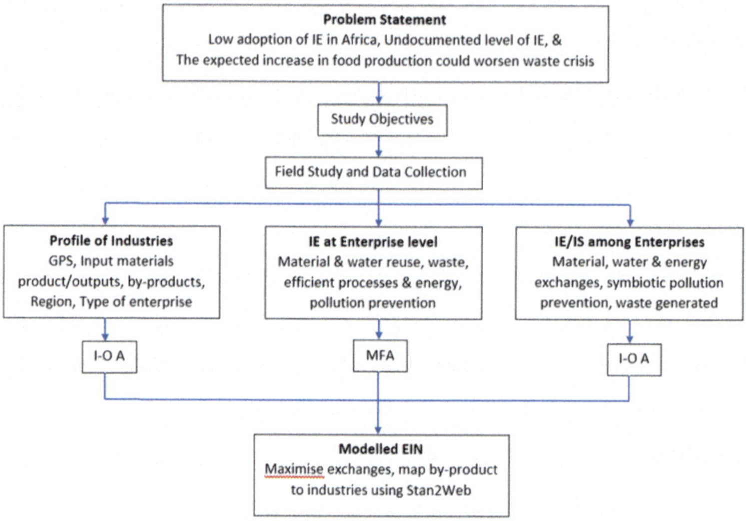

Fig. 3 Research framework (*Abbreviation: IE = Industrial Ecology; IS = Industrial Symbiosis; I-O A = Input–Output Analysis; MFA = Material Flow Analysis; EIN = Eco-Industrial Network*)

Qualitative responses were triangulated to support the quantitative data and vice versa to mitigate the weaknesses of each method [5]. Stan2web (Stan), a material flow analysis (MFA) software, was used to model a potential Eco-Industrial Network (EIN). For instance, if an assessment revealed that by-products of an enterprise could be reused, reduced or recycled by another, the said resource would be mapped to the potentially receiving enterprise.

3 Results

3.1 Industry Profile

The study reveals several clusters of industries within the agro-food value chain. This includes alcoholic and non-alcoholic beverages, food, packaging and waste management. The dominant enterprises within the agro-food industry are food-related enterprises, constituting 50% of the total enterprises sampled. This is followed by non-alcoholic, alcoholic, waste management and the food packaging industry in descending order. Table 1 presents the categories of enterprises surveyed.

Table 1 Industry types within the agro-food value chain

Industry/Cluster of enterprises	Percentage (%)
Alcoholic	13
Food	50
Non-Alcoholic	29
Packaging	3
Waste Management	5

3.2 *Knowledge and Application of Environmental Management at the Firm Level*

Overall, more than 88% of respondent firms were knowledgeable about environmental management, with over 78% engaging in environmental management initiatives (IS/IE). Further, the study showed that 11.29% of respondent firms had no knowledge of applying environmental management within their firms. Although 11.27% had knowledge regarding environmental management, they did not apply it in their firms. Figure 4 shows the degree of knowledge and engagement in environmental management initiatives by various enterprises within the agro-food value chain. It was revealed that among non-alcoholic, food and alcoholic industries, 26.31%, 14.63% and 83.33%, respectively, had knowledge in environmental management (IE/IS) and yet did not apply it at the firm level. Figure 5 highlights some of the environmental management practices by firms. Such practices include regulating the use of material and energy as well as practices that ensure waste reuse within and among enterprises. Figure 6 presents the summary results of IS within enterprises in the study area. At the firm level, 78.86% of enterprises implemented environmental management initiatives, including internal water production, reducing material and energy waste leakages, and constructing eco-friendly factories. Examples include IS40, an alcoholic beverage production company in Accra, reusing tanks as water reservoirs, and IS75, a waste management company in Medea, recycling wastewater for irrigation and converting faecal matter into biochar.

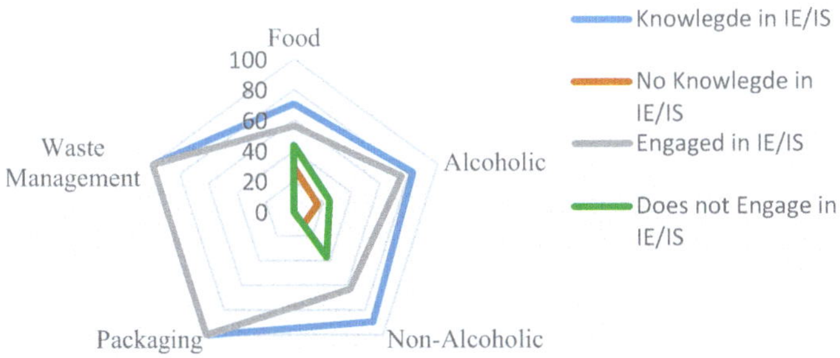

Fig. 4 Knowledge of and engagement in IE/IS among industries

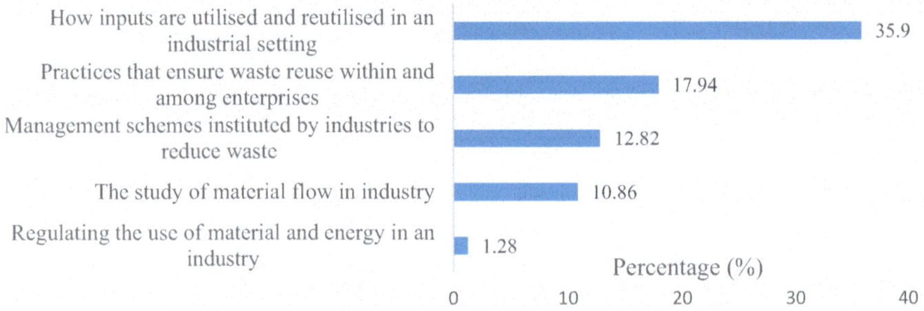

Fig. 5 Environmental management practices undertaken by respondent firms

Fig. 6 Environmental management initiatives within enterprises in the agro-food value chain

3.3 *Input–Output Analysis of Enterprises*

The results of the input–output–by-products analysis for the industries are shown in Figs. 7–11. The P1 represents the process the inputs undergo, while W1 is the process by which waste is discharged in the industry.

3.4 *Industrial Symbiosis Among Enterprises*

The study reveals that on average, about 53.84% of the respondent enterprises practice industrial symbiosis. These include exchanges with waste management enterprises. Table 2 details all identified exchanges among enterprises.

The study further revealed that there was one energy-based interdependency constituting 1.3% of the surveyed enterprises. However, most of the firms relied

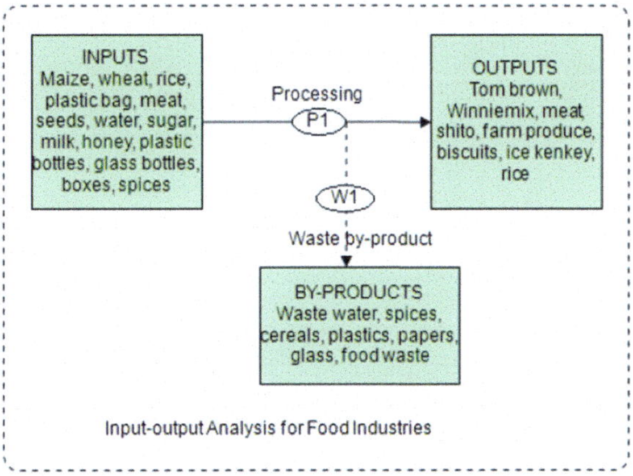

Fig. 7 Input–output analysis for the food industry

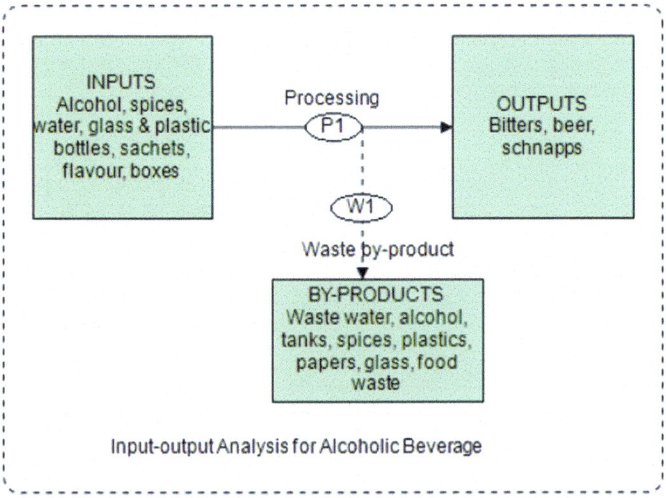

Fig. 8 Input–output analysis for the alcoholic industry

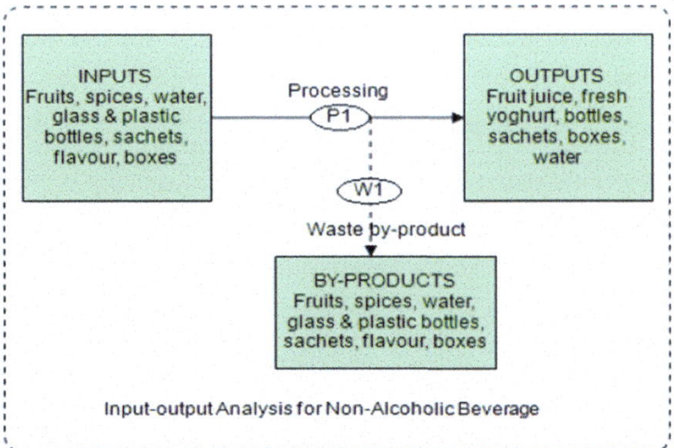

Fig. 9 Input–output analysis for the non-alcoholic industry

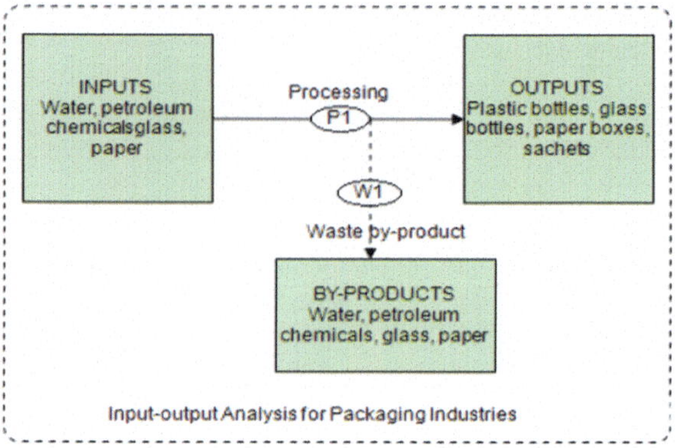

Fig. 10 Input–output analysis for the packaging industry

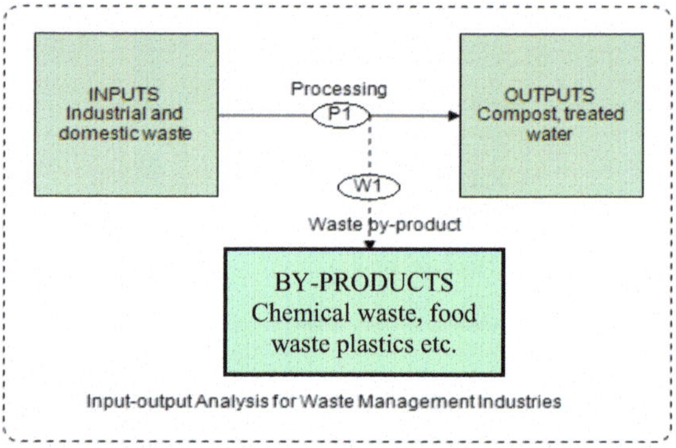

Fig. 11 Input–output analysis for the waste management industry

Table 2 Existing exchanges among enterprises

Primary firm	Dependent firm	By-products exchanged
IS54	6 non-alcoholic enterprises, Out-grower farms, local markets	Waste fruits, rejected fruits, compost
IS06	3 non-alcoholic enterprises, Farms, local markets	Waste fruits, rejected fruits,
Packaging Companies (Plastic/Paper)	17 enterprises depend on the Packaging companies	Waste bottles and sachets, waste paper boxes
Waste management companies	42 enterprises depend on the waste management companies	General waste materials
IS01-IS74	Waste management companies	Waste and by-products
Cocoa Processor	IS25, Briquette company	Waste cocoa, Cocoa husk
Briquette company	IS59	Briquette
IS70	Local farmers, market	Waste and rejected fruits
Fish processor	IS36	Fish for animal feed
IS40	Residential facilities	Alcohol Tanks

partially on the national grid for their energy needs. Additionally, a substantial portion of these enterprises, specifically 68% of food-related businesses, 58% of alcoholic beverage producers, and 53% of non-alcoholic beverage manufacturers, relied on diesel generators to supplement their energy requirements. Furthermore, it was observed that all packaging and waste management enterprises also operated diesel generators in addition to their reliance on the national grid. These findings indicate a diversified energy strategy among these businesses, incorporating both grid-based electricity and on-site diesel generators to meet their energy demands.

On the issue of by-product reuse, a substantial number (76.1%) of the respondent firms expressed concerns about potential negative customer reactions if their enterprises were to adopt the use of by-products. This observation reflects cultural barriers where people frown upon the reuse of materials perceived to be waste.

3.5 Modelling Potential Exchanges Among Enterprises

Based on the input–output–by-products and material flow analyses, a model was developed showcasing interdependencies among enterprises in the agro-food value chain (Fig. 12). The model took cognisance of the Synergy Compliance, Synergy Characterisation, and Synergy Feasibility phases of the TVAIS framework. Observations were that the waste from the food industry, including wastewater, fibre/food waste, waste spices, paper, plastic, glass and sacks could be used as animal feed and compost manufacturing, wastewater treatment and paper, plastic, glass (PPG) manufacturing and recycling enterprises. By-products of non-alcoholic and fruit juice enterprises, waste management and PPG enterprises were also mapped. The mapping revealed that wastewater, steam and/or biogas, and alcohol treatment plants are essential to complete circularity within the agro-food industry in the country. Table 3 describes the modelled interdependencies in Fig. 12.

4 Discussion

4.1 Profile of Enterprises

The study highlights the diverse nature of enterprises in the agro-food value chain, leading to variations in inputs, outputs, and by-products. For example, food enterprises used a wide range of inputs, from cereals to fruits, spices, vegetables, meat, and fish, resulting in diverse outputs and by-products. Non-alcoholic and alcoholic beverages, as well as waste management and packaging industries, also displayed diversity, impacting their respective outputs and by-products. This high diversity laid the foundation for assessing the Synergy Compliance, Synergy Characterisation, and

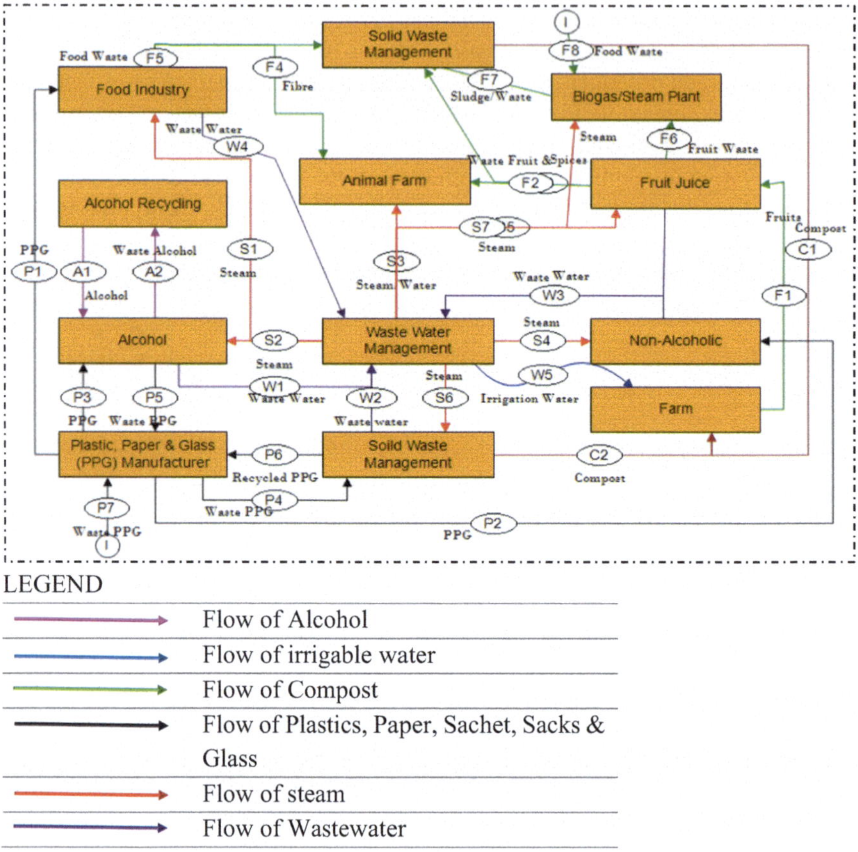

Fig. 12 Modelled interdependencies among industries

Synergy Feasibility phases of IS. According to van Capelleveen et al. [34], diversity in by-products can facilitate interdependencies by incentivising enterprises and redistributing synergistic advantages. Boons et al. [4] and Yeo et al. [36] reinforced this, stating that diversity during the preliminary assessment is a critical stage in IS creation, as it induces participation opportunities.

4.2 *Enterprise (Firm) Level Environmental Management Initiatives*

At the firm level, knowledge of sustainable environmental practices and pollution prevention was high. However, in terms of material exchange, there was widespread discomfort and potential backlash from consumers over the use of by-products for production and shareholders' low inclination towards environmental sustainability.

Table 3 Interpretation of modelled flows in Fig. 12

CODE	Interpretation of Synergy
A1	Waste alcohol from alcoholic industries is transferred to a recycling plant for treatment and reuse
A2	Treated alcohol is reused by alcoholic industries
C1 & C2	Compost from solid waste management industries is transferred to farms
F1	Fruit from farms utilising compost and treated water from other enterprises is supplied to fruit juice enterprises
F2	Fruit by-products or waste are converted to animal feed at animal farms
F3	Fruit by-products waste transported to solid waste management enterprises for the manufacture of compost
F4	Food waste or by-products are converted to animal feed at animal farms
F5	Food by-products waste is transported to solid waste management enterprises for the manufacture of compost
F6	Fruit by-products or waste utilised as feedstock by biogas plants for the generation of electricity
F7	Sludge or waste from biogas plant is converted to compost by the solid waste management industries
F8	Food waste from food enterprises and other sources is used as input for biogas plant for the generation of electricity
P1	Recycled plastics, sachets, glasses and papers are used as packaging material among food enterprises
P2	Recycled plastics, sachets, glasses and papers are used as packaging material among non-alcoholic enterprises
P3	Recycled plastics, sachets, glasses and papers are used as packaging material among alcoholic enterprises
P4	Waste plastics, sachets, glasses and papers are transferred to solid waste management enterprises for recycling
P5	Waste plastics, sachets, glasses and papers from alcoholic enterprises are transferred to plastic, paper and glass (PPG) manufacturers for recycling
P6	Recycled plastics, sachets, glasses and papers are transferred back to PPG manufacturers
P7	Waste plastics, sachets, glasses, papers, and other sources, including residential homes, are transferred to plastic, paper and glass (PPG) manufacturers for recycling
S1	Wastewater treatment facility supplies food enterprises with steam generated from wastewater
S2	Wastewater treatment facility supplies Alcoholic enterprises with steam generated from wastewater
S3	Wastewater treatment facility supplies Animal farms with steam or water generated from wastewater
S4	Wastewater treatment facility supplies non-alcoholic enterprises with steam generated from wastewater

(continued)

Table 3 (continued)

CODE	Interpretation of Synergy
S5	Wastewater treatment facility supplies fruit juice enterprises with steam generated from wastewater
S6	Wastewater treatment facility supplies solid waste management enterprises with steam generated from wastewater
S7	Wastewater treatment facility supplies Steam Plant for electricity generation with steam generated from wastewater
W1	Wastewater from alcohol enterprises is transferred to a Wastewater treatment facility, where it is treated and converted to steam or irrigable water
W2	Wastewater from Solid Waste Management enterprises is transferred to a Wastewater treatment facility, where it is treated and converted to steam or irrigable water
W3	Wastewater from Non-alcoholic enterprises is transferred to a Wastewater treatment facility, where it is treated and converted to steam or irrigable water
W4	Wastewater from Food enterprises is transferred to a Wastewater treatment facility, where it is treated and converted to steam or irrigable water
W5	Treated water is used for irrigation on farms and lawns

Studies on barriers to the circular economy in the Netherlands (Campbell-Johnston et al., [6] emphasised the importance of addressing customer concerns, as disinterest or indifference in environmental sustainability may deter customers from paying premiums for eco-friendly products. Other studies have opined that the adoption of IS can be enhanced by overcoming technical, economic and strategic barriers [13]]. Thus, firm-level initiatives, such as improving system efficiency and re-orienting enterprise design to optimise material flow, as well as public policy directions can influence consumer behaviour [18]. It is vital for firms to identify by-products that could replace or complement the raw input materials or develop new products using their by-products.

4.3 *Industrial Symbiosis*

A little more than half (53.84%) of the enterprises surveyed engaged in exchanging their by-products. However, the lack of insight on the quantities of waste actually exchanged was a challenge. Despite only one energy-based interdependency, some enterprises generate ample food waste convertible to biogas. For instance, IS36 converts internal waste to animal feed and compost, while IS25 and IS59 convert bio-waste to biogas or briquettes, demonstrating pathways to overcome technical challenges. Generally, there is room for enterprises to be innovative by diversifying their investment, including investing in biogas plants to help close material and energy loops associated with the generation of waste.

To improve IS, specialised enterprises to manage wastewater may have to be established, in addition to the promulgation of relevant legislation. Only one sampled enterprise had a wastewater treatment subdivision. The relevance of wastewater treatment and an enhanced system in deepening by-product exchanges or transfers has been highlighted by Madanhire et al. [22]. Indeed, over 50% of respondents in the study indicated their willingness to reuse their wastewater if they could overcome barriers. This necessitates an evaluation of barriers and relationships between enterprises and regulators. State agencies can leverage this relationship to enhance linkages, particularly in wastewater interdependencies, while removing administrative barriers, facilitating technology adoption, and providing strategic direction for IS in the country [19]. This 'win–win' approach collaboratively minimises risks and exposures among stakeholders, critical for driving IS [32].

4.4 Modelling Potential Exchanges

The findings of this study suggest that building physical exchange networks among enterprises may be unlikely and economically unviable due to their dispersed locations. Modelling industrial synergies revealed potential enhancements in exchanges among enterprises. An Eco-Industrial Network (EIN) could be established among food and fruit juice enterprises, compost manufacturers, farmers and local markets. This would enable the recycling, reduction, or reuse of by-products such as fruits, husks, and spices [21]. A study in Liberia highlighted the importance of IS for farms, where food waste from agro-based enterprises is reused in farms with limited intermediary processes [1].

Furthermore, packaging enterprises could establish synergistic relationships with other industries to receive plastics, sachets, sacks, glass and paper waste. Similar relationships could also be formed between industries and customers to enhance recycling. Due to the fact that the enterprises sampled are dispersed spatially, building physical exchanges may not be economically viable. Thus, a small-scale network like an eco-industrial park could be established for co-located firms anchored on a large-scale enterprise [7]. Alternatively, a virtual exchange system could be created, identifying available by-products and mapping them to enterprises in need of inputs, similar to the Nordic Industrial Symbiosis Network (NISN) and the National Industrial Symbiosis Programme (NISP) in the UK [21], [24].

5 Conclusion

The study assessed inputs, outputs, and by-products of agro-food enterprises in Ghana's value chain, analysing prevailing firm-level environmental management practices and industrial symbiosis (IS) among firms. Potential exchanges and synergies were modelled to make a case for the adoption of Industrial Symbiosis (IS) in the country. The focus was on enterprises in Greater Accra and the Eastern regions. The study established that the majority of the enterprises implemented interdependency and environmental initiatives at the firm level. The study further makes a significant contribution to modelling potential material and energy exchanges for resource sustainability among enterprises. In terms of recommendations, further investigation into the techno-economic potential of Industrial Symbiosis (IS) is proposed. Critical areas to evaluate include the quantities of by-products generated, economic viability for IS, and feasibility of building a wastewater treatment enterprise for industrial steam generation and/or biogas plant. Additional studies could focus on regulatory agency roles in deepening IS in Ghana. Formulating regulations to govern IE and IS, and encouraging consumer acceptability, are imperative. Government initiatives to facilitate interdependencies among industries and create adaptable transfer mediums for identified by-products should be prioritised.

References

1. Alfaro J., & Miller S. (2014). Applying industrial symbiosis to smallholder farms: Modeling a case study in Liberia, West Africa. *Journal of Industrial Ecology* 18: 145–154.
2. Arun, K. B., Madhavan, A., Sindhu, R., Binod, P., Pandey, A., Reshmy, R., & Sirohi, R. (2020). Remodeling agro-industrial and food wastes into value-added bioactives and biopolymers. *Industrial Crops and Products, 154*, 112621.
3. Aviso, K. B., Tan, R. R., Culaba, A. B., & Cruz Jr, J. B. (2010). Bi-level fuzzy optimization approach for water exchange in eco-industrial parks. *Process Safety and Environmental Protection, 88*(1), 31–40.
4. Boons, F., Chertow, M., Park, J., Spekkink, W., & Shi, H. (2016). Industrial symbiosis dynamics and the problem of equivalence: Proposal for a comparative framework. *Journal of Industrial Ecology*, 21(4), 938–952.
5. Bryman, A. (2006). Integrating quantitative and qualitative research: How is it done? *Qualitative research, 6*(1), 97–113.
6. Campbell-Johnston, K., de Munck, M., Vermeulen, W. J., & Backes, C. (2021). Future perspectives on the role of extended producer responsibility within a circular economy: A Delphi study using the case of the Netherlands. *Business Strategy and the Environment*, 30(8), 4054–4067.
7. Chertow, M. (2000). Industrial Symbiosis: Literature and Taxonomy. *Annual review of energy and the environment*, 25, 313–337. https://doi.org/10.1146/annurev.energy.25.1.313
8. Chertow, M. R. (2007). Uncovering" industrial symbiosis. *Journal of industrial Ecology, 11*(1), 11–30.
9. Côté, R. P., & Cohen-Rosenthal, E. (1998). Designing eco-industrial parks: A synthesis of some experiences. *Journal of cleaner production, 6*(3–4), 181–188.
10. Diasz, R., Azevedo, J., Ferreira, I., Estrela, M., Henriques, J., Ascenço, C., & Iten, M. (2020). Technical Viability Analysis of Industrial Synergies—An Applied Framework Perspective. *Sustainability, 12*(18), 7720.
11. European Commission. (2020). *Circular economy action plan for a cleaner and more competitive Europe*. European Union.
12. FISSAC. (2020). What is industrial symbiosis? Assessed on 22/01/2022 and available at https://fissacproject.eu/en/what-is-industrial-symbiosis/
13. Francasscia, L., Magno, M., & Albino, V. (2016). Business models for industrial symbiosis: A guide for firms. *Procedia Environ. Sci. Eng. Manag, 3*(2), 83–93.
14. Ghana Statistical Service (GSS). (2021). Ghana Population and Housing Census 2021, General Report; Volume 3E. https://statsghana.gov.gh/gssmain/fileUpload/pressrelease/2021%20PHC%20General%20Report%20Vol%203E_Economic%20Activity.pdf

15. Grant, R., & Oteng-Ababio, M. (2021). Formalising E-waste in Ghana: An emerging landscape of fragmentation and enduring barriers. *Development Southern Africa, 38*(1), 73–86.
16. Gu, C., Leveneur, S., Estel, L., & Yassine, A. (2013). Modeling and optimization of material/energy flow exchanges in an eco-industrial park. *Energy Procedia, 36*, 243–252.
17. Hamam, M., Spina, D., Raimondo, M., Di Vita, G., Zanchini, R., Chinnici, G., Tóth, J., & D'Amico, M. (2023). Industrial symbiosis and agri-food system: Themes, links, and relationships. *Front. Sustain. Food Syst.* 6:1012436. https://doi.org/10.3389/fsufs.2022.1012436
18. Hartley, K., Roosendaal, J., & Kirchherr, J. (2022). Barriers to the circular economy: The case of the Dutch technical and interior textiles industries. *Journal of Industrial Ecology*, 26(2), 477–490.
19. Henriques, J., Ferrão, P., & Iten, M. (2022). Policies and Strategic Incentives for Circular Economy and Industrial Symbiosis in Portugal: A Future Perspective. *Sustainability, 14*(11), 6888.
20. Kliopova, I., Baranauskaitė-Fedorova, I., Malinauskienė, M., & Staniškis, J. K. (2016). Possibilities of increasing resource efficiency in nitrogen fertilizer production. *Clean Technologies and Environmental Policy, 18*(3), 901–914.
21. Laybourn, P., & Morrissey, M. (2009). National Industrial Symbiosis Programme: The pathway to a low carbon sustainable economy. International Synergies Ltd.
22. Madanhire, I., Muganyi, P., & Mbohwa, C. (2018). Turning industrial area into an eco-industrial park in South Africa: case study. In *Proceedings of the international conference on industrial engineering and operations management.* Bandung, Indonesia.
23. Miezah, K., Obiri-Danso, K., Kádár, Z., Fei-Baffoe, B., & Mensah, M. Y. (2015). Municipal solid waste characterization and quantification as a measure towards effective waste management in Ghana. *Waste Management, 46*, 15–27. https://doi.org/10.1016/j.wasman.2015.09.009
24. Moodie, J., Salenius, V., & Leino, J. (2019). Industrial Symbiosis in the Baltic Sea Region: Current Practices and Guidelines for New Initiatives. Policy Brief 2019:1. https://doi.org/10.30689/PB2019:1.2001-3876
25. Morseletto, P. (2020). Targets for a circular economy. *Resources, Conservation and Recycling, 153*, 104553.
26. Neves, A., Godina, R., G Azevedo, S., Pimentel, C., & CO Matias, J. (2019). The potential of industrial symbiosis: Case analysis and main drivers and barriers to its implementation. *Sustainability, 11*(24), 7095.
27. Niutanen, V., & Korhonen, J. (2003). Industrial ecology flows of agriculture and food industry in Finland: utilizing by-products and wastes. *The International Journal of Sustainable Development & World Ecology, 10*(2), 133–147.
28. Nukpezah, D., Ofori, B. D., & Adu-Manu, K. S. (2019). Application of Industrial Ecology Principles to the Management of Industrial By-products in Ghana: A Conceptual Framing. In *Smart Cities/Smart Regions–Technische, wirtschaftliche und gesellschaftliche Innovationen* (pp. 563–572). Springer Vieweg, Wiesbaden
29. Oduro-Kwarteng, S., & Van Dijk, M. P. (2013). The effect of increased private sector involvement in solid waste collection in five cities in Ghana. *Waste Management & Research*, 31(10), 810–893.
30. Oni, O. O., Nevo, C. M., Hampo, C. C., Ozobodo, K. O., Olajide, I. O., Ibidokun, A. O., ... & Ikpeama, C. C. (2022). Current Status, Emerging Challenges, and Future Prospects of Industrial Symbiosis in Africa. *International Journal of Environmental Research, 16*(4), 1–15.
31. Sugri, I., Abubakari, M., Owusu, R. K., & Bidzakin, J. K. (2021). Postharvest losses and mitigating technologies: Evidence from upper East Region of Ghana. *Sustainable Futures, 3*, 100048.
32. Tsvetkova, A. (2014). Designing sustainable industrial ecosystems: The case of a biogas-for-traffic solution. Doctoral Dissertation, Laboratory of Industrial Management, Department of Chemical Engineering, Division for Natural Sciences and Technology Åbo Akademi University Turku, Finland.

33. United Nations Environment Programme (UNEP). (2021). *Food Waste Index Report 2021.* https://wedocs.unep.org/20.500.11822/35280
34. van Capelleveen, G., Amrit, C., & Yazan, D. M. (2018). *A literature survey of information systems facilitating industrial symbiosis.* In B. Otjacques, P. Hitzel-berger, S. Naumann & V. Wohlgemuth (Eds.), From Science to Society. Progress in IS. Cham: Springer.
35. Veiga, L. B. E., & Magrini, A. (2009). Eco-industrial park development in Rio de Janeiro, Brazil: A tool for sustainable development. *Journal of cleaner production, 17*(7), 653–661.
36. Yeo, Z., Masi, D., Low, J. S. C., Ng, Y. T., Tan, P. S., & Barnes, S. (2019). Tools for promoting industrial symbiosis: A systematic review. *Journal of Industrial Ecology, 23*(5), 1087–1108.
37. Zeng, X., & Li, J. (2021). Emerging anthropogenic circularity science: Principles, practices, and challenges. *Iscience, 24*(3), 102237.

Evaluating Architectural Design Decisions in Systems-of-Systems: Using the Energy Domain as an Example

Johann Schütz and Jorge Marx Gómez

Abstract In the era of digital transformation, new opportunities for data-driven value creation are emerging. These opportunities can only be fully realized through collaboration, transforming individual companies and organizations into Constituent Systems (CS) of a higher level System-of-Systems (SoS), which can be systematically engineered or emerge arbitrarily. Without adequate control mechanisms, the development of SoS can lead to unmanageable complexity and undesirable dependencies. This work introduces a methodology to ensure the future viability of SoS and assist individual CS in their design decisions to avoid costly consequences. It presents the special traits of an SoS environment and a Reference Designation System (RDS)-based approach to address these challenges.

Keywords System of systems · Interoperability · Standardization · Complexity · Evolvability · Technical debt

1 Introduction

In the course of the continuously advancing digital transformation and emerging technologies, more and more new and untapped opportunities are emerging. As the potential for data-driven value creation has just begun to be leveraged, the opportunities created by data-driven value creation and their associated business models become increasingly evident. However, these potentials cannot be leveraged by a single company or organization on its own; only in collaboration. In order to utilize the full potential, the individual companies and organizations need to collaborate based on their shared objectives towards their mutual benefits. This, however, depends on an ICT-based integration and collaboration between individual organizations. As a result, more and more companies and organizations are attempting to open their previously isolated systems and data silos.

J. Schütz (✉) · J. Marx Gómez
Carl von Ossietzky–Universität Oldenburg, 26129 Oldenburg, Germany
e-mail: johann.schuetz@uni-oldenburg.de

J. Marx Gómez et al. (eds.), *Advancement in Embedded and Mobile Systems*, Progress in IS, https://doi.org/10.1007/978-3-031-99219-3_34

1.1 Motivation

When independent companies or organizations collaborate in order to realize and provide joint mission capabilities, these become so-called *Constituent Systems* (CS) of a high-level *System (-of-Systems)* (SoS) [8]. An SoS can be engineered systematically or emerge arbitrarily. As this kind of systems (of systems) are additionally characterized by an immense co-development, co-evolution as well as co-innovation, an arbitrary development of the overall SoS architecture is inevitable without adequate control and evolution mechanisms as a rigorous guidance or framework. If the manifold solutions of the heterogeneous CS are developed in parallel and not viewed from a holistic point of view, innovations emerge locally and uncoordinated, resulting in an unmasterable complexity of the overall architecture—unwanted dependencies with a multitude of undesirable side effects for both the SoS as well as the CS are the inevitable consequence [18].

1.2 Problem Statement

While such strategical cost-considerations are well-known and commonplace business decisions in the domain of *Software Engineering* (SwE). If such costs could have been prevented, these additional costs are classified as so-called *Technical Debt* (TD). TD commonly consists of design or implementation constructs that are expedient in the short term but that set up a technical context that can make future changes more costly or impossible [1], impacting primarily, but not only, the maintainability and evolvability [4, 16].

In accordance with the fundamental systems principle of emergence and interaction theory, an SoS as a whole exhibits behaviours and properties that the CS do not have on their own [2]. These behaviours and properties as well as the new joint capabilities emerge only when the parts interact in a wider whole and do not belong to any of the individual CS. But when such emergence occur the reductionistic assumptions of the components no longer apply [7]. Due to this phenomena, not all properties of a system can be determined or explained by its components alone. As a result, the quality of the SoS as a whole cannot be derived based on an assessment of the individual CS. Hence, the integration of qualitative individual CS will not automatically lead to a qualitative SoS [3, 18]. Correspondingly, this contribution deals with the question: "*How to assess and evaluate architectural design decisions as a CS of a SoS*".

1.3 Objective and Methodology

The main objective of this contribution is to provide an overall framework to assure the future viability of an SoS and, simultaneously, to assist the individual CS in their design decisions to avoid costly consequences.

Considering the presented issue and the overall objective, this work follows the Design Science methodology that provides an appropriate framework, which in essence unites the scientific rigour with the practical relevance. While the practical relevance has already been presented and motivated, the scientific rigour is ensured by the inclusion of the state-of-the-art and standards from research and practice.

1.4 Related Work and Scientific Context

This contribution builds on earlier research and combines several previous conceptual contributions into one applicable approach. The foundations were laid (not exclusively, but significantly) by three individual works. First, [11] laid the preliminary groundwork required to fundamentally differentiate between the underlying paradigms for *TD Management* (TDM) in CS and TDM in SoS. Secondly, in [12], a general high-level concept to systematically analyse SoS architecture (using the energy domain as an example) was introduced, which takes the special traits and general framework conditions of an SoS into account. This concept facilitates well-established standards as the *IEC 65,229—Use Case Methodology,* as well as the Smart Grid Architecture Model (*IEC SRD 63,200—SGAM Basics*). And lastly, in alignment with [11] and [12, 18] provides a more in-depth introduction on how the complexity and, ultimately, the maintainability and evolvability of an SoS are impacted; especially by interoperability.

2 Background

2.1 Constituent System and System-Of-Systems

As the system term is highly recursive in nature and the engineering paradigms to consider are tightly coupled to the scope and context of the *System-of-Interest* (SoI), a clear definition is first required. The newer ISO/IEC/IEEE 21,839:2019-standard for "*Systems and software engineering—System of systems (SoS) considerations in life cycle stages of a system*" [8] provides adequate state-of-the-art definitions:

- System of Systems (SoS)—A set of systems or system elements that interact to provide a unique capability that none of the CS can accomplish on its own. Note: Systems elements can be necessary to facilitate the interaction of the CS in the system of systems.
- Constituent Systems (CS)—Constituent systems can be part of one or more SoS. Note: Each CS is a useful system by itself, having its own development, management goals and resources, but interacts within the SoS to provide the unique capability of the SoS.

2.2 The IEC 62,559 Use Case Management and Smart Grid Architecture Model Methodology

Although the CS are collaborating towards shared objectives, each CS has its own individual starting point with unique requirements, resources, restrictions, and understanding of the problem, leading to preferred solutions. Nevertheless, CS that are willing to provide their individual capabilities to realize joint SoS-level capabilities need to embed their respective systems into the higher level structures of the SoS. As each CS within an SoS environment no longer operates in isolation, the CS must meet its own requirements as well as the requirements of the SoS as a whole. The alignment between the heterogeneous CS, their individual perspectives, and the SoS, however, requires a common understanding and a common point of reference [18]. This is where the *IEC 62,559 Use Case (UC) Management* methodology and the *Smart Grid Architecture Model* (SGAM) methodology steps in. Both methodologies were developed to complement each other [20]. The dynamics of a static architecture with its processes and exceptions can be documented in an IEC 62,559 template, while the individual components can be referenced within the so-called SGAM baseplane [19]. Although both methods can be applied independently, they work seamlessly together due to their shared meta-model based on the ISO/IEC/IEEE 42,010 architecture standard [20].

The IEC 62,559 Use Case Management Methodology

As SoS initiatives are characterized by an enormous heterogeneity of the system landscape, stakeholders and actors from a wide variety of domains and disciplines, in various roles, they face additional challenges in jointly identifying objectives and mutual requirements [7]. Due to the interdisciplinary and heterogeneous nature of the SoS environment, the various stakeholders within an SoS use a wide variety of tools and standards for requirements elicitation and documentation. To enable comparability, analyzability, and evaluation across stakeholders, the IEC 62,559 standard emphasizes a structured and uniform methodology for capturing and detailing UCs. For this purpose, the IEC 62,259–2 "*Definition of the templates for use cases, actor list and requirements list*" offers a systematic and standardized template to document UCs and serves as a systematic framework for documenting UCs [15]. Table 1 provides a brief overview of the structure of the IEC 62,559–2 UC template.

The Smart Grid Architecture Model

Table 1 Structure of the IEC 62,559–2 use case template

Section	Description
1. Description	General information such as name, version management, objectives, description, assumptions, and prerequisites
2. Diagrams	Diagrams that illustrate connections of a content-related or temporal nature of the UC
3. Technical details	Collection and grouping of the actors involved and references on which the UC is based
4. Step-by-step analysis	Description of the scenarios of the UC with step-by-step illustrations
5. Information exchanged	Overview of all information exchanged in the scenarios with reference to their requirements
6. Requirements	Grouping and description of all occurring prerequisites and requirements
7. Common terms and definitions	Comprehensive glossary in which frequently occurring terms are defined
8. Custom information	Optional further structured information on the UC that could not be accommodated elsewhere

Traditionally, the energy value chain of the energy system consists of different domains with different areas of responsibility, which in turn are divided into different energy management zones. The different domains or zones are subject to different problems, which are accompanied by different approaches to solutions, standards, and the associated perspectives and ideas on the overall system. In order to realize an efficient overall system, the heterogeneous perspectives of the stakeholders and systems along a given value chain must be mapped and harmonized in a common "language" or model, e.g. to identify an overarching need for standardization and to promote a common vision. In order to cover all key aspects and to enable a comprehensive perspective on the SoS, or to be more precise on the energy system as a whole, the SGAM is represented as a three-dimensional cube (depicted in Fig. 1).

The value chain of the electric energy domain is subdivided in "*Bulk Generation*", "*Transmission*", "*Distribution*", "*Distributed Energy Resources*", and "*Customer Premises*" (based on the NIST conceptual model [21]). As each of these sub-domains was never designed to be integrated, these are characterized by individual requirements and needs along their respective automation chains (so-called zones) in "*Process*", "*Field*", "*Station*", "*Operation*", "*Enterprise*" and "*Market*" (based on the automation pyramid). The intersection of the two dimensions, i.e. domains and zones, constitute the core of the SGAM—the SGAM baseplane. Finally, the third dimension of interoperability is added to the base plan. Based in the so-called *GridWise Architecture Council* (GWAC) *Interoperability Stack* [6], this dimension adds the interoperability abstraction layers which enable a differentiation between viewpoints for the "*Component Layer*", "*Communication Layer*", "*Information Layer*", "*Function Layer*", and "*Business Layer*". In alignment with ISO/IEC/IEEE 42,010, all three dimensions provide a general framework that allows a comprehensive and unified

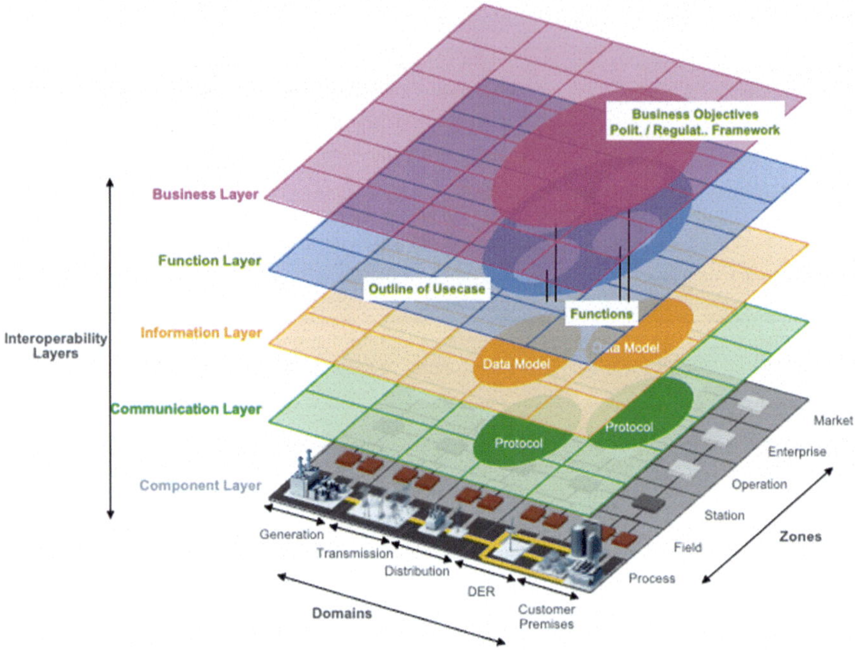

Fig. 1 Smart grid architecture model

description of all CS and their interdependencies within the SoS as a whole. Hence, the SGAM framework enables the creation of a domain-wide point of reference for all participating CS [18].

3 Methodology: Evaluating Architectural Design Decisions

The realization of joint capabilities and their accompanying shared requirements and functionalities necessitate a technically, semantically, and pragmatically adequate integration within the SoS. The extent of adequate integration is determined by the architecture of the respective SoS. For this purpose, a suitable architecture needs to establish well-defined integration points, clear interfaces, and interaction patterns that enable a secure and seamless connection or integration of cyber-physical automation components and business information systems [6]. Simultaneously, it is the architecture that gives a system its unique capabilities and properties by emphasizing and harnessing emergent effects between the elements [21]. To this end, a suitable architecture ideally defines the basic principles for the organizational interaction of the components involved in a given system at a high level of abstraction. This includes a description of the components with their functionalities and capabilities, their roles and areas of responsibility, their relationships with each other and with the environment, as well as the associated functional and non-functional requirements [10]. For this purpose, it is mandatory to differentiate between:

- The **target architecture,** which describes an ideal–typical architectural version of the respective system and establishes a common understanding of processes, data structures, technologies, and best practices, which are generally recognized and adhered to by key stakeholders.
- The **actual architecture,** which refers to the instantiated architecture of a given system, i.e. the internal structure of a realized system. This can follow a target architecture as a regulatory framework or emerge organically.

Ultimately, as introduced, the evaluation of a design decision requires a generally accepted target architecture, which serves as the common point of reference to evaluate all architectural design decisions of the CS. The overall objective of the target architecture is to keep the complexity of the actual architecture at a manageable level.

Any deviation from the desired target architecture leads to a so-called *Architecture Erosion* of the actual architecture [5]. *Architecture Erosion* is generally considered a main driver for the accumulation of TD and refers to the sum of all deviations between the desired target architecture and the actual architecture, and hence, can be regarded as the equivalent of excess complexity [5, 17]. While the general diversity and heterogeneity of the systems involved in the SoS and its underlying (technical) components represent a part of the essential complexity of an SoS architecture that cannot be influenced in principle, the relationships—the way in which the CS interoperate or collaborate—can be organized in a variety of ways. If there is no target architecture recognized by the key stakeholders that ensures the requirements of the superordinate SoS, interfaces between the actors are negotiated and implemented individually based on the individual requirements. The result is a self-reinforcing erosion of the architecture and a proliferation of the system landscape, which is characterized by a multitude of proprietary isolated solutions and leads to an unmanageable complexity of the overall architecture [18].

This is the starting point for a suitable methodology for evaluating architectural design decisions. As depicted in **Fig. 2**, the methodology mainly consists of two overlapping perspectives with three building blocks linked by the SGAM. The first perspective represents the UC-specific information that only applies to a specific UC, while the second perspective represents the domain knowledge related to the overall energy system that applies (to a certain degree) to all UCs.

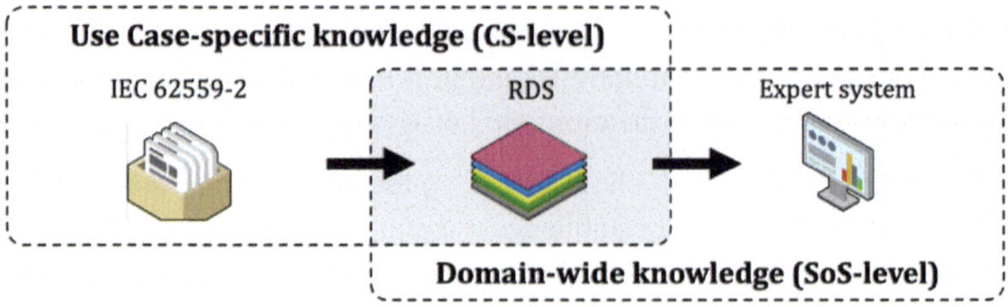

Fig. 2 Main building blocks (based on [12])

3.1 Domain-Specific Reference Designation Systems as a Pre-Condition

Reference Designation Systems (RDS) play a crucial role in integrating modern technologies such as IoT and Industry 4.0, promoting interoperability and standardization across different systems and platforms.

A reference designation in general provides an "*identifier of a specific object formed with respect to the system of which the object is a constituent, based on one or more aspects of that system*" and serves the unambiguous and exact identification and classification of technical objects within a given domain or area [9]. As presented by Uslar and Engel [22], RDS in general defines a baseplane that connects all sub-domains of a given value chain (of a given domain) with their respective automation chains, strictly following structuring principles and application rules [9]. The baseplane, which combines the (sub-)domains and zones that form the core of most RDS, creates a domain-wide point of reference for all participating CS. The SGAM provides a successful archetype, which has inspired the development and successful implementation of various derivatives in other fields. For instance, the fourth industrial revolution utilizes the *Reference Architectural Model Industry 4.0* (RAMI 4.0), and the maritime sector employs the *Maritime Architecture Framework* (MAF) [22].

3.2 Main Building Blocks for Evaluating Architectural Design Decisions

The separation between the UC-specific view and the SoS view is necessary to account for the duality of such an environment. The SoS can be viewed both bottom-up (from the perspective of the CS) and top-down (from the perspective of the SoS), with each perspective focussing on a different level, target system, and area of responsibility. While the UC-specific CS-perspective is required to assure that the individual requirements are taken into account, the SoS-perspective is required to assure that all decisions are aligned with the general target and reference architecture of the SoS to avoid further architecture erosion. Hence, to verify architectural design decisions of the CS, both perspectives are equally mandatory, as both are required to contextualize the individual UC of the CS within the SoS as a whole and, thus, to identify and evaluate discrepancies.

Building Block I: UC-Specific Knowledge Using the IEC 62,559–2 Template

As the IEC 62,559–2 standard provides a unified and systematically structured template to document UCs and their cross-organizational requirements from different viewpoints, as well as their relationships to each other, this template represents the first building block.

As UCs can be defined at different levels of abstraction, identifying the right system boundaries (in scope and context) and finding the appropriate level of abstraction for the identification, documentation, and analysis of UCs is often challenging. For this purpose, the guiding system's principle of abstraction states that UCs should be described "as generic as possible, as specific as needed" and demands a focus on essential aspects of a given system, thus allowing a simplification of complex problems by ignoring non-essential aspects. Usually, this still allows a lot of interpretation.

As it is not essential to understand all the details of each CS in order to understand the SoS as a whole, the focus here lies on the definitions of the interplay with external systems—on the interoperability. Hence, only use cases that require a cross-organizational data flow are of relevance. With this prerequisite in mind, each outgoing message of one CS represents an incoming message for another CS. As a result, all individual UCs and perspectives of the diverse CS can be consolidated into a single overall representation—the SoS. If a consolidation is not possible, meaning, the outgoing messages of a given UC do not match the incoming messages in another UC, this indicates a misalignment between the CS and needs further investigation.

Building Block III: Domain-Wide Knowledge Using Reference Designation Systems

Although the IEC 62,259 UC methodology, or more specifically, the IEC 62,559–2 UC template, supports the identification and harmonization of cross-system (interoperability) requirements of the CS involved in a given UC, this does not automatically prevent the development of proprietary solutions. In principle, the same UC can be implemented differently in different projects or initiatives by different stakeholders. While the CSs in a given UC are able to collaborate reliably despite using proprietary solutions, the associated lock-in effects generally make it more difficult to integrate other market participants. This means that changes in trading and communication partners are associated with additional (avoidable) costs due to the integration distance [18].

As the IEC 62,559 UC methodology "only" allows the direct comparison of two or more UCs, but not the comparison with the standards established within a given domain or demanded by the SoS, a discrepancy between the local requirements of the CS and the requirements of the SoS is still possible. This is where the SGAM's ability to act as an RDS can be utilized. One of the characteristics that makes SGAM a powerful tool is its ability for its domains and zones to act as an RDS [18]. As an RDS, the general knowledge of a given domain can be located according to the domains and zones of the respective RDS, which serve as a reference to map the domain knowledge to the UC-specific knowledge and, thus, to derive new knowledge by combining. The:

- *Smart Grid Information Security* (SGIS) for information security,
- *Confidentiality, Integrity and Availability* (CIA) requirements of the NISTIR 7628 and their *Logical Interface Categories* (LIC), and
- the *Seamless Integration Architecture* (SIA) for standardization and interoperability

are well-established examples of such higher level domain knowledge, which has already been mapped to the SGAM as an RDS [12]. Moreover, all components and their expected properties can be assigned to the respective domains, zones, and, if required, interoperability layers. These properties can include, for instance, existing regulatory requirements, safety requirements, and/or prevailing standards for communication protocols, information models, or functionalities [18].

Building Block II: Overlay of the CS and SoS Knowledge

The last building blocks serve the linkage and mapping of the UC-specific knowledge with the general domain knowledge. This convergence of the UC-specific and the general domain knowledge enables two types of analysis: metric-based analysis and gap analysis.

Currently, there are only a few metric-based analyses with a focus on the cross-system or SoS perspective in the literature [12]. Examples include the i-Score metric [13], which evaluates overall interoperability capability, and the SecMet metric [14], which assesses the *Smart Grid* architectures and their components to indicate the "Securitisation Need" based on individual risk assessments. Both examples apply generally established domain knowledge to the specific UCs and provide valuable insights into the decision-making process and require both building blocks as a pre-condition for their application.

The gap analysis, on the other hand, analyses the deviation between the actual architecture and target or reference architecture to assess the architecture erosion of the SoS as briefly introduced in [18]. A reference or target architecture, which is mapped onto an RDS allows a distinct contextualization of the role and functionality of each CS as a part of the SoS; hence, allowing an easy identification and shared understanding in which way every CS should be embedded within the higher level structures of the SoS [12]. By doing so, the RDS provides all information mapped to the designated domain and zone where the CS is located, including all required standards, integration profiles, information models, potential business models, and regulatory frameworks that are mapped to the respective reference designator.

As a result of the shared meta-model, all UC-specific information can be seamlessly translated into a corresponding SGAM as depicted in **Fig. 3**.

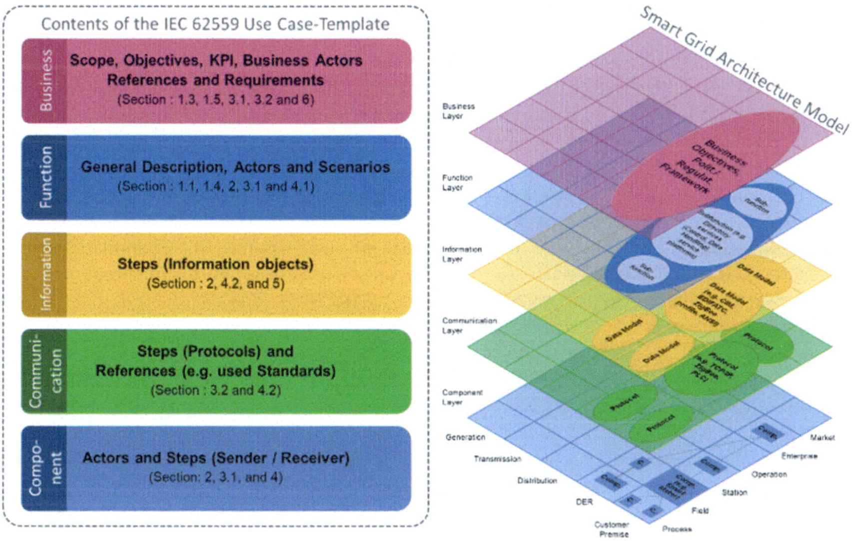

Fig. 3 Mapping of the IEC 62,559–2 UC sections to SGAM [13]

4 Conclusion

Although most CS have successfully mastered operating within their own system boundaries, data-driven and cross-organizational value creation is subject to new engineering paradigms. As CS within an SoS environment no longer operate in isolation, the implications of local technical decisions cannot be predicted nor adequately evaluated. Without an additional holistic SoS-level perspective, potential propagation and feedback effects on the interacting and mutually dependent CS may go unnoticed.

To provide an overall framework that assures the future viability of an SoS and simultaneously assists individual CS in their design decisions to avoid costly consequences, this contribution highlighted the underlying issue and introduced a high-level methodology to address it. Although the examples used have been derived from the electric energy domain, the overall methodology can be applied to any domain. However, applying it to other domains always requires a specific RDS that covers the given domain and specialized domain knowledge, such as potential reference or target architectures, relevant standards, or regulatory requirements.

However, the manual application of the proposed methodology may be time-consuming and challenging. In future, this could benefit from automation within an expert system. For this purpose, the IEC 62,559–3 should be investigated as a basis, as this standard already provides a standardized, interoperable, and machine-readable format or serialization of the UC template.

References

1. Avgeriou P., Kruchten P., Ozkaya O. and Seaman C. B.: "Managing Technical Debt in Software Engineering (Dagstuhl Seminar 16162)". In: Dagstuhl Reports 6.4 (2016). Ed. by Avgeriou P., Kruchten P., Ipek Ozkaya, and Seaman C., pp. 110–138.
2. von Bertalanffy L.: "General System Theory: Foundations, Development, Applications". International Library of Systems Theory and Philosophy. G. Braziller, 1968.
3. Billaud, S., Daclin, N., Chapurlat, V. (2015). Interoperability as a Key Concept for the Control and Evolution of the System of Systems (SoS). In: van Sinderen, M., Chapurlat, V. (eds) Enterprise Interoperability. IWEI 2015. Lecture Notes in Business Information Processing, vol 213. Springer, Berlin, Heidelberg. https://doi.org/10.1007/978-3-662-47157-9_5
4. Clemente Izurieta et al. "Perspectives on Managing Technical Debt: A Transition Point and Roadmap from Dagstuhl". In: QuASoQ/TDA@APSEC. 2016.
5. Dewayne E. Perry and Alexander L. Wolf. "Foundations for the study of software architecture". In: SIGSOFT Softw. Eng. Notes 17.4 (Oct. 1992), pp. 40–52. https://doi.org/10.1145/141874.141884.
6. The GridWise Architecture Council, "GridWise® Interoperability Context- Setting Framework v1.1," 2008.
7. Ian Sommerville, Dave Cliff, Radu Calinescu, Justin Keen, Tim Kelly, Marta Kwiatkowska, John Mcdermid, and Richard Paige. 2012. Large-scale complex IT systems. Commun. ACM 55, 7 (July 2012), 71–77. https://doi.org/10.1145/2209249.2209268
8. ISO/IEC/IEEE 21839:2019: "Systems and Software Engineering—System of Systems (SoS) Considerations in Life Cycle Stages of a System", 2019.
9. IEC 81346–1:2022: "Industrial systems, installations and equipment and industrial products—Structuring principles and reference designations—Part 1: Basic rules", 2022.
10. ISO/IEC/IEEE 42010:2022: "Software, systems and enterprise—Architecture description", 2022.
11. Johann Schütz and Jorge Marx Gómez. 2020. Towards collaborative Technical Debt Management in Systems of Systems. In Proceedings of the 3rd International Conference on Technical Debt (TechDebt '20). Association for Computing Machinery, New York, NY, USA, 87–91. https://doi.org/10.1145/3387906.3388620
12. J. Schütz, M. Clausen, M. Uslar and J. M. Gómez, "IEC 62559–2 Use Case Template-based Smart Grid Architecture Analytics," CIRED 2021—The 26th International Conference and Exhibition on Electricity Distribution, Online Conference, 2021, pp. 2935–2939, https://doi.org/10.1049/icp.2021.1909.
13. M. van Amelsvoort, C. Delfs, and M. Uslar, "Application of the Interoperability Score in the Smart Grid Domain," in *2015 IEEE 13th International Conference on Industrial Informatics (INDIN)*, 2015, pp. 442–447.
14. M. Clausen and J. Schütz, "Identifying Security Requirements for Smart Grid Components: A Smart Grid Security Metric," 2022 IEEE 20th International Conference on Industrial Informatics (INDIN), Perth, Australia, 2022, pp. 208–213, https://doi.org/10.1109/INDIN51773.2022.9976103.
15. Marion Gottschalk, Mathias Uslar, and Christina Delfs. "Case Studies". In: The Use Case and Smart Grid Architecture Model Approach: The IEC 62559–2 Use Case Template and the SGAM applied in various domains. Cham: Springer International Publishing, 2017, pp. 71–83. https://doi.org/10.1007/978-3-319-49229-2_5.
16. Philippe Kruchten, Robert Nord, and Ipek Ozkaya. Managing Technical Debt: Re- ducing Friction in Software Development. Pearson Education, 2019.
17. Ruiyin Li, Peng Liang, Mohamed Soliman, and Paris Avgeriou. "Understanding software architecture erosion: A systematic mapping study". In: Journal of Software: Evolution and Process 34.3 (2022), e2423. https://doi.org/10.1002/smr. 2423.
18. Schütz, J., Marx Gómez, J. (2024). A Brief Introduction into (De-)Coupling Lifecycles in Net-Centric Systems-of-Systems. In: Marx Gómez, J., Elikana Sam, A., Godfrey Nyambo, D.

(eds) Smart and Secure Embedded and Mobile Systems. ICTA-EMOS 2022. Progress in IS. Springer, Cham. https://doi.org/10.1007/978-3-031-56603-5_22
19. S. Faller, J. Schütz, A. Bogensperger und M. Uslar, "Anwendungshilfe SGAM—Smart Grid Use Cases modellieren", Energiewirtschaftliche Tagesfragen (et) 5/2020.
20. Uslar, Mathias, Sebastian Rohjans, Christian Neureiter, Filip Pröstl Andrén, Jorge Velasquez, Cornelius Steinbrink, Venizelos Efthymiou, Gianluigi Migliavacca, Seppo Horsmanheimo, Helfried Brunner, and et al. 2019. "Applying the Smart Grid Architecture Model for Designing and Validating System-of-Systems in the Power and Energy Domain: A European Perspective" Energies 12, no. 2: 258. https://doi.org/10.3390/en12020258
21. U.S. Department of Energy (DOE), "NIST Framework and Roadmap for Smart Grid Interoperability Standards, Release 3.0," *Nist Spec. Publ.*, pp. 1–90, 2014.
22. Uslar M., Engel D.: "Towards Generic Domain Reference Designation: How to learn from Smart Grid Interoperability". D-A-Ch Energieinformatik 2015, Karlsruhe.

The manufacturer's authorised representative in the EU is Springer Nature Customer Service Centre GmbH, Europaplatz 3, 69115 Heidelberg, Germany. If you have any concerns regarding our products, please contact ProductSafety@springernature.com

Printed and bound by CPI Group (UK) Ltd, Croydon, CR0 4YY
21/09/2026
02219965-0020